STUART

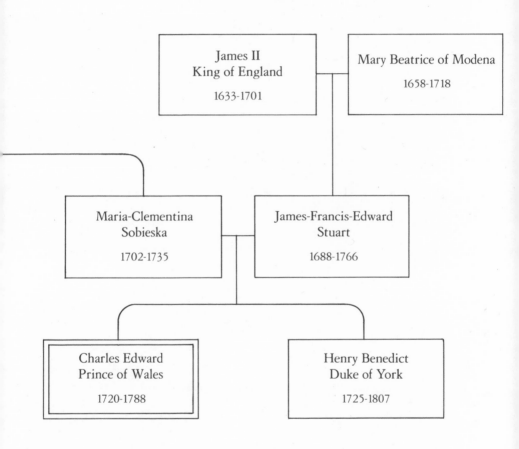

| James II
King of England

1633-1701 | Mary Beatrice of Modena

1658-1718 |

| Maria-Clementina
Sobieska

1702-1735 | James-Francis-Edward
Stuart

1688-1766 |

| Charles Edward
Prince of Wales

1720-1788 | Henry Benedict
Duke of York

1725-1807 |

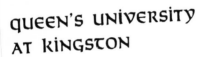

The Love of a Prince:
Bonnie Prince Charlie in France, 1744-1748

The Love
of a Prince

BONNIE PRINCE CHARLIE
IN FRANCE, 1744-1748

L. L. Bongie

UNIVERSITY OF BRITISH COLUMBIA PRESS
VANCOUVER 1986

The Love of a Prince:
Bonnie Prince Charlie in France, 1744-1748

© University of British Columbia Press, 1986

This book has been published with the help
of a grant from the Canada Council.

Canadian Cataloguing in Publication Data

Bongie, Laurence L.
   The love of a prince

   ISBN 0-7748-0258-8
   1. Charles Edward, Prince, grandson of
James II, King of England, 1720-1788. 2.
Louise, Duchesse de Montbazon and Princesse
de Rohan, 1725-1781. 3. Jacobite Rebellion,
1745-1746. I. Title.
DA814.A5B65 1986   941.0720924   C86-091172-1

ISBN 0-7748-0258-8

Printed in Canada

To all those who helped

Contents

Illustrations

PHOTO CREDITS

Plates 22 and 23 appear by gracious permission of Her Majesty the Queen; Plate 7 is by permission of the Duke of Buccleuch and Queensberry (Photo: Victoria and Albert Museum); Plates 2, 21, and 30 are from the National Galleries of Scotland, Edinburgh; Plates 20 and 33 are from the National Portrait Gallery, London; Plate 31 is from the Derby Museum and Art Gallery; Plate 34 is from the Mansell Collection, London; Plates 3, 11, and 24 are from the Rohan Portrait Gallery, Sychrov Castle, Czechoslovakia; Plate 26 is from the Mittelrheinisches Landesmuseum, Mainz; Plates 15, 16, 17, 19, 25, and 27 are from the Bibliothèque Nationale, Paris; Plate 32 is from the Uffizi Gallery, Florence; Plate 1 appears in Peggy Miller, *A Wife for the Pretender* (London, 1965); Plate 5 is from Bryan Bevan, *King James the Third of England* (London, 1967); Plates 12 and 13 appear in Paul Lacroix, *XVIIIᵉ siècle, institutions, usages et costumes* (Paris, 1875); Plate 9 is taken from A. Gieysztor et al., *History of Poland* (Warsaw, 1968); Plates 6 and 8 appear in Wanda Roszkowska, *Oława Krolewiczow Sobieskich* (Wroclaw, 1968); and Plate 14 is from *L'Encyclopédie,* article "Blason ou Art Héraldique," Planche XVIII.

Preface

This is not another life of Bonnie Prince Charlie although the reader will find in it much that is new about Scotland's legendary hero, especially concerning the critically important years that followed his escape to France after the debacle of Culloden. In fact, I have found the genre of the work particularly difficult to define, and the ambiguity of the title reflects that problem of definition. The "love" of Charles Edward Stuart refers certainly to the hitherto untold story of the Prince's first passionate affair during which he fathered a son whose existence has been unsuspected by historians to this day. But that key word is also intended to designate the object of his love—the Princess herself— and to mark the extent to which I have found it important to comment in a lengthy introduction on her anguished letters to the Young Pretender and on the essentially tragic story of an abandoned woman that they tell. Here, as with tragedy, the external realities of history and everyday events scarcely make themselves felt, and the letters almost become, in the old classical sense, vehicles of a timeless and universal human truth.

But tragedy, as Aldous Huxley once wrote, quite properly refrains from telling the whole truth, and as we read on through the Princess's letters and share in the poignancy of her internal crisis, we feel the need to ask the sort of questions that are more the province of the historian or the novelist. We want to know more about our protagonists and their circumstances. Who was this unfortunate Princess? How did she and the Prince come to meet? What became of their son? How did the affair end, and what happened after the final curtain?

This book does not pretend to tell the complete story. The Princess's tragic effusions end on a note of mystery, and although many new facts are presented in the main body of the work, ranging from important revelations about the Prince's early vow of chastity and the existence of his young son to trivial detail concerning the name of his dog and even the design of his wallpaper in Paris, I do not attempt to fill in the entire picture. The better known adventures of the

Bonnie Prince have for the most part been set aside. I have not, for example, looked at the '45 in itself but rather at certain less familiar perceptions of it that were current in France at the time. Similarly, I have dealt less with the Prince's failure at Culloden than with his subsequent inability to cope with that failure or with the even more devastating personal defeat that his arrest and his expulsion from France in December 1748 symbolized for him.

Not surprisingly, Bonnie Prince Charlie does not always play the hero in this story, any more, perhaps, than his tormented mistress emerges as grandly "tragic." Clearly, she was a more human than tragic figure. She was content to feel deeply and to write passionately obsessive love letters. Intellectually significant or profound epistolary literature was beyond her reach. As for the Prince, despite his early idealism, his fortitude and magnanimity, his heroic sense of sacrifice, he too reveals finally his all too human flaws in the face of unbearable pressure. During his two years in France after Culloden, he evolved into a different man. Charles Edward Stuart was a do-or-die sort of person, and the essential tragedy of his life is that, when the right time came, he managed neither.

I am most grateful to Her Majesty Queen Elizabeth II for permission to use the Stuart Manuscripts at Windsor and to Count Henri de Boisgelin for authorizing the reproduction of documents in the Archives Rohan-Bouillon (Archives Nationales, 273 AP). Very special thanks are also due Miss Jane Langton, Registrar of the Royal Archives, her colleague, Mrs. Sheila de Bellaigue, Mme Suzanne d'Huart of the Archives Nationales in Paris, and Dr. Marie Mzykova of the Czechoslovakian State Institute for the Protection of Historical Monuments. Without their valued assistance, completion of this work would not have been possible.

Vancouver   L.L.B.
March 1986

Introduction to the Letters

I F THE LOVE letters in Appendix A at the end of this book (the reader is invited to begin with them) had been discovered early on in the last century, they might well have attracted the colourfully romantic talents of a Walter Scott or a Victor Hugo. The latter, especially, would have been intrigued by a love story whose most passionate moments came alive in a bedroom of the very house he occupied in Paris for over fifteen years and which today is a museum devoted to his memory.

As befits the venerable conventions of high drama, the protagonists of this clandestine affair were both of noblest birth. The lover, ideally suited to the role of tragic hero, was none other than Bonnie Prince Charlie, the Young Pretender to the throne of Great Britain, twenty-seven years of age and freshly returned from an ignominious and bloody defeat at Culloden. The lady he loved and who loved him in return with equal passion was his twenty-two-year-old cousin, Marie-Louise-Henriette-Jeanne de La Tour d'Auvergne, Duchesse de Montbazon and Princesse de Rohan, the young wife of the even younger head of one of France's oldest and most powerful families, Jules-Hercule-Mériadec, Prince de Rohan, Duc de Montbazon, Prince de Guéméné. The father of the Princess, the Duc de Bouillon, a descendant of the great Turenne, was Grand Chambellan de France, a gambling and carousing crony of Louis XV and the head of another of France's three or four most powerful families who claimed their princely titles and prerogatives by the grace of God alone. In 1737, only ten years before the secret romance began, four of Europe's kings or would-be kings had personally intervened in early marriage plans for the Princess, who happened to be the great-granddaughter of Poland's legendary monarch, Jan Sobieski, as well as one of Europe's potentially wealthiest heiresses.

Nothing of this intensely emotional affair, very probably Prince Charlie's first—indeed, perhaps his only great passion—has found its way into the history books or the scores of biographies devoted in the last two centuries to every known detail of the Young Pretender's life. Even those accounts—and there are several such—that expressly claim to reveal all concerning the Prince and "his ladies" have been silent on the subject. No less astonishing is the fact that neither legend nor history has breathed the slightest word about a son born of this secret union. Genealogists will find no urgent need to chart the antecedents or eventual fate of yet another Stuart pretender among the various fraudulent claimants who continued to turn up in different places well into the nineteenth century—all hoping for a modest share of royal ancestry. The child was real enough; indeed, the Prince secretly "acknowledged" his paternity well before his son was born in Paris on 28 July 1748, a date that was preceded, however, by the definitive end of the affair. As it turns out, the infant was cleverly camou-flaged as a *bona-fide* Rohan-Guéméné, but, like many in those days, he died before reaching the end of his first year of life, on 18 January 1749. The child's name, Charles-Godefroi-Sophie-Jules-Marie, was ultimately scrubbed from all official genealogies of the Rohan-Montbazon family, which today record only the birth of an elder brother, Henri-Louis-Marie, Prince de Guéméné, whose famous bankruptcy shook the *Ancien Régime* to its very foundations on the eve of the Revolution.

Ignorant of these and other fascinating details, I confess that on catching my first glimpse of the Princess's hopelessly jumbled correspondence at Windsor, I was only mildly attracted by the notion of pursuing the matter further. Here, if something could be made of it, was certainly material for a few more footnotes to an already oft-told tale of Scotland's celebrated hero. But mild curiosity was soon transformed into a sense of intrigue and suspense as I read on through the tormented letters, all in the same hand, undated, unsigned, unpunctuated, and dashed off in frenetic haste by, as the card inventory of manuscripts correctly indicated, the Duchesse de Montbazon to her cousin Charles Edward Stuart (though obviously to several other recipients as well). There is evidence to suggest that at some time in this century a serious attempt was made to arrange the letters in some kind of chronological order, but apparently with little success. After closer examination of a microfilm copy, I decided to try my hand, and Appendix A is the result of many long hours of puzzlement and guesswork applied to the problems of deciphering, sorting, and dating of the letters. I am confident that most of them have now been placed in rough chronological order and that the identity of each recipient has been established. The difficulties of such an undertaking were not unexpected; originally intended for the fire, once read, all of the letters are couched in terms sufficiently anonymous and covert to hide, in case of interception, the identity of both the sender and the recipient. In fact, it is now clear that much of this correspondence and the physical love affair itself had to be carried on at great risk almost under the very nose of the Princess's husband, not to mention the acutely vigilant eye of her highly suspicious resident mother-in-law whose servants were, at one point, assigned round-the-clock surveillance duties and instructed to prevent communication of any kind between the suspected lovers.

Apart from the general problem of chronological ordering, assigning even an approximate date to individual letters has proved to be most difficult, so much having to depend on tenuous speculations concerning the probable permutations and combinations of a mercurial passion. Only rarely are direct references to external events provided. Such infrequent clues include the Princess's allusions to the New Year, Easter Week, the Opera season, and, more than once, the anticipated joys of trysting in the "month of May." What we might term the internal chronology of emotions progressing through a series of crises turned out to be a less useful guide than originally expected since there are many crises in the correspondence, and several resemble rather closely or overlap similar ones that precede or follow. We are sometimes left wondering, for example, whether we are dealing with the emotional peak of crisis number "two" or "four," the depressed depths of number "five" or "three," and so forth. The process, indeed, has been somewhat like trying to fit together a large jigsaw puzzle with too many pieces showing barely perceptible variations in shape or colour. An additional complication arises from the fact that a number of the puzzle's important "pieces" are missing.

They are missing, moreover, in several ways. We have, first of all, only one side or "half" of the correspondence: that of the Princess. As the affair—at least from the Prince's viewpoint—cooled, Charles Edward seems to have become far too clever (or too skittish) to entrust his own intimate and now ambivalent feelings to the treacherously vulnerable medium of the *billet doux*. In any case, the few written replies that he did send were destroyed at his request by a naively loyal Princess, artless enough to believe that he was regularly returning the courtesy. We are thus left with only one voice in the dialogue, that of the Prince's passionate, suffering mistress whose tortured thought processes must govern our perception not only of her own feelings, but those of her lover as well. The resulting gap in information is significant although, in another sense, to speak of a "missing half" of the letters is misleading since, toward the end of the affair (which was carried on between October 1747 and May or June of 1748), the Prince obviously did not match, despite the many pleas of his mistress, the frequency of her own feverish epistolary efforts.

That the Prince's letters are missing is no doubt especially regrettable to the historian. On the other hand, for those readers who (legitimately emboldened by the subject matter) may wish to go a little beyond history, that fact may have its aesthetic advantages since the missing voice imposes a poignantly tragic focus and concentration on the events related. We have only to consider such equally "one-sided" literary parallels as Guilleragues' *Lettres Portugaises*, the *Lettres de la marquise de M*** au comte de R**** of Crébillon *fils*, or, to take a modern example, Cocteau's *La Voix Humaine* to sense the enhanced power and intensity of expression that can result from similar presentations in fiction of an abandoned woman's sorrowful outpourings.

The mention of literary parallels reminds us that elements of the correspondence are "missing" in another and equally important sense, creating gaps that again dramatically enhance a collection of letters in which life often seems to imitate art. As with the psychological events of tragedy, we are here caught up only in the moment of crisis. Entirely "missing" in the correspondence is a conventional starting point or an identifiable end. How or precisely when the affair began or ended remains a mystery. We cannot be absolutely certain which is the first letter or which the last, and in presenting the correspondence, I have been only too aware of the potentially conflicting claims of scholarly history, on the one hand, and what I shall call "literature," on the other. Of course, since this is a real correspondence, the requirements of history must be served as faithfully as possible, and the bulk of my study deals extensively with the background of events and characters. But our respect for history must not, at the same time, allow another kind of truth to escape us, and the reader is invited to test out the notion that perhaps the greatest attraction of the correspondence resides in its value as a poetic human document, one that transcends the miscellaneous tidbits of history that require many pages of narration but little in the way of introduction. Seen in this light, the letters become vehicles for the kind of truth that is so well celebrated, for example, in the enduring triumphs of French classical literature and, more particularly, in the eighteenth-century epistolary novel. Indeed, life in the Princess's letters sometimes imitates art so cleverly, fusing with it almost, that readers familiar with the works of a Guilleragues or a Laclos may well suspect an elaborate hoax.

There are obvious dangers attached to even the provisional application of such quasi-literary considerations to a reading of the letters, but let us postpone for the moment our more solemn objections and consider, in just such a light, the "first" letter of the correspondence. Of course, even before we begin doing that, we are mindful of the dilemma: is our "first" letter in fact the first? History, unfortunately, is silent on that point. The demands of art, on the other hand, are eloquent and categorical. The reader will appreciate the editor's problem!

The opening note is short and joyous; it expresses in blissful innocence a young lover's affirmation that happiness can never end. No clouds threaten on the horizon. We are unaware of any difficulties, of any "triangular" complications such as the fact that there is a husband who is currently away with his regiment but who will soon be returning. The consummate artistry of the novelist Laclos building to the spontaneous tone, the attenuated detail of Cécile Volange's first letter in *Les Liaisons dangereuses* fifty years later will not surpass it:

Si vous avez été content de votre nuit, mon amour, je vous avoue que pour moi j'en ai été enchantée. Je me flatte que nous en passerons encore longtemps de même. Cela sera mon unique bonheur. J'attends de vos nouvelles avec impatience. Adieu, cher coeur. Je me porte très bien. A ce soir. Venez vivre dans les bras de celle qui n'aime dans le monde que son cher amour.

Unashamedly and exuberantly sensual, the two lovers go on to explore with abandon all the hidden by-ways of pleasure. There is more than a hint, however, that even in the beginning, the Prince, immature and inexperienced in matters of the heart, is apprehensive of being displaced by a rival. Were there lovers before him? The Princess is coquettishly reassuring: how delighted she is, for example, to hear him list the many wicked things the gossips say about her; they are, she swears, entirely false, and let that be a lesson to him to pay no more heed to idle tongues! Happiness thus continues. Before long, however, a darker shading invades the picture: winter is approaching, the military campaign in the Low Countries is drawing to its seasonal close, and the husband will soon be home. They make arrangements to continue meeting but there are grave risks: their former untroubled evenings together are now transformed into furtive (though far from hasty) assignations in the Princess's bedroom. These begin only after midnight, at first, then at one-thirty in the morning, and, finally, as late as 3:00 a.m. Coinciding also with the husband's return from his regiment, there is an almost unspoken, discreetly painful interlude when lover and husband must no doubt "share." Already the mother of a two-year-old son, the Princess realizes that she is carrying the Young Pretender's child. The practical problem of arranging some opportunity for the husband to "father" another heir has to be faced. But at the same time the Princess is careful to reassure her increasingly jealous and insecure lover: has she not already given him ample proof, after all, that she loves him more than ever, and that she loves only him? It will be business as usual then, till midnight, *cher roi—le comble des plaisirs*! Moreover, the very thought of *experiencing pleasure* now with her husband is out of the question: "Oui, cher amour je n'en peux avoir qu'avec vous." Later, presumably after all the awkward details have been attended to, she swears, on her honour, that the husband will not be allowed to come near her.

The Princess's soothing (and absolutely sincere) reassurances do little to ease the Prince's tortured imaginings. In fact, they leave him more troubled and more angry than before. Soon he grows defiant as well. He retaliates with the boast that he will go elsewhere, that he has *une femme toute prête*. The Princess is shattered; she points out that if he abandons her as he threatens, there will be no man *tout prêt* in her life: "je vous jure que si je vous perdois, jamais aucun homme ne me sera de rien et je vous puis assurer que cela me couteroit la vie" [no.20]. In fact, neither his possessive jealousy, her recurring morning sickness, the growing suspicions of a mother-in-law who is obviously no fool, nor even the normal presence of a young and probably naive husband, has the effect of abating the eager joys of their sexual relationship. The Princess complains often of being "sick as a dog"; she is even bled from time to time. With all that, she never fails to look forward to their scheduled meetings, knowing that at midnight, or even at 3:00 a.m., everything will be set right again: "je serai guérie de tous maux....Oui, cher amour, je ne suis contente que quand je suis dans vos bras."

Frustration arising from the mother-in-law's effective security arrangements within the Montbazon-Guéméné household finally brings the Prince's distrust, along with an angry sense of deprivation, to a point of extreme crisis. Perhaps not surprisingly, he responds by flaunting his determination to impose on his mistress even greater risks, insisting on spending the entire night in her bedroom, threatening otherwise to skulk in the Place Royale below or to beset the house and cause a public scandal. For one brief moment, we are led to imagine that the Princess will find the strength to break with her now insanely possessive lover. She begins a determined letter along appropriate lines, but that determination soon fades and turns into another message of reassurance: "Vous voulez donc toujours m'inquiéter, cher amour, en ne vous tranquillisant pas. De grâce, ne tuez pas qui vous adore. Je vous jure que nous nous verrons souvent.... Demain, à une heure et demie, nous serons heureux, et souvent si vous êtes raisonnable" [no.7]. She does, it is true, go on to hint at the possibility of refusing to see him ever again; it would cost her her life to make such an impossible sacrifice, but if he will not begin to trust her and to be reasonable.... Her threat, we soon realize, is empty. The Princess is no more able to break off the relationship than the Prince is capable of being reasonable.

It is not my intention here to provide a day-by-day summary of the correspondence; the letters, obviously, best speak for themselves. What is perhaps worth emphasizing, however, are their aesthetic dimensions. The story unfolds at first much as in a popular romance: in the beginning, spontaneous joys, manageable tensions, an exchange of locks of hair, of portraits....Then come brief but sorely felt privations that shatter the continuity of their regular nightly diversions. Both lovers initially think of the affair as an idyllic interlude, something that will inevitably come to an end with the return of the husband, a young and valiant officer, one of the Prince's closest friends. Along with the Princess's only brother, the Prince de Turenne, he had obtained special permission from Louis XV two years before to join the Young Pretender's campaign in the '45. Things would certainly have to change when he returned: "Vivons heureux," the Princess writes in one of her early letters, "le peu de temps que nous avons à être ensemble. Hélas, il ne sera que trop court" [no.12]. But the lovers soon become caught up in a deeper madness. The Prince's mistrust becomes daily more insistent. He grows harsh, unreasonable, and threatening; his movements seem unpredictable and capricious. He makes it clear that he must have all of her love; he cannot share her, body or soul, with anyone else. He will maintain an all-night vigil in the street and defy the spies that the mother-in-law, Mme de Guéméné, has posted to guard the great family home on the Place Royale. The threat to abandon her is repeated: other seductive women are no doubt anxiously awaiting the opportunity to spirit away the most celebrated hero of the day.

The lovers are frequently on the point of quarreling. Urged on especially by the Prince's taunting rashness and despite very real tensions and risks, they nevertheless pursue their passion, throwing caution to the winds. There are moments of quiet happiness too: they rejoice in the delayed discovery that, without realizing it, they have been secretly in love for nearly three years; it had all happened even before he set out for Scotland in July 1745 to regain the throne of his Stuart forefathers!... We are left not a little bemused, for that was when Louise was carrying her first child, born the following month. But now they perceive their love as a kind of narcotic, and they indulge their addiction even as they fear it will dangerously augment their desires. The unborn child only adds to this closeness: the Prince loves to talk to it in its mother's belly, and he makes it a solemn promise of love; he will love it for as long as he himself has life. Though constantly worried about discovery, the Princess accedes to his every whim. Love makes it all worthwhile. Who could have thought such a love possible! She worries frequently about his health. He must take care of himself, for her sake and that of his great cause: "Conservez-vous donc pour faire mon bonheur et vous devez songer que vous n'êtes pas à vous. Vous vous devez à trois royaumes et à la plus tendre et plus fidèle maîtresse" [no.26].

There are several narrow escapes. One night in a blind rage, he apparently shoots off his pistols in the Place Royale. On another occasion he manages to escape from the Princess's bed just in time to avoid catastrophic discovery — catastrophic since others besides the personal servants of the Princess would have become involved. Rumours begin to circulate as far away as Marly and Versailles that he is spending every night with her. Finally, the inevitable happens: the mother-in-law and the Princess's father (the husband, it would appear, remained happily ignorant throughout) decide that they must confront the daughter and put a quick end to her scandalous behaviour. The matter was, of course, delicate in the extreme: Charles Edward the hero-Prince was no ordinary intruder but the leading social lion of Paris! His regular attendance at the Opéra was routinely greeted with wild applause and carried out almost as a kingly function. All of the great families vied for the pleasure of his company. But the father and the mother-in-law nevertheless saw their duty as clear: the Prince had dishonoured his sweet and illustrious cousin, in her own house, as if she were no better than the lowest of fallen creatures. He had shown no respect for her, for himself, or for a family that had offered the greatest help and protection given him by anyone from the time of his first arrival in France. Certainly, the liaison would have to come to an immediate end. There could, first of all, be no more secret letters. All conniving servants would have to be dismissed. Naturally, it was hoped that the Prince would have sufficient self-respect to continue visiting socially, *at conventional hours*, to demonstrate to the world that all was normal and that the many nasty rumours in circulation were totally without substance.

We shall see that many of the details of this painful confrontation scene on 23 January 1748 along with the very words used by Mme de Guéméné and the Duc de Bouillon, were dutifully conveyed to the Prince (for a translation, see *Appendix B*, II, 8), almost as a command performance, by an eyewitness, Mlle de Carteret, a long-time friend and confidante of the Princess whom Charles Edward had bribed with a pension. The accusations, only too true, stung the proud Prince. He had indeed been guilty of disloyalty to the only true "family" left to him in the world, especially now that he was almost totally estranged from his father, not to mention his brother Henry, who, everyone agreed, had recently done the Stuart cause more harm by accepting a cardinal's hat than had resulted from the entire aftermath of Culloden.

The very deep but largely suppressed feelings of guilt in this, his first and cruellest love affair, somewhat akin perhaps to the unspoken remorse the Prince felt at having provoked the humiliation and ruin of the clans after the '45, soon began to have strange effects on the Young Pretender's thought processes. Perhaps his new-found love of the bottle also contributed. In any event, he categorically refused to accept any chiding in the matter. His ego discovered an easier solution: denial. He now simply denied—to himself as much as to others—what was clearly undeniable. We know that even before the final confrontation he had had jealous doubts, a gnawing conviction that he was being duped, that his mistress was unfaithful, that perhaps the child he had promised to love forever was not even his, that the Princess was blabbing the details of their relationship to any and all who cared to listen, and that she had shown his letters. And now he was being grossly insulted by the mother-in-law, by his *cher oncle*, the Princess's father, and to crown it all, the King of France was preparing to tear up a sacred treaty and threatening to expel him from the country in order to play toady to the Hanoverian usurper, George II!

In this context of suspicion and alienation, what has remained until now a puzzling composition hidden away among the Stuart papers at Windsor, suddenly takes on new meaning. It is a short and rather strange autobiographical fragment, told in the third person and done up in the fashion of the popular salon *conte* of the day. Composed apparently in the spring of 1748, it probably represents Bonnie Prince Charlie's only formal attempt at fiction. In bitterly alienated tones (and rather dubious French[1]), it relates, pseudonymously, the events of his disastrous love affair, set against the background of his disillusionment with the French nation. Disenchantment had followed quickly on the resounding hero's welcome accorded him in Paris after his miraculous escape from Scotland in October 1746. Nearly two years later, Charles Edward Stuart was making it clear that he wanted from the French, not empty praise, but the firm promise of troops to help him accomplish what he had failed to do in the '45. What he wanted the record to show concerning the Princess and her family, is even more obvious.

Since it represents one of the Prince's few direct comments on his great romance, the *conte* obviously holds a special interest for readers of the correspondence. Charles Edward's own letters to his mistress, with one or two notable exceptions,[2] were probably either burned immediately on receipt or eventually returned to him at his insistence. In the face of his repeated accusations that she was showing his letters around, the Princess could hardly have acted otherwise. Furthermore, contrary to his usual practice, the Prince seems also to have destroyed even his rough drafts, an action probably in keeping with his general attitude of denial at this time. The *conte* thus provides a useful glimpse into the workings of the Prince's mind, already impaired by a haze of self-protective distortion and, probably, incipient paranoia. We are especially struck by the acerbity of his denial, the crude attempt to dissociate himself entirely from his former feelings of tenderness toward his mistress, and by what we know to be a totally false account of how the secret of their affair became public. Also surprising is the evidence of a complete reversal in his feelings toward the Duc de Bouillon, who had been like a father and special protector to him from the moment he set foot in Paris in February 1744 after leaving his real father, James III, in Rome. It was also from Navarre, the Duc's country estate near Evreux, that Charles Edward had launched the '45. Of course, the Prince may have had other reasons for painting events in such dark colours, and among these could have been a perceived need to sacrifice a former flame to the approving giggles of his new love, the Princesse de Talmont. Mme de Talmont, a cousin of the Queen (as well as, by the way, of our own Princess) was to become the Young Pretender's first "public" mistress late in the spring of 1748.

Because the numerous orthographical peculiarities in this particular specimen of Charles Edward's French prose might prove more disheartening than quaint to the average reader, I have provided here a rough translation.

A TALE COMPOSED IN PARIS BY MR........
ABOUT A YOUNG FOREIGNER CALLED MR.........

This is the story of a man of excellent family who arrived from an exotic land, having been driven here by the enemies of his legitimate king. On his arrival at Genoa [Versailles], *he was welcomed most warmly and invited, by the nobility both high and low, to dinners and suppers in abundance. Such festivities are ordinarily the occasion of little more than shallow pleasantries and everyone was very curious to learn how he had managed to escape the many dangers that commonly follow on civil war. He remained there for a time but (and this is what usually happens to poor wretches bereft of power) realizing that the soup was growing cold and that once the first thirst of curiosity had been satisfied there was only boredom to be gained, he determined to take a change of air. He thus went from there to Avignon on his way to Spain where he was granted the same cordial welcome he had received in the beginning at Genoa* [Versailles], *only this time he was careful not to stay until the end and set out immediately for Paris where he placed himself in the hands and under the protection of the Robens, believing that was the best course to take in a land where he intended to stay as long as the war continued. Finally, he fell in love (being in a country house whose name now escapes me) with an agreeable person called Roudeboulon* [Rohan de Bouillon?] *(such was the name of the village where she was born), whose father was a fool and whose mother-in-law was an old lunatic (as we shall see in what follows). Everything took place in the greatest of secrecy, especially where our young traveler was concerned (for he was accustomed in his own country to being extremely cautious in affairs of the heart) a usage which is, in truth, little practised here where there is commonly boasting not only of what is but very often too of what is not. But to get back to our story, the mother-in-law, the father, and the unhappy daughter resolved, in spite of him, to make the affair public and in this they succeeded in some measure, such things being all too easily believed. I pity this unfortunate visitor for his misfortunes and I pity too our poor nation for the bad opinion that this young man will now have of it. I think I can safely conclude at this point the first volume of M.......'s adventures, since I believe he has been sufficiently mistreated in love to be disgusted with it for as long as he will do us the honour of remaining here. When he returns to his own country, I shall not fail to publish the second volume, which will no doubt deal with war.*

Those readers who have by now perused the entire correspondence and noted in detail the tender anxieties of the Princess, along with her many cautionary remarks concerning her lover's safety and welfare, will recognize the harshness and lack of good faith displayed in this curious literary exercise in princely self-deception. It must, in retrospect, have been apparent to the Prince that his insanely possessive behaviour, the indiscretion of his nightly visits at all hours, along with his noisy street vigils, could have led only to disaster for both of them. He must have realized too that the Princess was in all this far more vulnerable than he and least guilty, certainly, of betraying their secret. That the *conte* was written at all, however, added to the fact that the Prince carefully preserved his mistress's letters, probably speaks volumes for the depth of his original passion and any vestiges of it that survived the crisis.

What happened immediately after the family confrontation? Judging from references in the Princess's letters, the Prince probably wrote no more than one or two brief notes to his mistress in the subsequent months. She, on the other hand, always at great personal risk, continued to smuggle out agonizing epistles of ever-increasing length, persisting in her self-inflicted torture, pleading with him to love her, to write, to visit. More than once she threatens, though not convincingly, to kill herself and their child; she offers to defy her family and to meet him at Versailles, at Saint-Ouen, wherever he wishes....But the Prince had already begun to see his "humiliation" as part of a larger symbolic struggle. After three months of silence, cold and absolute, he at last relented and tossed her a small crumb of hope by consenting to meet her for an hour or two in a rented carriage at midnight. This assignation had taken the Princess weeks to arrange and was finally managed only by bribing one of Mme de Guéméné's spies. Louise, in any case, was thrilled at the opportunity, and we are led to believe from her excited account of their cramped encounter near the Pont Tournant that a good deal of intimate affection was exchanged. Curiously, even as he scolded her on this occasion for not being sufficiently independent and "grown-up" in her handling of the family, he told her that he still loved her, adding, however, that his fondness was now less intense. He assured her, nevertheless, that he would no more abandon her than he would give up his rights and leave France at the treacherous insistence of those who were preparing to sign a treaty of peace with his enemies. Now, also, he told her that he was seeing someone else, the Princesse de Talmont, no doubt equally beautiful and (since at forty-seven she was more than twice the Princess's age) certainly much more "grown-up"!

Heartened by this promise of renewed affection, the Princess was unrealistic enough, even at this late date, to ask the Prince for _all_ of his love, begging him to see less of her rival "Mme T...." who could not possibly love him as much as she did. She was also delighted that he had promised to write her every day! Of course, she believed him!...The very last letter in the correspondence, which seems to have ended abruptly approximately two months before their child was born on 28 July 1748, suggests, however, that little changed as a result of that meeting. In it the Princess continued to express the hope that she would manage to find other opportunities to see him. Did the idea of meeting again in a carriage displease him? Why then, she would risk everything and go as he requested to his house, dangerous as that was; but he was not to taunt her with accusations of childishness or waning affection if circumstances made that impossible. Soon she would be giving birth to his child; she might die in the process....None of that really bothered her; it was _his_ dear health that worried her! She would make every effort to see him, to minister pleasurably to his little comforts, and she would not talk about anything that annoyed him—if only he would keep his solemn promise to write!

In fact, nothing changed. The abandoned Princess continues her classical lament, having lost everything except the completely unwarranted hope that the clock can be turned back. Why does the correspondence suddenly end? Were more letters—now lost—written? Not many, one imagines; the dangers of such communication were very real. Perhaps one of her visits to the Prince's house (a convenience for him, certainly, but no doubt also a way of imposing a symbolic sexual constraint on his mistress) terminated in disaster, with Mme de Guéméné's spies finally managing a petty triumph. Perhaps the Prince simply imagined some new slight and exploded one day in a bombastic rage, forbidding all further contact. We are left to wonder....We last see the Princess yearning and pleading as usual—and dying of unrequited love, just as she had yearned, pleaded, and threatened to die so often before. We suspect that, come what may, she will remain totally devoted, ready to risk any danger to see him, to be able to tell him in person of her unbounded love, ever eager to purchase a few moments of his condescending attention by offering him other furtive interludes of pleasure, at his house, in a rented carriage at the Pont Tournant, or wherever he might wish. No doubt we would like to imagine the Prince at this point magically vanishing from her tortured thoughts, but again the precise details of the affair's final resolution are shrouded in mystery. For her there will certainly be more humiliation, more emptiness, and more pain before she manages to find her own way again. As for the Prince, perhaps the most we can hope for is that years later he will still occasionally recall through the murky layers of alcoholic oblivion the short-lived joys of his first great passion.

It is puzzling that not one word of this tragic romance seems to have seeped down through the gossipy annals of a century that generally loved to record such juicy incidents in intimate detail. Indeed, except of course in the case of the Prince, there is almost no published historical or biographical documentation relating to the characters involved. We shall see, for example, that not even the date of the Princess's death seems to have been known to historians. Happily, a number of useful manuscript sources, related mainly to Louise's early years, have come to light and these will be fully examined in due course. The new documents do not, unfortunately, tell us much about the essential character of the woman who played such an important role in the sentimental life of Charles Edward Stuart, and in our attempts to discover the basic nature of her character, we are again brought back to the letters in the hope of finding in their style or substance useful clues to what she was really like and how, as a member of France's highest nobility, she fitted into the social scene of the day. What, in short, would such letters tell us about her if they had been penned, not by the Princesse de Rohan-Guéméné, but by an eighteeth-century master of epistolary fiction such as the novelist Choderlos de Laclos?

One first and obvious truth becomes apparent as we examine these surviving relics of a long-spent passion from such a perspective: however many inviting parallels occur to today's scholarly reader familiar with the world of the eighteenth-century epistolary novel, we never find the Princess actually engaged in the business of being an "author" or trying to write a conscious species of "literature." Totally lacking in her letters is the all too common *ostensible* element frequently present in real as well as fictional writing. She makes no attempt to offer clever analysis or to achieve stylistic effect. Her letters are entirely spontaneous throughout. She emotes, she expresses, and despite the occasional well-turned *périodes* — surviving echoes, no doubt, of her romanesque readings or the happy consequence of a natural gift (the letters of her mother, Marie-Charlotte Sobieska, will impress us occasionally in much the same way) — she makes no attempt to sustain a literary style or to address a "reader." Her purpose in writing is to tell her lover what she feels. Self-expression and communication overlap in a single function. The letters are the direct and naive emotional outpourings of a joyful or suffering woman; they are never the studied rhetorical creations of a Crébillon *fils* or a Laclos concerned first of all with finding the means to create the illusion or "feeling" of that same reality. The Princess, unlike the fictional heroines whom she, in a sense, imitates (and who are, of course, themselves an imitation of her reality as imagined by the artist), indulges in none of the popular metaphysics of the passions. She provides no witty observations, paints no astutely balanced "literary" portraits of mutual friends, gives no gossip, and precious little everyday information (we learn that she occasionally sews and that she is studying English). There are no profound *maximes* in her epistles, no tidily precious moral observations to remind us of the salon, nothing at all, in short, for the benefit of an imagined audience. All that is vitally important to our assessment of her genuineness and personal integrity. The only reader she has in mind is her Prince, and her letters are written for him alone — to devour, cherish, weep over, and, finally, to burn.

Does she, even in small measure, possess the lucidity and detachment (perhaps even the insincerity) indispensable for conscious imitation of herself — that is, for "playing" her own role? The point is crucial, and the answer is that she probably does not. Not the slightest distancing will be found in her utterances. Her love is obsessive and total; her passion, an all-consuming form of madness. In short, we are here brought face to face with *true* love, as the romantics will have it. Louise is blinded by it both in a real and in a symbolic sense for she often cannot see her writing paper because of the tears that obscure her vision; similarly, her clairvoyance, her inner vision, is clouded by this constant welling of raw emotion. Her repetitious, overstated style becomes an integral part of this great obsession. How often do such expressions (we choose them at random) recur: "*le comble des plaisirs*," "*le comble de mes voeux*," "*le comble des malheurs*," "*le comble de l'injustice*"! Or again: "*mon malheureux enfant*," "*je suis comme une folle*," "*vous m'avez percé le coeur*," "*je me donnerai la mort*," "*rendez-moi la vie*," "*je baise mille fois votre main*," "*je baise mille fois tout ce*

que j'ai baisé hier," *"je suis la plus malheureuse de   toutes les créatures."*
Warmly *pleurnicheuse* in the style of some of her romanesque counterparts of
the day, she does make us uncomfortable at times by harping too much on one
injured tone. But such repetition should not be dismissed as merely obnoxious.
To say that she is a story-book cliché of herself is, indeed, fully to grasp the point.
Her passion is absolute and unchanging: "Love is not love which alters when it
alteration finds," the poet tells us. Her moods frequently shift from joy to
sorrow, desire to despair, but such superficial variation only serves to confirm
the tenacious nature of her passion, dignified throughout by what we know to be
her genuine tenderness, devotion, and fidelity.

Just as we find little analysis in the letters, we find even less morality. The
Princess never stands back from her writing table to deliver Richardsonian
sermons on virtue or duty, and she expresses no remorse. In even the better
novels of the day, the heroine might be fittingly called upon to die after so much
sinning or, at least, despite all redeeming proofs of tenderness and sincerity, to
suffer some drastic punishment. Guilty love does not go unresolved and morality,
at the end of the play, must be avenged. Perhaps the Princess is, indeed, secretly
haunted by such torments for we find her more than once mildly shocked by her
lack of any feeling of repentance and by her absurd willingness to risk everything,
to follow her lover anywhere...if only he had some place to go! But what no
doubt worries her more—and here she typically reflects the preoccupations of a
milieu and an age concerned with *paraître* more than *être*—is reputation.
However routine the game of lovers and mistresses may have become in
eighteenth-century French aristocratic circles, it still retained its ground rules.
Appearances, above all else, had to be kept up, and as we listen in on the
century's worldly gossip, we are sometimes prepared to believe that the first
words of a husband on discovering his wife *en flagrant délit* had to be: "What if
someone else had seen you!" In fact, the Princess is numbly aware, finally, of
having sacrificed everything to a guilty passion: she has put at risk her own
reputation, that of her family, a great family whose members were notorious on
both the Bouillon and Rohan side for insisting on marks of recognition second
only to those accorded members of the immediate royal family and the *princes
du sang*. We suspect, however, that the problem never really reaches her
innermost being and remains, in any case, a social rather than a moral concern.

With all that, other questions come to mind....We wonder about her marriage.
Was it unhappy? It was arranged, of course, and with the blessing of the King of
France, who had personally involved himself in plans for the Princess's marriage
on at least two earlier occasions. Such arrangements were a fairly routine part of
higher political, financial, or diplomatic policy and were quite often made
without consulting the individuals most immediately concerned. The fortunate
ones would eventually find pleasure and fulfilment in what was first embraced
as duty. As for the others, while it was officially assumed that husband and wife

would come to love each other, there was also in these Crébillonesque times a remarkable degree of unspoken freedom to seek one's diversions elsewhere: "Les infidélités courent à Paris prodigieusement," the fashionable novelist, no doubt with some hyperbole, tells us: "c'est comme une maladie épidémique. Dieu veuille nous en garantir, mais jamais les commerces amoureux n'ont été de si courte durée, soit que les faveurs se refusent avec trop d'opiniâtreté, ou qu'elles s'accordent trop promptement, tout est fini en moins de quinze jours."[3]

That rather well-known observation—and there are many others in much the same vein to be found in eighteenth-century French literature—may have applied in certain aristocratic circles. We are not easily convinced, however, that such was the private world of our two lovers. Prince Charles Edward, whatever his later amorous exploits and achievements, was, in 1747, not a seasoned roué. Not only was this his first romance, it marked as well the abandonment of a long-standing vow of chastity, taken years before as a gesture of dedication and single-minded commitment to his great mission—part of his preparations for the day when he, like a knight of old, would vanquish all his enemies. It may be true that the charms of the Princess found an ally as well in the Prince's currently disheartened state of mind, brought on by the continuing odour of defeat after Culloden and especially by the pious treason of his brother Henry, secretly abetted by his father. Here was indeed a perverse avenue of requital! Perhaps, too, there was the pragmatic notion that a little hell-raising with naughty French ladies could only help to shake from his image any clinging vestiges of a Romish piety that could cost him many red-blooded supporters in Protestant England. He would, after all, soon convert to the Anglican faith and make desperate efforts to seek out a Protestant marriage for just such opportunistic reasons! But we know also from the undoubtedly authentic reflections of his own tender sentiments conveyed in the early letters of the Princess, as well as more directly in one or two "outside" sources, that much more than a tactical affection was involved and that his awakening love for the Princess was, like hers for him, spontaneous, overpowering, and, for a time, total. The first stages of the affair remind us, in fact, far more of the early chapters of an old sentimental romance than the beginning of a novel by Crébillon *fils*.

As for the Princess, though she is young and impulsive, perhaps something of a social butterfly to begin with, possibly even the more innocent variety of coquette, she hardly corresponds to our notion of the sophisticated libertine; nor is there any evidence to suggest that she is brazenly *experte*. Although, like her royal lover, she is sensual in the extreme[4] and given to almost fervent indulgence of her sexual appetites (a minor violation, incidentally, of the normal literary *bienséances* since even in the Age of Elegance ladies were not really supposed to savour love in that virile fashion), one doubts that there could have been anything like a planned initial *séduction* by either party. How it began, who wrote the first note, stole the first kiss, who was the pursuer and who the pursued will, in all probability, forever remain a mystery. They are months into the affair by the time they make the delightful discovery that their love for each other was born even before the Prince's departure for Scotland, proof enough that nothing casually untoward had been articulated early on. Certainly, they are both rashly adventurous, with ardent high spirits, and both are open to reckless initiatives. It seems probable, nevertheless, that their "affair" remained for a substantial period of time a matter of awkward unspoken feelings. Charles Edward, especially, was ill at ease in polished society. One doubts somehow that their love came to fruition as the climax of a fashionably shallow courtship, complete with the mannered rituals of precious salon patter, hardened persiflage, discreet encounters in public gardens or masked balls, and culminating finally in the usual felicities of the *carosse de remise*. We sense much innocence and inexperience in the nascent love of these two cousins, overtaken one late summer evening in a magnificent château near Evreux or in a quiet country house at Saint-Ouen by an almost involuntary *surprise de l'amour*, much in the style of a Marivaux plot. Though they are helped along by clever conniving servants (his valet, Daniel O'Brien, was perhaps the only person in the world Charles Edward ever completely trusted), who again remind us of their counterparts in the love comedies of the day, their attachment does not depend for nourishment on any compulsion to rebel against an oppressive family structure— give or take one understandably perturbed mother-in-law and, possibly, the Prince's injured feelings toward his own father throughout. We can be fairly certain too that the obligatory cuckolding of an overweening or brutal husband is not at issue. Quite the contrary, the husband, barely twenty-one, strangely gentle and diffident, in fact, is also the lover's companion and comrade. Nothing we know about him—and we know very little—suggests that as a husband he was either notoriously unfaithful or incredibly *complaisant*. The Princess's father too is seen as full of understanding and is much loved and admired by both his daughter and, in the beginning at least, by his distinguished nephew.

The Princess's letters soon reveal how this idyll, or, to continue with our literary analogy, this *roman de l'amour goût* or *de l'amour divertissement* as critics of the age would have classified it, is transformed with fatal rapidity into a *roman de l'amour passion*, or, more fittingly still, a love tragedy, carrying us far away from Marivaux to the hazardous precincts of Racine. Certainly, Crébillon's promiscuous formula: "On se plaît, on se prend. S'ennuie-t-on l'un avec l'autre? on se quitte avec tout aussi peu de cérémonie que l'on s'est pris...Et jamais on ne se brouille....L'amour n'est entré pour rien dans tout cela,"[5] does not describe their passion. The initially enchanted Prince all too soon becomes the cruelly suspicious lover, and not with the sham jealousy of a confident gallant who expects to be answered in kind by the equally conventional coquettishness of a playful mistress. In fact, what must have been extremely distressing and angry scenes of jealousy and—to use the Princess's own words—*duretés* foretell the worst of the brawling public spectacles later with Clementina Walkinshaw, the drunken beatings, and even the delicately balanced little bells suspended from chairs surrounding the couple's bed to warn the jealous lover of imagined rivals in the night. We sense already that Charles Edward will one day more than merit his Alfieri! At heart, he was a soldier—made for war, not love. Unfortunately, in both love and war, his luck was abominable.

But that kind of retribution was still far off in the future. Relishing the freshness of the Prince's first romance, the Princess is only too willing to comply with her lover's every demand, never showing the slightest hesitation or artful coyness—and, some will say, without displaying a grain of legitimate pride, dignity, or self-esteem. Though he will deny it later on, and even assert the contrary, the Prince insists throughout on acting in such a way as to let the whole world know that the Princess has nothing more to refuse him. On the other hand, as the victim of an all-consuming passion, she is willing to pay whatever price is necessary. An aesthetic if not a moral requirement of the popular romances of the day was that the suffering heroine, if unlucky enough to be left unrescued by an opportune death, should be granted at least sufficient pride to carry her securely past such storms of cruelty and jealousy and safe too from ultimate debasement, unworthy tears, and all indecent pleas and supplications to an unreasonable and cruel lover. Something had to survive intact in the shattered ruins of a well-tested noble soul, the possibility at least of rebirth and growth, the bitter fruit of much suffering.

Was it the fate of the Princess to go on begging for crumbs of affection, groveling for her lover's pity, without ever experiencing a redeeming sense of anger, the power finally to tell the merciless object of her affection to be on his way? The letters make us aware of her many self-contradictions, and we know that she is capable of expressing both hope and despair in the same breath. But they leave us uncertain that her capacity for noble indignation matched her powers of submissive devotion. Did she, in the end, achieve a victorious *prise de conscience* after suffering the destruction of each tender illusion in the repertory of passion? Was there, at least for her, a salutary moral climax to the affair?

Without providing clear answers to those key questions, the sharply focussed tragedy of the letters is suddenly extinguished, and the heroine is torn, we know not how, from her lingering obsession. The once-converging elements of tragedy now broaden into a diffusely panoramic novel of everyday life: their child is born, is legitimized, and, not long after, dies; a new mistress for the Prince appears on the scene, more mature and experienced in the ways of the world and ready to entangle for a time her fortunes in the vicissitudes of the Young Pretender's hopeless cause; the war that Charles Edward so hoped would continue comes inevitably to an end; the Treaty of Aix-la-Chapelle is signed and the hero, much against his will, is suddenly and ignominiously yanked from centre stage. Several decades later it will all degenerate to the point where an aging, bloated Charles Edward, claiming the title "Charles III" but spurned as such even by the Pope, will send, from the other side of the Alps, routine and trivially affable New Year's greetings to his once passionate Princess.

But all that, for the most part, is the more imposing story of Bonnie Prince Charlie. Such diffuse external happenings—the stuff of history and biography—will be examined in the main body of this study. They have been ignored up to this point, wittingly and in full awareness of the risks, on the grounds of their irrelevance to the fated internal workings of the Princess's passion. They tell us nothing certain about the moral salvation of, not merely a *maîtresse délaissée*, but an archetypal *femme abandonnée*. Was that salvation achieved in struggle, and not simply thrust upon her by circumstance? Possibly, on balance, the Princess does not measure up to the full dimensions of a tragic heroine. Perhaps, because of her exalted rank and the enormous social risks she takes, we become too easily impressed by a merely quantitative notion of her final sacrifice? Perhaps nowhere in her being was there sufficient strength to resist the forces that worked to destroy her, nothing to ensure a final victory in defeat, through a process of growth in moral stature and dignity. A struggle too one-sided would leave us not with a noble tragedy but only the pathetic tale of a snivelling victim totally overwhelmed by meaningless circumstances. The Princess admittedly *felt* too deeply and rarely ever thought. Horace Walpole, a witty contemporary (and no friend) of the Prince once construed that as the essential distinction between the two major dramatic genres—the world being a comedy to those who think, a tragedy to those who feel. Doubt remains. And yet, in the end, many readers may find themselves willing to recognize at least some of the classical elements of tragedy in her brief story of despair and defeat. Not just a random happening, her struggle had its own fatal logic and was the inescapable consequence of a nature all too human, caught up in an overwhelming passion. We cannot, in aesthetic annoyance, dismiss it as banal merely because the heroine has the bad grace to survive catastrophe and continue on with the mundane events of a conventional life. The word *conventional* is not, moreover, entirely appropriate here: for her, spontaneity, joy, and innocence could certainly no longer form part of it. This may indeed have been nothing more than the Prince's first love affair; it was very probably her last. When, for example, we come to look at the Princess's final will and testament, written out over thirty years later in the same naive hand that composed these love letters, we experience little difficulty in imagining that a life of domestic duty, inner repose, and piety filled most of these intervening years. The tranquillity, the flatness of such quiet survival may be of little interest to those who have shared, through her love letters, her most secret moments of passion, torment, and crisis. The Princess nevertheless remains a touching figure, not entirely overshadowed by the legendary hero to whom she so trustingly gave all of her love and who, not six months after the birth of their son, would himself face—with greater defiance but certainly with less calm and dignity—another kind of exile and, ultimately, an empty destiny of wandering, diminishment, and final defeat.

rope in the Mid-Eighteenth Century
owing the Routes of the Princesse de Bouillon to Poland
d of Charles Edward Stuart to Scotland.

is-Zolkiew itinerary _____

e Prince's route to and from Scotland ....✕.....✕.....✕..

I

From Paris to Zolkiew

IN SEPTEMBER 1735, Marie-Charlotte Sobieska, Duchesse de Bouillon, *très haute et très puissante Princesse Royale de Pologne et du Grand Duché de Lithuanie*, left the safety and comfort of her imposing residence on the Quai Malaquais with the intention of returning briefly to her native Poland to attempt a reconciliation with her father, the Prince Royal, James-Louis Sobieski. She had come to France twelve years before, a prize catch in the marriage plans of the ambitious Bouillon family. The Sobieski name was legendary: her grandfather, King John III, had earned everlasting fame for himself and his countrymen by his personal triumph at Vienna in 1683. There, almost in the tradition of medieval knighthood, European civilization and Christianity had been saved from the Ottoman hordes.

Unfortunately, Poland had fallen on darker days since that famous victory, and now a civil war was raging. September 1735 seemed indeed an ill-chosen time for the Duchesse to be travelling back to her homeland: the signs of economic, cultural, and moral decline were everywhere. External terror and internal intrigue ruled a land that hovered perpetually on the brink of a new Dark Age. The war of succession sparked two years earlier by the rival claims of different nations and diverse national parties after the death of the Saxon King Augustus II had not yet ended. The French had backed, though not wholeheartedly, the renewed pretensions of Louis XV's father-in-law, Stanislas Leszczynski, against Russian and Austrian support for Augustus III. The conflict was, however, winding down, and only a few weeks after the departure of the Duchesse, a preliminary accord was signed. The final compromise settlement, granting recognition to Augustus III as King of Poland and titular rights to Stanislas in Lorraine, was not achieved for another year or more. In the end, France's honour was appeased, but official diplomatic relations between the two countries remained almost non-existent. Little help could be expected if there was trouble along the way.

But the Duchesse was no ordinary traveller. She was connected either by blood ties or marriage with most of the reigning families of Europe and could expect a warm reception at all the courts along her route. When she reached Mannheim, for example, she was given a royal welcome by her uncle, the Elector Palatine, who hastened to confer, in absentia, his highest decoration on her young son, the Prince de Turenne. From his camp at Heidelberg, Prince Eugene of Savoy even wrote a solicitous note to her husband, Charles-Godefroy de La Tour d'Auvergne, regretting his inability to come to meet with the Duchesse. Everyone was astonished at the daring of her travel plans: "On me fait trembler pour mon voyage pour la Pologne," she wrote to her husband in her somewhat approximate French, "a cause des tems presente, mais je marme de constance et de fermette; je de trop bon principe pour faire ce voyage pour que je puisse Craindre."[1] Readers familiar with the escape from British-inspired detention in 1719 of the Duchesse's younger sister, Maria-Clementina, on her way to marry James III, *de jure* King of Great Britain, will recognize in Marie-Charlotte's tone the stubborn courage of a Sobieski princess.

For the Duchesse and her husband the importance of undertaking this hazardous voyage could scarcely be exaggerated, and even though the war was not yet over, she had felt compelled to set out at the earliest possible opportunity. Maria-Clementina had died in January that year in Rome, leaving Marie-Charlotte as the only surviving child of the aging Prince Royal, whose enormous land holdings in Silesia and Poland, great sums of money owed by the Polish State, and family jewels (including the Polish crown jewels) had suddenly become a matter of grave concern and possible opportunity. There was also the likelihood that a royal marriage could be arranged for their ten-year-old daughter, the Princess Louise, either with the eldest or the second son of Augustus III. Finally, and perhaps most important of all, there was the prospect of securing through a Polish inheritance sufficient funds to settle the enormous debts of her profligate courtier-husband.

Despite those debts, the Bouillon family figured among the most honoured and prestigious in the country.[2] It had given France one of her most celebrated generals, the great Turenne, and from father to son the Dukes of Bouillon traditionally held the important position of Grand Chambellan de France. Emmanuel-Théodose, the Duc's father, had nevertheless felt the need to enhance the family's prestige by arranging for a brilliant alliance with the House of Sobieski. In his journal entries of the day, Saint-Simon snobbishly but grudgingly admitted that the old Duc had managed a triumphant coup by arranging for the marriage of his eldest son, Frédéric-Maurice-Casimir, Prince of Turenne, to a granddaughter of the great Polish hero "qui avoit occupé longtemps le trône de Pologne, et en avoit illustré la couronne par ses grandes actions."[3] The usually caustic Mathieu Marais also referred admiringly to the marriage, "qui devoit tant faire d'honneur à la maison de Bouillon, car cette princesse est alliée de fort près à toutes les couronnes de l'Europe."[4] Emmanuel-Théodose, who had recently lost his third wife, had himself been intent, in spite of her father's opposition, on marrying Marie-Casimire, the eldest of the three Sobieski princesses. She, unfortunately, died on 18 May 1723.[5] "Il arrive aux Bouillon ce qui n'arrive point à d'autres," Marais commented in September of that year: "Le duc de Bouillon et le prince de Turenne, son fils, doivent épouser les deux princesses Sobieski. L'aînée meurt, et voilà le père veuf sans l'avoir épousée; la cadette obtient, avec de la peine, le consentement de l'empereur, dont elle est cousine germaine." Marais' record of strange happenings continues: Marie-Charlotte arrived in Strasbourg in late September; the young Prince de Turenne rushed to join her but he was the victim of an accident almost as soon as he arrived: "Il épouse le lendemain; il se presse de consommer le mariage; il lui prend une rougeole causée par sa blessure et son épuisement, et il meurt le 1 octobre. Et voilà où a abouti ce grand mariage, tant désiré, tant souhaité." The chronicler's next comment, echoed in even greater detail by Saint-Simon, is rich with implications for our understanding of future events. Marie-Charlotte Sobieska had sacrificed much for this marriage: "Elle a refusé le Prince de Piémont; elle eût pu épouser le roi de France et est d'aussi bonne maison que l'Infante, hors qu'elle n'est pas fille de Roi. On la dit désespérée." In fact, one wonders if Marie-Charlotte, a tall, witty and very attractive redhead who was given to flirting outrageously with her many admirers at her father's court in Ohlau, would have been judged sufficiently submissive to become the wife of the young Louis XV. In his search for a royal bride for James Edward Stuart, Charles Wogan had earlier decided that she would probably be too much of a handful for the over-pensive and melancholic Pretender, and so he had concentrated his attentions on her younger sister.[6] Mme de Prie and her lover, the Duc de Bourbon, who had assumed power in France at the death of the Regent in 1723, no doubt had in mind someone more easily manipulated and humbly grateful. Certainly, Maria Leszczynska, the plain and unsophisticated daughter of the impoverished Stanislas, fitted their specific requirements rather more exactly, and her eventual marriage to the fifteen-year-old King of France in 1725 provoked much sneering comment in the French capital.[7]

But if Marie-Charlotte was well aware of her own worth, so too was her father. She came, first of all, with an extremely rich dowry made up of annuities and other credits amounting to well over one million livres. A counter-dowry was also part of the arrangement, however, and Marie-Charlotte was required to give up any further claims on the Prince Royal's estate, without prejudice, of course, to any additional bequests that his paternal love might later induce him to make in favour of a deserving daughter. James Sobieski further insisted that if his daughter died childless, or if her husband died and the Princess decided to remarry, the dowry would have to be returned. Her voyage to France was to be entirely without cost to her father; the Bouillons would be required to send a confessor, ladies-in-waiting, and all other servants needed to conduct the Princess in safety and comfort to Paris. That had been the arrangement when the Prince's sister, Theresa Cunegunda, had gone off in 1694 to marry Maximilian Emmanuel, the Elector Duke of Bavaria, and also when Maria-Clementina had set out for Rome to become the *legitimate* Queen of England.

The Bouillons were flattered to find themselves hobnobbing with such a distinguished class of royalty—Prince James's last condition must have convinced both father and son of that! "Je demande de fortes asseurances," the Prince Royal had insisted, "que la Princesse, ma fille, ne fera point sa cour aux Princesses du Sang, ny ne cedera le pas aux legitimées & qu'elle ne donnera la main chez elle à Personne excepté aux Princesses du Sang; ou bien pour eviter tous les inconveniens, Elle ne viendra à Paris qu'incognito & demeurera la plûpart sur les terres de la Maison de Bouillon."[8] Little wonder then that her arrival at Strasbourg was greeted by a 60-gun salute! "Toute la cavallerie et les dragons de la garnison depuis le pont du rhin jusqu'à la ville etoient le sabre a la main avec touts les officiers a la teste et depuis la porte de la ville jusqu'à la maison du prince Frederic, toute l'infanterie etoit rangée en haie"—So wrote the young Prince de Turenne to his father, Emmanuel-Théodose, on 25 September 1723, five days after the marriage ceremony. One week later, to everyone's consternation, he was dead, a victim of smallpox.[9]

The old Duc could scarcely have felt less despair than the widow. His reaction, nevertheless, was quick-witted and to the point. Saint-Simon takes up the narrative of the arrangements for her to marry the Duc's younger son:

> Personne de la famille n'étoit allé à Strasbourg que son frere (Henri-Oswald, later Cardinal d'Auvergne); la mariée y étoit arrivée en fort léger équipage; on comptoit l'amener tout de suite à Paris, quand la maladie de son mari les arrêta. Dès que la nouvelle en vint, le duc de Bouillon pensa aussitôt au mariage de son second fils, si elle devenoit veuve, et à tout événement dépêcha le comte d'Evreux[10] à Strasbourg pour lui persuader de continuer son voyage dans l'espérance de gagner son consentement. Ils y réussirent, et la gardèrent tantôt chez eux à Pontoise, tantôt dans un couvent du lieu, et n'en laissèrent approcher personne qui la pût imprudemment détromper des grandeurs qu'elle croyoit aller épouser. Ils négocièrent en Silésie pour avoir le consentement, puis à Rome pour la dispense, où il n'est question que du plus ou moins d'argent, qu'on n'avoit pas dessein d'épargner. Enfin le mariage se fit en avril 1724, fort en particulier, à cause du récent veuvage.[11]

Unfortunately, the marriage on 2 April of the twenty-six-year-old widow with eighteen-year-old Charles-Godefroy de La Tour, despite many tearful pleas, finally had to take place without the consent of Marie-Charlotte's father.

Cheated of his legal right to claim forfeiture of the dowry, the Prince Royal was outraged, and he retaliated immediately by cutting off all communications with his daughter. Thus, her prospects for a hoped-for reconciliation during the trip back to Poland eleven years after her second marriage were anything but certain.

But in 1724 it was clear to all that, with or without the Prince Royal's consent, Emmanuel-Théodose had managed another master stroke. By means of the unusual second marriage, the Bouillon family had been spared a punitive financial loss. It had not been easy to arrange. As Barbier rather delicately points out, it had required "une dispense très considérable de la cour de Rome."[12] Unlike the Pope, Marie-Charlotte asked for nothing although she clearly had the Bouillons at her mercy. Her alternatives, after all, were few: a life of tedium in one of her erratic father's castles or, worse still, in a Saxon nunnery. Besides, she had quickly come to like her late husband's brother.

The very next year Emmanuel-Théodose managed another triumph, taking, in his fourth venture into matrimony, Mlle de Guise as his bride. The new Duchesse de Bouillon, Louise-Henriette Françoise de Lorraine-Harcourt (1707-1737), was younger than his new daughter-in-law and ten years younger even than his surviving son. Trouble would eventually result, but at least the first twenty-four hours of the marriage were auspicious. Marais reveals a few of the details:

La goutte l'a pris par tout le corps, le jour de sa noce; on le portoit à quatre et il a dit: "Ou qu'on me fasse mourir, ou qu'on me laisse marier." Il s'est marié, a fort bien fait son devoir, et a envoyé dire à sa belle-mère qu'il n'avoit que vingt ans. Le prince de Conti a dit que c'étoit un cerf à sa quatrième tête. L'Allemande [sic] que son fils a épousée et qui est une grande princesse, veut trop l'être, et, pour l'humilier, on lui a donné une belle-mère qui la fait la seconde de la maison.[13]

Whether Emmanuel-Théodose equalled on his March wedding night the no less than seven "proofs of affection" offered to Marie Leszczynska by Louis XV on the night of 5 September that same year (as reported by the Duc de Bourbon to King Stanislas the following day),[14] Marais does not say. But court and town gossips were not long in detecting signs of strain in Marie-Charlotte's marriage with young Charles-Godefroy. Saint-Simon discreetly refers to her supposed dissatisfaction with her secondary status: "On supprime ici l'étonnement où elle fut de se trouver ici bourgeoise du quai Malaquais, comme elle l'osa dire, ayant compté d'épouser un souverain, et de tenir une cour."[15] In another entry describing Marie-Charlotte's first contacts with the social world of Paris, he is even more explicit:

Quand elle commença à voir le monde et à être présentée à la cour, elle fut étrangement surprise de s'y trouver comme toutes les autres duchesses et princesses assises, et de ne primer nulle part avec toute la distinction dont on l'avoit persuadée; en sorte qu'il lui échappa plus d'une fois qu'elle avoit compté épouser un souverain, et qu'il se trouvoit que son mari et son beau-père n'étoient que deux bourgeois du quai Malaquais. Ce fut bien pis quand elle vit le Roi marié. Je n'en dirai pas davantage. Ces regrets, qu'elle ne cachoit pas, joints à d'autres mécontentements, en donnèrent beaucoup aux Bouillons. Le mariage ne fut pas heureux. La princesse, qui ne put s'accoutumer à l'unisson avec nos duchesses et princesses, encore moins à vivre avec les autres comme il falloit qu'elle s'y assujettît, se rendit solitaire et obscure.[16]

The tender sentiments expressed in Marie-Charlotte's letters to her husband from Poland more than a decade later suggest that Saint-Simon may have exaggerated her dissatisfaction somewhat. Still, any such feelings would have been augmented by knowledge of her father's continuing disapproval of the marriage and her awareness of the contrastingly brilliant situation enjoyed by her sister Maria-Clementina who was indeed married to a sovereign of sorts and who held court in Rome. Perhaps it was some comfort to Marie-Charlotte, to learn in November 1725 that even in the Eternal City things were not going all that smoothly, Clementina having suddenly abandoned husband and children in order to retire to a convent for a two-year period of huff and hysteria, thereby doing serious damage to the personal image of James III and to the political cause of the Stuarts. On the other hand, Saint-Simon's description of Marie-Charlotte's life as *solitaire* and *obscure* seems entirely accurate. The birth of Louise on 15 August 1725 (no one wanted a girl!) and that of her brother, Godefroy-Charles-Henry in 1728 appear to have been the only notable events in her career during this period. We learn from the gossip of servants later on that her husband stopped sleeping with her sometime around 1730,[17] showing, in that respect, less endurance and devotion to duty than Louis XV, who apparently did not give up marital relations with the Queen of France until the birth in 1737 of Madame Louise, baptized by the King himself as "Madame *dernière*."[18]

In 1730 the old Duc Emmanuel-Théodose died. Now two *Duchesses de Bouillon* reigned in the palatial residence on the Quai Malaquais, the newly widowed dowager duchess and Marie-Charlotte. But if the life of Marie-Charlotte could be fairly described as *solitaire et obscure*, that was hardly the case with Charles-Godefroy's attractive and lively young stepmother. Unfortunately, despite marked differences in character, the two women were occasionally confused by chroniclers of the day.[19]

Readers familiar with the life of the famous eighteenth-century actress, Adrienne Le Couvreur, will have by now recognized the dowager duchess in question. A veritable *Messaline moderne*, she had already achieved notoriety before the death of her aging and gouty husband. Beautiful and dazzlingly cynical, she had rapidly accumulated a long list of lovers, including the Comte de Clermont, a *prince du sang*, the celebrated Maurice de Saxe, the actors Quinault-Dufresne and Grandval, the Opera singer Denis-François Tribou, and apparently many others, not excluding, it was rumoured, the occasional *bateleur*, knock-about comedian, or well-muscled street acrobat as ready to perform his tricks in the Duchesse's bedroom at the Hôtel de Bouillon as in the square in front of Notre-Dame. Voltaire held a very high opinion of her ability as a drama critic, and he cited her example to his friend de Moncrif in January 1732 as proof that there was "bien plus d'esprit et de goust dans ce siècle qu'on ne croit."[20] Lovers of opera will recall the most serious charge brought against Emmanuel-Théodose's last duchess, namely, that she had poisoned her rival for the Comte de Saxe's affections, Adrienne Le Couvreur.[21] The confusion in some minds as to which de Bouillon duchess was involved must have been especially disturbing to Marie-Charlotte! Barbier, noting the death in March 1730 of the Comédie Française's greatest actress, recalled at the same time the poisoning story of the preceding year and clearly referred to the suspect as the daughter of Prince James Sobieski.[22]

Opinion concerning the probable guilt of the de Bouillon Messalina has to this day remained somewhat divided. Not long after her death in March 1737, d'Argenson recalled not only her numerous affairs but also described her as *mégère et noire*: "cette princesse...était empoisonneuse et assassineuse."[23] Voltaire, who had much respect for the Duchesse and a great love for Mlle Le Couvreur, arranged for an autopsy immediately after the death of the famous actress, but it produced no evidence of poisoning and he finally dismissed the assassination story as based on nothing more than "bruits populaires qui n'ont aucun fondement."[24] There seems to be little reason today to question Voltaire's verdict. The story, however, does help to convey something of the unsavoury atmosphere of daily life at the Hôtel de Bouillon from which the devout Marie-Charlotte eventually sought escape. Moreover, although the poisoning charge may have been totally without foundation, other rumours circulating about the nymphomaniacal young widow, soon to become a sister-in-law of the Duc de Richelieu, were not. De Maurepas' *Tableau* of town and court scandal for the year 1732 took detailed note of her activities and cited a satirical song on the subject, apparently sung to the tune of *Margot la ravaudeuse*:

> Dufresne elle agaça,
> On n'en voudra rien croire;
> Mais Tribou l'engrossa,
> L'ingratte prit Grandval
> Qui bien-tôt la quitta;
> Mais Gilles la fixa.

It is unlikely that Mme de Bouillon ever bedded Gilles—the traditional buffoon character being no doubt mentioned only in order to hint at the great lady's wide-ranging taste for players. The last verse contains, however, a reference to Marie-Charlotte's husband and mother-in-law that must have been more disquieting for the distinguished granddaughter of King John III:

> On ne peut se méprendre
> En parlant de Bouillon,
> Qui met beau-fils et gendre
> Dessous son cotillon
> Et bien sottement folle,
> Se livre à tout venant
> Mais sans tempéramment.

Maurepas added that the new duke, "beau-fils de madame la duchesse dont il s'agit, et M. le duc de la Trémoïlle, son gendre,"[25] passent pour aimer leur belle-mère qui sans véritable passion donna des preuves de beaucoup de penchant pour la variété."[26]

Though the *Mémoires* just quoted are somewhat apocryphal, the reported liaison between Charles-Godefroy and his stepmother was authentic enough. Even before he reached his mid-twenties, Marie-Charlotte's husband had become notorious for his wenching, gambling, and general penchant for drunken revelry. Maurepas records, for example, a much talked-about brawl which took place in November 1731 at Navarre, the famous Bouillon country seat near Evreux, between the young Duc de Bouillon and the Duc de Durfort. Both parties suffered serious knife wounds in the incident.[27]

Such disorderly behaviour, however mortifying it must have been for Marie-Charlotte, was apparently not enough to keep the young Duc from his functions at Court where, succeeding his father in 1730, he now enjoyed the triple prerogatives of Grand Chambellan, Grand Maître and Grand Ecuyer, along with the privilege of being able to take leave without the King's permission. The *Mémoires* of the Duc de Luynes, the most detailed and reliable chronicler of day-to-day happenings at the court of Louis XV, contain frequent references to Charles-Godefroy's official activities and testify as well to his close personal friendship with his royal master. It was not uncommon, for example, later in the decade, for Louis to invite his Grand Chambellan *en tiers* to intimate suppers with the current royal mistress,[28] and we frequently hear of the Duc joining the King in a game of *quadrille, piquet, trictrac*, or *cavagnole*.[29] Stakes at the royal gaming table were high and Charles-Godefroy does not seem to have been the luckiest of gamblers. De Luynes notes that on one occasion the Grand Chambellan lost nearly 100,000 livres to the King[30] even though he already had debts amounting to well over one million. That financial burden, inherited partly from Emmanuel-Théodose, went hand in hand, however, with ownership of many fine properties, including the Hôtel de Bouillon, then one of the most impressive noble residences in Paris. Such was the splendour of its location and its spaciousness that in 1729 the King of Spain asked to make use of it for a celebration intended to be "au-dessus de ce qu'on a jamais vu en Europe,"[31] in honour of the Dauphin's birth. The Duc's most prized country residence, the Château de Navarre, was even more impressive and constituted a unique show place where the King was happy to be invited to the stag hunt. To mark such distinguished visits, the roadway through the forest would be brightly illuminated for several leagues. As a final touch, the many canals, waterfalls, courtyards, and gardens traced out by Le Nôtre, as well as the huge building designed by Mansart in 1686 and rivalling in dimensions and magnificence but not in beauty and grace the royal residence at Marly, would also be "prodigieusement éclairés."[32]

Such then were some of the ambiguous elements in Marie-Charlotte's life left behind when she set out for Poland. Her young husband, eight years her junior, was obviously a man of many contradictions. Though something of a hell-raiser, he found himself in good company, being not very different from his master, Louis XV. In general, he was thought of as a man of honour and integrity. All of Paris had heard in December 1730, for example, how Emmanuel-Théodose before his death had informed Charles-Godefroy of a long-forgotten peccadillo. The old Duc, many years before, had fathered a bastard son, and he had kept sight of him since his birth. The son was now a hosier in Paris and completely ignorant of his noble ancestry. Emmanuel-Théodose, not wishing to grant him an official bequest in his will, had discreetly placed 10,000 livres in the hands of the Curé of Saint-Sulpice to be paid anonymously after his death. Charles-Godefroy had agreed to see to it that the order was carried out faithfully. True to his word, he stopped one day by the hosier's shop only to discover, after a number of inquiries, that the tradesman lived in rather modest circumstances. Further questioning revealed that he had indeed recently received a small anonymous inheritance of between 500 and 1500 livres, brought to him by an unknown priest. A noisy confrontation between the Duc and the Curé of Saint-Sulpice followed, and soon the hosier received the balance of his legacy.[33]

The anecdote is probably true. However, as we turn now to follow the course of Marie-Charlotte's lonely adventures in her Polish homeland over the next several years, there will be more than one occasion when the Duc's conduct toward her may cause us to wonder whether the story does not, in fact, flatter him a little.

Saint-Simon implies that the Duchesse's departure was the direct result of her unwillingness to tolerate any longer her difficult marital situation in Paris, adding that Marie-Charlotte's husband was only too glad to get rid of her so easily.[34] De Luynes, in almost daily contact at Court with the Grand Chambellan, confirms that view. On the other hand, such assertions are difficult to reconcile with the affectionate tone of Marie-Charlotte's letters, which refer constantly to her apparently much-loved husband and the two dear children she has had to leave behind. She also expresses deep regret at having to leave her uncle, the Comte d'Evreux, who had been her mentor and special protector ever since her arrival in France.

Accompanying the Duchesse was the Duc's right-hand man, Messire Antoine-Guy-Henri Guéroult de Bacqueville, Governor of the *duché* and *souveraineté* of Bouillon (which the eighteenth-century dukes of Bouillon almost never visited) and a Knight of the military order of Saint Louis. More than a decade earlier, he had gone to Rome to arrange for the difficult papal dispensation which had allowed Charles-Godefroy to marry his brother's widow. Much delicate work of a similar nature no doubt awaited him in Poland, but he was not looking forward to it. He had already spent many years in the service of both Emmanuel-Théodose and Charles-Godefroy, and he would have preferred not to leave the solid comforts of life on the Quai Malaquais. A confirmed gastronome, he was worried that war-torn Poland would have little to offer in the way of good food, good wine, and good tobacco. The truth was that he was getting to be a bit of a fuss-budget. Already he was uneasy about who would be running the show with old Prince James: himself or the Duchesse? He neither trusted nor liked Marie-Charlotte. His role would be to see that the Duc's interests (not to mention his own) were well served. He knew very well that the Duc cared nothing for his wife. Charles-Godefroy had made that clear over the years. He was to report everything, in detail, directly to the Duc. That, at least, pleased him for he did like to write letters, the more long-winded, the better. Finally, if along the way there was an opportunity to play Iago, he understood that he was to seize it. His master, of course, had not told him that in so many words, but the bluff Chevalier was anything but slow-witted and took broad hints without difficulty. Already he was looking forward to the rewards that would await him on his return.

The Duchesse also wrote letters to the Duc during the long journey. They were shorter, far less grammatical, and less frequent than de Bacqueville's, but it is essential nevertheless to catch something of the emotional flavour of Marie-Charlotte's style and to note how much (religious fervour aside) that of her daughter Louise, writing to her lover Charles Edward Stuart twelve years later, was to resemble it. The first, from Mannheim, presents a good example:

> Je nait qu le tems que de vous dire mon Roy que plus je mesloigne, plus je sent lesloignement Cruelle davec toy mon Coeur. Je fairoit mes désvotion a Prague pour prier Dieu qu'il fasse que mon absence soit cour et que je fasse les affaires selon nos desieres et pour de pouvoir donner des preuves de mon sincere et tendre attachement pour toy trop heureuse si dans la suitte je pouvez te faire connoitre combien je t'aime....

Adieu, cher mary, je t'embrasse de tous mon coeur et ame et suis toute a
toy pour la vie. Noublie pas ta pauvre fame.[35]

A second letter followed within a few days. The Elector at Mannheim was
being more than kind, but she would leave all of those details to de Bacqueville.
What she had to say of her love for her husband was more important:

> Je veut te parle que de toy et de moy cher Roy. Je te jure si je suis encor
> longtems absent de toy je ne viveray pas....Donne moy a Breslaw de tes
> nouvelles et conte sur ta famme plus que sur toy meme. Je ne vous ay pas
> encor fait mes remerciment sur ce que vous mande a Baqueville ou vous me
> temoigne une entiere confiance. Je vous jure que vous le devez, jose le dire,
> par les sentimens que je pour toy et nabusant pas de tes bontes et confiance.
> Adieu cher mary, noublie jamais ta famme qui taime plus quelle ne te peut
> dire. De tes nouvelles et souvent. Mes compliment a mes amyes. Qu'il
> veuille bien ce souvenir de moy.[36]

Their parting in Paris had apparently generated the tenderest of scenes: the
Duc, overburdened with a crushing debt, was filled with great hopes that the
Duchesse's visit to her father would provide a solution to his financial problems.
Since her marriage to Charles-Godefroy had resulted in Marie-Charlotte's
catastrophic repudiation, reconciliation was certain to be difficult. On the other
hand, with the death of her sister, Maria-Clementina, there was no time to lose
since the aging Prince Royal might decide to leave everything— his rich
possessions at Ohlau in Silesia, along with enormous land holdings in Poland—to
his two grandsons in Rome, Prince Charles Edward Stuart and his brother
Henry, Duke of York. Some means had to be found to restore Marie-Charlotte's
legitimate rights of inheritance, if not directly, then perhaps indirectly through
their daughter Louise who would soon be eligible for a brilliant marriage.
Louise's grandfather was naturally anxious that the Sobieski bloodline not die
out with him, and he had offered to sponsor her marriage to a son of the Polish
King. The mission on which Marie-Charlotte and de Bacqueville had embarked
would thus involve arduous negotiations and require the utmost secrecy. Code
names only were to be used in de Bacqueville's correspondence with the Duc:
the Duchesse would be referred to as *ma tante*, the Duc, *son Neveu*; Prince
James was *Renaudin*, and his negotiator, Canon Mocki became *la Mouche*.
James III was *Jules Romain*, and the Stuart princes were to be called *les Jules*.
As for the central figure of the piece, Marie-Louise-Henriette-Jeanne de la Tour
d'Auvergne, Princesse de Bouillon, she would be referred to as *Mlle d'Orveaux*—
not a little confusing since that also happened to be the real name of the niece of
Mlle de Minières, Louise's governess.

Despite the many opportunities to enjoy lavish receptions and receive honours along the way, the travellers made as much haste as possible, arriving finally on 10 October in Breslau. There they stopped to await developments before pushing on to Zolkiew,[37] the Polish residence of Prince James Sobieski, not far from the city of Leopold or Lvov. Conditions for travel were grim: the war was not yet over and the harsh Eastern European winter threatened to be soon upon them. They had suffered countless vehicle breakdowns, had been forced more than once to go on foot in the rain, and sometimes they had even been obliged to sleep on straw in dilapidated shelters. Thought had been given originally to taking Louise along since she would necessarily figure in any negotiations, but the hazards of such a long and dangerous journey had seemed too forbidding and in the end she had been left safely behind in the care of the nuns at her convent in the Rue du Cherche-Midi.

On reaching Ohlau, Marie-Charlotte was extremely disappointed to discover that no letter awaited her from Prince James, welcoming his daughter back at long last. The old man's fury had lasted for more than eleven years and was not to be so quickly dissipated. She then sent a letter appealing directly to her father, but it went unanswered. Finally, it was decided that de Bacqueville should be sent on ahead to try his luck. The Duc's emissary arrived in Zolkiew in mid-November and was granted an audience on the strict condition that the subject of the Prince Royal's daughter would not be brought up in the conversation. Matters progressed well, and soon the old man began to ask questions about his grandchildren, especially the young Princess. Why had Louise not come along? Yes, he had in mind the possibility of marrying her to the eldest son of Augustus III of Saxony, King of Poland. As for the *grande princesse*, his daughter, she had better keep her distance! It was presumptuous of her to turn up like that without her daughter. In fact, it has been reliably reported to him that she had had a cheerful and laughing look about her at Ohlau. What kind of repentance was that! Great care had to be taken and nothing could be rushed, de Bacqueville reported to the Duchesse. Meanwhile, he would do his duty, but he had to watch his step "car je suis," he continued, "à la Bastille et à l'Inquisition."[38] On the following day, the Duc's agent wrote to Saint-Gervais, his master's secretary in Paris, that he was obliged to spend hours everyday talking to the old Prince about Louise and her brother. He had now been invited to stay at the castle and took every meal with the Prince. Gaining entry for the Duchesse would, however, still require time. It was a horrendous error not to have brought along the little Princess! Her portrait had to be sent immediately, and perhaps the children could also be asked to write a little note to their grandpapa. Tears came to the old man's eyes every time they were mentioned. The Chevalier Ramsay's newly published *Histoire du Vicomte de Turenne*, dedicated to Louise's seven-year old brother, had arrived safely and was much appreciated. De Bacqueville had not yet dared, however, to hand on the Duc de Bouillon's letter.

The Duchesse, meanwhile, was growing worried and impatient. Almost no news had arrived from her husband: "Les absents ont toujours tort," she chided him, echoing the currently celebrated line from Destouches. Much to her credit, she had other complaints too: Charles-Godefroy, according to information she had recently received, had turned out one of their servants without a penny. Would he not, on humanitarian grounds, give the poor wretch a pension of some sort? "Donne-moy cette marque d'amitié. Dieu vous le rendra d'une autre côté. Ne me refusez pas cette grace ny celle d'estre persuadé de mon tendre et inviolable attachement pour vous." Soon after, she sent her husband another letter which again seems to give the lie to rumours that she had no wish to return to the Duc:

Je reçu ta cher lettre mon Roy, laquelle ma fait verser un torent de larmes. Je ne say ou j'en suis. Je ne m'acoutume point a un si cruelle esloignement. Ouy, mon coeur, si je ne fini rien jaime mieu entreprendre de men retourner par les mauvais chemin que destre si longtems absent de toy. Dieu donne que je puisse bientost exsecuter et revenir avec toy a Navarre.

Marie-Charlotte closed with the injunction that the Duc was to love their children. She was being scolded from every quarter for having left the Princess at home. In truth, she admitted she was not in any great hurry to get rid of their daughter so soon. They could afford to hold out for a good marriage. There was now specific talk, according to de Bacqueville, of marrying Louise to the eldest son of Augustus III, but he was still rather young. She had also heard other, less flattering suggestions made, but her reply was that "nostre fille est asse riche et asse de bonne maison pour faire de meilleur mariage sen sortire du pays." As soon as there was a firm commitment from the Polish king, they could give their consent, "mais sur des promesses en laire, point. Tene bon sur sa quand on vous demandera votre fille, je t'en prie, car pour estre privez d'elle pour quelle soit malheureuse jespere que vous ne consentire jamais." She was ill and uncomfortable, but she asked nothing better than to help him out with his great financial problems. Why did no one send her news of their children? He was to have portraits made of them right away and sent to her. "Je t'embrasse du fond de mon ame et suis a toy pour la vie."[39]

De Bacqueville, for the moment a loyal helper in negotiations on behalf of both the Duchesse and her husband, continued his efforts with Prince James and did his best to temper the intense stubbornness and even hatred the old man felt toward them. Leaving aside the question of the Duchesse for the moment, the Duc's envoy pointed out that Louise and her brother were not at fault and that it was not right to dishonour and debase them in the face of all Europe. Would not the Duc their father have done better to marry a poor bourgeoise if that was to be the situation? He was, after all, a grand seigneur in his own right.

De Bacqueville by then had handed on the Duc's letter, but the Prince Royal had refused to open it, and that, surely, was a mark of the greatest scorn! Not so, the old Prince had replied, "Je l'aime et je l'estime pour sa personne...mais pourquoy a-t-il laissé partir sa femme sans une permission de moy et ne m'a-t-il pas envoyé sa fille que je demandois?" It was at this point, no doubt, that de Bacqueville began to sense that the Duc's interests (and his own) diverged considerably from those of the Duchesse whose presence in the wings seemed to be more a hindrance than a help. The conclusion of his report to the Duc was categorical: "Il est inutile de se flatter de rien faire sans le moien de la petite princesse. La grande s'est trop flattée de réussir par elle meme."[40]

At least some of the blame for the Duchesse's difficulties was being attributed by rumour to local agents of James III, who were actively pursuing the rival interests of the two Stuart princes. But whatever the cause, Marie-Charlotte's health had begun to suffer. On 17 December, she reported that she had already fainted four times, "par foiblesse, ne faisant que pleurer....Je seroit saigne lundy. Ah, cher coeur, qu'on a du male dans ce monde mais je mon esperance en Dieu quil ne mabandonnera pas dans tous ceci." Now her father had apparently let it be known that he would have welcomed her with open arms if only she had brought Louise to him; the Duchesse, however, again warned her husband that their daughter's happiness was not to be sacrificed to mere financial gain: "Je t'en conjure de tenir bon, que tu ne l'enverra pas n'ayant de surte sur de son sort." Now also a new note of complaint was sounded: all of her letters from the Duc were being opened first by de Bacqueville as the primary recipient. It was obvious that this would cause trouble. Success with her father, on the other hand, was not far off: her illness had come to his attention and she was informed that he would shortly take pity on her. It would not be a moment too soon! She was nearly out of money, and she had many servants and horses to feed. She had gone to Jaroslaw, only twelve leagues from Zolkiew, travelling incognito as a countess; even so, she had been recognized. The Duc could rest assured that if all of these hardships had been for her benefit alone, she would long since have abandoned the undertaking and returned to the side of her beloved husband. Poland was a horrible place: "quel chien de pays!" she exclaimed, "je ne voudroit pas y demeurer. J'aimere mieu estre, si Dieu me pardon, chien a Paris que estre Reyne ici!"[41]

At last, fortune smiled upon the Duchesse. On 22 February 1736, de Bacqueville informed Saint-Gervais that they were now all residing with the Prince Royal in the palace at Zolkiew. The old man had finally relented! But what had happened to the portraits of the children? Surely, from the time he had requested them, the entire Last Judgment could have been executed! There was a severe shortage of everything at Zolkiew. The Duchesse had promised to send some good Burgundy wine to her father. Good cooking oil was also in short supply. The mails were dreadfully slow! On 4 April he repeated his request for the portraits:

"Avez-vous songé au vin pour le prince et aux portraits des enfants? On devroit les faire écrire souvent au grand papa. Ce sont de petites choses avec quoy on l'amuse mais vous négligez tout."

The Prince Royal's marriage plans for Louise continued, but now there was talk only of a marriage with Augustus III's second eldest son, Prince Xavier, who was not yet six years old. The Duchesse, finding the disproportion of ages unsuitable, reminded Charles-Godefroy that Louise should not be sent without a firm commitment. Now, too, the Duc's special envoy began to insert subtle notes of hostility towards the Duchesse in his letters, suggesting to Saint-Gervais, for example, that Marie-Charlotte's reluctance to send for Louise was based on a desire to keep her father's inheritance entirely for herself. He simply did not believe her when she told him she had no wish to die in Poland, however sensible that seemed! Living there was bad enough! Everyone was tired and bored. The winter had been dreadfully long. It was mid-April: how he missed all those delicious spring vegetables that everyone was now gobbling up in Paris!

What troubled de Bacqueville not a little was that the Duchesse and her father rapidly developed a great affection for each other in spite of their long estrangement. She was constantly worried about her *cher papa*'s health; he, in turn, now spoke of including her along with the young Princess in his will. Why, she complained to her husband, did he not write? Why was it that only de Bacqueville received letters regularly? She would either hear from him soon or she would depart for France, provided her father was better.

It was not long after that Marie-Charlotte capitulated to her father's request to send for Louise. She informed Charles-Godefroy that she would leave the detailed arrangements up to de Bacqueville; but the Duc was not to take the decision lightly: "Tout ce que je a vous dir sur sa ce que si vous donne votre parole a mon Pere de la faire partire, de ne point changer de sentimens, parceque sa seroit afreux." If the Duc agreed to send Louise, it was to be with only a small retinue: a reliable governess (if Mlle de Minières, her regular governess, did not wish to undertake such a long journey), the maid, Lorence, and another female servant "qui sache coeffer parfaittement," two footmen, and a priest if possible. The Duc was to consult her *cher oncle*, the Comte d'Evreux, on all points. There was good news as well: a total reconciliation with her father had now taken place. She had handed on to him the Duc's letter, and he had accepted it with great joy. The Prince Royal had also instructed her to convey his most tender sentiments to the Duc and had drunk his health in great ceremony. As a result, unfortunately, she would now have to stay on in Zolkiew a little longer: "Je craint que vous ne vous accoutumée a mon absence et que vous m'oubliere entierement....Dieu donne que je puisse contribuer a votre tranquillite et rendre mes enfans heureux. Je seroit contente apres de mourire. Adieu cher mary; aime un peu ta fame, elle taime de tous son coeur."

Rumours of an impending marriage contract between Louise and Prince

Xavier had by now become European news. The Dutch gazettes even reported on some of the supposed details, stating that one of the clauses would require Prince James to make over all of his Polish lands to the young Princess. Between Zolkiew and Paris, communications continued to be extremely haphazard. On 2 May the Duchesse wrote to inform the Duc that she had just received (opened first by de Bacqueville as usual) a letter from him sent in January, at the same time as another dated 5 April! The children's portraits had still not arrived. She was astonished by his recent offer to come to Poland: much as she wanted to see him, she hoped that he would not. The boredom at Zolkiew was deadly and they were all ill. Her valet, in fact, was unlikely to survive and she herself seemed to be dying "à petit feu." She had heard that he intended to sell her *grand carosse*. He had promised that he would not do such a thing without her consent! She might be back earlier than expected, and she would need it. Would he please hug their children for her? How she looked forward to her return! Why did it seem as if she had to be absent to be loved by him? She would always prefer being with him, even if he hated her. She had had her fill of Poland: "Grand Dieu, quel pays!"

With hostilities throughout the country drawing to a close, some improvement in the physical conditions of life in Poland were, however, becoming apparent. Toward the end of May, de Bacqueville reported that regular mail services had been re-established but that the roads remained a nightmare. The difficulties of travel for anyone who was not a *grand seigneur* could not be imagined! He was, he wanted it known, extremely reluctant to stay on. If he had to he would, of course, but he would need warm clothing and a good supply of Dutch tobacco. The Duchesse was hateful! She did not really want the young Princess to come to Poland. If Louise did come, the maid Lorence would surely be accompanying her: that was some consolation, for Lorence would be able to smuggle his precious tobacco across the border under her ample skirts!

Marie-Charlotte had good reasons for hesitating to bring her daughter all the way from Paris to Zolkiew. She had been away now for nine months, and she was beginning to sense that her husband was using her as a mere pawn in the affair. She found it increasingly difficult to trust him. He had asked her, for example, to send him a document whereby she legally gave up her property rights; it was to be purely a matter of form or convenience, and for her protection she was to receive from him a *contre-lettre*, secretly cancelling out the effect of her renunciation. For some reason, however, the Duc was unwilling to send the *contre-lettre* first, and in retaliation, Marie-Charlotte, to her husband's great irritation, decided to withhold the needed document. How little he seemed to care about the sacrifices she was making for him! Moreover, she was certain that it would all be a wasted effort. She had heard from the Abbé Mocki, her father's negotiator at the court of Augustus III in Dresden, that a royal marriage for Louise was probably not in the offing. Old Prince James had been deceiving himself all along, and only humiliation for the House of Bouillon would result:

Ainsi voye quelle honte pour nous et dans quelle danger on auroit mis nostre pauvre enfant. En verité, il veau mieu qu'elle me reste pour estre ma consolation dans mes vieu joures. Adieu ingrat, malgre tous tes defauts je taime et suis a jamais toutes a toy. Envoye moy le papie en question autrement je ne te renveray point ceux que jay. Je veut que vous ayez confiance plus que vous avez en moy.[42]

In the coming months, accusations and counter-accusations would be exchanged between the palace at Zolkiew and the Hôtel de Bouillon, and, little by little, the Duc and his agent would manage to isolate the Duchesse entirely from her daughter and most of her servants. And yet it had been Marie-Charlotte who had clearly shown the greatest foresight. From the beginning, she had had her suspicions that the proposed marriage with a Saxon prince would not take place. She had also warned the Duc not to make promises lightly to her father concerning Louise. The whole business, she sensed, had not been thought through carefully enough.

Marie-Charlotte, a true Sobieski, frequently looked on the gloomy side of things, but events too often proved her right. Even her premonition that she would never see her beloved Navarre again but would die in that unforgiving land she had given up forever a dozen years before was to come true.

II

Louise

O N 13 JUNE 1736, accompanied by her father's *maître en chirurgie*, Jean-Henri Bourgeois, her governess, Mlle de Minières, and a small retinue of servants, the Princesse de Bouillon, not yet eleven years old and fresh from the convent of Chasse-Midi, set out from Paris on the long and hazardous journey to her grandfather's royal palace at Zolkiew. The precise purpose of the trip had been made clear to her. She would be marrying a son of the King of Poland; negotiations were going on at that very moment! The family had earlier decided against sending her along with her mother for reasons of protocol: "Il ne convient pas à la dignité de Mademoiselle d'Auvergne qu'elle fut conduitte a la cour de Pologne avant que l'on eut pris pour son mariage toutes les assurances par ecrit que l'on peut prendre avec le Roy et la Reyne de Pologne." Such had been the grave decision of her father's Council.[1] Many questions must have passed through her mind as she looked out at the summer landscape from the window of their light and rather uncomfortable carriage. Her first letter back to her father, written from Nuremberg, was dated eleven days after her departure:

> J'aurai deja eu l'honneur, Mon cher Papa, de vous ecrire sans que Mr Bourgeois vous a donné de mes nouvelles de Strasbourg ou j'ai été tres bien recû de Mr le Marechal du Bourg et de Mde de Lusbourg[2] qui m'a menée a la comedie. Je suis arrivé ce matin a Nuremberg, ce nest pas sans fatigue car nous avons eu de mauvais chemin depuis Strasbourg et nôtre voiture est tres rude, et le chagrin que jai de vous avoir quitté, Mon cher Papa, est la plus grande de touttes mes peines. Jespere que vous voudrez bien me les adoueir en me conservant toujours vos bontés. C'est la grace que vous demande vôtre petite fille.
>
> L. De Bouillon

A Nuremberg
Ce 24 juin, 1736

Je ne veux pas manquer, Mon cher Papa, de vous mander que Mon cher oncle ma donné 40 louis en partant de Mousseau[3]

It is not difficult to find the later Princess in those tidy lines, carefully revised no doubt by her governess. Easy contact with the great was a normal part of her life as were the flattering attentions and expensive gifts of her powerful relations. But even taking into account the enormous wealth of her granduncle, the Comte d'Evreux, we must be impressed by the generosity of his parting gift of nearly 1000 livres in pocket money! Obvious too is the fact that the young Princess was very much her "daddy's girl." No mention is made of Marie-Charlotte whom she hadn't seen for nine months and who was anxiously awaiting her daughter's arrival.

As the small party proceeded eastward, the difficulties of travel increased considerably. The roads deteriorated and there were torrential rains. Finally, de Bacqueville, who had come to meet them in Silesia, was able to report their safe arrival in Breslau on 6 July. The Princess, he noted, was accompanied by a group of attendants as strange and ill-assorted as could be imagined: no one had thought to include a cook, for example, but a useless cabinet-maker had been brought along! Everyone was in good health although somewhat the worse for wear. Their carriage was in an extremely battered condition. Farther on, in the direction of Ohlau, the roads would be quite impassable, and they would all have to wait out the bad weather in Breslau. Even at the height of summer there was a threat of famine in the countryside. So many flour mills had been destroyed by floods that a pound of bread could not be had anywhere, even for 100 ducats. Damage in the province of Silesia alone was estimated at 29 millions. But some of the news was good: Saxon and Russian occupation troops would soon be getting out of Poland. As for the Princess herself, she was not the slightest bit homesick or bored. Her governess was very nervous about going on to Zolkiew; de Bacqueville had been able to reassure her and had taken advantage of the opportunity to slip some discreet advice to the little Princess but without, of course, being too "preachy" about it....The exact nature of that advice will become only too clear when we note his increasingly hostile references to Marie-Charlotte in letters to the Duc. The process of alienating Louise from her mother, no doubt already well begun in Paris by Charles-Godefroy, would be continued and reinforced in the months to come. The young Princess listened carefully and stored everything away for future reference. That she was not in any way alarmed, however, is evident from the tone of her next letter to her father:

Malgré touttes les fatigues que nous avons eu, Mon cher Papa, nous sommes arrivez a Breslau en tres bonne santé. Nous avons eu des chemins abominables et une voiture on ne peut pas plus mauvaise et tres rude. Je croi que nous ne pourron pas aler sitot a Olo. Les chemins sont impraticables et les equipages du Prince Jacques ne sont pas encore arrivez. Quand il le seroient nous ne pourrions pas partir. Cette ville ici est charmante par la bonne compagnie. Je dine presque tous les jours chez son Excellence, Mde la comtesse de Chafcot.[4] Elle a une fille et deux nieces chez elle charmante. Elles sont de mon age. La grace que je vous demande, Mon cher Papa, c'est de continuer toujours vos bontés et votre amitié a vôtre petitte fille.

L. De Bouillon

a Breslau
ce 15 juillet, 1736

A note from the governess accompanied the letter. Louise was indeed well; she had been going out in "grande et bonne compagnie" and everyone found her charming. Their departure date was still not known, however: "Je désirerois que ce fût dans peu; la route qui reste à faire est encore plus mauvaise que celle que nous avons faite. C'est beaucoup dire."

It was not until 29 July that de Bacqueville decided the roads were safe enough to travel. Marie-Charlotte, meanwhile, waited impatiently in Zolkiew. On 18 July she had written to the Duc's agent asking him to send her daughter as soon as possible and to convey to her "cent choses tendres....de ma part." Three weeks later, on 8 August, she wrote to the Duc complaining somewhat coyly that since de Bacqueville's departure for Breslau, she had heard nothing at all from her dear husband. No doubt he was pleased to be rid at last of his wife and daughter: "Vous ne pensez plus qu'ils sont au monde et vous laissez tout a l'abandon." That was not what he had solemnly promised her just before she had set out on her lonely mission! Their daughter had not yet arrived: "Je l'atens a bras ouverte et feroit pour elle que mere au monde ne feroit pour ses enfans. Sa sera ma consolation." Marie-Charlotte, not entirely in her father's good graces, was well aware that she and Louise had been handed competing roles and that she might be required to give up all of her own inheritance claims in favour of her daughter's marriage. The situation was made worse by knowledge of her precarious position back in France. She had just learned, for example, that Charles-Godefroy was threatening to turn out one of her *filles d'honneur* without paying her wages! How could he even think of doing such a thing! She had also been told that he was spending most of his time at Navarre and that his dear *belle maman* was constantly with him. The Duchesse, not unaware of the rumours concerning her husband's liaison, added a sarcastic comment: "Faites luy ma coure et prie la qu'elle vous permette un quart d'heure pour repondre a mes lettres."

Finally, the great day arrived. On the afternoon of 25 August, the entire population of Zolkiew turned out to greet the little Princess. Even someone as accustomed to public honours as Louise must have felt a thrill of excitement at the reception awaiting her in front of the royal palace. Prince James, de Bacqueville reported, was swept quite off his feet. He found his granddaughter totally charming and would not let her out of his sight. Even the nervous and grumpy Mlle de Minières admitted that she was impressed, and she wrote to the Duc on the following day that Louise "a estes recue de la part du prince roial et de Madame la duchesse avec la plus vive tendresse. Toutte la ville est venue au devant de la princesse avec les drapeaux et tambours."[5]

Despite the parade atmosphere, de Bacqueville was extremely worried. Shortly after his arrival, the Duchesse had told him of a recent angry exchange with her father. The old man, anticipating possible difficulties in Dresden, was already looking around for alternatives and had made the claim, in Marie-Charlotte's presence, that he was the complete master of any marriage arrangements for the child, independently of the mother's wishes. The Duchesse had protested vigorously but the Prince Royal seemed unconvinced by her arguments. The fact was, de Bacqueville hinted, that Prince James doted on the young Princess, cared not two pins for her mother, and could easily be persuaded by mischief makers to send the Duchesse packing. Mischief makers, moreover, were not in short supply at the palace, and de Bacqueville himself felt surrounded by much local hostility: "Je me trouve au milieu des rochers dans une barque fragile dont je n'ay pas seul la conduite; bien des gens me regardent icy come un home qui fait venir des Etrangers pour prendre leur heritage."[6] Fortunately, though he resented her role in the whole affair, he and the Duchesse were on speaking terms, at least for the moment; everything now depended on the success of negotiations at the court of Augustus III.

More stormy scenes with the old Prince followed. On one occasion he had asked to see a copy of the Duchesse's marriage contract. When de Bacqueville respectfully inquired why he was making that request, the Prince Royal exploded with twelve years of pent-up resentment and indignation: "C'est, me dit le Prince, qu'on a oté a ma fille la moitié de son bien par le second mariage et que le Duc de B. est debauché et boit et joue beaucoup!"[7] But the Duc's agent was quick to defend his master: the Duchesse, after the untimely death of her first husband, Frédéric-Maurice, could have crossed back over the Rhine, taking all that was legally due her and leaving a great hole in the finances of the Bouillons, who, after their enormous expenses, would have received in return only the honour of an eight-day alliance with the House of Sobieski. Would it have been fair for the Duchesse to insist on pressing her advantage? As for the Duc's behaviour, "il a fait comme touts les jeunes gents qui sont de bone heure maistres de leur conduite et de leur bien. Il a un peu depensé. Si il a joué, il a payé et s'en est corrigé." The Duc, moreover, was not a drunkard: "Il ne boit que come les honestes gents a sa table ou avec ses amis & le roy meme." And women? De Bacqueville was bluffly categorical: "Je ne sache pas qu'il depense son bien avec les femmes, et ceux qui tiennent ces propos à V.A.R. sont bien mal instruits ou bien mal intentionnés." Finally, de Bacqueville drove home his strongest rebuttal which was that even if the Duc were guilty of all those things and impoverished to the point of being down to his last shirt, Prince James's grandson, the Prince de Turenne, would still have a guaranteed income of 400,000 livres from legally protected property, and the Duchesse could not be deprived of even *one sou* of her own wealth since in France a marriage contract was sacred.[8] Finally, he had managed to convince the old man, who was now feverishly making plans for settling his huge holdings on his granddaughter and speculating about other possible marriage arrangements. What about the son of the King of Prussia, for example? Demurring at that particular suggestion, de Bacqueville was nevertheless happy enough to join in the discussion and was obviously in his element as he tossed around kingdoms and fortunes. Ah, if only he had been given a free hand and sole control of negotiations without the interference of Prince James's hateful priest, Mocki, and, of course, the Duchesse! His bitterness and bluster increased with every new letter to Saint-Gervais, and even his letters to the Duc—which, he insisted, were to be burned—are filled with ill-natured insinuations that the Duchesse was merely looking after her own interests and that his poor innocent master was being duped. Obviously, de Bacqueville knew what his master wanted to hear!

That Marie-Charlotte was viewed by her husband as little more than an instrument for getting rid of the family debt became increasingly clear as time passed. A sensitive and intelligent woman, Louise's mother was conscious of being exploited in this way. Her affectionate letters to the Duc suggest, nevertheless, that she accepted the situation—probably in the fond hope that by bringing back a large sum of money and repairing the Duc's finances she could regain his love as well. In their exchange of correspondence, Charles-Godefroy did, in fact, occasionally toss his wife a cynical crumb of affection. He wrote, for example, on 11 August, assuring her that he most certainly loved her. She answered on 12 September, offering him an opportunity to prove it by not turning out yet another of her servants and, instead, by driving from the house a certain demoiselle Lombard, a new little favourite she had got wind of. "Je veray si vous maime," she continued, "je ne veut point vous parle d'autres torts que vous avez avec moy car je ne finire point, mais je peut avec justice vous dire que vous estes l'home du monde le plus ingrat." Canon Mocki and de Bacqueville would be leaving in a week's time for Dresden to settle the marriage. Perhaps, she added sarcastically, in the absence of his dear de Bacqueville, "unique possesseur de votre confiance et protecteur de la gloire de nostre maison," she could be trusted to carry on usefully in Zolkiew. Their daughter, thank goodness, was well. As for Charles-Godefroy's hypocritical fears, expressed in an earlier letter, that his cherished wife might be tempted to stay on in Poland once a marriage had been arranged for Louise, Marie-Charlotte astutely pointed out that perhaps that was exactly what he wanted: "Il ne tiendra qu'a vous pour me determiner." Two lines further on, she shifted to a stylistic intimacy that betrayed her true feelings: "Il ne tient qu'a toy que je t'adore."

De Bacqueville and the Abbé Mocki left for Dresden on 24 September, and the Duchesse continued to express dismay at not being involved: "Je me tourmente pour tirer partie de tout sa pour nous mettre a nostre aise et que tu puisse estre quitte de tes creanciers." The primary motive for her journey to Poland could not have been made plainer. With equal clarity she assured the Duc that she would rather be back in France, even if it meant that they would have to be paupers: "Ne m'oublie point. Je te proteste que je voudrois bien estre avec toy si je devois allez a pieds. Je me meur d'ennuye. Adieu. Je t'embrasse de tout mon coeur. Dieu donne que je puisse bientost le faire moy meme. De tes nouvelles, autrement je croyere que tu ne maime point. Pour moy je t'adore et suis ta constante femme, jusque a la morte."[9] Louise was to come very honestly by her passionate nature and style!

That the Duc was himself capable of rising to somewhat less authentic waves of rhetorical passion is evident in a wrathful letter he sent to the Duchesse on 7 October. Charles-Godefroy described himself as furious that she had refused to send along a legal *renonciation* without first receiving the *contre-lettre*. How dared she not trust him! He would not remind her of all the ways in which she had already failed him. What ingratitude! He had sent his daughter to Poland only because he had learned on good authority that the Duchesse would otherwise have been driven from her paternal home. He was indeed pleased if not entirely dazzled by the grandeur of the proposed marriage. The interests and splendour of the House of Bouillon were, however, less important to him than his great and abiding affection for his dear wife: "Je vous voyé prete de recevoir le comble de l'affront, renvoyée sans ressources. Je ne balance pas. Je fais partir ma fille ou, pour mieux dire, je l'immole a ma tendresse pour vous. L'embarras de mes affaires, mon amitié pour elle, en un mot, rien ne m'arrete. Je vous la sacrifie."[10] But she had not cooperated; she had not honoured his trusted emissary de Bacqueville with her full confidence. She had, moreover, wickedly suppressed a letter he had given Louise for her grandfather. As for the letter of renunciation, she simply *had to* send it; he *demanded* it: "Sinon je redemande ma fille et dussai-je partir et l'aler chercher, je jure sur mon Dieu de qui seul je depends maintenant que je l'iray prendre moy meme." Marie-Charlotte was not to forget that he had the means to punish her, even at a distance, and that he could arrange matters so that she would never be able to receive a penny of her money from France. "Je le feray avec tout le chagrin possible, je vous le répète, je te le jure sur mon Dieu.... Je suis outré de vos procedés a mon egard et rien ne peut faire changer mes resolutions que le retour sincere de votre amitié que toute autre que vous n'auroit pu refuser a la tendresse que je vous avois vouée pour le reste de ma vie." The letter continues in the same warmly grandiloquent style, leaving us to wonder how the Grand Chambellan managed to choke back his giggling as he wrote. His reference to the suppression of a letter is not clear in the remaining correspondence but the accusation could well be true since he seems to have been kept well informed (probably by Mlle de Minières) concerning all the Zolkiew gossip. He had also learned, he warned the Duchesse, that she wished to remove the valet St. Amand from Louise's service. That was out of the question! "Je le luy ay donné comme un garçon sage. Je le connois pour tel et je veux qu'il reste avec elle." We shall hear more of that worthy young servant later on.

Negotiations meanwhile continued in Dresden. On 23 October, de Bacqueville reported that he had gone to see the Prince Royal, Frederick-Christian-Leopold, the eldest son of Augustus III.[11] Unfortunately, the young man was sickly: "Il est beau et aimable et c'est un domage qu'il ne puisse se soutenir sur ses jambes. Le prince Xavier, que je n'ay point été voir, est petit et assez joly."[12] Little progress was being made, however. There was also a sinister and ubiquitous papal legate hovering in the background, concerned, naturally, with defending the interests of James III. Finally, an agreement of sorts was reached and reported in somewhat puzzling syntax by Canon George Mocki in a letter to the Duc dated 28 October 1736:

> Leurs Majeste de Pologne...acceptent avec plaisir les propositions de S.A.R. le Prince Jaque concernantes le mariage entre le Prince Royal de Saxe leur fils et la Princesse de Bouillon, mais il n'en veuillent point finalement decider, mais le laisser a la liberté de leurs age, que chacun luy choisisse sans le forcer avant leurs distinction, ils ne veuillent non plus en decider la moindre chose, en cela consiste la reponse que jay eu.

The Duc's puzzlement on receiving this particular example of Mocki's prose several weeks later was not surprising. Was the priest saying that the proposal had been accepted or rejected? "Tout cela est pour moy un fatras qui me semble difficile a debrouiller."[13] In desperation, Charles-Godefroy asked his agent to try to find out directly from the King of Poland what decision, if any, had been reached.

What Mocki had intended to convey in his turgid account to the Duc is clarified somewhat by the parallel announcement he sent to the Duchesse not long after. Having convinced Augustus III that Prince James's failing health would not allow for any delay, Mocki had received the reply that things could not be rushed. To begin with, there were a number of competing propositions to consider. In any case, a contract could not be drawn up since their Majesties did not wish to force their son's decision and intended to leave him free to make his own choice once he had reached the âge de discretion, that is, twenty. Nothing more could be decided or put in writing, and Prince James was obviously free to make other arrangements.

It was thus all a great disappointment. Many such would follow for Louise, whose marriage prospects were to become in the next half-dozen years a constant preoccupation underlying nearly all of Charles-Godefroy's financial dealings. Undeterred by failure, Mocki immediately began casting about for other suitable matches. There was little time to secure the Sobieski estates for the young Princess, and all of Europe seemed to be waiting to see what would happen. The situation had become so public, in fact, that de Bacqueville had to beg the Duc on 6 November "de garder un secret inviolable de ce qui se passe, car on a esté scandalisé icy de voir touts les projets dans les Gazettes et on soupçone avec justice qu'ils en transpirent du Quay Malaquais."

The Duchesse, who had firmly opposed sending Louise to Poland without a solid commitment, was not flattered by such public attention or by what she saw as a shameful rejection. Without delay, she forwarded Mocki's letter to the Duc, indicating that her worst fears had been realized:

> Enfin mon cher Coeur, voyla a la fein la determination de la negociation come je l'avois dit, Voyla la copie de la lettre que je vous envoye de l'abbé Moski. Enfin Dieu a voulue me faire encore souffrire cette disgrace. Quelle honte pour nostre maison et quelle joye pour nos enemies. Vous navez pas voulue vous rendre a mes prieres et larmes pour ne point risquer denvoyer cette enfans pour rien et encor courire risque de la perdre.

But that, she recognized, was water under the bridge. What was to be done now? Everything was up in the air, and she was at the end of her patience: "Je me meurt de chagrin et d'ennuye ici." No worthy alternatives seemed to be in the offing. The son of the King of Prussia? One of the Radziwills? All of the Polish lands would have to be sold, of course, "et Dieu sait quand et qui et coment on les vendera, et moy et mon enfant nous perissons ici." The Duc simply had to decide what she was to do. She would sacrifice even her life for her poor child, "trop heureuse au depends de ma vie de la rendre heureuse, ainsi ne me ménage point sur ce que vous, mon Coeur, et mon cher oncle me jugeront capable. Mais pesez bien les choses auparavant." She would need a prompt reply. Her own suggestion, if she dared make it, was that a marriage be negotiated with the Prince de Conti or one of the Radziwills or some other distinguished prince, but the arrangements would have to be ironclad and there could be no further risk of a shameful rejection. "Voyla ma pensee. Je ne sais come elle sera recu de mon cher oncle et de vous. Je vous laise le maitre de faire l'usage come vous voudrez. Il est vray que jaimeray mieu le P Conti[14] et meme toute autre a Paris." Money would not be a problem; if Prince James kept his promises, Louise would have a large dowry. "Enfin tache de nous tirer du bourbier ou nous some tombez.... Je suis trop heureuse de pouvoir estre bon a quelque chose a ma chere famille et sur toute a toy mon Roy, dut-il m'en couter la vie.... Adieu mon cher mary...mande moy des nouvelles de mon fils."[15]

Despite Marie-Charlotte's offer, the Duc preferred the help of de Bacqueville. He wrote to his agent on 18 November, urging upon him the need to persuade Prince James to leave all of his property directly to the young Princess. He was now quite indifferent to the Duchesse's own inheritance rights, and he gave his envoy the unwelcome news that he would absolutely have to stay on in Poland for some time yet to counteract any undue influence the Duchesse might have on her father: "Ce qui me fait tout craindre, c'est que Made de Bouillon, restant seule aupres du Prince, peut nous porter des coups que nous ne scaurons parer....Voyez de quelle importance il est que vous soyez sur les lieux. Si quelqu'un peut empecher les menées secrettes de ma tante,[16] c'est vous." To Marie-Charlotte he sent a rather different message: he wanted her to know how hurt and irritated he was by her attitude toward de Bacqueville. The dear man was guilty of no crime, and to him had to go all the credit of her reconciliation with her father. He promised to do everything possible to prove to his wife "que vous avés dans votre mary le plus fidelle et le plus tendre amy et qu'il vous est attaché par des noeuds indissolubles." As for Louise's future, Canon Mocki had recently transmitted a new scheme of which he warmly approved: Augustus III had agreed that if Prince James willed all of his Polish land holdings to Louise, he would make her his official ward and take charge of her education. "Ce projet est, je vous l'avoue, si fort de mon gout, que je ne desire autre chose qu'il soit egalement gouté de S.A.R. Nous avons assez de biens pour pouvoir vivre heureux ensemble." In such a scheme, Louise would benefit from the highest possible protection and have the advantage of being well placed to receive excellent marriage proposals.[17] As for the Duchesse's suggestion concerning the Prince de Conti, however advantageous such a union with a prince of the blood might seem, it was financially out of the question: "Nous n'avons pas assez d'argent pour pouvoir y penser." Such uncharacteristic modesty on the Duc's part was followed by a renewed plea to the Duchesse to work in close harmony with de Bacqueville and to give up any thought of her own interests in favour of her daughter. He promised to be eternally grateful to her for the sacrifice: "Je n'auray pas assez de jours pour vous prouver l'estime que j'auray d'une pareille action. Je vous proteste que je n'ay jamais eu d'autres vues que votre gloire et celle de la maison et, en vérité, de vous donner des témoignages assurés de la plus vive tendresse et amitié."[18]

Four days later the Duc wrote to de Bacqueville and made less tender references to the Duchesse. He did not want her meddling in any way in their daughter's marriage negotiations. De Bacqueville was to keep his eyes open for a wealthy German prince; he himself had in mind the half-brother of our Messalina, the Prince de Guise, "a qui je la donneray volontiers."[19] But the Grand Chambellan favoured most of all the scheme whereby Louise would be endowed with the

Sobieski estates in Poland and brought up at the court of Augustus III. He now gave de Bacqueville full powers to negotiate such an arrangement.[20] On the same day the Duc also wrote to Prince James Sobieski, urging him to accept the Polish King's proposition. The letter was deferential and seemed to leave all decisions regarding Louise's future in the old Prince's hands:

> Si j'ose prendre la liberté de faire de mes reflections sur cette affaire a V.A.R., j'auray l'honeur de luy dire qu'il me semble que la proposition du Roy n'est pas a rejeter, la délicatesse de sa conscience et de l'amitié paternelle ne lui permet pas de lier les Princes ses enfans par des serments qui, en grandissant, leur seroient peut etre desagréables. Mais se déclarant tuteur de l'Enfant, elle met V.A.R. hors de toute inquietude. De plus, l'honeur que ma fille a d'appartenir a la Reyne est encore un point capital pour determiner V.A.R. a ne point rejetter la proposition que Mr le Chanoine Moski a eu l'honeur de faire à V.A.R. de la part de leurs Majestés et V.A.R. estant tranquille sur ses biens cela luy donne le tems de trouver des Partis convenables si le mariage en question ne peut avoir lieu.
>
> Je supplie V.A.R. de me pardonner l'aveu de mes sentimens qui, toutefois, seront toujours soumis aux volontés et aux désirs de V.A.R.[21]

Prince James was indeed on the point of changing his will and naming Louise sole beneficiary of all his Polish lands, "heritière de toute ma substance, meuble et immeuble." There is also no doubt, judging from his instructions to Mocki, that he too approved of the Polish King's proposal. He insisted, however, probably at Marie-Charlotte's urging, that no proclamation of the will be made and no letters of commitment be sent before solid assurances were received from Dresden. An additional difficulty pointed out in the Prince Royal's instructions was that, by Polish law, execution of the will in favour of Louise could not be guaranteed unless she were married or at least engaged to be married to a Prince who either was Polish or possessed the *indigenat* of Poland.[22]

This last point, confirmed by legal experts as eminent as François-Maximilien, Duc de Tenczn Ossolinski, Grand Maître at the court of Stanislas in Lorraine, now became a matter of utmost concern to de Bacqueville who saw it as yet another sinister means by which the Duchesse could attack the will and lay claim to her father's vast properties.[23] The chaotic state of Polish affairs also presented another source of worry since there was great risk that rival magnates might simply seize the estates at the Prince Royal's death, especially if the Duchesse was not at hand to defend the succession. Thus, for both the Duc and his wily emissary, a delicate balance had to be struck between ensuring Marie-Charlotte's full cooperation and continuing presence in Poland in order to protect Louise's inheritance, and depriving her, at the same time, of any power to influence events or assert her own legitimate claims. The King of Poland, himself concerned that the Sobieski estates might be pillaged after the Prince's death, issued orders to the Palatin of Kijowie, Grand Général de la Couronne, to have military forces in readiness to protect the lands and interests of "une princesse mineure."[24]

Prince James had insisted that negotiations with Augustus be completed by the feast of the Epiphany, after which time his offer to place Louise and his lands under the tutelage of the Polish Crown would be withdrawn. As it turned out, the proposal did not come to fruition, probably to Marie-Charlotte's delight. Indeed, she later protested to the Duc that sending their daughter to Dresden would have been equivalent to admitting that they were themselves incapable of caring for her or providing her with a dowry.[25] She also told him that she had had quite enough of Poland and intended to set out on the return journey to France in April. For Charles-Godefroy the situation could not have been worse, and he spared no effort in his attempt to dissuade her. He was not at all worried about the breakdown of negotiations; he had entrusted his daughter to Prince James, who would decide what was best. If his wife were to leave, she would irreparably harm both her daughter and her husband. The Duc's zeal knew no bounds: he even gave Marie-Charlotte news of her son—something she had been vainly requesting for months: "Rendez-moy un peu plus de justice," he pleaded, "et croyez que je vous aime plus tendrement mille fois que je n'en puis vous le dire. Votre fils vous presente ses respects. Il se porte à merveille et grandit etonamment. Donnez moy de vos nouvelles, je vous en conjure!"[26] An advance copy of that prize effort was, as usual, sent confidentially to de Bacqueville for whatever strategic use he could make of it.

Though it is concerned almost entirely with Louise's hoped-for marriage and inheritance, this extensive exchange of correspondence between the palace of Zolkiew and the Quai Malaquais unfortunately provides little information that relates directly to her. A December 1736 letter from one of the palace officials to Mocki in Dresden assured the priest that the little Princess, "laquelle devient de jour en jour plus belle et plus charmante, a entierement gagné le coeur de Monsgr Son Grandpapa qui ne cherche que de lui faire du plaisir et des presents." The writer added confidentially, however, that Louise's mother was, on the other hand, not really in her father's good graces. The extent to which Louise herself was aware of the great fuss going on around her is not directly revealed in the charmingly social letter she wrote to her father in February, although the influence of Mlle de Minières and of de Bacqueville probably lies behind the total absence of any reference to her mother and her well-coached promise that in all things she would submit always to her father's orders:

Je suis tres sensible, Mon Tres cher papa, de l'honneur que vous m'avez faite d'avoir bien voulu prendre la peine de m'ecrire. Les sentimens d'amitié dont vous m'honorez me font esperez que vous me les continuerez. C'est la grace que vous demande votre petitte fille qui sera toutte sa vie, Mon Tres cher papa, occupée de vous plaire et suivre tous vos ordres avec soumission. Je ne manque pas, comme vous me l'ordonnez, de faire ma cour A Son Altesse Roïalle, mon cher grand papa qui a toujours milles bontés pour moi.

J'ai prié Mon cher frere de vous supplier de ma part, Mon Tres cher papa, de vouloir bien avoir la bonté de m'envoyer deux habits de tafetas. Je n'ai osé prendre la liberté de vous faire tout ce détail. Il est dans la lettre de mon cher frere. Si vous avez cette bonté, il faudroit que la boete ce trouvas a Breslaw la semaine d'apres la mi-careme. Il y a une ocasion ici pour l'aporter. Vous m'avez permis tant de fois, Mon Tres cher papa, de prendre la liberté de m'adresser a vous, quand j'aurai besoin de quelque chose, c'est pourquoi j'espere que vous le trouverés bon de la part de votre petite fille, qui vous baisse la main de tout son coeur, Mon Tres cher Papa

L. De la Tour D'auvergne De Bouillon

Mlles des minieres et d'orvaux prennent la liberté de vous faire leur cour

a Zulkiew
ce 6 fevrier, 1737

One week later the Duchesse wrote to the Duc that, although she was as impatient as ever to rejoin him in France, she was doing her best to help out: "Je suis comme une ange avec mon pere, et nostre enfant aussi, laquelle, grace au ciele, ce porte bien. Elle grandie a vue d'oeuille." Her own situation, Marie-Charlotte admitted, was becoming more and more desperate; she would try to cooperate and be friendly with de Bacqueville when he returned, but Charles-Godefroy was to know that his agent had deliberately done them much harm and had tried to divide them. She was, at the time, engaged in a confidential attempt to collect the large debt repudiated by Augustus III[27] and hoped to have the matter raised at the next Diet by an important senator of her acquaintance. Another piece of news was that her father secretly intended to leave additional monies to the Stuart princes ("les Jules") in his will. Finally, without reminding her husband that he had opposed her earlier wishes to remove the valet St. Amand from Louise's immediate service, she now begged the Duc's clemency for this servant whom Mlle de Minières had just decided to send away penniless into the cold because he had married the governess's maid. This was not the first time Marie-Charlotte had shown more compassion for the weak than those around her. Mlle de Minières was right, the Duchesse conceded, not to want married servants with Louise, but St. Amand had committed no crime, and the punishment of being reduced to begging for alms in a foreign country was out of all proportion to the offence: "Ayez la charité," she pleaded, "de ne le point abandonne. Il a este a nostre enfant, il a eu du male come un chien en chemin. Enfin, je vous en prie, cette une grace que je vous demande. Vous n'auroit pas la cruauté de me la refuser."[28]

The full extent of Marie-Charlotte's clemency becomes clear only when we examine a letter from Louise's female attendant, Lorence, who wrote indignantly to the Duc's secretary Saint-Gervais about the outrageous behaviour of the dismissed valet. The lusty young man, had turned out to be a most unworthy personal servant for the Princess:

> En premier lieu il a passé par la Casrolle, en segond il a fait un enfant a la femme de chambre de Mell deminier qui est depuis six mois a la princesse. Cela a fait un tres mauvais efait dans la cour que la princesse ait eut a son service un verole et une efronte. On les a fait marie le vingt huite ou 20 neufs de janvier. On les renvoy tout les deux. Ils doivent partir a la fin de ce mois...deux miserable que l'on tire de la miser; ils n'ont pas voulu en profiter. Le vilain Limousin netoit point propre pour etre a une prince. Il est grossier comme du pain dorge, il ne scait ny lire ny ecrire. Nous norions peut etre pas eut tant d'affront si on avoit eut affaire a quelqun desprit. Il norois pas manques de respect jusqua ce point dans un voyage d'aussi grande importance a la suite d'une jeune princesse.[29]

Lorence included other colourful details in her confidential February report, providing a fresh perspective on the tedium of events at Zolkiew. Life in the palace, far from friends and relatives, was worse, she maintained, than in any convent. De Bacqueville was still away. His presence was certainly needed in order to persuade the old Prince to sell his land and endow Louise with the money. Otherwise, there would be no getting around the legal impossibility of leaving land to a foreigner. It was really all a great mess. "Il y a des personnes qui tache de prolonge et ils font acroire a madame la duches quelle sera leritiere et moy je scait tres sertainement que si le prince royal venoit a mourir avant un arangement elle norois pas seulement un tableaux." Lorence was equally forthright in giving her own negative views on some of the suitors suggested for Louise: "Je ne vois rien d'avantageux pour la maison. Il est question du fils du grand marechal mais par luy meme il nest que staros(te), c'est a dire, simple jantilhom, c'est sa charge qui le distingue." There was also a Radziwill prince, "mais apres avoir espere aux fils de la couronne ce serois une grande chute d'avoir recour a ces sujets. Si cetois ma fille jaimerois mieux quelle pouris dans un couvent que de fair de pareill mariage. On nous a fait faire un voyage bien presipité. Un peu de reflection pour des affaires daussi grand consequence norois pas ete inutile." Servants of the Great, we see, easily matched the exalted pretensions of their masters! Louise's maid closed her valuable letter by noting that her young mistress was in very good health and that she had made her first communion at Christmas. As an afterthought, she added a note of caution: "Je vous prie, Monsieur, de ne pas dir par qui vous saves ces choses, pour plusieurs raison."

III

"Toujours dans la balance"

D E BACQUEVILLE returned to Zolkiew from the court of Augustus III on 26 February 1737. It was a certain sign that all hope of successfully negotiating a marriage for Louise with one of the royal princes of Poland had been abandoned. Now began a period of intense dispute and dissension among the various members of the Bouillon party who had set out on their troubled mission already a year and a half earlier. Differences between the Duc and the Duchesse, no doubt present but still unspoken when Marie-Charlotte left for Poland in September 1735, now became open and obvious to all concerned; Marie-Charlotte and the Duc's trusted agent de Bacqueville were barely on speaking terms. The conflicting interests of wife and husband, mother and daughter, were taken for granted and matter-of-factly discussed even by the servants. To make matters worse, Prince James, on his last legs physically, was also fast approaching mental infirmity. Everyone agreed that something had to be arranged quickly or all would be lost. Alternative marriage proposals came to mind; none were entirely satisfactory.

Daily living was much harder in Poland than amid the comforts of the Hôtel de Bouillon. De Bacqueville, who had contracted a fever, lost no time in sending a graphic account to Saint-Gervais of the harsh conditions he had just encountered on the road back to Zolkiew. The weather had been so cold that even his wine froze. Death and starvation stalked the countryside. A servant he had sent one day to buy bread discovered four corpses in the first house he approached and two in the next. Children fought desperately with ferocious dogs over the bones cast from hostelry tables.[1] St. Amand and his pregnant wife must indeed have been grateful to the Duchesse for her humanitarian sentiments!

On his arrival, de Bacqueville found that little had changed at the palace. Prince James was growing weaker by the day: "C'est un demy squelette dont les vautours mangent le reste des chairs en attendant qu'on l'embaume." Still, the old Prince managed a warmer greeting than the Duchesse. The Duc's emissary was now more convinced than ever that she and the priest were conspiring to destroy him. Louise and the governess had, on the other hand, remained loyal to his instructions. In a letter to her father, the young princess herself makes that clear:

> je n'oublirai de ma vie tous ce que vous m'avez fait l'honneur de me dire en prenant congé de vous. Vos bontés sont gravés dans le fond de mon cœur. Mon cher grand Papa contoit recevoir la reponse d'une lettre quil vous a ecrite pour scavoir la desission de mon sort. Je suis toujours dans la balance. J'espere que vous donnerez ordre a tout cela par Mr de Bacqueville qui se porte mieux. Mon cher grand papa a toujours de bonnes intentions pour moi. Je crains fort qu'ils ne s'accomplissent pas. Toutte ma consolation seroit de vous revoir en parfaitte sante. Soyez persuadé, Mon cher papa, du profond respect de vôtre petitte fille.[2]

Now only a few months from her twelfth birthday, Louise was fully aware of the problems surrounding efforts to establish her in Poland, and her pessimism contrasts sharply with the tone of earlier letters concerned exclusively with social activities, the presents she had received, or the delicate taffetas she needed for the next fancy party. Completely alienated from her mother, she explicitly urged her father to deal with the situation through de Bacqueville alone. For good measure, her governess added a postscript, attacking the Duchesse by innuendo. De Bacqueville soon confirmed the open hostility between mother and daughter by reporting that the Duchesse had informed him of her wish to return to France *but without Louise*, "qui étais si maussade et si mal elevée qu'elle lui faizoit honte."[3]

With the failure of negotiations at the court of Dresden, it became urgent to get down to a serious exploration of other possibilities. The Duc began by asking Prince James for three months' delay, until August, in order to make his choice among the various distinguished Polish candidates who had declared their interest. Meanwhile, another idea had suddenly come to him, and he shared it with his agent in a letter of 26 April: what would the Prince Royal think of marrying his granddaughter to one of her Stuart cousins? De Bacqueville was to sound him out discreetly on the subject. Prince James and James III would be allowed complete freedom, of course, to arrive at any suitable arrangement. Charles-Godefroy stipulated only one condition: the Duchesse was to be told nothing of the scheme! It would be their little secret for the time being. Much pleased with the notion, the Grand Chambellan closed his letter with the warmest assurances of his *constante amitié à toute epreuve*. On the same day, the Duc wrote to Marie-Charlotte, saying only that he had asked her father for a three-month delay, assuring her at the same time that he yearned for her return.[4] Reading his advance copy, de Bacqueville must have smiled a little...

In letters that reached the Duc in Paris only after Charles-Godefroy had sent along his proposal for a Stuart marriage, de Bacqueville had already reviewed the various aspirants. He was able to report that the Duchesse, on hearing Mlle de Minières repeat what was originally the Duc's suggestion concerning the suitability of the Prince de Guise, "se mit en fureur, et donna à ce jeune prince touttes les mauvaises qualités de son pere." In fact, according to the governess, Marie-Charlotte had declared "quel aymerois mieux donné sa fille a un paysan."[5] Marie-Charlotte's rejection of another dubious suitor, Prince Wisniowiecki, Castellan de Cracovie, as a *vilain bègue* and a *débauché* again showed the same concern to avoid placing her daughter in a situation rather too similar to her own. Other suitors included le Petit Général, a fine looking man, de Bacqueville reported, perhaps forty-six or forty-seven years old, who would probably be appointed Grand Général after the death of Potocki.[6] The Petit Général had already been married twice, first to a Radziwill who died, it was rumoured, under mysterious circumstances; his second wife had run off with Count Lowendal, the future Maréchal de France, currently a general in the Saxon army. That marriage was now dissolved. The Petit Général came well recommended and was said to be wealthy. The Grand Général, Potocki, had also placed his name on the list for his grandson and there were several Radziwill princes and various members of the Polish aristocracy of lesser rank or fortune. It was imperative to make a choice. Moreover, if Prince James did not sell his lands immediately, he would be reduced within the year, de Bacqueville insisted, to little more than the palace at Zolkiew and a modest revenue from Ohlau. Not enough money would remain to put even a pound of bread or a scrawny chicken on his table! And if (God forbid) he were to die suddenly, the situation would be even worse, for the Radziwills would probably attempt to seize the Prince's lands by military force. The prospects were dizzying. He would ask nothing better than to bring the young Princess back to France if none of the Polish arrangements worked out. As for the mother, he would not accompany her on the return trip for all the money in the world!

Not surprisingly, Marie-Charlotte espoused the opposite view, advising that the lands not be sold: the proceeds, she maintained, would be quickly dissipated, and then they would have nothing. She too asked for clear instructions from her husband: did he want her to stay on with their daughter or not? Her health was not good, and though she would give up Paris if she had to, she would regret not being able to confide in her uncle, the Comte d'Evreux, before she died. She assured her husband that she loved their daughter: "Je fais tout ce que je peux faire pour luy marquer ma tendresse maternelle et je crois peu de meres fasse autan. Je ne suis non plus ingrate. Je me souviens fort bien que c'est le premier gage de votre amitié." Again she pleaded with him to trust her. It was imperative, in any case, that he write as soon as possible to her father, giving him his unambiguous instructions concerning Louise's marriage.[7]

In the weeks following, she even made an effort to reconcile with de Bacqueville. Her olive branch was spurned.[8]

At the end of April, news reached Zolkiew that Emmanuel-Théodose's notorious young widow had died suddenly. Writing to the Duc a few days after learning of the event, the Duchesse twitted her husband on the loss of his dear stepmother. He was not to take it too much to heart, she added ironically, although she herself had been very remiss in allowing her rival to precede her to the other world![9] Having delivered that uncharitable remark, Marie-Charlotte returned to her conciliatory efforts with de Bacqueville. She had offered to hand over any legal papers the Duc might require, but he no longer seemed interested. Her only regret was that she had not been allowed to be of any use to her husband: "Tout mon chagrin ait que je ne vous suis bon a rien. Soyez, je vous conjure, assure et convaincu, mon adorable mary, de mon tendre et sincere attachement pour vous et que je suis tout a vous pour la vie, votre fidelle fame."[10]

The uncharacteristically ardent tone of the Duc's next letter to the Duchesse, almost makes us believe he had suddenly converted to the ways of peace. First of all, he informed his wife, he had now totally decided against any Polish marriage—of any kind. Louise was to be brought back to France where she would be "established." The Duchesse, he assumed, would be pleased, both for herself and for the daughter she loved. Nothing was to be said to Prince James for the next two months, however. She was to keep his intentions secret and let him know how best to proceed so as not to harm her interests in Poland. He wished it were already the moment when he could see her again: "Que de choses j'aurois a vous dire et quel plaisir j'aurois a vous voir partager les horreurs que j'essuye de la part de Mr le Comte d'Evreux que je ne vois plus depuis deux mois."[11] We begin to understand! From the time she first met him in Strasbourg in 1723, Marie-Charlotte had developed a warm relationship with the Duc's uncle, whose great wealth and senior position in the Bouillon family gave him substantial power over Charles-Godefroy's affairs. The Duc was hoping that his wife would be able to intervene in their recent dispute: "Pourray-je me flatter que mes chagrins puissent vous donner quelque moment d'amertume contre un homme qui me persécute et qui, sous pretexte d'amitié, cherche mon mal personnel et ma ruine?" What was the occasion of this serious dissension? No hint was given in the Duc's letter, which closed with even more mysterious references to great riches and mountains of affection in the offing: "Enfin je suis a la veille d'estre en Etat de me passer a jamais de toute succession si mon affaire reussit. Je partageray avec vous une fortune Brillante et ne la trouveray douce qu'en la partageant avec vous." The Duc's cynicism toward his wife was limitless. Only a week before he had sent the following secret message to de Bacqueville: "Sur toutes choses, faites en sorte d'empecher le retour de ma tante."[12]

Ironically, the explanation of the great mystery is revealed in a letter from the Duchesse to the Duc, written before the Duc's strange epistle arrived at Zolkiew. Her father, she stated, was delighted that Charles-Godefroy was finally conducting some of his business through her. He had agreed to the three months' delay and was pleased at the prospect of having the little Princess married in Poland, thus preserving in Sobieski hands his own estates and those that had belonged to his illustrious father. In her view, the best choice seemed to be the Petit Général. Her father approved, but the Duc would be wise to make his consent conditional on assurance from Augustus III that the Petit Général would indeed be appointed Grand Général after the death of the incumbent. The position of Grand Général, the Duchesse explained, was extremely important since it constituted "un beau chemin pour la Couronne." Louise could thus become, one day, Queen of Poland! Of course, it was all up to the Duc to decide; she would not insist one way or the other.

Marie-Charlotte next turned to a subject related to the Duc's enigmatic promises of a brilliant fortune to come. She had heard that he was selling the *vicomté* of Turenne, the jewel of the Bouillon family's properties, but she had refused to believe it for if he did that, Charles-Godefroy would be dishonouring his ancestors! Were others now to bear that great name? Did he not realize that he would be robbing their son to whom the estate was entailed? "Au nom de Dieu, ne faitte pas," she begged; "Dieu nous donnera d'autre moyen pour arranger nos affaires."[13] The Comte d'Evreux, as it turned out, actively shared the Duchesse's concern to protect the legal rights of her son, the Prince de Turenne, and it had been precisely the uncle's opposition to the scheme that had caused the heated dispute and a rift that was to last for several years to come.

The unusual sale of the property bearing the name of France's most celebrated general of the preceding century was a momentous event. The purchaser was none other than the King of France, and the Duc de Luynes noted in his journal for 10 June that the proposed arrangement had been the subject of court gossip for some time:

> l'on prétend que ce seroit un bon marché pour le Roi. Ce marché mettroit M. de Bouillon à portée de payer toutes les dettes de sa maison et les siennes, et de jouir encore d'environ 400,000 livres de rente, sur quoi, à la vérité, il y a 160,000 livres de rente à payer, mais viagère. M. le comte d'Evreux croit avoir droit de s'opposer à cette vente.[14]

The Zolkiew mail was, meanwhile, just catching up with the Duc's earlier proposal of a possible marriage arrangement with one of the Stuart princes. De Bacqueville reported on 3 June that Prince James, whose affection for the children of Maria-Clementina was great, wept tears of joy on learning of it. Louise might one day be Queen of England! A letter was immediately sent off to

Rome. The Duc's agent, following instructions, had also insisted on secrecy, reminding the old man that there had already been more than enough scandal in the gazettes related to the earlier fiasco in Dresden. That was the good news de Bacqueville had for his master. The bad came not more than two days later: the secret, unfortunately, was already out, the old Prince having blissfully blabbed the Stuart proposal to all and sundry, Marie-Charlotte as well. She, of course, was furious at their little deception.... Trapped in a series of lies but feeling no guilt and filled with sham indignation, de Bacqueville now did his best to make mischief. Entire letters to the Duc were devoted to descriptions of a Duchesse planning nefarious schemes; he had it first hand from Mlle de Minières, for example, that Marie-Charlotte was doing everything possible to destroy her daughter in the eyes of the old Prince. Nor was her husband spared, he could be certain! His faithful emissary more than once had been obliged at the dinner table to defend the sale of Turenne (although he too admitted to certain qualms about the unfortunate loss of a great name to the family). The Duchesse was clearly out to gobble up the inheritance entirely for herself. Much luck to her! He hoped she would never return to France; he wanted nothing more to do with her. Henceforth, he would see her only if urgent business required it.

Long delays in the mail between Paris and Zolkiew, aggravated by contradictory and constantly shifting instructions from the Quai Malaquais, added to the confusion in the court of Prince James. The Duchesse was reported to be already worried about another "refus honteux" if the Stuart proposal failed. Wild rumours circulated that Louise would have an enormous annual revenue of 600,000 livres as her dowry from France. The Petit Général, rich in land but probably poor in money, was still hopeful. So too was the Grand Général, who was rich in money but stingy; he had settled little wealth on his son, the Palatin of Smolensko, father of one of the suitors. Even King Stanislas had now entered the competition with a strong personal recommendation in favour of the young Staroste Buski, a Jablonowski who had only a name and no money.[15] But what could one think of a candidate with an income of no more than 30,000 livres to his name?

Meanwhile, though his memory was failing, Prince James had not forgotten the time limit he had granted the Duc to decide on which of the various suitors would be most appropriate for Louise. On 19 June the Prince's secretary, de Lauro, handed de Bacqueville a note reminding him that the Grand Chambellan's decision had to reach Zolkiew no later than 10 August. The Duc's envoy was now faced with a dilemma, having just received a secret letter dated 29 May from the Duc giving him official authority to oppose any Polish marriage, even if Prince James insisted otherwise. He knew that the Prince Royal would be furious at the Duc's apparent lack of good faith.

De Bacqueville, in fact, managed the bad news brilliantly, proving once again that he was worth every penny the Duc was paying him. First of all, he solemnly and soothingly promised, the deadline *would be met*; yes, the Prince Royal could be certain on that point! But, to be perfectly truthful, there *was* one small worry that had been troubling his master the Duc for some time now and this involved the extremely tender age of his children, especially the Prince de Turenne. If the young lad were to fall prey to an illness and die, would Louise not suddenly become the richest heiress in Europe? Marriage to a foreigner under such circumstances would be unwise. In any case, Prince James could rest assured that whether Louise's marriage ultimately took place in Poland or in France, it would take place *only* with her grandfather's formal approval. Moreover, was there not still some hope of an alliance with the Stuarts?

All in all, the interview had gone well, de Bacqueville reported to the Duc. The old man had indeed raged for a time and the Duchesse afterwards was none too pleased at the deception; but it had got him through a hard day, and he felt the storm would soon blow over.

The storm did not blow over. De Bacqueville soon heard from de Lauro that Prince James was again furious with him and with Mlle de Minières too. They had apparently been maligning the Petit Général and, indeed, had talked openly against *any* Polish marriage. Protesting his innocence, the Duc's agent asked for an audience to justify himself. He was refused, but he managed to communicate with the influential Palatine de Russie, Prince James's cousin (and mother, incidentally, of the Princesse de Talmont), who agreed to act as an intermediary. She reported that the Prince Royal had now resurrected all of his old grievances: Marie-Charlotte had married without his consent and that gave him the right to do what he pleased with Louise. De Bacqueville's account of his proxy-counterattack, though probably somewhat overblown, was a masterpiece of eloquent rage in defence of the Duc's interests:

Je repondis a S. Ex.[16] que lorsque Madame La Duchesse s'etoit remariée, elle etoit majeure, veuve et maitresse de son bien et de ses volontes... mais qu'aujourd'huy l'espece etoit bien differente; que la princesse n'avoit que 12 ans et peu,[17] et qu'elle et sa mere etoient en votre pouvoir, que S.A.R. n'auroit sil vouloit l'exercer de droit que la violence, que je le croyois trop sage et trop eclairé pour violer en la persone de sa petite fille le droit de la nature et des gents, mais que s'il en venoit a cette extremité, 50 ou 60 homes de garde qu'il avoit ne me feroient point trahir mon devoir : que je me ferois hacher en piece avant d'abandoner un enfant qui m'etoit peut estre autant confiée qu'a la princesse sa mere; que j'attendois du courage et de l'attachement de Mademoiselle Deminieres la meme chose et que quand on commenceroit par m'assassiner, j'instruirois si bien la jeune princesse de ses devoirs qu'elle n'y donneroit jamais son consentement, qu'elle apartenoit à l'Empereur, qu'elle etoit fille de V.A. et sujete du Roy de France qui sait bien proteger ses sujets de moindre rang contre les violences... que finalement on me rendît et a sa gouvernante dans ce moment l'enfant en chemise et que je trouverois bien les moyens de la rendre a V.A., que j'estimois d'ailleurs que je m'adresserois a Made la Palatine elle-meme, sa tante pour avoir chez elle azyle contre la violence si on en venoit la.[18]

If we are to believe de Bacqueville's own description of the Prince's temper, it was perhaps fortunate for him that all this had been said to Prince James's cousin rather than to the old man himself. During the exchange, the Palatine expressed regret at being obliged to pass on Prince James's harsh messages, but she assured him "qu'elle adouciroit mes reponses en adoucissant le prince." De Bacqueville, of course, insisted that he was prepared to repeat every word directly to the Prince's face. He then informed the Duc of his next move—instructing Louise in her duty to her father:

J'allay de suitte chez la jeune princesse que je pris en particulier avec Madle de Minieres. Je dis en peu de mots a cette pauvre enfant ma situation et luy fis conoistre qu'elle devoit obeir a V.A. come a Dieu dans les choses de Droit et qu'elle devoit dire resolument toujours non et encor plus au pied de l'autel si on l'y menoit par force, jusqu'a ce qu'elle vît un ordre de la main de V.A.

The eleven-year-old Princess must have been duly impressed if not terrified! It is equally probable that in the course of de Bacqueville's dramatic exhortations, the Duchesse was not spared; certainly, she was not spared in subsequent references to her in his letter to the Duc! She was still conspiring with the priest and, full of false tears, now talked only of leaving Poland and even of entering a convent. He was not enough of a fool to believe all that! She was up to some trickery. The Duc was to be congratulated for buttering her up so well in his last letter.[19]

Buttered up or not, the Duchesse hastened in her next letter to tell her husband a few home truths. She would say nothing of his incredibly deceitful practice of writing, as she had finally discovered, one thing to her and another to de Bacqueville. She could not, on the other hand, remain silent concerning his reprehensible conduct toward her father: "Vous avez tres male fait d'avoir flatte mon Pere que le mois daoust vous ferez donne la resolution finale sur le choix de la personne ici en Pologne et aujourd'huy vous ecrivez brusquement que vous ne voulez pas la marier en Pologne. Bacqueville l'a dict a mon Pere lequel est furieux.... Vous vous etes bien male pris, vous faittes tous de votre teste."[20] He had undone all her good work; she had gone to Poland to be reconciled with her father and regain his good will; she was being gratuitously isolated in her role as daughter, wife, and mother; now everything was lost forever. They would be sent back in August or September. She had sacrificed everything for him, her health, all hope of fortune, and she was left with only his cruelties.

Although Prince James had indeed decided to send everyone back to Paris if the Duc's final decision was negative, the situation in the palace at Zolkiew grew even more uneasy. Scarcely one week after vividly narrating his angry proxy exchange with Prince James, de Bacqueville felt obliged to write again with even more alarming news. The Prince, he reported, had now regressed to his former position, insisting that, no matter what decision the Duc came to, he could still proceed on his own authority and marry Louise off in Poland. Once it was done, it would be done, and no one would have a word to say. De Bacqueville had apparently countered that murder too was done when it was done, but there was still justice in heaven and on earth to consider. Moreover, was it not best to send Louise back to France? Her education was being sadly neglected, and she was forgetting everything she had previously learned. Calm had ensued, but at dinner that same day there was another explosive discussion, during which the Duchesse, de Bacqueville was generous enough to admit, had attempted to reason gently with her father. Prince James had remained unmoved; moreover, he had had enough of the Duc's agent incessantly "breaking his ears." The Duc's letter to him had been clear enough, the old man declared, and he was thus authorized to proceed.

De Bacqueville was now genuinely alarmed: the Prince was a weak old man, "mais il est aussi furieux, et capable dans cette fureur de doner des ordres violents a des brutaux qui les executeroient."[21] How would he be able to defend the Princess and Mlle de Minières if he were set upon by fifty or sixty guards and an even greater number of servants? There was only one way out: it was time for the Duc to ask the King of France to intervene. Cardinal Fleury had to write a letter on behalf of Louis XV, requiring that the Princess be returned immediately to France. Appropriate threats of punishment for non-compliance would have to be included. As for the Duchesse, the Duc's agent had already made it perfectly clear to her that he would rather jump from the castle parapet than have anything to do with her *and he was not alone in that sentiment*: only her valet de chambre and the hated priest supported her: "Je n'avance rien icy que Mlle de Minieres et Mlle d'Orvaux, et la jeune princesse elle meme n'ayent vu et entendu."

De Bacqueville had already expressed his complete satisfaction with Mlle de Minières and her niece, whose loyalty to the Duc he now singled out for special praise. Strangely enough, even Marie-Charlotte seems to have felt somewhat intimidated by Louise's formidable governess. The following letter, from de Minières to the Duc, fully sharing de Bacqueville's fears for Louise's safety, adds to our knowledge of a woman who probably had more direct influence on the formative years of the Princess than her own mother:

Monseigneur,
Permettés moy de prendre la liberté de remercier tres humblement vôtre altesse de la bonté qu'el vient de marquer a mon neveu, de le mettre aux nombre de ces gentilhomme.[22] Jespere, Monseigneur, qu'il ne ce rendera pas indigne de la protection dont vôtre altesse veut bien l'honorer. Mr de Bacville a rendu comte a vôtre altesse des inquietude ou nous avons este par tous les mauvais conceil que lon avoit donnes au prince roial.[23] Mr de Bacville et moy ne soufririons qu'au peril de notre vie que l'on entrepris aucune chose sans un consentement precis de la part de votre altesse. Je ne quitte pas un moment la princesse qui assure de son tendre et profond respect votre altesse. Si c'es son intention de rapeler la princesse, je desirerois fort qu'el eü encore un apartement au Chasse midi. C'es une maison ramplie de bons example et souvent tous les couvent ne sont pas de meme. J'ose dire a votre altesse qu'il es de consecances de bien choisir sa demeure.[24]

> Jatens les ordres de Monseigneur.
> des Minieres
> A Zulkiew ce 17 juillet

Rather than being married to a great prince—perhaps a future King of either Poland or England—Louise would be going back to her convent! De Bacqueville had already alluded to Mlle de Minières' request for accommodation there in his letter to Saint-Gervais of 10 July: "Elle voudra bien ravoir l'appartement du Cherche Midi où trepassa la deffunte."[25] Adding a note to the outside of her governess's letter, Louise expressed her usual affection for her father and mentioned the death of the Abbess in terms that lead us to believe she was a polite and deferential pupil. True to her rigid conditioning, however, she avoided any mention of her mother:

Je gronde Mlle Desminieres, Mon Tres cher papa, de cacheter sa lettre sans que je vous assure moi meme de mon profond respect et de l'envie que jay d'avoir l'honneur de vous embrasser. Je trouverai bien mauvais, Mon cher Papa, si vous ne me faites pas un compliment sur la mort de Madame l'Abesse.

That the Duc's final decision would be negative and that Louise would be sent back to her convent was a foregone conclusion for everyone at Zolkiew except, possibly, the Prince Royal, who, despite de Bacqueville's broad hints, still awaited a formal statement. Much the same situation obtained with regard to the Stuart marriage proposal, even though that particular suggestion had, in fact, already been tentatively explored by the Duc earlier in the year and politely declined in Rome. Everyone thus waited around pretending there was something to wait for.

The Duc, meanwhile, had found de Bacqueville's quick-thinking arguments against a Polish marriage so plausible that he decided to adopt them holus-bolus as his own. To Prince James he expressed his delight that the Stuart marriage proposal had been forwarded from Zolkiew to Rome. Of course, if he were to consult only his own interests, he would not marry Louise to anyone at all until her young brother was settled, he being "encore dans un age a craindre un malheureux evenement."[26] But he would not be so selfish: "Je laisse a part mes sentiments et regarde ce qui peut convenir a V.A.R. Aussy elle peut estre assurée que je suivray exactement les ordres quelle me donnera pour finir cette affaire, mais j'ose luy en demander, par toutes les bontés dont elle me comble, de ne point exiger de moy d'etablir la jeune Princesse de Bouillon en Pologne au cas que la lettre que V.A.R. a escritte au Roy[27] n'eut pas tout l'effet que j'en espere." Moreover, since he would certainly not want his daughter to be a burden on the Prince, de Bacqueville had been instructed, in the case of a negative decision, to bring her back to her father, who would naturally seek the Prince Royal's approval for any future marriage arrangement.

Charles-Godefroy wrote to Marie-Charlotte on the same day, using the same blandly comforting arguments. He had thought the matter over carefully and could not agree now to a Polish marriage since the risk that Louise might become "en un moment la plus riche heritiere de l'Europe semble luy devoir assurer un sort plus brillant que celuy ou ceux que l'on me propose."[28] He acknowledged the distinction and illustrious birth of the various Polish candidates and would forever be grateful for their interest, but his position was final. Even the Stuart suggestion was acceptable to him only because it had pleased Prince James so much and would be advantageous to his dear wife! Yes it was indeed true that if the Stuart proposal failed, de Bacqueville was charged with *sole* responsibility for bringing Louise back to her father, but even there Charles-Godefroy was thinking only of his dear wife's welfare. She would no doubt want to stay on. He had carefully instructed his agent to carry out his orders "en ménageant les choses de façon que vous puissiez demeurer si cela vous convient, comme il me le paroit, sentant combien il vous est important de vous trouver sur les lieux en cas de malheur." That particularly brilliant idea he had hit upon himself. It only remained now for the Duc to assure his wife that his feelings of tenderness for her were eternal *and had never wavered.* As an afterthought, he informed her that the Queen of France had just given birth to a girl "ce qui a bien affligé le Roy et, en vérité, tout le monde."

Formally announcing the final bad news to Prince James presented a risk. Not wishing to jeopardize further the position of his agent, the Duc hit upon the notion of enclosing his negative letter to the Prince Royal in that of the Duchesse. No doubt it could be construed as more evidence of his great affection for her! The Duchesse's reaction was predictable: the honour of presenting such a letter, she immediately replied, should obviously be left to de

Bacqueville! By his cruel and insulting behaviour, Charles-Godefroy was making it obvious that he did not want to see her again! She would be obliged to wander from place to place if her father refused to keep her. For the first time ever, she allowed herself a frosty closing formula: "J'ay l'honneur d'estre, Monsieur votre tres humble...."[29]

Two days later, de Bacqueville confirmed that Marie-Charlotte had refused his repeated requests to show the old Prince her husband's letter. Her reluctance, he thought, was quite incomprehensible! Finally, Mocki, the priest, had agreed to bell the cat. The Prince had reacted with predictable fury, but he was now strangely calm. De Bacqueville felt nervous and worried. He would not feel secure until he and the Princess were safely in Austrian territory.

Only one last question remained to be answered before the move back to Paris, or at the very least to Ohlau, could take place: would the Stuart King, James III, finally approve of a marriage between one of his sons and the Princesse de Bouillon? The answer came from Rome almost at the same time as the Duc's disappointing communiqué arrived from Paris, and de Bacqueville was duly handed a copy. Not unexpectedly, the *de jure* King of England, needing to keep his options for future alliances open, found himself unable to acquiesce in the proposal:

> Rien n'est plus naturel que le desir qu'a le Duc de Bouillon de faire épouser sa fille à un de mes enfants. Mais il est vrai que je m'étonne qu'il a entammé a present une négociation avec vous sur cette matiere; car il m'en a fait presenter il y a deja du tems, et il ne pouvoit ignorer les difficultés que j'y trouvai. Les motifs que j'ai d'estimer et de considérer avec une amitié distinguée la Maison de Bouillon sont grands. Mais quand ils seroient encore davantage, je croyerois veritablement manquer a ce que je dois a mes enfants d'engager ma parole pour eux dans une pareille matiere avant qu'ils ayent atteint l'age que l'Eglise a fixé pour cela. D'ailleurs, Mon Cher Pere, vous sentirés bien que mon retablissement pourroit un jour dependre de quelques alliances avec mes enfants, et que je ne pourrai repondre ni à Dieu ni aux hommes si par des engagements prematurés je me privois de telles resources pour le retablissement de ma famille dont le retour au Trône de nos ancestres doit être par toutes sortes de raisons le principal, et on pourroit quasi dire, l'unique objet temporel qui doit m'occuper. Je suis persuadé, Mon Cher Pere, que vous vous renderez aux raisons que j'ai de ne pas entrer a present dans vos vieüs par rapport au Duc, mais avec tout cela je ressens une vive peine de ne pouvoir vous complaire la dessus, et je suis bien persuadé que votre tendresse pour mes enfants n'en sera pas affoiblie puisqu'ils tacheront toujours, aussi bien que moi, d'en mériter la continuation par notre constant et tendre attachment pour vous.[30]

The proposal, so fitting in many ways, had come at the wrong time. Jacobite hopes were on the rise again by 1737; Charles Edward, the handsome young Prince of Wales, had just completed a triumphant tour of the northern Italian cities where he had been feted royally at balls and assemblies given in his honour. There was talk, even, of prestigious marriage prospects—for example, with an Infanta of Spain— and no doubt James III had every right to look forward to a brilliant destiny for his two sons.[31] Who could have foreseen that only a decade later it would become James III's gloomy duty to inform his eldest son, fresh from defeat at Culloden, that a Spanish or French princess was now wildly beyond reach—as was, probably, even a minor princess from the same family as James's own mother?[32] Ironically, not long after that, Charles Edward Stuart himself was to begin a desperate search through all the usual almanacs for a suitably minor bride. But before that search began, he was destined to fall in love with the Duc de Bouillon's daughter, already married, and, as it turned out, a distinguished princess from *his* own mother's family.

IV

Prisoners in Poland

THE DUC DE BOUILLON'S decision against any Polish marriage and the unambiguously negative response from James III should have removed all uncertainty from the situation of the beleaguered Bouillon party in Zolkiew. Their hope was that they would now be sent home or at least be allowed to await any further developments at Ohlau in Silesia, well beyond the Polish border. With that end in view, de Bacqueville even signed an undertaking in the Duc's name pledging that Louise would remain at the old Prince's castle in Ohlau for as long as her grandfather desired.

Unfortunately, Prince James had not made up his mind to accept a humiliating defeat. He had in good faith publicly accepted candidacies for his granddaughter's hand from the most distinguished and powerful members of the Polish aristocracy. It was now an embarrassing and delicate problem to inform such a dazzling array of aspirants that the whole thing had been a mistake. His affection for his granddaughter was deep and genuine; tears came to his eyes and his voice broke with emotion when he finally told Louise how much he regretted that she would probably have to return to some dismal convent in Paris.[1] A move back to Ohlau would not be so easy to arrange, moreover. Land would have to be sold to meet the additional expenses. Worse still, it amounted to abandoning the Prince Royal's cherished dream of keeping his vast Polish estates in the family. To the moody autocrat (who had barely four months to live), it all seemed extremely improper and unjust.

Paradoxically, much of his resentment was now turned against his daughter. Why had she not been placed in charge of his granddaughter rather than that confounded windbag and interfering pest, de Bacqueville? The obvious contempt shown her by her husband, by the servants, and even by her own daughter, far from exciting the old man's compassion, served merely to remind him that Marie-Charlotte had long before given up all right to his blessing by marrying a dissipated and debauched Frenchman. When it came to ordering people to leave, she deserved to be among the first to go! As for her worthless husband, who did he take himself for anyway, giving orders from Paris about what was or was not to happen at his court in Zolkiew! Such indignant musings were, of course, reserved mainly for those occasions when an irritating incident triggered a royal tantrum. For the most part, however, life was fairly calm at the palace, and from time to time members of the group, though feeling more like prisoners than guests, became caught up in the excitement of rumours that everything was being made ready for their impending departure.

Alarmed by de Bacqueville's highly dramatic reports that Prince James seemed prepared to resort to violence, the Duc had meanwhile enlisted the support of powerful friends to force Prince James to release Louise from "imprisonment." One such appeal was made to the King of France and a second to the King's father-in-law, Stanislas, whose own recent misfortunes in Poland had sufficiently convinced him that it was a country of violence where people would not hesitate to take the law into their own hands. In a letter cogently presenting his case but totally lacking in candour, the Duc set out the "facts" of the matter: he had never, he solemnly informed Stanislas, given consent, either directly or indirectly, for the settlement of his daughter in Poland. His father-in-law had deliberately sought out a quarrel with him in order to justify a scheme to marry the Princess to the Petit Général. The proposal had never received his blessing, and it would be useful if Stanislas informed the Prince Royal that the Duc de Bouillon was asking only that his daughter be returned to him — unless, of course, the old man succeeded in *his* plan to marry Louise to one of the Stuart princes. "Mais si ce mariage ne peut réussir, je le laisse le maître de frustrer mes Enfans de toute sa succession, et borne mes desirs a ravoir ma Fille."[2] As for his wife, he had generously agreed to allow her to stay with her father as long as that suited her interests.

A reply from Lunéville was not long in coming. The proposed Stuart marriage, Stanislas declared, would indeed be logical and natural since it would unite the two branches of Prince James's family, thereby eliminating future inheritance problems; the only difficulty arose from the fact that, as foreigners, neither of the two English princes would be able to own land in Poland. Nor would it be possible for them to acquire the requisite *indigenat* because of collateral Polish claimants to the estate. The best solution was, therefore, to sell the land while the Prince Royal was still alive and to transfer his wealth afterwards in the form of money. But, Stanislas continued, Prince James was so much in favour of the Petit Général, Branicki, that the Duc was quite right to fear the worst. The old man might very well try to ram through a marriage without the Duc's consent: "La Pologne est un Pays ou on croit que tout est permis, ainsy prenez vos mesures la-dessus."[3] He would certainly do his best to deal with his cousin, but his final advice was that the Duc should get his daughter out of Poland at the earliest possible opportunity.

In fact, the urgings of the Polish King in exile were superfluous, the Grand Chambellan having already appealed to Louis XV to make a formal request to Augustus III to intervene directly in the dispute. Just as in his appeal to Stanislas, the Duc in his presentation to the King of France took substantial liberties with the truth. He explained how, with the approval of Louis XV and Cardinal Fleury, he had sent his daughter to Poland at the request of his father-in-law, Prince James Sobieski, who had informed him of Augustus III's intention to marry Louise to one of the Polish royal princes. Negotiations had failed. Subsequently, Prince James had proposed other possible Polish matches, but the Duc had insisted that he would not under any circumstances give his consent. Now, Prince James was intending to ignore the Duc's wishes and was determined to take advantage of the fact that he had the Princess in his custody in order to marry her to whomever he pleased. The Duc was thus appealing to the King of France to ask the King of Poland to forbid any marriage planned without the express written permission of the Duc de Bouillon.[4]

In Zolkiew, meanwhile, Mlle de Minières and the Princess had been explicitly instructed by de Bacqueville to resist at all costs. Louise wrote to her father on 4 September to assure him that she would not be lacking in the courage to do her duty, even if it were to cost her her life:

> Vos ordres seront toutte ma vie une loi pour moi. Je soufrirois plus aisement la mort que de m'eloigner un moment de votre volonté. Je prie Mr de Bacqueville de vous faire un plus long detail de tout ce qui se passe ici. Je suis encore incertaine du tems que j'aurai le bonheur de baizer la main de Mon cher Papa et de l'assurer du profond respect et entiere soumission de sa petitte fille.

Throughout September there was as much talk as ever about possible marriages. Suitors continued to turn up, including one of the Radziwill princes, who even de Bacqueville thought was a good match. What really seemed to be worrying the Duc's agent now was not the danger that Prince James might force a marriage but rather the Duchesse's mounting anger toward him. He became more and more convinced that some of the comments he had made about her in his secret correspondence with the Duc had somehow been "leaked" back to Marie-Charlotte by her friends in Paris. She had apparently even made threats, saying, as de Bacqueville reported to the Duc, that "malgré son aversion à faire du mal, elle se vengeroit d'un coquin comme moy, qu'elle prieroit, avant de partir, le Prince son père d'en écrire à V.A. et qu'elle ne remettroit pas le pied dans l'hotel que je n'en fusse chassé, etc."[5] De Bacqueville, we sense, was not really worried about losing in a close battle with the Duchesse for the Duc's affections! But while he had no need to fear expulsion from the Hôtel de Bouillon, he did come close, near the end of September, to being unceremoniously thrown out of the Sobieski palace in Zolkiew! His vivid account of one of the Prince Royal's epic rages, this time apparently caused by Louise's failure to learn Polish, is to be found in a letter to his friend Saint-Gervais. While it is drawn out and obviously enhanced by de Bacqueville's habitually dramatic posturing, the story does provide an intimate glimpse of Louise, traumatically entangled in a web of dissension and intrigue that must have left its mark on her later character:

Le 20 au soir apres souper où l'on avoit parlé de polonais et de langues, j'allay a mon ordinaire chez la jeune princesse comme j'ay coutume de faire touts les soirs, mais celui la un peu plus tard a cause d'une visite que je fis dans le chateau. Je trouvay cet enfant en pleurs et sanglotante. Le sujet etoit que le prince Royal, apres la table...demanda a la jeune princesse pourquoy elle n'aprenoit pas le polonais. Elle repondit que cette langue etoit tres difficile. Le prince se mit alors en colere et luy dit c'est ce...cavalier (parlant de moy) qui en est la cause mais j'y mettray fin. L'enfant se tourna et vint a la gouvernante. Come je causois avec M. le Chancelier, je ne vis rien de tout cela et le P.R., au lieu de doner sa main a l'ordinaire a la petite fille et luy doner sa benediction, la repoussa. Je la consolay et m'allay coucher. Elle passa la nuit assez mal et Mlle Deminieres, qui jugea a propos de la faire aller a la messe (jour de St Mathieu) et la faire remettre ensuitte dans son lit, m'envoya demander si je voulois aller a la messe a la chapelle et me conta que Mlle avoit fort mal passé la nuit. La mere prit cela pour une incomodité jouée, et le P.R. encore mieux et me voila criminel pour avoir été a la messe avec Mlle de Bouillon. De plus, quelqu'un des honestes gents qui entourent le prince lui avoit dit que la petite princesse m'ayant dit le soir en haut la reponse qu'elle avoit faite, j'avois dit qu'elle avoit fort bien fait, lesquels deux faits sont exactement faux et bien conus pour tels, mais ils ne laisserent pas de produire un bel effet, car vers le midy, M. de Lauro vint me dire de la part de S.A.R. qu'etant la cause de touts les troubles qui arrivoient, j'eusse a prendre mon parti pour sortir le lendemain du chateau & m'en aller & que si quelqu'un des femmes netoit pas contente, je pouvois la prendre avec moy. De plus que je pouvois faire afficher et enregistrer mon diplome d'opposition au mariage partout où je voudrois et que le Duc de Bouillon n'avoit point d'ordre a envoyer dans son chateau et qu'il garderoit la petite fille tant qu'il voudroit. Je repondis que je n'aportois aucun trouble icy, que je ne pouvois mais, et ignorois parfaittement ce qui s'etoit dit la veille, et que j'avois su par Mlle la gouvernante et les domestiques que Mlle de Bouillon avoit été incomodée, que du reste je parlerois a Made. la Duchesse.[6]

The Prince Royal's fury was finally calmed by Marie-Charlotte, to whom, much to his chagrin, de Bacqueville was obliged to appeal. He would be allowed to stay on, he informed Saint-Gervais, on condition that he never mention even the name of the Duc de Bouillon. On that same occasion, old Prince James had solemnly informed his daughter that he no longer regarded the Duc as his son-in-law, "en quoy elle s'est mise a portée de se faire repondre par son page et par sa femme de chambre qu'elle est donc la maitresse de M. de Bouillon et sa fille une batarde. Elle en est quitte pour dire que son pere ne sait ce qu'il dit et elle a grande raison. En attendant, point de depart".

In spite of her intervention on his behalf, the Duc's agent remained staunchly unforgiving toward his benefactress. His letter to Saint-Gervais closed with a slanderous hint that Marie-Charlotte was greedily raking in an under-the-table fortune—perhaps as much as 100,000 livres, in *pots de vin*—through the sale of her father's land. She was also still trying to worm her way into his good graces, but, he assured the Duc's secretary, he was having none of it and had refused to hand over papers that she had requested. Their departure for Ohlau would apparently not take place now until the following spring, in order to give the Prince time to arrange for the sale of his lands. He and Mlle de Minières both agreed that this was only another pretext for delay, and he hoped that the Duc would take immediate and severe counter-measures. He himself intended to stay on in his "purgatory" at Zolkiew for no more than two additional months; then, no matter what happened, he would leave. He preferred the Duc's everlasting displeasure, and the "galleys" even, to remaining there.

De Bacqueville's confidence in the strength of his position with the Duc was well-founded. Scarcely more than two weeks later, Charles-Godefroy congratulated him warmly on his intrepid display of steadfastness and courage which, the Duc felt, had probably saved Louise from ruination. The Grand Chambellan also indicated that if ever it came to choosing between the Duchesse and his agent there would not be the slightest hesitation: "Soyez tranquille, mon cher Bacqueville, sur les menées de vôtre tante....Je suis trop satisfait de votre conduitte pour que ses discours puissent me faire quelque impression."[7] In the same letter the Duc revealed that Augustus III, thanks to Cardinal Fleury's representations, had agreed to look into the situation in Zolkiew. Louise, meanwhile, would be safe enough once in Ohlau. In fact, if her grandfather wished, he was free to explore possibilities for a German marriage. A Polish marriage remained, however, quite out of the question.

Prince James, along with his entourage, nevertheless continued to hope— Louise had attracted such worthy suitors! Admittedly, the Petit Général was perhaps a little old, but did the Duc de Bouillon not realize that he was the richest and most distinguished nobleman in Poland? How could that dissipated French fop imagine that Branicki himself was not good enough for a Bouillon Princess! His own reputation at Zolkiew was certainly not impressive: "Toute la maison," de Bacqueville complained to Saint-Gervais, "retentit icy de la mauvaise conduite du prince notre maistre: qu'il a des maitresses, qu'il joue et perd, et que depuis plus de six ans il ne couche pas avec sa femme."[8]

With such tidbits of gossip, de Bacqueville no doubt hoped to increase his master's irritation with the Prince Royal and consequently to reduce the length of his own dreadful sentence in Poland. Unfortunately, a newsy item forwarded to the Quai Malaquais nearly six weeks earlier was already causing more mischief than even he had intended. He had reported vague suspicions that the old Prince intended to drive him, the governess, and Mlle de Minières' niece from the castle. Embellished *à la Bacqueville*, this passing reference had been enough to set the entire apparatus of the French Foreign Ministry in motion. Vague rumour was transformed by the Duc into scandalous fact, and the King of France himself now felt obliged to intervene personally, in the belief that Prince James had actually dismissed all of the Duc's servants. Louise, now publicly represented as a helpless prisoner in a foreign land, suddenly became a European *cause célèbre*!

Though couched in the usual diplomatic niceties, Louis XV's letter to the King of Poland was firm and to the point:

Tres haut, tres excellent & tres puissant Prince, notre tres cher & tres aimé bon frere, Cousin allié & Confédéré. Vous avez deja du etre instruit, par un mémoire remis en notre nom à Vienne,[9] des justes sujets d'inquiétude de notre Cousin, le Duc de Bouillon, sur le projet formé par le Prince Jacques Sobieski de faire faire à sa petite fille qui est actuellement pres de lui, un mariage peu convenable & sans le consentement des Pere & Mere. Ces inquiétudes sont encore augmentées par la nouvelle que le Pce Jacques vient de renvoyer tous les Domestiques dont il a crû que la presence pouroit gener l'execution de son projet. Dans cette situation, voulant donner a notre Cousin le Duc de Bouillon des marques particulières de notre protection dans une circonstance aussi intéressante pour lui, & ne pouvant etre indiférente sur le sort d'une personne, notre sujete, nous avons voulu nous adresser directement a vous pour vous demander, comme la chose qui peut nous etre la plus agreable & qui nous intéresse le plus, que vous veuillez donner les ordres & faire prendre les mesures les plus efficaces par tout ou il sera necessaire pour qu'aucun mariage de la dite personne ne puisse etre fait sans un consentement par ecrit de ses Pere & Mere. Nous sommes persuadés meme que si cela etoit necessaire pour prevenir tout inconvenient, vous seriez le premier a desirer que nous reclamassions en forme cette personne come nôtre sujete. Nous vous saurons un gré particulier de concourir avec nous aux moiens les plus surs de nous procurer la satisfaction que nous attendons de votre amitié pour nous. Sur ce nous prions Dieu qu'il vous ait Tres Haut, Tres Excellent & tres puissant Prince, Notre tres cher, & tres aimé bon Frere, Cousin Allié et Confédéré, en Sa Ste et digne garde. Ecrit a Fontainebleau, le 27 8bre 1737

Votre bon Frere
Cousin Allié & Confédéré
Louis

On the preceding day, also from Fontainebleau, the Duc had addressed an angry appeal to the Duchesse: "Quoy, Made! Vous ne fremissés pas des procedes que j'essuye et vous avés le coeur de me laisser déshonorer publiquement non seulement par les propos injurieux que votre Pere tient de moy, mais encore dans la violence dont il use en gardant ma fille malgré moy et en traittant avec la derniere indignité celuy qui me represente!"[10] He could not believe that his own wife shared in her father's nefarious schemes. Once more he reminded her of their tender parting when she had left for Poland more than two years before: "Souvenés-vous Made de nos adieux et voyés quel prix vous donnés à ma tendre amitié. Je ne puis vous en dire davantage, tant jay le coeur percé d'amertume et de douleur." But in a letter to de Bacqueville, strategically mailed two days earlier, the Grand Chambellan referred to his spouse in a somewhat different tone. Irritated to the point of fury, he dropped all pretence of affection. All his hopes rested on his faithful de Bacqueville. His trusted envoy simply had to stay on in Zolkiew: "Enfin mon Cher Bacqueville, si vous m'abandonnés je n'ay plus de ressource et je vais donc essuyer le plus sanglant affront et par le sacrifice le plus barbare et le plus affreux pour moy."[11] Henceforth, he would have full powers to deal as haughtily as required with the Prince Royal and, especially, the Duchesse: "Si j'en croyois mon ressentiment, elle fremiroit du sort qu'elle se prepare....Vous luy pouvés annoncer que si elle retient ma fille ou qu'elle n'obtienne point que le Prince la renvoye, elle peut renoncer a la France et a jamais recevoir un sol de moy ny de son bien et, puisqu'elle me force d'eclater, je vais prendre de si justes mesures que je luy feray connoistre jusqu'où va l'horreur qu'elle m'inspire." So much then for the financial guarantees of a French marriage contract!

It was at this point that Charles-Godefroy realized there was something even better than money to be had from the situation. The Duc's agent was to tell Marie-Charlotte that she could have her money after all *if she agreed not to return to France*. Yes, if that were understood, he would generously agree to any separation arrangement she wished, and provided the little Princess was returned, de Bacqueville was to hint (*but only to hint*) at the possibility that the Duc would even be prepared to add something of his own to her personal funds. She would, of course, have to agree formally to stay away. Even so, no *definite* promise was to be made with regard to extra money: "Cecy est une idée," he added, "dont sourdement vous pouvés vous servir." At the same time de Bacqueville was to persist in Louise's catechizing: "Redittes-luy mille fois combien elle m'est chere et combien elle me fait repandre de pleurs." As for her mother, she would meet ill fortune if she did return to France: "J'abandonne a jamais son indigne mere et elle peut compter que si elle revient en France, elle n'y sera traittée que conformément a ses infames procedés."

Thanks to the slowness of the mails, neither Charles-Godefroy's fearful recriminations nor echoes of Louis XV's solemn warnings reached Zolkiew before December. The month of November thus turned out to be fairly quiet. The Prince Royal continued to behave erratically, changing his mind almost daily on whether the Bouillon party should leave or stay, but there was no sign of a forced marriage or impending violence in the offing. The tedium continued and even the usual diversions failed. De Bacqueville informed Saint-Gervais, for example, that he had withdrawn from all card games because of the interminable arguments and bitter quarrelling. He saw the Duchesse only at mass or at dinner and avoided the Prince Royal entirely. The servants at the Quai Malaquais would be interested to learn that the old Prince had just given Louise one hundred ducats for her everyday expenses. No doubt it was to make up for the fact that her wicked mother refused to pay the costs of having her daughter's linen washed! The prospect of spending another winter in Poland was horrifying. If the Duc only knew what he was going through, five hundred leagues away from his comforts and his friends! One thought worried him especially: there was bound to be a gigantic explosion of anger when the King of Poland's letter of admonition arrived. Already he had promised himself to take shelter, if necessary, with the Palatine de Russie in Leopold. If only he had twelve grenadiers and a day's head start! He could easily rescue the Princess, and he would not worry about being pursued by the Prince Royal's guards either! At least he had been able to get to Leopold to purchase his own private stock of wine and supplies. Meals at the castle were simply inedible. He no longer brought up the subject of their leaving. The Duchesse, moreover, was always finding some new excuse for delay.

Meanwhile, huge land sales were being discussed, some of significant value, like Tygenhoffen in Polish Prussia, potentially worth an annual income of 40,000 livres to the Duchesse and revertible to the young Princess on her mother's death. Prospective buyers and suitors continued to drift through. Some were financially quite out of their depth but others had enormous estates and wealth. There was still much talk of the Petit Général whose candidacy was now backed even by King Stanislas and by the Palatine de Russie. De Bacqueville intended to keep his counsel on all that and maintain a low profile. The important thing was to get out of Zolkiew. Once they were in Silesia, he could easily get the Princess back to her father. But the mother remained a problem: "Je voudrois de tout mon coeur que la mere restat et j'y ay fait de mon mieux, mais cela ne me paroit pas aisé sans l'enfant et je demeure toujours dans cet

Enfer par l'attachement que j'ay pour Mgr. le Duc de Bouillon dont je n'ay encore pu me resoudre d'abandoner la fille, mais au nom de Dieu, Monsieur, que S.A. pense un moment que voila deux ans revolus que je suis en Pologne!"[12]

Occasionally, de Bacqueville's normally captious letters provide a grudging glimpse of happier events at the palace, reminding us that the little Princess was in fact less a prisoner there than the centre of attraction at one of Poland's antique royal courts. Joyously intimate celebrations were held, for example, on 4 November, the feast day of St. Charles, patron saint of the Duchesse. Even the old Prince had joined in the merriment and had drunk the health, albeit "un peu solicité," of the Duc, his son-in-law, and "tout seul, de luy meme" the health of Louise's brother, the Prince de Turenne. After a festive dinner the two Princesses, mother and daughter, had joined in the dancing. The musicians for the event had been engaged and paid for by Marie-Charlotte, and a concert was held later in one of her antechambers "où elle assista avec haut et bas domestiques."[13] Much food and drink was made available, but de Bacqueville had remained sourly unimpressed: "Je me retiray chez moy ou je suis reduit plus que jamais." His gloomy mood continued throughout the succeeding weeks. Marie-Charlotte annoyingly persisted in her efforts to be pleasant and even shared with him a gift of fine game she had received from a distinguished visitor. He had accepted, but, as he informed his friend Saint-Gervais, "tout cela ne me ramene point chez elle."[14] Another dreaded winter was nearly upon them, and the nights came early: "Nous voilà bientot reduits à la nuit à cinq heures, à ne savoir ou doner de la tete que vis a vis chacun de son feu." To the Duc, on the same day, he wrote: "On se tient toujours icy mordicus au projet de mariage." There were now dozens of proposals for Louise's hand, but everyone realized that the Duc's consent would be required and the Grand Chambellan could rest assured that nothing untoward was going to happen. Indeed, there was now really no need to hurry Louise out of the country. The trip in winter would not, moreover, be without its dangers: "Encore une fois, Monseigneur, pesez vos dernieres resolutions.... Ma persone ne tiendroit a rien pour partir quelque temps qu'il fît, mais la santé de la jeune princesse n'est pas la meme chose."[15]

Throughout November the Duc's envoy pursued his endless gazette. As Charles-Godefroy's representative, his function was, of course, to offer little or no hope for a Polish marriage, but, at the same time, did he not have to keep abreast of all the offers? The Duc might, after all, change his mind, and then where would he be without detailed information on the candidates? Potocki, the Grand Général, had come back to Zolkiew again and was much taken with Louise as a prospective bride for his grandson, described as "une petite fouine assez jolie et bien de l'argent comptant." But then again, would he be to the young Princess's taste? Certainly, enormous wealth was involved in that quarter, and the Grand Général was both widely respected and feared—feared even at the court of Augustus III! The Sobieski and Potocki estates contained many fortresses and towns and hundreds of villages. If united through the marriage of Louise and the "pretty weasel-face" those acres would equal half of Normandy! Naturally, it was up to the Duc to decide; but if there was the remotest possibility that a Polish marriage might be approved, no time could be wasted. The old Prince was definitely on his last legs and as likely, on any given day, to die as to live. The Duc could count on his loyal agent to implement any new system and even to give it a respectable appearance of consistency with whatever had already happened. Perhaps a soothing letter could be sent from the Duc to the Prince Royal expressing profound appreciation of the old man's very understandable sorrow at having to separate from his dear little granddaughter. How regrettable it was, too, to see the great Sobieski heritage swallowed up by hostile strangers....There was the problem of a royal thunderbolt arriving any day now in the Zolkiew post as a result of his earlier complaints, but perhaps he could even hit upon some means of suppressing it. Yes, the Duc would be wise indeed to weigh the Polish option one last time. Of course, he would have to keep his agent strictly above the fray and totally uncompromised![16]

It was in such an atmosphere of relative tranquillity, with only de Bacqueville aware of impending catastrophe, that various members of the Bouillon party sent off their New Year's greetings to Paris at the end of November. The tone of Louise's letter to her father reflects the change in mood, contrasting markedly with her doleful note of 4 September:

Mon Tres cher Papa

L'esperance ou j'ai ete longtemps d'avoir l'honneur de me rendre aupres de vous me flatoit sensiblement. Je vois presentement qu'il n y a plus d'aparances. Je vous suplie, Mon cher Papa, de vouloir bien recevoir les assurances de mon profond respect et parfaitte soumission au commencement de cette nouvelle année. J'ose esperer que vous ne refuserez pas vos bontes a une enfant qui en connoit tout le prix, qui sera toutte sa vie, Mon cher Papa, attaché a vos volontés.

J'ai recu hier l'ordre de l'Imperatrice que S.A.R. mon grand Papa a demandé pour moi. Recevez s'il vous plait, Mon Tres cher Papa, les assurances du profond respect et tendre attachement de vôtre petite fille qui prend la liberté de vous baiser la main.

L. De La Tour D'Auvergne De Bouillon.

A Zulkiew
Ce 27 9bre 1737   Mlle des Minieres prend la liberte de
                                         vous faire sa cour.

That, unfortunately, is the last available example of Louise's early epistolary style. It is a little wistful, to be sure, but the tone is not unhappy and even the address recalls the charmingly naive little traveller of the year before. It reads as follows:

> A son Altesse
> Monseigneur Le Duc De
> Bouillon, Mon cher Papa
> A Paris

In a letter to the Duc on the preceding day, de Bacqueville had also made reference to recent festivities in honour of Louise's award: "Le pere de famille laisse boire la santé de V.A. au bruit du canon mais il ne la boit pas. Il a celebré aujourd'huy avec grand plaisir l'arrivée de la croix de l'Imperatrice Amélie pour la jeune princesse. Pareils evenements l'intéressent et l'amusent beaucoup."[17]

No doubt it was Marie-Charlotte who faced the most difficult task when it came to composing New Year's wishes to the Duc in Paris. Spelling excepted, she managed, under the circumstances, rather well:

> Quoyque je voye pas avec peu de Chagrin que vous moubliés entierement, sa n'enpeche pas que je fait san cesse de voeux au Ciele pour votre Conservation et lequelle je augmente pour vous faire avoir Cette nouvelle année plus de bonheur et de satisfaction et que dieu vous conserve des longs année en santé, esperant que Dieu vous ouvriera les yeux sur les torte afreu que vous faitte a mon coeur pour vous, ne voulant que votre bien et votre amitié laquelle vous ne me pouréz en consience me refuser. Toute ou tard je me flatte que vous me la redonnere et que vous verez que je la merite par le tendre attachement que je vous ay vouez pour ma vie, mon adorable mary; quand vous voulez. Je vous embrasse du fond de mon ame et suis a vous pour ma vie, votre fidelle fame. Un most de votre main pour que je voye que je ne suis pas toute a fait esfase de votre memoire[18]

Writing that same week to the Comte d'Evreux, Marie-Charlotte, in a letter that is particularly valuable for the rare light it throws on her relationship with Louise, also demonstrated that she was prepared (though just barely) to give even de Bacqueville a second chance—however reprehensible his conduct had been. He had deliberately trampled on her rights as a mother. Worse still, he had done his utmost to alienate her daughter, "luy ayant inspire des sentimens de mefiance et de desobeissance pour moy."[19] The young Princess now took absolutely no notice of her mother and the Comte d'Evreux would surely appreciate how grief-stricken she was to see even her own flesh and blood thus turned against her. "Je ne trouve nulle consolation que dans l'espérance que Dieu aura pitié de moy et qu'il voudra bien me prendre a luy."

There were others at Zolkiew and nearby who hoped for a positive resolution of the Sobieski-Bouillon conflict. Among these the Palatine de Russie, a supporter of the Petit Général and the mother of King Stanislas's mistress, made sincere efforts to persuade the Duc to change his mind. She had earlier chided him for misleading her old cousin, Prince James, on the question of a Polish marriage. In his deferential reply of 5 December, Charles-Godefroy showed himself to be irrevocably committed to a draconian solution. His letter—important because it sets out the "official" version of his separation from Louise's mother as it was accepted later on by such memorialists as Saint-Simon and de Luynes—is a masterpiece of deception, perhaps even of self-deception. It rises to heights of ingenious rationalization, equal to the best that even his agent could offer.

Going back to the very beginning, the Duc explained, first of all, the true reason why he had sent the Princess, his dear daughter, to the court of Prince James. He had done it, as Heaven was his witness, for the sake of his wife! The Duchesse, who had gone to Poland to reconcile with her father, would otherwise have been sent away. It was only later that the question of a royal marriage proposal had come up, but this had not worked out for some mysterious reason. He had then agreed—*solely* in order to please his father-in-law, who wanted to tidy up his succession before his death—to a marriage between Louise and one of the Stuart princes. The fact remained, however, that both reason and family honour had always argued against any foreign marriage. Then there was the problem of his only son, "qui n'ayant encore essuyé aucune maladie qui me mette en seureté sur sa vie, et d'ailleurs d'une complexion délicate, si malheureusement je venois a le perdre, quel chagrin n'aurois-je pas de voir passer tous mes biens entre les mains d'un gendre que jamais je ne seray à portée de voir."[20] Besides, if he had been foolish enough to give his consent, the King of France would certainly have refused to approve such a marriage.

Having been so totally frank with his correspondent to that point, the Duc now promised to open his heart entirely to her. She must know of the odious litany of discourtesies he had suffered at the hands of his father-in-law: "Me menacer de procéder et d'user de violence; refuser de lire des lettres remplies de respects et de veritables tendresses; me reprocher d'avoir épousé sa fille malgre luy, moy *qui a peine avois quinze ans*,[21] et elle qui estoit Veuve et Majeure; vouloir chasser la personne qui m'a representé." Would not the Palatine herself have reproached him one day if he had given in to such shameful treatment? The answer was obvious, and Prince James was free to cut the Duc's children off without a penny if he wished!

But there was worse: the Palatine was no doubt aware of the many vicious rumours that had been circulated at Zolkiew about his character— that he was "joueur, dissipateur, et tout ce qu'on peut etre de pis." But he was prepared to show that he had in no way dissipated the Duchesse's dowry. In fact, he was prepared to return every penny of it, "car il est bien vraysemblable qu'à ce qu'elle fait et dit elle-même, elle ne compte pas revenir en France, ni revivre avec moy."

He was heartbroken that she no longer wanted to live with him, of course, but if that was how she felt about him and his family, he wanted nothing more from her, only the return of his daughter! It was for that reason that he was now throwing himself at the mercy of Prince James. That was why he begged the Palatine, on his knees, to intercede on his behalf. The tears he had shed while writing his letter would prove his sincerity. It would surely arouse her maternal compassion: "J'ose assurer que si V.E. connoissoit la tendresse extreme que j'ay pour cet enfant, bien loin de me presser de conclure un mariage qui doit à jamais me separer d'elle, elle joindroit ses prieres aux miennes pour obtenir la grace que j'espere." Oh yes, and would she also please assure the Petit Général that there was nothing personal in his refusal to allow a Polish marriage?

Charles-Godefroy apparently belonged to that happy race of men who can be more fairly described as sincere hypocrites than true deceivers. Whatever the case may be, by December 1737, he was in grave danger of believing his own (or de Bacqueville's) propaganda. In one of his last letters to his agent in Poland, the Duc piously confirmed the position adopted in his letter to the Palatine. He was also able to announce that the long period of waiting for a response from the King of Poland had ended. Louis XV had now received a promise from Augustus III that stern measures would be taken. Prince James, the Duc was pleased to note, would soon find out that his son-in-law was not to be trifled with! Indeed, he would not consent to a Polish marriage for Louise even if the crown of Poland were joined to Prince James's entire succession! His orders to de Bacqueville were formal: Louise was to be moved from Zolkiew *immediately*, "sans avoir aucune consideration pour sa santé ny pour la saison."[22] If absolutely necessary, they could stop at Breslau and await better weather. Any letters received from Prince James would be returned unopened. And Marie-Charlotte? Her future was not his concern: "Tout ce qu'elle peut faire ou dire me devient totalement indifferent; ainsy, qu'elle reste en Pologne ou qu'elle aille a la Chine, j'en suis egalement d'accord." Things would be made very unpleasant for her if she returned: "Assurément, si elle y revient, ses morceaux seront courts, et nous n'aurions pas grande accointance ensemble." Charles-Godefroy ended by directing his agent to read an important postscript to the young Princess, placing him *in loco parentis*, "afin qu'elle soit prête a vous suivre partout ou vous voudrés et a suivre vos ordres comme les miens."

Fortunately for Louise's health and safety, the Duc's letter did not reach Zolkiew until weeks later. By that time a rapid series of events had rendered obsolete its instructions for an immediate departure in the dead of winter. Most of the Polish correspondence seems to have ended around this time, and it is not possible to reconstruct from its remnants many details of what occurred at the court of James Sobieski after the first week of December 1737. It is apparent, nevertheless, that by the time the Duc's order reached Zolkiew, de Bacqueville had already been evicted from the palace, leaving Mlle de Minières and Louise to fend for themselves.

Without doubt, the long-awaited arrival on 10 December of Augustus III's humiliating letter to Prince James was the direct cause of de Bacqueville's sudden departure. Not only did it shatter the calm that had prevailed in the palace at Zolkiew during October and November, it also hastened the old man's death which occurred soon after, on 19 December.

Augustus III had understandably hesitated before taking such a drastic step, but the arrival in Dresden of Louis XV's warning of 27 October left him little choice. Indeed, the direct intervention of the French King in a "domestic" matter must have provoked a certain amount of respectful astonishment in several quarters. Action had to be taken. Without further delay, Augustus fired off a no-nonsense order to James Sobieski to cease and desist:

Monsieur mon Cousin,

Il y a quelque tems que le Duc de Bouillon m'a fait connoître ses apprehensions sur ce que vous voudriez vous prevaloir, à son préjudice, de vôtre autorité comme aieul maternel de la jeune Princesse sa Fille qui se trouve aupres de vous pour la marier malgré lui & sans son consentement en Pologne. J'ai d'abord regardé ces inquietudes du pere comme des craintes peu fondées, n'aiant pû m'imaginer que vous voulliez vous porter a une resolution si opposée aux lois divines, au bon ordre dans la societé civile, & aux usages reçus même parmi des Princes, & j'ai toujours encore de la peine à croire une chose si peu conforme a Votre Sagesse ordinaire. Neanmoins, comme le Roy de France vient de m'ecrire la-dessus lui même dans les termes de la copie ci-jointe, en me faisant les instances les plus pressantes pour l'interposition de mon autorité Royale a vous detourner de l'Execution d'un tel projet, je ne saurois me dispenser de vous faire par ma presente des remonstrances aussi amiables que sérieuses, pour que, en cas que tel eut eté votre dessein, ou le fut encore, il vous plaise d'y faire l'attention convenable de mieux entendre avec le Duc de Bouillon sur l'etablissement de sa fille, sans user de contrainte pour la marier & de bien reflechir sur les chagrins et suites facheuses auxquelles vous vous exposeriez & Votre petite fille, par une demarche precipitée et contraire a ses veritables interets

En attendant Votre reponse qui renferme une declaration positive de vos intentions telle que je puisse la produire & communiquer a la Cour de France, je ne demande pas mieux que d'avoir souvent occasion de vous donner des marques de mon affection & estime, & vous souhaitant la continuation d'une parfaite santé, je prie Dieu qu'il vous ait, Monsieur mon Cousin, en sa sainte & digne garde.[23]

Though firm, the Polish King's politely phrased letter was manifestly intended to cause the least hurt and humiliation for the great John Sobieski's son. What must have rankled most, however, was the totally false accusation, relayed by Louis XV, that Prince James had dismissed Louise's servants in order to remove all obstacles to a forced marriage. This time, clever footwork and rodomontade were insufficient to meet the situation, and it appears that de Bacqueville was taken into custody and finally sent packing because of his carelessly vivid and malicious words. The few details known about the entire incident come from a pitiful letter sent by the Duc's agent to his friend Saint-Gervais on 11 December. It is uncharacteristically short. The tone is that of a condemned man, totally dejected and waiting for the inevitable, but not, for all that, overcome with remorse:

> Je vois bien qu'on a recu icy des lettres qui font grande rumeur. Elles sont naturelles; on devoit s'y attendre plus tost. On m'a ordonné en espece d'arret chez moy. Peut estre seray-je demain finalement chassé. Nul ne me dit mot et je ne dis rien a persone. J'attends la fin de quelque conseil violent et plains le pauvre prince qui en est tourmenté. Je faisois tout pour le mieux, sans le dire. Il faut que cecy prenne fin. Je ne puis vous en dire davantage. Peut-estre ne recevrez-vous pas ce mot.[24] Adieu mon cher amy. Plaignez moy. Assurez Monseigneur et Maistre de tout mon respect et mon attachement a toute Epreuve. Je suis veritablement abbatu de tout cecy, sans marquer ny sentir cependant la moindre foiblesse contre mon devoir.[25]

Released from confinement a few days later, the Duc's ambassador returned to Paris but under what circumstances precisely is not revealed in the few remaining letters. Ironically, he would soon be back in the land he had grown to hate with such fervour, this time to settle the affairs of his enemy, the Duchesse, after her death in May 1740. Additional details concerning what happened at the palace after the intervention of Augustus III are provided in a fairly lengthy note also written on 11 December by the Duchesse to the Comte d'Evreux, her only remaining influential friend in Paris. Her tone is understandably bitter. She was writing under nearly as much of a cloud as de Bacqueville and had once more become a convenient target for her father's wrath. The letters from Augustus III and Louis XV, copies of which she enclosed with her note to the Comte d'Evreux, would provide proof enough of the evil the Duc's man had managed to perpetrate. The leading courts of Europe had been induced to take unjust action against her father on the basis of de Bacqueville's absurd lies. The shock of it might kill him for he was at an age when such outrages had deadly effects. The Duc's ambassador had, moreover, destroyed any hope that the Bouillons would ever inherit from the old man since the King of France had imposed the specific humiliation of claiming Louise as a French subject, and this had revived the Prince Royal's ancient resentment about her own marriage. It was really all too much: "Admire, mon cher Oncle, ma triste situation! La religion ait mon soutien en verite....Et tout sa par ce ministre qui a brouillé la fame avec son mary, le pere et le beau fils, la mere et la fille."[26] What was to be her fate now? The Duc's agent had passed on his master's threat to cut off her money: "Je ne...veut estre a ne savoire que devenire et de quoy vivre." She begged the Comte to do what he could. She had reached the point of desperation: "J'en suis la premiere punie de venire a cette extremite mais il est tems de ne plus vivre come jay fait entre la crainte et l'esperance." Another obstacle to her return was, of course, the matter of how de Bacqueville, "ce magnanime ministre," was to fit in at the Quai Malaquais. His reception there would demonstrate how much friendship and consideration the Duc had for her, and she would act accordingly.

It thus became easy for Charles-Godefroy to prevent his wife's return. De Bacqueville had already been given fervent assurances that a warm place awaited him in the Duc's heart as well as at the Hôtel de Bouillon. Indeed, there he would remain for many years to come, in a fine apartment overlooking the Seine, the trusted friend and adviser of France's Grand Chambellan.[27] In contrast, the Duchesse's pension, an allowance of 40,000 livres drawn from her own money, was cut off. It was now a simple matter for the Duc to explain to his friends at court, almost with a deferential solicitude, that his dear wife had decided for her own private reasons to stay on in Poland. Indeed, he had suspected almost from the beginning that she had never intended to return to France!

In a postscript to her letter of 11 December, Marie-Charlotte threw additional light on Prince James's reaction to Augustus III's letter. Her father had not, contrary to what the King of France had written, dismissed anyone. In his impatience, he had said that he could have done so, "car il ne depend de personne que de Dieu." Nor had the old Prince ever intended to marry his granddaughter in Poland (although the Duc's letter specifically authorized such a course of action) without her father's consent, "de quoy je vous jure," the Duchesse continued, "et vous pouvez me croire. Il me l'a encore dit les larmes aux yeux que [c'étoit] bien mal recompenser les tendres sentimens qu'il avoit eu pour cette enfant et qu'il ne se seroit jamais attendu d'une pareille chose de la part de Mr de Bouillon. Il en est penetre au vif et toute sa douleur rejaillit sur moy."

Prince James Sobieski's grief was probably genuine enough. When the Duchesse wrote those words, she could not have known that her father would be dead within the week. The remaining half-dozen letters in the correspondence for this period leave many questions unanswered. On 9 January 1738, the Comte d'Evreux answered Marie-Charlotte's letter. News of Prince James's death had not yet reached Paris,[28] but the Duc's uncle did not hesitate to reassure her that all would be well on her return. He was not, he confessed, very well informed of the Duc's activities for he and Charles-Godefroy had not spoken a word since the sale of Turenne. Surely her husband would not suppress her pension! "Ainsy tranquilisez-vous; bien loing de penser a rester ou vous estes, au nom de Dieu revené Princesse, quand le Prince votre Pere le trouvera bon." She still had in him a most faithful friend: "Compté sur moy solidement, vous ne serez pas trompée."[29]

Marie-Charlotte had not heard such warm words for some time! They were probably sufficient, coming after the shock of her father's death, to convince her of the wisdom of returning to France. Charles-Godefroy had only to offer the smallest sign of encouragement! The signal never came.

The Duc's categorical order that Louise be returned immediately, even in the dead of winter, presented a difficult problem. On 15 January, the dowager Palatine de Russie wrote to the Duc, assuring him that everyone would be extremely sorry to see the young Princess leave. Her mother would, of course, see to it that his orders were obeyed to the letter. "Mais il me semble," cautioned the Palatine, "que la saison d'a present est bien mauvaise pour exposer ce cher Enfant au froid extreme."[30] Marie-Charlotte, who had suffered incredibly throughout the entire affair, would thus await confirmation regarding Louise's departure. The Prince Royal had been quite impossible to live with: "...que pouvoit-elle dire de contraire a un Pere que la moindre contradiction mettoit en danger et a la derniere extremité?" His fatal illness had come on very suddenly; the letter from the King of France had been an especially crushing blow. The Palatine was happy to report, however, that in the old man's last moments he had tearfully tried to undo all the effects of his cruelly unforgiving conduct toward his daughter: "Il a fait voir en meurant une grande tendresse pour Madame vostre famme. J'espere que les marques de la vostre adoucira la perte qu'elle vient de faire."

We come finally to the last two letters from Marie-Charlotte. The first is undated but addressed to the Duc in Paris, probably as late as April or May 1738. Louise was still in Zolkiew,[31] and none of the urgent matters relating to Prince James's succession had yet been settled. Marie-Charlotte had heard nothing from her "cher Roy" except for a note of condolence mailed in mid-January (along with an eager inquiry about the will!). It can be safely presumed that any residual warmth or sympathy he may then still have felt for his wife had completely vanished after the arrival of de Bacqueville in Paris. What a litany of windy recriminations must have followed and how naive it was of Marie-Charlotte to imagine that there would ever be room for her again at the Hôtel de Bouillon!

And yet the desire to return seems to have remained uppermost in her mind. The April-May letter refers anxiously to her husband's silence: "Vous ne voulez donc plus me donner de vos nouvelles, mon Roy; je vous et escrit plusieurs foies sent pouvoir avoir aucune reponse. Je ne sait ce que j'en doit croire."[32] He had inquired about Prince James's will but she really knew nothing about it or even if there was a proper will. She knew only that the Abbé Mocki had certain papers locked up for safekeeping in a strongbox in his room and that he was awaiting instructions from the Court at Dresden.[33] The Court was her legal guardian, "et come cette cour est lente, tous le reste va de meme. Tous ce que je peut vous assure ce que je me meure de chagrin de ne pas pouvoire finire ici pour vous allez bientost rejoinder et finire mes joures en repos." If she did not die in Poland, if one day she managed to get back to Paris, he would not recognize her, so much had all her torments and suffering altered her appearance. And yet he was still gratuitously adding to those torments! He had not written to her, and just when she was in the greatest need of funds, he had cut off her pension even though he had promised on his honour never to do such a thing! One day, surely, he would realize how unjust he had been.

A mysterious reference to Louise follows. Although she was still in Zolkiew, it was obviously no longer because of bad weather: "Je vous ay mande les raisons pourquoy je [ne] vous renvoy pas encore ma fille; je croy que vous devez avoir recu ou vous receverez du lieu meme sur sa des chose positive et les meme raison font que je ne peut pas encor la renvoyez jusque j'ay quelque chose de positive de l'endroit. Voyez ma fason de pense si elle et come on vous la mande. J'atens ses joures cy des nouvelles. Je vous mande sa en Secret."

Perhaps what Marie-Charlotte called a secret remains one today, but in all likelihood she was alluding to a possible marriage arrangement for Louise with the Prince of Sulzbach.[34] Such a proposal was highly flattering, and even James III, when he got wind of it in Rome from the Palatine de Russie, was duly impressed, as was his *chargé d'affaires* in Paris, Daniel O'Brien. But O'Brien, who had already sniffed at the notion of a marriage between Charles-Godefroy's daughter and one of the Stuart princes, remained sceptical: "Le mariage de Mlle dauvergne avec le Prince de Sulzbaq na point encore transpiré ici," he informed the Old Pretender on 23 June. "C'est un grand evenement pour Mr de Bouillon de voir sa fille a la veille d'etre Electrice palatine, mais si la chose etoit aussi avancée que la palatine de russie le pretend, je ne conçois pas pourquoy Mr de Bouillon n'en auroit pas deja fait part a 106 [i.e. James]."[35]

O'Brien, like James, could not appreciate the extent to which communications between Zolkiew and the Hôtel de Bouillon had broken down. Whatever the nature of Marie-Charlotte's secret business involving Louise, the negotiations fell through. News of their failure, possibly accompanied by evidence of the Duc's lack of support for the proposal, apparently reached her as she was about to post her own letter to the Duc. Such, at least, may be the explanation of a second mysterious passage near the end of the Duchesse's letter. It reads as follows:

Je rouver ma letre et vous envoye une letre par ou vous verez les tromperie de celuy qui m'a jouez mais qui nous jouera plus et sa mettera fein a tous mes affaires, j'espere en Dieu. Je vous renvoye votre fille, puisqu'il vous a plue ainsi, et de laquelle je ne veut attendre parle dornavant. Adieu. En exsecutant vos ordres je me satisfait. Voyla le mister decouvert. Ce l'abbée qui et lautheur qui embrouille tous les affaires.

Marie-Charlotte was referring no doubt to the self-seeking activities of the Abbé George Mocki who, in the months following the Prince Royal's death, demonstrated to everyone's satisfaction his thoroughly unscrupulous character. Having failed to obtain what he wanted from either the King of Poland or the Duchesse (whom he later accused in a letter to James III of having tried to steal her father's will from him, in order to suppress it!), he next proposed to sell his services in Rome, offering to place at the Pretender's disposal important Sobieski papers which he had secretly hidden away. James, he implied, would find these most useful in pressing his legal claims against the Duchesse de Bouillon. To his credit, the Old Pretender declined to take advantage of the Abbé's offer, especially when it became clear that Mocki wanted a bishopric as part of the bargain! Not long before Marie-Charlotte's death, the wily Abbé managed for a time to ingratiate himself once again with her and she even supported his renewed request to James for the appointment! After her death, he solemnly tried to convince the Duc that his only object in everything he had done had been to protect the interests of Charles-Godefroy from the rapacious and plundering activities of his wife![36]

More important to our immediate purpose, however, is the stark evidence provided by Marie-Charlotte's letter of the intense estrangement between mother and daughter on the eve of Louise's departure from Zolkiew. The finality of her remark, totally washing her hands of the Princess, leaves us puzzled and wanting to know more. Unfortunately, no record of any direct communications between them seems to have survived and there is nothing to reveal the precise nature of their everyday relations. Marie-Charlotte obviously considered her daughter spoiled and ill-mannered, and Louise most certainly detested her mother. Equally certain is the fact that Louise did not refrain from voicing her hatred when she and Mlle de Minières took their leave. A bitter letter of recrimination, found among Marie-Charlotte's papers after her death and mailed by de Bacqueville to the Duc in 1740, leaves no room for doubt. Now lost, it is referred to by the Duc's agent in the following terms: "Je joins icy, Monseigneur, ce fameux papier de Mademoiselle de Bouillon qui luy attira et a Madle de Minieres a leur depart un si terrible orage et le pretexte d'une hayne continuée jusqu'à la mort. V.A. en portera son jugement."[37] We try to imagine the situation: did they, for example, speak to each other at table? When she left for France did Louise say goodbye? What must it have taken for the sentimental Marie-Charlotte to say that she never wanted to hear her daughter's name mentioned again? Whatever it was, we know only that, with hopes of yet another brilliant marriage shattered, the young Princess was back in her con-

vent on the rue du Cherche-Midi by the summer of 1738. Between her and her
mother there would be no further contact.

Louise probably left Zolkiew around mid-May. From a letter addressed to the
Duc by Marie-Charlotte in August, we learn that the Duchesse had been unable
to raise the ready cash to pay for her daughter's trip: "Dieu est mon temoin que
je navoit pas un sol et que je ne peut pas engage rien moy meme, ayant bien de la
peinne de vivre."[38] This was the wealthy princess who only fifteen years before
had set out on the same journey to marry Charles-Godefroy's brother, bringing
with her a dowry worth over one million livres!

In spite of everything, the Duchesse still looked forward to her eventual
return to France, a fact attested to by others at this time.[39] But the simple truth
was that Charles-Godefroy had cleverly made such a move financially impossible.
Her total accessible wealth consisted only of the personal effects she had fallen
heir to in the palace at Zolkiew, and from these she generously selected token
gifts of jewelry and ceremonial decorations to offer to the Duc. She had taken
the liberty, she noted, of sending him a fine diamond ring and two snuff boxes:
"Je vous conjure de garde sa pour l'amour de moy. Si vous pouviez avoir la
Toison," she continued, "je vous en garde deux superbe, un tous de diamant et
l'autre de ruby et diamant, tous deux tres beau. Mande moy si vous voulez que je
le demande pour vous ou mon fils a l'Empereur." Marie-Charlotte still had
powerful friends and relatives! Her chief problem amidst such empty trappings
of wealth was the absence of ready money for daily expenses. She had not been
able to draw a penny from her father's inheritance and nothing had been settled.
The servants' wages had not been paid, and she had been obliged to let most of
them go. There was not even enough money available to give her father a proper
burial or to carry out any of his charity bequests, let alone pay off the estate's
many angry creditors! And now, incredible as it seemed, her husband had cut off
her allowance! But with all that, what she still wanted most from him was his
love: "Mon cher coeur, ayez pitié de votre fame dans tous ses peinnes et rendez
luy votre coeur laquelle elle estime mieu que tous les Richesse du monde et
croyez la toute a vous pour la vie." There is more involved in those pleading
words than strategic begging for the restitution of a misappropriated pension!
Ironically, ten years later, her estranged daughter would echo the plaintive tones
of an abandoned woman in equally pitiful letters to Prince Charles Edward
Stuart, evincing at last an emotional kinship with the mother she had earlier
hated so much.

In these final letters, Marie-Charlotte also offered to continue working on her
husband's behalf in Poland. That, after all, had been the purpose of her mission
when she had set out for Zolkiew nearly three years before. Of course, if the Duc
wanted to send someone else to take care of his business and to represent him he
was perfectly free to do so. She had only one reservation in that regard:
Charles-Godefroy was not to suggest de Bacqueville: "Je ne puis en consience ny

pour mon bonheur y consentire."

Charles-Godefroy did not choose to send a representative to Poland, prefer-ring apparently to give up any immediate claim on the Sobieski estate in exchange for being well rid of his wife. In any case, with the sale of Turenne, the state of his finances had improved immeasurably. Now he had his daughter safely back in her convent in Paris. The search for an advantageous marriage could begin again, and this time the candidates would have to be French!

As for Marie-Charlotte, there was no way for her to know that before very long her old enemy de Bacqueville would indeed be back in Zolkiew seeing to Charles-Godefroy's interests in the affairs, not of his dead father-in-law, Prince James Sobieski, but rather of his late wife, the unhappy Duchesse de Bouillon.

V

A Death and a Wedding

LIFE IN ZOLKIEW after her father's death brought only more misery and discomfort to Marie-Charlotte. The situation of the heavily mortgaged Polish lands was precarious, and the endless conflict over inheritance matters with her brother-in-law James III now began in great earnest. Her first impulse was to propose an equal division of the Prince's entire estate, both in Poland and in Silesia, between herself and the Stuart heirs of Maria-Clementina,[1] but James, thinking that more could be gained for his children through litigation, refused to compromise. As a result of that short-sighted decision, both the Stuarts and the Bouillons eventually lost out.

Two years after the Prince Royal's death, the situation had not changed. Nothing came from France, and money was still in such short supply that none of the old Prince's debts had been settled. Even his body was still in deposition and "not in a very decent manner," according to some opinions.[2] All that was not, however, for lack of trying on Marie-Charlotte's part! On several occasions she had asked her brother-in-law for help, pointing out that the Sobieski jewels already in his possession in Rome were worth more than everything that remained unencumbered in Poland and that her sister Maria-Clementina had received three times as much from their father as she had. Her pleadings were to no avail. When pressed by the old Palatine de Russie to help Marie-Charlotte provide at least a worthy burial for the Prince Royal, James replied that he simply could not afford to contribute. He had not yet drawn a sou from the Sobieski estates; indeed, he had actually lost revenue as a result of his father-in-law's death! He assured the Palatine that he would, of course, prefer to do something for the old man's body and, yes, even more for his soul, but was the Prince's own daughter not already on the spot and thus in a better position to attend to the problem? Besides, although he was unfamiliar with the custom in Poland, was there really that much of a rush? Did the Palatine know that in Rome, for example, even the bodies of dead Popes were sometimes left for years, temporarily walled up in some little corner of a church, awaiting appropriate burial?[3] It was a fine performance. One would have to search for a long time among the Pretender's thousands of letters before finding another such miserable note![4]

Prudently stingy, James was at least willing to maintain contact and to let the courts decide (albeit with the help of his friend the Pope). The attitude of Marie-Charlotte's husband was, however, less charitable. The Duc continued to ignore her appeals for the restitution of her pension and by the end of 1738 all regular correspondence between Zolkiew and the Quai Malaquais seems to have ceased.[5] Early the following year, the Duchesse coldly informed the Duc that his livery was no longer in use at Zolkiew, she having decided to return to her own. Charles-Godefroy was furious.[6] Their separation was now complete.

Along with penurious living and the loneliness of being cut off from her family and friends, Marie-Charlotte in the last year of her life had to contend with bad health as well. The first signs of serious illness had come on her return to Zolkiew after she spent the winter of 1738-39 in Warsaw. Soon it became apparent that she was suffering from an acute case of consumption, and in January 1740 she was forced to take to her bed. By spring, she had grown so thin that she was almost unrecognizable to her close friends.[7] Tormented by the fact that the Prince Royal's affairs had still not been settled and fearing that she herself might die before the inheritance rights of her children were assured, she sold all the Polish lands to Prince Michael Radziwill, her closest eligible relative, asking him at the same time to work out an accommodation with James III. The move was important since her children, after her death, would be in the same vulnerable position as the Stuart princes, that is, aliens unable to inherit Polish land. By converting into ready money what equity remained in the Sobieski estates, she managed to salvage something for her family out of the five disastrous years in Poland.[8] Payment, unfortunately, did not follow immediately, and monies were still owing as well on the Prince Royal's holdings near Danzig, which had already been sold to the dowager Ordinate, Antoinette de Zaheron Zamoyska. Four days before her death, Marie-Charlotte drew up her will. Apart from various special bequests, she left everything to her children.[9]

On 8 May, at 10 o'clock in the evening, Marie-Charlotte died, after receiving the last rites of the Church. Her body was placed in the palace chapel and afterwards transported incognito (to save on costs and to escape the interference of Canon Mocki) to Warsaw for burial, dressed according to her last wishes, "comme les Filles du St Sacrement dans leur Eglise de Varsovie dont la Reine Sa Grande mere est Fondatrice."[10] Meanwhile, her heart, which even at the end of her life she hoped would be welcomed back to Paris, was solemnly deposited in the parish church of Zolkiew to await Charles-Godefroy's instructions— "qu'il reste ici, ou bien qu'il soit envoyé a Paris," wrote the Grand Chancellor of Poland to the Duc, "pour y etre placé dans le Tombeau de Votre sérénissime

Famille."[11] Predictably, Charles-Godefroy was unmoved, and Marie-Charlotte's heart remained in Poland. As for James, he recorded his extreme satisfaction on learning that his sister-in-law had died a model Christian.[12] It thus only remained for him and his two sons to go into deep mourning, which they did for six months until 30 November, St. Andrew's Day. In the meantime, the Bouillon-Stuart lawsuits continued uninterrupted.

News of the Duchesse's death reached Paris in June, and de Luynes made use of a delicately brief and attenuated formula in his reference to the event: the wife of the Grand Chambellan "paroissoit avoir pris le parti de ne plus revenir dans ce pays-ci. M. de Bouillon n'étoit pas content d'elle depuis longtemps."[13] The Duc de Saint-Simon was retrospectively more blunt in his assessment and noted her husband's relief at her death: "Son mari ne demandoit pas mieux que d'en être honnêtement défait. Il ne la pressa point de revenir, et au bout de peu d'années elle mourut en Silésie, au grand soulagement de M. de Bouillon, qui ne laissa pas d'en recueillir assez gros pour ses enfants."[14]

No attempt had been made by the Duc in Paris to conceal his estrangement from Marie-Charlotte, nor did he, on Louise's return, try to hide the fact that mother and daughter had also been at loggerheads. Even the King of France had taken that circumstance openly into consideration when he granted Louise a special pension in mid-March 1740, less than two months before her mother's death. The Duc de Luynes noted that the annual allowance of 12,000 livres had formerly been attached to a tobacco concession in the *vicomté* of Turenne but was no longer payable after the sale. It had been graciously reinstated by the King in favour of Louise specifically on the grounds that she was not "à portée d'avoir rien à présent de Mme de Bouillon, d'autant plus qu'elle est en quelque manière brouillée avec elle depuis son départ."[15]

Although there is little documentation specifically concerning Louise in the Bouillon papers, we do find several accounts for this period that show on what kind of footing this diminutive descendant of the First Crusader lived at the fashionable Chasse-Midi convent. Apart from her governess, the young Princess had among her attendants a *valet de chambre*, a *valet de pied*, a maid, a *femme de garde-robe*, a cook, and various other servants! In 1741 the bill for work on her teeth by Monsieur Capron amounted to 500 livres.[16]

Exploration of possible marriages for Louise had continued and chief among the likely candidates mentioned after her return to Paris was the young Prince de Guise, half-brother of Old Emmanuel-Théodose's merry widow. Marie-Charlotte had already rejected in March 1737 a suggestion, repeated by Louise's governess, that he might make a good candidate.[17] It was a notion that the servants had been bandying about at the Hôtel de Bouillon for some time. The Duc himself, probably in concert with his young stepmother, had also brought it up as a possibility to de Bacqueville late in 1736.[18] The dashing young prince was generally viewed as a good catch for Louise. Certainly he could boast of the finest connections! When he was presented at Court, for example, his sponsors were none other than Prince Charles of Lorraine and his own brother-in-law, the Duc de Richelieu. Here, finally, was the kind of son-in-law Charles-Godefroy had had in mind from the beginning! An alliance with the Prince de Guise would reinforce the House of Bouillon's connections at Versailles, the very centre of the Universe, where precious little time was wasted thinking about frozen wastelands five hundred leagues to the East!

Active negotiations with the de Guise family began in earnest late in 1738, and they had reached a successful conclusion when the young prince's father — himself about to embark at the age of sixty on a last matrimonial fling with Mlle de Joyeuse—died quite unexpectedly on 29 April 1739. Suddenly there was no more talk of marriage with the Princesse de Bouillon for the freshest gossip had it that Charles-Godefroy's daughter had lost out to Mlle du Maine, Louise-Françoise de Bourbon, thirty-two years old but a *princesse du sang*! De Luynes noted on 26 May the Grand Chambellan's displeasure: "d'autant plus qu'il n'a entendu parler de rien de la part de M. de Guise."[19] In July, rumours were still flying; the Prince de Guise was indeed going to marry Mlle du Maine, and the Duchesse du Maine, her mother, Louise-Bénédicte de Bourbon-Condé, had generously consented to the alliance, asking only that the young man's credentials (that is, proof of 50,000 livres *de rente*!) be shown to her. Unfortunately, the financial assurance provided left something to be desired, the old Prince de Guise having departed this world leaving behind a great many debts.[20]

Not yet fourteen, Louise had now suffered four rejections in a series of marriage proposals that had included the Royal Princes of Poland, of the House of Stuart, and even the future Elector Palatine! We know nothing of her feelings in the matter. What is certain is that much worse still lay ahead.

As it happened, Louise may well have been fortunate in this particular loss for scarcely more than a year later it was announced that the Prince de Guise would be marrying an entirely different member of the Bouillon family. The young lady in question was the Prince's own niece, Marie-Sophie-Charlotte de La Tour, the only child of Emmanuel-Théodose and his last Duchess. De Luynes noted in January 1741 that, owing to her age, the union would not be taking place immediately: "On attend qu'elle ait quatorze ans," he explained, "et elle en a treize passés."[21] But even this marriage between the half-brother and the daughter of the Messalina was not to be, for the Prince suddenly decided, three years after his official engagement, that he could not go through with the ceremony, having just noticed that his fiancée was slightly hunch-backed! It was a forgiving age for fastidious princelings, and even though the King and Queen had given their blessing, de Guise's decision seems to have caused little scandal. De Luynes, usually the soul of discretion, did allow himself an expression of mild surprise at the Prince's awkward timing: "On peut être étonné qu'il ne s'en soit aperçu que dans ce moment; mais M. de Guise est l'homme du monde le plus distrait; on en rapporte une infinité d'exemples qui prouvent une distraction singulière et peu commune."[22]

Charles-Godefroy had, of course, other things to think of now besides his daughter's marriage, and chiefly the problem of Marie-Charlotte's estate. An important family council was arranged with the Comte d'Evreux, with whom the Duc had been at odds ever since the sale of Turenne in 1737. With Marie-Charlotte gone, Henri-Louis decided it was best to reconcile with his nephew, and he generously marked the occasion by resigning his position as Colonel Général de la Cavalerie (valued at more than half a million livres) in favour of his twelve-year-old grandnephew.[23]

Uncle and nephew, acting as joint guardians for Louise and her brother, were not long in deciding on the need to dispatch a representative to Poland immediately. Thus it was that, not long after Marie-Charlotte's death, the Duc's trusted ambassador, Antoine-Guy-Henri Guéroult de Bacqueville, Capitaine de Cavalerie, Chevalier de l'Ordre Militaire de Saint-Louis and Gouverneur du Duché de Bouillon, reluctantly set off once again on the long road to Zolkiew.

De Bacqueville's assignment threatened to be anything but simple: inventories had to be drawn up, and debts owing to the estate had to be collected. Formal consent was to be granted to the execution of all clauses in the Duchesse's will that were deemed not to be contrary to the interests of her children. He was to take possession of all diamonds, precious stones, pictures and furnishings located in the castle of Zolkiew at the time of her death as well as any other articles of value there or elsewhere that had been in her direct or indirect possession. Anything judged to be too costly to transport back to France was to be sold.[24]

The Duc's emissary arrived in Zolkiew on 22 June and soon a stream of indignant correspondence describing the situation there began arriving at the Hôtel de Bouillon. The food was as putrid as ever, and just as he had expected, everything was in a total state of chaos. The Duchesse, his mortal enemy to the last, would most certainly have set fire to the château or ordered his assassination on the road had she known that he would be turning up again! After her death, some of her unpaid servants and attendants had been taken in by the old Palatine de Russie in Leopold, but they were all thieves who had been robbing the Duchesse blind. Several had sought payment of their wages by selling off valuables at the local pawnbrokers and one had even sold Louise's jewelled dog collar, a gift from the Staroste of Halicz. What a scandal it was that the mighty Sobieski fortune of well over ninety millions had been squandered in only forty-three years! The Duchesse had done her share of the damage by making ridiculously generous bequests to her servants and stipulating outrageous sums for her father's burial as well as for repairs to the parish church in Zolkiew. The two executors, Prince Radziwill and Chancellor Zaluski, had been given the Zolkiew paintings and library. Mme l'Ordinate had received a fine watch, and the Palatine de Russie, a beautiful ruby and a holy relic. He would, of course, be trying to get all those items back! It was indeed true that Marie-Charlotte, contrary to what he would have expected, had left everything to her children but he had it on the best authority that she had really wanted to leave nothing to Louise—or was it almost nothing? How typically petty of her! He had intercepted all incoming mail and had carefully gone through Marie-Charlotte's private papers. He had found nothing compromising; was that not proof enough that someone had been very quick to destroy *the evidence*? He had managed to snatch back from one of the thieving servants, Claude LeBlond, a sum of money supposedly given to him by the dying Duchesse. Was it not possible that some kind of sexual favours were involved? All in all, the Duc de Bouillon should praise God that the Duchesse had died when she did for had she lived another year or two the entire estate would have been eaten up![25]

After only a few short months, de Bacqueville's work in Poland was done. Eleven large bales containing everything of value at Zolkiew that could be easily transported were on board ship in Hamburg, ready to be transported to Rouen and, finally, to Navarre. The Duc's man trusted no one in this delicate enterprise: nothing was to be unpacked until he himself arrived back in France, inventory in hand!

He next turned his attention to the much-contested Sobieski holdings in Silesia, having already sent on ahead a magnificent stable of thoroughbred horses, the gift of Prince Michael Radziwill to the Duc. He himself intended to reach Ohlau by the end of January 1741. Unfortunately, a little more than one month before that, misfortune struck when the new King of Prussia, hoping to exploit the confusion in Austrian affairs resulting from the death in October of the Emperor Charles VI, decided to invade Silesia. At the end of a lightning campaign in December, Frederick's self-styled army of "liberation" had triumphed. The population was expected to rejoice. It was even said that in Breslau the Prussian King had danced with the burghers' daughters! What, de Bacqueville wondered, would be his attitude toward the Duc de Bouillon's just claims on the autonomous Sobieski possessions in Ohlau?

One additional piece of bad news worried the Duc's agent: the biggest storm in several decades had come howling down on Northern Europe; many ships were lost at sea, and the Hamburg vessel carrying the Zolkiew possessions was reported overdue. In Paris, the worst flooding since 1711 was taking place. The Seine had overflowed its banks, and as Claude Linotte, the Duc's steward, reported to de Bacqueville, "on va en Bateau dans les Champs Elisées."[26]

But Linotte had good news too: finally, after nearly five years of uncertainty and delicate negotiations in so many different quarters, the future of the young Princess Louise was at last assured! She would be marrying the Prince de Monaco, the fabulously wealthy son of the Duc de Valentinois. De Luynes, always careful to list the assets of both parties, noted in his diary that Louise, now fifteen and a half years of age, had 22,000 livres *de rente* of her own, plus an additional sum of 200,000 livres, not including what she would probably realize from her mother's estate which, it was optimistically estimated (how quickly the gossip had changed!), might go as high as forty or fifty thousand livres *de rente*. It was a considerable sum but scarcely to be compared with what the future bridegroom had to offer! First of all, the young Prince would have the revenue of the principality of Monaco, conservatively estimated at 72,000 livres *de rente*. The Duchy of Valentinois was worth another 88,000 livres annually, and over 100,000 livres of additional income was produced by several other estates. Included also would be ownership of the magnificent Hôtel de Valentinois in Paris.[27] There was one slight hitch: the Prince did not have a normal rank, and marriage to someone as distinguished as the Princesse de Bouillon would obviously make it necessary for M. de Valentinois to resign his dukedom in favour of his son. Linotte informed de Bacqueville that Louis XV had not yet given the father permission to do so and consequently the news was not yet public. However, in a postscript of 1 February, Linotte noted that the King had finally agreed and that the Duc de Bouillon would be setting out that very day for Versailles to give official notification of the wedding. There were to be great celebrations, and de Bacqueville was being asked to return immediately to Paris for the festivities! Such was the express wish of both the Duc de Bouillon and of the prospective groom's father. Moreover, given the unsettled situation in Silesia, surely there was not much for him to do in Ohlau. He could, if it was safe, bring along with him via Dresden any of the Duchesse's effects already in his possession. There was no need to rush. The wedding was planned for May or June since the construction going on at the Hôtel de Bouillon, where the young couple would be residing, would not be finished until then.[28] De Luynes, also referring to the upcoming marriage, noted that Mlle de Bouillon would be presented at court for the *tabouret* ceremony before, rather than after, the wedding. It was one of the important traditions of the Bouillon, Lorraine, and Rohan families who demonstrated their superiority of rank over run-of-the-mill dukes and duchesses by such practices. De Luynes also predicted that such a distinguished marriage would most certainly be celebrated in the *cabinet du Roi*.[29]

Ever the victim of delayed postal communications, de Bacqueville would have been thrilled if he had learned on reaching Ohlau on 26 January that he was to return immediately to Paris to attend a happy wedding ceremony. Unfortunately, the scene awaiting his arrival was much less pleasant. To his dismay, he learned that when the Prussian invaders reached Ohlau, the colonel commanding the troop of three hundred Austrian defenders garrisoned in the town had decided to retire to Prince James's castle to mount a more effective defence. That strategy proved unproductive, however, when it became apparent that the Prussians were prepared to reduce it to rubble with canon and mortar fire. A quick surrender followed. Not long after, the King of Prussia himself rode into the town, and, still on his horse, graciously presented the castle *and all its contents* to his Major General Von Kleist.[30] Protests from the concierge that only the walls belonged to the Queen of Hungary and that everything else was part of the late James Sobieski's estate and under legal seals were to no avail. Locks were forced and seals were broken. Soon, packing cases filled with Sobieski treasures were on their way to Prussia.

With some difficulty, de Bacqueville managed to arrange a meeting with the redoubtable Major General, "vieux militaire âpre et raide," only to discover that the Prussian was completely indifferent to the inheritance rights of Mlle de Bouillon and the Prince de Turenne. No, he really could not be bothered by such legalistic quibbles! All of these possessions, the Duc's agent was informed, had become part of the Major General's personal estate. And in truth it was little enough! A stream of fiercely righteous rebuttals rushed silently through de Bacqueville's mind. When it came to the Duc's fine horses, however, he was determined to speak out. Was it not contrary to the laws of war and the laws of nations to seize the horses of a representative of the Duc de Bouillon who was peacefully traveling under the protection of the King of France's passport? The Major General surely realized that neither the Duc de Bouillon nor the King of France were at war with the King of Prussia! To this, the Major General retorted that the Austrian colonel who had surrendered the castle had also surrendered all of its contents, including the fine horses which seemed to be causing the French gentleman so much excitement. But, surely, de Bacqueville countered, the Austrian colonel had simply not been in a legal position to surrender the horses; indeed, he had asked nobody's opinion before doing so! The subtle force of that last point having totally escaped the new owner, the Duc's agent then asked only for assurance that he would be allowed to go safely about his legitimate business in Ohlau and Breslau. The Major General was now pleasant, almost jovial: of course, the gentleman from France was free to travel in the countryside; why, he should act exactly as if he were at home in Paris! And did he, by the way, wish to have a guard assigned to him to carry his personal luggage? Declining politely, de Bacqueville beat a hasty retreat, having decided to put up at de Lauro's residence in the town. As he was leaving, one or two additional thoughts crossed his mind: was the Major General aware that various art treasures from the castle had already been sold? If such sales continued and were open to the public, he, on behalf of the Bouillon family, would like to purchase all of the family portraits or other similar objects to prevent their dispersal. Now the beaming Major General spoke kindly and soothingly: there was no need for concern: he, in fact, intended to keep all such portraits together himself, *for his own satisfaction*.... Scarcely heartened, the Duc's agent desperately begged one last favour. Would the Major General at least hand on to him the many family papers in the castle? These could be of no possible interest to the good Major General but they were of vital importance to the heirs of the estate.... At this, the good Major General pretended to be both amused and a little shocked: was the French gentleman surreptitiously trying to purloin documents relating to a contested estate! No, it would not be possible to hand over those dusty old papers. De Bacqueville, indignant at the accusation, pointed out that he needed no help or any additional documents, to prove that the estate was owed over 400 thousand florins! Clutching his passport and not a little reminded of his epic interviews with the old Prince Royal, he hurried from the castle. At least he had gained a last-minute promise that the Major General (who had heard so many good things about the Duc de Bouillon) would see what could be done about the horses!

On the same day that he sent Linotte an indignant account of his interview with Von Kleist, de Bacqueville decided to take the bold step of appealing directly to the King of Prussia. In a respectful note dispatched to Berlin, he acknowledged that a great king would want to reward his officers for services rendered, but the late Prince Royal's treasures, not to mention the Duc de Bouillon's horses, surely deserved special consideration. His plea was specific:

> Je supplie V.M. au nom de Mr le Duc de Bouillon et du Prince de Turenne, [de la] Princesse de Bouillon, ses enfants, d'envoyer ses ordres pour me faire remettre tous les effets, qui sont dans le chateau ou les remettre sous le scellé de V.M., et me donner la liberté d'emporter tout ce que j'ay envoyé ou apporté de Pologne, et de pouvoir aussi faire sortir de Breslaw pour France, les effets qui y sont encore appartenants a la Succession, sans passer a la Douane.[31]

Although he had omitted any mention of Stuart interests in the Ohlau possessions (these had been, after all, in dispute long before Frederick's troops took over the castle), de Bacqueville congratulated himself for having taken such a bold initiative on behalf of the Bouillon family. It therefore came as something of a shock when he learned from Linotte that deeper calculations had been going on at the Quai Malaquais in the meantime. His note to Frederick had been a mistake: "On ne croit pas icy," Linotte explained, "qu'il convienne trop de faire des demarches et d'écrire."[32] The Duc was now taking the position that Prussia's seizure of Ohlau was really a problem for the Stuarts and not for himself or the children of Marie-Charlotte since, in an October letter composed well before the invasion, James III had by implication accepted a compromise position: the Stuarts would give up any claim to the Polish movables in return for full rights on those at Ohlau.[33] By protesting the Ohlau seizures, de Bacqueville might inadvertently have given the Stuart Pretender an excuse for reneging on his agreement. It was plain bad luck for the Stuarts that the Prussian army had become involved; nevertheless, it was best to let sleeping dogs lie. In Linotte's subsequent letters, the point was repeated with even greater emphasis: "Les Princes d'Angleterre n'ont rien à demander dans les meubles de Pologne, et...le hazard des meubles d'Ohlau est pour leur compte."[34]

But again Linotte had good news as well: information had finally reached Paris that the Hamburg vessel had arrived safely at Le Havre. The bales would soon be in Navarre, and none would be opened before de Bacqueville returned. Plans for the wedding were proceeding smoothly although renovations at the Hôtel de Bouillon were even more behind schedule than before. Finally, the two guardians wanted de Bacqueville to know that he was not to worry about events beyond his control. "On est bien éloigné icy," Linotte reassured the fretful envoy, "de vous rien imputer sur la prise du Chateau d'Ohlau et des meubles. On ne vous a pas donné une armée a commander pour conserver Ohlau et ses dépendances et vous ne pouviez rien faire au dela de ce que vous avez fait pour faire rendre les meubles."[35] The Duc was not, of course, pleased at what the Prussians had done, but, with respect to Silesia, he would be quite satisfied with just the return of the horses. De Bacqueville was to forget about the lost chattels, but he was to continue his attempts to obtain the family papers and portraits.

Linotte scarcely dared mention the next item he had to report: it was that de Bacqueville's new apartment in the Hôtel de Bouillon would not be ready in time for his return. The porter was occupying it temporarily, but other suitable accommodation would certainly be found. With Louise's wedding not far away, the Grand Chambellan himself was in despair and talking gloomily about renting the Hôtel de Hollande because of the constant delays.

De Bacqueville was bitterly disappointed at the low-key response from Paris. If the children's guardians were not surprised to learn that the King of Prussia intended to keep the Ohlau chattels, he, for his part, wanted it known that he was *extremely* surprised, and he was even more astounded that Cardinal Fleury and the French Ministry had not been informed of this snub to the person of the Duc de Bouillon and, yes, to the French nation itself. How astonishing to take the position that it was best not to stir things up because the problem concerned only the Stuarts! "N'étoit-ce pas," de Bacqueville objected with uncharacteristic magnanimity, "une raison pour les aider? M. le Duc de Bouillon ne pense qu'à ses chevaux." Those damned horses! "Je voudrois n'en avoir jamais ouvert la bouche pour le mal qu'ils me donent et me doneront." Finally, was no one giving any thought at all to where he would be lodged? Truly, one got the impression at times that with *Son Altesse*, "les absents [ont] toutes sortes de torts."[36]

Other serious problems for the Bouillon family had meanwhile developed in Paris, and had de Bacqueville been aware of these, he might have tempered his criticism somewhat. In March, a minor scandal had suddenly jolted the ritualistic boredom of court life at Versailles, and the young Princesse de Bouillon, through absolutely no fault of her own, was involved. Was ever a young Princess so unlucky! It had all begun with an anonymous letter delivered to her at the

Chasse-Midi convent—a poisonous note containing the cruel boast that her future husband secretly loved another. The note went on to say that it was within the power of that person, at any time she wished, to break off the dazzling Monaco-Bouillon alliance, even though it had already been gazetted and ratified by the King and Queen!

Such were the perils of arranged marriages, but the effect on Louise of a fifth public "failure" was probably deep. Investigations soon confirmed that the claims of the mysterious letter were true. On being questioned by his father, the young Prince de Monaco broke down and confessed that he was passionately in love with a young widow, Mme de Néri, and that he had signed the articles of the engagement contract with Louise only with the greatest reluctance, indeed with bitter mental reservations. He had tried, but without success, to overcome his guilty passion.[37]

In fact, it was not, as de Luynes pointed out, the first time that the widow, "agée de vingt-six ou vingt-sept ans, fort petite, mais assez jolie," had disrupted official marriage plans. The affianced nephew of the Bishop of Verdun had earlier succumbed to her charms, but then she had acted responsibly, insisting that the young man honour his contractual obligations. The case with the young Prince de Monaco[38] was very different. Indeed, it was suspected that Mme de Néri herself had sent the malicious note to Louise. The Duc de Bouillon had no choice but to break off the marriage, and on 19 March, Louise's uncle, the Duc de la Trémoïlle, Premier Gentilhomme de la Chambre, along with the Duc de Valentinois, the errant Prince's father, travelled to Versailles to inform Louis XV of what had happened. Linotte, writing to de Bacqueville three days later, noted that the Duc de Valentinois was grief-stricken by the sudden turn of events: "Il n'a pas cessé dans tout le cours de cette affaire de donner a Mongr Le Duc de Bouillon et à sa maison tous les témoignages d'une sincere amitié et du désir extrême qu'il avoit de s'allier avec elle."[39] Linotte added that, unfortunately for Louise, the affair was creating a good deal of noise in Paris. Mme de Néri had been living as a guest in the household of Mlle de Sens, one of the *princesses du sang*,[40] who, though no better than she should be herself,[41] immediately expelled the pretty widow from her house. Commenting on the intensity of public anger towards the temptress, Linotte noted as well that "le public est déchaîné contre Made De Nery, et on ne scait pas si elle en sera quitte pour avoir été chassée de la maison de Madelle de Sens." Everyone was being very kind to Louise, including Mlle de Sens, who had acted in a most obliging manner "pour la Maison." As for the wayward Prince's father, he had remained on intimate terms with the Bouillon family: "Il aime Madlle de Bouillon," Linotte explained, "aussi tendrement que si Elle etoit sa fille, et dit hautement que son Fils n'etoit pas digne d'elle."

That the Duc de Valentinois meant what he said about his son's unworthiness was soon confirmed by action. On 19 March, the very day Louis XV was given the bad news, he obtained a *lettre de cachet*, ordering that his twenty-one-year-old son be locked up in the Citadelle at Arras, there to meditate on the follies of ungoverned passion. Commenting on the *lettre de cachet*, de Luynes revealed the harsh exchanges between father and son that accounted for it: "Ce n'est pas parce qu'il n'a pas voulu se marier, mais parce que, n'écoutant que la violence de sa passion et parlant comme un homme ivre ou qui a le transport au cerveau, il a été inflexible aux larmes et aux prières de M. de Valentinois et lui a dit même des choses extrêmement dures."[42] We are not a little reminded of Prévost's hero, des Grieux, "*enflammé jusqu'au transport et à la folie*"! Mme de Néri proved more caring than the beautiful Manon and made desperate efforts to take the blame upon herself, but her repeated attempts to see Cardinal Fleury were rebuffed: "Elle avoit apparemment entendu parler de lettres de cachet; elle demandoit que, s'il y en avoit une, ce fût [pour] elle. Barjac, à qui elle parla et qui avoit déjà averti M. le Cardinal, ne voulut jamais la laisser entrer; elle trouva M. de Bouillon en revenant de Versailles; elle l'arrêta et chercha fort à se disculper de la rupture du mariage."[43]

The effect on Louise of this highly publicized and extremely embarrassing breach of contract, provoked by an older rival's apparently superior charms (Louise seems to have always lost out to older women!), was long-lasting, if not permanent. Muffled reverberations of her hurt can be detected in the anguished and painfully insecure letters she wrote later on in a similar situation to Prince Charles Edward Stuart. The effect on the young Prince de Monaco was less damaging. By December of that same year, he was back in circulation on the fringes of court life.[44] Reconciliation with his father, on the other hand, did not come until the death of Mme de Néri early in 1744. Even then, the old Duc had hesitated: "Le premier jour d'après cette mort, M. de Valentinois avoit trop montré sa joie et sa satisfaction; mais présentement il agit avec toute la douceur et l'amitié possible à l'égard de son fils."[45] Only after the pretty widow's demise was it learned for certain that no secret marriage existed between them although the Prince apparently had made a commitment to marry his mistress as soon as he attained his majority. Out of affection for his Grand Chambellan, Louis XV let it be known that forgiveness would not come too easily, and it was some time before the passionate young Prince was allowed to re-establish his full credit at Court.[46]

Meanwhile in Ohlau, de Bacqueville's work—such as it was—had come to an end. Frederick the Great finally agreed to release the horses, but the only joy the Duc's agent derived from that minor victory was in witnessing the consequent annoyance of the Major General. "Kleist est enragé," he informed Linotte, "que les chevaux luy ayent echappé. Je luy ay ecrit une lettre fort peu humble, quoy que dans les termes convenables."[47] The Major General retaliated by sending, along with the Duc's horses, a large bill for their upkeep! De Bacqueville's feelings of bitterness had scarcely subsided, however. Even the news that the Monaco marriage was broken off scarcely moved him: "Je ne plains à tout cela," he grumbled, "que le pauvre M. le Duc de Valentinois."[48] He was, in any case, more worried about his housing in Paris: "Je vous prie pour la derniere fois, Monsieur, de me mander a Strasbourg les intentions de Mgr le Duc de Bouillon pour mon logement en arrivant."

In that respect, only a few problems remained. Linotte was soon able to report that emergency lodgings were being arranged for him at the Hôtel d'Auvergne. Louise's valet, Chavray, would move in whatever furniture and personal effects he, his two servants and his own valet required.[49] By the time de Bacqueville reached Paris in May, he had regained his good spirits. He had with him the Duchesse's remaining chattels and jewelry and could congratulate himself on a difficult job well done.[50]

With the certainty that new revenues would be coming to her from her mother's estate, Louise now had an even more attractive dowry to offer a prospective husband. By the following year, the Monaco scandal was nearly forgotten and with the family fortunes once more on the mend, the Duc de Bouillon again set about actively looking for a suitable match for his daughter. He was now an even more powerful figure at Versailles, having become one of the closest personal associates of the King. Other dukes and duchesses could grumble all they liked about the pretensions of the Bouillons, the Rohans, and Lorraines (and de Luynes' *Mémoires* provide frequent examples of such complaints), but the three or four leading families, always "sticking together," managed without real difficulty to impose their haughty ways on the French Court. What was common wisdom in the matter is typically summed up in the pseudo-memoirs of the Marquise de Créquy: "La première famille de France, après la maison royale, est évidemment celle de Lorraine; la seconde est, sans contredit, celle de Rohan; et la troisième est celle de la Tour d'Auvergne ou de Bouillon-Turenne, si vous l'aimez mieux; la quatrième est, à mon avis, celle de la Trémoïlle."[51] As good luck would have it, the Duc could scarely have improved on the brilliant marriage arrangements he soon had the pleasure of announcing for both of his children: in February 1743 an important alliance with the Rohans was formed by the marriage of Louise to Jules-Hercule-Mériadec de Rohan, Prince de Guéméné; in November of that same year, the Prince de Turenne was married to Louise-Henriette-Gabrielle de Lorraine.[52]

De Luynes first speaks of the contractual arrangements relating to Louise's upcoming marriage in December 1742, and the financial details he provides show that distinctly less money was involved than with the earlier Monaco proposal. Still, there was more than enough, and now there was much more prestige![53] Of particular interest (and foreboding significance for later events), is a special clause that was written into the contract at the insistence of Louise's future mother-in-law: the young couple, Mme de Guéméné stipulated, would be required to live with her at her residence in the Place Royale. "Elle l'a demandé," de Luynes explains, "comme une condition essentielle du mariage"; Prince Jules, it was noted, was only fifteen and still at the Academy.[54] No mention was made of the young Prince's father, Hercule-Mériadec de Rohan, Duc de Montbazon (1688-1757), who had married Louise-Gabrielle-Julie de Rohan-Soubise (1704-1780) on 2 August 1718,[55] but we learn from later references in de Luynes that Mme de Guéméné's husband was *interdit* and hence never seen in public. The truth of the matter was, however, well known: Louise's father-in-law suffered from serious mental illness and fits of brutish insanity. He lived sequestered on one of the family's many properties at Sainte Maure near Montbazon, an arrangement that did not prevent his presumptive siring of five of his nine offspring after the formal *arrêt d'interdiction* dated 19 December 1726.[56]

Contractual matters having been settled between the Duc de Bouillon and the prospective groom's mother, the effective head of the Guéméné household, the next order of business was to seek formal permission from the King, and this was done on 31 January 1743. Arrangements for Louise's presentation at Court before the wedding ceremony then had to be made in order to mark the Bouillon's claim that they were princes *by the grace of God*. De Luynes noted on 10 January that the Duc was planning to have his daughter presented on 27 January. The engagement ceremony could then take place on the 28th with the wedding held subsequently at the home of Cardinal d'Auvergne, the bride's great-uncle. The couple would then go on a honeymoon trip to Navarre.[57] Unfortunately, the death of Cardinal Fleury on the 29th necessitated a slight change in plan, and it was not until a week later, on 6 February, that Louise was presented by her aunt, the Duchesse de la Trémoïlle. The occasion was not without moments of tension, it being Mme de la Trémoïlle's first appearance at Court since the death of her distinguished husband. In fact, Charles-Godefroy's sister had agreed to participate at the last minute only because her old enemy, the Cardinal, was now dead, the wily old minister having several years earlier manipulated events so cleverly that it was his nephew, the Duc de Fleury, rather than her own young son who had succeeded to her late husband's position.[58]

Even the presentation of the bridegroom on 9 February was not without complications. He was the eldest son of the Prince de Guéméné, and his mother had always felt that he should bear the title *Prince de Rohan*. That suggestion had never sat well, however, with Mme de Guéméné's father, Hercule-Mériadec de Rohan-Soubise (1669-1749), himself known as *le Prince de Rohan*. It was tentatively agreed, therefore, that for the wedding, the bridegroom would be called *le prince Jules* and his wife, *la Princesse de Rohan*. The simplicity of such a solution seems to have overwhelmed protocol experts at Versailles, and, in the end, it was rejected out of hand: "M. de Gesvres fit l'observation, *avec raison*, qu'il ne pouvoit être présenté au Roi sous le nom du prince Jules, et enfin l'on est convenu qu'on lui donneroit le nom de duc de Montbazon, et c'est sous ce nom qu'il a été présenté."[59] Such were the earth-shaking challenges of daily life at the most powerful court in Europe!

Finally the great day arrived, Sunday, 17 February! De Luynes recorded the momentous event in minute detail: after the evening benediction, Louis XV, attended by the Dauphin and the *princes du sang*, the Comte de Charolois, the Prince de Dombes, and the Duc de Penthièvre, proceeded to the Oeil-de-Boeuf salon where the King stationed himself to the right of a small table in front of the great marble fireplace. Meanwhile, another group had assembled in the Queen's apartments. The gathering included the *princesses du sang*, Mme la Princesse de Conti, Mlle de Conti, Mlle de la Roche-sur-Yon, and Mlle de Sens. In attendance also were approximately fifty distinguished ladies of the Court, all soon to be joined by Mesdames, the royal princesses, and by Louise. The arrival of the bride was the signal for the Queen to lead off the procession, and soon all the ladies made their grand entrance into the Oeil-de-Boeuf. The Queen immediately took up her position on the left. The Dauphin and the *princes du sang* joined the King on the right. The royal princesses and the *princesses du sang* stood with the Queen on the left. Everything was now ready for signing of the marriage contract.

The King signed first, even before the bride and groom, as was the custom. He was followed by the Queen, then the princes and princesses, in the order of their rank. Then came the turn of Jules, followed by Louise. Finally, the Duc de Bouillon and Mme de Guéméné added their signatures. It was a glittering scene: the young Duc de Montbazon wore a costume of silver brocade, trimmed with gold lace. Louise was dressed in black and gold and wore a mantle of gold netting, the train of which was carried by Jules's cousin, Mlle de Montauban, the very ugly daughter of one of the Queen's ladies-in-waiting. The ceremony ended without a hitch, although the Marquis de Dreux, Grand Master of Ceremonies, later pointed out to the young groom that he too should have been dressed in black and gold. Fortunately, the lapse was deemed to be of no great consequence.

After everyone had signed, Cardinal de Rohan, the groom's great-uncle and Grand Aumônier de France, entered the room, solemnly preceded by various priests, among whom was the curé of Notre-Dame. The engagement ceremony was then performed, after which the Queen withdrew, followed by all of her ladies. The King remained behind for a moment to converse with the young couple. Now the Duc de Montbazon was positioned to his right and Louise to his left.[60]

It was all over except for the simple wedding ceremony, which was performed two days later at the residence of Cardinal d'Auvergne.[61] To some it seemed a curious choice of setting for the celebration of holy matrimony since Louise's aging great-uncle was notorious for his everyday neglect of ecclesiastical duties and was commonly accused of having forgotten how to say even the simplest prayers.[62] Moreover, his sodomitical proclivities were no secret and had been the subject of much angry criticism when, to the surprise of everyone, including himself, he was appointed in December 1737 (with the help of James III) to the College of Cardinals. At least one ribald wit of the day noted that the appointment demonstrated in a curious way the truth of the old proverb that "tous les chemins mènent à Rome"![63] Undoubtedly, such considerations were also borne in mind by the usual gossips who allowed themselves to speculate on precisely how Louise and her husband spent their wedding night in the Cardinal's bed. Crébillon's novel, le Sopha, had been published not long before, and it was obviously not entirely forgotten in the following anecdote about that blissful occasion, recorded in de Maurepas' apocryphal *Mémoires*:

> Le mariage de mademoiselle de Bouillon avec le prince de Guémenée a été fait chez le cardinal d'Auvergne qui leur prêta son lit.
>
> Ce lit, dit-on, alors parla, et voyant leurs amours antiques avec des procédés nez-à-nez, il leur dit qu'ils étoient sans expérience, et que M. le cardinal ne s'y prenoit pas de cette façon.[64]

VI

Enter the Hero-Prince

A FTER their brief honeymoon, the young couple returned to Paris and dutifully took up residence with the groom's mother at the Hôtel de Guéméné on the ancient but still fashionable Place Royale.[1] Louise made a ceremonial appearance at Court on Sunday 31 March when she was formally presented as Duchesse de Montbazon, her earlier presentation having been only to ensure recognition of the Bouillon family's pretensions. Keeping up such appearances was equally important for the family she had married into. Its motto: *Roi ne puis, duc ne daigne, Rohan suis* was well illustrated a few weeks later, for example, when the groom's distinguished relative, Cardinal de Rohan, found himself in the ridiculous position of having to leave a solemn Good Friday mass before the Veneration of the Cross because of a trifling infringement of Rohan prerogatives by lesser princelings.[2] Happily, with the unexpected arrival in France the following year of her royal cousin, Prince Charles Edward Stuart, Louise was soon to have matters of much greater moment to preoccupy her thoughts!

Despite their polite but nonetheless determined and unending legal disputes over the inheritance of Prince James Sobieski, the Bouillons and the Stuarts had carefully kept in touch over the years on such routine items of news as family deaths, births, and marriages. James, it is true, remained rather suspicious of the Duc. He had never quite understood why Charles-Godefroy seemed *si peu au fait*, to use his words, concerning his late wife's business. He was also not certain that it was proper for the Grand Chambellan to address him as *beau-frère*. It was a delicate point of protocol, but since the Duc was anxious about it, O'Brien, the Pretender's chargé d'affaires in Paris, was assigned the task of investigating all relevant historical precedents. James agreed to conform to whatever practice had been normally followed by the kings of England and France over the centuries, but he rather had his doubts....[3]

Correctly amicable relations prevailed, for all that. On 9 January 1743, for example, the Duc had written to the exiled Stuart king to announce Louise's forthcoming marriage.[4] James offered his congratulations on 7 March and expressed particular satisfaction that his niece had married into the distinguished Rohan family, "à cause de l'estime toute singuliere que j'en fais, et de mon amitié personelle pour le Cardinal de ce nom, et Le Prince son Frère, Grand Pere du nouveau marié."[5] He was equally impressed and full of congratulations on the occasion of the Prince de Turenne's subsequent marriage to a member of the house of Lorraine.[6] No doubt he still recalled Charles-Godefroy's offer in 1737 to marry Louise to one of his sons....What the future now held for Charles Edward and his younger brother, Henry-Benedict, he was still unable to tell. The new wind blowing might soon require the marriage of one or both of the princes to cement a union with France or Spain and assure the restoration of his family to its rightful place on the throne of Great Britain.

How, precisely, to regain that throne was, of course, an increasingly anxious concern of James Edward Stuart. France, he knew, held the key to the problem, just as she had in 1715 when he had made his last concerted effort to rally supporters to his standard. By the early 1740's, the situation was in fact looking more favourable than it had in years. The recent death of Cardinal Fleury and the hope that he would be succeeded as chief minister by Cardinal Tencin (who owed his red hat to James), the news of growing dissatisfaction with the Hanoverian government, and glowing accounts of widespread Jacobite support throughout the British Isles all helped generate an atmosphere of cautious optimism at the Pretender's court in Rome. Here at last was the basis for firm hope that France could be persuaded to organize a descent on England, coinciding with an effective rising of Jacobite supporters in the North.[7] By 1743 there were many signs that Jacobite prayers would be answered, and, indeed, by December of that year, a definite invasion plan was in place. Louis XV wrote to Philip V of Spain on 10 December to announce his scheme for a military expedition. It was to be carried out without warning or formal declaration of war. The King of France had, of course, a dynastic purpose that went well beyond merely reaffirming the principles of Stuart legitimacy. As he informed Philip V, he was interested in destroying "tout d'un coup, par les fondemens, la Ligue des Ennemis de la Maison de Bourbon."[8] Planning and detailed preparations had been carried out in such great secrecy, Louis XV explained to his confrere, that it had not been possible to inform him of the project sooner. The undertaking was not without risks, but he had every reason to believe it would succeed: "Les circonstances presentes et les eclaircissemens que j'ai pris avec le plus grand soin en rendent le succès tres aparent." In his reply, Philip V was highly approving; it would be, he declared, a glorious undertaking for France.[9] Naturally, the presence at some time during the campaign of a representative of the House of Stuart was required to lend an air of legitimacy to a Bourbon war against, not the British nation, but the House of Hanover. Meanwhile, parallel planning had been going on in Rome as well. Two weeks after Louis XV sent his letter to Spain, James granted a Commission of Regency to his elder son, authorizing him to act on his behalf in all matters related to the undertaking, it being "absolutely impossible," as the document asserts, for the King to be in Great Britain in person "at the first setting up of Our Royal Standard, and even some time after."[10]

The invasion had originally been scheduled to begin on 9 January 1744, but various delays allowed extra time for Charles Edward to slip out of Rome undetected by the ever vigilant Hanoverian spies. Both Louis XV's plans for an expedition to be led by the Comte de Saxe and the arrival of the Young Pretender in France turned out to be remarkably well-kept secrets. Barbier, a generally reliable gauge of town opinion and information on most matters, seems not to have picked up his first rumours of military movements until early in February when he noted with a certain degree of scepticism a report that the Brest fleet was leaving for Scotland and that Charles Edward had joined it: "Si cela étoit," he commented, "cela donneroit bien de l'ouvrage aux Anglois: ce prince légitime de la maison de Stuart, *et plus brave que son père*, peut avoir un gros parti dans les royaumes d'Ecosse et d'Irlande, même dans l'Angleterre."[11] But all that was conjecture, he admitted, although it was certain that the Chevalier de Saint-George's son had been seen arriving at Antibes. Soon after, the news of vast military preparations at Dunkirk became more definite. It was the talk of the town, Barbier noted, and had become a matter of public enthusiasm: "Tout le monde est charmé et admire ce grand projet, et l'on attend de jour en jour des nouvelles intéressantes."[12] Even the famous prophecies of Nostradamus seemed to augur well for the mission's success, and, in all seriousness, the French chronicler cited the pertinent quatrain:

> De l'aquilon les efforts seront grands,
> Sur l'Océan sera la porte ouverte,
> Le règne en l'île sera réintégrant,
> Tremblera Londres par voile découverte.[13]

Charles Edward's departure from Rome and his arrival in Paris on 8 February 1744 after a hard ride from Antibes had been so well hidden that not even Cardinal Tencin, the man generally (and quite erroneously) credited with originating the idea, was aware of what was going on. After only two days' rest, the Prince was champing at the bit to continue. To his father he wrote on 10 February that he was now ready to travel as far again if necessary. He very much looked forward to the campaign, "which will be a great pleasure to me who had desired so long to see and understand Millitary matters, as they best become my situation." His incognito had, of course, to be total since his very presence on French territory was a flagrant violation of solemn treaty agreements between

England and France, including, specifically, article 5 of the Treaty of the Quadruple Alliance of 1718, which forbade the harbouring on French territory of the person who called himself James III and of any of his descendants as well. Moreover, it would be still more than a month before France was to declare war on her old rival across the Channel.

Events of the next few weeks, while no doubt exciting for the apprentice warrior, were to prove in the end extremely disappointing. By 25 February, Charles Edward had set out from Paris for Dunkirk, where a French force of more than ten thousand men awaited orders to embark. The story of what happened between that date and 13 March, when the project was officially suspended, is well enough known: bad weather and bad luck, not to mention a certain amount of mismanagement and hesitation, soon dashed Jacobite hopes and convinced the French Ministry that the essentially well-planned expedition would have to be postponed. "Vous ne pouvez, Monseigneur, accuser que les vents et la fortune des contretemps qui nous arrivent," de Saxe wrote to the Prince on 13 March; the expedition's commander went on to give assurances, however, that the King of France was "dans la ferme résolution de ne point abandonner ce projet, mais de le suivre jusqu'à son entière exécution."[14]

De Saxe left the coast for Versailles on 16 March and was reassigned to the Army in Flanders, where he soon won his *maréchal*'s bâton. Charles Edward remained on at Gravelines, hoping against hope. He had written to his father on the 13th, telling him of the violent storms that had destroyed so many transport vessels and prevented the French forces from sailing. As it turned out, the storms had been providential since Admiral de Roquefeuil had not effectively blocked the movements of Sir John Norris's squadron, and, consequently, capture of the French invasion force, himself along with it, would have been a certainty. No one was discouraged, the Prince continued somewhat naively, not even the Comte de Saxe. With "the weather now becoming favourable upon the change of the Moon," the expedition would soon be reinstated.[15]

Much to Charles Edward's dismay, Louis XV issued instructions that he too was to leave the coast. In a long letter to Lord Sempill of 15 March, the Prince earnestly requested that the King's decision be reconsidered. It was still possible, he argued, to organize something, if not a descent on England, then at least a smaller expedition that would land in Scotland. The matter was most urgent: this was not solely a campaign to recapture a lost throne; it was also a war of liberation to free an oppressed nation from foreign bonds. He was ready to sail off on his own, but he realized that without the support of an invasion force to give his loyal followers sufficient time to come forward and declare themselves, there could be no hope of success. A botched mission would result in even greater oppression by the Hanoverian government. He had thus set aside all such thoughts. It was important, nevertheless, to remember that the entire expedition would be viewed by everyone as his first great effort in the Stuart cause and, although he was incognito in France, the eyes of the world were upon him. If he withdrew without making any attempt, it would encourage everyone to think that he was just another of those unlucky Stuarts, a family dogged by misfortune from one generation to the next. It would dishearten his followers and give comfort to an enemy that only a week or two before was ready to panic. A French landing in Scotland would find many supporters, and he was himself familiar enough with the situation there to know that even if he were to turn up alone and unaided, most of the Highlanders would immediately rally to the cause. Would it not be more fitting for him to go there now and perish if need be at the head of those good and brave people, than to continue to lead the abject and dreary life of an exile? The time to act was now![16]

Charles Edward's letter, obviously written to be shown to the King of France,[17] holds the key to much of his future behaviour, and it deserves more attention than historians of the Stuarts have generally given it. After reading it, no one, least of all Louis XV or Lord Sempill, should have been surprised at the daring step the Prince was to take in July of the year following when he did sail for Scotland, almost on his own and without really consulting anyone. For the moment, however, he had decided to be patient, and he dutifully stayed on at Gravelines, waiting for a miracle. On 26 March, he again wrote to James, assuring him that whatever happened, nothing would ever "slacken" him in his duty: "I have lerned from you how to bere with disappointments, and I see it is the only way, which is to submit oneself entierly to the will of God and never to be discouraged. You need not be in pain for me whatever hapens, for nothing will ever hinder or discourage me from applying and minding my business."[18] Such solemn expressions of filial obedience and dedication to the cause came easily to the Prince at this time, and he was submissive as well in his assurances to Cardinal Tencin, a man he already distrusted and soon grew to hate.[19] Good-naturedly, he was even able to see the humour of his strict incognito: "No body nose," he wrote to his father on 3 April, "where I am or what is become of me, so that I am entierly Burried as to the publick, and cant but say but that it is a very great constrent upon me for I am obliged very often not to stir out of my room for fier of some body's noing my face. I very often think that you would laugh very hartelly if you sau me goin about with a single servant bying fish and other things and squabling for a peney more or less."[20]

In his reply of 15 April, James, as usual, counselled submission to the "decrees of Providence"; it was right for Charles Edward to look to the future and not be cast down; "yet," he urged his son, "you must let yourself be overruled & governed by the King of France, in whose hands you now are, & on whom alone you must depend, and who will, I am persuaded, never approve of rash undertakings." The suspension of the expedition was a misfortune, but it was not irretrievable, "except we should make it so ourselves, by pursuing precipitate & desperate measures, & undertake some rash & ill concerted project which could only end in your ruin & in that of all those who joyn with you in it."[21] James knew his son well, and though the younger Henry had always been, and would always be, his favourite, he clearly held the more impulsive Charles Edward in great affection also, now discovering a tenderness for him which, he admitted with curious candour in the same letter, was "much greater than I thought it was."

Whether, on the other hand, Charles Edward *knew Charles Edward* as well as James did is a question well worth puzzling over for a few moments. The young Prince's emotions during this period were certainly more complex than those generally attributed to the *héroïque étourdi* so often described by biographers familiar only with his later exploits, misdeeds, and failings. The secretiveness and alienation, the irrationality and defiance, the paranoia even, of the post-Culloden and, especially, the post-Aix-la-Chapelle hero—that pathetically desperate outlaw who had been unlucky enough to survive the butchery of Drummossie Moor—seem nowhere in evidence. Perhaps there was already in him a hidden vulnerability, the makings of a tragic flaw that would eventually allow catastrophic failure to turn all of the very genuine virtues of his youthful character inside out. Even so, the young Charles Edward's openness and simple idealism, his exalted sense of duty, of filial obedience and virtue, have too often been overlooked. Especially, we have forgotten the extent to which these qualities were fortified by a deeply ingrained religious sensibility. Charles Edward was a Sobieski, his mother's son, as much as he was a more adventurously pragmatic Stuart. Maria-Clementina had been exasperatingly saintly[22] during her few years with James, and though she had been gone for nearly a decade, indelible traces of her pious influence on both of her sons remained. It is significant that the Prince asked his father, as soon as he was able to write freely from Dunkirk, to send him a copy of his mother's portrait in miniature, along with his own and Henry's.[23] No doubt his mother's frequent exhortations to seek virtue, submit to Providence, "to love the Virgin Mary and her Divine Son," echoed still in his post-adolescent psyche. Perhaps he could even recall his promise to say everyday a special office of prayers to the Virgin, "qu'il ne faut jamais abandoner," Maria-Clementina had urged, "jusqu'o dernier soupir de votre vie, car par son intercession vous pouvés esperer qu'elle vous obtiendra du Seigneur la grase de ne jamais plus l'ofenser."[24]

It is thus likely that Charles Edward continued, despite his recent setbacks, to trust in Maria-Clementina's God and perhaps even in the efficacy of her schedule of prayers. The lonely isolation of his incognito was to persist for a long time, but with it continued also the strength of his single-minded commitment to the family's sacred cause. Everything else was a matter of total indifference: "Whether I am free from company or diversions, its all alike to me," he wrote to James on 10 April, "for I can think of nothing or taste nothing but your service, which is my duty."[25] Two weeks later, he stressed again his acceptance of sacrifice: "I think of nothing but your service, and cante enjoy anything till the business is done. I trust in God and hope that he will have mercy on us."[26]

By May, Charles Edward was back in Paris, very privately, as required by Louis XV's personal instructions. The Prince's fortitude and patience at Gravelines had much impressed the French monarch who, before leaving for Flanders on 2 May, expressed his regrets at not having seen the Pretender's son personally. He even hinted that Charles Edward might soon be allowed at his side, with the Army. Short of being actually on his way to Scotland, the young Prince could have desired nothing more, and he made no attempt to hide his resentment when he later learned that Lord Marischal had managed to block any such move by persuading the French Ministry that the Stuart cause would be seriously harmed in Britain if it became known that the Young Pretender—even in the strictest incognito—was actually engaged in fighting Englishmen.[27] The incognito continued then, despite the Prince's hope that he would soon "be free of this lurking."[28] Nothing changed, and as the days passed, he felt more and more imprisoned by the King's order, "not being able so much as to breth the fresh are as often as I would wish for fear of being seen by some body that should know me."[29] Yet his readiness to submit to the Divine will remained strong: "all adversitys pas esily with me and I am shure that by my doing my duty before God and man I will have the reccompence in next Life, which is nothing to be compered with this Life."[30] Thus, during this long summer of 1744, he seemed well on his way to following submissively in his father's and grandfather's footsteps, convinced that the French King would call on him at any moment to join once more in a renewed expedition. He waited and prayed while even James, who had much more experience with "lurking" and waiting, began to grow irritated at what seemed a purposeless confinement. On 1 June, the Prince reported that he would be doing his devotions the following week, the fourth time he had done them since arriving in France: "Your Majesty may be fully persuaded that I neglect nothing of that kind nor will never with Grace of God."[31] Like an obedient schoolboy writing home, the twenty-year-old Prince even added a postscript apologizing for the "Blots and faults" in his letter. Again, on 29 June, he reported having done his devotions. He hoped too that with the grace of God he would never fail in his duties.[32]

We now know—but more on this later—that one of those duties included being faithful to a youthful vow of chastity, a vow he seems to have conscientiously kept until the summer of 1747 when, in Balhaldy's words, he abandoned "the resolution he had taken of being singular in that virtue."[33] The months continued to pass without any sign from the French King that a new expedition was being planned or that the rigid incognito, now labelled even by James as "indecent in all respects,"[34] would be mitigated. In June, Charles had moved "like a hermit" to an isolated house about a league from Paris.[35] He had already taken on George Kelly as a secretary and acquired several servants, including a *valet de chambre* who, he noted significantly, was "given to no vice."[36] Even Kelly, the non-juring parson who had spent fourteen years in the Tower before escaping to the Continent, was reputed to be, although somewhat gossipy, fairly straight-laced and disapproving in matters of dalliance. His former employer, the aging Duke of Ormonde, had been only too happy to transfer his secretary to Charles since the clergyman's presence was "a great constrent to his Amoors."[37]

Devotion and resignation, interspersed with occasional sprinklings of suspicion that the French were playing him for a fool and giving him only fair words and cheap promises, continued to be dominant themes in the Prince's letters to James during the remaining months of 1744. The Almighty remained truly his "only hope."[38] In November, after doing his devotions, he assured his father that he was being careful to observe "as much as possible the doing of them as often as at Rome, and on the usual Holidays. I hope the Almighty will have mercy on us at laste; in the meantime I will always say *fiat volontas tua...* submitting entierly to his will."[39] Perhaps one small sign of incipient rebellion came in November when he decided to change confessors. His usual spiritual adviser, the Abbé Sempill, brother of Lord Sempill, was "a very exemplary and good Eclesiastic," but since his incognito presence in Paris was already *le secre[t] de la Comedie*, he had decided that he would henceforth do his devotions in a church rather than a private chapel and go to a common confessor. "I made good enquieris to go to one of noted Caracter for lerning and wright way of thinking," he assured his father, "and have founde one to whom I go ho has all these Quallitys. He is called Kelly...at the Convent here called Le Grand Cordelie. He is releted to Kelly that is with me. I here on all sides of people that dose not no I go to him a great Caracter of him. I recommended to him to say to nobody untill I tell him otherwise that I confess to him."[40] It was the first time since his arrival in France that the Prince had asserted his independence from James's official Jacobite establishment.

Charles Edward's doubts and suspicions increased significantly as the year 1744 drew to a close with still no sign that his prolonged seclusion would end. He had blindly followed instructions and waited patiently for Louis XV's permission to show himself in society, but all in vain. Finally, at the end of November, he confided to James his private belief that the French King thought little of him. He was getting "out of youmer at all these prosidings." He was distressed too by the petty and destructive bickering that was going on among the Jacobites in Paris and complained of being "plagued out of my life with *tracasrys* from our own People." His letter ended on a depressed note: "The more I dwell on these matters, the more it makes me Melancholy."[41] But one week later he demonstrated how well-armed against such fits of depression he really was: "I can begin to say that I finde by experience that thô one meets with adversitys, they are much sofened to one that resignes himself entierly to the will of God, and bears them with Patience. I made my Devotions on St Andrews

Day, recommending my self particularly to him as ower Protector. I hope the Almighty will always give me grace to do all my Dutys. Doing that, I reccon it to be the only, and solidest confor one can have in this Life, to have nothing to reproch one self with."

During the whole of this period, the Prince had not been allowed to look up his French relatives, the Bouillon family. The Duc, as Grand Chambellan, had accompanied the King to the Army and was with him at Metz when he fell gravely ill on 8 August. To the enormous scandal of many, the royal mistress, the Duchesse de Châteauroux, and her sister, the Duchesse de Lauraguais (popularly rumoured to have jointly provoked the King's illness through sexual exhaustion on the preceding evening),[42] remained at the King's bedside. Convinced at last that he was at the point of death, Louis XV was persuaded to send the sisters away and to make a public act of contrition for his wicked ways. At the same time he publicly begged the Queen's forgiveness for the scandal and grief he had caused her. Even on what he thought was his death bed, Louis XV had not been brought to such actions easily. The final decision to drive off the royal playmates and to summon the King's Jesuit confessor, le Père Pérusseau, had been a matter of exquisitely delicate timing—largely the work of the Bishop of Soissons, Charles Edward's cousin, and, unfortunately, of his uncle, the Duc de Bouillon, to whom the King had finally called out in words now famous: "Mon Bouillon, mon Bouillon, adieu; je me meurs, je ne vous reverrai plus; le P. Pérusseau."[43] So great was the anger and indignation of the inhabitants of Metz that the sisters had to be smuggled out of the city behind the closed shutters of the governor's carriage.[44]

Back in Paris Charles Edward was perhaps more worried about the King's health than anyone else. For all his trust in God, he knew that without the backing of the French monarch, there could be no realistic hope of a restoration: "It would be a terrible stroke to Mr Howel [himself]," he wrote to his father, "if Mr Adams [Louis XV] dys, for he would not know what would becomme of him."[45]

As it turned out, Charles Edward did not become a casualty of the King's illness, although the Duc de Bouillon eventually did. Not surprisingly, Louis' death-bed remorse was of the less enduring variety, and with the rapid recovery of his health, he soon found himself bitterly regretting the indignity of his act of contrition in front of the gaping masses at Metz and his panicky repudiation of fleshly joys. For his part in the affair, the good Bishop of Soissons eventually lost his chance at a cardinal's hat (thus lending a cruelly ironic twist to Charles Edward's expressions of happiness that his cousin[46] had gained "a great dele of honour, on this occasion, and is much in favour with the King who sed these words to him, squeezing him by the Hand: *Je n'oublierez jamais les services que vous m'avez fait.*"[47] Charles-Godefroy, on the other hand, suffered the more visible pains of actual disgrace when the two sisters returned to royal favour only a few months later. The Duc had been particularly vociferous in his protests concerning their presence in the sickroom, and he had been abrupt with the King's physician for shirking his responsibilities. As with the Bishop of Soissons, Louis XV did not seek his revenge immediately,[48] but soon little signs of royal displeasure began to appear. The Grand Chambellan had, for example, been soliciting a regiment for Louise's husband, at the time a mere captain of cavalry in the Royal-Pologne regiment. To become the colonel of his own regiment was the next logical step for Jules, and the Duc de Bouillon chose the auspicious occasion of a battle near the Rhine, at which his son-in-law had been wounded, to bring the matter once more to the King's attention. Several regiments had recently been awarded, and Charles-Godefroy made known his keen disappointment that the Duc de Montbazon had been passed over: "Il en fut vivement peiné," noted de Luynes, "et crut devoir dire au Roi que les circonstances présentes l'affligeoient...que les intérêts de son gendre étoient les siens et qu'il se flattoit de mériter un traitement plus favorable."[49] The Grand Chambellan's appeal was unsuccessful although the King's rejection of it was gentle and friendly: Jules was still very young; he would certainly be kept in mind, and the Duc de Bouillon "verroit incessamment combien il étoit touché de l'attachement et de l'amitié qu'il lui avoit marqué."[50] In the end, the King made good his words, whether taken ironically or *au pied de la lettre*: within two months Charles-Godefroy was in exile, and less than one year later, Louise's husband had his own regiment.[51]

The Duc's unsuccessful overtures on behalf of his son-in-law had been made to his convalescing master in Metz. Not more than ten days later he again found reason to suspect that the King was unhappy with him. On the journey from Metz to Lunéville, where the royal party arrived on 29 September, the Duc found himself obliged to sit *facing the rear* in the King's four-seater carriage, alongside the Duc de Villeroy, captain of the *Gardes du Corps du Roi*! Worse still, M. le Premier, the King's *premier écuyer*, had been allowed to occupy the rear seat next to His Most Christian Majesty! That particularly galling arrangement was continued through several days of travel, and Charles-Godefroy was not pleased. M. le Premier maintained, of course, that it was a privilege of his particular office to ride facing forward. In his solemn reflections on the problem, De Luynes confirmed that protocol indeed sanctioned M. le Premier's presence in the King's carriage; he was not at all certain, however, that the *premier écuyer* had to be on the forward facing seat.... It was, indeed, a matter of the first importance. And what was the King's own opinion? "Le Roi dit," de Luynes noted, "que personne n'a droit d'avoir de place dans son carrosse, qu'il y fait monter ceux qu'il veut. M. de Bouillon est furieux; le Roi a dit de ne lui en point parler pendant le voyage, qu'il examineroit cette affaire à Versailles."[52] History has perhaps been harsher on Louis le Bien-Aimé than he deserves!

De Luynes, a veritable Boswell of the French court, also recorded at the time his disappointment that the King's reconciliation with the Queen at Metz had somehow cooled, possibly as a result of an angry conversation during which the Dauphin had allowed himself to speak unfavourably of the Duchesse de Châteauroux. "Le froid est aussi grand que jamais,"[53] de Luynes noted, recording also his suspicion that the dazzling proofs of religious fervour demonstrated by the King at Metz a few weeks earlier were now much less in evidence: Louis, for example, had stopped praying on his knees. Perhaps, the court diarist speculated charitably, the King was still too weak to do otherwise.... No doubt he now said his prayers in bed. The pity was that the public could not be touched or edified by the example of royal devotions carried out so privately!

In fact, the King of France was beginning to feel a renewed inclination to engage in less solitary activities in his bed! Full proof of that came on 26 November when it was learned at Court that the two exiled sisters had been invited back to their Versailles apartments. The King of France had even apologized to them for the indecent treatment they had been subjected to. Charles-Godefroy received the news even earlier and with it a royal command to leave the Court immediately and betake himself, not as might be expected to his beloved Navarre, but rather to a chateau in the far-away *duché* of Albret that had not been lived in for two hundred years! The peculiar nastiness of the order is explained by the smouldering rage and vindictiveness of an injured mistress. Happily, the Duc was not without friends, one of them being the Duchesse de Châteauroux's aunt, Mme de Lesdiguières, the longtime mistress of his uncle, the Comte d'Evreux. The elderly woman had practically reared Mme de Châteauroux from childhood, and she managed to plead successfully on the Grand Chambellan's behalf, threatening otherwise to have nothing more to do with her niece. Soon after, Louis XV reduced the sentence of his old gaming crony to simple exile at Navarre.[54] When the royal mistress died in December, Louis XV was grieved beyond words, but it was only a matter of weeks before his Grand Chambellan was allowed back to Paris. It had been a brief punishment and not a disgrace, after all.

The French King still had another thorny problem on his mind—deciding what to do with his Grand Chambellan's nephew, the young Stuart Pretender. He had promised to take a decision on his return from the Army, and even Cardinal Tencin was now pestering him on behalf of the sequestered Prince. There was some talk of sending Charles Edward to Avignon and that turned out to be Louis XV's expressed preference, but the Prince, dedicated to winning the hearts of English Protestants, was understandably opposed to the thought of taking refuge in the Pope's dominions. It was finally agreed that he would be allowed to escape his Parisian "imprisonment" by going to the nearby country seat of Fitz James, situated north of Paris on the high road to Calais, where his cousin, the Duke of Fitzjames, resided.[55] Charles Edward was now also granted a small pension of 1000 livres per month (soon increased to 5000), but it was made clear at the same time that the King of France felt no financial obligation for his maintenance since he had not sent for him in the first place.[56] Unfortunately, the Prince had already built up by this time a considerable debt, the secret reasons for which were to become clear only after his departure for Scotland six months later.

Busy arrangements to leave for Fitz James began in January. However, except for the prospect of shooting and hunting, Charles Edward was not looking forward to the move, seeing it as merely trading one form of imprisonment for another. The isolation of a country house, away from his "real business" and entirely separated from the company and diversions of Paris would, he feared, give him the spleen. All that was of no consequence, however, as long as it advanced the family's "Great Lawsuit." He was ready, if necessary, to put himself in a tub, like Diogenes,[57] but before going he was determined, *incognito or no incognito*, to see his own relatives, the "familys of Bouillon and Berwick" as well as any other persons who might legitimately expect to be received by him.[58] The Duc de Bouillon had himself been waiting impatiently for an opportunity to pay his respects to his royal nephew. His exile cut short, Charles-Godefroy was back in the capital by the last week of December, and a week later he was asking to be allowed to wait on the Prince. Until now Charles Edward had been restricted to socializing only with the Jacobite exiles of Paris and only in the most discreet manner at the house of Colonel O'Brien, James's most trusted representative. With the Prince on the point of leaving for the country, Louis XV had let it be known through Cardinal Tencin that he would allow Charles Edward to meet briefly with his French cousins as well. The great day came on Friday, 8 January 1745. At last he was able to talk with his uncle, the Duc de Bouillon, and with his cousin, the Prince de Turenne! The following day, 9 January, precisely one year after his departure from Rome, he called on the Prince and the Princesse de Turenne at the Hôtel de Bouillon. There too he met the Prince de Turenne's sister, Louise. He saw her again on Sunday at a dinner party in the same house. Thus began, *avant l'Ecosse*, a fond relationship, later recognized by both of them as having been, from the very beginning, unspoken love.

Writing to his father the day after, Charles Edward was almost ecstatic in his account of the evening, his very first social outing since leaving Rome:

Paris ye 11th Jan. 1745

Sir,

As I have received no other paket since my Laste Letter I have not much to say. Thank God I am very well and much plesed with making and receiving visits of all those that are anyways my relations and that desier it on that consideration, which I do on Writ's[59] saying I may do so. I have already seen the D. of Bullion, the P. of Turain and his sister, and Last night I supt with all that family and after supper I went to the Opera Ball in mask, along with the P. of Turein, Mr Mombason and P. Camill. I am mightely well plesed with the D. of Bullion and his family, with their sivilitys and expressions towards me, and am very fond of the Prince de Turein, ho is really a very well behaved prety yong man every way. I have nothing more particular to add but that I am every Day now in a great hurry with one thing or an other for to be able to part as soon as possible to my Country House. I lay myself at your majestys Feet most humbly asking your Blessing.

> Your Moste
> Dutifull Son
> Charles P.[60]

Having been allowed to taste some of the normal pleasures of social life in the great city, Charles Edward became more reconciled to the thought of living in retreat. Fitz James was not impossibly distant. He would be able to cover the fourteen leagues between there and Paris in about six hours, whenever he wanted to. Perhaps it would even be amusing. He had always had a genuine fondness for country life and as he prepared for the move he joked with his old *caccia* companion, James Edgar in Rome, about not having handled a gun for months: "I intend to begin again to Shute, but not when it rens. You see by this that according as one advances in years one gets reason."[61] In a letter to his father of the same day he was less cheerful and not a little annoyed with French officialdom. The news of his having attended a masked ball at the Opéra had apparently reached Louis XV's ears and provoked immediate disapproval. Soon a message filtered down through the Comte d'Argenson's War Ministry, warning him to keep out of the public eye. Even Cardinal Tencin now recanted his earlier hints that the French Court was prepared to be more permissive concerning his incognito. Of course he would submit; such annoying constraints were easier to accept when one knew that they were directly related to advancing the Great Cause.[62]

The Prince arrived at Fitz James on Thursday, 18 February, and quickly sent out invitations to his friends in Paris to visit him. The Duc de Bouillon and the Prince de Turenne were among the first to accept and also among the first to offer the kind of moral support Charles Edward so urgently needed. The full meaning of his ten months of virtual imprisonment had begun to sink in: the French, it was clear, were not going to put aside their own interests or rearrange their European strategies and commitments merely to restore the House of Stuart to the British throne! He would himself have to see to matters in such a way that, confronted with a *fait accompli*, they would have no choice but to throw their support behind him.

Not surprisingly, his letters now speak less and less often of the virtues of patience or the need to submit to the decrees of Providence. Providence was, after all, perhaps nothing more than fate. In a letter to James of 25 January, he gloomily referred to the family fortunes being in a "bad Constellation."[63] There had been a lot of plain bad luck for the Stuarts in the past and he was determined to reverse their long and unhappy tradition of patient failure.

The Prince was determined also to take more liberties with his incognito than the letter of Louis XV's law seemed to allow. Five weeks after his arrival at Fitz James, he was back in Paris, passing himself off as a German Baron, much hurried "between Balls and business," and regretting all the while that he had so little "real business" on his hands.[64] But real business was on its way. By the beginning of the year, he had secretly begun to gather money and arms for a possible summer expedition to Scotland. Fearing that James would forbid any rash initiatives, he said nothing to his father although he candidly informed him that he was holding back certain information: "There are several things that are impossible to be writ," he advised James on 7 March, "on account of the risque, and others which I do not care to writ for fear of not meeting with entier credit, on account of my Age and want of experience. This makes me silent and catious in several things."[65] In a subsequent letter, he again referred to his lack of experience and his wish to acquire it as soon as possible, "for to be able," he told James, "to serve you, and our Country more effectually and to purpose, which is all that I am putt in this World for."[66] He continued to find the bickering among his followers in Paris distressing, and several times he expressed his determination to avoid getting embroiled in "politicks." On one amusing occasion his fears in that regard had been needless. He had been cornered at a masked ball by Mme de Mézières—reputed to be the greatest mischief-maker and nuisance among the Paris Jacobites—and had persisted for some time with the claim that he was a German baron newly arrived in the capital. It had been to no avail, however, and he was finally forced to admit who he was. To his great surprise, not a word of "politicks" was mentioned; Mme de Mézières—apparently better than her reputation—had merely wished to pay him a great many compliments, which he was able to return with equal civility.[67] Bals masqués at the Hôtel de Ville, the Opéra, and at Versailles were much in fashion during this pre-Lenten period in 1745, and Charles Edward, now constantly accompanied by his Bouillon cousins, attended as many as possible. Since thousands of disguised revellers were generally present, often until 7:30 or 8:00 o'clock in the morning, there was little risk of discovery, and, in any case, he was developing a taste for tempting fate. On Thursday, 4 March, he attended a bal masqué in the galerie at Versailles where, after a while, he sat down near the Queen. The tall, handsome Prince cut a striking figure, and it was not long before Her Majesty asked one of her ladies-in-waiting, the Marquise de Bouzols, who the audacious reveller was. In connivence with the Grand Chambellan, who had already let her into the secret, Mme de Bouzols informed her royal mistress that the person in question was her brother. Only a week later was the true identity of the mysterious guest learned. By then, de Luynes was able to report that Charles Edward had attended all of the balls at Versailles, "dans le plus grand incognito," including one given by the King's daughters. It became known too that he dined frequently at the Hôtel de Bouillon.[68] The Prince seemed completely taken with his uncle. The fact that the Duc was in such intimate daily contact with the one person in the world who held the key to the Stuarts' fortunes no doubt had its special importance for him. No one was in a better position to know Louis XV's private views on political matters even before these were communicated to the Ministers. For example, the Grand Chambellan had been able to tell his nephew that the King was as concerned as he was about the degree of squabbling going on among the Paris Jacobites.

But more than politics was involved in the Prince's extraordinarily warm attitude toward his uncle. In a letter to James, written while the Duc was visiting him in the country, Charles Edward's praise for Louise's father was boundless: "Really I must say that the more I am acquainted with him, the more I like him, for he has the best Hart in the World and I believe is thoroly attached & willing to do anything to serve me. So he has repeted to me several times, and he is nown by everybody to be cincere, which I no for certain not to be the case in ceveral People 380.440.530.225.305.362.306. 602.520.575.484.378. 282. 277.357.309.433.534.659.422.[whom I dare not risque to name in writing]."[69]

The "old fool" of Charles Edward's fable of 1748[70] was as distant in the future as Marie-Charlotte's tormentor was now forgotten in the past!

While pursuing his secret preparations for Scotland, borrowing money and arranging to have some of the Sobieski jewels pawned in order to buy broadswords and military supplies, Charles Edward continued to yearn for action in France. The war with the Elector of Hanover, whatever others thought, was his war too, and it was hard to sit around reading or hunting when everyone else was preparing for the glories of battle. He thus again offered his services to the King; all his friends, including the Duc de Bouillon and even the Duc's amusing associate, de Bacqueville, offered encouragement. Surely Louis XV could only applaud the Prince's efforts to join the campaign! But on 5 April, the Prince wrote that it now seemed highly unlikely he would be allowed to do so. James would thus see the many reasons he had for being "out of umer." He would be patient, nevertheless, and continue to hope in the Almighty.[71] His patience, however, went unrewarded and on 9 April, Charles Edward received the King of France's final word: permission would not be granted. To James he now complained bitterly: "I cannot conceive what it is that makes them refuse me, unless it be the expence, and iff it be only that, its very shamful and poor of them, supposing that to be the reason, which is the only Good one the[y] can have and Bad is the best can be said safely."[72] The Duc de Bouillon, meanwhile, had been doing his best to persuade the Ministers to allow his nephew to participate. He himself was setting out for the Army on 10 April, and Charles Edward had come down from Fitz James to say good-bye. Another reason for the visit, the Prince explained to James, had been to thank the Duc for offering him the use of Navarre. It would be an opportunity to see the stag hunt, which was quite new to him: "I have accepted of his offer, which was not to be refused, it being offered so civilly."[73] He would not be leaving for some time, however, since much work remained to be done in Paris and at Fitz James; also, the problem of getting the King's permission to make such a move had to be dealt with.[74]

Still unaware of the Prince's secret plan, James now began to worry that the French intended to make his son stay on for another summer in his "odious incognito."[75] He had also been hoping to arrange for the promotion of his nephew, the Bishop of Soissons, to the rank of Cardinal, but on making inquiries, he discovered that Louis XV for some reason (everyone was too discreet to mention the Metz affair) had developed an intense dislike for the Bishop and had stated that he would never allow the promotion. To compensate for this family disappointment, the Stuart King thought it would be appropriate to confer the Garter on the Bishop's brother, the Duke of Fitzjames, although he was somewhat reluctant; if it became known, he would be "teized and tormented" by other pretenders to the distinguished order.[76] Charles Edward's reaction to the proposal was immediate and once again demonstrated the unusual depth of his affection for his new-found friend, the Duc de Bouillon. If James gave the Garter to the Duke of Fitzjames, he clearly would have to give it also to the Duc since it would be "of the greatest mortification" to the Grand Chambellan if he were treated differently. Promising to keep the matter absolutely secret, Charles Edward "intreted" his father to honour his beloved uncle in that way: "I cannot but repet how good a man is the Duke of Boulion, and how attentive and civil he is to me, which one can see esely is without affectation, et de Bon Co[e]ur."[77] The Duc was now with the Army, but Charles Edward continued to visit his cousins in town. When Lent ended, the bals masqués resumed with a vengeance. The Prince needed very little persuading to attend. Other things remained unchanged as well: he had been careful to do his Easter duties at Notre Dame, and he was still half hoping to be called by Louis XV to the Army. Soon, news of the great victory at Fontenoy, and especially the gallant role played by the Irish Brigade in French service, made him envy even more the opportunity others had to prove their valour. King George's troops had finally shown their vulnerability. It was time to act. He could not wait forever for the French.

The move to Navarre finally took place on 29 May. Charles Edward had delayed his departure, still hoping that the King of France would call him to the campaign. He even left instructions in Paris that he was to be advised immediately if anything new concerning his "cerving" was heard. He also informed his father that before leaving Paris he had again made his devotions, "recommending myself to the Allmighty to give us better days and have mercy on uss."[78] With no more hope of seeing action in Flanders, Charles Edward now knew that he would be putting into effect his secret plan. He would leave for Scotland on his own. His prayers for "better days" anticipated deeds of valour and glory to be accomplished across the sea.

The next several weeks at Navarre were filled with preparations for the expedition. At the same time he anxiously awaited confirmation from Antoine Walsh, the Irish ship-owner at Nantes, that the vessels needed to ferry him and his small party to Scotland were ready. The exact date of departure had not yet been set, but the Prince decided to compose his parting letters to James and others well in advance. Though dated 12 June, they were to be posted only after the tiny expeditionary force was safely on board ship and ready to sail, carrying with it all the guns, broadswords, powder, ball, flints, dirks, and supplies of brandy he had been able to scrape together on borrowed funds.[79]

To James he penned a detailed eight-page letter setting out his intentions and the grounds of dissatisfaction with his situation in France from the time of his arrival. He was going at the invitation of a group of loyal supporters in Scotland, who were convinced that a restoration of the Crown to the Stuarts and of liberty to themselves could be achieved only by such a daring move. These same supporters had concluded from the scandalous treatment he had received from the French during the preceding year and from the fact that during the winter and spring of 1745 no new expedition was organized that the original venture under de Saxe had been nothing more than a feint. They were therefore determined to rise on their own. The worst that could happen to them was death on the field of battle, but that was preferable to living any longer in misery and oppression. The Prince assured his father that he had done his best to convince these Scottish friends that their view of French intentions was incorrect, and he had patiently waited for Louis XV to prove him right by inviting him to join the campaign or showing some other sign of committed support. No sign had come and he was now inclined to agree with his Scottish friends' interpretation of events. He had therefore resolved to place himself at their head "and Dye with them rather than live longer in such a miserable way here, or be obliged to return to Rome, which woud be just giving up all hopes."[80] James would understand that his son could hardly expect to command the loyalty of his Stuart supporters if he himself did not show that he had some life in him: "Your Majesty cannot disapprove a sons following the example of his Father; you yourself did the like in the year 15." There was, however, one important difference: now the situation across the water was much more promising. He had not let his father in on the secret for fear that he would have forbidden the venture, but James could be certain that he had not taken the decision lightly. He had done his best to persuade the French; he had tried every means to get access to the King or to the Ministers, but without the least success. Louis XV, the one person in whom, "after God Almighty," Charles Edward knew his destiny lay, was "timerous" and unable to make up his mind. Of course, he intended to continue his efforts and would be writing to different people urging them to try to convince the French King to make his move. As for James's "orthodox" representatives in Paris, Sempill, Tencin, Balhaldy—they had been kept completely out of his planning. Cardinal Tencin was not much trusted by Louis XV, and as for Lord Sempill and Balhaldy, they had been less than candid with him and would no doubt do everything they could to represent the affair as a rash and desperate venture, led by a mere child who was himself guided by silly and indiscreet advisers. He had allowed them to go on thinking that he was blind to their duplicity, but he knew them better than they knew him. James would now understand why he had asked that his share of the Sobieski jewels be pawned and why he had gone into so much debt in Paris, having borrowed 60,000 livres from Old Waters, the Stuart banker, and 120,000 from Waters *le jeune* in order to buy arms and supplies. So favourable was the situation now with recent British defeats in Flanders that the enterprise was virtually guaranteed success. If he indeed achieved his goals, he would have more glory than he deserved; if he failed, all the blame would be placed on the French "for having push'd a young Prince to shew his Mettle, and rather dye than live in a state unbecomming himself." But whatever the outcome, his action would oblige the French to enter the conflict and support the Stuart cause.

It was not, of course, Charles Edward's wish to die, and despite his heroic rhetoric, we are allowed to doubt that he really believed his death would be necessary, as he expressed it, "to save my Country & make it happy." What is certain is that he did not intend to come back defeated: "Let what will happen, the Stroke is Struck. I have taken a firm resolution to Conquer or to Dye, and stand my ground as long as I shall have a man remaining with me."

Here then is our Prince *avant l'Ecosse*. How frequently he had been able to meet with the Princess since first seeing her five months before in Paris and what they talked about are questions that cannot be answered. Certainly, she and her brother, proud descendants of King John Sobieski and the great Turenne, would have heard him in full rhetorical flight, expressing the same heroic sentiments, the same great sense of mission that we find in his 12 June letter to his father. Charles Edward had grown to trust the Bouillons as he trusted no one else in France. His meeting with them in January had been like the sudden discovery of a friendly oasis after months of aimless wandering in a hostile desert. For an entire year before that meeting, he had been sequestered and constantly obliged to deny his own exuberant sense of identity. In contrast, the Bouillons had become his family away from home. It is not surprising then that only one day after he wrote his long good-bye message to his father, the Prince composed another letter for James, a brief note this time, devoted almost entirely to praising once again the "many civilitys and attentions" of his French family.[81] To his uncle the Duc he also wrote a special letter, dated, like the first one to his father, 12 June and posted after he was safely on board ship. It too spoke the brave words of a young hero on his way to war, but its purpose was not merely to say good-bye. The Prince also asked Charles-Godefroy for additional help, implying that the Grand Chambellan had already done a good deal. With what satisfaction the Prince's letter must have been passed around at Court and admired by his proud uncle and adoring cousins! Composed in much better French than Charles Edward was able to muster on his own, the letter was obviously intended to be shown by the Grand Chambellan to his royal master as well. Since, unlike most of the Prince's celebrated 12 June letters, it is not known, I shall reproduce it here in its entirety:

Navarre Le 12.Juin, 1745

Mon Oncle & Mon Cousin,

Comme vous savez ce qui m'a fait passer en France, vous ne devez pas vous étonner de m'en voire sortir de la même maniere que j'y suis entré, c'est a dire, a la derobbée. Je n'y suis venu ny pour voire le Pais, ny pour ètre a charge au Roi Tres Chretien, mais uniquement pour me trouver plus a portée des Etats sur lesquels ma naissance me donnent des Droits si connus, et que je suis resolu de soutenir du moins en faisant voire que je n'en suis pas indigne. C'est presque tout ce que j'y puis contribuer de ma part. Comme vous avez l'honneur d'approcher Sa Majesté de si prés, je vous prie de prendre les momens les plus favorables pour lui représenter la situation dans laquelle je vais bientot me trouver, et l'occasion que cette situation lui donnera de faire eclater sa generosité en m'accordant une Assistance dont je lui serai a jamais redevable. Quelque disposition que l'on ait deja faite pour les Operations de la Campagne, l'on ne sera pas obligé d'y faire de grans changemens pour me preter les secours que je demande; et quand ces changemens devroient etre plus grands, on les verroit bientot plus que compensez par les Avantages qu'on en retireroit. Voila — Mon Oncle, le service que je me flatte de recevoir presentement de votre Affection pour moi. Vous m'en avez deja donné des Marques qui me font esperer que vous ne negligerez rien de ce qui peut avancer mes Interets. Je vous ecris cecy de votre Chateau de Navarre, que vous m'avez preté de si bonne Grace. J'en trouve le sejour charmant, et j'y gouterois volontiers tous les agremens que vous m'y avez procurez, si le dessein dont je viens de vous faire part ne m'appelloit ailleurs; en quelque lieu que je me trouve, vous pouvez compter sur l'Amitié et l'Affection que j'aurai toujours pour vous.

Votre Affectionné Neveu & Cousin
Charles P.[82]

Navarre Le 12: Juin, 1745:—

Mon Oncle & Mon Cousin,

Comme vous savez, ce qui m'a fait passer en France vous ne devez pas vous étonner de m'en voire sortir de la même maniere que j'y suis entré c'est à dire a la derobée. Je n'y suis venu ny pour voire le païs ny pour être a charge au Roi Tres Chrétien mais uniquement pour me trouver plus a portée des Etats sur lesquels ma naissance me donnent des droits si connus, et que je suis resolu de soutenir du moins en faisant voire que je n'en suis pas indigne c'est presque tout ce que j'y puis contribuer de ma part. Comme vous avez l'honneur d'approcher la Majesté de si près je vous prie de prendre les momens les plus favorables pour lui representer la situation dans laquelle je vais bientot me trouver, et l'occasion que cette situation lui donnera de faire eclatter sa Generosité en m'accordant une assistance dont je lui serai a jamais redevable. —

Charles Edward to his uncle, the Duc de Bouillon, on the eve of his departure for Scotland.

Time would add a curiously ironic twist to the Prince's solemn assurances of eternal friendship for his uncle, just as it would for the warm sentiments James himself conveyed to the Grand Chambellan that same month, thanking him for the many kindnesses he and his family had shown his son: "Je suis persuadé," James assured his brother-in-law, "*que vous aurés lieu d'être toujours content de lui*, au moins Je le suis des sentiments que Je remarque en lui envers Vous."[83] Within a few years, at the end of the Prince's disastrous love affair with the Duc's daughter, the bitter recollection of such cordial sentiments must have starkly underlined his betrayal of so much family trust. That, of course, would be the work of a different Prince, of Charles Edward *après l'Ecosse*.

The Duc answered James in kind from the French Camp at Tournai, regretting that his personal negotiations, undertaken with the Ministry to gain permission for the Prince to join the campaign, had been unsuccessful. At any rate, he had afterwards done what he could to soften the blow by making Charles Edward as comfortable as possible at Navarre, where he was at least able to enjoy the hunting and all kinds of excursions. "Je n'auray jamais," he added, "de jours plus heureux que ceux que me procureront des occasions de luy prouver mon attachement autant fidèle que respectueux."[84]

Now, of course, Charles Edward had other excursions on his mind though it would not be until 16 July, after many difficulties and some "ancyety," that the Prince, with Walsh and the "Seven Men of Moidart," finally managed to put out from the French Coast on the *Du Teillay*, bound on a desperate and lonely mission. Almost immediately, the venture grew even more lonely and more desperate for their escort vessel, the *Elisabeth*, was obliged to turn back after losing a running battle with the British man-of-war, H.M.S. *Lion*. But the *Du Teillay*'s luck held, and she finally got through, "not with little trouble and dangir," to the Hebrides where the Prince landed on 3 August (23 July Old Style). The following day he wrote to his father that he had been joined by brave people, as expected, although their numbers could not yet be determined. Uppermost in his mind was still the critical role of France: "The worst that can happen to me iff France dos not succor me, is to dye at the head of such Brave people as I finde here iff I shoud not be able to make my way, and that I have promised to them as you no to have been my resolution before parting. The French Courte must now necessarly take of[f] the maske or have an Eternal sheme on them for at present there is no mediom, and wee, whatever happens, will gain an immortall honour by doing what wee can to deliver our Country in restoring our Master or perish with sord in hand."[85]

VII

"Sword in Hand"

MUCH has been written on Bonnie Prince Charlie's campaign of 1745 and there is little need here to add to the well-known chronicle of events. More important for our purposes are the delayed and distorted echoes of it that drifted back to the Continent, causing much excitement and anxiety among supporters and friends who awaited the outcome of the Young Pretender's daring initiative.

On first learning of his son's bold move, James was dismayed and astounded. He could scarcely believe that the Prince was capable of coming to such a decision on his own. Then he thought better of it: "Je ne pouvois qu'admirer," he wrote to O'Brien in Paris, "ce que Je n'aurois jamais conseilé."[1] Charles Edward's move was quite understandable, given the fact that he had been treated almost like a prisoner in France for more than a year, had been refused permission to go to the Army, and was not once received by the King. He had also been constantly teased with vague hopes for another expedition. Eventually, peace between England and France would have obliged him to return ignominiously to Rome. It was thus not surprising, James continued (displaying far more understanding now than he would after Culloden), that such a young man, "vif & ardent, & qui a, Dieu Merci, des sentiments nobles & genereux, se soit laissé emporter a des resolutions extremes & violentes, lesquelles pourtant une fois prises & executées, ne scauroient que faire honneur à son caractere personel." In truth, Charles Edward's father could not help feeling proud: despite his youth and inexperience, the Prince had managed to plan and execute in the greatest secrecy an important project. He had demonstrated that he was both an "homme de Coeur et de Tete."[2] Now it was of the utmost importance to support him. To that end James immediately set about writing letters to Louis XV and to all of the Ministers.

Wildly exaggerated reports of the Prince's amazing progress in Scotland and his immediate success in gathering an army of thousands soon became the talk of Paris. Everyone agreed that Charles Edward had gone at the request of the

Scottish nation.[3] By August, it was being rumoured that he had been crowned King of Great Britain at Edinburgh and was at the head of an army of seventeen thousand Highlanders! The timing of his initiative was seen as especially favourable. The British Army was heavily committed on the Continent, and there were reports that fewer than two thousand regular troops remained on the entire island. Even these would scarcely be enough to contain the London mob, which, driven by love of liberty, would doubtless welcome the Stuart Prince with open arms. It was known too (and this rumour at least was true) that the Hanoverian government, on the edge of panic, had put a price of £30,000—nearly three quarters of a million livres—on the gallant hero's head!

Though nothing like what was rumoured in Paris, Charles Edward's progress had been remarkable. By the end of September, he had been able to show himself to the inhabitants of Edinburgh from the balcony of Holyrood House, the ancient palace of his ancestors. That symbolic triumph was soon followed by a great victory over Sir John Cope at Prestonpans. The romantic saga of my darling Charlie, to be forever enshrined in song and legend, was born!

In France, too, he had become a hero overnight. Louis XV, who had studiously ignored him for more than a year, finding even his incognito presence in the kingdom a great embarrassment, now wrote him a very warm letter. It began with the salutation "Mon Frère" and stated that he was sending the Prince a special envoy, the Marquis d'Eguilles, for no particular reason other than to inform his dear brother how ready he was to give "en toutes occasions des témoignages de mon affection pour votre personne." The letter was signed "Votre bon frère, Louis"![4] D'Eguilles had, of course, a more specific intelligence mission than the French King's non-committal message seemed to suggest,[5] but sending him to the Prince along with a letter couched in such affectionately positive terms was evidence enough of personal support. No doubt the persuasive arguments of the young Prince's father, not to mention those of the Duc de Bouillon (from whom Louis had just won a small fortune at cards), played a part in helping the King to make up his mind. The French Court's new stance was also, undoubtedly, the work of French public opinion. Writing to James on 17 October, O'Brien expressed amazement at the sudden admiration France and all of Europe now had for the Prince. Charles Edward's reputation was assured forever, no matter what the outcome of his expedition: "En verité je n'exagere pas quand je diray qu'il fait oublier Charles XII, roy de Suede. On compare S.A.R. a Gustave Vasa. Mr de Voltaire ma demandé des memoires sur son arrivée en Ecosse, desirant etre son panegiriste."[6] France's great poet had already written a history of the renowned Swedish king and an epic *Henriade*; the recent battle of Fontenoy had given him an opportunity to celebrate the glories of Louis XV. Now a new epic hero had appeared on the scene![7]

The big question was how much help would the French send? Help, everyone realized, would soon be desperately needed. On 15 October (Old Style), the

Prince wrote to his father, telling him that he hoped to God he would find his brother Henry already landed in England when he got there with his army of eight thousand men. A French landing was needed in all haste, "for ... as matters stand, I must either conquer or perish in a little while."[8] To his uncle he wrote a similar letter, pointing out that the aid already received was totally inadequate. Interestingly, the letter reveals that the King of France had conveyed specific assurances of support through his Grand Chambellan well before the 24 September greeting delivered by d'Eguilles:

D'Edinbourgh le 25 Octbre [old style] 1745

Mon Oncle et mon Cousin,

Vous pouvez bien croire que la lettre que j'eu le plaisir de recevoir de vous il y a prés de deux mois, ma mis jusqu'ici dans une grande Impatience de voir les Effets de la Generosité de S.M.T.[C.] a mon egard. J'ai reçu dernierement il est vrai quelque secours d'Armes et d'Argent pour lesquels je vous prie de faire bien des remercimens de ma part. Mais ces secours ne repondent point a mes besoins et le tems presse. Mes Ennemis ont accru leurs Forces et ont amené autant de Troupes qu'ils ont voulu de dela la Mer, pendant qu'il ne m'est pas arrivé un seul Regiment. Si on songe encor a profiter d'une si belle Occasion, il n'y a pas un moment de tems a perdre. Pour moi, je suis resolu de pousser toujours en avant et de risquer au plutot une autre Battaille dont la Providence, qui m'a soutenu jusqu'ici dans les plus grands dangers, et la valeur de mes Troupes me promettent un bon succes. Mais cela ne m'empeche pas de souhaitter l'Assistannce des Princes sur lesquels j'ai tant de raisons de compter. Songez-y je vous prie et n'obmettez rien pour m'obtenir ce que je demande. Je me remets du reste au Chevalier Stuart que j'ai chargé de cette Lettre et a qui j'ai ordonné en même tems de vous assurer de mon Amitié particuliere pour vous.

Votre Affectionné Neveu et Cousin
Charles P.R.[9]

Unfortunately, the wheels of ministerial decision-making in Paris turned very slowly, despite the visible advantages the French Army had already gained from the Prince's "diversionary" activities in Scotland. Even individual gestures of support such as the Duke of Fitzjames's formal request for permission to join the Prince were denied[10] although by mid-October, largely as a result of the personal enthusiasm of Louis XV and the official support of such figures as the Duc de Richelieu, Cardinal Tencin, and the Marquis d'Argenson, firm plans for a French invasion finally began to take shape. On Sunday 24 October, the highly secret Treaty of Fontainebleau was signed by O'Brien and the Marquis d'Argenson.

It committed France to a policy of military support for Charles Edward "en tout ce qui sera praticable" in his war against the common enemy, King George, the Elector of Hanover.

It was on that same day that Henry Benedict Stuart, incognito as the Comte d'Albany, arrived in Fontainebleau from Rome. He was immediately granted an extended if somewhat awkward audience with Louis XV. The French King shyly embraced the young Duke of York and listened attentively to his passionate pleas in favour of immediate military support for his brother. Louis, ever embarrassed with strangers, remained silent for a rather long time but then began to speak "en très-bons termes et très-dignement," as de Luynes notes, "sur la justice de la cause du prince Edouard, ajoutant des assurances de la plus grande sincérité à l'aider et le soutenir et lui donner en toutes occasions des marques des mêmes sentiments que le feu Roi avoit eus pour le Roi son père."[11] Henry explained how much his brother had wanted to have the honour of seeing His Most Christian Majesty in person and how he had even made an unsuccessful attempt to speak with him during the masked ball at Versailles. After that more silence ensued,[12] broken occasionally by desultory small talk. Finally Louis XV hit upon the happy notion that the Dauphin should be sent for. Additional confusion followed since no one had thought to tell the King's son, who was even more bashful in society than his father, who the visitor was. Eventually, it was all sorted out and after an extremely friendly session of more small talk and silence, the Duc de Gesvres, Premier Gentilhomme de la Chambre du Roi, mercifully suggested that Henry was no doubt feeling tired. Henry quickly agreed, withdrew, and proceeded to get hopelessly lost in the dimly lit staircase leading to the Marquis d'Argenson's apartment. He had accomplished, on his first day, what Charles Edward had not managed in over a year of patient waiting!

Henry, in fact, had made a good impression, and he was well satisfied with his interview. Within a week, despite his incognito, everyone was aware of his arrival, and dinner invitations began to pour in. O'Brien informed James that "tout ce qui est de mieux à la cour" had been dropping by to see the brother of the heroic Stuart Prince. Soon, Henry himself was busy entertaining. His first dinner party, given at O'Brien's, brought together all of Charles Edward's dearest friends: the Duc de Bouillon, the Prince and Princesse de Turenne, the Princesse de Guéméné, and, finally, the Duc and Duchesse de Montbazon.[13] We may be certain that the conversation did not languish! Plans were made for the baptism of Louise's infant son, Henri-Louis-Marie, born 30 August. Henry agreed to act as godfather and Mme de Guéméné was chosen as godmother.[14] If we are to believe Louise's love letters, her heart must surely have fluttered a little as the unbelievable exploits of the handsome prince with whom she was already secretly in love were discussed! Her brother and her husband also talked enthusiastically about their plan to join the impending invasion force as aides-de-camp to His Royal Highness, the Duke of York. A new day was dawning at last for the House of Stuart!

For now it was official: Louis XV had given the order that everything was to be in readiness for an embarkation by 19 December. The momentum of victory seemed unstoppable. The Prince had already marched into England at the head of a huge army, composed, according to some reports, of as many as thirty thousand determined men (he, in fact, had by then fewer than five thousand!) and, with the expected rising of his English supporters, encouraged by the presence of the Prince's army, everything would be over quickly—perhaps even before the Duc de Richelieu arrived with his expeditionary force of twelve thousand.

In this atmosphere of heady optimism, no less a person than Voltaire was commissioned by the Marquis d'Argenson, the Foreign Minister, to draft a gracious manifesto to be proclaimed in the name of the King of France on behalf of Prince Charles Edward, the very moment the Duc de Richelieu set foot on English soil. No major difficulties were expected, for Richelieu's mission was purely one of liberation. The reason for the French invasion was simple: the Prince, having landed in Great Britain with no other support than his own courage had, by his remarkable progress, gained the admiration of all of Europe as well as that of all true Englishmen. It was thus *at the request of the Prince's loyal subjects* that the King of France had now graciously sent along his forces; they were there only to help the Prince bring liberty, peace, happiness, and legitimate government to his country.

The manifesto, which was printed up in three thousand copies, in both English and French, is today a quaint reminder of a certain state of mind in French history. Even more than thirty years later, in his third-person autobiography, Voltaire could not help expressing deep satisfaction with what must be the most bizarrely polite invasion proclamation ever issued.[15]

Meanwhile, news of Charles Edward's progress continued to be favourable. Carlisle had now fallen to the Prince, and for many Frenchmen, the speed of his army's advance toward London seemed a guarantee that he would be in the English capital by the Christmas holidays.[16] Richelieu's precise date of embarkation, on the other hand, seemed less certain; some spoke of 20 December, others of the 24th. One thing was evident in any case: the great secrecy that had surrounded preparations for the aborted expedition of 1744 was now completely absent. De Luynes even wondered whether so much loose talk about military preparations on the French coast meant that no real intention to execute the project existed.

Such, however, was not the case, and there is ample evidence that the King of France was determined to see the venture through. That the Duc de Richelieu had been picked to head the expedition and that a number of France's most distinguished nobility were going along provided additional proof of his resolve.

Everyone knew, for example, that the Prince de Turenne and the Duc de Montbazon had been granted special permission to accompany their cousin Henry as aides-de-camp, and Barbier recorded a little joke that was current on the subject: "les Anglois sont bien malades, puisque nous leur envoyons notre dernier bouillon."[17]

On the coast, despite various delays, there was no lack of enthusiasm. J.P. Stafford, writing to Edgar, describes the triumphant arrival in Dunkirk of Henry and his two cousins. On the road they had encountered several French regiments who drew up as they passed, showing their colours and beating the general salute. The Duke was charmed with their repeated acclamations of *God save the King, God save the Prince, God save the Duke*, which were so hearty that tears came to his eyes. Henry, Stafford remarked in closing, carried "victory in his face."[18]

But stalemate rather than victory was soon the order of the day. Military preparations had been only half-hearted in several quarters. Then came the news, received on 29 December, that Charles Edward had retreated from Derby. No help had arrived from France, and no popular uprising had occurred in England to support the Prince's army of "liberation." Everyone realized that there was not a moment to lose, but now the British navy, not to mention bad weather, had the French embarkation force tightly bottled up at Boulogne. No one, however, doubted the sincerity of French intentions: from Versailles, Louis XV continued to insist that there was to be no turning back, no repetition of what had happened nearly two years before. In fact, he was particularly worried that Richelieu seemed to be finding one excuse after another for delaying the project's execution. The Comte d'Argenson was called upon to remind the Commander-in-Chief of the King's concern. On 8 January, the War Minister conceded that the news from England was unfavourable: "Le Prince Edouard commence à se rallentir dans les progrès qu'il avoit faits, et semble par là avoir plus besoin de la diversion qu'il seroit utile de pouvoir lui procurer....Ce qu'il y a de plus facheux, c'est que plus notre opération se retarde, plus elle devient publique, et donne encore plus de tems aux Ennemis pour s'opposer à nos desseins."[19] In a touching letter, written the following day from Boulogne, Henry appealed to Versailles for immediate action: "Si le Prince mon frere n'est pas secouru, quels perils ne coura t'il pas? Je tremble quand j'y pense. Que deviendra le Royaume d'Ecosse? Le Duc d'Hannover s'affermera si bien sur le thrône par l'abattement des Partisans de notre Maison, qu'il seroit vain dans la suite de vouloir l'ebranler. Le Roi T.C. m'a deja donné tant de preuves de sa bonté et de sa generosité, que Je ne puis pas douter qu'il ne previenne de si grands malheurs en achevant son Entreprise."[20] Finally, Louis XV was reduced to giving Richelieu a direct order to sail at any cost. But still the blockade held, and even Kelly, the Prince's secretary in France, conceding that the French had done everything they had promised towards the embarkation, saw no way out.[21]

Perhaps no one summed up the weary frustration of the situation better than Hérouville de Claye, the Duc de Richelieu's liaison officer with the War Ministry. Writing to d'Argenson from Dunkirk on 7 February 1746, he pointed to the inevitable failure of a project that only a month before had seemed destined for easy success:

> Les vents, la mer, et surtout les Anglois ayant jusqu'à present rendu nos tentatives d'embarquement inutiles, il y a lieu de croire que les mesmes obstacles existeront tant que cela sera necessaire, et que le roy Georges, parfaitement instruit de toutes nos manoeuvres, n'en aura plus de crainte qu'elles ne meritent. Tout l'univers doit estre aujourd'huy plus convaincu que jamais de l'impossibilité qu'il y a d'envahir sans marine une puissance située dans une isle, et plus riche en vaisseaux que tout le reste de l'Europe.[22]

Impatient to get on with the real war in Flanders, the future *encyclopédiste* clearly implied that the expedition should be set aside and begged permission to leave as soon as possible to join Marshal Saxe "pour tascher d'y reparer le temps que j'ay perdu sur la coste, et que j'employerois bien mieux devant Bruxelles."[23] Sentiment aside, France's military realities demanded that the Young Pretender's cause be abandoned.

The news of Charles Edward's victory at the Battle of Falkirk (28 January, New Style) reached Versailles on Saturday, 12 February, one day before the Duc de Richelieu returned from the coast, ill and depressed. For some, Falkirk revived hopes that the Prince would be able to hang on in Scotland even without French help. The victory did little, however, to restore confidence in the eventual execution of Richelieu's project. After recording details (highly exaggerated, as usual) of the recent battle, de Luynes noted in his journal for 14 February that "l'embarquement est toujours dans le même état, et il y a lieu de croire qu'il est impossible, ou qu'on ne juge pas a propos de le faire."[24] No one knew, moreover, quite what to make of the puzzling news that the great victory at Falkirk had been followed by the Prince's continuing retreat into the Highlands. Barbier wondered if it was on the orders of France, now rumoured to be seeking accommodation with George II in the interests of ending the European war. Anticipating the situation in Paris two years later, Barbier astutely commented that, although the people wanted peace, the notion of abandoning the Young Pretender was not at all to the public's liking.[25]

While Richelieu was back in Paris being comforted for his failures, Henry, who had not got on at all well with the Commander-in-Chief, remained in Boulogne, glumly awaiting developments. He was desperately worried about his brother's fate, and as if that were not enough, a series of petty annoyances had come to plague him. Mysterious rumours had followed him from Rome, mocking his supposedly neurotic religiosity, and hints were circulating too that he was somewhat lacking in normal "manliness." He had also learned of an extremely impertinent letter sent by Louise's mother-in-law, Mme de Guéméné, to O'Brien, complaining that he was keeping her son in Boulogne to little purpose. Beside himself with indignation, Henry brought the matter up directly with Louise's husband: "J'en ai dit mon sentiment tres clairement a son fils," he wrote to O'Brien haughtily, "lui faisant voir la lettre qu'elle vous a ecrite, et lui faisant sentir combien de certaines expressions convenoient peu a elle et moins a moy."[26] Thoroughly embarrassed by his mother's interference, Jules sent his own letter of protest, to what effect we do not know. Mme de Guéméné, accustomed to running house and family, was obviously a strong-minded individual but it is possible that in the future cardinal she found her match. For the moment, in any case, both of the Duke's aides-de-camp remained with him cooped up in Boulogne.

That is not, however, where James imagined them to be when, on 24 January, he addressed a letter to his young nephews from Rome: "Je me flatte," he wrote to the Prince de Turenne, "que celle-cy vous trouvera en Angleterre, où votre bon coeur envers nous vous a fait accompagner Mon Fils le Duc."[27] To the Duc de Montbazon he expressed equally cordial sentiments. Finally, he penned an affectionate note to Louise, choosing words that no doubt held far richer meanings for her than for him: "Tout ce que nous avons de plus cher au monde se trouve engagé dans la présente expédition d'Angleterre. J'ai une ferme confiance dans la Providence que nous pourrons recevoir bientot des nouvelles qui nous consoleront des facheux moments que nous passons a present."[28]

Unfortunately, the news from Scotland was getting worse rather than better. In a letter to O'Brien of 8 February (19 February, New Style), Sir Thomas Sheridan tried to put the best light on the Prince's retreat into the Highlands after his unsuccessful siege of Stirling Castle. Falkirk had been an important victory, but time was on the enemy's side. The Prince desperately needed immediate help of various kinds, engineers, artillery—but especially fresh troops and money. And yet the French were not moving! "Pour l'amour de Dieu, à quoi pense-t-on? Regarde-t-on la réussite de nos desseins comme une chose indifférente à la France? Ou veut-on à quelque prix que ce soit que nous périssions? Si ce ne sont pas là les intentions de la Cour, qu'on mette sérieusement la main à l'oeuvre et cela sans perte de tems.' "[29] Among the items captured at Falkirk, Sheridan continued, the Prince's men had found a letter from General Cope stating that London was no longer taking the threat of a French invasion seriously: "Cela seroit bien désolant pour nous, et bien déshonorant pour la France, apres ce qui s'est passé aux yeux de toute l'Europe, et je me flatte qu'il n'en est rien." Rumours that France had abandoned the expedition were rife in the Jacobite camp, Sheridan warned, and morale was rapidly deteriorating. "Il faut donc des faits réels, et des secours considérables pour nous soûtenir, et non des promesses vagues et des miettes de pain."

By the beginning of March, Henry too had abandoned all hope for an expedition, and he was growing desperately bored with his situation in Boulogne. His best plan, he felt, was to join the campaign in Flanders, but the whole tedious business of waiting for authorization from the King of France had to be gone through. One thing was certain: he was not going back to Italy! But Boulogne was intolerable! No purpose was being served by his presence there: the British were not in the least worried about the threat of a landing. His health was suffering; there were not even good opportunities to go walking or riding. Why should he stay? "Donné-moy une bonne raison," he exclaimed to O'Brien, "je ne demande que ça et je me soumet a tout cesy avec bien du plaisir."[30] Both of his aides-de-camp were on the point of leaving for their regiments. If only he were allowed to go with them, if not to the Army, at least to Navarre or Pontoise![31]

Ten days later Henry was in total despair: Boulogne was nothing but a "vilain trou." He had been stuck for three months with nothing but bad news and the unpleasant society of "des gens comme les notres" (his gruff fellow Jacobites were presumably lacking in the future Cardinal's social graces). It was a joke to imagine that while the Duc de Richelieu rested comfortably in Paris, the Elector of Hanover would be worried about Henry Stuart on the French coast! "Nos ennemys scavent mieu que nous que nous n'y pouvont rien faire pour l'Angleterre."[32] Henry was not made of the same stern stuff as his brother. Like his father James, he was inclined to choose, in the face of hopeless situations, "realistic" solutions. For this he was to suffer his rasher brother's suspicious criticism, even before he eventually decided that going back to Italy would not be such a bad idea after all....

Henry's hopes for a prompt response to his request to join the campaign in Flanders were held in abeyance for a long time. Louis XV had let it be known in April that he would give the matter some thought, but when he himself left for the Army at the beginning of May, he had not yet reached a decision. The Duke, meanwhile, had received what seemed like a very honourable invitation from the Maréchal de Saxe to join him privately as an aide-de-camp or élève, if Versailles approved. The Prince de Turenne had received a similar offer and was already on his way. Although O'Brien saw it as a pis aller,[33] Henry was delighted at the prospect of learning the art of war under the most celebrated general of the age.[34] In the end, because of the King's hesitations,[35] nothing came of de Saxe's proposal, but at least it got the Duke as far as Navarre. Then, on 20 May, he was allowed to go to Antwerp as aide-de-camp to the Comte de Clermont, a prince du sang who was commanding at the siege of the Citadel.[36] Once the siege was over, Henry was ordered back to Navarre.[37] French relations with the Jacobites were entering a familiar phase: His Most Christian Majesty, having finally given up his plan to invade England, was once more distancing himself from the Stuarts. Whatever his genuine sympathies for their cause, Louis had to bear in mind the peace—near or distant, no one knew—that would eventually come and the predictable objections of George II. Moreover, as it was pointed out to the King, even the withdrawal of his support could be rationalized as a form of kindness: when the day of peace came, would the Stuarts not have a shorter distance to fall if the King of France refrained from gratuitously raising them too high?

This same preoccupation with what King George II would think or say or do was also to cost the Duc de Bouillon his Order of the Garter. Deeply grateful for the many proofs of affection and family solidarity offered by the Bouillons to both of his sons, James had finally decided to grant Charles Edward's request. It was decided that June would be the best time to approach Louis XV on the subject, when he and Charles-Godefroy were scheduled to return from the Army for the Dauphine's lying-in. O'Brien thought it would be a good stroke for the Jacobite cause: "Il seroit a souhaitter que le roy luy permit de porter la jarretiere donné par le roy Jacques, et cela ne sçauroit que produire un bon effet de voir le Grand Chambellan de France, ou son fils, l'arborer."[38] O'Brien warned, however, that there might be difficulties: "Cela ne se peut obtenir qu'en un temps ou le roy tres chretien se trouve en guerre avec l'Angleterre." James had similar doubts: "La cour de France ne permettra certainement jamais au Duc de Bouillon de porter la Jartierre tant qu'elle suivera le systeme de ne pas nous appeler de nos propres noms."[39] To Henry, James expressed much the same fear: "When you see your uncle," he wrote on 4 July, "make him a great many kind compliments from me. . . I am glad he was pleased with the offer you made him of the Garter, but as long as the Court of France acknowledges the Elector of Hannover for King of England, they will, to be sure, never allow him to wear a Garter given by me."[40] The Old Pretender's pessimism proved justified: in August, the Marquis d'Argenson made it clear that the King could not allow one of his highest officers to receive such an honour,[41] and even Charles Edward's subsequent efforts on his uncle's behalf were to prove fruitless.[42]

Throughout this period there were, of course, matters of much graver concern. The weeks it took for news to travel between Charles Edward's camp and Paris made it difficult to know how things stood with the Prince. At a greater distance still, James was even worse off. It was, for example, with great relief, that he finally received in Rome on 19 April, long awaited dispatches sent by Charles Edward on 8 February! At last the strategic motives of Charles Edward's retreat from Stirling were explained, and he again began to hope that his son would be able to hold out in Scotland long enough to give the French time to provide effective aid. Realizing, however, that the Prince, even in victory, would be extremely bitter that the projected French landing had not taken place, and knowing that the Stuarts in exile could never afford to show their displeasure with France, he cautioned his son. While it was quite true that the French had shown insufficient zeal for the Stuart cause before Charles

Edward's departure for Scotland, they had from the time of Henry's arrival been "hearty and sincere." But they could not do the impossible: "Their not having a Fleet to cope with that of England, their operations by Sea must naturally be difficult, & dangerous in the execution & more uncertain in the success."[43] Thus, he and his sons had no choice. They could not apply elsewhere for help. With undeniable prescience, James already knew that his son would act toward the French precisely as he eventually did after escaping from the Highlands. For the good of the cause, long-term perspectives had to be borne in mind: "Whatever they may be, or however affairs may end, it would be acting against all the rules of policy & prudence not to dessemble our dissatisfaction for their former conduct, & not to express at present the greatest confidence in, & relyance upon them. By this means We may hope for good from them."[44]

Continuing in the same vein, James showed remarkable foresight in another matter as well, anticipating the rift that would eventually develop between Charles Edward and his brother, who was already being maliciously accused of not having done everything possible to bring help to the Prince. It would depend in great measure on Charles Edward himself to remove the sting from such wicked accusations by showing on all occasions his affection and deference for his father and his love for his brother: "As long as we are all three united...we shall render abortive the malice of our enemies, & get the better of them at last with God's assistance. But should any disunion get in amongst us, or even the least appearance of it, it would be the ruin of us all."[45]

James wrote this long letter to his "dearest Carluccio" on 19 April. Eight days later, any realistic hope for a restoration of the Stuarts to the throne of Great Britain was forever destroyed when his son, stunned by disaster, was led weeping from the field of battle at Culloden. Ironically, the final defeat came when the Prince's many friends and supporters in France still had the most sanguine hopes for his ultimate success. Such hopes had just been dramatically renewed by the deliberately exaggerated reports of the Prince's victory in the "Rout of Moy" skirmish. These had been brought to Versailles at the end of April by the Prince's aide-de-camp, Richard Warren, in a desperate last effort to galvanize the French into immediate supportive action. The strategy had even begun to work! On 4 May, De Luynes recorded as gospel Warren's account of many enemy prisoners taken and of wholesale desertions to the Prince's army.[46] On 1 May (New Style), four days after Culloden (although the Duke of Cumberland's genocidal butchery was still going on in the surrounding countryside), O'Brien had sent James a report very similar to that found in de Luynes. According to Warren, the Prince was preparing to attack Cumberland's forces with an army of fifteen thousand men that thought itself invincible,[47] whereas there was only terror and panic in the ranks of the enemy. O'Brien noted too that Sir Thomas Sheridan's letters confirmed Warren's report.[48] This last detail brought to O'Brien's mind an annoying thought: Warren had delivered letters from Sheridan, writing in Charles Edward's name, to the Duc de Bouillon and the Bishop of Soissons. How was it, he wondered, that the Prince had time to write to his French cousins and not to the King of France? Cardinal Tencin, moreover, had recently complained in O'Brien's presence that Sheridan's (that is, the Prince's) letters to Versailles betrayed "trop de hauteur et de secheresse."[49] Unlike James, Charles Edward saw no need to "dessemble"! But O'Brien's complaint enlightens us on another point as well: the Bouillon family had, if anything, grown even more important to the Prince since his secret departure from Navarre the summer before.

Like O'Brien's letter to James, hailing the Prince's victories when a great many of his brave Highlanders in fact lay dead and mutilated in heaps sometimes three and four deep on Drummossie Moor,[50] much of the Jacobite correspondence from the Continent at this time confronts the reader, caught up in a time lag of several weeks, with the bleakest of ironies. Five days after the battle, for example, James rejoiced in a letter to O'Brien that the news from Scotland was so reassuring. The Prince's situation seemed excellent, and France would now be certain to come through with powerful support.[51] From Versailles, the centre of the civilized world and a full two weeks after the battle, Cardinal de Rohan wrote to James that he believed the hand of Providence was guiding the Prince's affairs, and he congratulated him on his son's continuing good fortune:"C'est une grand consolation...de voir les Princes, vos enfans, tels qu'ils se montrent a l'univers. Celuy que l'Ecosse possede est generallement reconnu pour un vray heros; ses succes estonnent; ce sont autant de miracles. Dieu le protege et l'on peut dire que cette protection est une justice que la bonté divine vous doit à bien des titres."[52] The Marquis d'Argenson, who was accompanying Louis XV in Flanders, wrote later still to Sheridan of his hopes and those of the King of France for the continuation of Charles Edward's success: "Nous attendons avec la plus vive impatience le succès du projet généreux qu'il avoit formé de marcher au Duc de Cumberland, et vous me devez, Monsieur, la justice de croire que personne n'y aplaudira plus sincèrement que moy."[53]

Finally, nineteen days after Culloden, on 16 May, vague echoes reached France via Holland that the Prince had suffered an important reversal. O'Brien wrote immediately to James. There was no doubt that there had been a battle and that the Prince's followers had come off second best. It was all rather puzzling. Perhaps Charles Edward had not had time to gather his entire army before engaging....In any case, British government reports were not to be trusted. They would have to wait and hope; James would need all of his resolve and all of his faith. O'Brien thought it likely that the Prince had retired with his Highlanders to Lochaber; if it proved impossible to hold out there, perhaps he could be persuaded to return soon to France on one of the French frigates recently sent over. "C'est tout gagner," the Jacobite colonel concluded, "que de sauver sa personne."[54] Cardinal Tencin, also writing to James, suggested that the reports of a great battle lost by the Prince were exaggerated. He was overwhelmed with grief, nevertheless, and he advised James to take consolation in the Prince's renown: "quelque chose qui arrive, le Prince se sera fait un grand nom dans le monde, qui tôt ou tard produira son effet, et jusque là, il ne sera certainement pas abbandonné."[55]

Now the long period of silence began. No cost was spared in French efforts to locate the defeated hero and bring him back to safety, for O'Brien's was the common sentiment: if the Prince's person could be rescued, everything could be rescued. Hanoverian belief in the truth of that same notion explains as well the even greater efforts made by Cumberland's forces to hunt down the Young Pretender. With his capture the last threat of rebellion would be forever destroyed.

As soon as he recovered from the first shock of defeat (although in a sense it remained with him for the rest of his life), the Prince made up his mind to return to France as quickly as possible, there to prepare again for battle. Following a fast escape to the West Coast where he hoped to be picked up by a French ship, he drafted a post-dated letter "For the Chiefs" to be handed on by Sheridan after his departure. This farewell address and its covering letter to Sheridan constitute the earliest of the Prince's post-Culloden writings that seem to have survived in the precious collection of Stuart papers at Windsor. They are significant "watershed" documents, and their greatest importance for us lies in the evidence they provide of a radical transformation that had suddenly come over the Prince. To Sheridan, for example, he now hinted darkly that treachery had been the hidden cause of his defeat. "We have traitors among us," he declared. It was for that reason he had decided to return immediately to France.[56] At the same time, his letter for the chiefs also betrayed a harsh new tone towards the French. Obviously, the trauma of defeat (and possibly the guilt of survival, for had he not promised to conquer or perish?) had deeply affected him. The references to traitors and his new acerbity were clear omens that, with the continuation of his misfortunes, Charles Edward would more and more seek a remedy for his misery, failure and guilt in the mistrust and blaming of others.

To the defeated chiefs, ruined and outlawed for their support of a cause that was only tenuously theirs, the introductory statement of high purpose in the Prince's farewell letter must have had a hollow ring. It is unlikely, however, that he was aware of this. Something deep inside him had given way, and never again would he be attuned to the resonances of his own insincerity:

When I came into this Country, it was my only view to do all in my power for your good and safety. This I will allways do as long as life is in me. But alas! I see with grief I can at present do little for you on this side the water, for the only thing that can now be done is to defend your selves till the French assist you.[57]

He would be leaving them, the Prince continued, to go to France, however dangerous that was (scarcely more dangerous than remaining where he was, one imagines!) and would engage the French to provide help. France had merely been using the Stuarts as pawns to keep the English off balance and to maintain "a continual civil war in this Country." Such a nefarious scheme could be countered only by his absenting himself from the country, leaving the French with no choice but to "strike the great stroke, which is always in their power, however averse they may have been to it for the time past." Otherwise, they would face the consequence of seeing the Elector grow as dangerously powerful (the Prince used the word "despotick") as Louis XV.

It is not entirely clear that Charles Edward believed that France had used him in that exploitative way. Certainly, the diversion he had created had proved very useful to the campaign in Flanders and ultimately contributed to the Maréchal de Saxe's victory at Brussels, where arms, ammunition, and treasure were extracted to a value of more than four times what France had expended in support of the Jacobites during the 1745-46 campaign.[58] There are also in the Archives of the Ministry of Foreign Affairs in Paris a number of highly cynical discussion papers which propose strategies and hypothetical courses of action that would have more than justified the Prince's worst suspicions.[59] But even if the French managed to turn a profit on the '45, it remains true that their efforts to support the Young Pretender had been in earnest. Those efforts had come to nothing, not because of deliberate neglect or duplicity but through ministerial squabbling, missed opportunities, and plain misadventure.

Meanwhile, on the West Coast of Scotland, no French ship managed to rendezvous with the Prince and so began the hunted fugitive's long summer of "skulking" in the heather. Those months, filled with danger and hardship, narrow escapes, concealments, and other adventures, have come down to us in the romantic legend of the beloved wandering Charlie, cheerful and courageous in the face of all adversity. For many years afterwards, his eventual return would be faithfully awaited by wistfully loyal followers. On the Continent, nothing was known of the Prince's fate, but persistent and risky efforts by the French to find and rescue him continued. Louis XV was determined to salvage at least *that* much of his image in the eyes of the Prince's supporters! Far away in Rome, and long conditioned to failure, James was rapidly losing interest in the politics of his own cause. All he could think of now was that Charles Edward had embarked on a rash venture without his permission or foreknowledge, and, what was worse, he had probably done so on the advice of men with evil intentions! These sinister advisers would no doubt try to shift the blame to the French and perhaps even to the supposed inaction of Henry, the more devoted and submissive (and, yes, really the more likeable) of his sons. Apart from the anxiety and pain he felt at not knowing whether Charles Edward was alive or dead, James's main worry now was that the Prince and Henry would no longer get along well and that

Charles Edward would make it impossible for the Stuarts to hang on in France and wait for better days.

James continued to write weekly letters to his elder son, hoping that somehow these expressions of concern and tenderness would reach their destination. Knowing the Prince's temperament, he tried to represent the defeat at Culloden as a personal victory. The honour Charles Edward had gained in his Scottish adventures would always "stick by" him and would make him respected abroad. As a result, the French would be committed at some time in the future to launching another project in his favour. But the Prince had to avoid all "rash or desperate measures" for these would ruin everything and take away from the honour he had gained.[60]

It has become a familiar enough cliché among Charles Edward's many biographers, embarrassed by the forty-two years of progressive decline and degradation that followed Culloden, to regret that he somehow did not die gloriously on the field of battle on that fateful April day in 1746. Given the outcome, an epic hero's death would have provided the most artistically pleasing conclusion to the Prince's story. But Charles Edward not only survived Culloden, he went on to outlive what everyone would like to think was his true self—that courageous, fair-minded and magnanimous young man who had sailed for Scotland filled with hope and a simple trust in Providence in the summer of 1745.

James very early on had grasped the essence of that cliché perfectly. Indeed, he was the first to recognize in the Prince those contingent flaws that, given failure, would engender the rapid degenerative process. The Prince's father thus continued to harp on the necessity of maintaining a prudent attitude toward the French: "You will know," he wrote in July, "all the French have done for your personal safety, for which they deserve all our acknowledgements; and if we have reason to complain of them in other matters, it behoves us to conceal our thoughts as to that, since we stand so much in need of them."[61] The following month, James expressed the hope that when Charles Edward returned to France, he would allow himself to be advised by Cardinal Tencin and O'Brien: "The first is the only sincere friend we can absolutely depend upon amongst those Ministers; you know my good opinion of the last."[62] Then James included another piece of advice: "Be always kind & loving to your Brother, & never...allow anybody to do the least thing that may tend to sow discord betwixt you." Unfortunately, almost as soon as he reappeared in Paris in October, Charles Edward would manage to do exactly the opposite of what, point by point, his father had recommended!

Meanwhile, accompanied most of the time by de Bacqueville (whose little house on the Quai Malaquais he eventually rented), Henry had gone reluctantly from the siege of Antwerp to Navarre. The Duc de Bouillon's country estate was better than the *vilain trou* of Boulogne-sur-Mer, but for someone whose tastes ran more to pious homilies, music, and devotional exercises than to stag hunting and body-punishing forest rambles, the experience was still unpleasant. Charles Edward had been happy there before he left for Scotland, but the two princes were as different in character as they were physically. The tall, handsome Charles was rather serious and sober; he spoke little and liked to play the rough Highland man. His brother was much shorter, his face less attractive; he talked a lot, laughed more easily and acted the part of the lively socialite.[63] Music and praying were his two main passions.

Praying especially! In their collection of selected Stuart materials at Windsor,[64] Alistair and Henrietta Taylor published a curious account of the Duke of York's daily routine, composed when he was seventeen years of age by James Murray (Lord Dunbar), who shared with Sir Thomas Sheridan the task of tutoring the Princes in Rome. Anyone who has read it and who is still prepared (along with the eventually embittered Charles Edward) to doubt the authenticity of Henry's religious calling when it declared itself the following year, requires a great deal of convincing indeed.[65]

In Boulogne with the French expeditionary force, Henry had found himself obliged to modify somewhat his daily schedule of devotions. It was nevertheless common knowledge that these had been a source of great embarrassment to the Duc de Richelieu, who was forced to great lengths to hide the Duke's "dévotion italienne" from his many Protestant supporters: "Il ne passoit jamais devant une croix ou un autel," the Marquis d'Argenson noted, "qu'il ne fît une génuflexion comme un sacristain."[66] Henry's extreme religiosity was not, however, seen by the Foreign Minister as a factor that impaired his courage; he had given a good account of himself during his brief time with the Comte de Clermont at Antwerp, and he had displayed, d'Argenson concluded, "une valeur naturelle et héréditaire."

At Navarre things went less well for the Duke. It is disconcerting to hear his constant complaints about being cold, uncomfortable, and bored at his uncle's magnificent country estate during exactly the same period that his brother, hunted by soldiers and with a reward of £30,000 on his head, resolutely faced the hardships and dangers of a fugitive's life in the Highlands. For Henry, the air at Navarre was "too thick"; he had no appetite.[67] Taking "physick" proved of some help. So did life's little luxuries. O'Brien was asked to send, along with his coach from Paris, a dozen shirts with plain ruffles (no sooty, tattered, or lousy Highland rags here!) and two periwigs made by that clever *perruquier* in Versailles. The company too (although it included de Bacqueville!) was dreadfully dull, despite the visit of a Monsieur Cambon, "a monstrous fat french who diverts his R.H. very much with his excessive sweating."[68] A more dramatic diversion came on 16 July with a violent wind storm that broke many of the windows in the château, uprooted huge trees, and killed a "basquet full" of swallows![69] After a brief period, O'Brien and James agreed that Henry could stay on at Navarre no longer. "Je tremble qu'il ne tombe malade, éloigné de secours," O'Brien noted. Once again, contrasting images of the Prince sleeping damp in smoky cowherds' huts or high in Cluny's cage come to mind....It would do Henry good, everyone agreed, to get away quietly to Paris: "He was saying the other day," his secretary Constable wrote to O'Brien, "that he coud like to see ye Bois de Boulonge and ye Chams Elisée."[70] When James complained of the hot July weather in Rome, Henry, in his 7 August reply, could not help but be amazed: "Your Majesty complains of heat, and wee are starving of coald in the begining of August"![71] Acknowledging that he was unable to judge the actual "thickness" of the air at Navarre, James was nevertheless certain that Henry's life there was "bien triste & bien solitaire."[72] Yes, he would be far better off on the outskirts of Paris where he could take a house. When Charles Edward returned, the two brothers could live happily together. Money was a bit of a problem, since such country houses were rarely put to lease for less than a year and Stuart princes lived, unfortunately, from day to day. But Henry had to be made comfortable as soon as possible, even in those hard times. When he finally did move from Navarre, first to Bagneux at the end of August, and then, in the first week of October, to the Clichy residence of Henri-Oswald, Cardinal d'Auvergne, he satisfied himself only with the best: La Tour was chosen to do his portrait, Astruc became his physician, and soon on constant call were Cupis and Alexandre, famous performers on the violin and harpsichord.[73] If ever a Stuart needed to become a Cardinal for both spiritual and material reasons, it was certainly Henry! As with Charles Edward the preceding year, the Bouillons, maintained with him throughout this time their special role as family away from home.[74]

The long and agonizing wait for news of the Prince continued and a great suspense had now built up throughout the whole of Europe, adding a powerful dimension to the heroic image Charles Edward already enjoyed. It was the opinion of Sir John Graeme in August that "all the dangers and hardships H.R.H. has undergone these four months past will add a great lustre to the character and reputation he so justly acquir'd whilst he was at the head of an army."[75] But that was cold comfort to James. Every week he continued to address a letter of hope and prayer to his fugitive son.

Prayer was certainly in order, for now was the time of the martyrs in Scotland, and there is little doubt that had he been captured, Charles Edward would have shared the fate of his unlucky supporters. Of course, he would have been given the privilege of the block rather than the common noose or that even more egalitarian instrument of justice, the English prison ship, where hundreds of captured Jacobites rotted away in stinking confinement. Every day during the summer, fresh reports of new repressive measures and more executions reached the Continent, heightening the dread of those waiting to hear that Charles Edward was safe. News of the atrocities also added to the ground swell of sympathy for the unlucky Prince, who, though he had failed to triumph in "an eminently just cause," remained even in defeat, as great a hero in the eyes of his followers as before. The words that old Balmerino wrote down before laying his head on the block on 18 August that year are proof enough. Indeed, they will be especially worth remembering when we come later on to examine the painfully obvious shortcomings of the embittered outlaw-prince who so quickly earned the right to be thrown out of France in December 1748. But that was still more than two years away. It was very different in the months that immediately followed the battle. The Jacobite prisoner, on the eve of his execution, could not find words good enough to praise his dear Prince: "I am not a fit Hand to draw his Character," he wrote; "I shall leave that to others, but I must beg leave to tell you, that the incomparable Sweetness of his Nature, his Affability, his Compassion, his Justice, his Temperance, his Patience & his Courage are virtues seldom all to be found in one Person. In short, he wants no Qualifications requisite to make him a Great Man."[76] Balmerino also chose the occasion to give the lie to the "wicked report" circulated by the English that the Prince "had given out in Orders that no Quarter should be given to the Enemy: This is such an unchristian a thing, & so unlike that Gallant Prince that nobody that knows him will believe it." The malicious report was being widely circulated, he concluded, to excuse the murders committed "in calm Blood after the Battle."[77]

In a letter written to James the day before his execution, Balmerino demonstrated in private the same degree of fervent support he would soon show in public for the young Prince who had led him into battle. He felt no dismay at his situation, only "great satisfaction and peace of mind to die in so righteous a cause."[78] It was the hero of that cause, the Charles Edward whom Balmerino invoked so tenderly on the scaffold, that the French saw when the Prince finally landed with Colonel Warren at Roscoff near Morlaix on the afternoon of 10 October. It was a time for national rejoicing: the Prince was rescued—delivered miraculously from his enemies! No one could possibly have got through such dangers and hardships without being in the special care of Providence!

That may well have been the returning hero's own view as well. But now he knew something he suspected his father had never learned: Providence had to be pushed at times. As he made his way to Paris, the Prince had but one thought in mind: to see the King of France immediately, in order "to bring things to a write head."[79] With luck he would be back in Britain in a month or two at the head of twenty thousand men! To his great dismay, unfortunately, he was soon to discover that at the Court of Louis XV everyone wanted to hear, over and over again, the story of his remarkable adventures, his concealments and his providential escape. No one seemed very interested in listening to the eager details of how he planned to return to finish off the job.

VIII

Compliments and Disaffection

BECAUSE of Charles Edward's extreme fatigue after his long ordeal, his rescuer, Colonel Warren, was sent on ahead to Paris to notify Henry and the French court of the Prince's safe arrival.

Now in the new house at Clichy, Henry was overjoyed, as were his two cousins, Louise and her sister-in-law. They immediately sent their excited congratulations. Louise's husband and her brother, the Duke's erstwhile aides-de-camp, were still with their regiments. The Grand Chambellan was with the Court at Fontainebleau.

By the morning of Friday, 14 October, Charles Edward had not yet reached Paris, but was expected at any moment. His instructions were that only Waters Junior, his banker, was to know where he was staying. It was understood, however, that the Bouillons would be among the first to see him. Even the general public was now aware of the central role the Bouillons played in the Prince's life. Shortly after the great defeat, for example, a rumour had circulated that Charles Edward had managed to make his way back to France on a smuggler's boat and was resting at the home of his first cousin, "Mademoiselle de Bouillon, princesse de Guéméné," on the Place Royale.[1] Barbier, for one, had immediately suspected a fabrication: "On ne sait si on ne fait pas courir ce bruit exprès, pour qu'on ne le cherche pas dans les montagnes d'Ecosse, ou par quelque autre trait politique." But as far as the public was concerned, it seemed only natural that the Prince would want to see the Bouillons the moment he returned. Had it not been from Navarre, after all, that he had launched his daring campaign! Similarly, there had been nothing odd about Sir Thomas Sheridan's asking the Duc de Bouillon to inquire whether it was indeed true, as Cardinal Tencin charged, that Louis had been angry, and therefore unhelpful, because the Prince had not written to him more often. Louis XV's answer had been reassuring and soon everyone learned of it: "Bien loin de cela," the King had confided to his Grand Chambellan, "ses lettres ne faisoient que m'embarrasser parce que je n'y pouvois pas répondre comme je l'aurois voulu."[2] No doubt it was because of such assurances passed on by Charles-Godefroy that Charles Edward trusted Louis rather more than he let on, and certainly far more than the King's ministers, whom he trusted not at all. Insofar as Jacobite affairs are concerned, thanks to the Prince's uncle, some form of *secret du Roi* procedure had probably already begun at Versailles as early as 1746.

Henry too had been informed by Warren that Charles Edward did not intend to see the King at Fontainebleau without first talking to his uncle, in order to be advised by him on how matters stood with the "timorous" monarch. Of course, another reason the Prince wanted to visit the Duc was to retrieve his pet dog, Marquis, whom he had regretfully left behind at Navarre sixteen months before. Immediately after seeing Colonel Warren, Henry wrote to the Grand Chambellan asking that Marquis be brought to Clichy: "Je crois," he explained, remembering his brother's fascination with hunting, "qu'il sera aise de le trouver a son arrivé icy. J'atten cett heureux moment avec bien de l'impatience, comme vous pouvez croire."[3]

On arriving in Paris, Charles Edward made straight for his banker's hideaway in the Rue du Roule.[4] The Prince then sent word to Henry to come and visit him and the two brothers subsequently arranged to dine together on 15 and 16 October. On the 16th, a Sunday, Henry brought Charles very privately to Clichy to see Marquis. The Prince, Henry wrote to his father the following day, had "as much goût for the *chasse* as ever."[5] But Henry had even more important news: Charles Edward had not uttered one word of recrimination or complaint that the Duke had not pushed the French hard enough. Their meeting was tender. "It is an unspeakable pleasure to me to see how much they love one another," Sir John Graeme reported to James, "and I hope in God it will always continue so."[6] Henry was equally delighted: "I defy the whole worled to show an other Brother so kind and so loving as he is to me. For my part, I can safely say that all my endeavours tend and *shall tend as long as I live*[7] to no other end but that of deserving so much goodness as he has for me." These words would come to haunt the future Cardinal less than a year later.

Colonel Warren, meanwhile, had hurried to Fontainebleau to bring the good news to the King of France, along with the Prince's urgent request for a private interview. Out of deference to the advice of his hypercautious ministers, who urged that no public sign of recognition should be accorded the Young Pretender, Louis hesitated; finally, he gave his answer: he would see the Prince, *along with his brother*, on the following Thursday, 20 October. There could, of course, be no official recognition of their presence and the usual incognito was *de rigueur*, but they would be granted an apartment in the Château for their stay. It was even hinted that no one would object if the Princes appeared resplendent in their various decorations and orders.

On learning about these only-too-familiar restrictions, Charles Edward was furious. For the moment, however, he decided to take his father's advice to "dessemble" (having by this time nearly caught up on the score of letters from James that had been waiting for him in Paris). Still it was incredible! He had expected—certainly he had earned—something better from a Court that had let him down so badly at the same time as it had so richly profited in Flanders from the sacrifice of his Highlanders! Louis XV should have been thinking rather of how to make amends! The popular view of the matter in the French capital was no different, even before the Prince's rescue. In June, Barbier had already recorded his suspicions that the courageous young prince had been sacrificed to the expediency of French foreign policy.[8] In August, he was even more severe as he repeated statements commonly heard about the city: "L'issue de cette rébellion n'est pas absolument bien glorieuse pour la France....On a profité de cette diversion dans l'Angleterre pour faire la conquête de la Flandre....La suite de cette politique jusqu'ici est de se jouer d'un grand prince souverain légitime de l'Angleterre et de l'Ecosse, et reconnu pour tel, de sacrifier plusieurs grands seigneurs d'Ecosse...nombre d'officiers et une partie des peuples de l'Ecosse, dont le pays a été ravagé par les troupes angloises....Cette politique est basse dans l'événement."[9] It would not be long before the Prince learned how to profit from such popular support in his struggle with the ministers and even with Louis XV himself.

But that was for later. Now it was more important to see how matters stood with the Court and to have the immediate advice of his uncle who had daily opportunities to speak privately with the King. Charles Edward therefore instructed Henry to send for Charles-Godefroy without delay:

A Clichy, ce Lundi [17 October] a 6 heures

Mon Cher Oncle

Je ne perd pas un moment de tems pour vous informer du desir ardent que Le Prince mon frere a de vous embrasser. Ce qui l'a empeché de vous avertir plutôt est qu'il a été bien aise de se tranquilliser ces jours cy, ne voyant personne que moi. Comme il desir de vous voir avant personne autre, il me charge de vous faire milles tendres amitiez de sa part, et de vous prier de venir a Paris demain. J'aurai soin d'informer a votre hotel, quand vous arriverez, ou il faudra venire. Mande moi aussy je vous prie a quell heure vous compté partir. Faits aussy milles excuses pour moi a mes Cousines si Je n'ai pas repondu a leurs lettres, mais en verité, Je n'ai pas un moment de tems a moi.

Adieu mon cher Oncle. Je vous embrasse de tout mon coeur et suis

Votre tres affectioné Neveu et Cousin
Henry[10]

What the Duc de Bouillon told his distinguished nephew on the following day is not recorded. In any case, the two princes set out for Fontainebleau on Wednesday, 19 October, and returned to Clichy on Monday, the 24th. Despite his annoying incognito, it was to be the most intense and brilliant period of socializing Charles Edward had ever known.

For most members of the Court, including Louis himself, this was a first opportunity to catch sight of the legendary Prince. All agreed that he looked every inch a hero—tall, very handsome, with "exceedingly noble features", much like Charles XII, King of Sweden. The few who had met him before he left for Scotland said that he was thinner now, but perhaps it was only because his hair was short. Even the first moment of the brothers' visit was a triumph: Louis XV interrupted the business of his Council and came to greet them! Next they saw the Dauphin, who asked to meet them again later that same day for there had not been enough time to talk; then it was the turn of the Queen, who left her card game especially to chat with the young hero. Various ladies whose gambling was thus interrupted now fluttered around excitedly; the Prince bowed deeply and gave each a kiss. On the following day, it was the turn of the courtiers: dinner with Cardinal Tencin and supper with de Maurepas; on Friday it was dinner with the War Minister, d'Argenson, and supper with the Spanish ambassador, the Duc d'Huescar; Saturday, it would be dinner with the Maréchal de Noailles (no great friend of the Stuarts) and supper with the Duc de Luynes. Sunday dinner was with the Contrôleur Général, Machault, and finally, on Sunday evening came the climax of the entire visit: supper with the Marquise de Pompadour! Louis XV himself turned up at 11:00 p.m.; he was suffering from a slight cold, but he stayed until two in the morning, informal and friendly, acting like an ordinary private citizen. Everyone was asked to remain seated. With Charles Edward he chatted on all sorts of subjects, but not a word about "business" was spoken. The Duc de Bouillon, the Princesse de Conti, the Duc de Richelieu, and the Marquis de Meuse were among the distinguished company.[11] It was all so incredible and amazing, everyone said! Here, at last, was the fabulous Prince whose fate had been so much on everyone's mind for so many months! Again and again, they begged him to tell the story of how he and three companions had been trapped for three days in the heather, surrounded by hundreds of English soldiers, so close that every word spoken by the enemy could be heard distinctly—and all that time with only a little cheese and oatmeal to eat and no water to drink! Of course, Highland streams were not in short supply, but the Prince and his companions had not dared to move a muscle for fear of being seen. Luckily, it rained heavily, and the Prince was able to catch enough water in his bonnet for everyone. And then there was that other time when a fifty-man patrol, guided by the traitor "Magdonel"—now, thank heavens, safely locked up on the Prince's orders in the prison at Morlaix—was closing in on them. No escape seemed possible, and so the Prince had ordered his companions to be ready to fire point-blank, for they could expect no mercy from the Hanoverians if caught: "I'll kill two with my two shots," he had told them, "you do the same." Luckily the soldiers went off in another direction!...And then there was the diverting tale of how Henry, on first catching sight of his brother in Paris, rushed forward with a great cry of joy, flinging himself at Charles Edward. It had very nearly been his undoing when an honest Highlander mistook him for some Hanoverian fanatic, come to assassinate the Prince!

It was all rather amusing, as O'Brien noted, but "nothing solid" had come of it. First of all, the Prince was still waiting for an opportunity to speak about military matters to the King in private....There was also the question of where the Prince would eventually be lodged: at one of the royal palaces, certainly, and O'Brien even speculated that the final choice would be Vincennes,[12] a notion that must have struck him as the cruellest of ironies when, two years and two months later, Charles Edward, bound hand and foot in silk cord, was in fact escorted by musketeers to the chilly *donjon* adjoining the château of that place and lodged there under guard and, yes, at the King's expense! If not Vincennes, then it would no doubt be the Luxembourg palace; it too was suitable. Already the Duc de Richelieu and the Archbishop of Cambrai had generously offered the Prince the use of their own Paris residences.

The Prince was officially introduced everywhere as Baron Renfrew, while Henry was still the Comte d'Albany. De Luynes noted, however, that the incognito seemed to bother Charles Edward a good deal: "Il sent ce qu'il est et quoiqu'il n'ait point de hauteur, il a de la dignité; il désire meme extrêmement d'être approuvé et de plaire."[13] The Prince also seemed ill at ease in the brilliant company of the court, and on several occasions he asked the Duc de Bouillon or Cardinal Tencin to handle some of the social pleasantries for him, he being, as he explained to his hosts, only a rough Highlander, unacquainted with the niceties and refinements of French manners. Naturally, everyone loved him all the more for that! The primitive delights of Rousseau's noble savage and the poetic mysteries of the Celtic warrior Ossian were only a few short years away.

For all that, it had not been possible to discuss business with the King. In desperation, Charles Edward finally wrote a private note to Louis, explaining that he had to see him, but without Henry being present: "Je voudrois eviter de lui donner aucune jalousie, comme je l'aime tendrement," he explained.[14] To make certain that his brother suspected nothing, Charles Edward even proposed having a "fainting spell" at one of the gatherings; he would be conducted as a result to the Comte d'Argenson's apartment, whence he could go to the King for a private talk. Henry would be none the wiser![15] Louis XV, however, failed to respond. The Prince's insistence on secrecy illustrates, nevertheless, the extent to which Henry's detractors among the Jacobite factions in Paris had already done their work. Trouble ahead was a certainty.

Henry and Charles Edward left for Paris on 24 October, having received an invitation from the King to call on him at Versailles as soon as the Court moved there later in the season. No one pointed out that it was the anniversary of the Treaty of Fontainebleau. In fact, Louis was already regretting the extent of his official hospitality. He had not intended that the two brothers should stay so long.[16] He was also getting worried about the common expectation that a royal residence, whether Vincennes, Luxembourg, or another, would be made ready for the Stuart princes. Such a gesture, his ministers protested, would be ill-advised. Serious peace negotiations were in the offing, and the old restriction about harbouring Stuarts on French territory was certain to be the first matter to come up.

Ill-advised or not, a royal residence *pour le prince Edouard* was the least that the public of Paris was expecting. Barbier speculated that Charles Edward was to have Saint-Germain, and he noted with apparent approval a rumour that the King at Fontainebleau had already presented Charles Edward with one of his little snuff-box mementos in which was discreetly hidden an order for 800,000 livres on the royal treasury. In addition, the Prince was to have a monthly allowance of 50,000 livres, not counting what the Pope and the Spanish King were no doubt anxious to supply! On the 28th, the Prince, accompanied by Charles-Godefroy and Henry, put in a much anticipated appearance at the Opéra. The place was jam-packed, and the public's applause, from the moment the Prince stepped from the Duc's carriage, was deafening. It was the kind of reception that the people of Paris were in the habit of giving the Maréchal de Saxe when he returned victorious from the wars. Now there was a new hero who had bearded France's enemy in his very den and had miraculously escaped. No wonder that the heroic Prince, standing next to his brother and his uncle in the Royal Box, was forced by the wildly cheering crowd to take so many bows![17] It was the beginning of the Prince's intense love affair with the Paris Opéra. From then until his arrest two years later, he attended regularly, often several times a week. Indeed, he was on his way there on 10 December 1748 when the final blow was struck and he was whisked off to prison, essentially for making a very serious miscalculation and imagining that it was the people of Paris, not the King of France, who governed the nation.

While he waited for the King of France to come up with a royal residence, Charles Edward moved in with Henry. Finally, on 1 November, came the bad news: Cardinal Tencin informed O'Brien that the Prince was not to have a royal residence after all, and certainly nothing like the lavish allowance talked about by the likes of Barbier. The two princes were to have a global monthly stipend of 12,000 livres, from 1 October. They would also be granted the use of the financier Pâris de Montmartel's great house at Bercy (so massive it was known as the "Pâté-Paris"), which would be furnished for them at the King's expense.[18] There was no mention of a snuff box, empty or otherwise.

Charles Edward could not believe his ears when the message was relayed to him by d'Argenson's *premier commis*, Le Dran, through O'Brien. Until he saw the proposal in writing, he would ignore the whole matter! He then dictated, in words that shocked O'Brien, a message to the French Foreign Minister: nothing, it said, could persuade him that there had not been a mistake. He would have to be given proof that this was indeed the King's recommendation, and he was prepared to make an issue of it. At the same time, he revealed the full extent of his anger to James: the verbal offer, delivered by a mere clerk, had proposed "a moste scandalous arangement"; he would not honour it with a reply.

No longer meekly prepared to accept such contretemps as the will of God, the Prince let his father know that he had had enough of waiting passively on his knees for the French to toss him a few crumbs. He would henceforth deal with them in a new way: "I find it, and am absolutely convinsed of it, that ye only way of delyng with this — Governement, is to give as short and smart answer as one can, at ye same time paying them in their own coin by Loding them with sivilitis and compliments, setting apart business; for that kind of vermin, the more you give them the more they take, as also the more room you give them, the more they have to Grapple at, which makes it necessary to be laconick with them, which is they only way of pussiling them, and putting all their sheme upon their backs."[19]

In the succeeding weeks, the Prince stubbornly refused to accept d'Argenson's explanation that what his *commis* had passed on to O'Brien was what the King of France had signified to him. The expressed will of the King of France was, by definition, not something to be debated or haggled about: "Tout ce que le Roy ordonne est bon, juste, digne, et conforme a des intentions aussy pures que le jour mesme; cessons, je vous prie, toutes discussions sur cela qui ne seroient bonnes à rien."[20] Charles Edward remained indignant and unyielding. D'Argenson next appealed to the Duc de Bouillon.[21] In the end, it was the Grand Chambellan who resolved the impasse by arranging for two fairly modest and quite separate residences for the Princes, next to his own grand residence on the Quai Malaquais. Henry's summer residence at Clichy was becoming quite unsuitable as winter approached, and de Bacqueville, who had been with him ever since Boulogne, was prevailed upon to make his own "petit hôtel de Bouillon" available to the Duke of York, for 3400 livres per annum. Charles Edward, on the other hand, took up residence in the former Hôtel de Transylvanie, just next door.[22] It was a cosy arrangement that brought the Bouillons and the Stuarts even closer together, not only physically but in an important symbolic sense as well.

It was precisely on this symbolic level that Louis XV's offer of a financier's mansion had gravely disappointed the Young Pretender, and that was something that Cardinal Tencin and, very probably, even d'Argenson did not understand. The Prince had not rejected the house and the monthly allowance because they were too modest; indeed, the Bercy house of France's richest financier, furnished at the expense of the King, would have been more lavish and comfortable than any of the royal apartments then available. Similarly, a monthly allowance of 12,000 livres, though not fabulous, was honourable, and it would have provided an annual revenue comparable to what some of the most distinguished members of the nobility managed on comfortably. But none of that really mattered to Charles Edward. Royal mistresses could be furtively hidden away in such a manner, but the Prince Regent of Great Britain required an unequivocal sign from his *ally*, the King of France, that gratefully proclaimed to the world France's recognition of the fact that less than one year before all of Scotland was at the Prince's feet and King George had trembled in his boots as Charles Edward approached London with his Highlanders! Instead, he was being asked by some functionary's clerk to sit quietly and play the part of a naively nameless refugee. For the Prince it was once more the case of a "timorous" Monarch— who had, after all, proposed the idea of royal lodgings in the first place— bending to the perfidy of his ministers. Charles Edward was getting fed up with the old excuse that the King of France was doing what he could do, not what he really would like to do.

The Prince had not forgotten, moreover, that he had yet to be granted a private audience to discuss business. It was now more than a month since his return from Scotland, and still his newest scheme had not been heard. Finally, by mid-November, he decided to set everything down in a three-page memoir, which he had delivered privately to the King. In it he warned that precious time was being lost. With the approach of winter and increasing Hanoverian repression, it would become more and more difficult to reawaken widespread revolt. His first venture had failed, not for lack of followers, but for lack of money, supplies, and just a mere handful of regular troops. Had any one of those three missing elements been provided in time, he would still be master of Scotland and, presumably, all of England too. It was still not too late; all he needed was eighteen or twenty thousand troops, immediately, and he would be able to use them effectively—exactly when and where was a secret he could confide only to His Most Christian Majesty in person. But Louis could be confident, nevertheless, that those troops would be used in the interests of France as well as of the Stuarts. Indeed, these were inseparable.[23]

Not surprisingly, Louis XV was not interested in going to war in the middle of winter, and the Prince waited in vain for an answer. He renewed his proposal two months later,[24] but again the French King failed to respond. Moreover, some of his ministers, Noailles and Maurepas, in particular, were already warning Louis that Charles Edward Stuart, to judge from his strange behaviour since his return, could well be more dangerous to France on the throne of England than the Elector of Hanover! O'Brien had got wind of the remark some time in December, but since he would not have been able to reveal his confidential source, he did not tell the Prince.[25] His source was probably Cardinal

Tencin, who, along with the Marquis d'Argenson, did support the idea of mounting another small expedition in the Prince's favour. But Tencin too was worried about the Prince's attitude, and he warned O'Brien that the Young Pretender was on a dangerous collision course with the French Court.[26]

The Prince continued his sullen brooding. The notion of returning to Britain with a body of French troops, small or large, was never far from his thoughts, and this was only the first of many proposals he would make in the next few years. He had not forgotten his farewell to the chiefs. Never would he allow himself to get caught up again in the consequences of French duplicity or have anything more to do with their teasingly vague offers of help! On this, his secret instructions to Sir James Steuart, whom he authorized on 29 December to treat with the French Court in the case of his absence, are brutally specific. Stuart was to suffer no prolonged negotiations or allow himself to be amused with vain appearances and hopes of succour: "If the Ministers pretend that the King has a mind to undertake something in our favour, you are to demand prooff of his Sincerity. Let that be either his Daughter in Marriage *or a large sum of money, not under a million.*[27] If you find them cold and backward, you are to communicate to them my orders to leave the Court until matters are riper....You are to concur in no measures which seem only to work the Affairs of France by occasioning a Diversion on the part of Great Britain, but on the contrary to take all possible measures to prevent and disappoint any such scheme."[28]

Equating a daughter of France with the sum of one million livres was an offensive suggestion that Charles Edward or one of his close advisers had the good sense to strike from the formal instructions he finally gave his plenipotentiary. Still, the Prince would obviously have been overwhelmed with joy by an invitation to marry one of Louis XV's daughters —whether such a proposal came with or without an accompanying offer to launch a French descent on the British Isles! The truth was that prospects for such a marriage were even poorer than the chances for a new expedition, and the Prince knew it. Marriage for him would have to wait. On the other hand, he was certain that an early marriage for Henry was an absolute necessity, and he mentioned it in a letter to James soon after returning from Scotland.

It had not been until 3 November that news of the Prince's safe return reached Rome, and James wrote immediately, both expressing his great joy and, predictably, warning his "dear child" that extraordinary efforts of patience and prudence would now be required of him in his dealings with the French Court. He was to put all of his trust in O'Brien and Tencin.[29] Ironically, by the time Charles Edward received his father's letter, he was barely on speaking terms with either of those gentlemen! It was all part of his new system of dealing "short and smart" with the French. Henry was caught in the middle and said nothing. Secretly, he agreed with Tencin and O'Brien on everything.

In his reply, the Prince demonstrated to James the style of his new system.

2

3

4

...nce James Sobieski (1667-1737),
...of Marie-Charlotte and
...Clementina. Engraving by
...iani.
...ria-Clementina Sobieska (1702-
... wife of James III, the Old
...der. From a portrait attributed
...visani.

3. Marie-Charlotte Sobieska,
Duchesse de Bouillon (1697-1740).
4. Entrance to town of Zolkiew,
Polish residence of Prince James
Sobieski (now Nesterov, Soviet
Ukraine), traditional print.

5

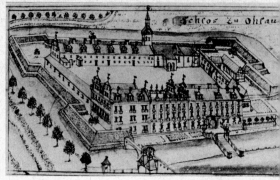

8

6

7

9

5. James Francis Edward Stuart
(James III and VIII, 1688-1766),
father of Bonnie Prince Charlie, *circa*
1735. From a painting by Louis
Gabriel Blanchet.
6. Detail from the tomb of
Marie-Charlotte (Lorenzo Mattielli,
1742; Sakramentek, Warsaw).
Unclaimed by Charles-Godefroy, her
heart remained in deposition in
Zolkiew.

7. The young Stuart princes,
Charles-Edward and Henry Bene
constant threats to Bouillon clai
on James Sobieski's riches.
8. Castle of Ohlau, Silesian resi
of James Sobieski, seized by Fred
the Great in 1740.
9. Bialystok, the "Versailles" of
and residence of *hetman* Branick
deemed, along with many other

10

12

Ball at Versailles

CHARLES GODEFROI DE LA TOUR
d'AUVERGNE DUC DE BOUILLON
VATER DER FÜRSTIN MARIE-LOUISE
HENRIETTE ROHAN-GUÉMÉNÉ
JULES-HERCULE-MÉRIADEC

BAL PARÉ
à Versailles
POUR LE MARIAGE
De Monseigneur Le Dauphin
Le Mercredi 24 Fevrier
1745
DeBouuval

Fig. 18. — Billet d'invitation pour le bal de la cour; d'après Cochin.

13

Grand Chambellan
Charles Godefroi Delatour d'Auvergne Duc
de Bouillon le Prince de Turêine
en survivance

11

14

ranking Polish aristocrats, to be
rthy of Louise.

ouis XV (1710-1774), from
rait by J.-M. Nattier. Though
le Bien-Aimé, he was not
s beloved by Charles Edward
t.

harles-Godefroy de la Tour
vergne (1706-1771), Duc
uillon and father of Charles
rd's first mistress.

12 and 13. Hurried "between balls
and business" (his secret preparations
for Scotland), Charles Edward attended
incognito many of the February and
March 1745 social events recalled in
these Cochin engravings.

14. Coat of arms of Charles-
Godefroy de la Tour d'Auvergne,
Grand Chambellan de France.

15

16

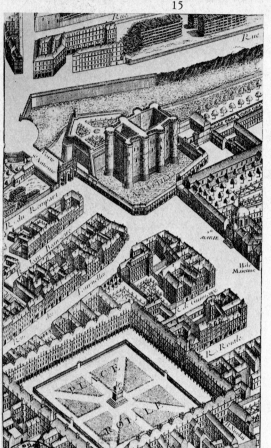

18

19

17

15. View of the Place Royale in 1752, from an engraving by J. Rigaud. Scene of the Prince's midnight trysts, it is better known today as the Place des Vosges.

16. The young Louise, from a contemporary portrait (*circa* 1740-42) after Lancret.

17. Detail from the Plan de Turgot (1739), showing the Bastille and the Place Royale. Louise lived in the corner house, known today as the Musée Victor Hugo.

18. Navarre, a surviving outbuild all that remains of the Hardouin-Mansart château from which Bonnie Prince Charlie laur the '45.

19. Charles Edward in 1744, fro engraving by J. Daullé.

20

22

21

23

enry Benedict Stuart, from a
t attributed to Pompeo Batoni.
pointment as Cardinal was
viewed as a disaster worse than
en.

eorge II (1683-1760), King of
d and Elector of Hanover, from
ing by John Shackleton.

22. William Augustus, Duke of
Cumberland (1721-1765). He gave
his name to the flower "Sweet
William," but he is remembered too
as "the Butcher."

23. Detail from David Morier's
battle scene of Culloden. Jacobite
prisoners apparently served as models
for the Highlanders.

24

25

26

27

Louise's age and quite her opposite
in character.

24. Louise, a later portrait, after
J.B.S. Chardin.

25. Charles Edward Stuart. J.G.
Wille's engraving of the Louis Tocqué
portrait given by the Prince to Louise
in early January 1748.

26. Mme de Talmont in 1741, from
a portrait by J.-M. Nattier. Twice

27. Charles Edward Stuart in 17
From an engraving by Michel Au
of Quentin de La Tour's pastel, g
by the Prince to his new mistress
Princesse de Talmont.

28. The *donjon* of Vincennes, sc
of the Prince's imprisonment in
December 1748. To the left can I

28

30

31

29

32

...e royal apartments which, two ...efore, Charles Edward had ...to occupy in modest splendour. ...iew of what was probably the ...'s cell.
...harlotte, Duchesse d'Albany ...1789), thought to be, until now, ...y child Charles Edward ever ...ortrait attributed to Hugh ...s Hamilton.

31. Clementina Walkinshaw (1720-1802), portrait attributed to A. Ramsay. In 1752 she became Charles Edward's mistress, replacing the 51-year-old Princesse de Talmont.
32. Louise of Stolberg (1752-1824), the last Stuart queen, portrait by F.X. Fabre. Thirty-two years his junior, she married Charles Edward in 1772 and fled to better things eight years later.

33   34

33. Charles Edward in later life: the
end of a dream. From a painting
attributed to Hugh Douglas
Hamilton, *circa* 1785.
34. Canova's monument in
St. Peter's, Rome; reunited at last
with James and Henry.

Tencin was "an absolute Roge & Rascal," almost universally hated and detested, even by the King of France, who, however, was himself "such a weke man that he has not the resolution of Banishing him and disgresing him publickly."[30] James might find that difficult to believe, but the Prince assured his father that his source of information was highly reliable although he would not be able to identify the person until he had a new cypher. No doubt the reliable source in question was none other than his uncle, the Duc de Bouillon. O'Brien, on the other hand, had all "the appearance of not being a rite man." He too was detested at Court and "heted by all our own people, both on this and tother side ye water."[31]

These were harsh attacks and quite unacceptable to James: Cardinal Tencin owed his appointment to the Stuart King and was his most faithful servant at Versailles, as was Colonel Daniel O'Brien in Paris. But the question of Henry's marriage was even more disturbing: "His marriage I take to be of ye Laste consequence," the Prince declared to his father on November 27th, "for my opinion is I cannot as yet Marry unless I got ye Kings Dauter, which is, in ven to ask at present, and am affrede will always be the same, untill ye Almighty restors yr Majesty."[32]

His own marriage could easily be put off. It would have to be part of a broader political strategy. For example, only a few months later, he would write to James about an ultrasecret (and absolutely hare-brained) scheme that had been rolling around in his head "ever since the unlucky Battle." Yes, he was thinking of making a confidential offer of marriage to Elisabeth, the Tsarina of Russia. Her dowry would be requested in the form of 20,000 soldiers, these to be sent immediately on an expedition against England. The entire operation had every hope of success, since the Tsarina was reputed to be of an enterprising nature and resolute, "as she well shewd it at her succession to the Crown."[33] "Enterprising and resolute" made her, despite her seniority, presumably a princess after Charles Edward's own heart! Unfortunately, as James pointed out, he had forgotten to investigate her current political inclinations, which leaned so much in favour of the Elector of Hanover that she had not long before refused Lord Marischal permission to stay in her country.[34]

Charles Edward's plan for Henry, grounded no doubt in unspoken fear of his brother's religious fervour, was more urgent. In fact, the Prince saw it as a case of accepting whatever was available. Henry "should not lose a minits time....If P. Ragevill has any Daughters of age, I shoud not think one of them to be an unfit match."[35] A Polish princess, he suggested, would be more agreeable to the English nation than any other, and Prince Radziwill would probably not refuse. On the other hand, there was no one suitable in France, "besides its being disagreeable to our Friends over ye sese."[36]

Far away in Rome, James saw every reason to be worried. His "dearest Carluccio" of happier days now seemed bent on acting in ways that realized his worst fears. His son had surrounded himself with "wicked advisors." One of them, Sir Thomas Sheridan, had providentially died in Rome before he could return to Paris. The Prince's old tutor had no doubt initiated the ill-advised departure for Scotland....Who knows what he would have suggested next! Another, the evil Strickland, had been brought down by the Almighty in Scotland.[37] But there were others now in Paris whom Tencin and O'Brien had warned James about, and he was especially worried by those in the Prince's household who seemed particularly hostile toward Henry. He sensed the rift developing between the two brothers. A crisis had nearly developed when Henry appealed to the French Ministry to intervene on behalf of Lord Derwentwater, to prevent his execution. Incredibly, this gesture provoked a very icy display of pique on Charles Edward's part; only the Prince was authorized to speak to the French Court, even on matters of mercy.[38] Charles Edward loved his brother, but in a domineering manner. James knew that the situation would bear watching.

It was no doubt with such fears in mind (and possibly because he already had a vague sense of his younger son's undeclared religious vocation) that James took strong exception to Charles Edward's proposal. There was no harm in delaying such plans for a while. The Stuarts were at a critical juncture: "If our great affairs should yet go well, you might both of you have the first Princesses of Europe, whereas perhaps now you could not have the last, & besides, naturally speaking, on all accounts methinks you should think of marrying yourself before your Brother."[39] James at the same time made it clear that he did not really want to hear any more on the matter.[40]

Another piece of news confirming the existence of trouble between the brothers was provided by O'Brien during the last week of December, and it was of such a disturbing nature that James decided that the two princes had to be separated without delay. Henry could perhaps go to Spain or even visit his father in Rome, leaving Charles Edward to take care of business in Paris. The Prince was obviously allowing himself to be governed by a "gang" of evil men whose wicked schemes would soon make him miserable in this life and probably in the next as well. Why, for example, had Charles Edward insisted, against his father's advice, on taking into his confidence the hard-drinking Anglican parson, George Kelly, whom James knew at first hand to be an indiscreet and scurrilous gossip and a person who had spoken disrespectfully of his King on several occasions and even of Charles Edward himself after he had left Rome.[41] And now, according to O'Brien, Kelly had dared to make light of Henry's devoutness and was even leading the hitherto virtuous Charles Edward down the path of moral turpitude!

It had begun over lunch at O'Brien's house. Kelly, no doubt in his cups, had had the effrontery to suggest to the aging O'Brien, in Charles Edward's presence, that he ought to do something about arranging a gallant affair for Henry, just as someone, Markam by name, had apparently promised to find a "girl" for the Prince. It was said jokingly, and O'Brien, swallowing his indignation, had answered in kind, remarking at the same time that such talk was unseemly for an Anglican minister. Charles Edward had found the response amusing, but a few days later he informed O'Brien that he really did wish the Duke were less devout for if one day he lost that excessive devoutness he might easily fall into the opposite extreme. "Can your Highness really be annoyed at the Duke's virtuousness?" O'Brien had asked in reply; "Indeed, I cannot," was the Prince's rejoinder, "and I'll even confess to you that in some things, I think myself as virtuous as he; but there's no harm in talking, or in allowing other people to talk socially about all that."[42] James would see by this, O'Brien warned, how Kelly was having a bad effect on the Prince's morals. He had gained credit with the Prince by playing the clown, being very clever at mimicking the various minis-ters of the Court, much to the Prince's amusement, although his unique source of information about such dignitaries could only be café soreheads and troublemakers. To O'Brien's certain knowledge, the Prince's secretary had never set foot in any of the *bonnes maisons* of the capital.

James was probably not much alarmed by O'Brien's suggestion that Charles Edward, at the age of twenty-seven, was finally developing an interest in "girls." But he was concerned that his elder son seemed on the point of abandoning his own devout convictions and was even playing the modish *philosophe* with Henry. There are indeed few references in the Prince's correspondence at this time to "doing his devotions" even though he occasionally does ask "the Almighty" for help and inspiration in gaining the Stuart cause.[43] The complaint to O'Brien about Henry's religiosity represented, moreover, the radical violation of a gentleman's agreement made in Rome in 1742 after Charles Edward had been prevailed upon by Strickland and others to speak to his brother on "very nice & delicate subjects" relating to religion.[44] James had reacted violently, and those subjects had, ever since, been taboo.

Still more bad news of a similar nature was relayed to the Stuart king two weeks later. The Prince had called at O'Brien's house on 13 January and forced the old man, though he was not feeling well, to go with him to dine at Henry's house. Kelly and about a dozen Jacobite exiles were present, and there had been an awkward scene when the Prince's secretary suddenly asked the Duke point-blank why, when he was at Boulogne in command of all the troops, he had not ordered the ships to sail for England, *at any cost*. Had he done so, at least some of them would have managed to get through, surely....The outcome for his brother would then have been very different. O'Brien, furious, immediately sprang to the Duke's defence: Kelly's remark conveniently ignored the fact that the Duke had no power over the invasion force on this side of the water, his commission having effect only after the landing in England. "Is that so?" remarked the undaunted Kelly, "and why was that, pray? For King James in 1708 had command of all troops then gathered at Dunkirk"—"Do you seriously imagine, then," O'Brien countered, "that if the King had had the troops at Dunkirk entirely at his command, he would have turned back without trying for Scotland, at all costs?" Charles Edward said not a word during the heated exchange. Henry, stung by an almost direct accusation of cowardice, *made in his brother's presence*, suddenly exploded. There was never a time, and Kelly knew it, when even Clancarty felt a crossing would have been possible! Moreover, when one was as ignorant as Kelly was on such matters, it was best to keep one's mouth shut: "A few months ago, you would not have dared to speak in this manner!" he screamed, putting an end to the discussion.

In the awful silence that ensued, the dinner guests merely shrugged their shoulders at Kelly's asinine performance. Still the Prince said nothing. Taken aback by the Duke's outburst, Kelly remained silent throughout the rest of the meal. Perhaps as serious as the events related in the letter was O'Brien's concluding statement to James: he had prepared his account of the incident *on the express orders of the Duke himself*. Difficulties, in other words, were now out in the open. The sooner the two princes were separated, the better.[45]

It is likely that George Kelly merely said on that occasion what an increasingly suspicious Charles Edward had been thinking for some time. In his correspondence with James, however, the Prince professed to be entirely puzzled by what he saw as Henry's withdrawn attitude toward him. "He dos not open his heart to me," he complained, "and yet I perceive he is grived which must proceed from malitios peoples putting things in his hid, and preventing him against me. Notwithstanding, I am persuaded He loves me tenderly, which is the Occasion of my Grife. God almity grant us better days!"[46] The Prince also defended the people he had gathered around him, including, presumably, Kelly; they were honest men, and there were so few of those in this world! He would be very sorry to lose any of them, but he had offered Henry the opportunity to name any that he "had a disgust for," promising to dismiss them immediately. Henry, it seems, had assured him that he did not dislike anyone and did not want anyone to be dismissed. What more could a loving and caring older brother do!

There were other Jacobites in Paris who would have gladly seized such an opportunity to express their disgust with George Kelly, as became more and more evident in the next few months. Balhaldy, for one, could not stand "Trebby" (one of the cant names for the secretary). He reported to James in April 1747, for example, that he had been thoroughly charmed, during a visit to the Prince's house, with Charles Edward's good looks and endearing manners; "but when I came to consider the animals about him," he continued, "my heart was torn to pieces, tho' most of them honest animals, I believe, all except Trebby." He had not been there for more than a few minutes, it seems, before he had caught Trebby out in some great lie.[47] An even more severe criticism of the Prince's secretary was sent to Rome by Kelly's kinsman, Father Myles MacDonnell, who at one time had risked his own life for "Trebby" and was himself in exile for the part he had played in helping his witty relative to escape from the Tower after fourteen years of confinement. Judging from MacDonnell's description, Charles Edward's secretary and court jester had apparently few redeeming qualities:

> He is indolent, lazy & careless, even to indifference. He has neither natural nor acquired parts tho he is somewhat shewy in both, false & faithless in his promises, making Nothing of disobliging your Mty's faithful subjects....The only talent I think in my conscience that Mr Kelly possesses in any perfection is Raillery & ridicule [which] he is very fond of exerting against your Sacred Majesty, & his R.H. the Duke, in sneers & sarcasms. He is downright scurrilous upon Mr O'Brien, Ld Semple & others employ'd, or at least in the confidence of Your Majesty. What needs I, Sir, arraign his honesty & integrity when I have added a sordid avarice to what I have said before? I tremble when I find myself forced to paint my countryman, my kinsman and the object of my care in this manner, but if my own father had been in his place & acted as he do's, I sho'd do the same.[48]

With relatives like Father MacDonnell, George Kelly hardly needed enemies! Curiously, another of Kelly's relatives, the Franciscan whom Charles Edward had sought out when he changed confessors in November 1744,[49] was being similarly denounced at this time in a letter from someone who signed himself "S," to Lord Dunbar, Charles Edward's old tutor. Also named Kelly, the Irish friar was still the Prince's confessor in 1747 (his services being rarely utilized, one gathers), and the letter accuses him of going about Paris, publicly ridiculing James and representing him as an old fool whose judgment had become clouded by the vapours. Since it was widely known that the Franciscan had privileged access to the Prince, the unidentified letter writer (perhaps the Prince's former confessor, the Abbé Sempill himself?) was worried that some might think the Prince shared the friar's offensive views. Furthermore, the confessor Kelly was probably having another kind of bad influence as well on the Prince: "The opinion prevails here," the writer continued, "that the Cordeliers in general are great drinkers, yet even among them this Kelly is infamous for his excesses; in fine, the wine of the Prince's table is term'd friar Kelly's wine, and the same person who governs his conscience is said to regulate his diversions, and his R.H.'s character in point of sobriety has been a little blemished on the friar's account."[50]

Charles Edward's character, "in point of sobriety," was to remain blemished till the bitter end. During the long months as a fugitive in Scotland, he had begun using brandy and whiskey on a scale that impressed even the best of Highland topers. The practice had continued after his return to France except that wine rather than spirits now became his favourite beverage—or so at least we must conclude from scrutiny of numerous suppliers' invoices that have survived. By December 1746, Sullivan, one of Charles Edward's closest associates, had already expressed concern to O'Brien that the Prince was abusing his health as much as he was harming his business affairs. At Charles Edward's birthday celebration on the 31st, O'Brien respectfully urged him to cut down on his long supper revels. Charles Edward promised moderation, but not convincingly.[51] The Prince was driving himself hard and drinking out of boredom and frustration. He needed action. Only the week before, O'Brien had given a large dinner party, followed by a concert for the two princes. Charles Edward had astonished everyone by leaving immediately after, at 1 o'clock in the morning, for an all-night ride to Navarre where he intended to spend Christmas with the Bouillon family.[52]

The Prince had not been neglecting his French family even though little is heard of them in the Stuart correspondence at this time, the reason being that around 10 November Louise had come down with smallpox, the disease then most dreaded by king and pauper alike. Charles-Godefroy immediately left the Court in order to share his daughter's quarantine. Several days later, Charles Edward sent the Duc a concerned letter which perhaps already betrays a special affection for his future mistress: "Il n'y a personne qui prens plus de part a sa convalescence que moi," he assured his uncle.[53] Louise's quarantine ended on 22 December, the very day Charles Edward left Paris for Navarre. He was taking advantage of the first possible opportunity to visit with his cousin in six weeks, and we can only guess at how impressed the young Duchesse de Montbazon must have been by such a display of solicitude. There is no evidence to suggest, however, that either she or the Prince had any inkling then of what their situation would be by the time the next Christmas festival came around.

Charles Edward was back in Paris, as planned, on the day after Christmas. The trip to Navarre had cheered him up, and he wrote a warm letter to his father, telling him about Navarre, "where," he declared, "I was to days, both to Chese away ye Spleen and for a Compliment to ye Good Duke of Boullion and his Family, ho are really all extremly attached to us."[54]

Fully recovered by the New Year, Louise returned from Navarre just in time to join in the round of Court activities occasioned by the arrival of the Dauphine, Marie-Josèphe, the fifteen-year-old daughter of Augustus III of Poland. As usual, along with the other ladies from the Houses of Bouillon, Rohan and Lorraine, Louise was very careful, at the great Choisy welcoming banquet in February, to see that she was seated at the King's table, immediately next to the *princesses du sang*. She had been well trained by her father to insist on taking precedence over all the ordinary duchesses![55] Various magnificent dinners and balls followed the wedding ceremony at Versailles. Louise took particular pleasure in waiting on the awkward young Saxon princess, who, everyone agreed, had a fine complexion and pretty blue eyes but who curtsied in that funny German way, like a nun, and whose nose was very unattractive.[56] That, however, was surely a small price to pay for the splendid victories of her uncle Maurice, the Maréchal de Saxe, as well as for the historic contributions she would herself eventually make by bringing into the world France's next (and very nearly last) three kings: Louis XVI, Louis XVIII and Charles X! Possibly because of Louise's Polish connections, the two women met several times during the feverishly busy week of festivities. They may even have found an opportunity to mention the fact that, ten years earlier, they had nearly become sisters-in-law. In any case, when the new Dauphine declared that she would very much like to see the *chasse du Roi*, a delighted Louis XV invited Louise, along with his daughter-in-law, to the hunt at Saint-Germain which began on 18 February. The company that day in the royal carriage was distinguished indeed! It consisted of the King, the Dauphin and his bride, two of the King's daughters, Anne-Henriette and Marie-Adélaïde, the Duchesse de Brancas, *dame d'honneur* of the Dauphine, the Maréchale de Duras, *dame d'honneur* of Anne-Henriette, Madame de Pompadour, royal mistress, and, finally, Louise, the only passenger without an official court function. De Luynes, who recorded the event, does not state whether the Duc de Bouillon's proud daughter was seated next to or opposite His Most Christian Majesty....

Charles Edward was not present at the celebrations for the simple reason that he had mysteriously left Paris on 24 January for Avignon and Spain. He thus avoided the awkward problem of how to attend both the great wedding and the ball incognito and yet be placed according to what was appropriate to the rank of a Stuart Prince. Henry and O'Brien agonized over the problem for weeks; everyone agreed that he could not be seated with the foreign dignitaries, *behind* the ambassadors! Happily, the duc de Gesvres had come up with a perfect solution which the King of France approved personally, and Henry was finally seated very decently in the chapel for the wedding, and for the *bal paré*, he was given the exclusive use of a balcony reserved for the Premier Gentilhomme de la Chambre. The problem of expense was also troublesome since it would cost, O'Brien estimated, between four and five thousand livres to dress properly for the event, and Henry did not have a sou! Still, O'Brien felt justified in borrowing 4000 from Waters, hoping that the French Court would eventually reimburse the Duke of York's costs.[57] In the end, Henry's bill for the wedding came to 6000 livres, and then there was the small matter of 1500 livres due for the recently completed La Tour portrait, plus 400 livres for doing up his decorations in gold and enamel (the jeweler kept hounding poor O'Brien about the money!). For someone without an income, Henry seemed to take it all rather calmly.[58] The princes were, of course, on a tight budget since Charles Edward had continued to scorn the joint pension of 12,000 livres per month offered by the French Court in October along with the "scandalous" housing arrangements.

The ball was an enormous success. The Saxon bride in whose honour it was given had unfortunately hurt her foot and was unable to dance, so the Dauphin opened the dancing with his sister, Anne-Henriette, then with Marie-Adélaïde. Not one of the ordinary duchesses was designated to join in, and, by order of the King, the first lady to be taken up after the two royal princesses was Mme de Turenne: it was another triumph for the House of Bouillon! From his vantage point, Henry glittered conspicuously. There had not been many opportunities for him to appear at Court since Fontainebleau; he and Charles Edward had gone to Versailles on 15 December to compliment the Dauphin on his forthcoming marriage,[59] and he had seen the King on his own on 31 January to explain his brother's sudden departure. According to de Luynes, Henry told Louis that the Prince had left because he was no longer able to bear the dreadful accounts that were still arriving daily of executions and atrocities being carried out against his followers in Britain.[60]

Charles Edward's disappearance was puzzling to courtiers and citizens alike. It was known that he had ridden off with several *milords* of his suite, had paid his household staff until the end of February, and had given no hint of his destination. Rumours abounded. Some said that he had gone to the Papal territory of Avignon because of dissatisfaction with his treatment in Paris; others claimed that it obviously meant that secret peace preliminaries had been signed at Breda and that the English had insisted on his departure as a condition; still others suspected that he had left to command a new expedition against England that was being organized at Brest.[61]

In fact, Henry had only a vague notion of the Prince's motives or of his final destination. O'Brien had been told that the Prince was fed up with waiting for Louis XV's response to his memo and that he was leaving for Avignon— perhaps indefinitely—to show his dissatisfaction. The Prince had fed the same story to Mme de Mézières, counting on her as the fastest way to get a good rumour circulating in Paris. It was thus all made to seem like part of his policy of dealing "short and smart" with the ministers. Henry had, in fact, gone to Versailles to smooth over ruffled feelings.[62]

Though he was glad to capitalize on rumours that he was leaving because of ungrateful and stingy treatment from the Court, the Prince's real destination was not Avignon but Spain, and he had already set down his intentions in a memo for his Jacobite supporters in England. He would stay only a few days in the Pope's territory and then go directly to Spain to appeal for support from the Court there. By mid-March he hoped to be back in Paris, fully informed on how much help his supporters in England could expect. He had already assured them that if George II (whose health was reported to be failing) should die, he was ready to put himself at the head of any attempt approved of by his supporters in England, *and he intended now to be entirely directed by them*. If the Hanoverian King survived and the great "stroke" could not be "struck," he would be glad of advice from his English friends on what steps to take next and what place they thought would be most proper for his residence. It would also be best if someone were sent over to serve as his minister in Paris since he had no confidence in his father's people. Similarly, he would leave it to his friends across the water to decide who was best suited to serve as his private secretary. His friends could be certain that no one, *without exception*, would know anything of his correspondence with them, except those they specifically authorized.[63]

The significance of this document and of the seemingly inconsequential charade of secrecy that preceded the Prince's trip to Spain has to some extent been overlooked by Charles Edward's biographers. It signals, in fact, a turning point in the Young Pretender's life, perhaps as important even as his dramatic departure for Scotland eighteen months earlier. He had been secretive then, it is true, and had not informed James in advance of his intentions; but his lack of candour had largely been a matter of unavoidable tactics and reflected the special difficulties of communicating safely and quickly between Paris and Rome. In any case, he saw his Scottish adventure at the time as something his father would basically approve of (and James's immediate reaction when he learned of the Prince's expedition showed that Charles Edward had been right). He had undertaken it in his father's name. He had nothing to hide then from James or from Henry. Differences of opinion within the family did occur, of course, but they were brought into the open. "Dessembling," later recommended as a tactic by James himself, was solely for the benefit of others. Now, however, and significantly well before Henry's red hat came into the picture, he suddenly abandoned that strong sense of family solidarity. It was being forced out of him by increasingly severe feelings of estrangement and mistrust. As the years passed, these would eventually cloud and distort even his everyday sense of reality.

That would be later on. For the moment, his feelings were less alienated: he simply knew that he had to adopt a covert, even conspiratorial stance with the members of his own misguided family. It was essentially the kind of secretiveness one maintains in the presence of enemies, and in some ways that is what James and Henry had suddenly become. If not enemies, they were, at the very least, liabilities. With their Italianate ways, their guilt-ridden servility toward the French, their superstitious insistence on not rocking the boat (and then all their praying and patient waiting!), they were destined to drown. It was time to cut them adrift before the entire enterprise was dragged under with them!

Charles Edward never told his father any of this; he merely stopped talking to him about anything that mattered. When his brother quietly gave up caring and became a Cardinal, the Prince simply ignored his very existence for the next two decades. But James did not have to be told: he sensed, perhaps even before Charles Edward did, what was going on in the Prince's mind and he set his views down in a remarkable letter to his son, dated 3 February.

The Stuart King began by assuring the Prince that his love and concern for him would never change, no matter what he or anyone else might do to diminish those sentiments. His criticisms were real enough, but they were intended solely for Charles Edward's temporal and eternal welfare. What especially distressed him, as he reviewed a long litany of complaints, was the growing evidence of his son's alienation, based, he suspected, on the malicious advice of others. It had started back in 1742 when wicked men had prevailed upon Charles Edward to speak reprovingly to Henry on the delicate subject of religion. Similarly, when the Prince undertook his "late unhappy expedition" to Scotland, without his father's approbation or knowledge, someone must have encouraged him. Only dismal consequences had ensued. When he returned to Paris, the first thing he had done was to exclude from his confidence anyone who was in the confidence of James himself and to substitute people who had "failed" James in one way or another. His conduct with the Court of France, his refusal to accept a pension, these were incomprehensible actions! Who was now supplying him with resources? Why all the mystery and concealment? It was as if Charles Edward was determined to will his own ruin, but James could hardly believe that; he therefore had to conclude that his son was being badly advised by others using specious arguments:

> It will probably have been represented to you that our chief interest lyes in the hearts of the people at home, & not abroad, that Foreign Powers will always pursue their own interest, & never attend to ours but when they can find their own account in it, and that therefore it is useless, as it would be mean, to sollicite & court them; it will, to be sure, have been represented to you that Our Religion is a great prejudice to our interest, but that it may in some measure be remedyed by a certain free way of thinking & acting, and in general they will have prevented you against anything that comes from me.[64]

James then proceeded to counter each of the arguments. Charles Edward surely knew that his father was not a bigot in religion; his Catholicism was of the kind that tolerated other sects; he merely asked that it too be tolerated. The cynical notion that the Stuarts could gain popularity in England by making light of religion was not only "unchristian & wicked in itself," but even manifestly contrary to honour and interest "for were you never so Irreligious & Libertine," he assured his son, "the name of Catholick would still stick by you, & be equally made use of against you by our enemies, while by such a conduct you would lose the esteem & deservedly acquire the contempt of all honest men of what Religion soever." As for maintaining a pleasant face with foreign powers, the answer was simple: "As matters now stand, & are like to continue, how can we be without them—either to subsist abroad or to obtain means of returning home, since, we see by a long experience, that cannot be effected without their assistance?" How could Charles Edward imagine, in any case, that these were true friends who were trying to alienate him from his father and his brother? It was only by close union and family solidarity that the three of them could hope to escape the snares of false friends and get the better of their real enemies. What arguments could possibly have been used to induce the Prince to suspect Henry and James? He had no better friends in the world! He would anxiously await Charles Edward's reply and judge from it what was to be expected in the future and take his measures accordingly "for your service & my own quiet, for I have been," the Stuart King concluded, "already too long in hot water on your occasion, & that without fruit or advantage to any of us."

James was in effect issuing a warning that if Charles Edward continued to act in such strange and unfriendly ways, he and Henry would have no choice but to drop out of politics and abandon him to his own devices. That is precisely what happened in the end, and though it has often been maintained that Henry's disloyalty in becoming a Cardinal was the cause of his brother's final disaffection, it may be more accurate to say that the Duke's red hat merely brought that alienation completely to the surface, for the anger and suspicion the Prince had been warmly nurturing since his return from Scotland was deeply rooted and quite sufficient in itself to drive his brother back to Rome and his father out of politics.

IX

"A Dager throw my heart"

THE PRINCE'S trip to Spain muddled matters in more ways than one for James and Henry. His sudden decision pre-empted Henry's own plans to go there, ostensibly on a mission to secure support for the Stuart cause. That was, of course, only a pretext thought up by Cardinal Tencin, James, and O'Brien to further their secret aim of separating Henry from his brother. When Charles Edward learned of Henry's travel plans, he was furious and wrote immediately to the Duke from Avignon, telling him in plain terms not to stir from Paris.[1] Henry's trip was cancelled as a result but the damage was done and the ensuing confusion only served to demonstrate to the Spanish Court (already notified of Henry's visit) that the two brothers were working at cross-purposes.

When Charles Edward left for Madrid, it was without any assurance that the King of Spain would even see him. What he hoped to accomplish there is not entirely clear. Along with a shopping list of military supplies, he took with him a copy of the Treaty of Fontainebleau, hoping that something similar could be arranged with Spain. He also intended to explore the possibility of marriage with one of the Spanish King's sisters, knowing, as he assured James in a letter from Avignon, "that France will never give any of her Dauters to any of us unles you was restored."[2] A Spanish marriage would, in any case, be more agreeable to his supporters in England "on whom we have all to depend upon now, for it is only they that can do the finishing stroke."[3]

Although Charles Edward tried to minimize the extent to which his Spanish mission had failed after he returned to Paris, his arriving unannounced at the Spanish Court had resulted in acute embarrassment for all concerned: "I thought there were not such fools as ye [French Court]," he complained to James afterwards, "but I finde it here far beiond it! Your Majesty must forgive me iff I spaike here a little out of umer for an Agill wou'd take ye Spleen on this occasion."[4] Charles Edward was far from having the patience of an "Agill"! He did manage to see King Ferdinand VI and the Queen, who made him "many sivilitys," but in the end they asked him to be so good as to go back to where he had come from and as quickly as possible. Charles Edward reflected that chivalrous nations in the old history books usually showed their generosity by the way they helped people in distress. Now the contrary "French fashion" seemed to be *à la mode* in Spain as well. Ferdinand, like his French counterpart, was only a tool of his ministers, too worried about what the English would think! Indeed, he was "a weak man, just put in motion like a clockwork."[5]

The Prince arrived back in Paris on 24 March and went immediately underground. Even O'Brien had to admit to James that he did not know where Charles Edward was living, being aware only that he could be reached through Waters *le jeune*. In fact, according to a secret report prepared for the Foreign Ministry, he had actually taken up lodgings in Waters's house on the Rue Sainte Anne, where he stayed very privately for the next month.[6] It was a foretaste of the cloak-and-dagger existence he came to enjoy so much after his expulsion from France in December of the following year.

The Prince wasted no time, however, in letting the War Minister know that he was back and ready for action: "La saison est belle et le tems à propos si l'on veut entreprendre quelque chose en ma faveur. Je suis toujours prêt et impatient pour cet heureux moment."[7] He wrote much the same message to Louis XV, adding the lie that he had received a good deal of encouragement from the King and Queen of Spain, whose most ardent desire was to help in whatever way they could. He also wanted Louis to know that his supporters in England were ready to rise at a moment's notice although, with every passing day, oppression and misery were on the increase in Britain and made such resistance more difficult. Louis had only to give the signal....[8]

Remaining in Paris totally hidden was not easy, and Waters was soon pestered by various people trying to arrange visits. To Madame de Mézières, for example, Charles Edward had to write (significantly on 1 April) that she should instruct her doorman to inform all would-be visitors that the Prince was not to be seen anywhere, being in "l'espase immajinere."[9] Henry was allowed to visit regularly, and the brothers got along well enough, but not one word of business was discussed between them and no mention was made of the Duke's cancelled visit to Madrid.

Money remained a problem. Henry's finances after the Dauphin's wedding were in a sorry state, and it was with great relief that he learned from Cardinal Tencin that his incognito spared him any need to borrow an additional 3000 livres to put himself in proper mourning for the Queen of Poland's death at Lunéville.[10] Charles Edward had no parallel need to worry about such trifles since he was supposedly not even in the city. He did, however, make one exception to his original plan of concealment, and on 6 April he informed his "cher oncle," the Duc de Bouillon, that he was back "en cachette." Nothing, however, was to be said to anyone! With Henry and James less supportive than he wished, it was a great comfort to have his substitute family close at hand, asking only to bring him the love, sympathy, and admiration he knew he so richly deserved.

The time was fast approaching when the Prince would need all of the Bouillons' comfort and support for, unbeknown to him, James and Henry had been busily plotting the Duke's secret return to Rome, and his elevation to the College of Cardinals. Effectively, it implied a moral abdication of their rights of succession. It signified as well that the Old Pretender and his younger son had stopped believing in the possibility of a Stuart restoration. Charles Edward would be allowed to dream on alone....

During the Prince's absence, Henry had written to James of his great happiness at having such a marvellous father.[11] The compliment was deserved for James, knowing full well the negative political consequences of Henry's move, not to mention Charles Edward's predictable reaction, set aside all normal objections and actively encouraged his younger son to follow his calling, insisting that he himself would take full responsibility. There was no real danger, he even assured Henry (who, to his credit, probably had his doubts in the matter), that accepting a Cardinal's hat would harm the Prince's cause. Charles Edward could not, after all, be held responsible for his brother's actions.[12]

The Stuart king then turned his attention to the delicate task of stage-managing the event. To prepare the way for Henry's departure, he wrote immediately to Charles Edward, telling him how concerned he was at the "uneasynesses & jealousies" he regularly found in Charles Edward's letters with regard to Henry. Given those unhappy circumstances, he was tempted to send for the Duke and had written to tell him that he could leave for Rome whenever he pleased: "It would be a comfort to me to have him here, were it but for a few months, and were he to stay here, he would be of the less expence to me & I could be better able to supply you on a pinch."[13]

The total lack of candour displayed in James's references to Henry's pre-arranged departure was matched only by his bluntness when it came time to discuss Charles Edward's own affairs. The Prince's marriage plans were, first of all, egregiously unrealistic: "As long as we are abroad, it would be a jest to think that you could have either a Daughter of France or Spain, and I should think that during our misfortunes we may be very well satisfyed if you can marry a Princess of the same Family as my Mother, & I doubt if you could have even one of them, except you nick the time in which the Court of France may be willing to do all in their power to soften the turning you out of France."[14] The best Charles Edward could hope for was one of the Duke of Modena's daughters and probably only if such a match were proposed while he was being whisked out of the country, with the inevitable peace treaty on the point of being signed! He reminded his son that in peace or war, France was still the Stuarts' only resource and it behooved Charles Edward to cultivate the goodwill of Louis XV and his ministers. Why was he being so obstinate about accepting the French pension? He should depend more on people like Sempill and O'Brien and less on his so-called English friends by whom he now seemed to be entirely governed.

In fact, James was now perilously close to giving up the struggle: "My age & infirmities encrease," he informed the Prince; "I am really unfit to do anything but to pray for you, and I am even under the necessity of taking the party to live & dy in this Country."[15] Rome, as it turned out, was precisely where Charles Edward was himself destined to die, but it would have taken a brave man indeed to suggest that to his face in the spring of 1747! He had better plans and every intention of taking up the heroic struggle against the enemy without further loss of time. The "exciting" military situation that spring made it especially painful for him to sit around uselessly in Paris. His gallant cousins, the Prince de Turenne and the Duc de Montbazon, had already left for a campaign that promised battles on an unprecedented scale between the world's most powerful armies, and he would be missing out on it! The fighting, he wrote to Lally, would be "curios to see." But he admitted that a lesser battle "would be not only curios but agreeable to us, were it tother side ye sea."[16] He was not alone, moreover, in that yearning. A number of senior French officers, like Lally, d'Hérouville, and the Duc de Richelieu, were also full of hope for a new expedition.[17] Even if an expedition were denied him, Charles Edward still wanted desperately to see action, and he again wrote to the War Minister, offering his services as an aide-de-camp to Louis XV. Predictably, the offer was turned down. It meant another frustrating summer of hanging about. Thank God there was at least *la chasse*! As for the notion that some of his idle hours might also be whiled away in rustic dalliance with the wife of an absent comrade-in-arms, it presumably did not even enter his head.

But it was time to get back to the countryside. Living arrangements at his banker's house were cramped and temporary, and he talked often now of finding it "impossible to breathe" in the city. Moreover, by the end of April, everyone seemed to know that he was in Paris, even though he had always been careful to travel about discreetly in a closed *fiacre*. Money would be a problem, however, for country houses were at a premium. He would have to find something fairly inexpensive.... Finally, he had a bit of luck: he was offered, rent free, a "pritty cuntry house" near Passy. Kelly and Colonel James Oxburgh were ordered up to Paris from Avignon, and his household servants soon followed. By 7 May everyone was ready to move in. The owner, Mme de Sessac, an independent and eccentric old lady, had apparently made her house available as a special gesture in honour of the Young Pretender, and it was said that she would not have rented even to the Dauphin of France if Louis XV himself had asked for it! Unfortunately, Charles Edward forgot to send her a word of thanks.[18] Following on a long family tradition, he was getting into the habit of taking free rent for granted.

In May the first in a series of family "betrayals" occurred. One week before the Prince's move to Passy, Henry, with the connivence of Cardinal Tencin's servants, sneaked out of Paris, saying not a word to his brother. That was how James and Tencin had planned it. Henry did leave a note to be delivered once he had reached a safe distance. It contained a profuse apology on the subject: "I begin by begging you ten thousand pardons for having gon away without acquainting you before hand. I own I deserve your anguer."[19] It was an honest enough beginning. But what followed was a minor masterpiece of soothing deception that damned the Duke forever in his brother's eyes, especially when, several months later, he learned the real reason for Henry's going to Rome. His only purpose, Henry explained, was to satisfy his great longing to pay James a visit. He might stay for only a fortnight. The trip would be good for his health. He had made particular inquiries about the condition and safety of the roads both for the trip to Rome *and for coming back*. Furthermore, now was really the best time to travel, before the violent summer heat took hold.

In imagining that merely by begging ten thousand pardons and inventing plausible lies he could escape the heat of Charles Edward's wrath, Henry had seriously miscalculated! On learning of his brother's surreptitious departure, the Prince flew into a rage. A special courier was immediately dispatched to warn James that Henry's presence in Paris was absolutely essential to the conduct of the Prince's affairs. At the same time, he informed his father that he wanted O'Brien replaced immediately by Sir John Graeme, and he now insisted that none of his letters be shown to the Duke. In another note he expressed bitter disappointment that the "tretor," Lord George Murray, still seemed to be travelling about freely; James had ignored the Prince's request that his general in the '45 be locked up. More and more, his thoughts on Culloden revolved around the notions of betrayal and treachery. Everyone was ignoring him and "making nothing of him"! In fact, the only good news he could think of was that he had had his bust executed by the famous sculptor, Jean-Baptiste Lemoyne. It was very well done indeed and could not have been "more like." The total cost amounted to 2400 livres![20] Where to find that amount was a problem, but the Prince, like Henry, was really above worrying about such details. It was a riddle for others to solve. Sir John Graeme, who had now joined Charles Edward in Passy, wrote to James describing the disastrous state of the Prince's finances: "I can compare our situation to nothing better than an immense Labyrinth without one ell of thread to conduct us out of it."[21]

Even in such penurious circumstances the Prince remained determined not to accept the French pension, despite his father's continual harping on the subject. It seemed indeed like a case of cutting off his own nose to spite his face, but there was a rough logic to his obstinacy. While accepting French support for his starving officers in Paris, he had cleverly retained the right to say that he was shifting for himself and had no money of his own to hand out in answer to the dozens of appeals received daily from Jacobite refugees. Moreover, he knew that it would not have looked good across the water for him to be receiving even a moderately fat pension from England's enemy, the King of France. He thus had the best of both worlds. What he especially liked was that the situation allowed him to put others "in the wrong." It was to become one of his favourite techniques and the key to most of his future behaviour. As for his choice of a bride, that too, he informed James, would have to be made with the preferences of his friends in England in mind. If marriage with a French or Spanish princess was impossible, he would try for a match in Prussia, Poland, or in one of the German states: "...it woud certainly be... more popular than any Italian Princess, as also living in any other Cuntry than Italy, on account of the great Prejugé they have against it."[22] It was the Prince's first hint to his father that he was seriously contemplating marriage to a Protestant. The next logical step—turning Protestant himself—was an idea still some distance away, but he clearly did not mind seeing James squirm just a little about that even now!

Charles Edward's special courier of 5 May arrived in Rome on the 19th, six days before Henry himself put in an appearance, but James left the Prince's letter unanswered for some time, failing, he later explained, to see the urgency of his elder son's frantic and terribly expensive message. Yes, what a pleasant and total surprise the news of Henry's impending visit had been! How petty of Charles Edward to begrudge a father the satisfaction of seeing at least one of his sons! In any case, how could Henry's absence possibly affect matters in Paris? The Prince had not been making any use of him for some time, and the two brothers had not even been living together, something that seemed very strange indeed, but that had been Charles Edward's choice. James also wanted the Prince to know that he rather appreciated his younger son's display of filial respect and tenderness. It was ridiculous for Charles Edward to be angry! And as for having Graeme instead of O'Brien, why the Prince could do exactly as he wished *and exactly what he could afford on his own* for James had no intention of meddling any longer in politics. In any case, he had understood that O'Brien, too, very much wanted to visit him in Rome....How nice it would be for everyone![23]

O'Brien was indeed thinking of leaving Paris, realizing that he no longer served any useful purpose. James was abandoning politics and the Prince was determined to ignore him completely. Charles Edward was also cutting himself off from all normal avenues of communication with the French Court, and he would soon suffer for it. Opinion there concerning his ability to serve as his own minister was not very flattering. According to O'Brien, the Comte d'Argenson, and even Louis XV, had let drop one or two uncomplimentary remarks. As for the Spanish Ambassador, he had said plainly that Charles Edward had no head for serious business and that his limited powers of expression impaired his reasoning on even the simplest matters.[24]

In his reply to James's letter, Charles Edward passed over his father's remarks concerning Henry: "This is so disagreable a subject to duel upon that your Majeste will, I hope, excuse me not entering in a further Detail of it."[25] He wrote those words on 12 June, assuming that his biggest problem would be in finding enough patience to deal civilly with Henry when he meekly returned to Paris. The day following, however, letters were posted by Henry and James in Rome that would bring far greater reasons for concern.

The time had finally come to tell the Prince the awful truth. It was not an easy task, and James must have pondered the matter for several days before coming up with just the right nuance of soothing equivocation:

> I know not whether you will be surprized, My Dearest Carluccio, when I tell you that your Brother will be made a Cardinal the first days of next month. Naturally speaking, you should have been consulted about a resolution of that kind before it had been executed, but as the Duke and I were unalterably determined on the matter, & that we foresaw you might probably not approve of it, we thought it would be showing you more regard, & that it would be even more agreable to you, that the thing should be done before your answer could come here, and so have it in your power to say it was done without your knowlege or approbation.[26]

Feeling guilty, the Old Pretender was clever enough to know that the best defence was to attack. Charles Edward, he warned, would be wise to suppress any sense of grievance about Henry's promotion and avoid making it a matter of scandal. Naturally, he was free to say he had had no part in it and even that he did not approve, but any *éclat* or fuss would *inevitably fall back on him*: "Your silence towards your Brother, & what you writ to me about him since he left Paris, would do you little honor, if they were known, & are mortifications your Brother did not deserve." Henry would be writing a word or two himself, but James had forbidden him to enter into any particulars with the Prince on the subject.

James must have been pleased with his letter. He and Henry had somehow emerged as the injured parties! Henry also wrote to his brother on the same day but, in comparison, rather amateurishly, and in the end James had to strike out most of it, drafting instead something more cleverly amiable and winning, which Henry dutifully copied.[27] Whatever Charles Edward's opinion of the step he had taken, Henry declared, he knew that he would be doing the Prince an injustice if he allowed himself to think for a moment that their brotherly love and affection would be altered as a result.[28] In the following weeks, at seven-day intervals, Henry sent two more letters. He was waiting for a response—not about his new office since it was too early for that—but for even the slightest reaction (angry but forgiving?) to his having departed from Paris without taking the Prince's leave. He hoped that Charles Edward would never do himself the wrong of breaking with a brother who loved him and was not unworthy of his kindness.[29] A final letter was sent on 27 June: Henry was still impatiently waiting, he confessed, for the arrival of the French post, in hopes that it would bring him the comfort of a reply: "I am sure you are too just and too good to exclude a Brother who loves you tenderly from that forgiveness and from that kindness which you offerd...to your greatest enemies while in Britain."[30]

The future Cardinal did not know Charles Edward as well as James did. Forgiving defeated Hanoverians in the first flush of victory was good politics and a normal act of storybook chivalry for a young hero; forgiving a brother was quite another matter. Henry would vainly wait an entire lifetime for it to happen; James waited for only one more week. It was important for the record to show that Charles Edward had been unforgiving and harsh well *before* he heard the news. The Old Pretender's final note on the subject, written the day after the ceremony took place, expressed great surprise that the Prince had remained so incensed with his brother for leaving Paris: "I own to you that in your present behavior towards your Brother, there is something so incomprehensible, & so contrary to your natural temper, & to that spirit of justice & mildness which gain'd you so much honor in Scotland, that I really know no more what to make or think of you, or what to write to you on his subject."[31] Since Charles Edward seemed determined to ignore Henry, James would no longer mention the Duke in his letters. Henceforth, the Prince would hear of Henry only by reading about him in the usual gazettes. Moreover, he had now forbidden Henry to write to his brother "till such time as you let him know that his letters will be agreable to you, since his silence is the only way you have now left him to show you his respect & tenderness."[32] In fact, he and Henry asked only to be left in peace. He regretted the inevitable ruin his elder son was bringing on himself, but he saw he could do nothing to prevent it: "All I have left to do is to pray for you."[33]

Having, in effect, now abdicated in favour of Charles Edward, James proceeded to wind down his affairs in Paris. It was almost as if the momentous decision Henry had taken was as much for James's benefit as for his own. Neither would henceforth be burdened with the prospect of succeeding to the throne, and somehow it was a tremendous relief: "Véritablement," the Stuart King confessed to O'Brien, "je songe avec plaisir que je ne serai plus exposé à des tracasseries dans ce pais-là."[34] Suffering the agonies of gout and no longer useful to his master in Paris, O'Brien too was preparing go to Rome where he would receive the title Earl of Lismore for his years of faithful service. His attractively skinny wife, mistress to the Archbishop of Cambrai,[35] would remain in the capital to take care of James's personal correspondence. Even Cardinal Tencin approved of the arrangement. By removing himself from the political arena and appointing a representative of only secondary importance in Paris, James was leaving the French ministry free to deal as it wished with his increasingly obstreperous son, all the while avoiding any formal act of hostility toward the House of Stuart. It was one more step in the relentless process of estrangement in which Charles Edward had enmeshed himself. The arrival at last of his father's letter of 13 June, announcing that Henry was to become a Cardinal on 3 July, was the last straw! After reading it, he was unable to utter even a word and immediately shut himself up alone for several hours.[36] Finally, on 10 July, he sent his answer:

> Sir
>
> I have received yrs of ye 13th & 20th June. Had I got a Dager throw my heart it woud not have been more sensible to me than at ye Contents of yr first. My Love for my Brother and Concern for yr Ca[u]se being the occasion of it. I hope your Majesty will forgive me not entering any further on so disagreeable a subject the shock of which I am scarce out of, so shall take ye Liberty of refering to next Post anything in yours to be answered. I lay myself full of Respect & Duty at yr Majestys Feet moste humbly asking Blessing.
>
> Your Moste
> Dutifull Son
> Charles P.[37]

One week later he wrote his final word to James on the subject: "Thô I cannot help Loving the Duke, which has always been, alongst with yr cause ye occasion of all our quarrels, it will be impossible for me now after this Last Step to have any Comerce with him."[38] Isolation from his family was now complete. Henceforth, little of consequence would be discussed in what became nothing more than a mechanical weekly exchange of perfunctory notes with his father. He warned James of his new laconic style by the very next post: "I cannot express the Concern at present I have of not writing anything worth but what woud be both disagreeable for me to write and for your Majesty to rede. This renders my Letters shorter than otherwise. I Lay myself at your Majesty's feet."[39] That was only the first of a long series of three-line communications, usually beginning with an acknowledgement of the last letter received from Rome (equally routine) and ending with a generally inane meteorological observation: "The weather here is turning to Winter and reccon yr Majesty will have found it Cold at Albano." Sometimes there was not even that much: "Having nothing particular to say this Post, I remain....etc."[40] The once generous and guileless Prince was prepared to withhold forgiveness to the bitter end, more so perhaps from his friends than his enemies.[41]

St. Ouen ye 10th July 1747

Sir

I have received yrs of ye 13th & 20d Jane
ad I got a Dager throw my heart it
oud not have been more sensible
o me than at ye Contents of yr first
My Love for my Brother and Conern
or yr Case, being the occasion of
it I hope your Majesty will forgive
my entering any further on so disagreeable
Subject the shock of which I am scare
out of so shall refer to next post
anything in yours to be answered I
say my self full of Respect at yr
Majestys Feet moste humbly asking
Blessing.

your Moste
Dutifull Son
Charles. P.

Charles Edward to his father, James III, on learning that Henry was to become a cardinal.

The general reaction in Paris to Henry's appointment was predictable. Although some, like O'Brien, saw no difficulty in what Henry had done (or at least they flattered James by telling him what he wanted to hear)[42] and even Louis XV expressed great confidence that Henry would become a central ornament of the Sacred College,[43] the vast majority of James's supporters viewed Henry's move as a catastrophe. Francis Fitzjames, Bishop of Soissons, wrote immediately to his uncle and pleaded with him to stop the appointment if there was still time, not only for the sake of Jacobite aspirations, but in the interests of Catholicism as well! The Elector of Hanover, he assured James, would be delighted since nothing could be more prejudicial to Stuart hopes for a restoration. If Charles Edward died, would the English accept a Cardinal for a King? And if he lived, as everyone of course hoped, would not the threat of having a Cardinal next in line be enough to cause all support for a restoration to vanish? The Stuarts could never return to England except by the consent of the English people, and the English people were much opposed to Rome. While keeping their faith, the Stuarts should have been busy severing their ties with Rome rather than the opposite! Such were the views of a zealous Roman Catholic bishop on the matter, dismayed that the Pope had agreed to such an *anti-Catholic* move. What, the Bishop asked, was there in it for Henry? Rank? But the rank of cardinal was so far beneath what Henry already possessed! Money? Surely, James and his family had already more than earned the Church's material gratitude, without having to make additional sacrifices. Flatterers might applaud the move, and those who were indifferent would say nothing; but sensible men who knew something about the English and who were at the same time James's true friends would not keep silent on such an important issue.[44]

The Bishop (who had sacrificed his own chances to become a cardinal to his zeal for religious decorum during Louis XV's illness at Metz) was only echoing the common sentiment of Jacobites everywhere.[45] One week later, Father Myles MacDonnell reported that everyone condemned the move as a "mortal deadly stroke to the cause," especially since it came at a time when the people at home were so hopeful that another attempt would be made: "All the old bugbears of Popery, bigotry &c. will be renew'd with (I am afraid) too much success."[46] The Jacobite banker, Theodore Hay, described the event as of "much worse consequence" than the Battle of Culloden and prayed that "the Great & Heroick Virtues of our Prince & his Behaviour when in England may remedy this fatall step, as he is ador'd by his friends and admired by his Ennemys."[47] Charles Edward's legend was alive! In fact, the initial reaction in Paris was overwhelmingly one of increased sympathy for the unfortunate young prince who had been sacrificed to the cunning self-interest of his brother.

The Marquis d'Argenson, an erstwhile ministerial ally of the Stuarts, now replaced by the less friendly Marquis de Puisieux, pretended to be not at all surprised: Henry was "tout Italien, fourbe et superstitieux, avare, aimant ses aises, et, de plus, jaloux et haïssant son frère."[48] D'Argenson was even prepared to believe that the whole business was a plot, cooked up by O'Brien and Tencin, in exchange for Hanoverian gold: "Il fallait à ces princes précisément le contraire; il fallait s'éloigner de Rome et de tout air de catholicité, pousser même cet éloignement à l'affectation."[49] Barbier, who did not have d'Argenson's political axe to grind, also makes it clear that popular sympathy in Paris was entirely in the Prince's favour and he began his own journal entry on the subject by noting that the Duc de Bouillon was much grieved by Henry's decision. Why, he wondered, had France allowed such a misfortune to happen at a time when public discontent with the Hanoverians in England was so widespread? Reflecting a more understanding attitude toward Henry (and probably echoing the views of the Duc de Bouillon whose opinion he had already quoted), Barbier wondered too whether Henry had simply grown tired of subsisting on French alms and of seeing the Stuarts used as pawns and bugbears in the war with the English.[50]

Henry had kept up social contacts with his uncle and cousins, especially Louise and her mother-in-law, Mme de Guémené, rather more even than Charles Edward, who was, theoretically at least, still in "imaginary space." It is quite likely, therefore, that the Bouillon family placed the most charitable construction possible on the Duke's "betrayal," reserving nevertheless their deeper sympathy for the Prince. But for Charles Edward, Henry's action was motivated by nothing more complicated than simple greed and the desire to "feather his bed" at his brother's expense.[51] He felt no sympathy with Henry's religious vocation, nor was he prepared to forgive the Church for its role in the affair. Now he would have to show his English supporters that he was prepared to counter Henry's move by moving in the opposite direction. More and more he began to speak of marrying a Protestant, and no doubt at this time too he began to think seriously of the need to abandon entirely one day the religion he had inherited. That day did not come until three years later when, in 1750, he went clandestinely to London, abjured Catholicism, and secretly became a member of the Church of England. It had been as a devoutly obedient son of the Church that he had first set out on his heroic attempt to restore the Stuarts to the throne in 1745. If he had chosen to be cynical about his religion then, he could probably have served his own interests and improved his chances of success by declaring himself a Protestant. The fact that he had not done so reflected to some extent the depth of his Catholic convictions but, especially, it mirrored his sense of filial duty. Now James's moral abdication, Henry's opportunism, and adversity in general had forced him to reassess those convictions, emotionally rather than theologically. Years later, he would speak of an intellectual process leading to his conversion and of having discovered, after much thoughtful searching and "aided by the grace of God," that the whole "artful system of Roman Infallibility" had to be rejected as nothing more than the invention of man. Eventually, he was even pleased to assert that the Roman Catholic religion had been the ruin of the House of Stuart and had very nearly destroyed the British Constitution as well.[52] Those sentiments form part of an essentially political platform drawn up in preparation for another projected expedition and, as such, represent something less than a personal credo. We can be certain, in any case, that in July 1747 (and largely because of Henry's actions), the bruised and alienated Prince was already looking seriously at the Protestant option, though concern with jeopardizing French and Spanish assistance, as well as the support of those Jacobites who would have remained narrowly loyal to James, still made him hesitate.

But betrayal by his father and his brother in the summer of 1747 triggered even deeper emotional trauma than is reflected in the transparent political calculations that underlie the Prince's talk of Protestant marriages or his eventual abjuration. The Stuart Papers at Windsor contain many bits and pieces bearing Charles Edward's undated scribblings and *obiter dicta* on various subjects. One of these, though composed after his expulsion from France in December of the following year, illustrates the deeply passionate anti-clericalism and total lack of filial devotion that would mark the period of intense disaffection brought to the surface by the July ceremony in Rome. The memorandum sets out an irreverent comparison of the deficiencies of two very important figures in Charles Edward's life: his father, James III, and his protector, Louis XV. Both, it seems, had failed him through blindness:

La Comparaison est egalle entre Le R[oi] J[acques] et L[ouis]. Ils sont touts deux des honest gens. Le premié dit-on est aveuglé par les pretres, et le secon par les Putins.[53]

X

A New Life and Love Eternal

THE SUMMER OF 1747 marked a major turning point in Charles Edward's career. Everything around him had come crashing down and needed rebuilding. He was feeling hurt and betrayed as well as politically frustrated and ignored. His father, though now prepared, in the wake of severe criticism, to admit that Henry's red hat had been acquired only at great cost,[1] seemed bent on keeping up the psychological and financial pressure. James Edgar, the Stuart King's private secretary, was forbidden to address any correspondence to Kelly, which meant that Charles Edward was now condemned to the drudgery of dealing with every trifling secretarial chore himself.[2] Sir John Graeme was in no position to help either since James, to punish the Prince for rejecting a French pension and the services of O'Brien, had refused to provide Graeme with a subsistence allowance, forcing him to retire in late August to the cheaper living accommodations of Avignon. In desperation, Charles Edward wrote to Lord Marischal, asking him to come to Paris to act as his general agent, but the old Jacobite warrior, who had never much liked Charles Edward anyway, declined, citing convenient reasons of "broken health."[3]

It was little wonder then that the Prince, who had been subject from his earliest years to psychosomatic reactions in moments of great stress, briefly lost his good health and fell into a state of melancholy serious enough to alarm everyone around him. Charles Edward managed to joke about the problem with Edgar, suggesting that his drooping spirits might be revived if a bonfire could be made of all those cursed cyphers!

Fortunately, the Prince's depression was short-lived. One circumstance that helped enormously was his move at the beginning of July to a fine country house in St Ouen belonging to the Prince de Rohan-Soubise, Louise's distinguished relative by marriage. Charles Edward had not been looking forward to the dismal prospect of leaving Mme de Sessac's house in Passy at the end of June and returning to town since, given his financial situation, it meant having to live out

Henry's unexpired lease in de Bacqueville's house. The thought of occupying Henry's former quarters was symbolically distasteful to him although he lost no time in commandeering his brother's coach, on learning that the Duke, before his furtive departure, had promised it to Cardinal Tencin![4]

As luck would have it, just as he was on the point of moving, the Princesse de Montauban, a sister-in-law of Mme de Guéméné and one of the Queen's *dames du palais*, sent him an intriguing note suggesting that it was not really proper for the Prince of Wales to be moving to Monsieur de Bacqueville's humble abode. Something better, she promised, was in the offing although she was not yet authorized to reveal the secret.[5] Not long after, an invitation to make use of the magnificent Rohan summer residence at St Ouen arrived. For someone with the Prince's genuine fondness for country living, the offer was a godsend, and the moment he saw the place he decided to stay "ye whole seson," it being, as he informed James, "a pritty situation on ye border of ye River and within to Short Leagues of Paris."[6]

The Prince had gradually abandoned his incognito after taking up residence in Passy, and by the time he was ready to move to St Ouen he had begun to socialize openly. Offers of help poured in from every quarter: the Princesse de Conti, on learning, for example, that the Prince wanted to see the castle and environs of St Germain-en-Laye, suggested that he simply take over her great country house at Luciennes near Marly and make it his headquarters during his visit. There, in traditional Jacobite country, Charles Edward had almost his first opportunity since arriving in France to entertain in the grand manner. He sent a carriage to St Germain to fetch Lady Derwentwater and her family and invited them to see the Marly waterworks. Mme de Mézières, mother of the Princesse de Montauban, Lord and Lady Ogilvy, and Sir William Gordon were similarly entertained in the Princesse de Conti's garden.[7] The Prince was in his element: the entire area was steeped in family history, and he wrote to Edgar the following day describing the surroundings of his grandfather's old castle at St Germain as "really very Pritty."[8]

It was not long before Charles Edward was deluged with social invitations from distinguished Parisian ladies. With everyone gone to the Army, dashing young celebrities were in short supply. Moreover, the whole town wanted to meet the mysterious hero who so obviously deserved comfort and sympathy after the ungrateful treatment his brother had just meted out to him in Rome! On 13 August he dined with his cousin Louise and her mother-in-law at the ancient and stately Guéméné residence on the Place Royale. Only a week before, he had been at Coupvray, amusing himself with "ye Shas" and dissipating his melancholy thoughts in the company of Prince Constantin, another of the Rohan clan.[9] Finally, toward the end of August,[10] his busy schedule took him on an extended holiday to Navarre, a place which already held many happy memories for him, and it is probable that his physical romance with Louise began there during this visit or soon after at St Ouen. He had actually gone down to the Duc de Bouillon's country seat primarily for the hunt, "ye shas" being still his greatest passion. Everyone was being so kind about trying to cheer him up! The Duc de Richelieu generously placed his exclusive game preserve, attendants, dogs, and paraphernalia at the Prince's disposal. It was a true gesture of friendship for not even a loving wife's virtue was guarded so jealously by great noblemen of the Ancien Régime! Even Louis XV let it be known that Charles Edward was free to hunt, if he wished, in the plain of St Denis. The Prince accepted but, unfortunately, he soon extended his shooting, in spite of several warnings to the contrary, to an area reserved exclusively for the King's personal use. Not even the Dauphin, it was pointed out, would have dared to hunt there! Louis, who was still with the Army, was not amused, and a sharp note was sent by his Foreign Minister, de Puisieux, to the Earl of Thomond, asking that the Prince be warned, though with as much discretion and delicacy as possible.[11] The King of France was also described as looking "somewhat angry"— a very strong reaction indeed![12]

Despite the joys of hunting, the Prince would have much preferred to be with the Army. His reaction to Cumberland's crushing defeat at Lawfeld on 2 July was nothing short of ecstatic! It had been a glorious slaughter, with thousands of brave men killed and wounded on either side. Another of Charles Edward's old enemies, Sir John Ligonier, had been made prisoner, and the fat Butcher of Culloden had himself escaped only by the skin of his teeth, thanks to a speedy horse! Forgetting for the moment that he was in one of his long-suffering snits, the Prince immediately sent off a spontaneous letter of congratulations to Louis XV, expressing genuine gratitude for the victory along with the fervent wish that he himself would soon have an opportunity to prove the great attachment and friendship he felt for the French monarch.[13] On the same day, he wrote to the Comte d'Argenson, reminding the War Minister of his impatience to return to battle and stating his hope that the victory at Lawfeld would lead to a renewal of French efforts on his behalf.[14]

Unfortunately, no call to arms materialized, and, once again, a Prince born only for glory found himself obliged to pursue a trifling life of idleness. The next two months were filled with news of the long siege of Bergen-op-Zoom which, against all odds, was finally taken by storm on 16 September. It is certain that by then Charles Edward had triumphed as completely in a less hazardous siege of his cousin Louise's heart. Whether it too was taken by storm, or simply by capitulation, we cannot say.

There is no need to review here our earlier conjectures[15] concerning the manner in which the Prince's very first love affair began. What is most important to note is that during this frustrating summer of 1747, Charles Edward was vulnerably caught up in a psychological crisis, and the act of yielding finally to the temptations of an illicit relationship with his beautiful cousin, like flirting with the notion of a Protestant marriage or even poaching defiantly on the King of France's sacred hunting grounds, was all part of casting aside the bruised persona of his former obedient self. Now he would rebuild, and defiance of everything his father stood for would be his guiding principle.

Details concerning the first stages of the affair are lacking, but the Prince's own strange autobiographical fragment refers to his having fallen in love in a *maison de campagne*, presumably Navarre in late August, or at St Ouen in September. St Ouen was especially easy for Louise to visit without attracting attention since her great uncle, the aging and increasingly senile Comte d'Evreux, owned a summer residence right next door to the house occupied by the Prince. A partially encyphered confidential letter from William Drummond of Balhaldy to James Edgar in Rome provides additional evidence of the timing and also lets us in on a secret that has too long been overlooked or ignored by Charles Edward's biographers. No ordinary mortal in matters of dedication and sacrifice, the Prince had devoted his youth to a rigidly self-programmed preparation for the day when he would succeed in regaining a throne where others before him had failed. We should thus not be surprised to learn that part of that early dedication had involved taking a vow of chastity, a vow which the Prince did not set aside until the summer of 1747, and then, the stern old Jacobite implied, only as a result of the wanton influence of those who had lately come to govern his actions and his conscience.

As a loyal member of James's camp and a confirmed denigrator of the Kellys and the other *distillers* (code name for the Irish) living with the Prince, Balhaldy may, of course, be dismissed as a hostile and unreliable witness. His explicit statement on the subject, made in February 1748 has, however, an authentic ring of truth to it, and it can be circumstantially corroborated.

Beginning with a complaint that the Prince was badly served by his various loose-tongued and quarrelsome advisers and that his interests both at the French Court and across the water were being neglected, Balhaldy went on to charge the distillers with even graver sins:

> they have at last succeeded in corrupting [the morals of the most] amiable [& most virtuous youth] was on earth. This commerce [with women] *begun in summer last* and continues yet to a great height, and explains the favor [Sheridan & Stafford] had which till now their stupid ignorance and worthlessness had made a mystery as well as their being the confidents [of H.R.H.'s] retirements and private parties. I could not venture to suspect it, *because of the resolution he had taken of being singular in that virtue*, untill I knew it certainly from the best possible hands, and therefore would not write of the danger he was in, in that respect, from those were about him, tho' many marks and hints of what is now certain fell in my way. I shall therefore say no more on the subject but to pray you to burn this, when the proper use is made of it.[16]

Balhaldy was writing at a time when the scandal of Charles Edward's affair with Louise, later so successfully hushed-up, had reached its height and before Louise's successor, the notorious Princesse de Talmont, came into the picture. As one who had taken a leading part in planning the events that preceded the '45, Balhaldy was, along with Edgar, uniquely well situated to know of any such vow long before the apparently total absence of whoring or dalliance in the Prince's life began to pique the curiosity of the public both in Edinburgh and Paris.[17] Charles Edward had himself always found it easy to counter good-natured teasing on the subject by retorting that affairs of state had to take precedence over those of the heart. In fact, he believed in that principle quite literally, and his contempt for Louis XV's practice of allowing royal mistresses to interfere in matters of government was never far below the surface of his discontent with the French monarch. We recall also that when Kelly had come to him from the Duke of Ormonde's service, Charles Edward and his new secretary had sniggered a good deal at the aging Jacobite's "amoors." Great heroes and great leaders were made of sterner stuff and there would be time enough one day for such frivolities!

Initially linked, possibly, with ambivalent memories of his "saintly" mother's dedication to the Virgin, this resolution became an important feature of the young warrior's self-imposed discipline, like the punishing joys he so deliberately sought out in his exhausting rambles through the Italian hills. Perhaps it is enough to say that the old novels of knighthood and chivalry were not unfamiliar to the Prince, and we should not be surprised that someone with his determination was capable of taking positive notions of self-discipline, fitness, and dedication to monastic extremes. The obsessive religiosity of his brother Henry suggests, on the other hand, a less innocent *raison d'être* and a self-horror nourished by less avowable erotic tendencies. But whatever the specific origin of the Prince's vow, it becomes clear from Louise's correspondence that, having once tasted the joys of physical love, Charles Edward soon developed an impressively healthy liking for it. In short, the all too usual view of an under-sexed Prince must be discarded forever.

And so it was that late in the summer of 1747 Charles Edward Stuart fell obsessively and insanely in love. For the next several months nothing else mattered: affairs of state, his own personal interests and safety, took second place. Later there would be other affairs, more, no doubt, than we will ever know about. But his love for Louise was unique, something that could never be repeated. When it was over, there could be no turning back to innocence.

Certainly it began casually and innocently enough: the hero wounded in spirit, found comfort and understanding in his cousin. At first, the affair was pursued in the greatest secrecy. Every precaution that common prudence demanded was observed. Louise lived miles away with a vigilant mother-in-law and was carefully watched over by servants, most of whom owed their first loyalty not to her but to the senior mistress of the house. In December, the Prince managed to move from St Ouen to the outskirts of Paris, but by then the lovers had to contend with the additional impediment of a husband, back from the wars. All of Charles Edward's cloak-and-dagger bag of tricks had to be brought into play, and evidence exists that the precautions taken during his nocturnal visits in October, even before Jules's return, had become so elaborate and mysterious that they finally attracted the attention of the police, both in Paris and in St Ouen. Lengthy surveillance reports may be examined today in the Archives de la Bastille,[18] and they provide a colourful description of the Prince's *modus operandi* during the affair, as well as amusing proof of the success with which he and his clever servant, Daniel O'Brien (not related to James's gouty agent), managed to frustrate the concerted efforts of Nicolas-René Berryer, Lieutenant General of the Paris police, and literally dozens of his agents and informers working round the clock for nearly a month!

The first report of suspicious movements involving the Prince was addressed to Berryer and the minister, de Maurepas, on 29 October 1747, by Rulhière, commander of the Maréchaussée de St Denis. For some time his men had noted the presence of a hired carriage which, two or three times per week, drew up at a rather suspicious distance from the Prince's house in St Ouen, sometimes at 9 or 10 in the evening but more frequently at 5 o'clock in the morning. A tall gentleman, sometimes dressed in a white frock-coat, would get out and disappear down a lane that led to the rear of the house located between the equally luxurious summer residences of the Duc de Gesvres, on the one side, and that of the Comte d'Evreux on the other. It was noted too that the morning coach would immediately head back to Paris. The matter had initially come to the attention of the police because of a complaint lodged by a local citizen who, on one occasion, had approached the vehicle out of curiosity and had been threatened with a pistol and ordered to keep his distance by one of the passengers. On reviewing the complaint, Rulhière recommended formal surveillance;[19] Berryer and de Maurepas agreed. Everyone knew that with Henry and James out of the picture, the Prince constituted the only real threat to George II's throne and that he was a good target for a Hanoverian assassination plot. Indeed, Maurepas was sufficiently alarmed that he ordered the creation of a second team of police agents and informers in Paris under the command of Poussot. Within two days, dozens of *mouches* were deployed at strategic locations in St Ouen and near the Paris barrier. Everyone now waited.

Unfortunately, after the pistol incident, the mysterious coach failed to appear again. Or so it seemed. A concerted plan of attack was drawn up by Poussot and Rulhière, and on 31 October the two men carried out a careful daylight surveillance of the area surrounding the Prince's residence. Discretion was the order of the day, and they hit upon the idea of casually strolling through the Duc de Gesvres's magnificent gardens, which were open to the public, in the inconspicuous company of several ladies. Everything seemed normal. They were even lucky enough to see the Prince of Wales in the distance, walking about with Mme de Montbazon, Milord Clare, and two unidentified gentlemen. The Prince seemed to be having a marvellous time, and every now and then he or one of his companions would take a pot shot at the partridges in de Gesvres's park.[20]

An even closer watch was maintained during the following week, but still the strange carriage did not reappear. Finally, Rulhière's sensitive detective's nose smelled a rat: the carriage was no doubt still turning up, but now, because of the pistol incident, its occupants were taking extra precautions and sneaking into St Ouen along the river road! Guards were therefore hidden in the meadow with strict instructions to lie flat on the ground, keeping entirely out of sight. Every other possible route leading into St Ouen was also covered.

Rulhière's hunch proved correct! On the evening of 7 November, at about 11:45 p.m., the same carriage was seen approaching the area by way of the river road. It stopped finally in the shadows near an avenue leading to the Duc de Gesvres's chateau. Luckily, one of Rulhière's *mouches* was nearby, and he immediately relayed a description of the vehicle to Poussot's men stationed at the Paris barrier. Approximately three-quarters of an hour later, the coach hurriedly took off on the road for Paris. Curiously, its departure seemed to have something to do with the appearance of a coach-and-four, blazing with torches, that suddenly emerged from the Prince's grounds. When the hired carriage reached the Paris barrier, Poussot's *mouches* were able to tail it to the Marais where it stopped in the Rue des Minimes. The street, which took its name from the nearby convent, ran parallel to the Place Royale on the side opposite the Hôtel de Guéméné and was completely deserted. More mysterious activities followed. After making absolutely certain that no one had followed and that the street was indeed as empty as it seemed, the coachman finally called out that it was safe, after which one of the passengers got out and disappeared immediately through the carriage doorway of a nearby residence. The coach then left for the Faubourg St Germain where a second gentleman got out at the Rue Sainte-Marguerite and entered the apartment of an English wigmaker at the sign of the Cornet d'Or. After fifteen minutes, the same man came down again and told the coachman that he could leave. The hired coach was then returned to Le Roux's livery stable on the nearby Rue de Seine.[21]

In his own report of the same date, Poussot corroborated Rulhière's observations and was able to add that the coach-and-four, whose departure had somehow constituted a signal for the hired carriage, had been carrying several passengers, including a lady, with three lackeys behind, two of them carrying torches. As for the hired carriage that had come up from the river road, the two gentlemen had obviously boarded it during the time it was stopped near the avenue but Poussot's men had been too far away to see anything. No effort would be spared to discover the identity of the two individuals who took so many strange precautions to ride into Paris with such regularity and at such odd hours.

Two days later another incident occasioned further concern on the part of the police. A drunken carter named Chevalier was wearily staggering home one evening at about 10:00 o'clock when he hit upon the notion of catching a ride on the back of a hired coach that had just passed him on the Paris-St Ouen road. No sooner had he managed to clamber aboard, however, when an enraged passenger, rapier in hand, threatened to run him through if he did not get off immediately! The carter complied, though not without shaking his stout walking stick at his angry assailant, whereupon the swordsman became even more furious and seemed ready to jump down to carry out his threat on the spot. The carter, frightened at last, ran on ahead to alert the local mounted constabulary, but too incensed to wait for their intervention, he caught up to the coach once more and drunkenly offered to do battle. At that, the same testy individual came down to meet him, ready to attack with a broadsword. The carter, shouting murder and calling for help, was saved from certain death only by the timely arrival of a mounted patrol, who immediately recognized the person with the sword as one of the Prince's valets. The armed valet angrily pointed out the carter as a scoundrel who was trying to prevent him from going about the Prince's confidential business. Satisfied with the explanation and only too happy to be of service to the celebrated Prince, the police offered to throw the miserable wretch into a prison cell, but at this the valet, later identified as one Daniel O'Brien, demurred, saying that it was now too late, that he had in any case missed his appointment because of the delay, and that he had to leave immediately to go to the Prince. The offer to imprison the drunken carter was repeated, but the valet now assured the *maréchaussée* that his anger had completely passed and that it would be wisest just to send the knave on his way. He also asked that no report be made of the incident since he did not want the Prince to hear of it. Emboldened at finding himself still alive, Chevalier next proceeded to denounce the valet again, claiming that his assailant had been reaching for a pistol in his pocket when the constables rode up and that if he had not grappled with him he would have been instantly killed. Rulhière's report notes that the police then questioned O'Brien further and that he admitted he did have a pistol on his person. "Ce valet de chambre paroist estre bien imprudent," concluded the St Denis police official, regretting at the same time that it had not been possible that night to follow the carriage past the Paris barrier.[22] Writing two days later about the incident, Poussot noted that his own men had been hesitant to follow the carriage that day since the passengers inside were obviously armed to the teeth with rapiers, broadswords, and pistols.[23]

Later reports indicate that the mysterious visits continued almost nightly except that the coach was occasionally exchanged for a less elegant fiacre. This had the effect of confusing Poussot's spies at the Paris barrier, and on several other occasions it had proved impossible to follow the vehicle which arrived at the Prince's place around 10:00 p.m. and left generally one hour later. The servant accompanying the passengers was, however, again positively identified as the Prince's valet. Curiously, after the incident with the carter, a second escort vehicle sometimes put in an appearance at the Rue des Minimes soon after the first arrived, but the same elaborate precautions to make certain that no one had followed were carried out. As before, one of the two St Ouen gentlemen would get out of the carriage and go through the usual entrance while the other, generally accompanied by O'Brien, would leave for the wigmaker's apartment in the Rue Sainte-Marguerite.

Finally, on 17 November, Poussot was able to report something new: he had managed to identify the gentleman who lodged in the Rue Sainte-Marguerite as an English Catholic by the name of "Staffort." The man was married, but it was not known whether his wife was also in Paris. Other occupants of the building reported being a little worried by their neighbour's puzzling nocturnal activities, but Poussot, who had now discovered that Stafford was attached to the Prince's household and was frequently accompanied by the Prince's confidential valet de chambre, thought it would be safe to discontinue intensive surveillance. He so recommended on 17 November, promising, nevertheless, to concentrate all of his efforts on identifying the person who mysteriously disappeared nearly every evening around midnight through the *porte cochère* on the Rue des Minimes.[24]

Rulhière, meanwhile, had also been making progress. By hiding his men in the vegetation near the Prince's house, he was able for the first time to determine what actually took place in the darkened lane once the mysterious coach arrived around 10:00 p.m. from Paris. One individual would get out and make his way to the rear of the Prince's house, using one of several back entrances, either on the side next to the Duc de Gesvres's house or beside the Comte d'Evreux's residence. After an hour or two, two persons would emerge from the rear of the house and enter the coach, which would then depart immediately. Rulhière's men, lying flat on their bellies in the wet field nearby, had been close enough on the last occasion to see that one of the men was, without any doubt, the fiery valet who had nearly sent the impudent carter to an early grave. As for the other, Rulhière's *mouches*, amusingly enough, were quite certain that it was the Prince himself — an absurdity, Rulhière hastened to point out, since he knew that on the evening in question the Prince had been entertaining the Princesse de Soubise, and she had not left the house until a good half hour after the mysterious coach departed for Paris. One could hardly imagine, the chief of the St Denis constabulary reasoned, that the Prince of Wales would desert a distinguished guest, beat a hasty retreat through the back door of his own house, and stumble through the dark to join a waiting fiacre in a distant meadow by the river! Unfortunately, Rulhière's men were so close to the vehicle that they had not dared to make the slightest movement. They were thus unable to signal a description of the coach to Poussot's waiting team, and it managed to slip past the spies Poussot had stationed at the Paris barrier. Two days later, the same thing happened again; only this time, the fiacre was successfully followed to its destination, again on the Rue des Minimes, next to the Place Royale. There the same strange ritual of making absolutely certain that no one had followed was carried out, and again one of the St Ouen gentlemen entered through the *porte cochère* while the other, the man called "Staffort," accompanied by the valet Daniel, proceeded as before to the wigmaker's quarters in the Rue Sainte-Marguerite.

Like Poussot, Rulhière now concluded that police surveillance could be safely discontinued since the valet's presence proved that the Prince knew of these strange activities: "Comme voila, Monsieur, cette affaire qui a inquiété St Ouen et moy aussi, je l'avoue, en quelque sorte éclaircie, que voila trois fois qu'on suit avec succes et qu'on voit descendre dans les mesmes endroits, qu'il n'est plus a douter qu'on n'en veut pas au prince puisque son valet de chambre est de l'affaire, et qu'il y a mesme lieu de croire qu'on luy parle et qu'on agit par ses ordres, je pense qu'on peut laisser de faire observer."[25] Poussot, who agreed with the recommendation, was not long in reporting another breakthrough: the house in the Rue des Minimes was apparently occupied by "M. de Dampierre et toute sa famille." He concluded, therefore, that the gentleman who returned clandestinely nearly every night from the Prince's house in St Ouen to the Rue des Minimes was M. de Dampierre's son, identified as a "lieutenant au Régiment des Gardes Françoises."[26] No attempt was made, of course, to determine whether the stranger from St Ouen actually entered the Dampierre house, or whether, with the discreet connivance of a well-bribed porter, he merely crossed through to a rear exit and made his way unobserved down one of the little streets that led directly to the Place Royale. There, in a large house on the corner diagonally opposite, another discreet attendant and a helpful valet waited at midnight, or later still, to admit the daring intruder and usher him quietly to the upstairs apartment of a waiting Princess. Completely forgotten too in Poussot's report was the mysterious early morning return carriage which, as a result of an inquisitive publican's complaint the previous month, had provoked the whole inquiry in the first place.

Rulhière and Poussot having, to use Rulhière's phrase, "more or less cleared up" the mystery, it remained only for Berryer to report to his minister, the powerful Comte de Maurepas. Both agreed that surveillance could now be ended. In addition, de Maurepas ordered that the matter be brought to the attention of the Prince through his secretary, George Kelly.[27] It was important to show how the French authorities had made every effort to ensure the safety and security of the Young Pretender while he was a guest in the country: "On a cru," Berryer concluded in his report to Kelly, "ne devoir négliger aucune précaution, même la plus legere, tant que l'on a pensé que cela pouvoit intéresser la Personne du Prince qui est cher a tous les Francois."[28] Omitted from the final version was de Maurepas' comment that the Prince, on learning of this intensive surveillance of his "associates," would no doubt be amused....[29] Charles Edward may have managed a smile anyway, and perhaps the thought even crossed his mind that de Maurepas, whose double portfolio included the French Navy, would have been better employed worrying about King George's seemingly invincible warships that had just destroyed the French West India fleet! In any case, there were many other ways to get from St Ouen to the Place Royale, and two days later Poussot reported that the carriage had now changed its route entirely and no longer went anywhere near the Rue des Minimes.[30] As for Kelly, probably never in on the secret and not a little puzzled by Berryer's cryptic report, he was simply instructed by the Prince to acknowledge the letter and to add a comment to the effect that His Royal Highness would soon be sending the Lieutenant Général de Police a private response.[31]

What Charles Edward eventually told Berryer privately is not recorded in the police file. Any number of plausible explanations were possible and perhaps a knowing wink sufficed. The rules of the game did not, moreover, require identification of the lady.

The Prince's style of living had now changed so much, in any case, that an affair of the heart would probably have been conspicuous by its absence. If he had pursued the matter, Berryer might have allowed himself one small question, nevertheless: *When did the Prince of Wales find time to sleep?* Louise worried a great deal about that, especially when their meetings were set for two or three o'clock in the morning![32] She herself, following the practice of most fashionable Parisian ladies of the day, rarely rose before the early afternoon, and it was not without a faint shudder that she refers on one troubled occasion to having got up *in the morning*![33] That lack of sleep was, indeed, a problem for the Prince is made clear by at least one good-naturedly catty letter addressed to him around January 1748 by an unidentified *grande dame*, obviously impatient with his dozing off in company when he was not simply mooning and sighing over what the correspondent regarded as the limited attractions of his Princess: "Vous ètes si obligeant, Monseigneur," the lady complained, "qu'apres vous ètre endormi hier en tres bonne compagnie, vous ne vous ètes reveillez et ranimez que pour parler de la pte p....Quand on na pas les gouts naturels lon a les bisarres et personne encore ne ce soit avisez de ce pendre de gout, ni d'amour pour une petite creature, a qui la nature semble avoir refusez l'espérence d'un etat d'humanité parfaitte et dont les charmes sont bornez jusque a present a ne faire plaisir qu'aux yeux tout seuls."[34] Louise, we see, had enemies only too willing to fuel the Prince's love-sick jealousies and doubts.

But that complaint comes from a later, much stormier period when the Prince's mistress had imposed the annoying rule that kept him from her bed until one half hour after her husband had settled down for the night in his own nearby apartment. Sometimes, as a result, their rendezvous could not take place until well past midnight! But in the beginning it had been very different, and there were times, especially at St Ouen, when they could peacefully spend entire nights together. Charles Edward had returned there on 24 October, for example, after an enjoyable stay at Rochefort, the country home of Charles de Rohan, Prince de Montauban. Again, he was simply overwhelmed by the kindness and hospitality of Louise's in-laws: "They are all good People," he informed James, "having all sorts of attentions for me." Much of the week following was spent with his mistress, and it was at St Ouen during the last days of October that their son, born on 28 July the year following, was conceived — perhaps even on the very day the two detectives, Poussot and Rulhière, saw Charles Edward and Louise shooting partridges in the Duc de Gesvres's garden....

But even without the testimony of Berryer's police officials, there is enough evidence in the Prince's letters to prove that he was seeing his mistress intimately at this time and that his infatuation knew no bounds. Indeed, he was prepared to give up almost anything for her. We recall how, from the time of Marie-Charlotte's visit to Poland, the Sobieski jewels had been a bone of contention between the House of Bouillon and the House of Stuart; legal wranglings over Prince James's inheritance promised to drag on endlessly.[35] Now Charles Edward knew that the squabbling had to cease. On 25 October from St Ouen, in a letter probably "corrected" by Louise, he promised her sister-in-law, the Princesse de Turenne, that he would appeal to his father to put everything right: "Je ne manqueray pas d'envoyer le Memoire au Roy mon Pere, et de le prier tres instamment de finir cette affaire. Je le souhaite tres ardemment, car je hais toutes sortes de proces, particulierement entre des parents, et vous pouvey conter que je faire tout ce qui dependra de mois pour vous procurer une entiere satisfaction."[36] True to his word, Charles Edward wrote to his father on 30 October, enclosing a memorial "relating to ye. inheritance of P. James" that Louise had just handed on to him.[37] James was flabbergasted. It was one of the Prince's first letters to him that dealt with personal matters of substance since the business with Henry. In it Charles Edward described how he and his French cousins had been talking about the manner in which the various Sobieski estates had been distributed between their respective mothers, Maria-Clementina and Marie-Charlotte, and also of the litigation that had gone on since Marie-Charlotte's death. It had been such a total revelation to him to learn how "extremely Ronged" Louise and her brother felt on the subject. James must surely have been misinformed as to the true circumstances.... He, for his part, was ready to do whatever he could to set things right: "I was not au fet of these Matters," he explained; "I telt them I woud send their Paper to you, recomending it ernestly to yr. Consideration, *and being entierly resolved to yeld my shere iff yr. Majesy thinks it resonable.*"[38]

No gesture could have been more generous, nor could we have any greater proof of the Prince's total infatuation! What James had struggled to protect for his children over the years, Charles Edward was prepared to give away in a trice for the woman he loved. He even asked James to reply in French so that he would be able to show the answer to his dear cousins and prove to them that he had appealed to his father in "ye strongest" terms. On 6 November, Louise herself wrote a warmly polite letter to James on the subject, to which James replied cunningly on 5 December, acknowledging receipt of the Bouillon document and assuring her that he had put his legal advisers to work on it. Their response would be forwarded to the Prince in due course. If after reading what his advisers had to say, the Duchesse de Montbazon and the Prince de Turenne still wished to pursue the matter, as was of course their right (for God forbid that he should in any way want to cheat them of what was theirs!), why then it should be up to the courts to decide. As to the choice of courts, for his part he thought (sitting snugly in Rome) that a tribunal established by the Pope would be best and fairest to all concerned and certainly most proper and seemly among friends. There were precedents too; why yes, he recalled that the Duchesse d'Orléans, mother of the late Regent, had chosen just such a method for settling a friendly dispute....[39]

James's letter to Louise scarcely measured up to what Charles Edward wanted, but at least it was composed in French! What the Stuart King had written on the subject to his elder son two weeks earlier reflected his sentiments much more accurately, however, and fell even more short of what the Prince wanted. James, it turns out, had an interesting counterproposal:

> By your continuing to refuse any Supplies from the King of France, & from what you now say of relinquishing your pretensions to your Grandfather's succession, to your Cousins, it would be natural & reasonable to conclude that you are easy in your private circumstances, & without any apprehension that they may alter for the worse. I heartily wish that may be the case, & if it be, I should much approve your kind & generous dispositions towards your Cousins, if you had not nearer Relations than they, who should be much dearer to you, & who are in want, while they are in plenty & riches....[40]

There can be no doubt that James had himself and Henry in mind when he referred to Charles Edward's "nearer relations in want." He was also aware that when Cardinal Tencin had asked the Prince what was to be done with the 72,000 livres of French pension that he had been quietly accumulating on Charles Edward's behalf, he had met with a severe rebuff. The Prince had been furious. By what right had the Cardinal dared to accept the money? A strong protest would be lodged with de Puisieux on the subject. It was not a pension but a new expeditionary force that the French owed him![41]

James, on the other hand, thought it a great pity that such riches would be lost through default. Swallowing his pride, he wrote to his elder son and informed him that he was thinking of asking Tencin to remit the money to him in Rome. He could make good use of it.[42] To that, the Prince replied with much dignity that he had nothing whatever to say on the subject for it really had nothing to do with him.[43] Two weeks earlier, however, not wishing to appear foolish in his father's eyes, he had lamely backtracked on the earlier offer to "yeld" his "shere" of the jewels. That was not what he had meant at all! "As to what yr. Majesty was pleased to Mention in yr. Last, in relation of P. James' inheritance, I must beg yr. Majestys Pardon, and believe you Misondrestood the sence of my Letter on that occasion, for I never intended to relinquish any of my rights but as far as it was found just and that if you agreed to it. I was entierly redy on my side to come to any such measurs as you thought fit."[44] James had obviously struck a masterful blow with his suggestion that Charles Edward might do better to pass on his share of the Sobieski inheritance to him and, yes, to his poor brother, the Cardinal! Still, as the weeks passed and the affair with Louise approached its catastrophic crisis, the problem of the Sobieski inheritance did not disappear, although the Prince moderated his earlier attitude of generosity and sacrifice considerably. On 16 January, James finally sent Charles Edward a response in Latin to the Montbazon-Turenne memorial.[45] By the time it and the Old Pretender's covering letter reached Paris in early February, Charles Edward was already in his grand post-crisis fury and merely readdressed the whole to Louise (who, trembling with joy at the sight of her lover's handwriting, initially thought that he had at last come back to her!)[46] Her formal letter of acknowledgement to the Prince, officially signed and dated, presents an extreme contrast in style with the pitifully desperate love notes she was managing to smuggle out to him at this same time. It reads as follows:

Monseigneur

Je suis bien sensible aux bontées de votre Altesse Royalle de la bontée quelle a eu de m'envoyée le memoire de sa Majestée Le Roy d'Angleterre. J'ai l'honneur de renvoyée a vôtre Altesse Royalle la lettre qui y etoit jointe. Je vous supplie, Monseigneur, De recevoir les assurances de l'attachement inviolable et du respect infini avec lequel je suis

Monseigneur
De Votre Altesse Royalle
la tres humble et tres obeissante
servante L. De la tour D'auvergne
Duchesse de Montbazon[47]

A Paris ce 10
fevrier 1748

Charles Edward filed the brief acknowledgement away but probably not with the growing pile of tear-streaked letters he had long since promised to burn. Several days later, he assured his father that he would forward to Rome any answer he might receive from the "Bouillon Family." However, an off-hand comment which must have puzzled James followed: "I have a Notion," the Prince added, "they will Let it drop."[48] But to the infatuated lover of October 1747, whether contentedly dozing in his hired carriage or shooting partridges, his adoring mistress at his side, all such troubles remained hidden in the future. For the moment he was happy beyond words, and no one could have convinced him that his passion might one day cool although both he and Louise were dreading Jules's return.

Even the Prince's political star seemed to be on the rise again. On 26 September, he had written to Louis XV and warmly congratulated the King on a triumphant campaign. Louis responded positively and invited the Prince to visit him at Versailles on 8 October. It was then that he had finally managed to obtain a regiment for Lochiel.[49] In fact, his credit with the French monarch now seemed so good that the Duc de Bouillon decided to ask his celebrated nephew to intercede with Louis on behalf of the Prince de Turenne, to ensure the eventual reversion of the high office of Grand Chambellan to his son. It was a thrilling moment for Louise. Her heroic lover—a king in his own right—was now also a family protector! Her father's request had in fact been received by her own *cher roy* while she was with him at St Ouen. What respectful terms the Grand Chambellan had employed! "Je suplie tres humblement votre Altesse royale, Monseigneur, de deigner adresser une lettre au roy par les mains de Mr de Maurepas ou Mr de Puisieux...." The closing formula was equally impressive: "Rien ne peut jamais augmenter ny diminuer l'inviolable attachement que je luy ay voué pour ma vie ny le respect profond avec lequel je seray toujours, Monseigneur, etc."[50] Charles-Godefroy had not lost his old touch....Three troubled months later, much less favourable sentiments would be voiced by the Duc de Bouillon concerning his nephew.

Charles Edward remained as much a hero in the public's eye as well. One of his supporters had put it in a nice way to Edgar: the Prince had gained little ground so far, but his heroism had gained him many hearts. And what hearts! It was rumoured, for example, that even Frederick of Prussia—anything but a political ally of the Stuarts—had been listening to an account of the Prince's adventures when, suddenly, he had felt compelled to cry out: "C'est un prince bien digne de vivre et bien digne de régner!" Frederick had also asked for the Prince's portrait; it was sent without delay.[51] Fortunately for the King of Prussia and other amateurs, Charles Edward was not one to neglect his iconography, and he had been keeping his artists busy. The famous sculptor Le Moyne, for example, in addition to the busts executed in both marble and bronze, was commissioned to turn out a life-sized medallion. The Roettiers, father and son,

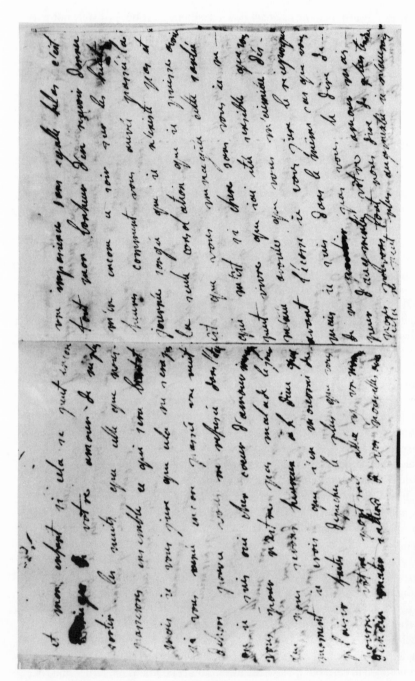

Louise writing to the Prince at the height of their passionate affair.

engraved a number of medals in gold and silver (examples of which Frederick again requested), not to mention hundreds of counters in silver and brass. Louis Tocqué, considered by many of his contemporaries the best portraitist of the day, completed a fine oil of the Prince in the first weeks of January 1748 (it was engraved by J.G. Wille that same year), and the celebrated pastel by Maurice Quentin de La Tour followed several months later. A number of miniature portraits and engravings were also made by lesser artists, and a popular gold ring bearing the Prince's likeness could be purchased in Paris for three louis d'or. Bonnie Prince Charlie was, we see, a lucrative trade item well before he became a Highland industry![52]

As the number of medals and counters indicates, the Prince's legend continued to grow in the popular imagination. Soon Voltaire, who rarely failed to exploit a good story, was busy composing his own saga of the Prince's exploits and provoking cries of admiration and tears of pity at gatherings in Mme du Châtelet's salon. Less illustrious persons were also concerned with the glorious Prince's destiny. One mad scheme drawn up in September 1747 by Ruginale De Rantzau, a resident of Marseilles, proposed that all the nations of Europe should join together to conquer an alternative kingdom (all Ottoman territories in Europe) for the worthy Prince. After an easy triumph over the Turks, Charles Edward would reign peacefully and prosperously as King of Macedonia and Albania! Even George II would be only too happy to supply the Prince with money, men, and arms, since the scheme would remove him forever as a threat to the Hanoverian throne.[53]

We do not know whether the Prince, blissfully consorting with a Princess who claimed the first Crusader as an ancestor, had a good laugh over the fanciful proposal. It certainly did not make him waver, in any case, from his more modest objective, the throne of his Stuart forefathers across the water. Louise continued to take English lessons with a tutor. She had no fantasies about becoming Queen of either England or Macedonia, but it no doubt seemed important to her to speak the language of the father of her unborn child.[54] The problem of what would happen once the war ended did not bear thinking about! Everyone knew that peace would mean the Prince's expulsion from France. Even more immediate was the problem of what to do when Jules returned. Louise's husband had been serving under the great Maréchal de Saxe and had been fortunate enough to survive the costly triumph over Cumberland at Lawfeld. If Charles Edward thought of him at all, it was probably more with envy than guilt, and one suspects that he would have gladly traded the joys of Paris for his rival's place at the front. As the year drew to an end, he grew more angry with the French than ever before. They possessed such overwhelming military might and yet refused to direct their attention to solving his problem! Of course, their neglect of the navy was scandalous and had twice cost him victory. The recent destruction of the West India fleet was infuriating but to be expected: "God grant that ye Blind may see at Last & see their own good!" he wrote to his father in November.[55] One week later, after informing James that he was "in perfect good health," the Prince again exclaimed that he would be still better "iff in action again and to porpose." That purpose he celebrated at a St Andrew's day dinner on 30 November at the Scots College, to which he invited fifty of his countrymen. But toasts to better days and happiness, perhaps even happiness in love, were not enough. In December, he once more expressed his frustration to his father: "There is nothing new at present here worth mentioning; God grant there may be soon a stir and to ye porpose."[56]

The reality of the husband's arrival turned out to be much worse than the vague threat it had represented for the couple during the uneasy weeks that preceded. Charles Edward, especially, was suddenly faced with a situation he had not entirely foreseen, finding himself quite unable to control his jealousy. For the first time in his life, he had let down his guard. He had held nothing back and had declared his love unashamedly and often.[57] Even the news of Louise's pregnancy had only intensified his passion, and he had taken a naive delight in "talking to" his unborn child, making promises to it even before it stirred in its mother's womb.[58] Like his mistress, he was now convinced that they had fallen in love even before he had left for Scotland. Their love was unique. How could he be expected to share with a husband! Within a few days of Jules's return, Charles Edward, lacking all experience and insecurely jealous, became insanely possessive. Constant reassurance by his mistress that he alone had her love and that she could never love another, only seemed to make matters worse, in fact, added to his suspicious imaginings and reckless determination. Jules's movements were unpredictable: like most young officers, he was out at all hours, either gambling at Versailles, attending balls at the Opéra, or simply staying on for late suppers in town. It was now December, and as the nights grew long and cold, the tedious drive from St Ouen became more and more fatiguing and hazardous. Finally, because of the season but also because of the ungodly hours he was now being forced to keep, Charles Edward decided to take a house closer in. Almost right away, he found what he wanted in the Rue du Chemin du Rempart near the Porte St Honoré. It was to be his last official residence in the French capital.

The Prince wrote the news to his father on 11 December. He began with his usual meteorological observations, but for once these were actually of significance: "The Weather now is beginning to be Winter Like, and dissagreeable for ye Cuntry. I have just got a litle house in ye scirts of ye Town which, Tho Litle, Will be very Convenient for me to see anybody privately and Lay in it when I cum to Paris."[59]

The new house, leased at a cost of 4000 livres per year from Denis Chartraire de Romilly, Chevalier Baron de Rochefort,[60] was indeed exactly what the Prince needed. He was now much closer to the Place Royale, but he could continue to take advantage of the luxurious Rohan residence at St Ouen whenver he wished! Although he described the new dwelling as "litle," it was a substantial three-storey structure with a small semi-detached wing, an inner courtyard, a coach house, porter's lodge, two stables, and sufficient room for the nearly thirty regular members of his household, including nineteen full-time servants.[61] Thanks to the meticulous inventory carried out at the time of the Prince's arrest, the Bastille archives contain today an unusually detailed description of the entire building along with its furnishings.[62] It was a house made for entertainment, and most of the ground floor was given over to facilities for feeding guests. The generously proportioned kitchen, presided over by the Prince's head chef, Barthélemy Chambaut, had a double-width fireplace with two roasting spits, and Chambaut always had at least two kitchen helpers to take care of the constant stream of visitors. A well-stocked larder, guarded by the Savoyard, Louis Reydet, was conveniently located nearby, and just below was the cellar where firewood and hundreds of bottles of wine were stored. The comfortable dining hall was dominated in the centre by a long marble table supported on stout legs that were gilded in the antique fashion. A large oakwood buffet stood along one wall, and on it was displayed the fine set of silverware by Gallien for which the Prince had made a partial payment of 13,052 livres only a day or two after moving in.[63] The wall opposite featured another double fireplace, gleaming with copper accessories. Panelled mirrors were set between two pilasters above the fireplace, and on either side of these, two more mirrors, each with six panels gave the room a bright and cheerful look. A third six-panelled mirror ran along another wall as well. Ten chairs, richly upholstered in fine Hungarian needlepoint, were set around the marble table. The walls were covered in gilt-inlaid leather. On the floor above, reached by a broad central staircase, was the games room with its green backgammon table; immediately adjacent was a reception hall which led to the antechamber of the Prince's apartment. The walls there were again covered with mirrors and decorated with hangings that depicted scenes and figures from classical antiquity. The Prince's bedroom was large. Two of its windows looked out on the Rue de Surène, and its cosy fireplace was flanked by richly panelled cabinets. The Prince's bed was located in a small alcove off the main room, on either side of which were doors. The door on the left led directly to Daniel O'Brien's small bedroom, and obviously not much could go on in the alcove without that trusted servant being aware of it. The door on the right led to a room of similar size which served as the Prince's wardrobe. A hidden stairway leading discreetly to a back exit could be reached through either the wardrobe or Daniel's bedroom. It was an ideal arrangement! The Prince could pretend to retire early, as at St Ouen, perhaps even before the last of his guests left the house; moments later, he and Daniel could be galloping off toward the Place Royale. The return trip, early in the morning, could be accomplished by master and servant with equal discretion. Not surprisingly, the

Prince's bedroom seems to have doubled as an armoury, and in December 1748, Berryer counted 25 muskets and 34 pistols there, most of them fully loaded!

Still within the general area of the Prince's quarters, off an adjoining common room, was the bedroom of Charles Edward's second most trusted servant, John Stewart. On the floor above was the apartment of the Prince's secretary, George Kelly. The former Tower of London prisoner also had a large office nearby in which he performed his official duties as the Prince's accredited representative to the French Ministry. Other rooms on the second floor, as well as on the floor above, where James Harrington slept, were reserved for officers and servants. Nearly half of the servants, including all of the stable grooms, lived in the other wing under the watchful eye of one of the Prince's gentlemen, Michael Sheridan, who had his own quarters on the outbuilding's second floor. The nearby porter's lodge, which commanded access to a *porte cochère*, was occupied by Aeneas Campbell. No fewer than ten horses, in the care of Jean Tardif, alias Jean Du Vergé, the Prince's coachman, were housed in the nearby stables. The coach house, finally, was large enough to house two carriages and four post-chaises. Clearly, the Prince had managed to come up in the world in the few short months since he had commandeered Henry's berlin under Cardinal Tencin's very nose! It had all happened, moreover, without touching a penny of French money or receiving anything from James. That alone must have been enough to reassure him that he had made the right decision in choosing to be subsidized (and guided) entirely by his new friends over the water.

Enormous grocery bills for this period are eloquent testimony to the Prince's new means as well as to his hospitality. The sum of approximately 500 livres was spent every month on meat alone (approximately 1200 pounds' worth), and that did not include the hundreds of game birds or domestic fowl consumed every week. Oysters, one of the Prince's favourite gastronomic delights, were ordered in quantities of ten or fifteen dozen every two or three days. Drink was not neglected either, and the bill for wine alone, from 9 December to 30 January, amounted to 1396 livres for 1200 bottles. The monthly bread account, on the other hand, though it represented a staggering quantity of that staple, amounted to less than 25 per cent of the wine bill, a proportion that Sir John Falstaff would have certainly approved![64] Most purchases were made and paid for by the ubiquitous Daniel O'Brien, sometimes described in official receipts as the Prince's *maître d'hôtel*. Curiously, it was Daniel who also paid the servants their monthly wages although, being unable to write, he could not acknowledge receipt of his own and was obliged to ask John Stewart to sign for him. On the Prince's behalf, Daniel even subscribed on New Year's Day for an optimistic full year of the *Affiches de Paris*, an indication perhaps that Charles Edward had no thoughts of leaving.[65]

It is ironic that while it has been possible to unearth so many details concerning the Prince's everyday life during this period, including the layout of his house, the design of his wallpaper, the names of all his servants, how much each was paid, and even the detail of his grocery bills right down to the last daily cabbage or onion, we remain so tantalizingly ignorant of the inner man and his evolving sentiments toward Louise. As a result, we are left to depend almost entirely on what her letters tell of his growing rashness, jealousy, and cruelty. From her anguished account we learn that the situation in December deteriorated rapidly and that, especially during the period of *privation* that followed her husband's return, a number of incidents took place that caused talk among Mme de Guémené's servants. One close call involved an attempt by the Prince to force his way into the house at night despite Louise's terrified pleas. For the most part, the scandal was successfully hushed up.[66] Other disturbances followed, and soon the jealous lover began to torment his high-strung mistress with the threat that he would abandon her forever (*and* cause a public fuss as well!) if she did not allow him access to her bedroom whenever it took his fancy to be there. Every gesture of prudent hesitation on her part he took to be proof that she did not love him. Worse still, as if a husband was not rival enough, he began to imagine that others were secretly vying for his mistress's affections. Not only was she required to give assurances, *parole d'honneur*, that Jules would no longer be allowed into her bed,[67] she also had to send word to at least one social caller, designated only by the letter "C," that his visits to the Guémené house had to be less frequent.[68] Driven to distraction by his crude emotional blackmail, the Princess several times threatened to do away with herself and their child.

Too trustingly, Louise burned all of Charles Edward's love letters.[69] He, on the other hand, despite her frequent requests,[70] carefully saved hers. The result is that nearly everything known about the Prince's conduct in the affair has filtered down through Louise's presumably highly subjective thought processes, and we wonder how much she may have exaggerated. Was he as childishly possessive and cruelly irrational as she suggests? Fortunately, a number of documents exist that amply corroborate the Princess's tormented complaints. Two are undated drafts, written by Charles Edward to his mistress probably late in December 1747 or early January 1748; both display remarkable insensitivity to her pleas that their meetings be postponed to safer times. The first refers to his having turned up at the usual place the night before, but the Princess's valet, who normally saw him safely into the house, had not put in an appearance. Fuming, the Prince had waited and paced about in the street long into the night. Louise had already tried to convince him that they had to be patient, that no more than a brief interval of deprivation was involved, and that soon they could be together again. But the following day his irritation was increased by the arrival of her usual request that he put in a social appearance during the *après-dîner* assembly that afternoon. They would thus have at least the consolation of seeing each other even if it meant only polite small talk in company. The Prince's categorical refusal, harsh and petulant, more than measures up to the impressions we gain from the Princess's own reproachful letters to him on the subject of his "duretés":

> Lundi a midi
>
> On ne puis pas etre plus Lase ni fache que je suis de toute les Cagotteris et Misers qui se font che vous. D'un Cote sa ma rendu du cervise en diminuent Mon amour qui etoit Extreme, mais de l'autre cote je suis en verité honteux d'avoir deja tant souffer. Mais je vous jure bien que celle cy cera bien la derniere et il n'y aura pas Pleurs ni Minoderis qui l'empechera s'il y arrive dorenavent la Moindre Chose. Je me trouverai se soire au rendevous de meme come hier et que votre hom my attend a onze heurs et demy. Je recois dans le Moment la votre et je nai autre a dire que mon parti est pri et inebranlable. Je viendrai se soire et pas avant, et si jy trouve la Moindre difficulte je jure revange et une Eclat Come il faut. A onze heurs et demy du soire a Nous revoir ou jamais de la Vie[71]

There can be little doubt that the Princess, despite her usual insistence on taking precautions, quickly buckled under his threat that he would never see her again if he was not admitted, just as she had so many times before.[72] Added to her fear of losing him forever was the obvious fact that she yearned to have him in her bed as much as he himself was prepared to bully his way past husband and mother-in-law to get there! When finally they would meet, all hesitation was forgotten; then there would be much tenderness and consistently memorable moments that Louise liked to call *le comble des plaisirs*. However, by the next day, at the first sign that her cautious hesitations might be renewed, the Prince would revert to his reckless and threatening ways. The process of moral extortion would begin again, and once more he would manage to impose his will. Louise really had told him too often of her unending adoration, despite all his *torts*.[73] He knew it was unnecessary for him to change. Was he even capable of doing so?

At least one other letter among the hundreds of undated and unaddressed miscellaneous notes in the Prince's hand at Windsor is a companion to the strange billet-doux just quoted, though it was probably composed a little earlier and no doubt in a more joshingly arrogant mood. In the end, however, the effect is equally chilling, and we can be certain that it too produced the desired effect. Seeing no other way out, the Princess would simply take it upon herself to fear and tremble for both of them and then surrender to her ecstasies. Only the grave, she felt, could ever separate them now, and, more and more, she resigned herself to the thought of risking her own life if it meant pleasing her lover. Pleasing him became her only function. As the following letter illustrates, that happened to correspond to the Prince's own sense of the fitness of things:

Dimanche a 4 heurs apres Midi

J'ai recu La Votre dans le Moment. Je ne suis pas fait d'attendre. Dites mois a quelle heur je dois etre se soire au rendevous et je my troverai. Et quoique je vous aime a la folli, aprené que je suis Metre de Moi Meme et quant je suis pousse au but il n y a rien qui tiene. Compare votre raison avec la miene. Alle Fame! Saché que vous n'ete agreable quotent que vous vous rende a nous plaire. Cecy peut etre est ma derniere visite. Adieu.[74]

Of course it was not Charles Edward's last letter to his mistress, nor was it yet time for him to say good-bye. That would not happen until the father and mother-in-law, perceived by the haughty Prince as mere intruders into his private business, had the audacity to take particular notice of the affair and to insist that it come to an end.

The Prince knew that a few outsiders were aware of what was going on, but they, in a sense, had his permission to know and so it was all right. Apart from Daniel O'Brien and one or two of the Prince's other servants, several officers in his household, including Stafford and Sheridan, were obviously in the Prince's confidence. At least one of Louise's servants, her footman Chrétien, was active in relaying messages back and forth. As Daniel's counterpart at the Place Royale, he was also responsible for meeting the Prince at a nearby rendezvous (probably no longer the Dampierre house on the Rue des Minimes after Berryer's solicitous letter to Kelly) and conducting him safely to the Hôtel de Guéméné where, at least in the beginning, perhaps only Mme de Guéméné's *suisse* and Louise's *femme de chambre* were in on the secret.[75]

Happily for us today, there was at least one keenly perceptive outside observer of the secret affair who was strategically well placed to see what was going on. This was Louise's friend and confidante, Anne-Françoise de Carteret. De Carteret had excellent Jacobite credentials, and in her assessment of the situation she seems to have given the Prince a fair hearing throughout. Anne-Françoise was the sister of Captain George de Carteret, who had served in the 1st Duke of Berwick's regiment before leaving France to join the Stuart household in Rome in the mid 1730's. In 1738, James rewarded de Carteret's meritorious service by granting him a commission of Colonel of Horse. He died in Rome on 18 February 1740. Louise and Mlle de Carteret probably met that same year when James asked Colonel O'Brien in Paris to recommend her in his name to the Comte d'Evreux as a governess to d'Evreux's orphaned niece and ward, Marie-Sophie-Charlotte de la Tour d'Auvergne (1729-63), the eleven-year old daughter of the notorious Duchesse de Bouillon. De Carteret was thus placed in charge of Charles-Godefroy's half-sister only a year before her young pupil, like Louise a resident at Chasse Midi, was engaged to be married to the Prince de Guise, her uncle.[76] De Carteret's placement had not been a matter of merely routine concern to James: "On m'assure," he informed O'Brien, "qu'elle est une Fille de merite et elle est certainement de bonne maison. Vous connoissez leur merite aupres de moy. Je voulois bien a Son Frere, et je regrete sa mort."[77] Charles Edward had known George de Carteret in Rome, and he would have felt well-disposed toward the sister when he met her later in Paris, probably through Louise. From Mlle de Carteret's few surviving letters it is clear that, although she visited the capital frequently, she was not living in Paris during the time Louise and Charles Edward were having their stormy romance.

The former governess, though of good family, was obviously of modest means, a fact that Charles Edward was quick to exploit for his own ends. Normally unable to assist the destitute Jacobite refugees that came to him for help in Paris,[78] he suddenly and unaccountably granted Mlle de Carteret a personal pension in late December 1747.[79] The Prince's generosity was not without an ulterior motive: quite simply, he needed someone he could trust to spy on his mistress.

In fact, Anne-Françoise was more of a friend than a spy during her frequent stays with Louise at the house on the Place Royale. She was there on that chilling occasion in December when Mme de Guéméné dropped a bombshell at the dinner table by complaining about the strange noises she had been hearing for some time in the house every night. Louise's mother-in-law had also made it clear that she would henceforth be posting one of her servants on guard and the entire household was instructed to be on the alert for "prowlers." Other knowing hints had been dropped in the course of the conversation that followed, and they had made Louise's heart sink. Her reckless lover, she knew, would turn up anyway![80] That, indeed, is precisely how Charles Edward met the new challenge and it had been a very close thing! It was no good asking him to be patient until May, when both Jules and his mother would be away, or at least until the Christmas holidays when the lovers could meet at St Ouen. A solution had to be found immediately, and de Carteret, "la pauvre Carteret," as Louise refers to her in her letters to the Prince, had volunteered to help find a way of getting around the problem of Mme de Guéméné's spies: "Nous avons cherché les moyens dy remediée," Louise informed the Prince.[81] Meanwhile, it was absolutely essential not to meet for a few days until things had time to settle down.

Louise's letters make it clear that de Carteret had been taken completely into the Princess's confidence and that she had been told not only about the child but about the Prince's unreasonable and erratic behaviour as well. The appellation "la pauvre Carteret," suggests that Louise's confidante had also been on the receiving end of Mme de Guéméné's remarks. The mistress of the house probably assumed that the former governess had been giving her daughter-in-law bad advice. In fact, after the scene at the dinner table, the atmosphere at the Hôtel de Guéméné grew so heavy and uncomfortable that de Carteret decided to cut short her stay and was reluctant to renew her visit later on despite repeated entreaties from her friend.

It was precisely at this juncture that Charles Edward, jealous of an imagined rival and feeling betrayed by a mistress who apparently cared more for her personal safety and reputation than for him, decided to capitalize on his recent investment in a pension. He wanted the truth, and he wrote to de Carteret on 10 January 1748, addressing her as one of his loyal subjects and "requiring" an explanation for her sudden departure. Obviously, he was hoping to discover confirmation of his darkest suspicions. The letter in question, unsigned and bearing no indication of its addressee, is the only dated document I have found in the Prince's hand that relates to his great love affair. It thus presents a rare opportunity to hear his voice directly on the subject:

ye 10th Janry 1748

I am sorry to have this Occasion to write this to you, but I find it necessary to satisfi my self and for yr Justification. When you was at Paris last, it was question of yr staing there with a friend you know I esteem; all was Chenged at once and you yourself told me the person in question wou'd explene to me the reason; but she always cut herself and never gave me a direct and write reason. I did then remarke it and kept it to myself; I have since herd ye reason and with concern, but with esteem for your self. This is now to requier of you to give me en entier explenation of this immediately, which you may be absolutely shure will be kept in my Brest, as I desier you may keep this, without exception and sacredly from every body whatsoever, and Burn this after reding. I am sory to have placed my affection to one that I have good reason deserves it so little as I am affraid [I] shall soon find to demonstration, but it shall be a Leson to me for ye future. I wish you joy with the pension you have lately got and you shall always find me ready to do you any cervice as occasion may happen.[82]

De Carteret's reply of the following day betrays a certain gratitude toward her new benefactor, not to mention some measure of awe at having been taken so intimately into the confidence of her royal master. In it she chose to flatter the Prince, not so much by telling him what he wanted to hear, but rather by adopting the tone of a concerned governess expatiating on the problem of how to deal with a difficult adolescent, which Louise (we have her dead mother's word for it!) certainly had been at one time and probably still was. But on the whole, the former governess, here as in a subsequent letter in which she gives an eyewitness account of the distressing scene that took place in the Princess's bedroom on 23 January, remains basically loyal to her convent friend. Between the lines, her own awareness of the Prince's disturbed behaviour filters through, and once again we have an "outside" perspective on the affair that confirms the general tenor of Louise's own tortured perceptions:

Monseigneur

J'execute les ordres de votre altesse royal et je vais luy dire avec la plus exacte verité quelles sont les raisons qui m'ont empeché de rester a Paris dans le dernier voiage que j'y fis. La personne que vous savez avoit fait son projet de me garder avec elle mais comme je connoissois le terein de la maison dans laquelle je ne voulois pas rester a cause de l'humeur de la mere, et je vous diray tout naturelment, a cause des enfances de la fille, je suposay plusieurs raisons pour m'en defendre. Je pris pour la premiere celle de ma situation mais v.a.r. y ayant pourveu je n'avois plus cette raison et je dis a la personne que vous savez que j'avois une Inclination dans ce pais cy que je ne pouvois pas me determiner a quiter. Elle se rendit a mes raisons et me dit quelle se chargeoit de trouver un pretexte pour que je n'y reste pas. Voila Monseigneur en vray comme cela sest passé mais la veritable raison c'est que jay cru que v.a.r. me soubsonnoit de la mal conseiller et je puis vous assurer que sy elle avoit suivi tous les conseils que je luy ay donne vous nauriez pas a vous plaindre delle et elle en seroit plus heureuse. Je vois avec douleur que vous nestes pas content. J'en ignore absolument les raisons car je vous donne ma parole d'honneur avec tout le respect que je vous dois quelle ne m'en a pas informe et que surement je la desaprouverez toujours de navoir pas menagé le bonheur de v.a.r. comme elle auroit deu. Il faut que je luy rende la justice quil luy est deu, c'est que elle ma toujours assuré quelle vous aimoit uniquement et quelle n'en aimeroit jamais dautre. Je la trouve bien malheureuse sy elle a pensé autrement. J'ose vous suplier Monseigneur de ne point me confondre dans les sujets de plainte que vous avez contre elle et de me faire la grace de me regarder toujours comme une sujette fidelle et Zellé pour votre altesse royal et qui naura jamais rien tant a coeur que de luy prouver mon profond respect.

Ce 11 janvier 1748 a quatre heures et demy du soir.[83]

Though he did not answer immediately, the Prince must have been fairly satisfied by de Carteret's response. She had managed to make him feel royally right in his injured sentiments, but she had provided at the same time assurance that there was no basis for his suspicions and complaints. His mistress, de Carteret was able to confirm, had told her confidante exactly what she had been constantly telling the Prince himself—that she loved only him and could never love another. An interesting sidelight of the letter is the revelation that Louise, whom the Prince constantly accused of blabbing, had actually got herself into trouble by an excess of discretion, having loyally kept to herself de Carteret's "reason" for not staying on with her in December: that is, a supposed affair of the heart.

The last week before the great crisis was relatively calm. Louise had earlier got herself into difficulties and managed to provoke the worst of the Prince's paranoid suspicions by making a last desperate effort to hold the line on his reckless visits. Perhaps at the suggestion of de Carteret (why should the former governess have otherwise worried that the Prince might suspect her of giving Louise bad advice?), she had sent the Prince an uncharacteristically firm letter, begging him to end his cruelties. Her plea was followed by an unusually resolute warning: if he was determined to continue, she would be forced to say goodbye forever.[84] The threat was probably de Carteret's idea. In any case, the letter had not ended on that note, and it was no doubt Louise who insisted on adding one more line, the effect of which cancelled the warning that had gone before: "Ne manquez pas," she pleaded, "de m'écrire cet après dîner!"

That ambivalent ultimatum had not worked, of course. Indeed, it would probably not have succeeded even without its ambivalence. The Prince counter-attacked with his own ultimatum. If she did not stop being so childish, if she did not agree to seeing him whenever he wished, he would cast all precautions aside and come barging into the house, causing whatever scandal he could. Either that or he would abandon her and her child (why should he believe anyway that it was his!) forever.

Again the Prince's strategy worked, only this time with an important difference: Louise was finally prepared to admit total defeat: "J'avoue ma foiblesse. Les larmes m'empêchent d'en dire davantage."[85] She would resist no longer, impose no further conditions. She could only hope that he realized how he was placing her very life in danger, for it would not go well with her if they were found out! Perhaps she would, with the Prince's permission, tell her father.[86] She had always trusted him implicitly from the time she was a little girl. He was a man of vast experience and would want only to be helpful to her. Perhaps he might even be able to make the Prince see reason. They simply had to stop the rumours that were beginning to circulate before they reached the Duc de Montbazon's ears.

Having totally sacrificed all that remained of her own will in the matter, the Princess's final act of submission purchased for the lovers some ten days of peace during the period immediately preceding the explosion of the 23rd. They even found it possible to return to their earlier routines. The minor crises of December and early January had only deepened and intensified their passion. Now they spoke of not daring to tell each other of their love for fear that by doing so they would dangerously augment it. Louise was surprised that she actually felt better about it, having decided to sacrifice her reputation, and even her life, for the man she loved.

Even the physical circumstances under which they met had now improved for it was the beginning of a new social season, and Jules was busy attending all the usual balls and suppers. In addition, after 15 January, the Court was scheduled to remove to Marly for its annual orgy of *comète*, *lansquenet*, and *cavagnole*, played always for high stakes. Jules would be spending at least a week there as one of the *salonistes* or *polissons* who crowded, often three to a room, into every available cranny of accommodation that the château or the town could afford. On Thursday 18 January, Charles Edward himself rented a coach and six and went down for a day's visit to the Princesse de Conti's place at Luciennes where a number of the Marly *salonistes* were staying.[87] As it happened, Jules's own departure for Marly, for some reason, was put off until Monday, the 22nd. Louise wondered for a time whether it would be worth trying to enforce her old rule about not seeing her lover while her husband was in residence; then she thought better of it. She had promised that they would see each other on the 21st, and so they would! But since Jules would surely not arrive home from a supper party before two or two-thirty in the morning, her dear Prince would have to wait until three![88] The Tocqué portrait had arrived at noon the day before, and she had been unable to take her eyes off it. She had even awakened herself early on Sunday morning to look once more at the object of her adoration!

That then was the situation of the two unsuspecting lovers on the eve of what turned out to be the Prince's last visit to Louise's bedroom in the Hôtel de Guéméné. Fate was about to deal the Princess a harsh blow and a bitter sense of the ironic accompanies our reading of letter 45 in which she anticipates not only the joyous hours that lay immediately ahead but also a hoped-for eternity of bliss. Only death could ever separate her now from her Prince: "Non cher amour, je ne me detacherai jamais de vous....Il n'y a que la mort qui puisse nous desunir....Soiée sure que votre fidelle maitresse ne cessera jamais de vous adorée. Vous verrée quand je serai dans vos bras si je vous aime. C'est a la folie!...De vos nouvelles tout a l'heure. Adieu tout ce que j'aime, et c'est pour la vie!"[89]

XI

End of the Affair

UNKNOWN to the lovers, someone else at the Hôtel de Guéméné was waiting just as anxiously for the young Duc de Montbazon to leave for Marly, but for an entirely different reason. For some time now, Mme de Guéméné had known about the torrid affair between her daughter-in-law and the Prince, and she had been hoping that it would burn itself out. She had tried every means, including special surveillance and ominous hints about prowlers, to put a discreet end to it and nothing had succeeded. Indeed, the lovers' apparent addiction to their passion seemed, if anything, to be getting more intense by the day! The situation required drastic measures, and she decided finally to risk open confrontation, with the help of Louise's father.

The Grand Chambellan, his attention monopolized by the Court, had only recently learned of the affair from his daughter, and he was enormously distressed. He and the Prince had been like father and son almost from the time Charles Edward had first arrived in Paris. His own son, the Prince de Turenne, and Jules, the unsuspecting husband, had eagerly proved their readiness to lay down their lives for the Young Pretender. Naturally, he could recall some rather high-spirited activities during his own youth, including the little escapade with his stepmother that Marie-Charlotte had not found amusing. But, in all decency, the Prince should have sought his diversions elsewhere or, at the very least, acted with greater discretion. Now the rumours were beginning to fly and tongues would be wagging, even among the most blasé, for the Prince was much in the public eye. It would be only a matter of time before the husband got wind of it, and then?...There was no accepted protocol in such cases. It was not quite the same thing as the King of France taking a mistress. Charles Edward had no throne....The only solution was to put an immediate end to the affair. At the same time, with the Prince's cooperation, every attempt to keep up normal social appearances had to be made. The public would be lulled into thinking that the rumours were without foundation, and soon everything would be forgotten.

Of course, to minimize the risks, it would be only prudent to wait until the husband was safely away from Paris.

Tuesday, 23 January, the day after the Duc de Montbazon's departure, was thus the first real opportunity the two parents had to act. Not surprisingly, the lovers had more joyous plans in mind. Louise was feeling unusually at ease. On the previous evening she had seen her friend de Carteret, who had finally responded to her pressing invitation to visit. They had talked for a long time, and she had told Anne-Françoise everything that had happened since her last visit in December. The former governess had been reassuring. Now Louise felt calm as she retired earlier than usual to her bedroom. She had a headache, but the impending arrival of the Prince would soon cure that! With Jules away it had also been possible to fix the rendezvous for a more reasonable time. She would have to wait until only one hour after midnight! Perhaps one thing did bother her...the unexpected visit of her father. The Grand Chambellan had taken leave of the King at Marly and turned up at the Place Royale; he had been closeted with Mme de Guéméné for what seemed like hours. Suddenly, she grew frightened. She was certain that it had something to do with her and the Prince! In fact, the two parents were still downstairs conferring secretly when de Carteret returned rather earlier than expected. Her friend came up to her bedroom, and they began to chat once more.

At ten o'clock it happened. In walked Mme de Guéméné and her father; de Carteret was politely but firmly asked to leave the room. Then came the dreaded decree, and Louise could hear herself screaming....

Mme de Guéméné did all of the talking. Strangely enough, she was not furious and she spoke softly, at least that is how it seemed in retrospect, for Louise at the time was in hysterics. Yes, her mother-in-law had known about her and the Prince for a long time. Now it had to end. Louise was to look upon her husband's mother as a true friend. She was not there to do her any harm. In fact, she would see to it that *no one* would ever find out. But there could be no more secret meetings with the Prince! Louise would have to write a letter. They would tell her what to say, and then she would have to promise solemnly never to write to the Prince again.[1] It was a moment of great emotion for all....Louise, sobbing uncontrollably, finally agreed. Soon, all three occupants of the room, daughter, father and mother-in-law, were in tears. De Carteret was called back, and everything was explained to her.

The letter Louise was forced to write that same evening[2] was dictated by the Duc, with occasional intercalations by the mother-in-law. It was couched in the mildest, most respectful language consistent with getting its firmly reproachful message across. The two kindly parents, the Prince was informed, knew everything about *his* actions. His Royal Highness would no doubt recall all of her previous warnings and hesitations. Now she owed it to her dear parents not to *see* him again (that is, in bed) and not to receive his *nouvelles* (that is, any private communication). To prevent her complete ruin (it was nearly complete already), His Royal Highness would do her the honour of visiting socially as usual in the afternoon. The last sentence, Louise was allowed to write almost completely by herself: "Adieu Monseigneur" (how strange it seemed to be calling him *Monseigneur!*), "c'est une rude épreuve pour ma tendresse pour vous qui ne finira qu'avec ma vie." Had she wanted to use the word *amour* instead?...It was agreed that *tendresse* would have to do!

Mild as it was, the letter infuriated the Prince. If there was anything he did not like, it was having people give him lessons or "laws"! Afternoon social visits, indeed! He was not going to be bullied by that interfering snoop, Mme de Guéméné, nor by the silly Grand Chambellan (much as he basically liked the fellow). Had they forgotten who he was? What right had they to meddle anyway? — to *know* even? Did husbands, or fathers, or mothers-in-law comment or feel injured when the King of France took a mistress? Already his mind was toying with the notion that they could not really know, it could not really be their business, since he had not given them his royal permission to take notice or to make it their business. He could simply ignore them.

During the next several days, the Duc, Mme de Guéméné, and Louise waited impatiently for the Prince's answer; Louise, in addition, waited for a secret love note from her *cher roi*. Surely, he would understand her predicament and find some way to send his assurances of affection just as he had in the past! But no answer, secret or otherwise, came. Finally, on Sunday, only one week after their last rapturous meeting at three o'clock in the morning, the Princess could bear the strain no longer. Breaking her five-day-old solemn promise to her father and Mme de Guéméné, she wrote to her lover, describing the events of that terrible evening and what had happened since. Her letter was four pages long and in the end proved difficult to smuggle out for she was being constantly watched. The Prince would know how frantic she was. The life that faced her now would be pure misery. She would have the will to survive, however, if only she was assured that he still loved her. She thought only of him; her days and nights were spent gazing at his portrait, holding all the while a lock of his hair close to her lips. She had not slept two hours in those five days and she looked terrible! Only a letter from him would bring her back to life. He must think often of their child, *his child*. Yes, *his*, and if it were not so, she would not keep it! A happier time would come for them. How cruel he was not to write! He had to visit socially, in the afternoon. Mme de Guéméné would welcome him as before. There was still time to prevent her total ruin. He must tell no one about her letter, not even Daniel! Her own Chrétien was going to be dismissed, and Mme de Guéméné's *suisse* had already been fired outright.[3]

It was a letter much more soothing to the Prince's ego than the one dictated to her five days before. Indeed, if his total knowledge of what had gone on at the Place Royale on that fateful Tuesday had been restricted to what Louise told him in her second letter, he might in the end have magnanimously allowed himself to forgive the Duc and Mme de Guéméné for their meddling, provided it was understood, of course, that he would be carrying on with his bedroom prerogatives.

Unfortunately, the Prince did not leave the matter of intelligence concerning what happened on the 23rd entirely to chance. Aware that his obedient and obliging subject, Mlle de Carteret, had arrived to stay with Louise the day before, he found it an easy matter to send someone to her, bearing a small gift of money in honour of the New Year, along with a reassuring comment in reply to her 11 January letter. No, she surely had no need to fear that he was accusing her of giving his mistress bad advice. But now something else had come up, and she would please be so good as to give him a full and exact account of everything that had gone on that evening at the Place Royale, *omitting absolutely nothing*.

De Carteret, intercepted by the Prince's courier as she was leaving Paris (having endured as much as she could of the nightmarish atmosphere at the Hôtel de Guéméné), had no choice but to obey. Unfortunately, her response, probably composed on 26 or 27 January, irrevocably sealed the fate of her former convent companion in the eyes of the Prince. That was not her intention, for despite the patronizing and critical tone she adopted in referring to her friend, she pleaded Louise's case rather cleverly. The Princess was young, impetuous, and inexperienced; somehow she had offended the Prince, and although her friend could not identify precisely what had been her crime, it must surely have been very wicked indeed if the effect was to offend so good a Prince! In any case, she, de Carteret, knew for certain that the Princess loved him faithfully, adored him even! Louise needed his help. Her situation with the child—the Prince's child—was desperate. Surely he would have the charity to forgive her immaturity and lack of prudence and visit her socially for fifteen minutes from time to time. Her reputation would be saved by it.

Knowing his character only too well, Mlle de Carteret deliberately avoided giving the Prince any "lessons," although she did allow herself the worldly-wise remark that many star-crossed lovers in the past had managed to survive similar difficulties and lived to see better days. But in her zeal to obey her royal patron's injunction to omit nothing in her report, de Carteret made the mistake of repeating the Grand Chambellan's uncomfortably accurate remarks about the Prince's conduct: Charles Edward had shown by his actions no respect either for himself or for his cousin; dishonouring Louise in her own house seemed truly a curious way to repay the Bouillons for their kindness and the many marks of affection they had shown him....De Carteret had no need to say more. The Prince's haughty sense of dignity, his now total incapacity to accept criticism of any kind, are enough to explain all of his subsequent behaviour toward his mistress and her family. The Duc's charges hit home and they hit hard, overwhelming the Prince to the point that he could cope with his guilt only by pretending that nothing had happened. The enormous sense of culpability he felt toward someone he had loved more than anyone or anything else in the world was thus made the equivalent of feeling no guilt at all, and the Prince's autobiographical fragment illustrates how well he managed to preserve his ego intact by that (perhaps largely subconscious?) stratagem.

De Carteret's letter has a value today that goes well beyond any explanation it may provide of the Prince's subsequent behaviour toward his mistress and beyond, too, the interesting sidelights it reveals concerning that distressing night at the Hôtel de Guéméné. It paints an acutely perceptive portrait of the heroine of our story and thus constitutes an indispensable appendix to her letters. Though long, it is worth quoting in full:

Monseigneur

La personne que v.a.r. ma envoié hier ma trouvé en chemin et par conse-quent hors detat de pouvoir vous remercier de vos bontés pour moy. Je me trouve bien heureuse que vous vouliez bien me rendre la justice que je merite et ne pas me confondre avec celle qui a eu le malheur de vous deplaire. Je puis bien jurer que je n'y suis pour rien et que je nay ete que le triste temoin de la plus horible cène qui se soit jamais veü. Je vais parler dans la plus exate verité à v.a.r. Il y avoit plus de 15 jours que la personne en question me solicitoit de venir la trouver en m'ecrivant les lestres du monde les plus pressantes. Elle m'envoia meme un carosse un jour, que je renvoiay, ne voulant pas absolument me mestre dans le cas de me trouver là car je prevoiois par les lestres quelle m'ecrivoit qu'il ariveroit incessament ce qui est arivé et je craignoit toujours que v.a.r. ne me soubsonna dy avoir part dont je jure estre bien innocente car sy cette personne avoit voulu suivre mes avis les choses nen seroit point ou elles sont et nauroit pas fait leclat horible et indecent qui s'est fait. Je suis donc arivé lundy, ne pouvant plus resister au solicitations, dans la ferme resolution de partir sy il arivoit ce que je craignoit. Vous veniez d'en sortir comme jarivay. Elle me dit quelle estoit la plus malheureuse creature du monde, que vous n'aviez aucun menagement pour elle, quelle estoit perdu, que vous l'acusiez de ne vous point aimer, quelle vous aimoit a la folie mais que vous ne vouliez pas en estre persuadé. Enfin il est vray que je la trouvay dans une douleur horible, me disant quelle avoit ete obligé de tout avouer a son pere afin quil fut vous trouver pour obtenir que vous ny alliez pas sy souvent afin de faire sesser les bruits qui courroit dans Paris que vous y passiez toutes les nuits. Il est vray que ce bruit la est public, non seulement dans Paris mais a Marly et partout. Enfin, le lendemain de mon arivé, je fus chez votre altesse royal pour avoir lhonneur de vous faire ma cour mais je fus assez malheureuse pour vous trouver sorti. En retournant le soir chez elle je trouvay le pere et la belle mere enfermé ensemble et je fus chez la belle fille que je trouvay dans le dernier desespoir, estant persuadé que la conversation que son pere et sa mere avoit ensemble la regardoit et que tout estoit eclaté. Efectivement, dans le moment apres, le pere et la mere monterent ensemble dans sa chambre. Jetois seulle avec elle. La belle mere me dit a moy en entrant quelle me prioit de sortir de la chambre parce que elle avoit des afaires avec sa fille et son pere. Je me retiray et dans linstant apres jentendis cette pauvre femme faire des cris et des pleurs teribles. Ils resterent tous trois enfermé ensemble au moins une heure et demie, apres lequel lon me pria d'entrer. Je les trouvay tous trois pleurant. Le pere me dit comme jentray vous n'ygnorez pas, mademoiselle, ce qui s'est passé entre le p.. et ma fille; elle est absolument perdu dans le monde. Le pr.. n'a pas eu pour elle le moindre menagement et en agi comme lon feroit avec la derniere des creatures, sans se respecter luy meme n'y sans re[s]pecter sa cousine germaine n'y sans aucune reconnoissance pour toutes les marques dattachement que sa famille luy a marqué depuis quil est dans ce pais puisque il est venu déshonnorer sa cousine dans sa propre maison. Il n'y a dautre parti a prendre dans un tel malheur qu'a rompre cette afaire brusquement et il faut que ma fille luy ecrivent sur le champ de ne plus venir et quelle rompe tout comerce dans ce moment. Il n'y a pas dautre façon de reparer la reputation de cette pauvre femme en faisant voir au public que tout ce que lon en a pensé estoit faux. Jespere, me dit le pere, que le p. aura assez de respect pour luy meme pour ne pas sesser d'y venir dans le jour car sy il ne se comporte pas dans lexterieur comme il a toujours fait c'est convaincre le public de tout ce qui sest passé et cest nous annoncer quil se soucie fort peu de la deshonnorer, ce qui seroit bien indigne de quelqun comme le p... Jetois plus morte que vive pendant cette conversation car la pauvre creature qui estoit dans son lit estoit preste a expirer. Je nay jamais veü un etat sy violent. Enfin lon luy fit ecrire la lestre quelle vous a envoié et en verite monseigneur, il faut que je sois vraye, elle estoit sy hors delle quelle ne savoit ce quelle faisoit et sy elle nest pas dans tout les termes de respect que lon vous doit vous deveriez luy pardonner cette faute car je puis vous certifier quelle estoit dans une situation sy violente quil luy auroit ete impossible decrire. Enfin la belle mere la traita avec un peu de douceur en luy disant que toutes les fautes devenoit pardonnable, quelle avoit pitié de son etat et quil faloit se tranquiliser. Pour tacher de la calmer un peu, tout les torts retomberez sur vous, monseigneur. L'on chassa le suisse des le lendemain, et le valet de chambre doit estre incessament re[n]voié. Ce n'est que par menagement pour elle que lon le garde encore quelque temp afin que cela ne fas[s]ent pas trop de bruit dans le public. Ils sont tous au desespoir que vous n'ayez pas repondu a la derniere lestre. Ils disent que cest un mepris trop marqué et que pour reparer les torts que vous pouvez avoir vous deveriez au moins observer les bienseances que tout honnette homme se doit a luy meme en respectant ce quil a aimé. La belle mere qui voit sa fille dans une douleur dont elle ne reviendra pas sy tot, sy elle en revient, luy parle avec assez de douceur devant elle mais il n'y a sorte d'horeurs quelle n'en dise quand elle n'est pas avec elle. Enfin vous pouvez compter que voila une femme qui va mener la vie la plus afreuse et la plus triste tant quelle vivra. Je conviendrez quil y a de sa faute et que sy elle setoit comporte comme elle auroit deü tout cecy ne seroit pas arivé mais elle est plus a plaindre qu'a blamer destre du caractere dont elle est, extremement vive dans ses passions, s'y livrant tette baissé, sans reflexion, fort jeune, sans aucune experience, s'en [croyant] beaucoup, pas le moindre usage du monde et voulant toujours suivre ses propres lumières qui sont tres borné; avec cela un tres bon coeur capable damitié et aimant ce quelle aime avec la derniere vivacite, mais dune imprudence quil faut que ceux quelle aime rectifie par la leur. Voilà, Monseigneur, ce que cest que le sujet. Mais ayez pitie delle: songez que vous lavez aimé passionement et que vous ne pouvez sy tot araché de votre coeur ce qui y a ete sy bien gravé. Ayez encore un peu de bonte pour elle. Ne labandonez pas a son desespoir qui est affreux. Ayez la charité pour elle d'aler de temp en temp chez elle lapres dinée, quand ce ne seroit qun cart dheure, afin de faire acroire au public qu'il s'est trompé. Quand lon verra que v.a.r. se conduit comme cela, cela la retablira dans le monde. Je suis desesperé de toute sa mauvaise conduitte envers vous. Je sens bien quelle sest comporté avec toute lextravagance et la folie posible vis a vis de vous, mais malgré cela elle vous adore, et j'en suis sure. Ayez, au nom de dieu, pitié de letat ou vous l'avez mise. Ne la perdez pas. Peut estre il viendra un temp plus heureux ou elle saura mieux se conduire et ou elle poura jouir avec tranquilité du bonheur de vous poseder. Vous nestes pas les premiers qui ayent trouvé des traverses dans pareils cas et qui avez essuié des orages mais sy lon saime bien veritablement cela ne fait point sesser et sans se voir lon peut saimer. Bien des gens l'ont eprouvé et leprouvent tout les jours. Mon respect et mon attachement me font parler a votre altesse royal peut estre un peu trop librement mais la confience dont vous voulez bien m'honnorer m'hautorisent a vous parler avec la verite et la bonne foy dont je suis capable. Pardonez a mon zelle et je vous suplie tres humblement destre convaincu que rien ne peut egaler le profond respect de votre plus fidelle et plus zellé sujette.

Jose vous suplier de jeter cette longue lestre au feu. Je vous demande tres humblement pardon de ce quelle est sy ample mais jay cru devoir rendre compte a votre altesse royal de tout ce qui sest passé devant moy.[4]

Despite her condescending references to Louise (astutely calculated to mollify the petulance and vanity of an arrogant benefactor), de Carteret sketched a portrait of her friend that has an authentic ring of truth and presents a needed corrective to the passive image Louise projects in her post-crisis letters. We are happy to be reminded that the Princess was not always the quintessential abandoned woman, ground down by despair. In many ways, her basic spontaneity, impulsiveness and recklessly passionate nature make us think of the Prince himself. In fact, mutual recognition, early on, of their emotional kinship probably helped to kindle their first feelings of attraction toward each other. Had Louise found it possible to continue on that boldly independent course, matching the Prince's own determination to kick over the traces, something more enduring might have come of their relationship. But particular circumstances allowed Charles Edward to cut himself off from parental authority to a degree that his mistress could scarcely hope to achieve even if she had wanted to, and, basically, nothing was farther from her mind. Her love for the Prince had never seemed to her inconsistent with a sense of duty toward her father, as we can see by her attempt to turn the Grand Chambellan into an ally and confidant. She was not the slightest bit interested in rebellion for its own sake. That kind of thing had ended with the death of her mother in Poland. Now a single emotion filled her entire being: an unquestioning love for her Prince. For Charles Edward, on the other hand, the affair itself had been part of an act of rebellion, and even as his relationship with Louise progressed, he continued to nurse along a deeply belligerent sense of alienation and personal hurt. Indeed, he nurtured it so well that it finally overshadowed everything else. No doubt de Carteret was right: he had loved passionately, and all traces of that passion could not suddenly be erased from his heart. It may even be that he loved the Princess on 30 January as much as he had loved her so possessively on the 23rd. But now that love was transformed into a kind of abstraction, something that he could turn off at will, just as he had been able to turn off completely his love for Henry after his brother's defection. Louise had not, of course, "defected," but she had been the occasion of his humiliation; because of her, certain authority figures had presumed to be critical of his conduct and to set down rules to govern his behaviour. By playing their game, Louise was as guilty as they were, and she had to be punished. She had wronged him just as the entire Rohan-Bouillon clan had wronged him. Amends had to be made and the whole sorry mess put behind him.

It was time, in any case, to turn his attention to matters of more strategic importance. There was already much talk about the imminent possibility of a negotiated peace. It was a worrisome thought that he tried to put aside, and he assured James on 5 February that people always talked about peace at that time of year. No preliminaries had yet been settled, and "the Cards being so well shuffled," he was not in any great apprehension of such an unhappy event.[5] Still the very notion that France and England might settle their differences, thus spelling the end of his stay in Paris, was disturbing. He would have to think of where to go, and it would not be easy for he was certainly not going back to Rome! Perhaps his move from the French capital could be best combined with a politically advantageous marriage. To counter Henry's betrayal he would, of course, have to find a Protestant bride. It was all the more important then to hush up any scandal with Louise for he could ill afford little stories circulating in every tidy German court about adulterous escapades and putative offspring. His next mistress (if ever he took another!) would have to be a little more clever about certain things! An older woman would be safer, more realistic in her expectations and even politically more useful....Certainly, in that last regard, Louise had been a complete liability. It was as if he had just wasted six precious months under the effects of some kind of spell! Now it was over, and he could think clearly again. He would stay entirely away from the Hôtel de Guéméné, write no more letters to the Princess, and take pains to show himself off as much as possible as the handsome, carefree idol of the town that he really was.

We can only speculate that by the end of January the Prince's thoughts ran along some such lines for he wrote not a word on the subject of his affair to anyone. But even if he had bared his soul in precisely such harsh terms in a letter to the Princess, one suspects that it would have made no difference to her! Her love was unshakable; she knew it would never change, just as she believed that one day he would come back to her.

Now the purely physical problem of communicating with the Prince became even more difficult for Louise. Mme de Guéméné's servants watched her like hawks, and even her own attendants could no longer be trusted. The example made of her valet and the *suisse* had brought the others smartly into line! Luckily, Chrétien had been taken in for the moment by one of the Prince's acquaintances and was able, for a time, to continue serving as an intermediary, along with the Prince's valet, Daniel. But apart from those two and a few friends who apparently agreed to act as "blind" messengers, Louise had no one. She was unable even to trust her own *femme de chambre*![6]

With the Prince now adamantly refusing to write or visit, Louise was soon on her knees again, engaged in that most self-contradictory of romantic absurdities, the act of *begging to be loved*! How unjust the Prince was to accuse her of wrongdoing! Surely he realized that she had had no choice about writing the offending letter! No, she had never, *ever*, shown his letters. He must love her or she would most certainly die! When that happened, as in the romances of old, others would bring her heart to him; it would speak the truth in her defence. She was dreadfully ill. Did he know that she was feverish and had lost all appetite? She worried constantly for the life of their child. How could the Prince not take pity at least on his own flesh and blood! Why did he not write?

Finally, during the second week of February, a letter did arrive. It was addressed in the Prince's hand, but it turned out to be merely James's answer in Latin to the Bouillon memorial concerning the Ohlau inheritance and the Sobieski jewels. The Stuart position had not changed after all.... How ironic that only three months before Charles Edward had lovingly told her that he wanted to give up his entire share to her!

As he forwarded the document, the Prince must have recollected with mixed feelings that week in October at St Ouen. But that was in the past and now he simply told James that he had a notion the Bouillons would let the matter drop. At least he had the satisfaction of knowing that his intransigent tactics with Mme de Guéméné were working. She had let it be known that he would be welcomed back to the Hôtel de Guéméné for social visits *as if nothing had happened*. He had only to send Colonel Oxburgh around to say, for example, that he had been feeling ill for a time. They were begging to see him! All the more reason to refuse, of course!

Though the Prince wrote only one note to the Princess during this time, he did use Daniel and Chrétien to communicate the occasional reproachful message. Once or twice he made an exception. Daniel was allowed on one occasion to hint that the Princess was still privileged to have his master's *amitiés* and that His Royal Highness might even consent to seeing her one day in private, *at his own house*. The real dangers and symbolic constraints imposed on Louise by such an impossibly risky arrangement appealed to him. It was a way of testing her affection, of making her openly choose him rather than her family. He was not, on the other hand, interested in Louise's pleading counterproposal that they meet instead in the absolute safety of her Versailles apartment. There was a time, she reminded him, when he would not have hesitated to travel that short distance to see her! Even in her distress, the Princess remembered to be generous: since it appeared, for the moment, impossible for them to "see" each other, she realized it would be too much to ask him to avoid "seeing" someone else. But even if his body had to be unfaithful, he must at least keep his heart for her. She was certain that better days lay ahead.

Unanswered, the Princess's letters grew longer and longer. Soon they were directed, not only to the Prince, but also to Chrétien and Daniel. It was natural that they should become her confidants for she had no one else to talk to and they had been involved in the affair from the beginning. Both had easy access to the Prince, and she could ask them to do for her what it was physically impossible for her to do herself. She could ask them, for example, to throw themselves at the Prince's feet for her, embrace his knees and beg him to be just, merciful and loving. Had he no pity at all? If not for her, at least for his child!

In turn, the two valets brought back, not direct messages, but echoes of his suspicious comments, his needling and indignant accusations. He was certain that she had shown his letters, that she had been unfaithful, that she loved another. She had revealed their secret to all and sundry....The Princess answered all charges with tearful indignation. Yes, it was true that all of the servants at the Hôtel de Guéméné knew of their affair but not because of anything she had said or done. Rather it was the Prince himself with his brawling insistence on reckless nocturnal visits who had let the cat out of the bag. She had never shown his letters. Had he, by the way, burned hers, as she had asked? As for the charge that she loved another, she deserved better from him than that! If ever she were to give her heart to someone else, it would be only to God. Her alternative to loving the Prince was a nunnery. She knew that she had vicious enemies who had made unworthy accusations to the Prince regarding her fidelity. But how could she defend herself? Daniel knew who her accusers were! Even if he had difficulty writing, he simply had to set down their names as best he could on a slip of paper, no matter how illegibly; she would be able to make out their identities. Why did the Prince snub her at the Comédie Française and the Opéra? She went only to see him! Why was he no longer wearing the waistcoat she had made for him? Was he getting rid of everything that reminded him of her? Where was the portrait she had given him? No doubt he had destroyed it too! If only he knew how often she looked at his! In fact, he must give her a copy in miniature so that she could have him with her at all times. And then there was the great question: had someone replaced her in the Prince's affections? Daniel was not to forget his promise to let her know the moment such a thing happened. He must also tell her if the rumour she had heard that the Prince would be going to the army in Flanders was true. She was unable to bear even the thought of her dear Prince surrounded by so much danger. She knew little and cared nothing about politics, but if the Prince had to leave France because of the peace that everyone was talking about she would surely die!

And so the weeks dragged on. Except for the brief note in February, accompanying James's memorial, and two or three hesitant letters written with great reluctance around 20 May after the two lovers had managed to meet one night in a carriage near the Pont Tournant, the Prince sent nothing. His silence was intended as a punishment for the unworthy treatment he had received at the hands of her parents. Chrétien and Daniel were several times specifically instructed to pass on that explanation to her. If Louise wanted to see him, she had only to act like a "grown-up" and cut away Mme de Guéméné's apron strings. She could visit him at his little house....Perhaps after that, he might even look into the possibility of resuming his social visits.

In spite of the insane risks, Louise did her best to arrange just such a rendezvous. Her most elaborate scheme involved a plan to visit her uncle on the evening of 11 April, Holy Thursday. She would arrange to go alone, without even her *femme de chambre*. She would leave early and send for a *carrosse de remise*, and as was the case when the Prince lived in St Ouen, it would be a carriage hired by Daniel; he would conduct her directly to the house on the Rue du Chemin du Rempart. If the Prince preferred, they could see each other for an hour or two in the carriage instead.

For all her planning, the scheme failed disastrously. Worse still, Mme de Guéméné was alerted, and there had been another ugly scene. Now the Princess would be watched with even greater vigilance, and spies were posted around the Prince's house. But less astonishing perhaps than the failure of that particular scheme, given the degree of surveillance Mme de Guéméné had ensured, was the Prince's reaction to it: Chrétien was instructed to let the Princess know that His Royal Highness considered the failure to be entirely her fault. The fact that Mme de Guéméné had got wind of the scheme and had dramatically foiled it by sending a carriage with Louise's maid and all of her other attendants to pick her up meant nothing to him. Why had she not simply stood her ground? Was she not her own mistress? And now Mme de Guéméné had forbidden her to go anywhere without her maid! That was not the sort of thing grown-ups accepted. By her actions, Louise had shown that she preferred to offer him an affront rather than risk the scandal of an open confrontation with her mother-in-law.[7]

It was the kind of argument the Princess was quite unable to deal with. How could he be so unjust? Why did he not simply send her a glass of poison, for her and for his child—a child that he had so often described as the pledge of his eternal love! Every means of action had been stripped from her, and yet he kept saying that she was her own mistress! She had seen him at the concert on the evening before. He had not even deigned to look at her! Her agony was such that she had fainted on the way out, and just thinking about it as she wrote made her feel ill. She would have to end her letter; she had strength enough only to add that she kissed his hands, a thousand times....

But even ten thousand kisses would not have been enough to budge the Prince. Moreover, it was not only Louise who had to be punished; other members of the Rohan clan needed a little shaking up—regrettably, even those "good People" who had arranged for the magnificent house at St Ouen where the whole business had begun. There could be no innocent bystanders in this affair!

Two members of the clan who had made especially devoted efforts to avoid becoming embroiled were the distinguished daughters of Mme de Mézières: the Princesse de Ligne and her older sister, the Princesse de Montauban, one of the Queen's ladies-in-waiting, who also happened to be the sister-in-law of Mme de Guéméné. Both women had inherited solid Jacobite sympathies from their mother and both had powerful connections at Versailles, in the Army and the Church.[8] One or the other had frequently made use of those connections on Charles Edward's behalf, and the Princesse de Ligne, in particular, had dedicated herself to advancing the Prince's interests at Court. Her good friend, the Duc de Penthièvre, was one of the *princes du sang* and very willing to divulge secret information about the peace talks and any pertinent discussions going on in the *Conseil des princes*. At her urging, early in February, he had spoken firmly to the Foreign Minister, de Puisieux, about the necessity of vigorously asserting the Prince's rights in negotiations with the British. She was delighted to be of such service and wanted nothing in return except more opportunities to prove her devotion.[9] Charles Edward clearly had a special gift for bringing out that kind of unquestioning allegiance in aristocratic French ladies. It was something he took for granted and exploited at every opportunity. It was, for example, to the Princesse de Ligne that he turned soon after the Hôtel de Guéméné blowup to find out whether people were still talking about the affair. On 10 February, he wrote her a discreet little note and invited her to a private supper to talk about "plusieurs bagatels qui ne se peuve pas mettre par Ecrit."[10] Four days later she managed to slip away from Versailles to the Prince's house. No other guests were present. They talked first of all about his latest instructions for the Duc de Penthièvre. The Prince was pleased to learn that there appeared to be no danger yet of peace being achieved, and she congratulated him for taking the trouble to call on Mme de Puisieux, the wife of the Foreign Minister. Such contacts might turn out to be very useful in the months ahead, and he was right to do everything he could to make himself *loved* in that way, *by everyone*. Of course, everyone already *admired* him!

It was at this point that the Prince brought up his "small matter of some delicacy." He was concerned, she might be surprised to learn, that exaggerated rumours regarding a silly little adventure he had had with the young Duchesse de Montbazon might be starting up, through no fault of his own, he might add. For his part, he felt it was best to ignore the whole thing and simply to go about his business. It pained him greatly of course to ask, but would his guest be so good as to tell him if she was aware of any such rumours? No stranger to scandal herself, the Princesse de Ligne was only too happy to oblige. Yes, rumours were rampant. The Rohans in fact were feeling very hurt, and, in that regard, she begged His Royal Highness not to take it amiss if she offered some sound advice. Quite simply, His Royal Highness should resume his normal social visits to save the situation. It was the only solution.

The Prince listened and grew angry. He found his friend's advice unacceptable. He told her as much.

Troubled by the blunt response, the Princesse de Ligne took her leave, but immediately on reaching her apartment at Versailles, she sat down and wrote the Prince a letter, begging his indulgence for bringing up the subject so soon again. The situation was far more serious than His Royal Highness thought: "J'ose encore lui repeté que le mesme honneur qui rand s.a.r. si discret doit la porté a faire une demarche qui est tout capable de finir les bruits qui l'afflige."[11] She and her sister (and also Mme de Guéméné, for that matter) were more than willing to do what they could to help. In fact, Mme de Montauban was hoping to give a supper and ball in the Prince's honour, on Shrove Monday, 26 February, just to demonstrate to everyone how normal everything was. All the Rohans would attend and would be glad to testify to their continued affection and loyalty. The Prince would be asked to make only one small conciliatory gesture, to do them the honour of attending. Would he please?...

The Prince, to everyone's relief, accepted. Yes, he would attend a supper, but not a ball. Delighted, Mme de Montauban immediately set about the arrangements.

Even her brother-in-law, Armand-Jules de Rohan, Archbishop of Rheims and *premier pair* of France, promised to come. The appointed day and hour arrived....Everyone waited. The hours passed. Still there was no sign of the Prince. Finally, shortly before 10 o'clock, Lord Lewis Gordon, one of the Prince's madcap *habitués*, arrived and informed the Princesse de Montauban and the august company assembled that the Prince had suffered a sudden attack of the colic at his banker's. Milord Gordon spoke nervously and, indeed, carried out his errand in such a strange way that everyone was immediately convinced the Prince's sudden malady was no more than a pretext and an additional affront to a family that had already been so mistreated in the Montbazon affair. The Princesse de Ligne waited with the others, horrified at the thought of more scandal and its potentially dangerous political consequences. Unable to bear the situation any longer, she sent a hasty note to the Prince begging him, colic or no colic, to put in a brief appearance. His absence was being interpreted by everyone as a deliberate escalation of the Montbazon business. He must not let her sister and the others imagine that to be the case.

It was past ten-thirty when the Princesse's lackey arrived at the house on the Rue du Chemin du Rempart and was admitted to the Prince's antechamber. The letter was taken in. Fully one hour later, the waiting footman was handed a note in Lally's handwriting. In it the Prince explained to the Princesse de Ligne that he had delayed her courier in the hope of recovering sufficiently to deliver a reply himself, "mais la colique dont je suis tourmenté me prive du plaisir de profiter de la bonne compagnie que je ne doute pas qui soit chez vous, et vous estes assez de mes amies pour que je vous charge de mes excuses aupres d'elle."[12]

Up to this point, the Prince's conduct toward the Princesse de Montauban and her guests, though cavalier, could be defended as acceptable, especially if his colic was genuine. Much of the difficulty had obviously stemmed from his messenger's manner of presentation and, though "Lewie Gordon" is still celebrated in Highland song, someone who required the services of a keeper was scarely the best person to send, given the circumstances.[13] Unfortunately, Colonel James Oxburgh, the aide who would normally have been charged with such an assignment, was out of town. It had been, moreover, a particularly trying day for the Prince: he had just sent off one of those disagreeably unfilial notes to his father who seemed still determined to keep open all the old wounds relating to Henry.[14] He had no wish to forgive Henry any more than he wanted to face all of those disapproving Rohans at supper, the very people who had no doubt been tittering and gossiping away for the last month at his expense.

On the very next day, the Princesse de Ligne sent another desperate note, reassuring him that her only desire was to rescue him from an intolerable situation:

L'atachement que j'ai pour votre altesse royal me donne la force de rompre un silence dont je crois que les suites pourois lui déplaire. Sa comision pour s'excusser du souper de lundi fut faite de façont que ma soeur et tous les Rohans on crut i trouver la confirmation du put de consideration quil pretendent qu'el a eu pour leurs famille dans laventur de Mme de M.... Cette idee les choquent tous vivement et la vivasité de leurs zel randerois leurs plaintes fondees, si reelement votre altesse royal n'avoit pas été forcee par une colique violente.[15]

Even before reaching that point in the Princesse's letter Charles Edward's temper flared! What right had anyone to doubt his belly ache if that is what he had said! Here, too, was graphic evidence to confirm the worst of his fears: the entire Rohan clan *had* been talking about him! The whole Montbazon business had not blown over, and what the Princesse de Ligne proposed he should do about it now made him angrier still. She begged His Royal Highness to go that very day to see Mme de Montauban, "lui parler avec la bonte qui lui est naturelle en lui marquant de la douleur davoir manquer cette partie." She also recommended that he do the same for the Archbishop of Rheims—everything, in short, to forestall "les cris d'une famille entiere qui ce croient méprisees." He was to say nothing of her letter; from that he could measure the hostility of her relatives: "Ils ne me le pardonnerois jamais, croyant estre blessé par un endrois trop sensible pour n'estre pas forcees a partager les mesmes sentimens. Si, par malheur, v.a.r. ne pouvoit pas sortir, il fauxderois qu'el eu la bonté d'écrire car il ne faut pas laisser aller ma soeur a Versailles avec l'idé qu'el a manqué cette partie sans raisons forcées."[16]

It would, in fact, have been difficult for Charles Edward Stuart to choose as the object of a deliberate affront a noble family of the Ancien Régime made up of a more politically influential collection of princes, cardinals, generals, and archbishops. Aside from the Bouillons themselves, it would also have been difficult for him to choose to insult a family better disposed toward him personally or that had tried to do more for his cause. In return for such devotion, as if answering the call of some twisted internal logic, he now set about doing his best to offend them even more. Filled with a sense of his many imagined injuries, he increasingly saw it as important to keep people "dans leurs torts." That was his way of coping with failure, and he would eventually turn it into a whole way of life. This time his reaction to the Princesse de Ligne's letter came quickly: No, he would not call on the Princesse de Montauban, nor the Archbishop of Rheims! He would not write either. In fact, politic or not, he would not even honour the Princesse de Ligne's plea with an answer.

Twice rebuffed, de Ligne might well have decided at this point to let her hero go to the devil, but with all the fortitude of a martyr she continued her work of salvation, and after two days had passed without an answer, she once more sent her lackey to the house on the outskirts of Paris, this time with a brief note of apology. She beseeched the Prince to forgive her if she had displeased him:

> Le silence de votre altesse royal me fait crindre que l'avis et le conseil que mon zel ma forcés a lui donné sur l'aifait du soupé manqué de lundi n'ait pas reusit aupres d'elle. Mon intention ne serois jamais de lui en donné aucune preuve qui puissent lui déplaire. Je la suplie de me mandé si j'ai eu ce malheur et de vousloir bien m'en garder le segret aupres de ma famille et de messieurs de Rohan d'un avis que mon respectueux attachement a put seul m'inspirée.[17]

Again there was no reply.

That was the state of affairs when de Ligne worriedly summarized events of the preceding week for James Oxburgh, a respected member of the Prince's household who was assigned to share some of George Kelly's duties. What was she to do? The matter had to be settled before she and her sister returned to their official functions at Versailles. "Eclairsisé moy s'il est possible," she pleaded with Oxburgh, "les raisons qui l'occasionne et la conduite et les propos que je doit tenir en consequence. Jusqu'a present nous nous sommes tenu, ma soeur et moy, dans le plus grand silence."[18] Her main concern was that the distinguished personages whom she had influenced favourably on behalf of the Prince's political interests might get wind of the difficulties. Would Oxburgh please advise her on how to behave and tell her the reasons for the Prince's attitude towards them: "Venes me dictée ma conduite;...J'eviterai jusqu'as que j'ait cette explication les conversations particulier sur son conte. Sil croit avoir des raisons pour rompre avec nous et pour ne nous les pas comuniquer il put tous jour estre persuader du respect profond dont mes reponses serons accompagné."

The Princesse de Ligne's letter was received by Oxburgh (and obviously the Prince) on Saturday, 2 March. No reply came on Sunday. On Monday she and her sister had to return to Versailles, but by 5 o'clock in the morning she was already up, composing another short note for Oxburgh. In it she expressed her fear that all of her zeal and eloquence might be insufficient to defend the Prince's strange behaviour. It would help enormously if she were given reasons to bolster her arguments. "Je suis bien affligé," she concluded, "des soins qu'il me parois prendre pour eloigné de lui tous ceux qui lui etoit le plus veritablement attaché."[19]

It is perhaps not surprising that de Ligne's pleading letters went unanswered. Their beseeching tone no doubt reminded the Prince too much of Louise's outpourings. But such, certainly, was not a failing of another brief and direct note sent to Colonel Oxburgh only a few days later by Mme de Guéméné herself requesting an immediate meeting. Since few examples of that formidable matriarch's correspondence seem to have survived, it is interesting to catch even a brief echo of the "epistolary voice" of the woman who managed to strike so much terror in the heart of her daughter-in-law and so much loathing on the part of Charles Edward Stuart. Why she felt impelled to get involved further at this point is not clear. No doubt her chief concern was to protect her son's honour and, consequently, her daughter-in-law's reputation. In five months, the child would be born, and it was of vital importance that the Prince do whatever was necessary to offset rumours now made even worse as a result of his most recent display of bad manners:

Ce 7 mars 1748

Je ne me rebute point, Monsieur, vous en serée peut être etonnée, mais vous ne le serée pas par la conversation que je veut avoir avec vous. Je vous prie que cela soit aujourduy. Cela presse et je vous prie de vouloir bien ny pas manquer. Faites moi reponse et soiée persuadée, Monsieur, que personne ne vous honore plus parfaittement que moi.

De Rohan, princesse de Guemene[20]

Mme de Guéméné's tone is in remarkably sharp contrast with that of the Princesse de Ligne, and Oxburgh must have shown her letter to Charles Edward with some hesitation, for the lady obviously meant business. But in the end, the Prince found Mme de Guéméné no more difficult to ignore than the others. Louise's mother-in-law had at last found her match, and the day was not far off when the two of them would clash publicly in an undignified and noisy quarrel. Her letter nevertheless confirms what we already know about the woman who, in the absence of her interdicted husband, ruled the Guéméné household with an iron hand. A few weeks later, after being caught trying to sneak off one night to the Prince's house, Louise would describe her as being "dans une fureur *horrible*."[21] The unfortunate Princess was obviously no more a match for Jules's mother than she was for the taunting barbs of the Prince who constantly accused her of lacking sufficient spirit and maturity to shake off her mother-in-law's leading-strings.

As for the Princesse de Montauban and the other Rohans, the situation did not change. Charles Edward's door remained closed to them, a fact that old Mme de Mézières complained about sorrowfully in a letter to the Prince written one month later. From her tenderest years, de Mézières had maintained a loyal, if somewhat fractious, commitment to the Stuarts, first to James and now to Charles Edward. Her family and her friends had always extended their unstinting support. She, as much as anyone else, had engineered events leading to the '45. Why then was he rejecting their friendship? "Pour coy," she asked (in a letter whose orthographical peculiarities equalled the Prince's best!), "votre porte metell fermee? Quege fet, permetez moy de vous le demander avec tout le respect qui vous est due? Cette fasons en bon Frances sapeille cheter ses vres amis par les fenetres pour amusement. C'est bien triste pour ceux qui pance comme moy."[22] Mme de Mézières had indeed been a special friend to Charles Edward, but nothing could compare to the intense devotion of her daughter, the Princesse de Ligne, who, despite repeated rejections, continued her fruitless conciliatory efforts to the bitter end. The eventual political costs to the Prince of her failure remain to be calculated.

The fact that Charles Edward seemed determined to cast aside his many staunch friends among the Bouillon and Rohan families did not mean, of course, that he had decided to abandon social activities in the capital altogether. Quite to the contrary, he now went about seeking public visibility more aggressively than ever, believing no doubt that it would put even greater distance between him and the Montbazon scandal and add as well to his bargaining strength at the inevitable peace conference. In March, Barbier noted the Young Pretender's increased attendance at the Opéra. By then, his daily appearance in the Tuileries had also become a public event, drawing crowds of admiring spectators anxious to catch a glimpse of the strikingly handsome figure striding along with his retinue of Highlanders, wearing the splendid new fur hat and large white plume that Daniel had purchased on his orders on St Valentine's Day.[23] Fashionable new hats were also ordered for his footmen,[24] and it was perhaps to enhance the Prince's dashing appearance during the Tuileries *promenades*, that Daniel was instructed on 3 March to purchase for his master no fewer than seven pairs of shoes.[25]

On March 9th, Balhaldy complained ironically of Charles Edward's new "image" in a partially encyphered letter to Edgar: "We have now given up all thought of business; even our favourite project [of declaring Protestant] is no more Spoke of; nor that [of a Protestant] mariage. We have no thoughts to mention of any kind but money. Our whole time is Swallowed up in a round of pleasure and could we be recovered out of this lethargick disease, we are assured that no discreet man [will have anything to do with us]."[26] Balhaldy noted too that there was a heavy cloud of suspicion hanging over the Prince's house. He had been obliged, for example, to hide the fact of his having gone to Versailles on private business, out of fear that Kelly or Lally, or the Prince himself, would imagine he was meddling with the Court—a Court which seemed to look upon all members of the Prince's household with a severely evil eye.

Balhaldy's observations were not far off the mark for the Prince had now given up on Versailles and begun to base his hopes on the Opéra. If there was a peace, he calculated, his chances of staying on in France would surely depend more on his huge public following in Paris than on anything else. Even his attendance at mass now seemed more a social than a religious occasion. D. Flyn reported to Edgar, for example, that on St Patrick's Day, the Prince, "with a great number of people of quality, assisted...at a sermon preached at ye Colledge of Lombard by the Curé of St Benoist."[27] It was a stirring sermon and contained a lengthy compliment to His Royal Highness. Admittedly, the feast day had fallen on a Sunday, but the contrast with the Prince's more private activities on St Andrew's Day, only a little over three months before, is probably worth noting.

It is unlikely that any of the Prince's old Bouillon or Rohan friends were among the great number of "people of quality" who helped him honour the Irish on March 17th. But now there were other friends. The Duc and Duchesse d'Aiguillon had become especially close, and, most important of all, the Prince, probably in April 1748, made a new conquest and acquired his first *public* mistress, the Princesse de Talmont.

The story of Charles Edward's stormy romance with the forty-seven-year-old Polish princess, a cousin of the Queen of France (as well as, more distantly, of Louise and the Prince himself) must be left for another time.[28] She was a woman of legendary beauty and wit, equally fluent in Polish and French. Her father, Jean-Stanislas Jablonowski (1669-1731) was Palatin de Russie (Ruthenia) and an uncle of King Stanislas Leszczynski. Her mother, whom we have already met in Lvov (Leopold),[29] died there in 1744. Young Marie-Louise Jablonowska had a younger, less attractive sister, Catherine-Dorothée, who married the exiled Polish King's *grand maître*, François-Maximilien, Comte de Tenczyn Ossolinski in 1732, but soon became, with the richly subsidized blessing of her aging husband, the mistress of Stanislas himself. Playing mistress to Stanislas had actually been one of Marie-Louise's own roles when, as Princesse Palatine de Russie, she had gone to live at Chambord in 1727 where the exiled father-in-law of Louis XV had taken up his official residence two years before. There, she became as well the public mistress of a handsome and dashing young officer, Charles-François-Marie de Custine, the celebrated Chevalier de Wiltz. Stanislas generously took it upon himself to find a suitable match for Marie-Louise, but her situation had become so notorious that one initially interested suitor, Louis-Henri de Bourbon, M. Le Duc himself, soon lost interest. Louis XV's father-in-law next tried to marry her off to the Comte d'Evreux, but again the lady's reputation cost her a golden opportunity. Less brilliant success came at last when the King of Poland's choice fell on Anne-Charles-Frédéric de la Trémoïlle, Comte de Taillebourg, the son of Frédéric-Guillaume, Prince de Talmont. At nineteen, Anne-Charles-Frédéric was ten years younger than the experienced Marie-Louise, and his family hesitated, but with the help of a generous dowry from Stanislas and a persuasive ducal title thrown into the bargain by the King of France, the marriage took place on 29 October 1730. Unfortunately for the tranquillity of the husband (whose tastes in later years seem to have run more to young men and extremely austere devotional exercises),[30] the new Duchesse de Châtellrault made not even a token effort to live up to her marriage vows. Her liaison with the gallant Chevalier de Wiltz continued without interruption as did, for a time, her affair with Stanislas. At the end of the War of Polish Succession, Talmont was enticed back to her cousin's new court in Lorraine where the Chevalier, now colonel of the Royal Pologne regiment, was appointed Stanislas's *grand écuyer* in 1737. He died of a leg injury in 1738, and his regiment was passed on at no cost to Marie-Louise's husband.[31] In 1739, on the death of Anne-Charles-Frédéric's father, the Châtellraults assumed the title of Prince and Princesse de Talmont. A son, appropriately named Louis-Stanislas, Comte de Taillebourg, was born in 1734. He was fourteen years of age when the liaison between his mother and Prince Charles Edward Stuart began, and he died the following year, on 17 September 1749, of smallpox. That event, along with his mother's tempestuous liaison with the Young Pretender, seems to have put an effective end to the Talmont marriage.[32]

Such then was the new paramour who replaced Louise in the heart of Charles Edward Stuart. She too was an admired beauty but there the resemblance stopped. The Prince's first mistress took no pride in wilful complexity; the Princesse de Talmont, on the contrary, was cerebral, articulate, and poised. Her wit and her mastery of the French language were such that even Voltaire felt obliged to celebrate her talents in one of his short verse portraits:

> Les dieux en lui donnant naissance
> Aux lieux par la Saxe envahis,
> Lui donnèrent pour récompense
> Le goût qu'on ne trouve qu'en France,
> Et l'esprit de tous les pays.[33]

In his fragments on the Abbé de Saint-Pierre, J-J. Rousseau also attests to the reputation of this formidable Princesse, "qui pensoit peu et parloit bien," when he records Saint-Pierre's admiring comment on hearing Mme de Talmont speak with great brilliance on a purely frivolous subject: "Que cette femme ne dit-elle ce que je pense!"[34] The Abbé de Saint-Pierre was, of course, praising style and regretting at the same time a lack of substance, a point emphasized again by the perspicacious *salonnière*, Mme du Deffand, in what was no doubt a perfidiously faithful portrait of the Polish princess:

> Madame de Talmont a de la beauté et de l'esprit; elle a une intelligence vive, et ce tour de plaisanterie qui est le partage de notre nation paraît lui être naturel. Elle conçoit si promptement les idées des autres, que l'on y est souvent attrapé, et qu'on lui fait l'honneur de croire qu'elle a produit ce qu'elle n'a fait qu'entendre....Elle se croit parfaite: elle le dit, et elle veut qu'on la croie. Ce n'est qu'à ce prix qu'on peut jouir de l'apparence de son amitié: je dis apparence, car elle n'a aucuns sentiments qui puissent s'épancher sur les autres: ils sont tous renfermés en elle-même. Elle voudrait cependant être aimée; mais sa vanité seule l'exige, son coeur ne demande rien.

The Princesse, Mme du Deffand continued, was as temperamental and capricious as she was vain. Above all, she scorned convention, and it was probably that lack of respect for the social norms that most attracted the Prince to her. His new mistress did not worry about what mothers-in-law or husbands thought! In her scheme of things, others counted for little. The world was a mad freakish place in which dullness deserved only to be ignored or crushed:

> L'heure de sa toilette, de ses repas, de ses visites, tout est marqué au coin de la bizarrerie et du caprice. Sans déférence pour ceux qui lui sont supérieurs, sans égard ni politesse pour ses égaux, sans douceur et sans humanité pour ses domestiques, elle est crainte et haïe de tous ceux qui sont forcés de vivre avec elle. Il n'en est pas de même de ceux qui ne la voient qu'en passant, et surtout des hommes. L'agrément de sa figure, la coquetterie qu'elle a dans les manières, la noblesse et le tour de ses expressions séduisent beaucoup de gens; mais les impressions qu'elle fait ne sont pas durables; son humeur avertit promptement du danger qu'il y aurait de s'attacher sérieusement à elle.

Perhaps it was the Prince's own sense of exhilarating danger that drew him to the older woman. But Mme de Talmont also had the virtues of her vices, and Mme du Deffand concludes her portrait of the Princess's good and bad qualities on an appropriately ambivalent note:

> Cependant parmi tant de défauts elle a de grandes qualités: beaucoup de vérité, de la hauteur et de la noblesse d'âme, du courage dans l'esprit, de la probité; enfin c'est un mélange de tant de bien et de tant de mal, que l'on ne saurait avoir pour elle aucun sentiment décidé: elle plaît, elle choque, on l'aime, on la hait, on la cherche, on l'évite. On dirait qu'elle communique aux autres la bizarrerie de son caractère.[35]

It was no doubt a great source of stimulation to Charles Edward to find himself suddenly caught up in the fast-moving, stylish world of such a dazzling creature! As February turned to March and March to April, he had grown bored with Louise's constant litany of woe. It is true that he had still not got her completely out of his system: his passion had run too deep for that to happen so easily, but he was careful to avoid giving out any signs of encouragement. Louise, on the other hand, was at a complete loss after the failure of her attempt to see the Prince on 11 April. Her only hope now was to see him at St Ouen after 20 May when Mme de Guémené was supposed to leave (Jules having already left for the Army by mid-March). At St Ouen it would be easy; it would be like old times....

Predictably, Louise's repeated attempts to elicit a response to her St Ouen proposal were ignored. If not St Ouen, she implored, would he at least see her at Versailles? If neither the one nor the other, then she would have no choice but to take poison. She would die, and he would be satisfied at last. Her only regret was that her death would be of no use in furthering his cause. Three months had gone by since their last night together. What happy moments they had enjoyed! Had he forgotten them? She still wore his lock of hair next to her heart, day and night. She still gazed adoringly for hours on end at his portrait. The very thought of seeing him at St Ouen during the summer brought back such a flood of happy memories. Was he being faithful? Her Prince must not take another! She had, it is true, thought herself capable of that sacrifice right after 23 January but she now was unable even to bear the thought of sharing. She begged him to remain faithful until they could meet again.

But what if it had already happened? Perhaps the Prince had already taken up with someone else? Yes, she confided to Daniel, she was certain of it now! Someone else had replaced her in the Prince's heart. She reminded the valet that he had promised to tell her if that happened. She poured her heart out to him. Talking to Daniel consoled her a little for not being able to talk to his master. With Easter gone and the Opera season again open, she had several times attended just to see the Prince. Each time he had averted his eyes. She had wept. She had not wanted to, but she had been unable to hold back her tears. She felt like killing herself. Daniel must tell the Prince.

Louise's tragedy continued. On Saturday 27 April she sent her usual note to the Prince.[36] Like so many before, it told him that he could not possibly imagine how much she adored him. She wanted him to know that she would be going to the Opéra again on the following day, *just to see him*: "De grace," she pleaded, "regardée moi avec ces yeux que j'adore."

Was it because of that special plea that the Prince decided, perversely, to show up at the Opéra the next day with his new mistress? It was their first time there together. Perhaps the older woman had recommended it as a way of curing once and for all that snivelling love-sick ninny of a girl who persisted in writing such hilariously pathetic letters. Perhaps she had even insisted on this deliberate humiliation of a former rival, exacting it as a token of her lover's commitment. Whatever the explanation, the effect on Louise was devastating.

For Charles Edward, going to the Opéra was like ruling over a fantasy kingdom. This was his territory, his fortress of safety and adulation! When he and his beautiful companion appeared in the royal box that commanded a sweeping view of the entire theatre, his thirteen hundred subjects rose to their feet, applauded and cheered. That was how heroes were welcomed. The Prince graciously took his bows. He was used to the public's little ritual by now, and he enjoyed it. Led on by a dozen or so members of his own household in the pit, the spectators continued to applaud wildly. *They* at least had not forgotten him, even if Louis XV's ministerial lackeys, obsequiously negotiating with the Duke of Hanover's envoys at Aix-la-Chapelle, were preparing to drive him out of the country!

On that day, at least one person in the audience did not applaud. She had probably wanted to but found herself too stricken with grief....Sitting in a box opposite, Louise was suddenly confronted with the proof of what she already knew instinctively, even though Daniel had told her nothing. *The Prince now had someone else.* Just by looking at him and his companion, she sensed their complicity and knew they were lovers. How she wished that she did not care, that she could tear herself away completely from him! She knew she would be happy if only she could manage that, but it was quite beyond her. She loved him to the point of helpless adoration. She was certain, too, that Mme de Talmont could not possibly love her *Cher Roi* as much; if she did, she would not be sitting there looking so radiantly well. Louise fought back her tears. She would at least deny them the satisfaction of seeing her totally destroyed. She had just time enough to reach an exit. Then the flood of anguish had begun. It had not stopped since.

All this Louise confided in a plaintive letter to Daniel. Yes, he must give her news of the Prince; it was her only consolation. No doubt she would soon die; for her it was an easy solution, but she feared for her child. Was it true that the Prince would have to leave France in a little while? Daniel would have to tell her the truth! The very thought made her deathly ill. Daniel must throw himself at the Prince's feet and plead for her. Would he like to hear about her newest scheme? It was foolproof! She would be able to visit the Prince in perfect safety in about two weeks, *at his house*. It was what the Prince had always demanded. He had only to give his consent, and she would see to the rest.

And so events continued into May with Louise becoming more and more frantic, not only about her rival but also regarding the possibility that her *Cher Roi* would have to leave the country. He simply had to agree to see her, at his house, around the 20th when everyone would be gone. It might be his last sight of her alive. Was it true, as everyone was saying, that he would not be allowed to stay?

Without realizing it, Louise, by insisting on this last point, may have stumbled onto the only certain means of obtaining, finally, the Prince's agreement to a meeting. She had managed it not by appealing to his love, his guilt, or his gratitude, but rather by accidentally goading his sense of vanity. Everyone was indeed talking about his *having* to leave because of the peace talks, and it infuriated him. Even James kept harping on the subject. He, for his part, was not at all certain he was going to leave! He certainly had no intention of allowing himself to be driven out. Had everyone forgotten the Treaty of Fontainebleau? He had his rights, and he intended to defend them to the end.

Apart from a defiant need to set Louise straight on the question of his rights, the Prince had another reason for agreeing to a meeting. The proposed rendezvous was, after all, to take place *at his house* and thus constituted that symbolic victory he had long been seeking over those members of the Bouillon and Rohan tribe who had presumed to give him lessons in good manners! Perhaps his gesture even represented a genuine act of love, an expression of sympathy for the plight of his former mistress and concern for the physical safety of his child. But whatever the explanation, his affirmative response, relayed in mid-May by Daniel, filled the Princess with joy. At last she would be able to prove to him how false all the malicious accusations he had heard about her really were! It would be her first moment of happiness in four months. How she looked forward to it! He would have to retire early that night so they could have more time together. He could rest assured that even his dear child would profit from her rejoicings when they finally met.[37]

The rendezvous was set for Saturday, 18 May, but at the last minute a change in plan had to be made. Mme de Guémené, apparently still in Paris and more vigilant than ever, had again posted spies around the Prince's house. It was thus not possible for Louise to go to the Rue du Chemin du Rempart after all. She would go instead to the nearby Pont Tournant at midnight, absolutely alone. It would be perfectly safe. She would finally meet her Prince (he was to bundle up in his great redingote, just as he used to at St Ouen). Daniel would take care of the *carrosse de remise*. She and the Prince would be able to see each other at leisure and without any danger....

Louise's next note[38] was written very early on Sunday morning. She was now safely back in her bedroom after seeing her lover for the first time in four months! Her excitement was such that she could scarcely write, but Daniel would tell her dear Prince what had happened when she and the valet had arrived back at the Place Royale. They had had a very narrow escape but nothing mattered now! A new era had dawned. Everything would be as before. She and her *Cher Roi* were once more inseparable lovers. They had talked about the press reports which hinted at his having to leave France the moment the preliminaries signed on 30 April were ratified. The Prince had thrilled her by solemnly swearing that he would no more abandon *her* than he would his rights. She needed no more assurance than that. His last words in the street as she drove off with Daniel had been that he would write *every day*. Again, she could ask for nothing better! Her excitement was almost too much: she had tried to sleep but all she could think of was how happy she was. She couldn't stop kissing her hands! She recalled how they had touched him....

As Louise reviewed in her mind the events of her meeting with the Prince in the carriage at the Pont Tournant, she remembered other things as well....Some of these, it was true, made her less happy. He had told her that he loved her still, but "not as much as before." He had spoken of his desire to take another. She would not be able to survive that now! She had urged the Prince to look at her portrait often and to see less of the Princesse de Talmont. He must not forget her. She would remain faithful to him as long as she lived. They had also talked about the possibility of seeing each other in St Ouen that summer. Why had the Prince hesitated? No doubt she had assured him that the Montaubans and the other offended members of the Rohan family would be more than willing to patch up their differences with him. It would all work out. The important thing was that they were back together again.

On Tuesday, 21 May, Louise waited for the first of the Prince's promised letters to arrive. Nothing came. It was a harsh blow, but she was consoled at least by the fact that one of Mme de Guéméné's spies had just been won over and had agreed to warn her in future when it was safe to visit. It would be easy now to arrange for more of those two-hour meetings in a hired carriage, and they could do all the joyous things they had done on the previous occasion. She would be able to give him as much of his *petit plaisir* as he desired....She had heard that de Puisieux had written and she was worried sick. She was desperate too at the thought of the Princesse de Talmont. It was Tuesday, an Opéra day again, and she knew that the Prince would be spending the afternoon with her rival. She was afraid, even though on Saturday he had told her that there was nothing to it, that he still loved his own little Louise *à la folie*. *A la folie*: those were his very words! Oh, he would have to repeat them to her again and again and tell her also that he would not be leaving.

Viewed from almost any angle, the Prince's behaviour on the night of 18 May seems difficult to explain. Despite his previous anger and disaffection, he had been strangely warm and confiding at the Pont Tournant. Louise had received many reassuring promises. He had told her that he would write every day, that he would not abandon her, that he loved her madly (though a little less than before, it is true), and that there was nothing much going on between himself and the Princesse de Talmont. In fact, all that turned out to be false. He very soon thought better of writing every day and even of writing at all, although he did send one or two brief notes. Typically, however, he used those occasions to accuse her of ingratitude and to tell her he did not want to love her any more because of her horrible relatives and the fact that she still clung so childishly to her parental apron strings. That was hardly love *à la folie*! As for his leaving, he did not inform her that he was already actively committed to finding a Protestant bride and had made preparations to take off for Lorraine or anywhere else at a moment's notice as soon as his agent, Sir John Graeme, turned up someone suitable. Finally, it was not true that nothing was going on between him and the Princesse de Talmont. That they were lovers was already old news by 20 May when, for example, Monsignor Durini, the all-seeing Papal Nuncio, wrote discreetly to Cardinal Valenti on the subject.[39] Indeed, on the very Wednesday that Charles Edward wrote to Louise (22 May),[40] he had arranged for the delivery to his new mistress of a beautifully trimmed jacket purchased for 240 livres at the Lyon d'Or on the rue Saint Honoré. It was not a terribly expensive gift, costing only slightly more than what he had paid for putting eight of his horses out to grass, but it was the thought that counted.[41]

Still we remain puzzled: although the Prince warned Louise that he now loved her less and that he felt an inclination to take another mistress, those reservations were outweighed by his reassuring promises. By how much was his love diminished if it still remained *à la folie*? Why did he promise *never* to abandon her? Why, too, did he agree to continue their meetings and to write every day? Was it a short-lived effect of their *petits plaisirs*? A bit of soft soap to silence her entreaties? In any case, the Prince was soon back to complaining that Louise was still "immature," still incapable of open rebellion against Mme de Guémené, and still unwilling, in short, to choose total ruin to satisfy his whims. Her prudence and her deference to parental authority remained, as before, an important stumbling block, and the last two or three letters of the correspondence, before it suddenly ended, echo his persistent sarcasms regarding Louise's *enfances*, her *leading-strings*, and her relatives. When it finally proved impossible to meet at his house, the Prince rejected her appeal for a repeat performance in a *carrosse de remise*. If she was to prove her love, her only choice was to court extreme danger. Taunted once too often, she complied, bringing the entire affair to a sudden and catastrophic end.

In fact, Charles Edward may well have miscalculated by underestimating the determination of his mistress. Louise, in the end, was prepared to do anything and to give up everything to follow him—if only he had some place to take her! Her last letter, probably written on Wednesday, 29 May, acknowledged his final message, sent via Daniel, informing her that he would no longer meet with her in a carriage. That being the case, no matter what the dangers, she was resolved to do the impossible and to visit him regularly at his house. She would prove to him that she cared only for him and that she was not just a child, afraid of taking risks. In two month's time, their child would be born; she might die in the process....But it did not matter anymore. Life without him was not worth living.

The correspondence ends at that point. By now Louise knew, even if Charles Edward still did not, that Mme de Guémené was deadly serious. She knew, for example, that there was every probability that she would be caught one night on her way to the Prince's house and conducted back to the Place Royale, there to be confined to her quarters during the remaining weeks of her pregnancy and longer still if it proved necessary. Mme de Guémené had no need to worry about gossip in that regard: the "confinement" of an expectant mother at Louise's stage of pregnancy would have sounded plausible enough. D'Argenson's puzzling reference to a "ridiculous" public scene that took place sometime in June[42] between Mme de Guémené and Charles Edward Stuart probably hints at the rest of the story. Perhaps it is not even puzzling that the erstwhile foreign minister mistook their vociferous confrontation for a lover's quarrel: one juicy rumour, Mme de Guémené might well have reasoned, was as good as another! The story of an older "unattached" princess unashamedly throwing herself at the hand-some Prince (Mme de Guéméné was three years younger and every bit as "distinguished" as the Princesse de Talmont) was perhaps even more plausible than the truth of the matter, and what better way could she have hit upon to throw the gossips off the scent? In fact, after her open quarrel with the Prince, the rumour could easily have got started on its own. Either way, the honour of her son was protected and that was all that mattered to her.

Perhaps the spontaneously muddied or even deliberately manipulated events that lay behind d'Argenson's story help to explain the Prince's subsequent complaints in his autobiographical fiction about false representations. A rumour to the effect that he *and Mme de Guéméné* had had a lover's quarrel would have angered and revolted him, for he hated Louise's mother-in-law with a passion. But given the circumstances, it would have been a difficult move for him to counter. He could hardly go around earnestly denying that the Princesse de Guéméné had thrown herself at him, offering instead the correction that no, it was her daughter-in-law, soon to give birth to his child! For Mme de Guéméné's scheme to work, only the quarrel had to be real, and of its reality we can be absolutely certain. We can be certain too, from d'Argenson's choice of words, that it was also very noisy and public: "Le Prince Edouard," he noted, "s'amuse à faire l'amour, Mme de Guéméné l'a presque pris à force; ils se sont brouillés par *une scène ridicule*, il vit avec la Princesse de Talmond."[43] By *une scène ridicule* we must understand a fairly violent altercation in front of witnesses, though scarcely the equivalent, one hopes, of another "histoire ridicule," described by d'Argenson on the very same day, involving the Prince de Conti and his mistress, Mme d'Arty, which culminated in an exchange of blows, hair pulling, and near defenestration of the lady!

As tasteless, brawling, and unpleasant as it must have been, Mme de Guéméné's final encounter with Charles Edward at least had the advantage of clearing the air. It freed him to get on with more important matters and to these he now turned his attention.

Apart from the emotional trauma related to his fast-fading affair with Louise, Charles Edward had two great gnawing concerns in the early spring of 1748. He was uneasy, first of all, about the outcome of the peace talks at Aix-la-Chapelle. After so many years of alternating stalemate and heroic butchery, the War of Austrian Succession was threatening to come to an end. Talk of peace was like a death knell for the Prince. While there was war, there was hope, hope that the French would again attempt something to further Jacobite dreams. He knew too that one of the first conditions the British would insist on in any peace treaty was his expulsion from France.

But if the fact of his having to leave was not in doubt, the location of his next place of retreat certainly was. He had not the faintest idea where he would go, except that he knew he would never return to Rome, not even for a visit. He also knew that Rome was precisely where the British would insist on sending him—"that young Italian," as they liked to refer to him in their official diplomatic protests.

The Prince thought often about the problem, but he did not view it as a matter of great urgency. More critical was his second concern, namely, how to go about finding a suitable, that is, *Protestant*, wife. Marriage to a Protestant, he was convinced, would go a long way toward repairing the damage caused by Henry's treachery. It would also have a more immediate advantage. Since, in all likelihood, his Protestant princess would have to be from east of the Rhine, marriage would provide him at the same time with a safe and honourable retreat in one of the many little German states, should an "outbreak of peace" make that necessary.

The Prince had been thinking about the possibility of finding a Protestant bride for some time, but it was only after his January catharsis that he began to take serious steps in that direction. After allowing himself a week or two to convalesce emotionally, he sent off in mid-February a highly confidential letter to Sir John Graeme in Avignon, inviting him to come to Paris for an important mission. Graeme replied on 26 February,[44] agreeing to come, but he cautioned that some method had to be found to prevent James from taking umbrage. The Old Pretender had renewed Sir John's pension the previous summer only on the condition that he not become a member of Charles Edward's household. Finally, after the appropriate ostensible letters had been exchanged for James's benefit,[45] Graeme turned up in Paris on 1 April, ready to offer his services.

The Prince lost no time in telling him his plans and again impressed upon him the need for absolute secrecy. Not even Kelly or Oxburgh were to know what was going on. On 4 April, he dictated formal instructions to his envoy, who finally understood the reason for all the hush-hush. He was being sent on a major diplomatic mission to the Court of Prussia to propose a marriage between Charles Edward and the King's sister and to hold out the possibility, as well, of an informal political alliance with Frederick himself. The Prince's directives were concise and to the point: Sir John would go incognito to Berlin, where he would wait until he hit upon some discreet means of informing the King through one of his ministers of his presence in the city. If Frederick agreed to see him, Charles Edward's emissary was immediately to convey (and to repeat at each succeeding royal audience) his master's sense of Frederick's "eminent Qualitys and distinguish'd merit, the great confidence we have in him and our ambition to make ourselves known to him and to concur with him in every step that may be for our common interest."[46]

After a generous dose of such pleasantries, Sir John was to get down to business. Not surprisingly, Charles Edward's first thought related to Henry:

You are to acquaint His Majesty that upon the late step the Duke our brother has made, our friends in Great Britain very pressing with us to marry without loss of time, and that they desire nothing so much in the world as our marriage with the Princess his sister, representing how agreeable that alliance would be to our own Inclinations, and how much it would strengthen our Party at home and facilitate our return thither.

Should the King of Prussia reject our marriage with his Sister, you are to tell him our resolution of marrying none but a protestant Princess, and that since we cannot have the satisfaction of being so nearly allyed to him as we most earnestly wish, we flatter ourselves he will chuse for us and facilitate our making a proper match, we being thoroughly convinced of all the advantages which must ensue not only for Great Britain and Prussia but for the general tranquillity of Europe from a strict friendship betwixt His Majesty and us.

In other instructions, Charles Edward did not bother to hide his growing sense of disaffection with France. Sir John could let it be known that the Prince's friends no longer trusted in promises of the Court of France since it had neglected "so many fair occasions of assisting us." His friends regretted too that Frederick had not been part of any earlier attempts launched in favour of the Stuarts, "so great is the opinion which all true and sensible Englishmen have of His Majesty's Integrity and Shining Qualitys."

Finally, Sir John was to bring up the matter of the Prince's future place of residence: "You are to do your endeavours to engage the King of Prussia to give us a Retreat in his Dominions in case we should upon a peace be forced to leave France." In return, the Prince was prepared to give assurance that if, with Frederick's protection, he succeeded in finally recovering the crown of Great Britain, there was nothing he would not be ready to do "to obtain from a free Parliament all encouragement for his shipping and commerce and the guarantee of his Possessions." Graeme was also to point out, if the subject arose in his discussions with the King, that Charles Edward had not accepted any money from France and even that he had not touched any of his father's money since leaving Rome. "Should he enquire," the Prince continued, "if we receive any Remittances from Britain or what other way we have of subsisting, you may tell him that we live decently, but that our Fund is a secret which we trust to nobody about us."

In his instructions to Graeme, Charles Edward spoke on 4 April of the possibility of his being "forced to leave France," but he obviously did not think such an event likely. Indeed, he was highly sceptical of the possibility of a peace treaty being signed at all. On 15 April, he informed James that he saw "no Likelyhoud of Peace just now."[47] By 6 May, after the great French victory at Maestricht, the Prince noted that "people talke now of Pease again," but he doubted that it could be "Composed so soon."[48] Even as late as 3 June, with preliminaries long since signed, he remained optimistic: "The Peace thô Concluded *id est* ye Preliminarys between France, Holand and England, seems to be much aflote, but iff even they shou'd prove to fix at present, it wou'd be little Lasting, in all appearence."[49] His fervent hope was that the "politicians" would fail, and in a letter to Edgar, he compared them to an "Assembly of Fisitians disputing on a desperate Case, which generally ends in a Glister."[50] Such being the case, if Frederick proved unhelpful, there would be plenty of time to consider other marriage alternatives.

Sir John left for Berlin during the first week of May. As he waited for a report on the success of Graeme's mission, Charles Edward carefully reviewed his options. Peace might come after all, but would he necessarily be asked to leave? If asked to leave, would he necessarily go? As time passed, the notion of resisting any such pressure began to attract him more and more. No doubt his clever new mistress (unlike Louise, she knew *all* about politics!) had given him the benefit of her advice. It is unlikely, however, that the Prince would have needed Mme de Talmont's help. The more he heard people gossiping matter-of-factly about his having to leave, the more stubborn he became about staying. Much, of course, depended on the outcome of Sir John's mission, but by the time Maestricht had surrendered, the Prince was already beginning to draw up plans for a campaign of resistance. With the help of Kelly and Lally, he sketched out a formal protest against an eventual peace treaty. The King of France would not be allowed to escape the sacred responsibilities spelled out, in black and white, in the Treaty of Fontainebleau of October 1745. He would have to study its clauses carefully. Five days after Maestricht's surrender, Charles Edward wrote to Lally asking him to return the copy of the "Trety" in O'Brien's hand that Lally had borrowed.[51] Depending on how things went with Sir John, that piece of paper might have great importance in the months to come.

On 6 June, Charles Edward received Graeme's first report in the form of a partly encyphered letter, posted in Frankfurt five days earlier.[52] The mission had been a total failure. The only kindness Frederick had shown Charles Edward's envoy had been his forbearance in not placing him under immediate arrest! In fact, the Prussian King had refused to see him and sent word that Graeme was to leave his kingdom without a moment's delay.

Frederick, it seems, had just contracted a new friendship with the Elector of Hanover and did not wish to jeopardize it in any way. Graeme, knowing the impetuosity of his young master, counselled patience. It was especially important to remain on good terms with the French. It was simply not a good time to be looking around for a bride in Germany. The Brandenburgs would not dare take a step without Frederick's approval, nor would members of the House of Saxony without the blessing of the King of Poland. Those from the House of Denmark were either governed by a King who was Charles Edward's bitter enemy or dependent on some other hostile prince. Nearly every Protestant prince in Germany was obligated in one way or another to the Elector of Hanover. All thoughts of marriage should be put aside for the time being for there were more serious problems to think about: "This point of a [retreat for you] is at present of greater and of more immediate consequence than that of [your marriage]. [The Prince] is just now like a Bird upon a branch going to fly without knowing whither, and in such uncertain circumstances, how can one flatter himself that [any prince] in [Germany] will [listen] to the [proposal] of [a marriage with his daughter]."[53]

Graeme, who was not unfamiliar with the world of diplomacy,[54] had given Charles Edward good advice. He knew the Prince's determination, however, and being only six leagues from Darmstadt, offered to call on Prince Louis, the Landgrave of Hesse-Darmstadt, whose daughter Caroline-Louise he knew to be on the Prince's list of possible candidates.

Charles Edward's first reaction on receiving the disappointing news was to warn Graeme that his bad reception in Prussia had to be kept in "dipe silence." Spurred by his rejection, his next thought, even before receiving Graeme's suggestion of 4 June, was that the Prince of Darmstadt should be sounded out on a marriage proposal without delay. Graeme was to do his best to examine the daughter carefully and "every way as far as possible,"[55] but with the utmost caution and without committing the Prince. "If you finde her Fitting and to the Purpose," the Prince continued, "strive to get her Picture immediately." It was especially important not to waste a moment and to maintain a "Deade secret" in the matter. Both the necessity for secrecy (urged by the Prince no less than three times in his brief letter) and the importance of not losing time were related, the Prince implied, to the current peace negotiations. Still, he was happy to report, the latest accounts received from de Puisieux had been encouraging: "He assures me how much the K. of F. has at hart to do everything in his power agreeable to me, at ye same time to be esy at present and remain as I am, things as yet not being pressing."

In his reply to Graeme's second message, Charles Edward chose to ignore completely his envoy's advice to abandon the mission, and he again stressed that the search had to continue in absolute secrecy. More than purely political considerations were involved in the necessity to conceal his plan: "However well Inclined ye F[rench] C[ourt] be in regarde of me, I have certainely Enemys here or People that at present would not care for such en Event as my Marriage."[56] It is likely that the Prince was referring to his father's partisans in Paris such as Cardinal Tencin, but he may also have been thinking of Louise (in the "people" rather than "enemy" category), who, only a week or two before, had received his promise that he would never abandon her. His quarrel with an "enemy," Mme de Guémené, also occurred around this time. But whatever the reason for it, "secrecy and dispatch," he reiterated, were to remain Graeme's watchwords. His ambassador was to leave aside any worries about strategy: the Prince himself would decide whether it was opportune or not to proceed at this time. Interestingly, though he rejected Graeme's advice, he was much taken with his imagery and later adopted the comparison of his situation to that of a bird on a branch, ready to fly off he knew not where. But the little bird had to know soon which branch he would fly to, and there was no time to lose. If marriage with the Prince of Darmstadt's daughter proved impossible, Graeme was to begin a new search immediately, "and so on," the Prince insisted, "till I finde a right nest to build on."

From the changing tone of his master's letters, it must have been clear to Sir John that Charles Edward's sense of urgency regarding the marriage had been increasing by the day. On 7 June, he had insisted that Graeme study the situation but make no commitments. Five days later, he was implying that it was now his firm intention to accept a marriage with the Prince of Darmstadt's daughter "immediately iff she inclines and you think her fitting." Since he was not at the moment being pressed to leave France, his plan was to meet with the Princess in Lorraine and marry her there. Only the Darmstadt family and Graeme would know anything about it, although it was possible that he might tell the King of France privately, as a friend, just before leaving.

In his reply of 18 June, Graeme stuck to his guns. On the question of secrecy, it seemed to him unwise not to tell Kelly and Oxburgh of Frederick's reaction, especially since they had been earlier made aware, in general terms, of the purpose of his Berlin trip. He also begged leave to repeat the objection that it was "the most unreasonable time in the world" for him to be going about Germany on such a mission. He had felt from the outset that Frederick would not give Charles Edward his own sister. Had the King of Prussia given the least hint that he would countenance an alliance with a princess from one of the smaller courts, there might have been some chance of success. "But as things stand now," Sir John warned, "I am persuaded there is not a [Protestant prince in Germany] will [hear of it] and it would be unbecoming [you] to be [Baloted about and Refused from] one little [court to] another."[57] There was, he repeated, no necessity for haste in the matter. In a year or two the situation could change and doors might be opened that were at present absolutely closed to the Prince.

Sir John flattered himself that the Prince would now call him back to Paris. That was where he was really needed, and he once more cautioned his master not to displease the King of France, "the only Prince in Europe that ever did anything for you and on whose friendship you can any way rely."[58] But the Prince's reply of 19 June again disappointed his emissary. Charles Edward was adamant, and Graeme was again warned not to concern himself with the wisdom of the plan but to get on with its execution. Dealing with the Prince of Darmstadt merely required tact and the greatest secrecy. As to whether Prince Louis would be nervous about offending the Elector of Hanover, Charles Edward, still thinking of Henry's betrayal, suggested that his own bitter experience of family disloyalty argued otherwise: "I believe it is not new to you the Little Regard Relations have for one a Nother. The Duke, I think, is en instance. He has fethered his Bed, which P.D. may do, but in a different manner, thô it shou'd disoblige ye Elector. I am persuaded that Marriage will succeed, but at ye same time in a manner impossible if it has ye Least vent till it be concluded."[59]

That turned out to be the longest letter Graeme was to receive from the Prince for some time. Other brief notes followed at urgent three or four-day intervals, each more harpingly emphatic than the last on the need for secrecy and dispatch. By 10 July, Charles Edward, now sounding desperate, was ready to accept the marriage, sight unseen: "Iff you finde ye P[rincess] fitting and willing...I think you should Embrace it in any maner Rathere than Let it slip; Considering ye Diffucultys I may have of finding en other one to my Porpose, and ye Necessity of my marying immediately. This is of ye Last Consequence."[60]

The Prince's sense of urgency obviously had its source in the events taking place at Aix-la-Chapelle and in his increasingly uneasy concern with finding the "right nest" to fly to. It was indeed getting late in the day. James had written on 25 June already assuming that his son had left Paris.[61] By the end of the month, the Foreign Minister, de Puisieux, had made it known that Louis XV needed an immediate answer regarding his intentions. Hopeful that Graeme would soon be able to report progress at Darmstadt, the Prince decided to play for time, but de Puisieux refused to be put off, and on 5 July, he wrote a formal letter: His Most Christian Majesty was aware that Charles Edward preferred Lorraine as his retreat, but that had turned out to be impossible. The Comte de St Severin, the French delegate at Aix-la-Chapelle, had tried very hard, but England's Lord Sandwich had rejected the proposal out of hand, insisting that the peace of Europe required prompt and faithful execution of all clauses ratified by the preliminaries of 30 April. Switzerland remained the best possibility, and the King of France was confident that the Prince would graciously comply. He wished, especially, to assure his guest that everything possible would be done to make his new residence comfortable: "Sa Majesté s'intéressera toujours à son sort et tachera de le luy adoucir le plus qu'il sera possible."[62]

Unfortunately, Charles Edward was in no mood to worry about the peace of Europe or to bow, graciously or otherwise, to the inevitable, even with the King of France's personal assurances that he would not be forgotten in the shuffle. While he waited to hear something definite from Graeme, he decided to go ahead with his official protest which was published, finally, on 16 July. Two days later, the Prince wrote to Louis XV and enclosed a copy. His "Justes Droits," he warned, were being ignored. The long period of escalating struggle and resistance that eventually culminated in Charles Edward's ignominious arrest five months later had begun.[63]

Firm, yet respectful and moderate, the Prince's letter pointedly omitted an accusing reference to the Treaty of Fontainebleau which he had included in an earlier draft, dated 10 July.[64] The truth was that he still had very strong doubts about the likelihood of a final peace settlement. On the 15th, he informed James that the Congress at Aix-la-Chapelle seemed to be breaking up, "either to Conclude separately... or for Good and all, God grant ye Latter."[65] It also pleased him particularly to note in the same letter that James was misinformed as to his leaving the country. Nothing was further from the truth! Life in the capital thus went on as it normally did. On 22 July the Prince purchased a fine telescope from Passemant for 384 livres; on the 27th, the same instrument maker furnished the Prince with a smaller and more cunning device that allowed its user to view objects close up while appearing to be looking in another direction. Just the thing to study the admiring faces at the Opera! Three days later he bought a conventional lorgnette,[66] and on 1 August, a large delivery of winter wood arrived at the Rue du Chemin du Rempart house despite the imminent expiry of its distinguished tenant's lease.[67]

Meanwhile, Sir John Graeme's progress in Darmstadt had been alarmingly slow. On his arrival, he had learned that the Landgrave, an avid hunter, was off in the country and that his daughter, the Princess Caroline-Louise, had gone to the waters somewhere near Coblenz three weeks previously but was expected back soon. Remembering his instructions, Graeme made discreet inquiries regarding her reasons for making the journey and learned, fortunately, that her health problem was not serious: "I am told," the Prince's envoy confided, "nothing but what the Fair Sexe is much subject to, and for which Mariage is the Best cure. I mean Obstructions."[68] Naturally, he had been careful not to seem too inquisitive in order to avoid making his purpose known. All other reports on the Princess were, in any case, very favourable: she was reputed to be of a most amiable character, sweet-tempered, and polite. Another encouraging piece of intelligence was that the Hesse-Darmstadt family was perhaps not so closely allied to the Elector of Hanover as he had originally feared.

The days passed, not unpleasantly, for the Darmstadt Court had an excellent table and good music. Finally, on Sunday, 7 July, the Landgrave left off hunting for a few hours and came to town to receive Graeme's visit. The long-awaited interview was friendly and direct, and Prince Louis was quick to say that he felt honoured by the proposal. His only regret was that it came seven or eight months too late for he had already promised his daughter to someone else.

In spite of this unexpected difficulty, Sir John continued at his persuasive best, pointing out Charles Edward's personal merits and the advantages that might one day devolve upon the Hesse-Darmstadt family from such a marriage. Then it came time to show the Landgrave Charles Edward's portrait as well as the beautiful Roettier gold medal. After carefully studying both for some time, Prince Louis expressed the opinion that Charles Edward was indeed a handsome Prince. Graeme then offered the medal as a gift, but his host could not be prevailed upon to keep it. Charles Edward's emissary did, however, obtain the

Landgrave's permission to speak freely with the Princess Caroline-Louise when she returned and even to assure her that, whatever her decision, her father had let it be known that he would not oppose her inclinations in the matter. Before returning to his hunting, Prince Louis did, however, raise another problem: would the fact that his daughter was a Lutheran be seen as an obstacle in France? Sir John was able to answer without hesitation: "I reply'd," he informed his master, "that I could assure him that would not be the least [obstacle]; that [you] was indeed [Catholic] but extremely moderate, and [the prince] in the world the most remote from everything that lookt like [bigotry]; that [his daughter] would be every bit as [dear to you] as if [she] was [of] your [religion and] meet with no manner of [constraint] in the practice and [exercise of her own]."[69]

Everything thus seemed to depend on the Princess herself, and although Graeme, as before, still had little hope of success, Charles Edward remained optimistic. His confidence was understandable: he had already witnessed the magical effect of his portrait on the female heart!

It was not until 13 July, two days after her twenty-fifth birthday, that Caroline-Louise finally returned from the waters. During the next two weeks, Sir John waited impatiently for an opportunity to pay his respects. Unfortunately, the Princess's slight indisposition persisted, and she kept to her chamber, a sanctuary to which Charles Edward's emissary had little hope of being admitted—"for you know," he confided expertly to his young master, "the [fair sex] does not care to be seen for the first time in [an undress]."[70] But the days continued to pass, and by 26 July he began to suspect that there was more to the delay than a stubborn case of female "obstructions." The Princess had by then seen everybody, "both of the Court and of the town" in her chamber, and yet she still refused to see him "in her undress," even though he had requested that favour several times.[71] The Landgrave, Graeme suspected, was attempting to gain time until he could discover the reaction of Maria Theresa, the Queen of Hungary, to Charles Edward's marriage proposal.

On 29 July, Graeme could report only that the situation had not changed. Charles Edward nevertheless remained positive about the outcome: "You no I sume times guess well; I wish I may this time."[72] Overconfident as usual, he was simply not going to worry himself about the possibility that the Princess would say no; six days later, he wrote again but apparently only to pass on a rude comment about the Duke of Cumberland ("Fick"), who was rumoured to be contemplating matrimony with the Princess of Prussia ("Hac"):[73] "I here that Fick is gone to London to be Cured of the Pox, I suppose for a preparation to his Mariage."[74]

Along with his little joke, the Prince remembered to enclose a copy of his protest. It was a reminder that time was getting short, and he wanted the uncertainty to end. Unfortunately, Graeme's next letter, though it gave a detailed account of the meeting he had finally had with Caroline-Louise, still left

matters up in the air. The Princess, charming and attractive, loved her father
dearly and intended to defer entirely to his wishes. She spoke with the greatest
esteem of the Prince's character and reputation and had at least two long looks at
his portrait, but she was too polite and "virtuous" to keep the picture when
Graeme laughingly offered it to her. In short, Sir John had little hope that the
problem would soon be resolved: the Prince would have to be patient.[75]

When Charles Edward received his envoy's letter a week later, it became
suddenly clear to him that he was not prepared to wait any longer. At last, he
sensed failure, and he reacted with mixed feelings of desperation and anger.
Graeme simply had to force the issue and conclude one way or the other:

> Ye 11th August,
>
> Sir
>
> I receive yrs of ye 2d Current and as I have already Mentioned to you the
> Necessity of my Marriage and that some people here at present might be
> averce to it, my Absolute determination of marrying a Protestant and the
> good Caracter of ye Princess you mention, gives me a great inclination to
> Cunclude with her immediatly but I must now tell you Plainly to make this
> marriage now or not at all, my Circumstances admitting no delay on
> Ceverall accounts, So Desier you to make a hog or a Dog of them; I cannot
> Reccomend to Much Caution and Secrecy, as also how much I have at heart
> you shoud succeed where you are. Adieu.
>
> P.S. On recete of this, take yr Party and make D. take his, for I have taken
> mine which is that once you parte from thence I shall on no account Ever
> here from them even ware they to be on their nees. I am willing to give the
> Preference to so aimiable a Princess, which has even made me Delay so
> Long a thing that is so pressing to my interest, but cannot now put it off
> further, So Adieu.[76]

Four days later, the Prince received another letter from Graeme, written on 5
August. The situation was now almost without hope. The Landgrave had made
it clear to his daughter that he could not really give his blessing to the marriage,
although the Princess was free to do as she wished. She, in turn, would not
budge without her father's approval, her sense of duty towards him being such
that she was convinced the blessings of heaven would be denied anyone guilty of
filial disobedience.[77] Recalling his own recent "emancipation" and his impatience with Louise's "apron strings," Charles Edward was furious. The delay at
Darmstadt had used up precious time. Graeme was ordered to return to Paris
immediately to await further instructions. The search for a Protestant bride
would continue apace, and the Prince intended to scour Europe (and all the

catalogues) until one was found: "I Reccon," he warned his envoy, "you have already Purchesed The Almanaks that give the best detaill of ye P.s of Germany, Poland and Elcewhere."[78]

Although Charles Edward still refused to believe it, Sir John's work was over. Now the increasingly paranoid Prince set himself on a direct collision course with the King of France. In spite of his desperate efforts, the summer had brought him neither a Protestant bride nor an honourable retreat. He continued to put up a brave front, showing himself every day to the admiring throngs in the Tuileries or at the Opéra. He knew he was still a living legend to them, a hero of history in the making. The street trade in his memorabilia remained brisk, and he had even found time to contribute to the preparation of one item that sold in Paris toward the end of July for the handsome price of twelve livres. It was a map, with commentary, of all his adventures in Scotland and England and was "prity Exact" as he informed his father, "I having perused it before it was maid publick."[79]

Charles Edward sent a sample of his handiwork to James in the Roman post for Monday, 29 July, along with his usual perfunctory greetings. The date in itself is not significant, but we are left wondering whether the Prince had thought of including in his letter news of an event that occurred the day before, an item of probably greater interest to James than a map of the British Isles. This was the birth of Charles Edward's and Louise's son, baptized two days later on Tuesday, 30 July, in the parish church of St Paul as Charles-Godefroi-Sophie-Jules-Marie, son of "Très Haut, Très Puissant and Très Illustre Prince, Monseigneur Jules Hercule Prince de Rohan, Duc de Montbazon" and his spouse, "Très Haute, Très Puissante and Très Illustre Princesse, Madame Marie-Louise-Henriette-Jeanne De la Tour d'Auvergne, Princesse de Rohan, Duchesse de Montbazon." Acting as the infant's godfather was none other than "Très Haut and Très Puissant Prince," Monseigneur Charles-Godefroy de la Tour d'Auvergne, Sovereign Duke of Bouillon, by the grace of God. The godmother was "Très Haute and Très Puissante Princesse, Madame Marie-Sophie de Courcillon, Princesse de Rohan," Mme de Guéméné's young stepmother.[80]

The good news that the senior branch of the Rohan-Guéméné family could now boast of a second male heir was immediately relayed by special courier to Strasbourg where Mme de Guéméné was visiting with relatives in another of France's Rohan strongholds. By Wednesday, only three days after the birth, the proud grandmother in her own letter to James repaired Charles Edward's omission with the following announcement:

> Madame la duchesse de Montbazon vient de nous donner un second fils. La mere et l'enfant sont dans l'estat le plus desirable. Il est de mon respect et de mon devoir d'en faire part a votre majesté et il est peu de devoir et de respect auxquels je satisfasse avec autant de joyes et d'empressement remplie du

plus parfait desvoument. J'ay l'honneur destre Sire de votre majeste

de Strasbourg le 31
de juillet 1748

la tres humble et tres
obeissante servante
de Rohan princesse de Guéméné[81]

Mme de Guéméné, of course, knew a secret—one that would keep for centuries to come....

XII

The Outlaw Prince

THE BIRTH of Louise's second child went unnoticed in the usual social chronicles. De Luynes failed to mention it although he normally recorded such events and was careful to note, for example, the birth of Louise's nephew, the Princesse de Turenne's second son, the following year.[1] The court diarist did, however, continue to cite extravagant instances of the Bouillon family's haughty pretensions. Dining with the Queen five days before the delivery of Louise's child, the Grand Chambellan made yet another of his dogged attempts to extend the privileges of his high office: this time he formally requested that his daughter-in-law, the Princesse de Turenne, be seated (as the wife of a future Grand Chambellan) immediately next to Her Majesty. Marie Leszczynska hesitated. The Duc persevered, assuring her that it was a recognized privilege. Admittedly, his own wife, the late Duchesse de Bouillon, had never claimed it since she rarely came to the Court.... Flustered and unsure, the Queen objected that to her certain knowledge, the Duc's young stepmother had never mentioned the matter. Was it not obvious, moreover, that she needed her own attendants next to her at table? The debate continued. Maurepas, who was present throughout, said nothing. Later, the Queen asked the minister privately why he had not spoken: "J'écoutais Votre Majesté," responded the minister smoothly, "et je trouve, comme elle, l'idée de M. de Bouillon nouvelle et sans fondement." Others agreed that the idea was quite "new." Louis XV, confronted with the problem by the Queen herself, also judged the notion to be "très-nouvelle."[2]

There the matter rested and the King made no promise to think about it further. Even in an age of *new* ideas, he obviously had more weighty matters on his mind. Occasionally, he shared some of these with Marie Leszczynska. A few days later, for instance, news of the death of M. de Mailly, husband of his first public mistress, reached the Court: "M. de Mailly is dead," the King informed the Queen matter-of-factly one morning. "And which M. de Mailly would that be?" the Queen asked innocently. "Le véritable," replied the King. De Luynes, as usual, made a careful note.[3]

Louis XV had a number of even more serious problems to contend with that summer, and one of these was what to do about Charles Edward Stuart! Printed copies of the Prince's protest against the Aix-la-Chapelle peace preliminaries, despite ministerial orders that they be seized, were circulating throughout Paris. It was a traditional gesture for Stuarts in exile to challenge the legality of all formal treaties made with the British government of the day. James had himself issued a protest at Albano on 17 June, but at the "very wise" suggestion of Cardinal Tencin, he later withdrew it.[4] It is probable that even Charles Edward's more aggressive caveat would not have unduly alarmed the French authorities[5] had he not insisted that it appear with the indication: "Donné a Paris ce 16. Juillet 1748." As Maurepas pointed out to Berryer, that made it seem as though the French Ministry approved of the Prince's "illegal" presence in the country. As a result, five hundred copies of the first edition were seized. A second clandestine edition soon followed with the words "fait a Paris" now printed separately on little slips of paper designed to be glued, after purchase, to the main body of the text.[6] Official government policy still called for suppression of the work, but the pamphlet quickly became a bestseller. On 14 August, for example, d'Hémery reported to Berryer that the forbidden screed was being read publicly at the *Caffé de Viseux* in the rue Mazarine: "Il y en a meme une imprimée qui est sur le Comptoir et que tout le monde lit."[7]

No doubt what appealed most to the public in the Young Pretender's protest was that it went well beyond the usual legalistic rejection of negotiations with usurping authority. In his own routinely diffident statement, James had gone that far. His son, on the other hand, seized the opportunity to speak over the heads of the Aix-la-Chapelle negotiators to his own followers, many of whom were still suffering cruel persecution for supporting his ill-fated campaign. Moreover, no matter what de Puisieux and the other ministers thought, Charles Edward knew that his loyal Parisian public still felt a certain collective guilt at France's "treachery" in that glorious affair. The hero-Prince had performed miracles of daring despite Louis XV's failure to keep a solemn promise. In the end, Charles Edward Stuart had suffered an unlucky defeat, but his noble sacrifice had made possible the great French victories in Flanders. Now the King's ministers were corruptly squandering all those hard-won military advantages by mollycoddling England's negotiators at the peace table and by playing Judas to the unfortunate Prince. Aware of such public sentiments, the Prince did not hesitate to inject an emotional note into his protest. The struggle for freedom from a foreign yoke, he vowed, would be continued, if necessary, till the last drop of his blood was shed:

> Nous déclarons à tous les Sujets de notre très honoré Seigneur & Pere, & plus particulierement à ceux qui nous ont donné récemment des preuves éclatantes de leur attachement aux intérêts de notre Famille Royale, & à la

constitution primitive de l'Etat, que rien n'alterera l'amour vif & sincere
que notre naissance nous inspire pour eux; & que la juste reconnoissance
que nous avons de leur fidélité, zéle & courage, ne s'effacera jamais de notre
coeur; que bien loin d'écouter aucune proposition qui tende à anéantir ou
affoiblir les liens indissolubles qui nous unissent, Nous nous regardons, &
Nous nous regarderons toujours dans la plus intime & la plus indispensable
obligation, d'être constamment attentifs à tout ce qui pourra contribuer à
leur bonheur, & que Nous serons toujours prêts à verser jusqu'à la derniere
goutte de notre sang pour les délivrer d'un joug étranger.[8]

The promise was of course directed as much to the French public as to
Jacobite partisans, and Charles Edward made every effort to publicize it. To that
end, for example, he sent a copy to Montesquieu, whom he had come to know
through the Duchesse d'Aiguillon,[9] asking the celebrated writer to make it as
public as he could. The request was followed by the playful remark that profes-
sional courtesy obliged them as "fellow authors" to keep in touch about their
latest works.[10] Montesquieu replied in kind: Charles Edward's protest was, he
declared, written "avec simplicité, avec noblesse et meme avec eloquence, car
c'est en avoir que d'exprimer si bien ce que vous sentés pour ces braves gens qui
vous ont suivi et dans vos victoires et dans vos malheurs."[11] The Prince was
quite right, Montesquieu agreed, to call himself an author "et si vous n'estiés pas
un si grand prince, Madame la duchesse deguillon et moy nous ferions fort de
vous procurer une place a l'academie françoise."

Not everyone, however, was prepared to receive Charles Edward's prose as
warmly as Montesquieu. In an effort faintly reminiscent of Rousseau's later
attempt to consign the manuscript of a confessional work to the care of
Providence by placing it on the high altar of Notre-Dame, the Prince engaged
the services of several notaries to serve the chief magistrates of Aix-la-Chapelle
with an official copy. On the morning of 23 August, in front of witnesses, his
legal agent, Michel Ignace Lefevre, made four unsuccessful attempts to tender
the document. Four times it was politely thrown back. On the fifth attempt,
Lefevre managed to throw the paper onto a table, but before he could make good
his escape, it was picked up by one indignant official and forcibly stuffed into his
hat! At the same time, shouting and gesticulating, the process server was
roughly ejected from the Town Hall.[12] The message was clear: as far as the
governments of Europe were concerned, the Prince did not officially exist.

Charles Edward's failure to serve legal notice on the universe was a minor
setback, but it probably did not trouble him excessively since he had managed to
make his position widely known in France. The incident, however, does confirm
suspicions that by the summer of 1748, his thinking processes had become
seriously disturbed. Having warned the world, he now saw himself as magically
freed of responsibility for whatever mischief or mayhem might follow. Evil

consequences could henceforth be placed at the door of any who refused to take his words to heart, the governments of Europe having been neatly placed *dans leurs torts*. An early draft of the document provides a concrete instance of the Prince's agitated thinking: "Nous protestons enfin devant Dieu que nous serons exempts de toute faute ou blame, et qu'on ne pourra rejetter sur nous La Cause des Malheurs que les Injustices qu'on nous a faites ou qu'on nous fera cy apres pourront attirer sur le Royaume de la Grande Bretagne *et sur toute la Chrétienté*."[13]

The identity of the person who wisely persuaded the Prince to strike those alarming words from his declaration remains unknown. Unfortunately, in the months to come, no one in his entourage proved to have sufficient influence over him to calm the increasingly disordered spirit that had inspired those words in the first place.

On 20 August, Charles Edward received a formal but extremely polite eviction notice from the King of France, delivered by the Foreign Minister, de Puisieux. The written notice reminded the Prince that the Preliminary Articles, signed on 30 April, had solemnly renewed France's earlier promises not to harbour the Stuarts. It had been part of the price France had had to pay in the interests of European peace: "Sa Majesté n'a pu refuser en cette occasion aux besoins et aux voeux de toute l'Europe, de se prester aux stipulations qui ont esté jugées absolument nécessaires, pour concilier les Puissances Belligérantes, et pour rétablir Solidement la tranquilité publique." De Puisieux was thus being ordered to inform the Prince that he had to leave the country forthwith: "Le Roy en ordonnant au Marquis de Puyzieulx de faire cette Déclaration au Prince, luy a prescrit en mesme tems de luy demander sa réponse, et de luy renouveller les assûrances des sentimens d'estime et d'affection qu'Elle conserve pour Luy."[14]

In his reply, delivered the same day, the Prince did not so much reject as ignore Louis XV's request. His answer, he implied, could be found in his declaration. The King of France was invited to consider his position carefully and to remember that it was Charles Edward, not the ministers, who had the King's interests at heart:

Paris Le 20 Aoust 1748

Je Crois Monsieur avoire deja assé Marque, par Ma Declaration du 16 du moi dernier, come quoi je mopose, et m'opposerai, absolument a tout ce qui pourroite etre dit fait et stipulé a Aix la Chapell ou alieurs; j'espere que S.M.T.C. fera toutes Les refflections necessaires dans les resolutions qu'elle prendra a mon Egard; je Regarde cette conjoncture come etant plus Critique pour les interests de S.M.T.C. que pour les miens; assurez, je vous prie, Sa Majesté de tout mon Respet et Attachement. Rien ne m'est plus a Cour que de luy Devenir utille un jour et de luy prouver que Ses véritables interests me sont plus Cheres qua Ses Ministres.

Charles P.

A Mr de Puysieulx[15]

There the matter rested for a time. The final treaty after all had not yet been signed, and the Prince had shown open disrespect only toward Louis XV's ministers and not toward the King himself. Another minor crisis occurred at the end of September when the Prince's lease on the Rue du Rempart house (near today's Place de la Madeleine) expired. The new tenant, the Comte de Vintimille, was impatient to take possession by 1 October. To show the world that he had no intention of leaving Paris, Charles Edward attempted to rent an even larger and more luxurious residence, offering to pay the entire annual rental of 8000 livres in advance. The move was foiled, however, by discreet ministerial pressure. The Prince's subsequent attempts to purchase a house outright similarly failed, and, in the end, he simply refused to vacate the Rue du Rempart premises.[16] Outwardly, Charles Edward remained his routinely charming self, turning up with clockwork regularity to accept his ovations at the Comédie Française, the Opéra, or the Tuileries gardens. Even his attendance at Mass, normally at *les Feuillants*, had become a fashionable event. Though whispered about in some quarters, his resistance to the King's will was not yet seen as a public scandal although the Nuncio in Paris, writing to Cardinal Valenti on 7 October, noted that members of the high nobility were beginning to visit the Prince less frequently now out of fear of incurring the Court's displeasure. It was also Monsignor Durini's impression that the Court was trying to find a way to avoid the use of force since such a solution would neither look good nor sit well with the Parisian public.[17] Many, like the Marquis d'Argenson[18] (and probably even Louis XV himself), felt that the Prince would leave quietly once the final treaty was signed.

With that done on 18 October, the situation at last turned critical. It also became more complicated. Public dissatisfaction with the "stupid" peace, whose terms, incredibly, seemed to favour the English in spite of the final series of triumphant French victories, now became closely confused in the popular mind with sympathy for the heroic Prince, who had been so visibly sacrificed in the give-away peace negotiations. Charles Edward, of course, was only too happy to exploit that confusion. Probably too, he was already thinking of a clever new strategy whereby his popular image in England would be enormously enhanced if he could manage to get himself thrown brutally out of France. It would demonstrate to all red-blooded Englishmen that once the throne of his fore-fathers was secured, he would not be backward in showing a proper degree of traditional anti-French ferocity. As an image-improving move it was consistent with his recent efforts to acquire a Protestant bride. In short, whatever the outcome, whether he was eventually ejected from the country or allowed to stay, he could not in the end lose out, especially if he could also make it appear to patriotic Frenchmen that his quarrel was not with their beloved King, but rather with a corrupt ministry.

If such were the Prince's thoughts, he kept them to himself. His usual

Monday morning letters to James, every one a jewel of vacuous concision, betrayed not a hint of concern. On 4 November, for example, the very day that Louis XV dictated a final letter of eviction and with all of Europe waiting to see what would happen, Charles Edward sent off the following typical missive to his father:

> Sir
>
> I receive yrs of ye 15th October. Having nothing Worth mentioning at present; I lay myself at yr Majestys Feet moste humbly asking Blessing Your
>   Moste
>   Dutifull Son
>   Charles P.[19]

Along with that masterpiece he enclosed a note to James Edgar, asking for an exact list of all the books he owned in Rome: "I amuse myself here," he explained to his father's secretary, "in bying the Choisest of such trumpery, and as I may sume time or other have occasion to send for what is at Room, dupplicats is dissagreeable."[20]

In Fontainebleau, meanwhile, Louis XV finally reached a painful decision. He had waited patiently for several weeks to see whether the official signing of the peace treaty would induce the Prince to leave voluntarily and nothing had happened. Knowing the risks of sending de Puisieux to see the Prince again, he adopted a different approach. Since the Prince saw the Foreign Minister as an enemy, the King's new messenger would be one of the Prince's most trusted friends, the Duc de Gesvres, Charles Edward's old next-door neighbour at St Ouen. It is possible that before designating his Premier Gentilhomme de la Chambre, the King had considered asking the Grand Chambellan, Charles Edward's uncle. If that was the case, a few whispered words of embarrassed explanation about recent events would have been enough to excuse the Duc de Bouillon from such an unhappy task.

It was with much hesitation that the Duc de Gesvres, a gentle and likeable soul with a long-standing affection for the young Prince, set out from Fontaine-bleau early on the morning of 5 November to deliver the King's letter. It was to be only the first of half a dozen such trips. The royal document he carried with him on this occasion was signed personally. Its message, while still very friendly, was unambiguous:

> Mes ministres plenipotentiaires aiant signé a Aix la chapelle le 18 du mois dernier, le traitté definitif de la paix generale, par lequel toutes les puissances de l'Europe ont renouvelle les engagements qu'elles avoient déja contractées en differentes occasions, par raport a la succession au throsne de la Grande Bretagne, mon intention est d'executer ce qui a eté stipulé a cet

egard. J'attends du Prince Charles Edouard qu'il m'en facilitera les moiens en se retirant incessament des etats de ma domination. J'ay trop bonne opinion de sa sagesse, et de sa prudence pour adjouter foy aux bruits qu'on a affectes de repandre sur la resolution dont on lui attribue le projet. Mon Cousin le Duc de Gesvres lui expliquera plus en detail quels sont mes sentiments. Je souhaitte que la reponse du prince Charles Edouard justifie de plus en plus l'afection que j'ay pour lui, et la disposition ou je suis de lui en faire eprouver les effets.

A Fontainebleau ce 4e 9bre 1748   Louis[21]

The Duc de Gesvres arrived on the evening of the 5th at the Prince's house on the boulevard. Charles Edward greeted him with warmth and eagerly chatted about the joys of shooting partridges at St Ouen.[22] Then the conversation got onto a more serious footing. De Gesvres spoke eloquently of his royal master's tender sentiments toward the Prince and reviewed the difficult situation Louis XV was in. It had not been possible to conclude a peace treaty without first renewing the old prohibition. Regrettably, the Prince would have to leave, but he could rest assured that Louis would do his best to help him settle in Switzerland. If the Prince defied the order, he would make the King's position intolerable. The King had to be master in his own kingdom....

The old man was almost in tears by the time he finished. Charles Edward had listened patiently. In the end, he said only that he knew very well the King of France was master in his own kingdom; just the same he was not leaving, at least not alive and in one piece. If the Duc cared to return the next day at 8:30 p.m. he would have his answer in writing for the King.[23]

True to his word, on 6 November, the Prince delivered the following blunt message to the King's emissary:

C'est avec beaucoup de regret que je me trouve forcé par mes interest de resister aux intentions du Roy dans cette occasion. J'en avois deja prevenu S.M. par une Lettre que jay ecrite a Mr de Puysieulx Le 20 Aoust dernier. Je prie instament Mon Cousin Le Duc de Gesvres d'assurer S.M.T.C. dans les termes les plus forts de tous les sentiments de Respect et d'Attachement que je lui ai voues pour toute Ma Vie.

Paris Le 6 Novembre, 1748   Charles P.[24]

De Gesvres left Charles Edward's house convinced of the Young Pretender's determination to resist—if necessary to the death. Adding force to the Prince's threat was the sight of what the Duc took to be an arsenal of weapons in the Prince's antechamber, described as "toute pleine de fusils, de sabres et de machines, comme pour soutenir siége dans sa maison."[25] Clearly, evicting the occupant would not be easy.

After hearing de Gesvres's report, Louis XV quickly concluded that the only
way to make Charles Edward leave without using force was to enlist the aid of his
father in Rome. If James III, in his son's eyes *de jure* King of England, *ordered*
the Prince to leave France, he could hardly refuse by arguing that it was contrary
to the interests of the House of Stuart! A courier was immediately dispatched,
and it was not long before news of the stratagem reached the Prince's ears. He
knew exactly what his father's reply would be, and in an effort to block the move
he informed everyone that he already had secret instructions from James to
ignore any letters from Rome that required him to act contrary to his interests.[26]
It was a desperate ploy, and by the time James's letter reached Paris, Charles
Edward had abandoned it for something better: he would, he decided, simply
refuse to read any letter from James forwarded to him by the French Court.

The Prince continued to think of other schemes as well. One private memo of
this period sets out his thoughts on how best to isolate de Puisieux from the
King and even from his fellow minister, de Maurepas. De Puisieux, he knew,
was his greatest enemy, and he was determined to prove that the minister was a
secret enemy of Louis XV as well.[27] Unfortunately, the Foreign Minister had
himself gone on the attack: in answer to another of Charles Edward's dubious
claims that he had in his possession written assurances, signed by the King of
France, guaranteeing him safe haven in France for as long as he wished, de
Puisieux challenged the Prince to produce the evidence and also to point out
where in the Treaty of Fontainebleau it was specified that such protection was
guaranteed.[28] Even the Marquis d'Argenson, who was basically sympathetic to
the Prince and who hated de Puisieux with a passion, felt compelled to discount
the claim.[29]

By Tuesday, 26 November, the Duc de Gesvres was on his third trip to the
Prince's house, Louis XV having asked him to try one last time to reason with
his young friend. This time de Gesvres had no written message, but he spoke
earnestly to Charles Edward for nearly two hours. The Prince was much moved
by the older man's entreaties, and the Duc, who on his previous visits had never
remarked anything more than invincible resistance in Charles Edward's facial
expression, now noticed that the younger man's eyes were filled with tears. "Ah,
Monseigneur," de Gesvres cried out, "puisque vous êtes si sensible à l'attachement
que je vous ai toujours marqué, ne serez-vous point ébranlé par ce que le Roi
vous a mandé et ce que je viens de vous dire de sa part?"[30] But he had once more
underestimated Charles Edward's unyielding character. No, the Prince replied,
despite his personal gratitude for everything the King had done for the Stuarts,
his decision had to remain the same; nothing would make him change his mind.
Realizing that there was no more to be said, de Gesvres regretfully communicated his latest orders. He had offered Charles Edward in the King's name a safe
haven in Fribourg and a generous living allowance, entirely appropriate to his
rank. He had also offered the King's apologies for requiring from the Prince

what the imperatives of peace in Europe had imposed. Now he was obliged to inform the Prince, without ambiguity, that if he continued to resist, he would be seized, bound hand and foot, and taken to Rome, where he would be placed in the custody of his father. No threat could have been more chilling. On hearing it, Charles Edward turned pale. Then, in a quiet, matter-of-fact voice, he told the King's messenger:

"You may be certain that I will not be taken there alive!" The interview was at an end. This time the awful truth hit home; posing and bravado aside, the Prince knew now that he truly would prefer death to the ultimate humiliation of being trussed up and taken back to Rome. His reaction was similar to what he had experienced after receiving the news of Henry's defection: he shut himself up in his room and refused to see anyone.[31]

The news that Charles Edward intended, if any attempt was made to arrest him, to use the two loaded pistols he always wore concealed on his person, the first on the arresting officer, the second on himself, was a commonplace of café gossip even before de Gesvres' third visit.[32] The Prince himself had started the rumour, and he displayed no hesitation in repeating his threat even at public gatherings. On 3 December, for example, d'Argenson saw Charles Edward at the Opéra, "fort gai et fort beau, admiré de tout le public." The Prince had made no secret of his intentions: "Il a dit que si on l'arrêtait, il y serait tué, mais qu'il n'y mourrait pas le premier."[33] No one took the threat lightly, not even those who saw it as part of a clever strategy to impress the now constant stream of English tourists in Paris. The Prince had indeed become one of the major attractions of the capital for visiting English ladies who, now that peace was officially at hand, were making special excursions to Paris just to see the handsome hero at the theatre. D'Argenson tells of seeing Charles Edward at the Comédie Française on 30 November. When the Prince arrived in the *première loge* with his Jacobite retinue, the entire audience, including two rather astonished Hanoverian *milords* sitting opposite, stood up and applauded. It was a mark of respect, the former minister noted, usually reserved for the princes of the blood!

Much of the blame for the Prince's ostentatious resistance to the King's order was at first placed on his wilful and notoriously unorthodox mistress: "Mme la princesse de Talmond," d'Argenson recorded on 18 November, "s'est emparée de son esprit et le gouverne avec folie et fureur, sans qu'il y ait le sens commun aux objets que l'on s'y propose; mutinerie, hauteur déplacée, voilà tout."[34] But even Talmont, whose close affiliation with the Queen's party was the mainstay of her haughtiness, was becoming convinced that she was on dangerous ground. Rumours that the King intended to exile her to Lunéville had been circulating for some time.

It was no doubt with that particular threat in mind that toward the latter part of November the celebrated Princess did her best to persuade her lover to obey the King's order to leave. By then, however, it was too late; "la tête anglaise," as d'Argenson noted, "était allumée."[35] Soon she was faced with trouble from a less expected quarter as well: her normally diffident husband, taking advantage of the fact that Louis XV himself was known to be unhappy with her latest lover, screwed up sufficient courage to complain to the Court about Charles Edward's constant visits to his house at all hours of the day and night. Not content with haunting the inside of the premises, the Prince was eternally roaming around in the Talmont garden as well or else prowling under his windows—and all without any invitation! In response to the grumblings of a beleaguered husband whose private feelings and public image had not been spared by either his wife or her royal lover, one highly placed court official apparently encouraged the poor man to make a stand. As a result, strict orders were left with the porter to deny the Prince access to the house. On the very next day when the Prince turned up for his usual 2:00 p.m. visit, he was crisply informed that no one was at home. His Royal Highness raged and threatened to no avail. To avoid scandal, the Princesse de Talmont made a point of inviting herself to supper with the Queen at Versailles that evening and piously informed Her Majesty of the incident, adding that it was only right a husband should be master in his own house. Yes, she entirely agreed, and it was her clear duty under the circumstances to obey her spouse. In fact, she would unhesitatingly deny access to Louis XV himself if M. de Talmont took it into his head to insist upon it! Marie Leszczynska was impressed. How unreasonable it was of Louis to be so irritated with her dear cousin from Lorraine!

Meanwhile, Charles Edward was saving up for a major tantrum, the likes of which he had not managed since his battle with Mme de Guéméné. By eleven o'clock the following morning, he was back at the Talmont residence, fully armed and pounding at the gate. The porter, adamant still, again refused him entry. This time the Prince's rage exploded, and he was on the point of attacking the door when Francis Bulkeley, the senior Jacobite in French service, arrived on the scene. After much persuasion, the respected *lieutenant général* managed to calm the Prince, and by evening Charles Edward's mind was once more at rest. He attended the Opéra and made his way as usual to the *grande loge du Roi*, followed by a contingent of his officers. A large number of his supporters were also in the audience, and when he appeared, all stood up and applauded. The rich symbolism of the event was unmistakable: the Prince, surrounded by a guard of honour, his private army standing at attention nearby, was defiantly holding court within the precincts of a powerful sovereign's dominions. Even the many Parisians who remained warmly sympathetic to their unfortunate hero-Prince felt uneasy, sensing the implications of such disrespect toward the King in the very heart of his own great capital! Louis would have to act. The Princesse de Talmont (whose husband had by now fled to Lorraine)[36] herself did not hesitate to challenge the Prince's threat to break down her door: any attempt on his part to repeat the bullying tactics earlier displayed at the Place Royale would be met with measures that would remind him in the end more of Mme de Guémené than of his soft and sweetly timid former mistress! "Je crois," she warned, "que vous voulez donner à mon occasion le second tome de Mme de Monbazon que vous avez déshonorée avec vos deux coups de pistolet."[37]

How that little reminder struck the Prince is not clear. It is unlikely that he had given his abandoned sweetheart a single thought for months. The entire Rohan clan, moreover, like the members of France's other leading families, had begun to drop him socially. Mme de Montauban deliberately stayed away from Paris to avoid any problems, and Mme d'Aiguillon stopped seeing the Prince in early November, once it became clear that he was intending to play the outlaw.[38] The Duc de Bouillon found the spectacle of his nephew showing such disrespect especially distressing, and his concern may even have contributed to the severe illness he suffered in late November. By the 28th of that month, everyone thought the Grand Chambellan was at death's door, and an emergency will was drawn up. The Duc survived the night and on the following day the notary, de Bougainville, was called to the Quai Malaquais to prepare a more formal document. There, in a room of the ground floor apartment whose windows looked out on the gardens, the Duc lay abed, "malade de corps, toutefois sain d'esprit, mémoire et jugement." Perhaps we should not be too surprised that in the nine-page testament drawn up on that day no bequest was made as an expression of the dying man's esteem for his nephew, Prince Charles Edward Stuart.[39]

As November drew to a close, public suspense rose to new heights. Everyone waited to see what James would write to his son in response to the King of France's request—everyone, that is, except Charles Edward. On 2 December, a Monday and consequently his day for mailing off a note to Rome, the Prince calmly wrote his usual "letter":

Sir

I receive yrs of ye 12th November. The Weather here is fine for the season being Noways Cold; having nothing further to add at present, I lay myself at yr Majesty's feet moste humbly asking Blessing.

Your Moste
Dutifull Son
Charles P[40]

The next day, James's long letter to his recalcitrant son, sent by courier from Rome on 23 November, finally arrived at Versailles. Included with it was, of course, a copy for the King of France. The Duc de Gesvres was immediately sent for and ordered to deliver the sealed original to the Prince on the following morning.

When he arrived on 4 December at the house on the Rue du Chemin du Rempart, Charles Edward refused to see him. De Gesvres then spoke with Sir John Graeme, George Kelly, and Colonel James Oxburgh—by now the three coolest heads in the Prince's immediate entourage. He asked them to hand the letter on to the Prince, and he also requested that they let him know the Prince's reaction. De Gesvres then withdrew and sent a progress report by courier to de Puisieux in Versailles. When, later that same day, he called again, he was informed that Charles Edward had merely put James's letter in his pocket,[41] its seal unbroken, and that it was highly unlikely he would ever open it. Emergency consultations with de Puisieux followed, and it was decided that a duplicate of the King of France's copy would have to be made and its contents read out to the Prince by one of his officers. By 10:00 p.m. de Gesvres was on his way again to Paris with the neatly scripted duplicate in his pocket. One hour later, the weary messenger deposited it at the Prince's house; he left as well a stern warning that Louis XV had now given the Prince three days to leave Paris and nine to leave France. It had been a long day!

We can only guess at the difficulties Graeme, Kelly, and Oxburgh experienced in their attempts to make the contents of James's letter known to the Prince. To begin with, Charles Edward refused to see them, except individually.[42] Whether or not they succeeded in actually reading to him the five-page letter, written entirely in French, is of little importance. Charles Edward already knew what the letter said from the mere fact that it had been addressed to him in care of the King of France.

Though he was reluctant to write such a letter in the first place and had little hope of being obeyed,[43] James adopted his most disapproving tone for the occasion. How could Charles Edward have imagined that he would be allowed to remain in France in spite of the King's orders? He was obviously being manipulated by evil advisers whose purpose was to destroy the French Court's sympathy for the House of Stuart. Charles Edward would have to admit, James continued, that his father had patiently refrained from intervening in his affairs. But now the Prince was simply going too far and he had to speak out: "Je ne scaurai plus me taire. Je vous vois sur le bord du précipice et prêt d'y tomber, et Je serois un Pere denaturé si Je ne faisois au moins le peu qui depende de moy pour vous sauver, et c'est pourquoi Je me trouve meme obligé de vous Ordonner, comme votre Pere & votre Roy, de vous conformer sans delai aux intentions de S.M.T.C. en sortant de bon gré de ses Etats."[44] If he did not leave France willingly, he would probably be conducted under guard to Rome, an event that would be neither to his liking nor in his interests. Indeed, all that he could gain from further resistance was a loss of reputation and credibility in the eyes of his true friends who might one day be in a position to help him.

James concluded his letter with assurances that it was written by a loving father "qui ne respire pour vous que tendresse et qui est uniquement occupé de votre véritable bien et de votre véritable gloire." Perhaps Charles Edward managed a bitter smile when that was read out to him. Had James also been thinking of his son's true benefit when he connived with Henry to make the Duke a Cardinal? The letter was just one more good reason for digging in his heels even if cowardly deserters like Kelly, Oxburgh, and Graeme chose to use it as an excuse for withdrawing from his service before the three-day grace period elapsed.

Seeing, meanwhile, no indication that the Prince intended to change his mind, Louis XV gave the order to make James's letter public. It was a clever move since it enabled the French monarch to banish the recalcitrant son even as he was carrying out the wishes of the father. By 6 December, there could not have been a single Jacobite in Paris still unaware of the orders of the King in Rome.[45] On Saturday the 7th, Francis Bulkeley, one of the Prince's most highly placed and staunchest supporters, sadly took his leave, declaring that he was obliged to obey the order of the King in Versailles as well as the one in Rome. On that same day, he warned the Foreign Minister that Charles Edward was indeed threatening to blow himself up with gunpowder when it came time for his arrest.[46]

The deadline passed. On Sunday, 8 December, Louis XV summoned the Duc de Biron, colonel of the French Guards, and gave the order to arrest the Prince at the earliest possible opportunity. Because of the Young Pretender's highly publicized murder-suicide threats, de Biron gave a good deal of thought to the assignment. The Prince would have to be taken by surprise and under well-controlled conditions. The notion of arresting him in his house was quickly rejected because of the supposed arsenal of weapons and explosives stored there and because the Prince's many live-in supporters might offer resistance. Taking him into custody during one of his showy walks through the Tuileries was equally unsuitable because of the constant crowd of sightseers and admirers; there was also the danger of rioting that the public arrest of such a popular figure might provoke. Finally, it was decided that the best solution was to arrest the Prince quickly and quietly at the Opéra as he made his way down the narrow and gloomy pedestrian access off the Rue St Honoré.[47] Unlike the Comédie Française, which was open every day of the week, the Opéra held performances only on Tuesday, Thursday, Friday, and Saturday. Tuesday, 10 December, was thus the earliest opportunity. As he planned his move, de Biron thought of the many potential repercussions. The Prince's arrest would create a sensation. Most certainly it would eclipse even the current gossip about the *fermier général*, La Popelinière, who had discovered behind a mirror in his wife's bedroom a doorway communicating with an apartment belonging to the Duc de Richelieu in the building next door![48]

Contemporary accounts of the Prince's arrest, most of them tendentious and unreliable, abound. One of the most vivid and detailed of these was probably composed in large part by the Prince himself after his arrival in Avignon and circulated widely in manuscript under the title, "Lettre de Madame de XXX à Monsieur de XXX." Like his earlier autobiographical tale, the Prince's narrative is well worth reading and provides excellent proof of his genuine talents in the art of fiction and mythomania.[49]

Before looking at this pamphlet, we would do well perhaps to review briefly the bare facts of the famous incident: Charles Edward was taken into custody on his way to the Opéra on 10 December at 5:15 p.m., three days after the expiry of the King's deadline. With him at the time were Sir James Harrington, Sir Henry Goring, and Michael Sheridan, three of his most loyal officers. They, unlike Graeme, Kelly, and Oxburgh, had decided to stay on with the Prince in spite of orders from Rome and Versailles.

Every conceivable precaution was taken by the Duc de Biron during the arrest. A total of some twelve hundred troops were deployed throughout Paris, and detachments of French Guards were scattered all the way from the Porte St Honoré area, near the Prince's house, as far as the Porte St Antoine and beyond. Such massive preparations were designed to make certain, first of all, that the Prince did not succeed in carrying out his threat to do himself (or anyone else) in and, secondly, to ensure that any popular demonstrations in his favour could be easily contained.

As the Prince left his carriage in the Rue St Honoré, in order to proceed on foot, walking slightly ahead of his three companions, he was suddenly tripped and seized by five burly sergeants from de Biron's regiment, dressed in civilian clothes. In a matter of seconds, he was carried out bodily through a gateway at the end of the passage and into a courtyard of the Palais Royal. There, pale and astonished, he was formally arrested in the name of the King of France by M. de Vaudreuil, Major of the Guards. After being disarmed, searched, and finally bound up with a seemingly endless length of silk ribbon (it was all for his own protection, he was assured), he was hurriedly bundled off to a waiting coach and driven to Vincennes, where he was kept under constant guard in one of the small corner rooms of the *donjon* or tower, but he was also given free access to the less spartan comforts of a large adjoining chamber. His much distressed jailer was the Marquis du Châtelet, Governor of His Most Christian Majesty's state prison of Vincennes and one of Charles Edward's personal friends. Sheridan, Goring, and Harrington, meanwhile, were taken off to the Bastille, as were, in the course of the next several hours, a total of thirty-six persons arrested by Berryer in the Prince's house, which had been simultaneously invested by a detachment of French Guards under the command of the Marquis de Rochegude.[50]

Beyond reviewing those bare facts, there is some merit in examining the Prince's own highly subjective version of events for evidence that a cleverly reasoned strategy lay hidden beneath his otherwise puzzling and self-destructive line of conduct. In fact, it is not at all certain that Charles Edward had *any* strategy in mind. Is it possible that after the failure of his Protestant marriage plans, he sincerely believed he would not be forced to leave? Was he quietly counting on Louis being too weak or too grateful or too guilt-ridden to carry out the dreadful deed? To what extent did he hope to be shielded by popular support in Paris long after he had squandered or thrown aside the more exclusive protection afforded by such great families as the Rohans? But even if we assume that the Prince did know his expulsion was inevitable and conclude that his ostentatious resistance was calculated merely to sensationalize the event and invest it with as much exploitable public emotion as possible, doubt remains whether, in the weeks immediately preceding 10 December, he saw himself as playing the victim's role more for an English audience than for a French faction of superpatriots embittered by what was considered to be a shameful ministerial sell-out to the English at Aix-la-Chapelle. Presumably, any prolonged attempt to capture simultaneously the sympathy of both groups would have entangled him in an unmanageable labyrinth of contradictions. But in the confused short run, the key element common to both strategies—a dignified martyrdom—could work in his favour. Whether he was perceived as a sturdy "Englishman," brutalized and bullied by the French King, or as simply an honest and loyal ally of that same King, victimized at Aix-la-Chapelle by a corrupt Ministry, Charles Edward stood to gain points on either side of the water. The widespread indignation of Parisians on hearing the details of his arrest is proof enough that his strategy to capture the sympathy of the French had worked, even as he hoped, by the same token, to improve substantially his anti-French image in England. One week after his arrest, it was the Duc de Biron and not the Prince who had emerged as the villain of the piece! Similarly, despite Bulkeley's genuine fears, Charles Edward's threats to commit murder and suicide may have been no more than part of an elaborate scheme of provocation; if so, that too had worked well, as the spectacle of twelve hundred French Guards being deployed for the arrest of *one* man suggests. Consistent with that strategy, it would have been equally important to deny, after the event, that such murderous threats had even been made, and earnest denials to that effect are to be found in the "Lettre de Madame de XXX à Monsieur de XXX." The important trick would have been first to provoke the massive use of brute force and, afterwards, to cause evidence of its provocation to vanish. James's letter had been a good countermove on the Ministry's part, but everyone except de Puisieux and Louis XV forgot about it after 10 December, and the Prince's cleverly orchestrated narrative makes no mention of it. What it does mention, with obvious relish, is an accumulation of supposed atrocities inflicted by barbarous captors cunningly made to look like agents in the pay, not of Louis XV, but of the Elector of Hanover. The supposed cruelty of the arresting officers is amplified and enhanced even more in the "improvements" and revisions personally inserted by the Prince in the final draft. Several versions of the scene in which he is disarmed and searched were obviously tested out before a sufficiently horrifying final account was concocted, probably with a view to exonerating the Prince, after the fact, for breaking the solemn promise he had made before witnesses, as he was being escorted from Vincennes, not to go to Lorraine or Avignon. As Charles Edward had learned from the plots of so many of the tragedies and operas he had attended, it was important even for outlaw heroes to be seen as honourable men!

The "Lettre de Madame de XXX a Monsieur de XXX" is thus an attempt to set the record "straight." Under the cover of an impartial third-person observer's account (the Prince must indeed have collaborated with several other persons in the preparation of this "inside story" of events, if only for the spelling!), we are told that the hero of the '45 had, in good faith, refused to leave the country because of his trusting belief that he could count on the King of France's personal assurances, the written guarantees of his treaties, not to mention his gratitude and kinship. Charles Edward's firm resistance on being ordered to leave had come as a surprise to everyone, and that was why rumours were deliberately circulated, suggesting that he had threatened to kill the arresting officer and himself. That falsehood was also used as an excuse by the ministers to seize him on his way to the Opéra. The Prince had been deliberately showing himself in public as frequently as possible in order to force the ministers to commit their atrocities in the open, thus preventing them from saying afterwards that he had voluntarily given up the asylum France had *promised* him. In a later revision, feeling perhaps that mere "promises" might seem insufficient, the Prince inserted instead a reference to his *legal treaties* with France.

Having dealt with the Ministry's perfidious decision to strike, the narrator then goes on to describe how twelve hundred men and ten ells of crimson silk cord were ordered up. The Palais Royal was surrounded, troops were posted all along the road to Vincennes, hatchets and scaling ladders were prepared and locksmiths were ordered to attend in case the Prince took refuge in a house or attempted to stand a siege. A doctor and three surgeons were also commanded to be present in order to care for the wounded.

Very much the people's hero, the Prince, early on the morning of that fateful Tuesday, had received several notes at his house, warning him of the danger. More warnings came that afternoon from well-wishers in the Tuileries, and even as his carriage proceeded later along the Rue St Honoré toward the Opéra, he had heard a loyal Frenchman shout out: "Prince, retournez, on va vous arrêter, le Palais Royal est investi." The Prince, of course, paid no attention and bravely went on.[51]

As he reviewed the section in the original narrative which relates how he was seized by the sergeants and carried off down the narrow passageway, Charles Edward decided that it would be useful to insert additional details to enhance the savagery of his captors and show at the same time how he had faced danger with calmness and courage. Now, not only was he seized, but ropes were immediately flung round him by guards "faisant en meme tems des Cris, tout come Les Sauvages font." According to another later insertion, the Prince remained amazingly cool and even had the presence of mind to make the following ironic comment: "C'est réellement beau et magnifique ce que vous faites la; si jetois a La Tete de mes Montagniards, il ne vous seroit pas si aisé de me prendre." His captors then assured him that they wished him no harm: "Prince ne crenies rien, nous ne voulons pas vous faire du mall." To which the Prince disdainfully replied: "Mardi non, je vous crain pas, mais je vous plain."

Changes of a similar nature were also made to the original description of the scene in which the Prince is disarmed. The first draft notes that after he was formally placed under arrest by M. de Vaudreuil, "on luy demanda ses armes." This was later changed to "on commensa a le foulier [fouiller]." In the original version, de Vaudreuil urges the Prince not to make any attempt on his own life or that of others, and the Prince obligingly gives his word. De Biron was consulted, however, and insisted that the prisoner be bound for his own protection, and this was carried out with apologies from de Vaudreuil. "The shame is not on me but on your master," was the Prince's comment. In the later version, such civilities are nowhere to be found. Instead, after being relieved of a sword, a double-bladed knife, and two pistols, the Prince with great dignity offers to spare his captors the infamy of searching him further by giving his word that he has no other weapons. His guards pay no heed, however, and continue their brutal probings, provoking the following indignant comment from the Prince: "Je suis outré de voire de si braves gens employes a une telle ministaire. Que vous auries eté bienvenu en Ecosse, et plus honorablement!" Then began the humiliation of his being tied up, hand and foot. The silken cord was wound round and round and, already in the first version, the Prince was given the opportunity to ask de Vaudreuil the disdainful question: "En trouvez-vous bientot assez?" To which the vile officer venomously replied: "Pas encore!" And so the winding was continued. The Prince answered by giving the Major a withering look.[52]

The Prince, now "tide Neck and Hils"[53] was carried like a corpse to a waiting coach. From a safe distance, the Duc de Biron watched the heavily guarded vehicle move off; then he left in his own coach to go and report to the King.[54] At the Porte St Antoine, the Prince's carriage stopped for a change of horses. The Prince, who had remained silent until then, seeing such preparations, asked: "Ou allons-nous, a Hannovre?" In his revised version Charles Edward thought of an even more devastating barb: "Je croies [croyais] etre a Paris mais je vois bien que je ne suis pas avec des François." The Duc de Vaudreuil explained that the change of horses was intended only to make the tedious voyage less long for His Royal Highness, and the Prince said no more. Finally, after what seemed like hours, the slow-moving procession reached its destination. It was well past seven o'clock, and through the darkness he could just make out the sinister outline of the *donjon* of Vincennes towering beyond the dimly lit compound.

Perhaps it did not even cross his mind as they drove past the nearby château that scarcely more than two years before he had been eagerly hoping that Louis XV would invite him to take up residence there!

The Marquis du Châtelet had just received his orders to place the Prince in the *donjon* rather than, as might have been expected, in one of the comfortable apartments of the château.[55] Du Châtelet, horrified at seeing his friend tied up like a common criminal, immediately ordered that he be released from his bonds. It was now the Prince, still according to his own narrative, who found himself obliged to comfort his jailer, and he took the lead as they mounted the fifty steps which brought him to the *chambre* he was to occupy. (In the revised version Charles Edward substituted the word *cachot*.) The Prince entered and began a gloomy inspection of his cell. For furniture it contained only a wicker chair and a nasty-looking cot. The walls were covered with inscriptions. Out of curiosity he asked the Governor what the marks represented and was informed that they had been made by a priest imprisoned for many years in that room. Still itching to be nasty, de Vaudreuil at this point informed du Châtelet that the Prince had not been thoroughly searched. The Governor, as a result, asked Charles Edward if he had anything left on his person with which he could do himself harm. The Prince responded by handing over a compass and gave his word that he had nothing else. Not satisfied, de Vaudreuil insisted on a complete search and proceeded to examine even "les endroits les plus secrets" of the Prince's garments. The Prince nobly mastered his indignation and said nothing. A wallet was found and not returned to the Prince.[56]

Remarking that the room was small, the Marquis du Châtelet next expressed the hope that the Prince, so accustomed to vigorous exercise, would not fall ill by being confined in such a small space. The Prince reassured him: he would merely go around it four times more often. The Governor then offered him the use of a large adjoining room if the Prince gave his word....But Charles Edward, with great dignity, did not even let him finish. No, he would not give his word; he had given it once and they had not believed him; he would not give his word again. At this, the Governor fell to his knees, broke into tears, and cried out in despair that it was the unhappiest day of his life. His royal prisoner rose to the occasion: with great kindness he extended a forgiving hand to his jailer. The Governor was comforted.

After a time, Charles Edward asked about his companions. Had his English gentlemen also been tied up? He was much concerned. Then he added a comment presumably intended to be overheard mainly in England: "Un Anglois n'est point accoutumé a etre lié; il n'est pas fait pour l'etre." A few moments later he brought up the subject once more: "Si vous avez traité le chevalier Harrington comme moy, je plains bien le pauvre homme; il est fort gras et il aura beaucoup souffert." But seeing that no answer would be made, the Prince finally went around the room exchanging pleasantries with the officers. Of course, he said not a word to the hateful de Vaudreuil! Finally, he threw himself on his bed, fully dressed, and slept in a troubled and agitated manner until six o'clock the following morning.

All of these details had been given to the narrator, the text explains, by an officer of the Guards who was present throughout the arrest and had stayed with the Prince at Vincennes until ten o'clock the following morning. We are not surprised to learn that the man in question, like all of his fellow officers, was filled with respect and admiration for the natural nobility of the royal prisoner: "Dans ce moment affreux il ne luy echappat aucun mouvement de foiblesse. Il montroit dans ses discours autant de moderation et de noblesse qu'un si grand homme en pouvoit avoir au sein meme de la prospérité. Il sembloit dans sa prison le monarque de l'univers et nous ses sujets faits pour recevoir ses ordres." In his later revisions of this particularly fulsome section of the initial draft, the only changes Charles Edward felt it necessary to introduce were spelling errors....

All of Paris, the narrative continues, soon fell into a state of shock on learning of the Prince's arrest: "Le Prince Edouard y est aimé, on y respecte ses vertus, on croyoit qu'il avoit merité un azile en France." Everyone saw it as a public calamity: "Dans quelque maison qu'on allat on trouvoit tout en larmes—hommes, femmes, tout pleuroit." It was the glory of the King, of the nation, and of every single Frenchman that was being universally mourned. Each felt, personally, an overwhelming moral guilt. Of course, a cynical Ministry had tried to fight back. False rumours were circulated to suggest that before the second pistol was found, the Prince had given his word of honour that he had no other weapon on his person.[57] Worse still, the Prince's guards had been ordered by their superiors to say that additional bonds had been placed on the Prince only because he had attempted to throw himself from the coach on the way to Vincennes. However, all but two of the guards admitted afterwards that the story was untrue. The French Ministry had also claimed that the Prince (who was now safely revising his story in Avignon) had, as a condition of his release, given his word of honour not to go to Avignon or Lorraine. In a conclusion to the account, entirely composed and not merely revised by the Prince, that particular charge (in fact, true) is hotly denied, and in an expanded and even more polished third version of the "Lettre de Madame de XXX,"[58] the denial is made even more explicit. Apparently, in spite of threats and blandishments from the Ministry, Charles Edward had in fact *dictated the terms of his own release*! He had agreed to leave the country with the escort provided *and nothing more*.[59] He had even made it clear to his captors (now, it seems that six thousand men had been deployed during his arrest!) that they could either give him liberty on those terms or give him death. In the last words he added to the revised edition of the "Lettre de Madame de XXX à Monsieur de XXX," the Prince rounded off his story with a fitting conclusion. Everyone, it seems, now praised the merit of the Prince and condemned with one voice the way he had been treated. He might be exiled from

France, but he could never be banished from the hearts of the French, who, "dans l'attachement qu'ils ont fait voire pour lui, sembloit avoire oubliés qu'il s'opposoit a La Volonté de leur Roy."[60] The implications of his last remark are disquieting. Had the Prince all along believed that by manipulating the discontent of "patriotic" factions and appealing to popular sympathies, he could actually force the most powerful monarch in Europe to bend to his will?

In his account, Charles Edward had not focussed much attention on the thirty-six persons arrested at his house except to suggest that no one was afterwards left there to care for his fine horses. They might have died as a result. He states too that the soldiers broke down various doors, in particular the one leading to the cellar, in their search for explosives. Not finding the supposed arsenal of gunpowder, they proceeded to drink up the Prince's wine "out of fear that it might spoil." Not one of his servants, moreover, was allowed to attend him at Vincennes during his entire imprisonment there.

Such then was the Prince's own sanctioned history of his arrest. The facts as they may be examined today in various archives present a somewhat less sombre picture, but there can be no doubt that incarceration in the Bastille of those arrested at his house must have been especially unpleasant in spite of both Maurepas's and Berryer's instructions to the Governor that everyone was to be treated with "politeness and humanity."[61] Curiously, over two-thirds of those arrested entered the Rue du Rempart house voluntarily, well after de Rochegude's troops had invested it and during Berryer's placing of the seals. Among these latecomers was the Princesse de Talmont's lackey, whose release was almost immediately demanded by his mistress in a wittily impertinent note to de Maurepas: "Monsieur, voilà les lauriers du roi portés a leur comble, mais, comme l'emprisonnement de mon laquais n'y peut rien ajouter, je vous prie de me le rendre."[62] Along with a dozen other French nationals, he was released on the following day, but at the same time de Maurepas mischievously circulated the Princess's note at Court, thereby almost causing her immediate exile to Lorraine.

The charge that doors were broken down and that much damage was done seems unfounded. Berryer is careful to note in his report to the Minister that everything went very smoothly: "J'ay eu grande attention que tout se passât avec décence et sans aucune curiosité indiscrète. On n'a point examiné, ni déplacé le moindre papier, on se contentoit de fermer les Bureaux, Commodes et Secretaires et d'apliquer dessus les bandes de papiers necessaires aux sçellez, le tout avec ordre et tranquillité." Daniel, described as the Prince's confidential valet, was present throughout, and, indeed, it was he who directed Berryer regarding the items to be sealed. Anything of value that could be easily moved was locked up, including the twenty-five muskets and thirty-four pistols. Daniel, meanwhile, was asked to select from among the Prince's effects whatever clothing his master would need at Vincennes, and several bundles were prepared for delivery to M. du Châtelet early the next morning. As Berryer's long list of the items sent suggests, the Prince at least did not lack for high fashion in his *donjon*. Meanwhile, as Berryer proceeded with his work, more visitors or servants arrived, and after being taken into custody, they were sent to join the prisoners already waiting in the dining room. All were searched and relieved of knives, scissors, "et de tout ce qu'ils pouvoient avoir d'offensive sur eux." Documents were found only on the person of Charles Stewart of Ardshiel, who had stayed on with a group of five or six gentlemen after dining that day with the Prince. Stewart had been playing backgammon when the house was surrounded. His papers were carefully placed unexamined in an envelope, which was then officially sealed and retained in Berryer's custody. According to a letter from de Maurepas to Berryer, written late on the night of the arrest, the Prince was more worried about his own papers than about anything else. The minister therefore urged Berryer to make certain that the Prince's officers were present when any documents were handled: "Vous entendez assez la consequence de cet article," Maurepas added, "pour que je n'aye pas besoin de m'y etendre davantage."[63]

Finally, Berryer's official report was complete. When it came time to ask the chief valet Daniel O'Brien to sign the inventory of items secured, the Lieutenant Général de Police found himself faced with a strange problem: Daniel adamantly refused, declaring that his unwillingness was based on the express orders of the Prince, "qui luy a deffendu de jamais rien signer de ce qui le regarde." It was only on the following Sunday that the fiery and proud valet, when he was again asked to sign the discharge document after the removal of the seals, admitted that he could not write. Stewart, Reydet, and Chevillon attested to his illiteracy and signed in his place.[64]

After completing all formalities late on the evening of 10 December, Berryer placed his thirty-six prisoners in the custody of d'Hémery, Lieutenant de Robe Courte, who was directed to conduct them to the Bastille. As for the safety of his house and the well-being of his horses, the Prince had no need to fear: when he departed for the night, de Rochegude left everything in the care of two sergeants and twenty guards who remained on duty in the days to come. In addition, one groom, Claude Dupierre, apparently on loan (along with four horses) from the King's *Grande Ecurie*, was not taken into custody. A special problem arose when Lady Clifford the next morning wrote to Berryer to ask for the release of her coachman, Michel Grout. She was worried too about her little dog "Charlot" (a gift from the Prince) last seen at the Prince's house on the 10th. To everyone's relief it was discovered that the dog had neither wandered off nor been taken to the Bastille, the Marquis de Rochegude having had the presence of mind to take it back to his own home for the night.

More serious letters of distress, however, soon began to flood out of the Bastille, and one of the most curious of these was sent by Daniel O'Brien to Berryer, obviously with the secretarial help of John Stewart. Betraying a spirited yet desperate temperament (not unlike his master's), Daniel made it clear that he had no intention of lingering long within prison walls:

from the Bastilles Xbre. 13. 1748

Sir

For to present you my Station in this place is Thus. If I be kept Longer here I do not expect to live four and Twenty hours Longer. Therefore I humbly begg of your honour to take it into consideration to relive me. If you be in any doubt of me, Mr. Kelly and Collonel Oxbourg will be answerable for me. I am Sir with all Respect

Yours.

O'Brien the Princes
Valet de Chambre.[65]

Luckily for all concerned, Daniel was indeed released the next day, his master having requested that he and Stewart, along with Stafford and Sheridan, be allowed to accompany him out of the country. Other prisoners were not so fortunate, but they remained fiercely loyal to their Prince nonetheless. One pathetic letter from the unemployed clerk, William Brennan, asked that two shirts and a cap be sent to him. Brennan, like other destitute Jacobites in Paris who had tasted misery in George II's prisons, obviously depended in great measure for his subsistence on the hospitality of the Prince's table. His note also requested that word be sent "to the person that has my Watch & Buckles in pledge to sell them, was it even for no more than what's on them rather than it shou'd be any Longer unpaid." His own predicament, however, did not deflect his main attention from the grief he felt at the Prince's situation: "It Touches my heart more than all the Confinements and Dungeons I felt with Barbereity from the ville Whiggs in Scotland."[66]

Equally moving is a letter from Sir Henry Goring, the scion of an old Jacobite family who had been arrested at the Opéra at the same time as the Prince. He and Charles Edward had been friends from the time they had toured through northern Italy in 1737. Following the Prince's expulsion from France, Goring would become Charles Edward's principal aide and companion during five years of difficult and ill-rewarded service. Now he and Sir James Harrington were in the Bastille and under threat of special penalties for having ignored the order that Kelly, Graeme, and Oxburgh had prudently obeyed. Why had he and Sir James risked the King's displeasure by staying on? Their motives had been entirely innocent. They had never counselled opposition to His Most Christian Majesty's orders nor had they carried weapons. "Je vous assure," Goring declared, "que nos souhaits & nos larmes etoit les seuls armes que nous avions pour le service de notre maitre." The Bastille in December was a cold and cheerless place. He appealed for linen, the right to take a little exercise, and the privilege of being allowed to see his fellow prisoners from time to time.[67] Goring's release came only on the 19th when he and Harrington were exiled fifty leagues from Paris.[68]

Simple imprisonment until 19 December turned out to be the punishment for all of the remaining foreign-born prisoners. Termination of their detention was dependent entirely on the timing of the Prince's decision to leave, the Ministry having directed that they could be released only after Charles Edward was well on his way to the frontier. One of these last, Charles Stewart of Ardshiel, wrote to Bulkeley on 12 December, asking the General to intercede on their behalf. He explained that he and the other penniless gentlemen who were arrested with him were in the habit of dining almost every day at the Prince's house, out of necessity. No general prohibition against going there had been circulated, and in any case it was surely less criminal for them as subjects of the Prince to go to his house than it was for all of the "Ladys of Quality, officers of the Army… Bishops and other Eclesiasticks of all degrees" who had kept turning up "to the very last" with impunity. He and the other gentlemen had not advised the Prince to stay on in France: "I can assure the Contrair, both for myself and any others of us of my acquaintance and that I used the freedom both in writing and by word of mouth to disapprove of his resolution as prejudiciall to H.R.H. & his friends that suffer'd in his behaf."[69]

Meanwhile, in his cell at Vincennes, Charles Edward had finally grasped the basic elements of his situation. His choices were clear. He could, first of all, leave voluntarily, that is to say, quietly and without resistance, after making a solemn promise to abide by the conditions laid down. He would, in that case, be accompanied by only one guard plus any of his servants and officers (to a certain maximum number) that he chose to take along. His escort would be the Marquis de Pérussi, Maréchal de Camp and Enseigne of the First Company of Musketeers; their destination would be Pont-de-Beauvoisin on the French border. His other choice was to leave Vincennes for a destination beyond the Alps, probably Civita Vecchia, and in a manner that would certainly remind him very much of his recent trip from the Cul-de-Sac de l'Opéra to Vincennes. As an "involuntary" prisoner, he would, moreover, be escorted by an entire detachment of musketeers, under the command of the same Marquis de Pérussi. In the end, he chose to go quietly.

Charles Edward signified his agreement in a face-saving letter to Louis XV on 12 December. Its message was as before: Louis was his friend; it was his ministers who were his enemies and it was they who had caused the problem in the first place: "Je ne puis exprimer a Votre Majesté l'inquietude dans lequelle j'ai eté tous ce tems de ne pouvoire pas luis exprimer directement mes panses, ne le pouvent pas a ces Ministres; j'ai trop de Confiance en ces bontes pour Croire quelle puise douter un Moment de mes Sentiments, et de mon inviolable attachement pour Sa Sacre personne; j'espere bien de le prouver un jour. En attendant je suis pret a partire immediatement de ces etats, puisquelle le desire."[70]

The Prince, suffering from bouts of coughing and vomiting, was obviously not feeling well. On the 13th, he nevertheless asked that his escort be sent for as soon as possible. Du Châtelet for his part tried to make his prisoner's stay as painless as possible. No expense was spared to keep the five fireplaces roaring (the Prince having relented on the question of moving from his corner cell), and the table was well served. Meals were eaten in ceremony with du Châtelet, another gentleman, and seven officers of the guard attending the Prince. "La table est servie comme il convient pour le Prince Edouard," du Châtelet reported on the 14th. "Le vin est le meilleur bourgogne. Il s'en boit honnestement."[71]

On the 14th, at Charles Edward's request, Stafford, Sheridan, Daniel O'Brien, and John Stewart were released from the Bastille and taken by carriage to Vincennes. O'Brien and Stewart were allowed to sleep at the Prince's house that night, still under guard, and they were present the following morning to witness Berryer's removal of the seals. The untouched condition of all the Prince's personal effects was verified and then everything, guns, broadswords, rapiers, kitchen utensils, silverware, clothing, papers, cupboards, horses, harnesses, carriages, etc., was left in the custody of Daniel, who, along with the other witnesses, Stewart, Chevillon, and Reydet, gave a formal acknowledgement that nothing had been disturbed.

After hearing mass, the Prince set out from Vincennes with the Marquis de Pérussi on Sunday, 15 December, at seven o'clock in the morning; by two o'clock that afternoon, he and his escort reached Fontainebleau where the Prince declared that he was too ill to continue.[72] Although he was often enough troubled with such bouts of illness after an emotional crisis, it is quite possible that on this occasion he had merely decided to delay de Pérussi's progress long enough to allow his servants time to catch up, since he had only the valet Richard Morrison with him.[73] Daniel O'Brien and John Stewart were still winding up his affairs at the house on the Rue du Chemin du Rempart and were unable in fact to leave Paris until the 16th. That was the case with the other two servants, Stokes and Gillsenan, who also benefited from an early release. Despite elaborate precautions to hide the precise date and time of the Prince's departure from Vincennes, the information leaked almost immediately, and the Princesse de Talmont lost no time in asking de Maurepas for permission to visit Charles Edward in Fontainebleau. The Minister wrote directly to Louis XV:

15 Xbre 1748

Sire

Je recois un courrier et une lettre de Me la Psse de Talmont qui me presse d'obtenir de Votre Majesté la permission d'aller avec Me de Bulkeley voir le Pce a Fontainebleau. Elle affirme que le Prince a a lui parler. J'attends les ordres de Votre Majesté pour lui repondre.

Maurepas.[74]

The King's negative answer, written in the margin of de Maurepas's letter, was swift and categorical: "Je ne veux pas que personne voie le prince. S'il a quelque chose a dire, il n'a qu'a ecrire." Louis was getting rather fed up with the Princess, and some of the ministers were suggesting that a *lettre de cachet* ordering her into exile in Lorraine was what was needed. De Maurepas, basically her friend, spoke against the suggestion, pointing out that she was the Queen's cousin and that it would seem as if she were being punished merely for her involvement in a romantic intrigue. It was decided, instead, that her husband (still brooding nervously in Lorraine) should be told to get her out of Paris as quickly as possible, but, as the Marquis d'Argenson wryly noted,"le pauvre mari y a moins d'autorité que son laquais, et cette dame prend le parti de rester à Paris, avec toute la fermeté même qu'y a apportée le prince Edouard."[75]

But if the Princesse de Talmont failed in her bid to see the Prince at Fontainebleau, she and Charles Edward's numerous supporters in the capital soon achieved major victories in the battle for public opinion. Much was made of the fact that the Prince had been placed in bonds during his arrest, and it was widely reported that the Dauphin had wept publicly on hearing the news. Court politics also played a part in the controversy, and some members of the Queen's party openly placed the blame for what happened not only on the personal enmity of de Puisieux toward the Prince but on the royal mistress as well — she whom the Dauphin and Mesdames now referred to only (albeit very much behind her back) as *Maman p*[utain].[76] D'Argenson went so far as to predict that the *garrottement* of the Prince would remain an indelible stain on France's honour: "On nous mettra sans doute à côté de Cromwell, qui a fait décapiter son roi, et nous, nous avons garrotté inutilement l'héritier présomptif et légitime de cette couronne."[77] Even Louis XV was shocked, apparently, by the manner of the arrest: "L'on dit que le tout retombe sur le duc de Biron, qui n'était pas déjà trop bien à la cour."[78]

By the last week of December, the reputation of de Biron's regiment itself had come under harsh attack, as the following sample of verse illustrates:

Cet essaim de héros qui sert bien son Roi
A Malplaque, Etinghen, Fontenoy,
Couvert d'une egale gloire,
Des gardes en un mot le brave regiment
Vient, dit-on, d'arrêter le fils du Prétendant.
Il a pris un Anglois, Ah! Dieu quelle victoire!

> Muses gravez bien vite au temple de mémoire
> Ce rare événement
> Va déesse aux cent voix, va l'apprendre à la terre,
> Car c'est le seul Anglois qu'il ait pris dans la guerre.[79]

Such abusive denunciations probably arose more from general dissatisfaction with the state of the nation than from specific indignation at the Prince's arrest. But the Cul-de-Sac incident somehow brought all of that general dissatisfaction into focus, and with the Jacobite exiles eagerly fanning the flames, the campaign of vituperation nearly got out of hand. Though pleased enough to see things falling apart in an administration which had seen fit to dispense with his services, D'Argenson was perturbed: "Je vois, dans le public et dans les bonnes compagnies, des discours qui me choquent, d'un mépris ouvert, d'un mécontentement profond contre le gouvernement: l'arrêt du prince Edouard y a mis le comble. Tout choque aujourd'hui: la paix paraît plus mauvaise qu'elle ne paraissait ci-devant, toutes les mesures pour la suite, l'exécution de la paix, la finance, les grâces, la nombreuse promotion, ce qui se passe à la cour, le choix, le crédit de la maîtresse, tout attriste, tout révolte; les chansons, les satires pleuvent de toutes parts."[80]

Examples of the many lampoons that were circulated are cited by de Luynes, Barbier, d'Argenson, and other memorialists of the day,[81] and it is not surprising, judging from the violence of some of the satirical pieces, that the government made a concerted if futile attempt to forbid discussions concerning the Prince in the cafés of Paris.[82] Some of the attacks were directed personally against the King. Louis XV, it was suggested, had become a lackey of the Elector of Hanover:

> François, gémissez tous, que l'Ecosse en frémisse,
> George d'Hanovre a pris Louis à son service;
> Et Louis devenu d'un électeur exempt,
> Arrête par surprise et lie indignement
> Un second Annibal, d'Albion le vrai maître,
> Et qui de l'univers mériteroit de l'être[83]

At Aix-la-Chapelle, France had been cheated of the spoils of a hard-won victory, a victory to which the imprisoned Prince had contributed in great measure:

> Peuple jadis si fier, aujourd'hui si servile,
> Des Princes malheureux vous n'êtes plus l'asile.
> Vos ennemis vaincus aux champs de Fontenoy
> A leurs propres vainqueurs ont imposé la loi.[84]

Violent satirical attacks on the King and Mme de Pompadour had occurred well before 10 December 1748 and continued long after, proof enough that the Prince's arrest represented only the pretext of the hour for venting an almost permanent state of public discontent with the Régime. But the ferocity of some of the lampoons directed against Louis XV, specifically in retaliation for his treatment of the Prince, is undeniable. One of the most violent appeared at the beginning of 1749. It will be the last example cited:

Incestueux tyran, traître, inhumain faussaire
Oses-tu t'arroger le nom de Bien-Aimé?
L'exil et la prison seront donc le salaire
D'un digne fils de roi, d'un prince infortuné?

George, dis-tu, t'oblige à refuser l'asile
Au vaillant Èdouard; s'il t'avait demandé,
Roi sans religion, de ta P[utain] l'exil,
Réponds-moi, malheureux, l'aurais-tu accordé?

Achève ton ouvrage, ajoute encore un crime:
Dans ton superbe Louvre élève un echafaud;
Immole, tu le peux, l'innocente victime,
Et sois, monstre d'horreur, toi-même le bourreau![85]

It was not only in Paris that tears of sorrow and dismay flowed for the Prince. At Lunéville, even the smoothly ambivalent Voltaire, who was working on his *Histoire de la Guerre de 1741* and praising the glories and triumphs of Louis le Bien-Aimé, was touched by the news of the Prince's arrest. He had just been reading to King Stanislas those parts of his work that dealt with Charles Edward's noble exploits and heroic sufferings. Many of the Prince's men had fallen. Defeat at Culloden had crowned the long series of calamities that had cursed his family for centuries. After finally escaping his pursuers in Scotland, he had taken refuge in France, where the English still hounded him, insisting, as a condition of peace, that he be driven out. The Prince had refused to comply: "son courage, aigri par tant de secousses, ne voulut pas plier sous la necessité. Il résista aux remontrances, aux prières, aux ordres, prétendant qu'on devait lui tenir la parole de ne le pas abandonner." Years later Voltaire would continue the story:

On se crut obligé de se saisir de sa personne. Il fut arrêté, garroté, mis en prison, conduit hors de France; ce fut là le dernier coup dont la destinée accabla une génération de rois pendant trois cent années.

Charles-Edouard, depuis ce temps, se cacha au reste de la terre. Que les hommes privés, qui se plaignent de leurs petites infortunes, jettent les yeux sur ce prince et sur ses ancêtres![86]

That is how Voltaire eventually wrote of the Prince whose career he had been following with great interest since 1745. But on that December evening in Lorraine when Stanislas informed him of the arrest, France's most celebrated author reacted less philosophically and in much the same manner as the Parisian public. According to his secretary Longchamp, he immediately grew very disturbed, crying out to the assembled company: "O ciel! Est-il possible que le roi souffre cet affront, et que sa gloire subisse une tache que toute l'eau de la Seine ne saurait laver!" Everyone present reacted in the same grief-stricken way, and when Voltaire returned to his apartment later that evening, he is said to have thrown his unfinished manuscript into a corner in disgust.[87]

The Ministry in Paris did its best to fight back, providing its diplomatic representatives abroad with a detailed account of the many steps that had been taken to try to convince the Prince to leave, as required by the peace treaty. There was ample evidence, going back as far as June, to show that the King had been more than patient. In the end, and to his great regret, Louis XV had been forced to act, especially when Charles Edward deliberately began to flaunt his scorn for the King's orders by showing himself off in public as much as possible and boasting to all who would listen that if it came to the use of force he would neither be taken alive nor be alone in dying on that day. Such desperate talk explained why so many precautions had been taken during his arrest, and that he was carrying concealed weapons when he was arrested showed only too clearly that those precautions had been justified.[88] In fact, despite all the rhymed diatribes, Louis XV eventually emerged from his contest of wills with Charles Edward Stuart and the Jacobites pretty much unscathed. Already by January, d'Argenson was able to note that even "bad Frenchmen" were disgusted with the satirical verses that attacked the King personally,[89] and Barbier earlier still had pointed out that the same public which protested the Prince's arrest would have certainly protested even more if the King of France had taken a hard line with the English at Aix-la-Chapelle on the clause requiring the Prince's expulsion and chosen instead to prolong the war for another two years.[90] His remark takes on a special significance and force when we read in his journal, less than one year later, that the Prince had become yesterday's news: "Une chose étonnante, c'est qu'on ne parle plus dans aucune *Gazette* du fils du Prétendant, le prince Edouard....On ne sait en aucune façon où il habite; cependant il existe et est quelque part incognito. C'est un fait bien singulier pour ce prince héritier légitime du royaume d'Angleterre, apres avoir fait tant de bruit dans l'Europe, de s'y trouver sans asile permis chez aucun prince, hors à Rome où il ne veut pas retourner."[91]

But as fate would have it, there were even more immediate ironies to the situation! When the outlaw prince and his escort reached Fontainebleau on the afternoon of 15 December, he was put up at the Cabaret de la Poste for the night. Almost at the same moment, another distinguished traveller arrived from the south and took a room immediately above that of the Prince. It worried de Pérussi (and it later worried de Puisieux and Louis XV even more!) when the identity of the traveller was discovered, for he was none other than General James St Clair returning from a military mission at Turin. With him was his secretary and aide, a rather fat, broad-faced, simple-looking man who seemed very much out of place in his ill-fitting scarlet uniform. The coincidence was simply too strange. Why would the General who in September 1746 had commanded a daring but largely symbolic landing of five thousand British troops at Lorient in Brittany, in retaliation for France's earlier token aid to the Pretender, suddenly turn up in Fontainebleau, on the same day as the prisoner, at the same inn, and *even in the room directly above?*[92] What Louis and his ministers were worried about is not exactly clear: a secret plot to abduct the prisoner? Or, more likely, an anti-French conspiracy entered into by a disaffected Pretender in exchange for the support of a new English faction? They were, in any case, too close to the situation to grasp the deeper, symbolic meaning of the event. Here was a man who had recently landed an enemy invasion force on French soil now peacefully enjoying the comforts of the best inn Fontainebleau could afford, on his way to Paris, perhaps to take in an opera or two before leaving to spend a cheerful Christmas at home in England; while in the room below, ill, under guard, and humiliated (though far from admitting it), was the erstwhile hero of the French nation, whose ragged band of five or six thousand badly disciplined and poorly supplied Highlanders, only three years before at Derby, had thrown the entire English nation into a state of panic. There was in fact nothing sinister about their purely coincidental meeting in Fontainebleau, but it symbolized unmistakably the end of Bonnie Prince Charlie's world. For him, there really could be no more serious hope. Ahead lay only illusion, disappointment, and the accelerating process of self-destruction that had already begun to set in. The General and his secretary, better known today as the philosopher David Hume, had been on the road from Turin since 29 November and knew nothing of what had happened in the Cul-de-Sac de l'Opéra on 10 December. At the Cabaret de la Poste, they had noted the presence of a young prisoner: "His Attendants said he was a Prince, but did not name him," St Clair reported in a letter to the Duke of Bedford from Paris on the 18th, but "as he wore a Star & Garter, he was soon known to every body." To underline the fact that the Prince's time of glory had indeed ended, the former invader (or more likely his philosophical secretary, a Scot but no friend of the Young Pretender) allowed himself the luxury of drawing a moral to the tale:

Thus by his rash Attempt in Britain, many of his Friends & Followers lost their Lives & Fortunes; and those, who had been so lucky as to escape to France, & to get into the Service of that Crown, he has now ruin'd their Fortunes, by his unaccountable Behaviour, which seems equally void of Temper & Common Sense. This I hope will open the Eyes, even of the most blinded, and let them see their Folly in engaging themselves in such desperate and criminal Enterprizes.[93]

Charles Edward, had he known about it, would have put such moralizing down to the wishful thinking of a vile Whig. He had lost the battle of Culloden, and now the battle of Paris, but he had not yet lost the war, nor his stubborn confidence that he would one day occupy the throne of his forefathers. In fact, the more he thought about it, the more his spirits began to pick up. Even before leaving Vincennes, he had started joking with his guards, asking what was happening at the Opéra and whether or not Jéliotte had sung well. On the 16th, before leaving Fontainebleau, he dashed off a short note to Bulkeley that summed up everything rather well: "Je vous prie de dire a tous mes amis que je me port bien. Ma tete n'a jamais eté hors de mes Epole. Il y est Encore."[94]

Seven days later Charles Edward said goodbye to the Marquis de Pérussi at the half-way point on the bridge at Pont-de-Beauvoisin. Before they parted, on Monday, 23 December, at eleven o'clock in the morning, the Prince asked his escort to convey the expression of his deep respect to the King, the Queen, and the Dauphin. Then, he moved off. Pérussi wrote immediately to Maurepas that he was "très persuadé...que ce prince ne rentrera pas dans le Royaume et nira point a Avignon. Il m'en a assuré plusieurs fois."[95]

Four days later, at seven o'clock in the morning on 27 December, Charles Edward Stuart was nevertheless in Avignon, standing at the bedside of his old tutor, James Murray, Earl of Dunbar, who was staying with his widowed sister, Lady Inverness. The Prince was dressed in the uniform of an Irish officer in French service.[96] It was only the first of many disguises and incognito identities he would adopt in the years of solitary wandering and "skulking" that lay ahead. But despite the ever-changing masks he would assume, his inner being had already fixed on a more permanent image of himself. It had to do with something Sir John Graeme had told him in a letter from Frankfurt back in June — such a long time before! Yes, he was indeed a poor bird searching for a nest. Until he found one, he would be forced to wander.

Would he in those years of wandering be forgotten? The thought did not even cross his mind! Already he was busy writing to his followers in Paris, attempting to establish a new base of operations. His mistress, the Princesse de Talmont, did not waste time either, and before a month had passed, she had organized an effective network of clandestine communications for her lover's benefit, and all with the help of an entirely new set of devoted friends. Soon he would join her secretly in Lorraine and even back in Paris. There would be many passionate quarrels followed by equally passionate reconciliations.

The Prince kept his goal of a Stuart restoration unswervingly in mind. Unfortunately, he now had no idea how it could be achieved. Later still, he would conduct himself as if it no longer mattered.

And his first mistress? We can be certain, I think, that she too had not forgotten. In fact, remembering the panic and anxiety she had experienced in May and June at the mere thought of his having to leave the country, we can only imagine the agonies of suspense and suffering she must have (silently now) endured at the time of his arrest. In her heart, she was still totally his; no doubt she would remain so till the end of her days, but there would never again be any way for her to give direct expression to her feelings for him. She, better than anyone else, knew what effect the humiliations and indignities of 10 December would have had on the vulnerably proud Prince. She had witnessed his secret reactions to defeat before. And now he was gone. Perhaps she consoled herself with the thought that at least his child was safely with her. On 29 December, she sent a New Year's greeting to James in Rome. No one knew where the Prince was or where he was headed. But her message to the father obliquely and discreetly included fond best wishes for the son as well:

Sire

Permettez moi d'assurer Votre Majesté au commencement de cette nouvelle année des voeux ardents que je faits pour elle. J'ose me flatter qu'elle doit estre persuadée de la sincérité de mes souhaits et combien je m'intéresse a tout ce qui peut regarder Votre Majesté. J'ose donc la suplier de recevoir avec les mêmes bontées dont elle m'a toujours honorée, les assurances d'attachement et du profond respect avec lequel je suis

Sire
De Votre Majesté
la tres humble et tres obeissante servante

L. De la Tour D'Auvergne, Princesse
De Rôhan, Duchesse de Monbazon

A Paris ce 29 Xbre 1748[97]

Postscript

W E HAVE REACHED—or very nearly—the end of our story. What
follows is not so much a conclusion as a combination of postscript and
potpourri. Far too many years remain in the lives of Louise and Charles Edward
to be summed up and "concluded" in the usual sense. The Princess did not die
until 1781, and the Prince lived on for seven years after that. When Charles
Edward's arrest took place at the Opéra on 10 December 1748, Alfieri was not
yet born, and Louise of Stolberg, Charles Edward's future wife, whom he
eventually lost in a humiliating manner to that handsome poet, did not come
into the world until 20 September 1752.

But in a certain aesthetic sense, the life of our main protagonist ended long
before his death. What touches us most about the Prince, his essential character
as revealed in times of moral crisis, is already rounded off and fully displayed by
the time he rode out from the Château de Vincennes to that symbolic bridge on
the border between France and Savoy. To trace his subsequent progress through
the dreary years of drunkenness, bad faith, and degradation would add little to
our appreciation of the tragedy of his life. After his arrest, the die was cast. What
happened in the Cul-de-Sac de l'Opéra that December afternoon was the
culminating point of his tragic misfortune and represented for the Prince a
defeat personally more devastating even than Culloden. After the unlucky battle
on Drummossie Moor, Charles Edward, though embittered, was capable still of
coping with failure. After Vincennes, he abandoned all honest contact with the
realities of his situation, sustaining himself mainly on self-delusion. The admirably passionate, eager, and generous apprentice warrior who had sailed off for
Scotland in the summer of 1745 was no more. Gone too was the celebrated hero
who, after his return from the Highlands, had allowed himself to fall innocently
and deeply in love with his charming cousin. Before that love affair was over,
and by the time he reached the Pont-de-Beauvoisin, every defect of character
identified with his later years was apparent. Only a long, frenetically aimless

game of hide-and-seek, followed by years of cheerless stupor, quite unredeemed by the commission of a single praiseworthy act or the attainment of even a hint of composure and serenity, lay ahead. The full story of the Prince's fall from glory, though pathetic and sometimes moving, belongs elsewhere. It remains peripheral, bereft of moral impact. The years after Vincennes—indeed, after the end of his only great love affair—led not to growth but to oblivion, the oblivion, first of all that the Prince now found all too frequently in his cups and, finally, to that great void revealed today in the popular memory of Bonnie Prince Charlie's legend, which has, by a restorative process of renewal, sloughed off the last forty years of its hero's life.

For the Princess, the story ends rather differently. Much less is known about her, of course, but we have turned up enough information to suggest that, unlike the hero she loved more than anyone or anything else in the world, she emerged from her own crisis of failure in 1748 enhanced and augmented in spirit, at ease with her friends and family (despite a brutal humiliation) and, most important of all, basically at peace with herself and her world when the moment eventually came for leaving it.

But all that is too quickly said. We have spent too many hours sharing in the daily lives and secret concerns of our characters not to try to capture an additional glimpse or two of their ghostly figures receding into the distant past. Moreover, there are still a few loose ends to attend to.

The first is the fate of the love-child, Prince Charles Edward Stuart's first offspring and only son. As we have already noted, the boy died young, on 18 January 1749. In those harsher times, it was common for children not to live through their first year, and generally no period of mourning was observed by the family. On the day following young Charles-Godefroi's death, at nine o'clock in the evening, the usual funeral prayers were recited in Louise's parish church of St Paul. Then the young prince's body was taken for burial to the crypt of St Louis in the famous convent of the Feuillants, where members of the Rohan-Guéméné family were traditionally buried.[1] Lovers of sentimental stories will seek in vain for vestiges of his tomb today. The famous church was razed early in the nineteenth century to make way for the Rue de Castiglione and the Rue de Rivoli.[2] From documents in the Rohan archives, however, we know that the child's epitaph read as follows:

> Ci gît Charles-Godefroi-Sophie-Jules-Marie, agé de 5 mois 21 jours; fils de très haut et très puissant et très illustre prince Monseigneur Jules-Hercule, Prince de Rohan, Duc de Montbazon, et de très haute et très puissante et très illustre princesse Madame Marie-Louise-Henriette-Jeanne de la Tour d'Auvergne, Princesse de Bouillon, son épouse: décédé le 18 Janvier 1749.[3]

The event must have left Louise (though perhaps not Mme de Guéméné) heartbroken. As for the Prince, he was in Avignon when his son's death occurred, and I have found no evidence to suggest that he even took note of it. Instead, he was busily planning his revenge and polishing up his narrative of the "unherd of Barbaros and Inhuman tretement"[4] he had so recently met with in Paris. Little hostile scribblings dashed off on the subject of Louis and James, on priests and *putains*, are found in his scrap papers of this period, along with various drafts of what he remembers telling his guards, such as the following: "Ses [c'est] Loui qui vous pey et c'est L'Electeur qui vous commande. Jugges si je me soumetterez a ses Lois."[5] Occasionally, he also tried his hand at scatological doggerel:

> Hier j'ai prie un Emetique severe
> Pour se soire je prens un ver de Biere
> Et demain je me purge par Deriere.[6]

Other profundities in a similar vein flowed from the pen of the man described only a few months before by the great Montesquieu as an author worthy (were he not so great a prince) of the Academy, but these are perhaps best left forgotten. One or two scribblings suggest that the exiled Prince was at last making significant progress in wisdom and self-knowledge. "Si je n'etoit pas Mois," he solemnly wrote, "je serois plus heureux."[7] Closer examination of the context of that insightful gem unfortunately reveals that the Prince meant only to flatter himself by stating that all of his problems had stemmed from the fact that he was a too-shining example of virtue and integrity. He had suffered because he was, fundamentally and unshakably, an honourable and honest man. Pragmatic men like Louis or James, less honest and less honourable, would never know what to make of such puzzling behaviour. It was a comforting thought. Soon it became one of the Prince's favourite notions, and he returned to it frequently in the next few years, especially when money was in short supply: "Je n'ai jamais fait fortune," he complained, "avec Les Cotillion [i.e., women]. Les pretres sont mes Enemis, et je suis trop malheureux ou honet home pour avoir de L'Argent."[8]

With such amusements the Prince whiled away some of the long hours of concealment. In the beginning, the game of hide-and-seek which he played with great skill for roughly a decade after riding out from Avignon with Henry Goring on 25 February 1749 was as much his way of taking sweet revenge on Louis and James for the humiliation of 10 December as it was an integral part of his covert strategy to keep the Hanoverians guessing about when, where, and how he would next strike. It pleased him mightily to be able to taunt the French King with rumours (generally true, but sometimes quite false and deliberately circulated by associates like Lally) that he regularly visited Paris, in spite of his promise not to return to French soil and, especially, in spite of a nation-wide alert of French internal security forces, provided with standing orders to apprehend the royal outlaw on sight. Indeed, it is probably fair to suggest that for a number of years after January 1749, Charles Edward had more to fear from the French in this respect than from George II's largely ineffective agents. Louis, moreover, had not found it difficult to grasp the point that the Prince's little game of concealment was meant to be a continuation of the nose-thumbing that had preceded his arrest. Harsh orders were consequently given out that he was to be offered none of the usual courtesies if apprehended, whether in disguise or otherwise. In fact, if the Prince did formally declare his identity after capture, he was still to be treated with exemplary severity as an impertinent adventurer who was obviously going around impersonating a worthy member of the House of Stuart, it being understood that the real Prince was a man too honourable to break his word to the King of France. Charles Edward, as it turned out, proved too clever to be captured in spite of the guards posted on roads and border crossings, the distribution of "wanted" posters bearing his likeness, and the frequent police searches carried out in Paris and Lunéville. Often he was rumoured to be in three or four different countries at the same time. The truth is that for the first few years, apart from a few short trips, he managed to live quietly and comfortably enough at Lunéville near the Princesse de Talmont or in Paris or Marly with her closest friends, the Comtesse de Vassé and Mlle Elisabeth Ferrand.

The Prince's romance with Mme de Talmont, though it had soured momentarily when she chose to comply somewhat too zealously with the Versailles-inspired order to deny him admission to her house, soon flourished again, even before his arrest. In the following year, with the death from smallpox of her only son, the fifteen-year-old Duc de Taillebourg, the Princess's long-troubled marriage finally collapsed, and there was no further need to exercise caution with respect to a husband who had, in any case, now retreated to his solitary devotions. Though a little tarnished by the open scandal of her relationship with the Prince, Talmont's reputation at the Court of Versailles as well as at Lunéville seems to have remained essentially undamaged, and her determination to maintain her status in both of those places soon provoked no end of suspicion and anxiety on the part of the Prince. At times, a curious reversal of roles developed in their correspondence. Though she too spoke of the Prince as her adored monarch, Talmont categorically refused to cater to his extravagant whims. Now it was his turn to complain of "duretés"—ironically, much in the style of his former sweetheart, well illustrated in the following *cri du coeur*: "Je me meurs, je vous aime trop et vous m'aimez trop peu....J'ai passé une nuit affreuse!"[9]

Such familiarly snivelling echoes of Louise's correspondence — infrequent but strangely incongruous in the Prince's prose—did not always instantly melt the heart of an experienced mistress who was serenely untroubled by doubts regarding her own worth. Her political influence at Lunéville with Stanislas and at Versailles with the Queen was not inconsiderable, and although she never hesitated to place it entirely at the Prince's disposal, she, unlike Louise, nevertheless always knew how and when to call his bluff and how to deal with his tantrums. She had put herself in Louis XV's bad books because of him; she had willingly sacrificed for him her own peace of mind, her health and even her fortune. For the most part, Charles Edward, now more self-centred than ever, simply took her for granted. Perhaps what eventually angered the Princess most was the fact that, ultimately, he had robbed her of a worthy "final affair." She had had many important lovers in her lifetime, but one especially, the long-dead Chevalier de Wiltz, had retained a unique place in her heart. Charles Edward should have been a worthy successor; regrettably, he often failed to live up to his own heroic image, and when the Prince chose to be disappointing, he could be very disappointing indeed! At one stage his paranoid suspicions even drove him to question Talmont's personal loyalty to his cause, and he accused her of wanting to betray him to his enemies. The Princess's response was withering: "Je ne puis jamais vous souhaiter aucun mal, encore moins vous nuire. Sortez de vos indignes inquiétudes. Votre secret est en sureté. Il n'y a que vous qui le trahissiez."[10] That particular letter, like a number of others in the same vein, closed with a formal *Adieu*, but, for all that, their relationship raged on well into 1751, even after she had suggested to him that he should seek his victims elsewhere: "Car ce n'est pas des amis qu'il vous faut, mais des victimes."[11] The affair ended only when the Prince in the following year turned his attentions toward a fresh victim, Clementina Walkinshaw, the eventual mother of his second child and probably the first of his ladies to experience routine physical (in addition to psychological) brutality at his hands.

Stormy as their relationship had been, Talmont never forgot the last of her distinguished lovers. Years later, though she continued to maintain a nodding acquaintance with the worldliness of Court life, her thoughts turned more and more to gloomy spiritual matters. It was noted by several of her friends that she often wore a rather unusual bracelet in which was set a miniature portrait of the Prince. By pressing on a hidden spring, one could cause a matching portrait of Christ to appear alongside it. The explanation was, of course, that the kingdom of neither of the two figures portrayed was of this world![12]

One last glimpse of this remarkable eighteenth-century woman deserves to be recorded. In January 1766, her friend the Duchesse d'Aiguillon asked if she might bring the English eccentric Horace Walpole to visit her in her Luxembourg Palace apartment. The Queen's cousin, because of her continuing loyalty to the Prince and a consequent dislike of Englishmen, hesitated, but she finally agreed. In a letter to Gray, Walpole describes how he found the aging beauty "sitting on a small bed hung with saints and Sobieskis, in a corner of one of those vast chambers, by two blinking tapers." "I stumbled," he continued, "over a cat, a foot-stool, and a chamber-pot in my journey to her presence. She could not find a syllable to say to me, and the visit ended with her begging a lap-dog."[13] In a letter to Montagu two months later, the same writer reported that she had just sent him a wretched painting of two pug dogs and a black and white greyhound; it was the latter, the dearly departed Diana, that needed replacing, and he was also to send back the precious picture immediately. "She is so devout," Walpole added, "that I did not dare send her word that I am not possessed of a twig of Jacob's broom, with which he streaked cattle as he pleased."[14] Even her death on 20 December 1773 was acted out in style. She had prepared for it well in advance. A magnificent blue and silver dress had been ordered for her burial, and even with one foot in the grave, she was concerned to leave behind a worthy epigram. On the evening of the 19th, her physicians, her confessor, and her steward were summoned to her bedside. To the first she said: "Gentlemen, you have killed me, but you did it in conformity with your rules and principles." To her confessor she declared: "You have done your duty by causing me great terror." And, finally, to her steward, she added: "You are here at the solicitation of my servants who wish me to make my will. You are all of you," she continued, "playing your parts very well, but you must grant I am not playing mine badly either!"[15] Afterwards, the Archbishop of Paris, sensitive to the requirements of his own role in such matters, ordered that the silver dress be sold, with the proceeds given to the poor.

Never too plentiful, money was in even shorter supply for the Prince after his association with the Princesse de Talmont came to an end. Stafford and Sheridan, who had been left in charge of his threadbare household in Avignon, regularly sent frantic reports on their financial difficulties. Finally, in May 1752, Charles Edward decided to dismiss all of his French servants, sell his horses and coach, and place his possessions in storage. Among the servants retained was, we are not surprised, his Irish valet, Daniel O'Brien, although it is clear that, given a choice, Stafford and Sheridan would have preferred to see the quarrelsome Irishman among the first to go. Some of the servants had already run off, citing Daniel's wicked temper and ill-treatment. Complaints of his "bad language" were also frequent, and it was suspected on at least one occasion that he had been wearing the Prince's linen and stockings.[16] Several months later, a further report informed the Prince that his fiery-tempered valet had been quarreling with Lady Inverness's maid and was threatening to leave.[17] Knowing the Prince's special liking for him, the two gentlemen stewards persuaded him to stay, but by the summer of 1752 the illiterate servant who had acted as Louise's confidant throughout the affair (with how much good faith we do not know) was imitating his master in ways that went well beyond the wearing of his clothes. The sad tale is made clear in the following letter sent by Stafford to James Edgar in Rome:

Dear Sir

The Intention of serving any body belonging to H.R.H. is a sufficient
Excuse for this trouble. One of his Valet de Chambres, named Daniel O
Brian, got a girl of this Town with child, she was of a bad character & almost
common before he knew her. In the beginning she seem'd satisfied to send
the Child to the Charity house, he paying the Expences, or that he woud
take the Child & give her more money than he could well spare, all which he
agreed to, but nothing will satisfy her now but his marrying her. You must
know that her father is one of the greatest rogues in this Town, two or three
Sisters of hers followed the same trade. They have done all they coud to no
purpose in this part of the world. The Mother & daughter set off for Rome
yesterday. If they shoud make any application to H.M. you'll be so kind as to
represent the affair in its proper light. It woud be cruel to oblige a Man to
Marry the rest of one third of the Town. He'll quit his bread & fly the
Country sooner than be pushed to that Extremity. He is a good Servant &
am persuaded that H.R.H. is very well satisfyed with his Service therefore
deserves your protection. You'll lay me with the greatest respect at H.M.'s
feet.

I am very sincerely, wishing you all health & happyness

Dear Sir

Your most obedient humble servant

Avignon   H. Stafford
August the 4th 1752[18]

From Rome a few weeks later came a reassuring reply. Edgar had consulted
James on the problem and found His Majesty inclined not to meddle in so
delicate a matter. "So I really think," the King's secretary continued, "poor
Obryen may be at ease as to any apprehensions he may have of H.M.'s giving ear
or encouragement to the complaints & instances of the Mother & Daughter you
mention to be coming here." There was the possibility that the two women
would go directly to the Pope, but, there again, Edgar believed they would not
meet with much success.[19]

Daniel's gratitude on hearing the good news knew no bounds. Although he
was by now busy learning to write, it is clear that he had more than substantial
help in penning the following expression of his appreciation to Edgar:

Avignon Sept 9 1752

Sir

As M. Stafford was pleas'd to communicate to me what you were so good
as write him with regarde to my affaires, not to appear ungrateful I thought

my self in Duty bound to give you the trouble of this, to Express my thanks and beg the continuation of your protection.

You will easily belive me when I assure you I am Extreamly Sorry to have given you trouble on this account as it is an affair has given me a great deal of uneasiness. But this never woud have happen'd had the Girl been of a fair Character. But as I have certain knowledge of her being quite the contrary, I was oblidged to stand on my own defence, for before they came to those Extremitys, I had offer'd to do every thing for her that was in my power and even more than was well in it, but nothing wou'd Satisfy them but what must absolutely have ruin'd me. Whatever Issue it may have, I Shall ever Retain a most grateful sense of your Goodness and Shall ever wish for an opportunity to shew how much I am with all Respect Your most gratefull

Most Oblig'd and most
Devoted humble Servant
Daniel O'Brian[20]

As it turned out, Daniel was soon rescued from his domestic dilemmas by the providential arrival of a mysterious letter from the Prince, asking Stafford and Sheridan to send him without delay and most secretly to Paris. There, under an assumed name, he was to hole up and await further instructions concerning a long journey he would be making.[21] The Prince's valet leaped at the opportunity to be once more back in action, cloak-and-dagger style. We are, nevertheless, left wondering about the nature of the very special relationship that existed between the Prince and his servant as well as the extent to which Daniel's own cynicism (and mischief-making inventiveness?) on the subject of women may have helped to poison the Prince's suspicious mind against Louise during the very time she was placing so much trust in him as her principal confidant. That he was indeed cynical in his attitude toward women and affairs of the heart is more than suggested by Lord Dunbar, who, having had sufficient opportunity over several years to observe the behaviour of Charles Edward's valet, warned Edgar that marriage to Daniel would be only a "second misfortune" for the poor girl in question, he being a "mauvais sujet" who, if dismissed by the Prince, would never find the means to maintain a wife.[22]

Our postscript should obviously include a word or two regarding James, but after it has been noted that Charles Edward's relations with his father continued at much the same low ebb until the Old Pretender died on New Year's Day, 1766, there remains little to add. After his son's arrest, he finally gave up trying to understand the Prince or what he was up to. For a time he was even convinced that Charles Edward, long before he left Rome in 1744, had somehow been "controlled" through a mysterious English correspondence whose purpose was to exclude James and the Catholic religion from any restoration scheme. The Prince had thus been conforming to a secret master plan all along! Just thinking about such a possibility made the old man thank God that at least Henry had become a Cardinal and a priest.[23] Mostly, however, James was now content to express only puzzlement. Fully one year after the Prince's expulsion, for example, he conceded that he could not criticize his son's conduct for the simple reason that he was totally ignorant of the motives that might be behind it. "But I own to you," he confided to his son, "I do not comprehend it, & I comprehend yet less what motives you can have to behave as you do & as you have done for more than four years towards your friends in this part of the world."[24]

The Old Pretender's uncertainties and questions went unanswered. Even when Charles Edward in July 1750 sent his valet Daniel to Rome on a special mission related to the renewal of his commission as Regent, it was made clear to James that the valet was under strict orders from his master to reveal nothing of the Prince's current whereabouts or activities. James was merely expected to grant the commission and to pay the courier's expenses as well! "As to the new Power of Regency you want," James pursued on that occasion, "you must be sensible that you have acted towards me for these five years past in a manner which noways deserves so great a mark of trust & kindness, but far be it from me to act, especially towards you, by picque or resentment. It is true the treatment you give me is a continual heartbreak to me, but it excites my compassion more than my anger, because I will always be persuaded that you are deluded. If you seem to forget that you are my Son, I can never forget that I am your Father."[25] In fact, Charles Edward would have been just as happy to forget even that particular truth. In the years to come, despite many pathetic appeals, he refused to visit his father although he was not above taking money from him specifically for that purpose. He eventually did turn up in Rome, but only after James's funeral, hoping, of course, to be recognized by the Pope as Charles III, titular King of England. Taking his lead from France, the Pope refused to comply, and Charles Edward was outraged. At least his brother Henry, to whom he now deigned to speak, was willing to treat him like the true King of England—in fact, the Cardinal Duke even made over one of his pensions to him! The Pope's decision did not, in any case, prevent him from styling himself as he pleased and now "Charles. R." replaced "Charles. P." as his signature to all letters. One such he wrote to his uncle, the Duc de Bouillon, expressing great shock and indignation at the Church's shabby treatment of one so deserving. Now, too, he professed great sorrow at the loss of his dear father:

Monsieur Mon Oncle et Cousin,

J'ai bien senti Monsieur combien vous auriez eté penetré de la perte que j'ai faite du Roy Mon Pere. Votre attachement pour mois que je me flatte pouvoire exprimer sans bornes, me fonte voire aussi Combien vous aurés eté chocké de l'endigne reception que La Sainte Eglise ma faite jusquasteur—

Contraire a tout droit de jens et Religion. Mon Cour est trop plen pour vous en dire davantage, je suis

Votre affectionné Neveu et Cousin
Charles. R.

Rome Le 25em Fev.er 1766[26]

It can be seen from this letter that by the time he became "King," Charles Edward had managed to improve his spelling only a little. His syntax, too, retained its old flavour. It is only the underlying tone of bad faith and hypocrisy that seems to have reached a new degree of perfection.

As for the Duc de Bouillon, it is worth noting that he and his family suffered no appreciable loss of favour at Court because of his nephew's escapades. In September 1749, for example, Louis XV paid the Grand Chambellan the honour of a visit at Navarre, where he was received in magnificence and splendour. A royal stag hunt was organized but went off only moderately well, the dogs having been distracted by the intrusion of an immature buck. Fortunately, Louis was able to play several games of piquet while matters were sorted out, and the incident did not prevent his joining in the kill later on in the day.[27]

Other things remained unchanged as well. When Madame Henriette, Louis XV's second daughter, died in February 1752, the Rohans and the Bouillons were presented with yet another excellent opportunity to insult a royal corpse by insisting as usual that they could not participate in the holy water ceremony unless allowed to assert their preeminence over ordinary dukes and duchesses. Representatives from both families, including Louise and her sister-in-law, stayed away as a result. When the Dauphin turned up to pay his respects to his late sister, the Duc de Richelieu, Maréchal de France, and the Duc de Fleury, Premier Gentilhomme de la Chambre du Roi, together carried his ceremonial cloak. Denied the privilege of carrying it entirely on his own, the Grand Chambellan finally declared to the King that he could attend only if ordered to by His Most Christian Majesty.[28] Louis, with exquisite delicacy, left the matter unresolved.

Ironically, a very different kind of incident involving the Duc, his daughter, and a rather larger quantity of unblessed water became the talk of Paris only a few months later when Charles-Godefroy, Louise, and ten other persons, including several servants, were bitten by the Duc's little dog at Navarre. Fear that the animal was rabid compelled all to leave immediately for the seaside where the traditional saltwater immersion treatment was administered to each by a party of sailors. Things took a comic turn when it came time for the Duc to be plunged into the sea. Stripped and nervously waiting to be called, the Grand Chambellan suddenly panicked and ran off naked through the town with a half-dozen sailors, similarly unclad, in hot pursuit. "Ils donnèrent," Mme O'Brien reported to her husband (now Lord Lismore) in Rome, "un spectacle assez ridicule à toute la ville; enfin on ratrapa Mr de Bouillon, et malgré sa peur, il a esté plongé dans les flots." It will be recalled that the writer, Margaret Josepha O'Brien, had not long before been sufficiently astute to turn down the opportunity for a brief romp with Louis XV in favour of a more stable adulterous relationship with the Archbishop of Cambrai. Now she added a remark that showed her wit in other ways as well: "On peut dire de cette scene comique, que le sang de Mr de Turenne ne craint pas le feu, mais l'eau."[29]

In spite of such inopportune occurrences, the Duc and his family prospered. In January 1753, the Grand Chambellan's uncle, the Comte d'Evreux, died. He had been senile for several years, but he had made out his will in 1745 while still mainly of sound mind. Seven codicils followed, granting generous bequests to all of his relatives with the notable exception of his grandniece.[30] The exclusion reflected d'Evreux's long-standing disapproval of Louise's disaffection with her mother, and de Luynes noted the omission in his journal.[31] Soon after his death, the Comte d'Evreux's house (it survives today as part of the Elysée Palace) was purchased by Mme de Pompadour for 500,000 livres.

The year following his uncle's death gave the Grand Chambellan a foretaste of the Revolution to come. In the best style of an Ancien Régime nobleman, he had always been as protective of his hunting privileges as he was jealous of his ceremonial rights at Court, and he had, for some time, been especially zealous in practising systematic game conservation in all of his many jurisdictions. Harvests over a large area suffered as a result, and local farmers complained bitterly. Finally, in the Mantes-Meulan region, discreetly urged on by two parish priests, eight hundred angry peasants armed with sticks assembled one day in March 1754 for an enormous *battue*. Every partridge and rabbit for miles around was destroyed while the Duc's game wardens, overwhelmed by the force of numbers, looked on helplessly. Only after the *maréchaussée* intervened and arrested twenty-seven leaders of the unholy sedition was the Grand Chambellan able to regain his peace of mind and the assurance that his favourite sport could continue undiminished.[32]

With the passage of time, though he still had a number of outstanding debts dating back to his days of high-stake gambling and youthful folly, the Duc gave proof of having learned how to practise conservation in other important ways as well. More and more of his attention was devoted to business and the accumulation of productive wealth. The estate at Navarre, enormously rich in forest resources, was generating by the mid-fifties an annual revenue of nearly 400,000 livres. In 1757, Charles-Godefroy distinguished himself by becoming the first head of the Bouillon family in his century to visit the duchy from which the family name was derived. Charles Edward himself benefitted from his uncle's new interest and spent the last of his wandering incognito years at the Château of Carlsbourg in the Duc's territories before returning, finally, to Rome after James's death. It was from Bouillon in 1760, that Clementina Walkinshaw, by then in almost constant fear of being beaten or choked to death by a Prince who was every day growing more violent and less charming, fled to a convent, taking with her their seven-year-old daughter Charlotte.

With the outbreak of the Seven Years' War, and especially when things began to go badly for France, Charles-Godefroy again found himself playing the role of intermediary between the Prince and Louis XV in matters of high policy. Charles Edward had not, of course, forgotten the humiliations of Vincennes or, for that matter, what he had told the Chiefs in Scotland about promised military expeditions and French bad faith. He was not interested in being duped a second time. If the French wanted to make use of his services, they would have to grovel a little. Then they would have to prove their sincerity by signing a binding treaty before any action was undertaken. A vague correspondence ensued and under such secret code names as "Newland," "Fisher," and "Le Faucon," the Duc eventually found himself playing the role of sole negotiator for his nephew in dealings with the Court of France. To the Grand Chambellan it must have seemed like the beginning of an exciting and important era. But even though the Prince finally agreed to correspond directly with Louis XV, not to mention his old enemy, Mme de Pompadour, assuring them that a mere thirty or forty thousand men would make him master of the whole of Britain in less than six weeks, it is highly doubtful that his heart was in the enterprise or that he really believed anything serious would come of it. The indomitable spirit of the '45 had long since died in him, destroyed by inaction, self-pity, and drink.[33] Before long, in any case, the victories of Boscawen and Hawke put an end to prospects for an expedition against England.

And Louise? There does not seem to exist, first of all, much in the way of documentation for our postscript. Indeed, even the most recent biographical references to the Princess, all of them sketchy, show her as living twelve years longer than she actually did and as losing her head to the guillotine in 1793.[34]

We nevertheless know a few facts. First of all, the departure of the Prince and the death of their son did not drive her to a nunnery or turn her into a devoutly solitary recluse. She still made infrequent appearances at Court, although, in that regard, her life does seem to have been unusually uneventful. The search for clues is complicated by the fact that during the period 1749-1756, there were two persons actively using the title "Princesse de Rohan"—Louise and Mme de Guémené's young and very attractive stepmother, Marie-Sophie de Courcillon (1713-1756), the widowed second wife of Hercule-Mériadec de Rohan-Soubise (1669-1749). Like the two Duchesses de Bouillon in Marie-Charlotte's day, the two Princesses de Rohan were occasionally confused in the public mind although their life-styles were quite different. Renowned for her exceptional beauty, Marie-Sophie (the godmother of Charles Edward's son) had already, by the time her husband died at the age of eighty in 1749, cultivated a number of intimate friendships among members of the capital's artistic and literary community, and her name occasionally comes up in the scandal sheets of the day. Writing to her husband in Rome about a reception that she had attended one evening in St Ouen at Prince Charles de Rohan's fine residence (Charles Edward's old summer house), Mrs. O'Brien mentions that among the guests were the celebrated Mlle Fel (who according to the Nuncio sang more beautifully than the finest performers of Rome), the poet de Moncrif, and the Princesse de Rohan, additionally described as "La belle ou la Courcillon," to distinguish her from her presumably less-favoured namesake.[35] On the occasion of Marie-Sophie's death, de Luynes recalled her legendary beauty and her skill at dancing. Unfortunately, she seems to have been notable, as well, for a distressing ability to detect *risqué* double entendres in the simplest and plainest of statements, and even in the *Kyrie eleison* at mass! Her final will and testament directed that no less than twelve thousand masses be said for the repose of her soul,[36] proof enough, no doubt, that beauty can be a greater obstacle to salvation than wit.

But if there seems to be no evidence to show that Louise fell into a life of reckless dissipation after her disastrous affair with the Prince, there is, on the other hand, a fair amount of documentation that suggests she did go on with a life of quiet domesticity. The few letters of hers that we have show her as remaining on very good terms with her father, her husband, and even her mother-in-law. Indeed, the tone of her letters to the Grand Chambellan reminds us almost too much of the young adolescent girl who wrote such affectionate notes from Poland twenty years earlier. Here is a sample, composed ten years after her tragic affair:

> Que je suis reconnoissante, Mon cher papa, de la bontée que vous avée eu de me mander votre montre. Elle reglera la mienne. J'yrai vous attendre a Versailles et de la repartirai en même tems que vous pour vous aller faire ma cour et j'espere que cela sera pour quelque temps. Cela fera tout mon bonheur, n'en connoissant pas de plus grand pour moi que de pouvoir estre avec vous.[37]

The occasion of this particular note is soon made clear: Mme de Guémené had asked Louise to send the Duc a copy of a letter just received from the Maréchal de Belle-Isle in which it was regretfully announced that Jules had been passed over that year for promotion to the rank of *maréchal de camp*: "Elle est furieuse et avec raison," was Louise's comment, reminding us of other times when Mme de Guémené's fury was not something that her daughter-in-law would have sympathized with. It was, she agreed, quite unjust: "Il me semble que l'on ne suit plus l'ordre du tableau et qu'il auroit pu mériter meme comme grace le grade de Maréchal de camp. Cela est désolant." Of course, family vanity rather than true wifely affection might explain Louise's keen disappointment. On the other hand, nothing could be more unambiguous than her obvious fondness for her father. Her letter concludes: "Adieu, cher papa, je me fais une bien grande feste de vous revoir jeudi et vous renouveller les assurances les plus tendre de mon attachement pour vous, cher papa, que j'aime et embrasse bien tendrement."

Mme de Guéméné too seems to have remained unchanged with the passage of time. Fifteen years after her favourite son's marriage, iron-willed and possessively matriarchal as ever, she was still running the family, defending its honour and seeing to its welfare:

> Jai reçù ce matin votre lettre Monsieur le Marechal; je ne puis vous cacher quelle ma fort afligée sans cependant m'oter la reconnoissance que je dois avoir de la façon dont vous avié bien voulu parler au roy en lui representant les injustices que lon a fait a Mr de Rohan et en lui faisant valoir la façon dont mon fils s'est toujours distinguer dans touttes les occasions. C'est bien malheureux pour mon fils quil soit le seul qui ne peut eprouver les bontés du roi....Puisque je nai pas la satisfaction de le voir recompenser pour le grade de marechal de camp, voici Mr le Marechal ma façon de penser que jay lhonneur de vous communiquer: je trouve en veritée que M de Rohan a assée bien servi pour sa gloire et celle de sa maison pour songer a present de venir se reposer auprès d'une mere qui l'aime tendrement.[38]

As it turns out, Jules did not leave the army to join his mother; he fought gallantly for the duration in a war that ended so disastrously for France, receiving his promotion to the rank of *maréchal de camp* in 1759 and to *lieutenant-général* in 1762. Two of his letters to the Duc, written from Germany in June 1760, give us our first real glimpse of the man who was Louise's husband. Though a military leader of unquestioned bravery, he, like Louise, is revealed as dutiful and tender; indeed, his style almost drips with family sentimentality:

Ce 17 Juin 1760, de Camberg

> Je veux réparer touts les torts que J'ay eû durant Les dernieres campagnes et vous assurer, Mon Cher Papa, que vous avez en moy un gendre qui vous est on ne peut pas plus attaché. Nous sommes icy dans la plus grande inaction. Nous ignoronts tottallement notre début de Campagne. Lont parloit Beaucoupt de paix ces Jours cy. Ces Bruits ce sont presques èvanouis. Ce quil y a de rèel, c'est que nous avonts La plus Belle armé et artillerie que l'ont puisse voire. Je croiois, cher Papa, que nous aurions marché sur Le Chateau de Dilimbourg ces Jours cy. Cependant, Jusquas l'heur nous sommes ancore dans nos quartiers. Je commande six battaillons allemans qui forment ma Brigade compose des Regs de La Marck et de Nassau. Je aurois desiré

pouvoir avoir votre regt mais Le sort en a disposé autrement. Voila Cher Papa pour le moment present tout ce que J'ay a vous mander....

Adieu Cher Papa; recevé avec Bonté Les assurances du plus sincere attachement et de l'amitie la plus tandre, qui ne peuvent finirent quavec ma vie, pour un Cher Beau pere que j'aime a la folie.

Le Prince de Rohan[39]

Not long after, probably following on a brief trip to Strasbourg where he was able to visit with his mother before she set off to join the Grand Chambellan at Navarre, Jules wrote again to his father-in-law. He very much regretted not being able to accompany Mme de Guéméné there:

Mon Cher Papa,

J'ai eu un furieux regret en voiant partire Maman pour Navarre de ne pouvoire point l'y suivre. Ce qui m'a consolé, c'est l'esperance que vous m'avez donnée d'y aller cette année. Vous n'avez qu'a m'ordonnez, Cher Papa, je partirai... sur le champ, meme a pied s'il le faloit.... Souvenez [vous], je vous supplie, Mon Cher Papa, d'un fils qui a et qui aura pour vous tant qu'il vivra le respect et l'atachement avec lequel j'ai l'honneur d'etre,

Mon cher Papa,
votre tres humble et tres

Ce 25 Juin 1760   soumis fils
Guéméné de Rohan[40]

Several letters from Louise to her father composed later that same year indicate that she was as anxious as her husband to join the Duc at Navarre. Again the tone is of particular interest: "Je vois arriver le moment de vous faire ma cour, mon cher papa, avec bien de l'impasience," she wrote from Versailles on 8 September 1760.[41] By 31 October her visit was over, and on her return to Paris she sent the Duc another letter: "Je me flatte, mon cher papa, que vous ne douttez pas de touts les regrets que j'ai eu de vous quitter. Je voudrois passer ma vie avec vous et ne convoite pas de plus grand bonheur." Then, after bringing him up to date on all of the family news, she begged her father to write soon: "De grace, cher Papa, donnez moi de vos nouvelles. Celle de votre retour me comblera de joie. Votre grosse fille vous aime a la folie et ose vous en assurer."[42]

At thirty-five years of age, Louise remained spontaneously and unashamedly affectionate and submissive, and still something of a "daddy's girl." For certain readers that will be proof enough that Charles Edward was right all along to complain of her fundamental inability to rebel or to act like a "grown-up." The Prince's accusation would, of course, have been more convincing had it been made by someone who was not himself displaying at the time all the characteristics of an arrested adolescent,[43] rushing headlong into total family alienation. Still, as we read her letters of this later period, we almost need to be reminded that she was already the mother of a fifteen-year-old boy, Henri-Louis-Marie, the Prince de Rohan-Guéméné, whose marriage the following year to his cousin, Victoire-Armande-Josèphe de Rohan-Soubise, daughter of Charles de Rohan, Prince de Soubise, was celebrated at Versailles with as much royal pomp and ceremony as the wedding of his mother and father eighteen years before.[44] The subsequent lives of the newlyweds turned out to be as publicly noisy and notorious as those of Jules and Louise had remained discreet and unchronicled. Victoire-Armande, Gouvernante des Enfants de France and a favourite of Marie-Antoinette, was not above dabbling openly in political intrigue. As for her husband, the Prince de Guéméné, it was not long before he managed to set the entire nation in an uproar by playing the starring role in one of the country's most resounding bankruptcies. Even his youthful upbringing, if we are to believe Voltaire (and there are times when it seems best not to), was not without its distressing incidents. In March 1765, writing to his fellow Jesuit basher, d'Alembert, the philosopher of Ferney asked about the fate of a former teaching member of that Order: "Est-il vrai que le jésuite qui avait enfondré le cul du prince de Guéménée est mort? ne s'appelait il pas Marsy?"[45] A note by Condorcet, later quoted by the editor Beuchot, enlarges on the issue but suggests, on the other hand, that things may not have gone that far. The problem had been revealed one day when Louise consulted her young son about an appropriate New Year's gift for his prefect: "Mon ami, dit la princesse à son fils, quelles étrennes faut-il donner à votre préfet? —Maman, il faut lui donner un pot de chambre.—Que voulez-vous dire?—Maman, c'est qu'il me pisse sur le dos, et je n'aime point ça."[46]

Louise was mercifully spared the worst of the continent-wide scandal of her son's 33,000,000 livres bankruptcy, since she died the year before, on 24 September 1781.[47] Fortunately, Henri-Louis's proud grandmother, Mme de Guéméné, had already passed on the year before that, on 20 August 1780.[48] It was thus left for Jules, the young bankrupt's father, to bear the brunt of the financial disaster and ensuing scandal. Hounded by creditors, penniless, and suffering from deep depression, he eventually withdrew at the invitation of Godefroy-Charles, Louise's now totally dissolute brother, to Bouillon where, ironically, he lived out his last days in the Château de Carlsbourg, the former residence of his old rival, Charles Edward. It was at Carlsbourg castle that Jules expired on 10 December 1788 in the presence of such friends as the local curé, one of his former captains from the La Marck regiment, and his spiritual director. He had gone to Bouillon to seek obscurity and the extent to which he succeeded is well illustrated by the fact that the date of his death is incorrectly recorded in most reference works as "vers 1800 en émigration."[49]

Louise's holograph will, dated 1 March 1780, is an interesting personal document that reveals a number of significant facts about her character and activities in her declining years. Charitable works and devotional pursuits seem to have preoccupied her a great deal toward the end, and even the manner in which her testament was brought to the attention of the legal authorities points to a perhaps immoderate influence of the Church in her later life. Though her death occurred in the evening, within one hour of her passing, Le Bossu, the curé of St Paul's parish turned up at the home of the notary Melchior Thomas Morin, carrying two sealed packages: one contained Louise's will; the other, her codicil. Curiously, both documents had been drawn up without the aid of notaries and left in Le Bossu's custody. The will itself began as follows:

> Au nom du pere et du fils et du saint esprit ainsi soit-il. Je soussignée, etant en pleine santée, occupée de la certitude de ma mort et de l'incertitude de l'heure ay fait mon testament et dispositions de mes dernières volontées de la maniere qui suit: Je recommande mon ame à Dieu; je lui fais le sacrifice de ma vie et je mets toutte ma confiance dans les merittes de Jesus Christ, mon bon ange et de tous les Saints; je veux etre enterrée sans nulle cérémonie aux Feuillants si je meurs à Paris ou, si je meurs ailleurs, dans le cimetierre de la paroisse du lieu ou je mourrai; je veux que l'on me fasse dire un annuel à ma paroisse, un aux filles de l'Ave Maria et un autre dans le lieu de ma sepulture.[50]

Louise was thus buried next to her infant son at Les Feuillants where, in his heyday, Charles Edward occasionally liked to attend a fashionable mass. The second convent mentioned, Les Filles de l'Ave Maria, was located in a less inviting quarter, very near the Church of St Paul, and it housed the most austere order of nuns in Paris: "Outre qu'elles ne portent point de linge," a contemporary description states, "elles se levent à minuit, & vont nuds pieds, avec l'étroite observance d'un silence perpetuel. Aussi est-il peu de maisons, où il y ait plus de vertu & un plus grand éloignement pour les choses du siecle."[51] For most of her adult life, Louise lived only a short distance from its forbidding walls and frequently passed by it. Knowledge of this fact entitles us perhaps to invest with deeper meaning her vow to the Prince that she could never give her heart to another man, but only to God.

Other stipulations of the will confirm our general impression. To her confessor Aubry, the curé of the Church of St Louis-en-l'Isle, Louise left the sum of two thousand écus "pour les distribuer aux pauvres selon sa volonté." To the curé of her own parish of St Paul, she left six thousand livres, also for the poor. Her next bequest was, however, less usual:

> Je donne et legue a la communautée des filles ouvrières de St Paul, dont je suis la protectrice, la somme de dix mille livres une fois payez...; j'exige qu'a

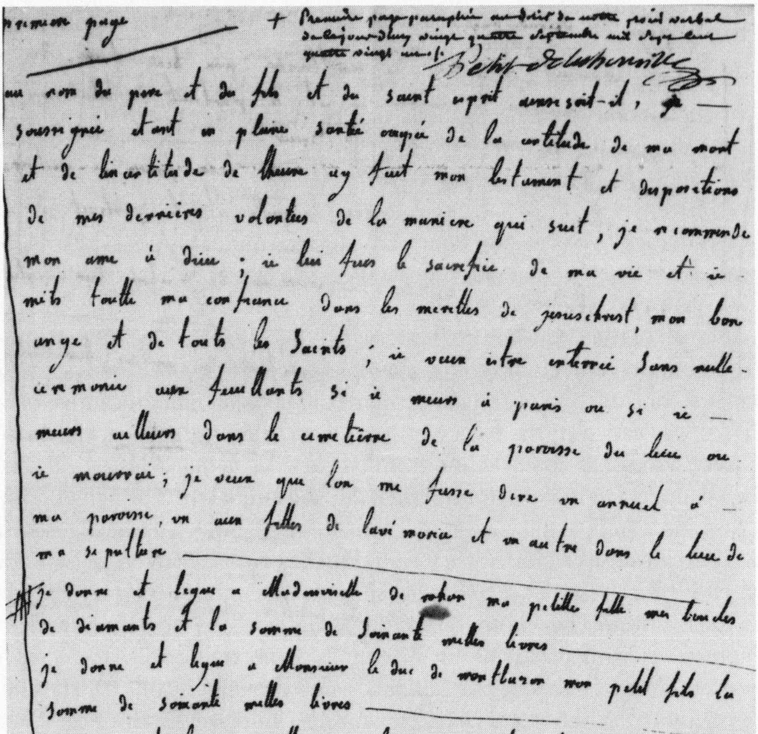

The first page of Louise's holograph will.

datée du jour de mon enterrement, les filles ouvrières de la communautée...
chantent au milieu de leurs travaux pendant l'espace d'un an les vêspres des
morts à mon intention et que touts les ans, au jour anniversaire de ma mort
seulement, le chapelain de la dite communautée celebre la messe à mon
intention, et qu'après la messe, le pretre recite avec les ouvrières le *de
profundis* pour le repos de mon âme.

In addition to charitable bequests made in favour of the poor in Paris, Louise's
will also stipulated that one thousand ecus be given to the poor in each of her
two country parishes.

Not all of the Princess's bequests were related to charitable or religious ends.
To her four grandchildren, for example, she left 60,000 livres each, and to
ensure continuation of the family name, a supplementary incentive of 90,000
livres was added to the legacy of her second eldest grandson, the 14-year-old
Prince Victor, to dissuade him from embarking on an ecclesiastical career. To
her daughter-in-law, Victoire-Armande, she bequeathed her emerald-studded
cross and watch, along with other costly items of jewelry. To her Jansenist aunt,
Marie-Hortense-Victoire de La Tour, Duchesse de La Trémoïlle (who lived on
until 1788), she gave her fine heart-shaped diamond ring. Of particular interest
is the bequest to her brother, Godefroy-Charles: "Je prie mon frere de vouloir
bien accepter ma boete dor emaillée ou est le portrait de feu ma mère." Louise
possessed many valuable portrait boxes, and it is significant that she chose as a
special gift for her brother one containing a miniature, not of the Duc, their
father, but rather of the woman she had so passionately hated and kept at a
distance in her youth. The ghost of Marie-Charlotte must have been cheered by
the gesture! Many other treasure boxes, in petrified wood, in shell or semipre-
cious stone, lacquered, enameled or studded with jewels, were left as tokens of
the Princess's esteem to relatives and friends, along with diamonds, pearls,
amethysts, emeralds—set in rings, bracelets, lockets, pins, and necklaces. Louise also possessed an extensive library (a miscellany of romances and *Lives* of the
saints, we imagine!), and Mademoiselle de Verneuil was given first choice of
two hundred volumes; Madame de Trente was granted the privilege of next
selecting half that number. The remaining titles were left to the Marquis de
Verneuil, along with Louise's diamond-studded cat's-eye ring and a fine amethyst.
No doubt because a large quantity of jewelry was involved, the will contains a
careful declaration regarding ownership: "Je declare," Louise wrote, "que les
diamants dont je dispose par le present testament m'apartiennent en propre, les
ayant...reçu en différentes occasions, de mon pere, de monsieur le Cardinal de
Soubise, de Madame de Mazarin, de Madame de Masseran."[52] Numerous
bequests to household servants followed, including a lifetime pension of 400
livres to her old nurse, "Madame Bacquet qui ma elevée." To Monsieur Dupuy,
her *homme d'affaires*, she gave a diamond worth 4000. Charles-Louis de

Barentin, Premier Président of the Cour des Aides, was named her executor, and, in return, he was begged to accept as a gift the Princess's lacquered and gold-trimmed writing desk, probably the very one that had been awash so often with her tearful letters to the Prince!

One last bequest in the will itself deserves mention. To her favourite brother-in-law, Louis-René-Edouard de Rohan, Louise bequeathed a fine jewelled box. It was only four years later that the recently created Cardinal would find himself caught up in the notorious affair of the Queen's diamond necklace, providing his eldest brother Jules with yet another reason to remain hidden in his lonely retreat at Carlsbourg![53] But the scandalous *affaire du collier* had more serious consequences than that. At a time when the façade of the Old Regime was beginning to crack, the arbitrary process by which a distinguished Rohan ended up in the Bastille did much to stiffen aristocratic resistance to the King. The monarchy was weakened, and no less an authority than Napoleon Bonaparte later saw the affair as one of the important causes of the French Revolution. Louise, of course, was not to know that her entire world was rapidly coming to a catastrophic end.[54]

To the March 1st will, a codicil was later added. Though also holograph, it was left unsigned and undated, and its provisions were not carried out.[55] Its terms, along with the way in which it came to light, nevertheless hint at the possibility of a confessor's undue influence on the mind of a dying woman. Her sizeable last-minute personal bequests to members of the clergy or their relatives are listed as follows:

> Jadjoute à ce que j'ai dit dans mon testament qui fut remis à Monsieur le curée de St Louis la somme de mille écus....
>
> Je donne et legue a Mademoiselle Le Bossu, soeur de Monsieur le curée de St Paul, la somme de dix milles livres, une fois payez.
>
> Je donne et legue à Mademoiselle Adelaide Le Bossu, soeur cadette de Monsieur le curée de St Paul la somme de dix mille livres une fois payez.

Our postscript is nearly at an end. There remains only the task of briefly tracing Charles Edward Stuart's declining fortunes in Rome and Florence. No doubt the highlight of that final period was the Prince's marriage to Louise, Princess of Stolberg, in 1772.[56] France, seeking to maintain the nuisance threat of a possible Stuart heir in the European scheme of things, had backed the arrangement with a pension (and the fact Charles Edward now had no compunctions about taking French money is a good indication of how much he had changed over the years). The marriage was consummated, as required by the bride's mother, on the very day of the ceremony, and although the Prince was described one month later as "drunk half the day, and mad the other,"[57] everything at first seemed to go tolerably well. Jacobites everywhere waited impatiently for news of a Stuart heir. Unfortunately, the twenty-year-old bride turned out to be barren, and it was not long before the new Louise in Charles Edward's life began to lose whatever affection she may have initially felt for a man who was thirty-two years her senior and still as insanely jealous and brutally possessive as ever. The marriage decayed rapidly, and after a short-lived experiment with moderation, Charles Edward soon returned to serious drinking. By the end of the decade, the state of his health, described in unsavoury but probably accurate detail by Sir Horace Mann, was quite deplorable: "He has a declared fistula, great sores in his legs, and insupportable in stench and temper, neither of which he takes the least pains to disguise to his wife, whose beauty is vastly faded of late. She has paid dear for the dregs of royalty."[58]

But Louise of Stolberg, who by then was eagerly waiting for the Prince, or rather, "King Charles III," to die so that she and the playwright Alfieri could get on with their own entertainment had not yet finished paying for the privilege of being the last Stuart Queen. Charles Edward, long known for his violence toward women,[59] outdid himself after a St Andrew's Day celebration on 30 November 1780. Mann, again in graphic detail, reports on an incident which eventually drove Louise from the marriage bed. Apparently, after imbibing "an extraordinary dose of wine and stronger liquors" for the benefit of Scotland's patron saint, the Prince forced his way into his faithless wife's bedroom, and, we are told, "committed the most nauseous and filthy indecencies from above and below upon her, tore her hair, and attempted to throttle her."[60] The lady's screams roused the household servants, who rushed to her assistance. So did, in the following weeks, the Grand Duke of Florence, as well as Henry and the Pope in Rome. After a series of clever manoeuvres and frustrating sojourns in various convents (crowned eventually by an official separation in 1784), Louise of Stolberg found herself free at last to spend her days and nights with her poet lover.

Charles Edward emerged from what he must have considered to be his only true defeat at the hands of a woman, an old man, bent and decrepit, impaired in memory and constantly repeating himself. But still he refused to die. The loneliness of his last years was eased considerably by the caring presence of his daughter Charlotte, whom he had made his heir in 1783. Subsequently legitimated by France as the Duchesse d'Albany, and fresh from her long affair with the Archbishop of Bordeaux (coincidentally Mme de Guémené's youngest son!), she joined her father in Florence in 1784. At the end of 1785 they moved to Rome where the Prince, now fully reconciled with his brother, returned outwardly at least to the fold of the Church. Much had happened to him since those early days when he would obediently do his devotions under the watchful eye of his mother, Maria-Clementina. But how little he could now remember of it! All of his early promise, the hopes, prayers, and single-minded sacrifices, the high sense of purpose, the courage, magnanimity and basic *fairness* of a true hero had now rotted away.

It had nearly all gone by the board a few months after Culloden. No doubt something of it had survived briefly for one or two years after his return to France. There the Prince had fallen in love for the first time. We recall his open-hearted generosity, his innocently selfless desire to give up his share of the family jewels, for example, and, more importantly, the total gift of himself that is evidenced in his promises of eternal love to his mistress and to their child during the early months of the affair. We even dare to hope for a time that he will recapture his former strength and bright determination. In the end, the hurt, suspicion and unspoken guilt that was born of failure won out and led to the shattering personal defeat of 10 December 1748 in the Cul-de-Sac de l'Opéra. After that, moral integrity and tranquillity of mind left him forever and not even the respite of a gracious twilight followed in old age. During the last forty years of his life, he who was once so ambitious to succeed (and who seemed in the beginning so richly deserving of success), attempted little that was commendable and accomplished even less. His days ended after a prolonged state of semi-consciousness on 30 January 1788, the anniversary of the execution of his martyred ancestor, Charles I. Having botched his epic and outlived his tragedy, the hero finally abandoned his ultimately meaningless role in life's novel of the absurd.

Notes

NOTES TO INTRODUCTION TO THE LETTERS

1. For the original, see *Appendix C*.
2. See pp.193-95, and translations, *Appendix B*, II, 5 and 6.
3. *Lettres de la Marquise de M*** au Comte de R**** (1732), Paris, 1930, p. 242.
4. The letters in this regard reveal an entirely new side to Bonnie Prince Charlie. For the generally accepted view of an "under-sexed" hero-prince, see, for example, David Daiches, *Charles Edward Stuart, The Life and Times of Bonnie Prince Charlie*, London 1973, p. 292; also Margaret Forster, *The Rash Adventurer, The Rise and Fall of Charles Edward Stuart*, London, 1973, pp. 297-99. James Lees-Milne, *The Last Stuarts*, London, 1983, p. 86, even speculates about the possibility of "partial impotence"!
5. *La Nuit et le Moment* (1755), Paris, 1929, p. 18.

NOTES TO CHAPTER ONE *From Paris to Zolkiew*

1. The Duchesse de Bouillon to the Duc, 18 September 1735, Archives Nationales (hereafter, A.N.), 273 AP 205, Dossier 1.
2. See Suzanne d'Huart, *Inventaire des Archives Rohan-Bouillon*, Introduction, Paris, ·1970, pp. 11-17.
3. Louis de Rouvroy, duc de Saint-Simon, *Mémoires*; texte établi et annoté par Gonzague Truc (Pléiade), VII, 339.
4. *Journal et Mémoires de Mathieu Marais*, edit. de Lescure, Paris, 1863, III, 24.
5. A.N., 273 AP 426. Pierre Boyé, *La Cour polonaise de Lunéville*, Nancy, 1926, p. 23, incorrectly gives 28 May as the date of death.
6. See Peggy Miller, *A Wife for the Pretender*, London, 1965, p. 33.
7. See, for example, Marais, III, 218-27.
8. "Copie des Articles de Mariage proposés par Monseigneur le Prince Jaques," RA SP Box 7/82.
9. A.N., 273 AP 426. He was buried in the cathedral.
10. Henri-Louis de La Tour (1679-1753), brother of Emmanuel-Théodose.
11. Saint-Simon, VII, 340.
12. *Chronique de la Régence et du règne de Louis XV (1718-1763)*, Paris, 1857, I, 349. The

dispensation did not in fact come cheaply. In February 1724, Mme de Tencin, acting as an intermediary for Emmanuel-Théodose, discreetly forwarded to her brother, the future cardinal, a bill of exchange for 50,000 Roman crowns. Tencin was actively supported in his negotiations with Pope Innocent XIII by Marie-Charlotte's brother-in-law, James III, ever mindful of the need for influential political friends at the Court of France (see A.N., 273 AP 204).

13. Marais, III, 162.
14. See Pierre Boyé, *Stanislas Leszczynski et le troisième Traité de Vienne*, Paris, 1898, pp. 65-66.
15. Saint-Simon, VI, 516.
16. Ibid., VII, 340.
17. A.N., 273 AP 205, letter from Antoine-Guy-Henri Guéroult, seigneur de Bacqueville, to Charles-Godefroy's secretary, Saint-Gervais, 16 October 1737.
18. D'Argenson, I, 265; also Boyé, p. 463.
19. See, for example, Barbier, II, 95; also, the apparent confusion in T. Besterman, *Voltaire's Correspondence*, General Index, Geneva, 1965, CIII, 346.
20. Besterman, D.453, Voltaire to François-Augustin Paradis de Moncrif.
21. A good account of this complicated affair may be found in Georges Monval, *Lettres de Adrienne Le Couvreur*, Paris, 1892, pp. 40-60; see also Paul Lorenz, "Adrienne Le Couvreur," *La Revue des Deux Mondes*, Sept.-Oct. 1956, pp. 302-9 and, especially, le Duc de Castries, *Maurice de Saxe, 1696-1750*, Paris, 1963, pp. 126-49.
22. Barbier, II, 95.
23. D'Argenson, II, 62.
24. Monval, p. 60.
25. Claude-Armand René de La Trémoïlle (1708-1741), Premier Gentilhomme de la Chambre, married in 1725 Charles-Godefroy's sister, Marie-Hortense Victoire de La Tour (1704-1788). Barbier refers to him as "sans contredit le plus grand seigneur de la Cour après les princes" (Barbier, III, 279), but notes his dissolute conduct, "n'ayant eu d'autre occupation, comme un des plus beaux seigneurs de la Cour, que de.....toutes les jolies femmes de la Cour et de la Ville" (ibid., III, 58). To the dismay of many, he had begun, however, by introducing the even younger Louis XV to what the age delicately referred to as *le péché philosophique* (ibid., I, 360-61; Marais, III, 114).
26. *Memoires du comte de Maurepas, Ministre de la marine, etc.* Seconde Edition, Paris, 1792, II, 250-52.
27. Maurepas, II, 231-32.
28. *Mémoires du duc de Luynes sur la cour de Louis XV*, Paris, 1860-65, IV, 152.
29. Ibid., IV, 276.
30. Ibid., VII, 115.
31. Barbier, II, 86-87.
32. For a brief description, see the article "Evreux" in Expilly's *Dictionnaire géographique, historique et politique des Gaules et de la France*, Amsterdam, 1764, II, 810; also, de Luynes, IX, 507 and XII, 23. In 1806 the Château de Navarre was confiscated by Napoleon, who later gave it as part of his divorce settlement to the Empress Josephine. It was largely demolished in the mid 1830's (see *Esquisses sur Navarre; Lettres à la comtesse de ****, par M. D'Avannnes, Paris, 1839, and Pl.18).
33. Barbier, II, 141-42.
34. Saint-Simon, VII, 340.
35. The Duchesse to the Duc, mid-September 1735, A.N., 273 AP 205, Dossier 1. Further correspondence relating to Marie-Charlotte's journey to Poland, unless otherwise indicated, is taken from the same source.

36. The Duchesse to the Duc, from Mannheim, 18 September 1735.
37. Zolkiew or Zholkva, now located in the Soviet Ukraine, was renamed Nesterov in 1951.
38. De Bacqueville to the Duchesse, from Zolkiew, 22 November 1735.
39. Duchesse to the Duc, 3 December 1735.
40. From Zolkiew, 7 December 1735.
41. To the Duc, from Jaroslaw, 1 February 1736.
42. To the Duc, from Zolkiew, 23 May 1736.

NOTES TO CHAPTER TWO *Louise*

1. A.N., 273 AP 427: "Mémoire instructif."
2. Léonore-Marie du Maine, comte du Bourg (1655-1739) (see Pierre Boyé, *Stanislas Leszczynski et le troisième Traité de Vienne*, pp. 29-30); Marie-Ursule de Klinglin, comtesse de Lutzelbourg (see frequent references in Voltaire's correspondence).
3. A.N., 273 AP 205. The Château de Mousseau, in Champagne, was one of the Comte d'Evreux's summer residences.
4. Presumably, Schaffgotsch.
5. Mlle de Minières to the Duc, 26 August 1736 (A.N., 273 AP 205; unless otherwise indicated, all subsequent references concerning Louise's Polish journey are taken from this source).
6. To the Duc, 29 August 1736.
7. De Bacqueville to Saint-Gervais, 12 September 1736.
8. Ibid.
9. To the Duc, 28 September 1736.
10. Quoted from de Bacqueville's advance copy—the Duc obviously believed in sharing his gift for drollery!
11. Frederick-Christian, born on 5 September 1722, was then fourteen years of age. Unfortunately, Louise had serious rivals. For some time, the Saxon minister of state, Count Alexander-Joseph Sulkowski, had been attempting to arrange a marriage between Augustus III's eldest son and one of the twin daughters of Louis XV, either Louise-Elisabeth or Anne-Henriette. He was finally married on 13 June 1747 to Marie-Antoinette de Bavière, daughter of the Emperor Charles VII (see Boyé, *Stanislas Leszczynski*, p. 500).
12. De Bacqueville to the Duc, from Dresden, 23 October 1736. Born in Dresden on 25 August 1730, François-Xavier, the second son of Augustus III, took up residence in France in 1771 where he was known as the Comte de Lusace. He died in 1806 (Boyé, p. 505).
13. The Duc to de Bacqueville, 14 November 1736. Canon George Mocki, though not at home in French, was the author of several books in Latin. (See Ludwik Finkel, *Bibliografia Historii Polskiej*, Warsaw, 1956, #8965, p. 484). He died at Zolkiew in 1747. A.N., 273 AP 423 contains copies of more elegantly worded but similarly vague letters dated 24 October 1736 from Augustus III to Prince James and from Queen Marie-Josèphe to Louise's mother on the same subject.
14. Louis-François de Bourbon, prince de Conti (1717-1776), who was to play an important role in Louis XV's secret diplomacy and who would later make a determined attempt to have himself elected to the Polish throne.
15. To the Duc, 14 November 1736.
16. I.e., the Duchesse.
17. Potentially similar, perhaps, to what was eventually arranged for Marie-Josèphe, the third daughter of Augustus III, who married the Dauphin, Louis de France, in 1747.
18. The Duc to the Duchesse, 8 December 1736.

19. Louis-Marie-Léopold de Lorraine-Harcourt (1720-1747), known as the Prince de Guise, was the son of Anne-Marie-Joseph de Lorraine, comte d'Harcourt, and Marie-Louise-Christine Jeannin de Castille.
20. The Duc to de Bacqueville, 12 December 1736.
21. The Duc to Prince James, 12 December 1736.
22. "Extrait des nouvelles informations de Monsgr le Prince Royal, données au Chanoine Mocki, son Commissaire, De Zulkiew, le 24 Novembre 1736."
23. De Bacqueville to the Duc, 28 December 1736.
24. Augustus III to Joseph Potocki, from Dresden, 14 December 1736.
25. The Duchesse to the Duc, 16 January 1737.
26. To the Duchesse, 2 February 1737.
27. The sum of 400,000 écus owed by Augustus II to James Sobieski, half of which was made over to Marie-Charlotte as part of her first marriage contract ("Partage entre le Prince de Turenne et la Duchesse de Montbazon, sa soeur," 19 May 1749, A.N., 273 AP 208). Maria-Clementina was to have received the other half of the former Polish King's debt (RA SP Box 7/82).
28. To the Duc, 13 February 1737.
29. Lorence to Saint-Gervais, 12 February 1737. De Bacqueville on his return to Zolkiew also comments on the incident to the Duc's secretary but rather in a tone of amusement: "le pauvre St. Amand qui, sans egard a sa verole, a la laideur et la pauvrete du Bachelie, luy a planté genereusement un enfant au grand scandale de Madl Deminieres qui en est aussi furieuse que si on luy avoit fait la meme chose" (27 February 1737).

NOTES TO CHAPTER THREE *"Toujours dans la balance"*

1. De Bacqueville to Saint-Gervais, 26 February 1737.
2. Louise to the Duc, 13 March 1737.
3. De Bacqueville to the Duc, 20 March 1737.
4. The Duc to the Duchesse, 26 April 1737.
5. De Bacqueville to the Duc, 20 March 1737.
6. Jean-Clément Branicki (1688-1771), who had become hetman in 1735, did indeed succeed Joseph Potocki (1673-1751) as grand hetman of the Crown in 1752. Both men were immensely wealthy and politically influential. Branicki's splendid residence at Bialystok was commonly referred to as the Versailles of Poland (Pl.9).
7. The Duchesse to the Duc, 20 March 1737.
8. De Bacqueville to Saint-Gervais, 16 April 1737.
9. She died "de la poitrine" (De Luynes, I, 208-9) on 31 March 1737 at the age of thirty.
10. To the Duc, 2 May 1737.
11. To the Duchesse, 24 May 1737.
12. The Duc to de Bacqueville, 16 May 1737 (A.N., 273 AP 423).
13. To the Duc, 29 May 1737.
14. De Luynes, I, 260-61. De Luynes gives a detailed account of the Duc's enormous debts in his entry for 19 March 1738 (II, 86-88).
    Because of the great family outcry surrounding the sale, instead of asking for the usual pot-de-vin, amounting to perhaps 100,000 livres for a transaction totalling 4,200,000, the Duc generously informed Louis XV that he would be happy with a simple little memento. Touched by his gesture, the King, in September 1738, presented his Grand Chambellan with a gold snuff box, encrusted with diamonds and containing the royal portrait, the whole worth approximately 1000 louis or 24,000 livres. That it was a century of style is made clear in de Luynes' account of the presentation: "Le Roi en la

donnant a M. de Bouillon lui a dit: 'Les petits présents entretiennent l'amitié' " (II, 246).
15. De Bacqueville to the Duc, 12 June 1737. A.N., 273 AP 423 also contains correspondence from Stanislas and his chief minister on the subject.
16. I.e., the Palatine.
17. Louise, in fact, was twelve only at her next birthday, on 15 August.
18. De Bacqueville to the Duc, 25 June 1737. The dowager Palatine de Russie (Ruthenia), Jeanne-Marie-Casimire de Béthune-Chabris (1677-1744), widow of Jean-Stanislas Jablonowski, was, in fact, the Prince Royal's cousin and not his aunt.
19. De Bacqueville to the Duc, 25 June 1737.
20. The Duchesse to the Duc, "Ce 26 Juin 1736"—an error for 1737. The Duc's letter of 26 April 1737 to the Duchesse entirely supports her interpretation of his request for a delay. To Prince James himself he had written in very similar terms, asking for a three-month delay "afin que je puisse estre exactement informé du caractere de ceux qui se presentent" (from Versailles, 26 April 1737).
21. De Bacqueville to the Duc, 3 July 1737.
22. In Charles-Godefroy's will of 29 November 1748 (A.N., Minutier Central, LXVIII, 437), reference is made to "M. de Minier, son procureur au Parlement."
23. Another veiled accusation against Marie-Charlotte.
24. Louise's convent, the Bénédictines du Cherche-Midi, known as "le Chasse-Midi," was founded by Marie-Eléonore de Rohan, the Abbess of Malnoue, in 1669 and was one of the most sought-after boarding establishments in Paris for young ladies of the high aristocracy. Closed in 1790, it was located near the present intersection of the rue d'Assas and the rue du Cherche-Midi (see Jacques Hillairet, *Evocation du Vieux Paris*, Paris, 1953, II, 335-36).
25. Louise-Emilie de La Tour, former Abbess of Montmartre, who died at the Cherche-Midi *prieuré*, at the age of 70, on 1 June 1737.
26. The Duc to Prince James, 25 July 1737.
27. I.e., James III.
28. To the Duchesse, 25 July 1737.
29. The Duchesse to the Duc, 12 August 1737.
30. Copy endorsed by de Bacqueville; dated from Rome, "ce 13 juillet 1737."
31. The marriage of Louise to one of the Stuart princes had seemed like a good idea to a number of the Duc's powerful friends at Versailles. James's chargé d'affaires in Paris, Colonel Daniel O'Brien, reported that he had been publicly blamed for the failure of the proposal by the Duchesse d'Estrées, one of the Duc's (and Louis XV's) intimates and that he had even been threatened with reprisals for it. But such a marriage, O'Brien claimed, "ne pouvoit être d'aucune utilité", and, he added somewhat mysteriously, he would have felt justified in opposing it for other reasons as well ("St. Quentin" [O'Brien] to James, 28 July 1738, Royal Archives, Stuart Papers (hereafter RA SP) 208/74 B). The year following, James wrote to O'Brien that Charles Edward was still too young to marry but that the prospect of a marriage with his eldest son "pourroit beaucoup encourager ou la France, ou l'Espagne a entreprendre mon Rétablissement" (15 April 1739, RA SP 215/54).
32. James to Charles Edward, 17 April 1747, RA SP 283/7 A.

NOTES TO CHAPTER FOUR *Prisoners in Poland*

1. De Bacqueville to the Duc, 14 August 1737.
2. The Duc to Stanislas; copy undated but probably end of July or early August 1737.
3. Stanislas to the Duc, 3 September 1737.

4. Copy undated, but filed with de Bacqueville's July 1737 correspondence.
5. De Bacqueville to the Duc, 11 September 1737.
6. De Bacqueville to Saint-Gervais, 25 September 1737.
7. The Duc to de Bacqueville, 11 October 1737.
8. De Bacqueville to Saint-Gervais, 16 October 1737.
9. Since France at this time had no diplomatic representative at the court of Augustus III, Cardinal Fleury had originally asked Amelot, the Foreign Minister, to lodge a strong protest through Vienna (Cardinal Fleury to the Duc, 1 August 1737: "j'en rendis compte au Roy qui entre parfaitement dans toutes vos raisons," A.N., 273 AP 423).
10. The Duc to the Duchesse, 26 October 1737.
11. The Duc to de Bacqueville, 24 October 1737.
12. De Bacqueville to Saint-Gervais, 30 October 1737.
13. De Bacqueville to Saint-Gervais, 6 November 1737.
14. De Bacqueville to Saint-Gervais, 13 November 1737.
15. De Bacqueville to the Duc, 13 November 1737.
16. De Bacqueville to Saint-Gervais, 20 November 1737; to the Duc, 26 November 1737.
17. De Bacqueville to the Duc, 26 November 1737.
18. The Duchesse to the Duc; no date but probably end of November 1737.
19. The Duchesse to the Comte d'Evreux, 4 December 1737.
20. The Duc to the Palatine de Russie, 5 December 1737.
21. My italics; the Duc was, in fact, eighteen when he married Marie-Charlotte!
22. The Duc to de Bacqueville, 15 December 1737.
23. Augustus III to James Sobieski, from Dresden, 21 November 1737.
24. It was in fact safely received in Paris, in record time, on 6 January 1738, according to Saint-Gervais' endorsement.
25. De Bacqueville to Saint-Gervais, 11 December 1737.
26. The Duchesse to the Comte d'Evreux, 11 December 1737, A.N., 273 AP 205, Dossier 2.
27. Comfortably wealthy, he died at what was called "le petit Hôtel de Bouillon" on the Quai Malaquais, 25 July 1765 (see Archives de Paris, DC6. 246, f.168). De Bacqueville's will, dated 13 July 1765 (A.N., Minutier Central, CXIII, 426; J.B.A. Dupré, Inventory 30 July), shows that he was a man of property and still the recipient, when he died, of a generous Bouillon pension. A fair number of servants are mentioned as well as a fine wine cellar, *porcelaines*, books, and paintings. His portrait, by Lemoyne, was bequeathed to Louise's brother, the Prince de Turenne.
28. On 18 January, de Luynes (II, 14-15) noted that the Duc de Bouillon had received "il y a cinq ou six jours," news of his father-in-law's death.
29. The Comte d'Evreux to the Duchesse, 9 January 1738.
30. The Palatine de Russie to the Duc, from Leopold, 15 January 1738.
31. A letter of 13 March 1738 from Augustus III to Marie-Charlotte makes it clear that the Polish King had no intention of interfering further in the matter of Louise's return to Paris: "Comme c'est une affaire purement de famille, Je laisse à Vous et au Duc Votre Epoux, de juger de la convenance de Vostre fille, et de faire ce que vous trouverez à propos là dessus" (A.N., 273 AP 204).
32. The Duchesse to the Duc, (?April-May) 1738.
33. On 17 April, the dowager Palatine de Russie confirmed in a letter to the Pretender in Rome that Abbé Mocki was refusing to make available (except to the King of Poland) the Prince Royal's will or any papers relating to the large debt owed by Augustus II, the previous king, to the Sobieski estate. Not long after, the will (drawn up in March 1737) was declared invalid by Augustus III, who also refused to make its contents public. (See the Palatine de Russie to James, 17 April 1738, RA SP 206/40; Abbé Mocki to James, 30

April 1738, RA SP 206/84; Owen O'Rourke to James, 21 June 1738, RA SP 207/105; Bishop André-Stanislas Zaluski, Grand Chancellor of Poland, to James, 27 June 1738, RA SP 207/115).

More details concerning the suppressed will can be found in letters from Bishop Zaluski and de Bacqueville to the Duc (8 June, 12 July 1740, A.N., 273 AP 423, 425). A longer account of it is provided by Jean-Chrétien de Lauro, the Prince Royal's former secretary, in a letter of 15 July 1744 (A.N., 273 AP 427). Prince James had apparently left all of his Polish estates to Louise on condition that she marry Prince Xavier, the second son of Augustus III. The Saxon king, believing that the Polish nobility would take umbrage at what could be interpreted as an attempt to establish his sons politically in Poland, simply suppressed James Sobieski's will. It is worth noting, as de Lauro points out, that Marie-Charlotte, even though she was acting against her own interests, attempted to have the will restored: "Feue S.A. Mde La Duchesse, nonobstant qu'elle savoit que le dit testament n'a pas été trop en sa faveur, mais bien la plus part à ce tems là en faveur de S.A. La petite Princesse, en a sollicité instamment la restitution."

A fair amount of detailed information relating to the House of Stuart's claims on the Prince's estate may be found in the dated Windsor papers for the period 1738-1741 and in RA SP Box 7.

34. Charles-Théodore de Bavière (1724-1799), who became Elector Palatine in 1743 and, in 1777, by the death of the Elector of Bavaria without heirs, sovereign duke of Bavaria as well. Boswell found him "very swarthy and very high and mighty" as well as singularly inhospitable during his visit to the Court of Mannheim in November 1764 (see, Frederick A. Pottle, *Boswell on the Grand Tour, Germany and Switzerland, 1764*, New York, 1928, pp. 165-74). In 1742, Charles-Théodore married Princess Elizabeth-Augusta, eldest daughter of the Count Palatine of Sulzbach.

35. "St. Quentin" (O'Brien) to James, RA SP 207/106; also O'Brien to James, 28 July 1738: "le mariage de Melle d'auvergne avec Mr le prince de Sulzbaq naura seuremt jamais lieux, et je doute fort qu'il en ait eté question" (RA SP 208/74).

36. See Mocki to James, 21 May 1738, 16 December 1739, RA SP 207/17, 218/179; Marie-Charlotte to James, 25 November 1739, 1 February 1740, RA SP 218/73, 220/64; James to Padre Giorgio Lascaris, 10 March 1740, RA SP 221/43; Grand Chancellor Zaluski to James, 16 May 1740, RA SP 222/91; Mocki to the Duc de Bouillon, 15 November 1740, A.N., 273 AP 205, Dossier 3.

37. De Bacqueville to the Duc, 31 August 1740 (A.N., 273 AP 425).

38. The Duchesse to the Duc, 19 August 1738 (A.N., 273 AP 425).

39. The Grand Chancellor of Poland, Bishop Zaluski, for example, wrote to James on 27 · June 1738 that the Duchesse was anxious to conclude, at the earliest opportunity, "les affaires de la succession qui la retiennent à contre coeur en Pologne, et qui luy causent tant de chagrin au quel Elle est nullement accoutumé, préférant son repos et la tranquilité" (RA SP 207/115).

NOTES TO CHAPTER FIVE *A Death and a Wedding*

1. Marie-Charlotte to James, 5 March 1738, RA SP 205/72.
2. James to Owen O'Rourke, 28 November 1739, RA SP 218/80.
3. James to the Palatine de Russie, 4 December 1739, RA SP 218/108.
4. Although Marie-Charlotte eventually made generous provision in her will, as well as in her agreements of sale with Prince Michael Radziwill, for the ceremonial burial of her father (see James to the Grand Chancellor, Zaluski, 21 January 1741, RA SP 230/80), nothing, in fact, was done after her death to carry out her wishes. During restoration of

the cathedral of Zolkiew, begun in 1862, a makeshift tomb was discovered in one of the walls. It contained the disintegrated coffins of James Sobieski and of his brother Constantin (who died in 1726). Also found was the heart of Marie-Charlotte, the last of the Sobieskis. On 16 June 1862, the various remains were reburied in small zinc coffins. (See article "Zolkiew," in *Slownik geograficzny krolestwa polskiego i innych krajow*, Wyd. pod red. Filipa Sulimierskiego et al., Warszawa, 1880-1904, XIV, 817.

5. O'Brien to James, 28 July 1738, RA SP 208/74: "Mme de Bouillon, a ce que l'on dit, n'écrit plus icy, et on m'assure que l'on ignore encore a l'hautel de Bouillon les mesures qu'elle prend au sujet de la succession du prince Jacques."

6. O'Brien to James, 9 February 1739, RA SP 213/117.

7. Monsignor Camillo Paulucci to Owen O'Rourke, 13 May 1740 RA SP 222/76.

8. Regarding the March 15th sale, see Michel-Casimir de Radziwill to James, 23 March 1740, RA SP 221/88; also, 20 May and 8 June 1740, Radziwill to the Duc (A.N., 273 AP 423).

9. James to O'Brien, 20 July 1740, RA SP 225/35. Chancellor Zaluski to the Duc, 28 May 1740 (A.N., 273 AP 423).

10. Chancellor Zaluski to the Duc, 28 May 1740 (A.N., 273 AP 423). See Pl. 6.

11. Chancellor Zaluski to the Duc, 29 June 1740 (A.N., 273 AP 425).

12. James to Padre Lascaris, 10 June 1740, RA SP 223/93.

13. De Luynes, III, 191 (3 June 1740).

14. Saint-Simon, VII, 340. Both de Luynes and Saint-Simon incorrectly give Silesia as the place of death, as does the *Gazette* account of 4 June 1740, which states that she died "en Silésie la nuit du 8 au 9 du mois dernier, dans la quarante-troisième année de son age, estant née le 15 du mois de Novembre 1697 (No 24, p. 282).

15. De Luynes, III, 155-56.

16. "Mémoire de ce que Mademoiselle de Bouillon doit au 1er juillet 1741" (A.N., 273 AP 427).

17. De Bacqueville to Saint-Gervais, 20 March 1737 (see above, p.53).

18. The Duc to de Bacqueville, 12 December 1736.

19. De Luynes, II, 433.

20. De Luynes, II, 469.

21. De Luynes, III, 317.

22. De Luynes, V, 190-91, 29 November 1743. Despite her handicap, Marie-Sophie-Charlotte, a close friend of Louise, married in 1745 the future academician and maréchal de France, Charles-Just, Prince de Beauvau (1720-1793). The Prince de Guise, a *brigadier* by 1745, died 20 June 1747 when he absentmindedly shot himself as he was loading his pistols! "M. de Guise étoit un homme fort singulier, très poli, mais extrêmement embarrassé et toujours distrait; il etoit assez instruit, mais on avoit peine à le déterminer à faire usage de sa science; et soit par distraction ou par son caractère, il étoit gauche à tout ce qu'il faisoit" (De Luynes, VIII, 252).

23. See de Luynes, III, 205-6. The Comte d'Evreux had already assumed responsibility for the education of young Godefroy-Charles, having hired the distinguished Chevalier Andrew-Michael Ramsay (1686-1743) as his tutor in 1732. Ramsay, a leading Freemason (as was the Duc de Bouillon) as well as a mystical follower and literary inheritor of Fénélon, is remembered as the author of various works including the celebrated *Voyages de Cyrus* (1727) and a two-volume *Histoire du vicomte de Turenne* (1735), which de Bacqueville took along in his baggage for presentation to Prince James in Zolkiew. In 1724, Ramsay had also acted as Prince Charles Edward's tutor in Rome but lost the position after about ten months as a result of James's suspicions concerning his connections with the Earl of Mar (see, Albert Cherel, *Fénélon au XVIIIe siècle en France (1715-1820)*, Paris, 1917,

pp. 31-93). That the Chevalier (who insisted on living apart from the Bouillon household with his young pupil) succeeded in firing the young Prince de Turenne's imagination with the old Jacobite legends is well illustrated in the following passage from a letter sent secretly by the 12-year-old Godefroy-Charles to James, 29 May 1740 (RA SP 222/161): "Les sentimens qu'on m'a inspiré pour Votre Majesté dès ma plus tendre enfance, se developpent tous les jours avec l'âge, et me donnent envie de meriter l'honneur de Sa protection; j'en ay besoin pour soutenir mon education, qui chancelle souvent par les degouts qu'on a donne a Mr de Ramsay, depuis les fatales discordes qui regnent dans ma maison entre mon cher Pere et mon cher Oncle, le Comte d'Evreux.

C'est à l'insçu de tout le monde que je prends la liberté d'écrire a Votre Majesté, pour la supplier dordonner à Mr de Ramsay de continuer de m'inspirer les principes et les sentimens qui me rendront un jour digne des bontez de Votre Majesté, du sang qui coule dans mes veines, et du nom que je porte."

24. Procuration (Bougainville), 24 September 1740, A.N., 273 AP 205, Dossier 3.
25. See various letters from de Bacqueville to the Duc, Claude Linotte, etc., from 28 June 1740 (A.N., 273 AP 425).
26. Linotte to de Bacqueville, 24 December 1740.
27. De Luynes, 26 January 1741, III, 316-17.
28. Linotte to de Bacqueville, 29 January and 1 February 1741.
29. De Luynes, III, 316 and VI, 258.
30. Jean Horguelen to Linotte, from Breslau, 26 January 1741.
31. De Bacqueville to Frederick II of Prussia, from Breslau, 29 January 1741.
32. Linotte to de Bacqueville, 22 February 1741.
33. James to the Duc de Bouillon, 10 October 1740, RA SP 227/35.
34. Linotte to de Bacqueville, 23 March 1741.
35. Linotte to de Bacqueville, 25 February 1741.
36. De Bacqueville to Linotte, from Breslau, 20 March and 6 April 1741. Marie-Charlotte, one suspects, would have savoured the irony of that last comment!
37. De Luynes, 20 March 1741, III, 346-47.
38. Honoré-Camille-Léonor Goyon de Grimaldi, later Honoré III. Born 1720, *brigadier* in 1745, *maréchal de camp* in 1748; he died in 1795 after a long and fairly uneventful reign.
39. Linotte to de Bacqueville, 22 March 1741.
40. Elisabeth-Alexandrine de Bourbon-Condé (1705-1765).
41. See d'Argenson, III, 372.
42. De Luynes, 25 March 1741, III, 347.
43. De Luynes, III, 346, note 1. Honoré Barjac was the Cardinal's valet and confidential factotum.
44. See de Luynes, IV, 92, note 2.
45. De Luynes, 5 February 1744, V, 319-20.
46. Before we leave the Prince of Monaco to the footnotes of minor history, a curious example of his conduct in later years is worth recording. In March 1751, his father, ill and at the point of death, called for his confessor, le père d'Héricourt. The celebrated Theatine preacher scolded the dying man for his sins and pointed out that his magnificent residence in the Faubourg Saint-Germain (today the Hôtel de Matignon) contained many paintings which, "quoique de grand prix, n'étoient pas soutenables dans la maison d'un chrétien, par l'indécence et l'immodestie des figures" (De Luynes, XI, 85). Accepting the priest's advice, the old man gave orders to destroy a fair number of the offending pictures. However, many of the most famous and most expensive belonged to his son: "Ces tableaux étant très immodestes...M. de Valentinois étoit absolument déterminé à les brûler et à faire ôter toutes les figures peu convenables; mais il ne le pouvoit sans le

consentement de son fils. Non seulement M. de Monaco a consenti à ce que son père désiroit de ces tableaux, mais il l'a fait exécuter devant lui. C'est aussi lui qui a averti son père de l'état où il étoit et qui s'est mis à genoux devant son père pour l'exhorter à songer à sa conscience" (De Luynes, XI, 85-86; see also, François Genard, *L'Ecole de l'homme*, Londres, 1753, II, 238).

47. De Bacqueville to Linotte, from Breslau, 27 March 1741.

48. De Bacqueville to Linotte, 6 April 1741.

49. Linotte to de Bacqueville, 25 April 1741.

50. The Bouillon correspondence (A.N., 273 AP 205 unless otherwise indicated) reveals one additional complication, arising from the Comte d'Evreux's suspicions that the Duc intended to keep Marie-Charlotte's jewels for himself rather than have them inventoried separately for Louise and her brother. The same protective attitude had motivated Henri-Louis' opposition to the sale of Turenne, as well as, no doubt, his unsuccessful attempts to restore Marie-Charlotte's pension (the Comte d'Evreux to the Duc, from St Ouen, 1 August 1741). Charles-Godefroy was not amused by what he saw as his uncle's *chicanes indécentes*: "Je ne veux ny torts ny graces; je ne demande que ce qui m'appartient de droit" (the Duc to Linotte, 23 August 1741), but, after much persuasion, he finally agreed to follow conventional practice.

51. *Souvenirs de la marquise de Créquy*, nouvelle édition, corrigée et augmentée, Paris, I, 210-11.

52. Perhaps to complete the Créquy formula, it is useful to recall as well that the Duc de Bouillon's sister had married in 1725 the Duc de la Trémoïlle, who died of smallpox in May 1741 (Barbier, III, 279).

53. Not to be overlooked, Louise's own annual revenues now totalled well over 40,000 livres.

54. De Luynes, 12 December 1742, IV, 296. Born 25 March 1726, the Prince de Rohan-Guéméné was, in fact, already sixteen.

55. An account of the marriage, incorrectly stating the bride's age, may be found in *Le Nouveau Mercure* for August of that year: "M. le Duc de Montbazon...épousa le deux de ce mois à Jouare, Mademoiselle Louise-Gabrielle-Julie, fille de M. le Prince de Rohan. Comme la jeune Epouse n'a pas encore 12 ans, on ne l'a laissée qu'un moment au lit avec M. son Epoux. Trois jours après son Mariage, elle a été conduite dans le Couvent de l'Assomption où elle restera jusqu'à ce que sa Famille juge à propos de la retirer" (p. 189). She died at Chevilly on 20 August 1780, in her 76th year (*Gazette de France*, Du Mardi 20 août 1780, No 69, p. 328).

56. See, A.N., 273 AP 7. One of Jules's brothers, Louis-René-Edouard, born in 1734, later achieved lasting notoriety as the Cardinal implicated in the famous *affaire du collier*. His youngest brother, Ferdinand-Maximilien, born in 1738, later became Archbishop of Bordeaux and the father of three illegitimate children born to Charlotte, Duchess of Albany (1753-1789), the illegitimate daughter of Clementina Walkinshaw and the hero of our following chapters, Prince Charles Edward Stuart (see, George Sherburn, *Roehenstart: A Late Stuart Pretender*, Chicago, 1960). It was a small world!

57. De Luynes, IV, 375, 391.

58. The son in question was Jean-Bretagne-Charles-Godefroi, duc de la Trémoïlle, Prince de Tarente, born 6 February 1737. The controversy over the Duc de Fleury's appointment as Premier Gentilhomme de la Chambre to what was a traditional la Trémoïlle office is discussed at length in Barbier, III, 279-82. Many influential members of the nobility, including the Duc de Bouillon, the Duc d'Orléans, and the Prince de Conti, attempted to intercede on behalf of the young prince, and Barbier notes that the Duc de Gesvres, "qui n'a point d'enfants, en qualité d'impuissant déclaré, a dit même au Roi qu'il étoit glorieux à Sa Majesté d'avoir pour premier gentilhomme un homme du nom de la Trémoïlle." All

such protests were to no avail, however, for the Cardinal had apparently found the cleverest of arguments to justify the exclusion: "Madame la duchesse de La Trémoïlle est grande janséniste, entourée de femmes et d'hommes de cette secte, gens même peu convenables pour elle; elle n'agit que par eux."

59. De Luynes, IV, 410.
60. De Luynes, IV, 412-14; *Gazette*, 23 February 1743, No 8, p. 96.
61. Henri-Oswald de La Tour (1671-1747), Premier Aumônier du Roi.
62. D'Argenson, I, 287.
63. De Luynes, I, 435; Barbier, III, 118.
64. Maurepas, III, 166. For a translation, see *Appendix B,* II, 1.

NOTES TO CHAPTER SIX *Enter the Hero-Prince*

1. Today it is No 6 Place des Vosges (Musée Victor Hugo). Acquired by the Rohan-Guéméné family in 1639, it remained in their possession until 1784. Victor Hugo inhabited the second floor of the building from 1832 to 1848. Purchased in 1873 by the City of Paris, it opened officially as the Victor Hugo Museum in 1902. A long-standing tradition that Marion Delorme lived there (Impasse Guéméné side) from 1640 to 1650 is apparently not entirely reliable (see Pierre Gaxotte's preface to *Le Marais*, Edition des Deux Mondes, Paris, 1964, p. 65).
2. De Luynes, IV, 460. A long list of the "Droits et prérogatives attachés au rang que tient en France la Maison de Rohan" will be found in A.N., 273 AP. These included such vital items as "la trousse de velours cramoisy non clouée sur leur carosse"!
3. James to Daniel O'Brien, 15 June, 10 August, 14 September, 7 December 1740, RA SP 223/135, 225/110, 226/70, 229/24; O'Brien to James, 21 November 1740, RA SP 228/155.
4. RA SP 246/178.
5. RA SP 248/20.
6. James to the Prince de Turenne and to the Duc de Bouillon, 12 December 1743, RA SP 254/50 and 51.
7. See on this general theme, the comprehensive study of F.J. McLynn, *France and the Jacobite Rising of 1745*, Edinburgh, 1981; I have also found Eveline Cruickshanks's *Political Untouchables: The Tories and the '45*, London, 1979, most useful.
8. Louis XV to Philip V, 10 December 1743, Archives du Ministère des Affaires Etrangères, *Mémoires et Documents* (hereafter AE, *M&D*), Angleterre, 82, f.80; see also, P. Coquelle, "Les Projets de descente en Angleterre, d'après les archives des Affaires Etrangères," *Revue d'Histoire Diplomatique*, 1901, XV, 594-95.
9. See Coquelle, p. 595, note 1.
10. Dated 23 December 1743, RA SP 254/94.
11. Barbier, III, 486; my italics.
12. Barbier, III, 492.
13. *Centurie IIe*, no. 68. (Translation, *Appendix B*, II, 2).
14. RA SP 256/122. See also, as a general reference on the de Saxe expedition, Marquis d'Argenson (Maurice), *Deux Prétendants au XVIIIe siècle, Maurice de Saxe et Le Prince Charles-Edouard*, Paris, 1928, pp. 112-42.
15. Charles Edward to James, 13 March 1744, RA SP 256/127.
16. See RA SP 256/131, "Traduction d'une lettre de Son Altesse Royale, le Prince de Galles, à my Lord Sempill, du 15 mars 1744."
17. See AE, *M&D*, Angleterre, 77, ff. 181-83.
18. RA SP 256/169.

19. RA SP 256/174.
20. RA SP 256/180.
21. RA SP 256/194.
22. Barbier in December 1748 noted that Charles Edward's mother was "déjà reconnue à Rome pour bienheureuse en attendant qu'elle soit canonisée" (IV, 334).
23. To James, 25 May 1744, RA SP 257/57.
24. RA SP Box 2/368, Maria-Clementina to Charles, undated. See also in the same box, letters 366 and 367.
25. RA SP 256/189.
26. To James, 24 April 1744, RA SP 257/7.
27. Charles Edward to James, from "Francfort" [Paris], 11 May 1744, RA SP 257/34.
28. To James, 18 May 1744, RA SP 257/48.
29. To James, 25 May 1744, RA SP 257/57.
30. Ibid.
31. To James, 1 June 1744, RA SP 257/68.
32. To James, 29 June 1744, RA SP 257/166.
33. William Drummond of Balhaldy to James Edgar, 8 February 1748, RA SP 289/120. Little notice seems to have been taken of this remark, and I shall have more to say on it in a later chapter.
34. James to Charles Edward, 20 October 1744, RA SP 259/141.
35. RA SP 257/68.
36. To James, 18 May 1744, RA SP 257/48.
37. Postscript, Charles Edward to James, 11 May 1744, RA SP 257/34.
38. RA SP 258/155.
39. To James, 16 November 1744, RA SP 260/62.
40. Ibid.
41. To James, 30 November 1744, RA SP 260/81.
42. See Barbier, III, 538.
43. De Luynes, VI, 62.
44. De Luynes, VI, 43; Barbier, III, 537-38.
45. To James, 17 August 1744, RA SP 258/139.
46. Francis Fitzjames, Bishop of Soissons, was the third son of the first Duke of Berwick, James's illegitimate half-brother.
47. To James, 24 August 1744, RA SP 258/155.
48. It was, rather, the revenge of the Duchesse de Châteauroux.
49. De Luynes, VI, 78-79. De Luynes mistakenly refers to "M. de Turenne" in his account.
50. Ibid.
51. Granted 26 May 1745 (see, La Chenaye-Desbois et Badier, *Dictionnaire de la noblesse*, XVII, 513).
52. De Luynes, VII, 93.
53. VI, 85.
54. De Luynes, VI, 167.
55. Daniel O'Brien to James Edgar, 20 December 1744, RA SP 261/1.
56. Charles Edward to James, 21 December 1744, RA SP 261/11.
57. To James, 3 January 1745, RA SP 261/109.
58. Sir Thomas Sheridan to Edgar, 21 December 1744, RA SP 261/12.
59. I.e., the Cardinal's.
60. RA SP 261/155. Prince Camille was the Princesse de Turenne's brother, Camille de Lorraine, second son of the Prince de Pons. He had been appointed Colonel of a regiment of cavalry in June 1743.

61. To Edgar, 16 January 1745, RA SP 262/1.
62. Charles Edward to James, 16 January 1745, RA SP 262/2.
63. RA SP 262/46.
64. To James from Paris, 28 February 1745, RA SP 263/24.
65. RA SP 263/51.
66. 19 April 1745, RA SP 264/70.
67. To James, 7 March 1745, RA SP 263/51A.
68. De Luynes, VI, 355-56.
69. To James, from Fitz James, 20 March 1745, RA SP 263/121. Word and number cyphers are a common feature of Stuart correspondence during this period. Subsequent quotations will give only the decoded form.
70. See *Appendix C*.
71. RA SP 264/1.
72. To James, from Paris, 9 April 1745, RA SP 264/32.
73. Ibid.
74. Sir Thomas Sheridan to Daniel O'Brien, 7 May 1745, RA SP 264/150.
75. James to Charles Edward, 13 April 1745, RA SP 264/55.
76. To Charles Edward, 26 April 1745, RA SP 264/97.
77. To James, 16 May 1745, RA SP 264/173.
78. 28 May 1745, RA SP 265/42.
79. Charles Edward to Edgar, 12 June 1745, RA SP 265/135.
80. To James, 12 June 1745, RA SP 265/129.
81. To James, 13 June 1745, RA SP 265/153.
82. A.N., 273 AP 206, Dossier 3. (Translation, *Appendix B*, II, 3).
83. James to the Duc de Bouillon, 1 June 1745, RA SP 265/86; my italics.
84. The Duc to James, 20 June 1745, RA SP 265/198.
85. To James, 4 August 1745, RA SP 266/174.

NOTES TO CHAPTER SEVEN *"Sword in Hand"*

1. From Rome, 11 August 1745, RA SP 267/1.
2. Ibid.
3. Barbier IV, 69; de Luynes VII, 17.
4. To Charles Edward from Choisy, 24 September 1745, RA SP 268/74.
5. The reader is once again referred to F. J. McLynn's book, *France and the Jacobite Rising of 1745*, for a detailed and comprehensive treatment of French ministerial discussions during this period regarding the feasibility of sending an expedition to England. See also, my "Voltaire's English, High Treason and a Manifesto for Bonnie Prince Charles," *Studies on Voltaire and the Eighteenth Century* (1977) CLXXI, 7-29.
6. Daniel O'Brien to James, RA SP 269/151A.
7. Voltaire, true to his word, was to devote many pages of his *Histoire de la guerre de 1741* and of the *Précis du Siècle de Louis XV* to the various victories and the final defeat of Charles Edward Stuart.
8. From Edinburgh, RA SP 279/122.
9. A.N., 273 AP 206, Dossier 3. The Prince's envoy was Sir James Steuart of Goodtrees (1713-1780). (Translation, *Appendix B*, II, 4).
10. Duke of Fitzjames to James, 22 October 1745, RA SP 269/196.
11. De Luynes, VII, 107.
12. Henry, in a letter to James, states that Louis XV several times expressed his regret at not having seen Charles Edward (from Bagneux, 1 November 1745, RA SP 270/88).

13. O'Brien to James, 21 November 1745, RA SP 271/15.
14. The ceremony took place on 9 December 1745 ("Extrait des Registres de St Paul, 9 Xbre 1745," A.N., 273 AP 399, 400).
15. See Voltaire's *Commentaire historique sur les oeuvres de l'auteur de la Henriade, &c.* (1776), in *Oeuvres complètes de Voltaire*, I, 71-126 and XXIII, 203-4.
16. Barbier, IV, 103.
17. Barbier, IV, 114. Charles-Godefroy, on 18 December, petitioned Louis XV on behalf of Louise's husband and her brother (AE, *M&D*, Angleterre, 78, f. 375).
18. 28 December 1745, RA SP 271/141.
19. Archives historiques du Ministère de la Guerre (Vincennes), 315/A1, f. 140.
20. AE, *M&D*, Angleterre, 79, f. 16.
21. Kelly to James Edgar, from Boulogne, 14 January 1746, RA SP 272/62.
22. Ministère de la Guerre, 315(2)/A1, f. 241.
23. D'Hérouville got his wish and was even wounded in the action that preceded the capitulation of Brussels on 20 February.
24. De Luynes, VII, 221.
25. Barbier, IV, 130.
26. From Boulogne, 23 January 1746, RA SP 272/89.
27. RA SP 272/93.
28. Ibid.
29. RA SP 272/146.
30. From Boulogne, 9 March 1746, RA SP 273/18.
31. Where another of the Duc de Bouillon's country residences (the scene of his honeymoon with Marie-Charlotte) was located; Charles Edward had gone there the preceding year during Easter week.
32. From Boulogne-sur-Mer, 19 March 1746, RA SP 273/32.
33. To James, 30 April 1746, RA SP 273/149.
34. Sir John Graeme to O'Brien, from Arras, 28 and 30 April 1746, RA SP 273/144 and 145.
35. Graeme to James, from Ghent, 6 May 1746, RA SP 274/43.
36. Graeme to O'Brien, from Ghent, 20 May 1746, RA SP 274/108.
37. De Luynes, VII, 329; James to O'Brien, 11 July 1746, RA SP 275/137A; Louis de Bourbon, Comte de Clermont, to James, 27 July 1746, RA SP 276/4.
38. To James, 25 April 1746, RA SP 273/135.
39. To O'Brien, 16 May 1746, RA SP 274/97.
40. RA SP 275/124.
41. O'Brien to James, 20 August 1746, RA SP 276/90.
42. Charles Edward to the Marquis d'Argenson, from Clichy, 27 October 1746, RA SP 278/33.
43. James to Charles Edward, 19 April 1746, RA SP 273/111.
44. Ibid.
45. Ibid.
46. De Luynes, VII, 302-3.
47. In fact, more than three times the number effectively available to him at this time!
48. O'Brien to James, 1 May 1746, RA SP 274/15.
49. O'Brien to James, 9 May 1746, RA SP 274/59.
50. Perhaps the luckier ones! I refer the reader to John Prebble's *Culloden*, a superb ground-level reconstruction of the battle and the long period of brutality and repression that followed it.
51. Letter of 2 May 1746, RA SP 274/22.

52. 11 May 1746, RA SP 274/76.
53. From Brussels, 12 May 1746, RA SP 274/81.
54. RA SP 274/99A.
55. 16 May 1746, RASP274/103.
56. Charles Edward to Sheridan, 23 April 1746 (Old Style; 4 May, New Style), RA SP 273/116.
57. Postdated 26 April 1746 (Old Style; 7 May, New Style), RA SP 273/117.
58. See McLynn, pp. 234-35.
59. See, for example, Mably's "Réflexions sur les affaires d'Ecosse," December 1745, AE, *M&D*, Angleterre, 78, ff. 375-78.
60. James to Charles Edward, 6 June 1746, RA SP 275/26.
61. 11 July 1746, RA SP 275/133.
62. 25 August 1746, RA SP 275/174.
63. See de Luynes, VII, 462.
64. *The Stuart Papers at Windsor*, London, 1939, pp. 106-9.
65. Henry's day, according to Murray, normally began at six with as much as one hour and a quarter of prayers recited aloud, followed by a ten or fifteen-minute breakfast. Then came an hour of lessons with Father Ildefonso and, on some days, a little fencing or dancing. After that it would be time to dress and to hear Mass in his Chapel. On holy days, Henry attended a minimum of two and as many as four masses (Charles Edward attended one, James two); often he would remain in the Chapel after the last mass for an additional fifteen minutes. Then came lunch, followed by an hour (and sometimes more) of prayers. Now it was time to go out, *generally to church*! At four o'clock, the Duke was back in his chapel for an hour or sometimes one hour and a half, and more devotions followed later in the evening. "It is to be remarked," Murray observed, "that in reciting or reacting his prayers, he puts his mind in agitation, pronounces his words aloud, and crowds them with great precipitation one upon another." Murray was naturally concerned at the possible effects of such a regimen on the young Duke's health as well as on the state of his education for it left him with "a blackness about the eyes" and little time to read. When he was not employed in prayer, Henry, it seems, was singing. It was all rather worrisome (see A. & H. Taylor, p.108).
66. D'Argenson, *Journal et Mémoires*, IV, 320.
67. J. Constable to O'Brien, 26 July 1746, RA SP 276/2.
68. Constable to O'Brien, RA SP 276/10.
69. Henry to James, 17 July 1746, RA SP 275/149.
70. 1 August 1746, RA SP 276/28.
71. RA SP 276/47.
72. 22 August 1746, RA SP 276/100.
73. O'Brien to Edgar, 12 June 1747, RA SP 284/92.
74. The Princesse de Turenne and Mme de Guéméné came to dine with him, for example, on 18 September (Graeme to James, from Bagneux, 19 September 1746, RA SP 277/43).
75. To James, 29 August 1746, RA SP 276/123.
76. "Lord Balmerino's speech upon the scaffold," 18 August 1746, RA SP 276/84.
77. Prebble (*Culloden*, pp. 125-26) gives an account of the "crude forgery" of Jacobite orders used by Cumberland and Hawley to justify the systematic butchery that followed the disastrous encounter.
78. Lord Balmerino to James, 17 August 1746, RA SP 276/82.
79. To Henry from Morlaix, 10 October 1746, RA SP 277/130.

NOTES TO CHAPTER EIGHT *Compliments and Disaffection*

1. Barbier, IV, 153.
2. Sheridan to Charles Edward, 19 August 1746, RA SP 276/86.
3. Henry to the Duc de Bouillon, 14 October 1746, A.N., 273 AP6, Dossier 3.
4. Belonging to a *marchand de galons*, according to a confidential Ministry report; he stayed there for three days (see AE, *M&D*, Angleterre, 82, f. 199).
5. To James from Clichy, 17 October 1746, RA SP 277/168.
6. From Clichy, 17 October 1746, RA SP 277/165.
7. My italics.
8. Barbier, IV, 161.
9. Barbier, IV, 178.
10. A.N., 273 AP 6, Dossier 3.
11. O'Brien to James, from Fontainebleau, 24 October 1746, RA SP 278/25. De Luynes also gives a detailed account of the visit (VII, 456-63).
12. To James, 22 October 1746, RA SP 278/1.
13. De Luynes, VII, 462.
14. Charles Edward to Louis XV, 22 October 1746, RA SP 278/3.
15. RA SP 278/4.
16. De Luynes, VII, 463.
17. Barbier, IV, 194; also O'Brien to James, 31 October 1746, RA SP 278/62.
18. Tencin to O'Brien, 1 November 1746, RA SP 278/72.
19. From Clichy, 6 November 1746, RA SP 278/113.
20. Marquis d'Argenson to O'Brien, 7 November 1746, quoted in RA SP 278/170. D'Argenson later referred to the problem in his *Mémoires*, pointing out that it was on the recommendation of such ministers as Maurepas that the King was prevailed upon to reverse his original intention: "Je n'ai point eu de part à ce dernier conseil; on a représenté au roi qu'il ne fallait pas choquer l'Angleterre par ce nouvel éclat, et que, moins on ferait pour les Stuarts en France, moins serait grande leur chute, lorsqu'à la paix générale nous les abandonnerions" (IV, 321; see also, V, 2).
21. Marquis d'Argenson to O'Brien, from Fontainebleau, 14 November 1746, RA SP 278/175; also, AE, *M&D*, Angleterre, 79, f.312.
22. See AE, *M&D*, Angleterre, 82, f. 199; also O'Brien to James 19 and 27 November, 1746, RA SP 279/9 and 279/34.
23. "Memoir to ye F.K. from me ye 10th November, 1746," RA SP 278/153.
24. Charles Edward to Louis XV, 12 January 1747, RA SP 280/69.
25. O'Brien to James, 26 December 1746, RA SP 279/171A.
26. Ibid.
27. The words in italics are crossed out in the draft copy.
28. RA SP 279/177.
29. James to Charles Edward, 3 November 1746, RA SP 278/75.
30. Charles Edward to James, 27 November 1746, RA SP 279/33.
31. Ibid.
32. Ibid.
33. Charles Edward to James, 3 April 1747, RA SP 282/128.
34. James to Charles Edward, 25 April 1747, RA SP 283/33.
35. Charles Edward to James, 27 November 1746, RA SP 279/33.
36. Ibid.
37. James to Charles Edward, 28 November 1746, RA SP 279/44.
38. O'Brien to James, 12 December 1746, RA SP 279/97. Charles Radcliffe, Earl of

Derwentwater, was decapitated on Tower Hill on 8 December 1746.
39. James to Charles Edward, 16 December 1746, RA SP 279/112.
40. See also, O'Brien to James, 7 and 14 January 1747, RA SP 280/49 and 89A.
41. James to Charles Edward, 28 November 1746, RA SP 279/44.
42. O'Brien to James, 26 December 1746, RA SP 279/171B.
43. See, for example, Charles Edward to James, 21 January 1747, RA SP 280/122.
44. James to Charles Edward, 3 February 1747, RA SP 281/34.
45. O'Brien to James, 14 January 1747, RA SP 280/89B.
46. Charles Edward to James, 16 January 1747, RA SP 280/94.
47. Balhaldy to James, 1 May 1747, RA SP 283/54.
48. Father Myles MacDonnell to James, 4 May 1747, RA SP 283/70. Others had a higher opinion of Kelly, a person of independent means, having a modest income of 4000 livres. He is described by d'Eguilles in 1748 as a cut above most of his associates: "Quoyque puissent dire les Anglois, les Ecossois et meme quelques Irlandois, c'est tout ce qu'il y a de mieux autour du Prince, et le seul homme après le chev. Harrington qui connoisse un peu le gouvernement et la situation des choses en Angleterre"(AE, *M&D*, Angleterre, 79, f. 238).
49. See above, p.108
50. "S" to Murray (Lord Dunbar), from Paris, 15 April 1747, RA SP 282/166.
51. O'Brien to James, 31 December 1746, RA SP 280/1A.
52. O'Brien to James, 24 December 1746, RA SP 279/163.
53. From Clichy, 14 November 1746, A.N., 273 AP 6, Dossier 3.
54. From Paris, 26 December 1746, RA SP 279/169.
55. De Luynes, VIII, 109.
56. De Luynes, VIII, 108.
57. O'Brien to James, 3 February 1747, RA SP 281/50A.
58. O'Brien to James, 20 February 1747, RA SP 281/118.
59. O'Brien to James, 18 December 1746, RA SP 279/124; de Luynes, VIII, 32.
60. De Luynes, VIII, 99.
61. De Luynes, VIII, 91; Barbier, IV, 216-17.
62. O'Brien to James, 21 and 23 January 1747, RA SP 280/118 and 129; Charles Edward to Mme de Mézières, 23 January 1747, RA SP 280/133.
63. "Instructions [to Sir James Harrington] for England," 22 January 1747, RA SP 280/127.
64. James to Charles Edward, 3 February 1747, RA SP 281/34.

NOTES TO CHAPTER NINE *"A Dager throw my heart"*

1. Charles Edward to Henry, 9 February 1747, RA SP 281/68.
2. Charles Edward to James, 12 February 1747, RA SP 281/89.
3. Ibid.
4. Charles Edward to James, from Guadalajara, 12 March 1747, RA SP 282/40.
5. Ibid.
6. AE, *M&D*, Angleterre,82, f. 199.
7. Charles Edward to the Comte d'Argenson, Paris, 26 March 1747, RA SP 282/92.
8. Charles Edward to Louis XV, 26 March 1747, RA SP 282/93.
9. RA SP 282/123.
10. O'Brien to James, 27 March 1747, RA SP 282/104A.
11. Henry to James, 20 March 1747, RA SP 282/71.
12. James to Henry, 14 April 1747, RA SP 282/163.
13. James to Charles Edward, 17 April 1747, RA SP 283/7.

14. Ibid.
15. Ibid.
16. Charles Edward to Lally, 16 June 1747, RA SP 284/116.
17. Lally to Charles Edward, 13 June 1747, RA SP 284/108.
18. O'Brien to James, 28 April 1747, RA SP 283/44.
19. Henry to Charles Edward, 29 April 1747, RA SP 283/45.
20. Charles Edward to James, 5, 7, and 15 May 1747, RA SP 283/72, 81, 121.
21. Graeme to James, 22 May 1747, RA SP 283/147.
22. Charles Edward to James, 23 May 1747, RA SP 283/155.
23. James to Charles Edward, 24 and 28 May 1747, RA SP 283/159.
24. O'Brien to Edgar, 29 May 1747, RA SP 284/1.
25. Charles Edward to James, 12 June 1747, RA SP 284/100.
26. James to Charles Edward, 13 June 1747, RA SP 284/103.
27. See RA SP 284/102.
28. Henry to Charles Edward, 13 June 1747, RA SP 284/101.
29. Henry to Charles Edward, 20 June 1747, RA SP 284/162.
30. Henry to Charles Edward, 27 June 1747, RA SP 284/207.
31. James to Charles Edward, 4 July 1747, RA SP 285/52.
32. Ibid.
33. Ibid.
34. James to O'Brien, 27 June 1747, RA SP 284/203.
35. See d'Argenson (V, 379), who notes with some scepticism that Mme O'Brien had declined a royal invitation, sanctioned by Mme de Pompadour, to join Louis XV's harem; also, de Luynes, IX, 310.
36. Father Myles MacDonnell to James, 15 July 1747, RA SP 285/126.
37. RA SP 285/104.
38. Charles Edward to James, 17 July 1747, RA SP 285/144.
39. Charles Edward to James, 24 July 1747, RA SP 285/184.
40. Charles Edward to James, 23 September, 21 October 1748, RA SP 293/123, 294/70.
41. See Charles Edward to Edgar, 24 July 1747, RA SP 285/185.
42. O'Brien to James, 3 July 1747, RA SP 285/40.
43. Louis XV to Benedict XIV, 24 June 1747, RA SP 284/172.
44. Francis Fitzjames to James, 6 July 1747, RA SP 285/78.
45. See also, Sir John O'Sullivan to Edgar, 14 July 1747, RA SP 285/125.
46. Father Myles MacDonnell to James, 15 July 1747, RA SP 285/126.
47. Theodore Hay to Edgar, 26 July 1747, RA SP 285/202.
48. D'Argenson, V, 99.
49. D'Argenson, V, 98.
50. Barbier, IV, 256-57.
51. Charles Edward to Graeme, 19 June 1748, RA SP 292/13.
52. See the Prince's declaration, drawn up around 1758-59, Box I, 454, Articles 33-39.
53. RA SP 316/225.

NOTES TO CHAPTER TEN *A New Life and Love Eternal*

1. James to Cardinal Tencin, 29 August 1747, RA SP 287/4.
2. RA SP 286/67.
3. Charles Edward to Lord Marischal, 14 August 1747, RA SP 286/109, and Lord Marischal to Charles Edward, from Treviso, 13 September 1747, RA SP 287/45.
4. See O'Brien to James, 3 July 1747, RA SP 285/40.

5. Catherine Eléonore de Béthisy, Princesse de Montauban, to Charles Edward, 24 June 1747, RA SP 284/174.
6. From St Ouen, 3 July 1747, RA SP 285/49. One of three famous summer houses at St Ouen (the other two belonged to the Duc de Gesvres and the Comte d'Evreux), the Rohan residence, according to a contemporary description, was "composée de quatre petits corps de logis, détachés l'un de l'autre, dont les dedans sont distribués avec beaucoup d'art; les meubles sont riches & d'un goût exquis, & chacun de ces corps de logis dans sa situation particuliere, jouit d'une vûe, qui quoique différente, est également délicieuse" (Germain Brice, *Description de la ville de Paris et de tout ce qu'elle contient de remarquable*, Nouvelle édition, Paris, 1752, IV, 349).
7. D. Flyn to Edgar, 25 June 1747, RA SP 284/189.
8. RA SP 284/200.
9. Charles Edward to James, 7 August 1747, RA SP 285/66; Mrs O'Brien to Edgar, 14 August 1747, RA SP 286/108.
10. Mrs O'Brien to Edgar, 28 August 1747, RA SP 286/174.
11. Marquis de Puisieux to Charles, Earl of Thomond, 27 July 1747, RA SP 286/4.
12. RA SP 286/8.
13. Charles Edward to Louis XV, 6 July 1747, RA SP 285/79.
14. 6 July 1747, RA SP 285/80.
15. See Introduction, pp.15-16.
16. My italics (brackets indicate decoded passages). Balhaldy to Edgar, from Hesdin, 8 February 1748, RA SP 289/120. Michael Sheridan (nephew of Sir Thomas) and Henry Stafford joined the Prince's household in 1747.
17. In a letter of 6 April 1746, Louis XV's special envoy, the marquis d'Eguilles, pointed out that most of the young and pretty women of Scotland were fervent Jacobites and that the Prince's not being *galant* endeared him all the more to the ladies who viewed him as "naturellement tendre" (AE, *M&D*, Angleterre, 78, f. 54).
18. Ms. Arsenal, 11658, ff. 84-120.
19. Rulhière to Berryer, 29 October 1747, Ms. Arsenal 11658, ff. 86-87.
20. Poussot to Berryer, 1 November 1747, f. 90
21. Rulhière to Berryer, from St Denis, 8 November 1747, ff. 93-94.
22. Rulhière to Berryer, 11 November 1747, ff. 102-3.
23. Poussot to Berryer, 13 November 1747, ff. 106-7.
24. Poussot to Berryer, 17 November 1747, ff. 108-9.
25. Rulhière to Berryer, 17 November 1747, ff. 110-11.
26. Poussot to Berryer, 19 November 1747, f. 112. Poussot was presumably referring to Pierre Picot, Chevalier Marquis de Dampierre (1722-1782) who, in 1748, married Emilie Le Prestre de Lézonnet. Their son, the celebrated revolutionary general killed at Valenciennes in 1793, was born in 1756.
27. Notation on Berryer's report to de Maurepas, 20 November 1747, ff. 113-14.
28. Berryer to Kelly, 21 November 1747, RA SP 288/73.
29. Berryer to Kelly, draft, 21 November 1747, f. 117.
30. Poussot to Berryer, 23 November 1747, f. 119.
31. Kelly to Berryer, 25 November 1747, f. 120.
32. See, for example, Letter 14.
33. Letter 8: "Je me suis levée dès le matin...."
34. RA SP 316/2.
35. A summary account of several lengthy disputes may be found in Box 7 (Group V, nos 87-95) of the Miscellaneous Papers at Windsor; see, also, the correspondence of Owen O'Rourke and James for the years 1738-1742.

36. A.N., 273 AP 427.
37. Charles Edward to James, draft, 30 October 1747, RA SP 287/76.
38. My italics.
39. James to Louise, 5 December 1747, RA SP 288/100.
40. James to Charles Edward, 21 November 1747, RA SP 288/74.
41. Tencin to Charles Edward, 31 October 1747, RA SP 287/202; Charles Edward to Tencin, 3 November 1747, RA SP 287/209.
42. James to Charles Edward, 12 December 1747, RA SP 288/109.
43. Charles Edward to James, 1 January 1748, RA SP 289/4.
44. Charles Edward to James, 18 December 1747, RA SP 288/72.
45. James to Charles Edward, 16 January 1748, RA SP 289/62; also James to the Princesse de Turenne, 5 February 1748, RA SP 289/108A. The memorial, along with a French translation, may be found in A.N., 273 AP 427.
46. Letter 52.
47. RA SP 289/126.
48. Charles Edward to James, 12 February 1748, RA SP 289/133. In fact, the disputation, never resolved, was to continue politely for many years to come. In May, Louise sent the following letter to James:
"Sire

Ayant fait consultée par les plus habiles avocats la reponse que Votre Majestée a bien voulu nous faire remettre par Son Altesse Royale, Monseigneur le Prince de Galles, au memoire que nous avons eu l'honneur de lui presentée, dès qu'ils m'auront communiquée leur avis, jaurai l'honneur d'en rendre compte a vôtre Majestée. Mon profond respect peut seul egalée l'attachement sans bornes avec lequel je suis

De votre Majestée
la tres humble et tres obeissante
servante

A Paris ce 29 Mai 1748   L. De la Tour D'auvergne, Princesse
                                          de rôhan, Duchesse de Montbazon"
(RA SP 291/109)
A similar letter from Louise's sister-in-law, who signed "Louise de Lorraine, Princesse de Turenne," was also sent to James around this time (RA SP 292/23).
49. Charles Edward to James, 16 October 1747, RA SP 287/122.
50. The Duc de Bouillon to Charles Edward, from Fontainebleau, 27 October 1747, RA SP 287/179.
51. J. Stafford to Edgar, from Amiens, 24 October 1747, RA SP 287/175.
52. Bachaumont's portfolio (Arsenal Ms. 3505, f. 199) presents a good contemporary summary of the best French art of the day relating to the Young Pretender. In addition, the financial accounts of the two Waters provide useful details concerning various costs and dates. Le Moyne, for example, received a total of 8000 livres in April and May 1747 for various busts and 224 livres on 4 May 1748 for gilding a large medallion. An additional payment of 1000 livres was made to him by Waters Junior on 14 November. In September 1747, the Prince sat for a miniature portrait by Georges Marolles, who turned out as well a tiny copy to fit a bracelet. Marolles received 800 livres for both from Waters Senior on 3 October 1747(RA SP 287/88). This miniature was sent to James, who found that it smelled so "strong" of musk that he finally had the frame changed (James to Charles Edward, 24 October 1747, RA SP 287/170). The portrait Louise waits for so impatiently in the secret correspondence was that by Tocqué for which the Prince sat late in 1747 (see Pl.25). Waters Junior paid Tocqué 744 livres on 20 January 1748 (RA SP

289/97). James Roettiers, Graveur général des Monnoyes de France, was paid a total of 1858 livres, 18 sols and 6 deniers for six gold and 100 silver medals on 3 May 1748 (RA SP 291/8). On 22 May, the same engraver received 1539 livres for 400 silver counters and 300 brass medals, plus an additional 584 livres on 26 September for ten more silver medals and two hundred in brass. Quentin de La Tour, for whom Charles Edward sat later in 1748 (see Pl. 27), received a payment of 1200 livres on 13 January 1749 (RA SP 296/161). James himself ordered one of the gold rings bearing the Prince's effigy on 3 December 1748, only one week before Charles Edward's arrest (Edgar to Waters, RA SP 295/81).

53. RA SP 287/66.
54. Letter 27.
55. Charles Edward to James, 20 November 1747, RA SP 288/72.
56. Charles Edward to James, draft (late December), RA SP 288/105.
57. Letter 27.
58. Letters 50, 80.
59. Draft, Charles Edward to James, 11 December 1747, RA SP 288/72.
60. See the account of George Waters, Junior, RA SP 289/97, and various legal documents in A.N., Minutier Central, VIII, 1078 (4 July 1748) and CXV, 577 (26 February 1749).
61. See accounts for servants' wages for January and February 1748, RA SP 289/90 and 182.
62. Ms. Arsenal 11658, Berryer's report of 10 December 1748: "Prince Edouard: Procès verbaux d'aposition et levée de scellés en sa maison du fauxb. St Honoré," ff. 153-80.
63. See RA SP 289/97.
64. See, for example, RA SP 289/6, 19, 30, 89, 91, 98, 119 and 177; 291/12; 292/89.
65. See RA SP 289/7.
66. See letters 24 and 25.
67. Letter 22.
68. Letter 27.
69. Letter 68.
70. Letters 76, 77.
71. RA SP Box 2/97. (Translation, *Appendix B*, II, 6).
72. It is possible, for example, that Letter 39 is her answer to the one just quoted.
73. Letter 20.
74. RA SP Box 2/98. (Translation, *Appendix B*, II, 5).
75. Letter 8.
76. And three years before that engagement was broken off (see above, p.88). Heir to her mother's wit, if not her beauty (or her morals), Sophie-Charlotte eventually married on 3 April 1745, Charles-Just de Beauvau (see *Souvenirs de la Maréchale Princesse de Beauvau... suivis des mémoires du Maréchal Prince de Beauvau*, Paris, 1872, Appendice, p. 9, "Lettre à M. le Prince de Craon"). The same letter, dated 3 April, provides an extremely rare glimpse of the Bouillon clan in 1745: Charles-Godefroy is described as "un homme très-aimable pour la société... mais son esprit et son caractère est si léger, s'il en a un, que l'on peut dire de lui, à quarante ans qu'il a: c'est un joli enfant et il ne sera jamais autre chose." The young Prince de Turenne is represented (rather accurately as it turns out) as not very promising. As for Louise: "La petite duchesse de Montbazon, sa soeur, est une très-bonne enfant, bon caractère, une inclination marquée pour la vertu, mais elle n'a point d'esprit, et elle est entre les mains d'une belle-mère, dont la compagnie, loin d'être recherchée, est à éviter pour une jeune femme" (p.10).

Anne-Françoise de Carteret, whose relationship with both of the young Bouillon princesses at Cherche-Midi was very close, was at least five years older than Louise, being described as a *fille majeure* (i.e., at least 25 years of age) already in 1744. On 11 January

1744, Sophie-Charlotte granted de Carteret a lifetime pension of 2000 livres, and a year later, an additional allowance of 1000 livres, accompanied by an invitation to de Carteret "de vouloir bien luy faire le plaisir et l'amitié de continuer à demeurer toujours avec elle" (see A.N., Minutier Central, LXXXVIII, 595, 28 April 1745 and LXXIX, 47, 22 March 1745). De Carteret is also mentioned in the Comte d'Evreux's will (A.N., 273 AP 423).

77. James to O'Brien, 15 June 1740, RA SP 223/135; also O'Brien to Edgar, 30 May 1740, RA SP 222/164, and Edgar to de Carteret, 1 February 1742, RA SP 239/157.

78. See, for example, the case of Mary Clark, the widowed sister of Sir Hector Macleane (RA SP 289/129).

79. See below, RA SP 289/46. The Prince kept the matter entirely confidential, and no record of the amount granted appears in his usual accounts. A letter from de Carteret to the Prince dated 15 February 1749 requests continuation of his "protection" (de Carteret to Charles Edward, RA SP 297/12).

80. Letter 22.

81. Letter 25.

82. [Charles Edward to Anne-Françoise de Carteret], 10 January 1748, RA SP 289/46. See also copy, 289/45. The recipient of this letter is mistakenly identified in the Windsor hand list for Volume 289 as Lord Marischal.

83. [Anne-Françoise de Carteret to Charles Edward], RA SP 289/47. The author of this unsigned letter has been catalogued as unknown, but a comparison of the handwriting with RA SP 297/12, de Carteret to Charles Edward, 15 February 1749, provides conclusive proof of the sender's identity. (Translation, *Appendix B*, II, 7).

84. Letter 38.

85. Letter 39.

86. Letter 40.

87. See Michael Sheridan's order of 20 January 1748 to Daniel O'Brien, authorizing payment for two days' hire of the coach. On the second day, Friday, 19 January, the Prince visited Versailles, returning to Paris late on the 20th (RA SP 289/68); also, de Luynes (VIII, 427-35), concerning the Marly festivities.

88. Letter 44.

89. Letter 45.

NOTES TO CHAPTER ELEVEN *End of the Affair*

1. Letter 48.

2. Letter 47.

3. Letter 48.

4. [Mlle de Carteret to Charles Edward, ? 27 January 1748], RA SP, Box 4, Folder 1/114. The letter is unsigned and undated. My conjectural dating is based on de Carteret's apparent awareness of the fact that the Prince has not answered Louise's "official" letter of 23 January, suggesting that at least two or three days have elapsed since it was sent. On the other hand, it is still the same week since she speaks of having arrived at the Hôtel de Guéméné "on Monday." (Translation, *Appendix B*, II, 8).

5. Charles Edward to James, 5 February 1748, RA SP 289/112.

6. It is possible that Lady Clifford was the person who offered shelter to Louise's valet on the Prince's recommendation. She was one of Charles Edward's most active social contacts at this time, and Louise, writing to her chief intermediary (no. 71) after the 11 April fiasco, reports that Mme de Guéméné had forbidden all further communication with "Mme C." As for the identity of the intermediary himself, the text makes it clear that it was a

servant, only too well informed about the unfortunate events of 23 January (no. 71), and that Louise, despite her father's understandable grouchiness on the subject (no. 68), was making every effort to arrange for a small pension through the Duc's *trésorier général*, Guillaume-Jean-Louis Maigrot (see letters 58, 64, 65, 68 and 77). Since her valet had been dismissed from a secure position because of her and the Prince, it would seem only normal that she should try to compensate him in some way. The Prince initially may have helped too, but later he seems to have abandoned Chrétien to his fate (no. 68).

7. See Letter 71.
8. See, for example, de Luynes, XVI, 154-55.
9. See [Princesse de Ligne to Charles Edward, ? 5, 8, and 9 February 1748], RA SP Box 4, Folder 1/102,104; also 289/109.
10. [Charles Edward to the Princesse de Ligne, ? 10 February 1748], RA SP Box 2/100.
11. [Princesse de Ligne to Charles Edward, ? 14 February 1748], RA SP Box 4, Folder 1/98.
12. [Charles Edward to the Princesse de Ligne, ? 26 February 1748], RA SP Box 2/103; see also, [Princesse de Ligne to James Oxburgh], 2 March 1748, RA SP 289/187.
13. See Oxburgh to Charles Edward, 15 February 1749: "Poor Lord Gordon will, I fear, fall into another fit of his distemper. He is at Versailles where, I am told, he acts very wildly"; also 21 February 1749: "Poor Lord Louis Gordon is under a guard as before and when he comes to himself will, I believe, be orderd to his regiment. I dont believe he will be permitted any more to go to Versailles." (RA SP 297/32). The condition eventually grew even worse: see, for example, William Hay to Edgar, 2 September and 15 October 1751, RA SP 324/109 and 326/32.
14. Charles Edward to James, 26 February 1747 (read 1748), RA SP 289/167.
15. [Princesse de Ligne to Charles Edward, ? 27 February 1748], RA SP, Box 4, Folder 1/95.
16. Ibid.
17. [Princesse de Ligne to Charles Edward, ? 29 February 1748], (delivered 1 March), RA SP Box 4, Folder 1/94.
18. Princesse de Ligne to Oxburgh, 2 March 1748, RA SP 289/187.
19. [Princesse de Ligne to Oxburgh, ? 4 March 1748], RA SP, Box 4, Folder 1/96.
20. Mme de Guéméné to Oxburgh, 7 March 1748, RA SP 297/80. This letter has been mistakenly catalogued as addressed to Colonel Daniel O'Brien and dated 7 March 1749. Several letters from Mme de Guéméné to George II and to the Duke of Newcastle, requesting the release of her son, Louis-Armand-Constantin, Chevalier de Rohan and *capitaine de vaisseaux du Roy*, held prisoner of war in 1758, are preserved in Brit. Mus. Add. ms. 32881, ff.248-51; 32885, f.513 and 32887, f.481.
21. Letter 71.
22. The Marquise de Mézières to Charles Edward, 6 April 1748, RA SP 290/107.
23. RA SP 289/142.
24. RA SP 290/198.
25. RA SP 289/190.
26. Balhaldy to Edgar, 9 March 1748, RA SP 290/13.
27. D. Flyn to Edgar, 4 April 1748, RA SP 290/96.
28. I am currently preparing a detailed study of Charles Edward's "obscure years," that is, the period following his arrest and expulsion from France when the Princesse de Talmont and her two friends, Elisabeth Ferrand and the Comtesse de Vassé, played key roles in the Prince's clandestine activities in Paris.
29. See above, pp. 57-58
30. See d'Argenson, IX, 243.
31. See de Luynes, II, 58, 95 and 106-7.
32. See Pierre Boyé, *La Cour Polonaise de Lunéville (1737-1766)*, Nancy, 1926, pp. 61-89.

33. *Poésies Mêlées*, #124, *Oeuvres complètes de Voltaire*, Paris, 1877, X, 520.
34. J.-J. Rousseau, *Oeuvres complètes*, Paris, 1964, (Pléiade), III, 661.
35. See *Lettres de la marquise du Deffand à Horace Walpole, etc.*, Paris, 1824, III, 47-49.
36. Letter 82.
37. Letter 87.
38. Letter 89.
39. See RA SP 291/71; de Luynes refers to the Princesse de Talmont on 14 May as "extrêmement amie...du Prince Edouard" (IX, 36).
40. See Letter 92.
41. See RA SP 291/78, 80 and 82.
42. D'Argenson's entry is for 4 July, but the context is retrospective and the item follows reference to a similar quarrel, first mentioned on 9 June, between the Prince de Conti and his mistress, Marie-Louise d'Arty, one of the illegitimate daughters of the financier Samuel Bernard (V, 226, 231-32).
43. D'Argenson, V, 232. My italics.
44. RA SP 289/168.
45. Charles Edward to Graeme, 8 March 1748, RA SP 290/10; see also drafts to James, 25 March, 1 and 8 April 1748, RA SP 290/5; Graeme to James, 18 March 1748, RA SP 290/40.
46. "Instructions...to Sir John Graeme", [4 April 1748], RA SP 290/98. See also, Charles Edward to Frederick the Great, RA SP Box 1/284.
47. RA SP 290/136.
48. RA SP 291/17.
49. RA SP 291/150.
50. Charles Edward to Edgar, 10 June 1748, RA SP 291/185.
51. RA SP 291/33, draft.
52. Graeme to Charles Edward, 1 June 1748, RA SP 291/124.
53. Graeme to Charles Edward, from Frankfurt, 4 June 1748, RA SP 291/153.
54. He had acted as James's agent in Vienna in 1725-27 and as his Secretary of State in 1727-28. At the death of O'Brien in 1759, James called him back to Rome where he acted as Secretary of State (but without the title) from 1759 to 1763. He was 56 years of age at the time of his mission to Berlin.
55. Charles Edward to Graeme, 7 June 1748, draft; RA SP 291/33.
56. Charles Edward to Graeme, 12 June 1748, draft; RA SP 291/33.
57. Graeme to Charles Edward, 18 June 1748, RA SP 292/10.
58. Ibid.
59. Charles Edward to Graeme, 19 June 1748, draft; RA SP 292/13.
60. Charles Edward to Graeme, 10 July 1748, draft; RA SP 292/13.
61. RA SP 292/50.
62. De Puisieux to F. Bulkeley, 5 July 1748, RA SP 292/104. Without attesting to its truth, de Luynes records the rumour that Louis XV eventually offered Charles Edward an annual pension of 800,000 livres to ease the pain of a move to Fribourg (*Mémoires*, IX, 259).
63. See, Charles Edward to Louis XV, 18 July 1748, RA SP 292/143.
64. RA SP 292/122A.
65. RA SP 292/127.
66. RA SP 292/177.
67. RA SP 292/180.
68. Graeme to Charles Edward, 29 June 1748, RA SP 292/84.
69. Graeme to Charles Edward, 9 July 1748, RA SP 292/117.

70. Graeme to Charles Edward, 22 July 1748, RA SP 292/148.
71. Graeme to Charles Edward, 26 July 1748, RA SP 292/155.
72. Charles Edward to Graeme, 1 August 1748, draft, RA SP 292/181.
73. A cypher of proper names, words, letters and numbers, used by Sir John Graeme in his correspondence with Charles Edward at this time, may be found in RA SP, Box 5/214.
74. Charles Edward to Graeme, 7 August 1748, draft, RA SP 292/181.
75. Graeme to Charles Edward, 2 August 1748, RA SP 292/183.
76. Charles Edward to Graeme, 11 August 1748, draft; RA SP 292/181.
77. Graeme to Charles Edward, 9 August 1748, draft; RA SP 293/1.
78. Charles Edward to Graeme, 14 August 1748, draft; RA SP 292/181.

    Princess Caroline-Louise of Hesse-Darmstadt, the only daughter of Ludwig VIII, was finally married in 1751 to Charles-Frederick, margrave of Baden-Durlach (1728-1811), whose enlightened and conscientious administration was greatly admired throughout Europe. The Princess and her husband devoted much of their energies to patronizing the arts and carried on an active correspondence with leading writers of the day, including Voltaire.

    One last problem must be mentioned before we leave the question of Charles Edward's plans to marry the Princess Caroline-Louise. Volume 297 of the Stuart Papers contains two unusually tidy drafts of letters in the Prince's hand addressed to Stanislas Leszczynski, the exiled King of Poland, and to Prince Louis, Landgrave of Hesse-Darmstadt. They were written on 24 February 1749, on the eve of the Prince's departure from Avignon where he had gone, in spite of a solemn promise to the contrary, after being released from Vincennes in December. The first, to Stanislas, is undated and speaks of the Prince having just arrived in Lorraine, accompanied by his wife, the Princess of Hesse-Darmstadt, "qui a bien voulu sunire a mois, et par consequent partage mon sort.... La Princesse, ma Fame," the letter continues, "desire et a intention de rester dans ce pais; d'autent plus quelle est proche de sa Maison Paternelle." On the reverse of the same sheet may be found, also dated 24 February 1749 a letter to the Landgrave, soliciting the hand of his daughter: "Je n'ai pas malheureusement une Couronne a lui offrir actuellement comme Elle le merite mais j'espere bien de l'avoir un jours, et d'etre alors en etat de vous prouver La Recconoissance due a un Prince qui m'auroit accordez une telle Grace pendant mes malheurs."

    A third letter in the same volume, again dated 24 February 1749, purports to grant full legal authority to "le Sieur Dugglas" (one of Charles Edward's frequently used aliases) to negotiate the marriage and even to marry the Princess in his name and to conduct her to his unspecified place of residence (RA SP 297/41). The letters have for years mystified Charles Edward's biographers, but in the light of what we know of the Prince's lack of success at Darmstadt six months earlier, it seems clear that they were written as ostensible documents, possibly for the benefit of Hanoverian agents and the French authorities who, in the next several years, did their best to track down the mysterious hiding place of the elusive outlaw prince.

79. Charles Edward to James, 29 July 1748, RA SP 292/165.
80. "Extrait des Registres de Baptêmes de l'Eglise Royale et Paroissiale de St Paul à Paris," Archives Nationales, 273 AP 3. Marie-Sophie de Courcillon (1713-1756) was the second wife (1732) of Mme de Guéméné's father, Hercule-Mériadec de Rohan-Soubise, duc de Rohan-Rohan (1669-1749).
81. RA SP 292/171.

NOTES TO CHAPTER TWELVE *The Outlaw Prince*

1. De Luynes, IX, 501.
2. De Luynes, IX, 219-20.
3. De Luynes, IX, 220.
4. See RA SP 292/4; also James to Mrs. O'Brien, 13 August 1748, RA SP 293/13.
5. In June the Prince had already asked that his protest be granted "tacit permission" to be printed clandestinely, "et qu'il soit insinué aux Magistrats de la Police de fermer les yeux à la publication et distribution qui en sera faite sous le manteau; Le dit Prince Royal promettant que le tout se fera avec une attention et des mesures si justes que personne ne sera Compromis." See Charles Edward's "Mémoire...Pour être présenté Aux Ministres de Sa Majesté Très Chrétienne" (May-June 1748 but incorrectly bound as RA SP 270/15 for 24 October 1745).
6. Berryer to Maurepas, 17 July 1748, Ms. Arsenal, 11658, f. 151.
7. Ibid.
8. RA SP 292/137, p. 3.
9. See Robert Shackleton, *Montesquieu, A Critical Biography*, Oxford, 1961, pp. 180-85 on Montesquieu's relations with the Duchesse d'Aiguillon.
10. Charles Edward to Montesquieu, [mid-June 1748], RA SP Box 1/286.
11. Montesquieu to Charles Edward, from Bazas, 19 August 1748, RA SP 293/31.
12. See notarized statement of Michel Ignace Lefevre, Liège, 26 August 1748, RA SP 292/132B.
13. See RA SP 292/133 B and 135 A; my italics.
14. De Puisieux to Charles Edward, RA SP 293/35.
15. RA SP 293/40.
16. Thereby exposing his agent, George Waters, Jr., to a costly lawsuit the following year (see AE, *M&D*, Angleterre, 82, f.236 and A.N., Minutier Central, CXV, 577, 26 February 1749).
17. RA SP 294/3.
18. *Journal et Mémoires*, V, 255.
19. RA SP 294/173.
20. RA SP 294/174.
21. RA SP 294/175.
22. De Luynes, IX, 260.
23. De Luynes, IX, 123.
24. AE, *M&D*, Angleterre, 80, f.87.
25. D'Argenson, V, 296.
26. De Luynes, IX, 141.
27. See "Memorandum of What to be Saide in case any new Remonstrance be Made," RA SP 294/177.
28. De Luynes, IX, 260, note 1.
29. D'Argenson, V, 278. It was d'Argenson who had signed the "Treaty of Fontainebleau" with O'Brien on 24 October 1745. The pact, following on Charles Edward's proclamation in Edinburgh as Prince Regent of Scotland in the preceding month, was conceived essentially as a wartime alliance between Louis XV, King of France, and Charles Edward Stuart, *de facto* Prince Regent of Scotland, both being effectively at war with a common enemy, the Elector of Hanover. Quite deliberately, no reference was made in the Treaty to the *de jure* pretensions of the House of Stuart and presumably the formal accord became a dead letter the moment the Prince ceased to be in effective control of what are described in the document as the "états qui sont ou seront soumis à la Régence du Prince Royal."

Obviously missing from that phrase, for Charles Edward's purposes, were the words *soumis de droit*. De Puisieux's challenge, in other words, would have been hard to meet. On the other hand, several of the treaty's clauses were couched in terms sufficiently loose and "inspirational" to allow the Prince to hint vaguely that more was obviously intended than was written down. Two copies of the Treaty in O'Brien's hand are to be found in RA SP 270/13 and 14. For a recently published copy of it, see F.J. McLynn, *France and the Jacobite Rising of 1745*, Appendix II, pp. 239-40.

30. De Luynes, IX, 259.
31. De Luynes, IX, 260.
32. See Barbier, IV, 321.
33. D'Argenson, V, 300. See also, Maurepas to de Puisieux, 22 November 1748, AE, *M&D*, Angleterre, 80, ff.95-100.
34. V, 278.
35. V, 284.
36. See AE, *M&D*, Angleterre, 82, f.240.
37. D'Argenson, 26 November 1748, V, 289.
38. D'Argenson, V, 318; de Luynes, IX, 257.
39. See A.N., Minutier Central, LXVIII, 437, 29 November 1748. The will, clearly drawn up "dans la veue de la mort," provides some useful information concerning the Duc and his household arrangements. After requesting a simple funeral at St Sulpice, he asked that his body be taken for burial to the Church of St Germain at Evreux. Five hundred low requiem masses were ordered in each of three different churches, along with one annual mass in perpetuity at another. All of his diamonds he bequeathed to his son, the Prince de Turenne, whose wife was to inherit the Duc's *porcelaines de Saxe* as well as his favourite ring, known as "le bateau," which he always wore. To his daughter the Duc bequeathed, "comme un témoignage de la tendresse qu'il a toujours eu pour Elle," a diamond valued at 10,000 livres and the most precious of his many jewelled boxes. Other family bequests were made to his old aunt, the Princesse de Montbazon, to his Jansenist sister, the Duchesse de la Trémoïlle, and to his young half-sister (the Messalina's daughter), Marie-Sophie-Charlotte, now Princesse de Beauvau. In addition to sizeable legacies granted his intendant, Claude Linotte, and his treasurer, Guillaume-Jean-Louis Maigrot, as well as other administrative officers in his household, the Duc made generous bequests to more than fifty domestic servants, each named individually.
    Louise's father was fortunate enough to recover from his November 1748 illness and went on to live for another twenty-three increasingly prosperous years. His final will and testament, dated 4 September 1769 (A.N., 273 AP 206, Dossier 2), shows him to be still conventionally anxious on the point of salvation, but somewhat more assured in his estimate of the number of masses required to effect the safe repose of his soul. Interestingly, his instructions in 1769 dictated that his heart be sent for burial to the parish church at Bouillon and that his body be buried next to that of his grandfather, Godefroy-Maurice de La Tour d'Auvergne, 3rd Duc de Bouillon, who had built the magnificent château at Navarre and died there in 1721. By 1769, the Duc's financial circumstances had improved sufficiently for him to provide his daughter with a lump sum of 50,000 livres as proof of his "tenderness and friendship," in addition to a *rente viagère* of 6000 livres. The Château de Montalet near Mantes, where he died of apoplexy on 24 October 1771, was left to his daughter-in-law, the Princesse de Turenne.
40. RA SP 295/69.
41. This document, certified by de Gesvres on 4 December 1748 as "pareille a l'original que j'ay fait remettre par ordre du Roy au Prince Charles Edouard," is preserved in the Stuart papers (RA SP 295/87).

42. AE, *M&D*, Angleterre, 80, f.114.
43. See James to Tencin, 4 November 1748, AE, *M&D*, Angleterre, 80, f.78.
44. James to Charles Edward, 23 November 1748, RA SP 295/34.
45. De Luynes, IX, 142.
46. AE, *M&D*, Angleterre, 80, f. 117.
47. Known as the Cul-de-Sac de l'Opéra. The year following, when management of the Opéra was given over by the King to the City of Paris, it ceased to be a *cul-de-sac*. Additional land was purchased allowing for a small exit at the end. See Henri Lagrave, *Le théâtre et le public à Paris de 1715 à 1750*, Paris 1972, p. 85 and plate No. 7).
48. See d'Argenson, V, 292-94, 299, 359; Barbier, IV, 326-29.
49. See RA SP 295/104, which is an early draft with major revisions in the Prince's hand. The final version, written out entirely in the Prince's hand, is contained, along with several other copies of the work, in RA SP 296; see also AE, *M&D*, Angleterre, 82, ff. 229-33.
50. Detailed information concerning the arrests made by Berryer at the Prince's house may be found in the Bastille archives (Ms. Arsenal 11658, ff. 153-264; see also partial—and frequently inaccurate—transcriptions in François Ravaisson, *Archives de la Bastille, documents inédits*, Paris 1883, XV, 445-89). Among the *gentlemen* arrested in addition to Goring, Harrington, and Sheridan, were the following: Louis Cameron, Richard Jackson, Alexander Macleod, David Murray, John Francis Nugent, Francis Stafford and Charles Stewart. Goring and Harrington were released on 19 December and exiled fifty leagues from Paris. Sheridan and Stafford were set free on 14 December and allowed to accompany the Prince the following day when he was escorted from Vincennes on his way to the frontier. The remaining six were released on the 19th. Eleven of the Prince's French servants and two natives of Savoy were liberated on 11 December. They were: Barthélemy Chambaut, Robert Chantepuis, Henri Chevillon, Jean Dunant, François Hubry *dit* La Rose, Killien Labbé, Toussaint Lalouette, Jean Marchand, Louis Reydet, Jean Tardif *dit* du Verger, and Pierre Titon. Also set free on the 11th were two other French nationals, Michel Grout, a coachman in the employ of Lady Clifford, and Jean-Nicolas François, the Princesse de Talmont's footman, who had gone that day to the Prince's house to deliver a miniature portrait of the Princesse. Charles Edward's two chief servants, Daniel O'Brien and John Stewart, were released at the Prince's request along with Stafford and Sheridan on 14 December, in time for their master's departure on the following day. Again at Charles Edward's request, two more servants, both Irish, were granted early release: these were, Edward Stokes and William Gillsenan, liberated on the 15th and 16th respectively. The Scottish servants, Duncan Cameron, Aeneas Campbell, Angus MacDonnell, and Alexander MacKenzie, along with Charles Delay, one of Lally's grooms, Laughlan MacLean, a servant of Sir Hector MacLeane and James Harrington's Swiss servant, François Willermaula, were allowed to go free only on 19 December, as were a mixed group of "found-ins", either residents or casual visitors, classified separately from the Prince's gentlemen and servants. These last were: Thomas Barton, described as one of the Prince's unemployed English supporters, William Brennan, a penniless clerk whose only worldly goods, his watch and buckles, were pledged, Robert Hackett, a fifteen-year old Scottish lad whom the Prince had been sheltering out of charity, Thomas Moncrieff, another penniless refugee from the '45, and James O'Farrell, a wigmaker and servant of a visiting gentleman named Wogan.
51. At this point Charles Edward inserted the following comment in an early draft: "Cela n'etoit pas étonnant car il s'etoit deja exprimes en plusieurs occasions qu'il n'etoit pas fait pour La Menase, et deja que l'on l'avoit, il yroit toujours a son ordinaire par tout, eut-il a rencontrer sans mille Diables."

52. In another fragmentary account in English, Charles Edward recalls having been rather more humorous on this occasion: "The Major Ordered More Cords Shou'd be Put about me; I asked him then joking wheather they had a minde to put me in Garters" (RA SP 295/182).

53. RA SP 295/182.

54. When the news was brought to him at Versailles, Louis was attending the opera *Tancrède* and enjoying a magnificent performance by Mme de Pompadour in the heroine's role (de Luynes, IX, 147).

55. D'Argenson, for example, on first learning of the arrest, made the comment: "On le traitera sans doute en prince à Vincennes, il sera dans le château où rien ne lui manquera; mais on craint qu'il n'attente à sa vie" (V, 309).

56. The revised version, however, makes no reference to a compass and concentrates rather on providing a justifiably outraged Prince with excuses for refusing to give his word of honour on anything since his captors had been so vile (and so right, as it turned out) not to believe him in the first place.

57. De Luynes, IX, 150-51. Was the earlier mention of a compass first brought into the Prince's narrative to confuse the public on that point?

58. See, RA SP 296/7, "Lettre de Mr Nugeon à un Anglois de ses amis sur l'Emprisonnement du Prince Charles Edouard." It would be more accurate to state, perhaps, that this last composition weaves the "Lettre de Madame de XXX" onto a broader canvas. John Francis Nugent was one of the gentlemen arrested at the Prince's house and released from the Bastille on 19 December.

59. In fact, though he managed to avoid signing any paper, he did make a solemn verbal promise to that effect, before witnesses (see AE, *M&D*, Angleterre, 80, ff. 163-64).

60. That is, "sembl*oient* avoir oublié qu'il*s* s'oppos*oient* à la volonté de leur Roy," RA SP 295/104; 296/11A.

61. Ms. Arsenal 11658, ff. 174, 196.

62. Quoted in d'Argenson, V, 320.

63. Maurepas to Berryer, 10 December 1748, Ms. Arsenal, 11658, f. 174.

64. Ibid., f. 168.

65. Ibid., f. 208.

66. Ibid., f. 212.

67. Ibid., f. 216.

68. Maurepas suggests that it was the King himself who singled them out for the additional penalty: "Je n'ay pas trouvé le Roy disposé a accorder la liberté, du moins sitot, a Mrs Harrington et Gorrein et je ne crois pas qu'ils puissent l'avoir que le Prince ne soit...sorti du Royaume," (AE, *M&D*, Angleterre, 80, f. 184).

69. Ms. Arsenal, 11658, f. 226.

70. Charles Edward to Louis XV, 12 December 1748, AE, *M&D*, Angleterre, 80, f. 145.

71. Ibid., f. 163.

72. Ibid., f. 156, 158. De Pérussi mistakenly dated his letter to Maurepas as "ce 14e dimanche."

73. Morrison, curiously, lived at a wigmaker's in the Rue de Seine and not at the Prince's house. He thus escaped arrest on the 10th (ibid., f. 160).

74. Ibid., f. 180.

75. D'Argenson, V, 320-21.

76. Ibid., V, 340.

77. Ibid., V, 314.

78. Ibid., V, 343-44.

79. Barbier, IV, 341; see also, Emile Raunié, *Chansonnier historique du XVIIIe siècle*

(Recueil Clairambault-Maurepas), 3e partie, Paris 1882, VII, 157.

80. D'Argenson, V, 343.

81. See also, Raunié, VII, années 1748, 1749. For a brief but well-documented account of public reaction to the Prince's arrest, see Adrienne Hytier, "An Eighteenth-Century Experiment in Historical Realism: The Marquis d'Argenson and Bonnie Prince Charlie," *Eighteenth-Century Studies*, III, 204-08. Box 3 of the miscellaneous Stuart papers at Windsor also contains many examples of these and other varieties of verse and songs relating to the Prince's misfortunes.

82. Barbier, IV, 335.

83. De Luynes, X, 87.

84. De Luynes, X, 86. For other examples, see RA SP Box 3/32, Folder 2.

85. Raunié, VII, 145-46.

86. *Précis du Siècle de Louis XV*, in *Oeuvres historiques* (Pléiade), pp. 1447-48. Readers of *Candide* will recall how the simple hero of that Voltairian tale meets up with Charles Edward in Venice, the Prince's misfortunes being cited as yet more evidence of the evils of the world.

87. Ibid., p. 1748, note 1.

88. See de Puisieux to the Maréchal de Belle-Isle, 15 December 1748, AE, *M&D*, Angleterre, 80, ff. 186-88; also, "Mémoire servant d'instruction au Sieur Durand [de Distroff], conseiller au Parlement de Metz, allant en Angleterre pour y etre chargé des affaires du Roi jusqu'à l'arrivée de l'Ambassadeur que Sa Majesté y enverra", 16 January 1749, in *Recueil des instructions données aux ambassadeurs et ministres de France depuis les Traités de Westphalie jusqu'à la Revolution Française*, XX-2 Angleterre, tome troisième, avec une introduction et des notes par Paul Vaucher, Paris 1965, pp. 326-30.

89. D'Argenson, V, 347.

90. Barbier, December 1748, IV, 340.

91. Barbier, November 1749, IV, 399.

92. See AE, *M&D*, Angleterre, 80, ff. 149, 157. The date is incorrectly shown as the 13th.

93. St Clair to Bedford, Public Record Office, SP 92/58; cited in Ernest Campbell Mossner, *The Life of David Hume*, Edinburgh, 1954, pp. 218-19.

94. RA SP 295/139.

95. AE, *M&D*, Angleterre, 80, f. 224; my italics.

96. Murray to Edgar, 31 December 1748, RA SP 295/198.

97. RA SP 295/187.

NOTES TO THE POSTSCRIPT

1. In a chapel immediately to the right of the main altar: see Germain Brice, *Description de la Ville de Paris*, I, 289-301.

2. Jacques Hillairet, *Evocation du Vieux Paris*, II, 60.

3. A.N., 273 AP 3.

4. Charles Edward to James, 1 January 1749, RA SP 296/46.

5. RA SP 316/173.

6. RA SP 316/190.

7. RA SP 316/278.

8. Back of RA SP 333/15; probably written around 15 June 1752.

9. See back of RA SP 316/103.

10. Princesse de Talmont to Charles Edward, undated, RA SP 316/100.

11. Talmont to Charles Edward, RA SP Box 4, Folder 1/56.

12. See Lucien Perey, *La Fin du XVIIIe Siècle, le Duc de Nivernais*, Paris 1891, pp. 34-35.

13. Walpole to Gray, 25 January 1766, in *Horace Walpole's Correspondence with Thomas Gray*, edited by W.S. Lewis, George L. Lam and Charles H. Bennett, New Haven, 1948, II, 157.

14. Walpole to Montagu, 21 March 1766, in *Horace Walpole's Correspondence with George Montagu*, edited by Lewis and Ralph S. Brown, Jr., New Haven, 1941, II, 208.

15. See *Lettres de la Marquise du Deffand à Horace Walpole*, Paris, 1824, I, 46-47.

16. Stafford and Sheridan to Charles Edward, from Avignon, 5 November 1751, RA SP 327/30.

17. Stafford and Sheridan to Charles Edward, 7 January 1752, RA SP 329/64.

18. RA SP 334/75.

19. Edgar to H. Stafford, 22 August 1752, RA SP 334/144.

20. RA SP 335/67.

21. Charles Edward to Stafford and Sheridan, 9 October 1752, RA SP 336/111.

22. Murray (Dunbar) to Edgar, 22 September 1752, RA SP 335/122.

23. See James to Colonel O'Brien, 23 June 1749, RA SP 298/143.

24. James to Charles Edward, 31 December 1749, RA SP 302/53.

25. James to Charles Edward, 4 August 1750, RA SP 310/14.

26. A.N., 273 AP 206.

27. De Luynes, IX, 507-8.

28. De Luynes, XI, 411-12.

29. Mrs. O'Brien to Colonel Daniel O'Brien, 20 May 1752, RA SP 331/119A. Similar reports of the incident are also found in the clandestine newsletters of the day.

30. See A.N., 273 AP 423.

31. De Luynes, XII, 326.

32. De Luynes, XIII, 185-86.

33. See RA SP Box 1/429, 451, 455, 458, 459, 469.

34. See, for example, Suzanne d'Huart, *Archives Rohan-Bouillon, Inventaire*, S.E.V.P.E.N., Paris, 1970, p. 45, note 2; Stephen Leroy, *Notice armoriale et généalogique de la maison de Bouillon-La Tour*, Sedan, 1896, p. 114; Georges Martin, *Histoire et généalogie des maisons de Rohan, de Chabot et de Rohan- Chabot*, Paris, 1977, II, 111.

35. Mrs. O'Brien to Colonel Daniel O'Brien, 16 October 1751, RA SP 326/23.

36. De Luynes, XV, 7-10.

37. Louise to the Duc, from Paris, 20 August 1758, A.N., 273 AP 206, Dossier 3.

38. Mme de Guéméné to the Maréchal de Belle-Isle, 19 August 1758, A.N., 273 AP 206, Dossier 3.

39. Jules-Hercule-Mériadec de Rohan-Guéméné to the Duc de Bouillon, A.N., 273 AP 206, Dossier 3.

40. Ibid.

41. Ibid.

42. Ibid.

43. The words belong to Margaret Forster whose penetrating summary (pp. 295-307) of Charles Edward's character in *The Rash Adventurer, The Rise and Fall of Charles Edward Stuart*, London, 1973, is one of the most cogent I have seen.

44. See the *Gazette*, No 3, 17 January 1761, pp. 31-33.

45. Voltaire to Jean Le Rond d'Alembert, 16 March [1765], *Voltaire's Correspondence*, Best. D. 12466.

46. Ibid., note 2. The Condorcet-Beuchot note continues: "Marsy fut chassé des jésuites, et Fréron, son ami intime, sortit avec lui." There are some obvious chronological difficulties with the story, as reported by Condorcet, since Fréron left the Society of Jesus in 1739, well before Henri-Louis was born (see Jean Balcou, *Fréron contre les philosophes*,

Genève, 1975, p. 12).
47. At approximately 9 o'clock in the evening, according to the deposition of Armand-Jean Petit de la Houville, Chevalier Conseiller du Roy au Châtelet de Paris (A.N., Minutier Central, VI, 828).
48. *Gazette de France*, 29 August 1780, no.69, p. 328. For a copy of her will, see A.N., 1969, 286 Mi, reel 2.
49. See, for example, such recent works as Georges Martin's *Histoire et généalogie des maisons de Rohan* (p. 111). Leroy, *Notice armoriale* (pp. 115-16), establishes the correct date. Examples of his correspondence for this period may be found in A.N., 1969, 286 Mi, reel 3.
50. Archives Nationales, Minutier Central, VI, 828; STATNI OBLASTNI ARCHIV LITOMERICE, pobocka DECIN, Archives de la famille de Rohan, No 421, Carton 170; also, Archives de Paris, DC6 277, f. 32.
51. Germain Brice, *Description de Paris*, II, 320.
52. Louise had presented Mme de Masseran at Court on 11 November 1752 (De Luynes, XII, 184).
53. Jules's only means of support at this time was, in fact, a small pension from the Cardinal.
54. Louise made several attempts to advance the ecclesiastical career of Prince Louis (1734-1803). Already in 1757 and again in 1759, she had unsuccessfully solicited his appointment to the College of Cardinals in letters to James in Rome (Louise to James, 5 June 1757, RA SP 371/147; Louise to Colonel Daniel O'Brien, 30 April 1759, RA SP 392/119). Prince Louis was not made a Cardinal, in fact, until 1778. In 1771 when he was appointed French Ambassador Extraordinary to the Court of Vienna, Louise initiated an exchange of letters with Charles Edward suggesting that joint Stuart-Bouillon negotiations, conducted by her brother-in-law, be pursued at Vienna to gain payment by the Austrians of the huge debt (with interest, well over one million florins) still owed the heirs of James Sobieski. (See Louise to Charles Edward, 23 July, 30 December 1771, 23 December 1773, 13 March, 2 August 1774, in RA SP 454/143, 457/13, 471/96, 473/99, 475/48; also, Charles Edward to Louise, 20 November 1771, 12 August 1772, 24 November 1773, 2 March, 30 March 1774 in RA SP 456/14, 461/120, 470/30, 473/87, 115.) A summary account of previous efforts to collect the debt may be found in RA SP Box 7/87; see also, B.M. Add. ms. 34638, vol. V.
55. Archives de Paris, DC6 277, f. 33.
56. Charles Edward was delighted to inform both Louise and the Princesse de Talmont of his marriage and wrote to them soon after. His letter to Louise (obviously corrected for spelling) is as follows: "Je ne puis douter, Madame, des plaisirs que vous ressentirez en apprenant mon mariage avec la Princesse Louise de Stolberg Guedern. La Reine vous fait ses complimens et je me flatte que vous serez toujours persuadée de ma constante et sincere amitié.

Votre affectioné cousin
Rome ce 6 May 1772.   C.R."

After the death of James, Louise and Charles Edward exchanged New Year's greetings for a number of years—entirely formal and routine in nature. In acknowledging her condolences of January 1766, the new *de jure* King did, however, allow himself a reference to the "tendresse particuliere que j'aurois toujours pour vous" (5 March 1766, RA SP 433/191). In her own greetings, Louise always made it clear that she continued to pray for a Stuart restoration (see, for example, Louise to Charles Edward, 29 December 1763, RA SP 448/120). In March 1774, Charles Edward sent two circular medallion engravings of himself and his wife to his former sweetheart (RA SP 473/101).

57. Mann to Horace Walpole, 9 May 1772, *Horace Walpole's Correspondence with Sir Horace Mann*, edited by W.S. Lewis et al., New Haven, 1967, VII, 406.

58. Mann to Walpole, 25 May 1779, *Correspondence*, VIII, 479-80.

59. See, for example, Boswell's interview with Voltaire at Ferney on 27 December 1764: "He is drunk every day. He kicks women, and he ought to be kicked" (Frederick A. Pottle, ed., *Boswell on the Grand Tour, Germany and Switzerland*, New York, 1928, p. 301).

60. Mann to Walpole, 12 December 1780, *Correspondence*, IX, 100-101.

Appendix A

LETTERS FROM
MARIE-LOUISE-HENRIETTE-JEANNE DE LA TOUR D'AUVERGNE
DUCHESSE DE MONTBAZON, PRINCESSE DE ROHAN
TO HER COUSIN PRINCE CHARLES EDWARD STUART,
THE YOUNG PRETENDER AND TO VARIOUS INTERMEDIARIES[1]

1.* (16)[2] To the Prince[3]

[? late November 1747[4]]

Si vous avée etée content de votre nuit mon amour je vous avoue que pour moi j'en ai etée enchantée. Je me flatte que nous en passerons encore longtemp de même. Cela sera mon unique bonheur. Jattend de vos nouvelles avec impasience. Adieu cher coeur je me porte tres bien. A ce soir venée vivre dans les bras de celle qui n'aime dans le monde que son cher amour.

2.* (22)

[? late November 1747]

Je n'ai pas encore recu de vos nouvelles cher amour mais j'espere quelles m'aprendront que vous viendrée passée la journée avec moi. Songée que je n'ai que ce seul plaisir là dans le monde. Adieu cher amour, je me porte tres bien. Venée soupée avec moi; de la a minuit je serai la plus heureuse de touttes les creatures.

---

*Translations of letters marked with an asterisk will be found in *Appendix B, I.*

3.* (19)

[*? late November 1747*]

Je vous avoue mon cher coeur d'amour que je suis enchantée que vous m'aiée dit tout ce que vous aviée contre moi. Comme tous les propos qu'on vous a tenû sont faux je n'en suis pas afligée. Au contraire cela vous prouve quil vous faut defiée des gens qui vous tiennent des propos. Je vous aime plus que jamais et je vous jure que c'êst bien sincêre et cela sera pour ma vie. Oui cher amour je viverai pour vous adorée. Adieu chere roi. A ce soir le comble de mes plaisirs.

4.* (51)

[*? early December 1747*]

Mon dieu cher amour que vous m'avée hier percée le coeur mais jespere qu'en vivant comme je vous ai supliée nous ne connoitrons plus le chagrin et nous jouirons des plaisirs sans peine. Je vous attendrai ce soir selon nos conventions sur les minuit. L'epoux arrive. Je suis aujourdhuy malade comme un chien[5] de l'etat ou jai etée hier mais j'espere que vous me guerirée ce soir. Soiée sure de mon amour et de ma tendresse. Elle êst sans egale. Adieu cher coeur vivons heureux le peu de tems que nous avons a êstre ensemble. Je vous embrasse milles fois.

5. (35)

[*? early December 1747*]

Un instant aprés que vous avée etée parti l'...[6] êst rentrée. Je conte que vous viendrée passée la soirée avec moi—cela fera une bonne journée et de bonne heure ce soir le comble des plaisirs! Oui cher amour je n'en peut avoir qu'avec vous. Je vous aime plus que jamais. Adieu chere coeur. Venée sur les six heures pour que l ...[6] soit sorti. Adieu coeur.

6. (30)

[*? early December 1747*]

Je suis malade comme un chien mon cher coeur. Il ne m'a pas etée possible de dormir ce matin mais cela n'êst rien. Ce soir a minuit je serai gueri de touts maux. C'êst l'heure la plus agreable de ma vie. Oui cher amour je ne suis contente que quand je suis dans vos bras; c'êst mon unique bonheur. Adieu cher roi. Je vous embrasse milles fois et vous aime plus que jamais.

7. *(8)*

[*? early December 1747*]

Vous voullée donc toujours m'inquietée cher amour en ne vous tranquilisant pas. De grace ne tuée pas qui vous adore. Je vous jure que nous nous verrons souvent et si vous ne vous en fiée pas a moi je ferai l'impossible dut il m'en coutée la vie pour me detachée de vous. Ainsi faites ce quil faut pour que je vous aime toutte ma vie. Donnée moi de vos nouvelles en arrivant ce soir. Demain a une heure et demie nous serons heureux et souvent si vous estes raisonable. Croiée cher amour que je vous aime plus que je ne peut dire et ne me mettée pas a portée d'avoir a me plaindre de tout ce que jaime qui êst mon cher amour.[7]

8. *(7)*

[*? early December 1747*]

Rien ne peut vous exprimer mon cher amour le mal que vous me faites en doutant de mon amour pour vous. Je n'ai pas fermée l'ouil et je me suis levée dés le matin.[8] Je ne m'accoutume pas a vous entendre dire que vous voullée vous detachée de moi et moi je veut vous aimée tant que je vivrois et mon dernier soupir sera en prononçant le nom de tout ce que j'aime. Oui malgré toutes vos duretées je sent que je vous aime plus que jamais et, je vous jure, uniquement. Au nom de dieu ne venée que sur les minuit! Personne n'etoit retirée hier. Mes femmes n'etoient pas rentrée ni Mde de g.....[9] retirée. Ce seroit vouloir me perdre que de venir plus tôt ainsi je conte trop sur votre amitié pour imaginée que vous ne voudrée pas ce que je vous propose. Je ne dormirai plus et je passerai mes nuits a baisée tout ce que j'aime. Mon dieu que je voudrois être avec vous actuellement. Je suis folle. Si vous pouviée venir un moment cet aprés disnée[10] cela me rendroit la vie. Je serai seule. Adieu cher coeur. Rendée moi justice. Aimons nous tant que nous vivrons. Que l'amour nous unisse a jamais. Recomendée a daniel[11] de ne pas restée ici toutte la nuit; c'est trop risqué. Adieu mon cher ange. Vene me voir tantôt.

9. *(37)*

[*? early December 1747*]

Je vous avoue mon cher amour que vous me faites un furieux chagrin de douttée de mon amour qui êst le plus tendre et le plus sincere. Je me porte tres bien mais je me porterois encore mieux si vous ne me dittes plus de duretées. Au nom de l'amour le plus tendre ne m'en dittes plus.

Adieu cher coeur, a ce soir. Jespere que nous jouirons des plaisirs sans peines. Je vous embrasse milles fois bien tendrement.

10. *(18)*

[*? early December 1747*]

Dimanche si l'... part comme j'y conte. J'avoue que cela êst encore long mais il le faut ainsi. De grace, menagée vous bien d'ici a ce tems la; tachée de prendre quelque chose, je tacherai aussi d'avalée quelque chose, et occupée vous du plaisir que nous aurons dimanche. Que ce plaisir nous soutienne dans nos malheurs! Vous m'en accablée en m'assurant que cela ne sera pas long. Je tenverrai demain de mes cheveux. Que ne puisje faire pour vous marquée a quel point êst mon amour! Envoiée ce soir un home et ecrivée moi et je vous ecrirai parcequil ne m'êst pas facile d'envoiée et je mourrois de douleur si je n'avois pas de vos nouvelles deux fois par jour. A dimanche; je ne scaurois trop vous repetée de vous en occupée. Soiée raisonable et tranquilisée vous et ne sortée aucune nuit si vous voulée que nous soions heureux dimanche. Je vous recomende mon portrait. Adieu cher ange. Je tadore; la têste me tourne, les larmes m'empêchent d'ecrire. Vous ne pourrée jamais vous imaginer a quel point je vous aime. De vos nouvelles ce soir, c'êst tout mon bonheur, et de grace menagée vous pour la plus malheureuse de touttes les creatures puisquelle sera peut êstre bientôt separée de vous. Adieu cher coeur. Je ne puis finir. Je vous baise mille fois.

11. *(4)*

[*? mid-December 1747*]

Jattend vos cheveux avec impasience. Je vous attendrai ce soir a minuit et demie. Quelque soit pour moi vôtre injustice, vous reconnoitrée dans tous les tems que je vous aime a l'adoration. Adieu cher coeur d'amour. Je vous embrasse milles fois.

12.* *(12)*

[*? mid-December 1747*]

Je n'ai pû lire vôtre lettre que dans l'instant mon cher amour et je ne perd pas un instant a y repondre. Oui je vous jure que mon amour ne finira jamais, que de la vie je ne me plaindrai plus jamais. Je n'aurai de la vie d'humeur. En un mot je ne vivrai que pour mon cher amour et pour lui plaire. Vivons heureux le peu de tems que nous avons a êstre ensemble—Helas! il ne sera que trop court. A ce soir a minuit. Venée vivre heureux dans les bras de celle qui vous adore et vous adorera toutte la vie. Mon dieu que je voudrois êstre dans vos bras!

13. *(39)*

[*? mid-December* 1747]

Je n'ai pas pû vous faire reponse plutôt mon cher amour. Je vous attend avec la [plus] grande impasience ce soir et vous n'aurée jamais a vous plaindre de moi. Je ne veut vivre que pour vous et pour vous plaire. Je vous le jure. Adieu cher coeur. A minuit je vivrai dans vos bras.

14. *(6)*

[*? mid-December* 1747]

Je suis fort enrhumée mon cher coeur mais cela ne sera rien. Je vous attendrai ce soir avec une impasience sans egale mais ne soiée au rendez vous qu'a 1 heure et demie. Si vous veniée avant vous seriée obligée d'attendre et cela m'inquieteroit. Il y a des gens dans la maison qui ne se couchent pas avant cette heure la. Adieu cher coeur. Tacher de faire un petit somme avant de venir, cela vous tranquilisera. Je suis plus folle que jamais. On ne peut aimée plus que j'aime mon cher amour.

15. *(52)*

[*? mid-December* 1747]

Je n'ai pas fermée l'oeil de la nuit. Jai etée d'une agitation affreuse aiant une impasience extrême d'avoir de vos nouvelles. Pouvée vous me refusée cette consolation cher amour? Je ne viverois pas si vous deveniez pour moi indifferent. Je vous aime plus que jamais et je sent que c'êst pour la vie. A ce soir, a une heure et demie comme la derniere fois. Je vous attendrai avec l'impasience de quelqu'un qui ne peut vivre sans voir ce quil aime. Rendée justice a ma tendresse et je serai trop heureuse. Elle êst je vous jure bien sincere. Je tembrasse milles fois tout ce que j'aime et aimerai toutte ma vie.

16. *(29)*

[*? mid-December* 1747]

Je suis toujours tres enrhumée et je n'ai pas pû dormir une minute apres que vous avée parti mais tout cela n'est rien. A ce soir a minuit, c'êst un moment que j'attend toujours avec une impasience sans egale, aimant plus que jamais mon cher amour, et je sent que si vous m'abandonniée je ny pourrois pas survivre. Adieu cher coeur. Aimée moi toujours et je serai heureuse. Je vous embrasse milles fois.

17. *(38)*

[*? mid-December 1747*]

Je suis toujours avec ma fluction mais cela n'êst rien. Je serois gueri de touts maux si vous etiée persuadée a quel point je vous aime. A ce soir cher amour—le seul et unique plaisir que jaie dans le monde. Je vous embrasse milles fois.

18. *(55)*

[*? mid-December 1747*]

Jai reçû vôtre lettre mon cher amour comme j'allois me mettre a table mais je vous avoue quil ne m'a pas etée possible davallée un verre d'eau. Vous m'avouée que vous comencée a vous sentir du froid pour moi. Cela me perce le coeur et je vous jure que vous serée cause de ma mort. Je ferai toujours l'impossible pour vous plaire mais, helas! je crains bien que rien ny fasse; mes larmes m'empechent. Je peine de tenir ma plume. Mde de g.... ne montera pas ici de la journée. Je vous demande en grace de venir. Je suis comme une folle. En verité, je tomberai malade si vous ne finissée vos duretées. Adieu cher coeur d'amour. Venée me voir Je n'ai de plaisir dans le monde que celui d'êstre avec vous. Oui, quoi que vous en croiiée, tout l'univers ne mêst rien. Je baise cette main qui me tue. Je suis dans un etat affreux.

19. *(36)*

[*? mid-December 1747*]

Je suis malade comme un chien mon cher amour. Je n'ai pas fermée les yeux depuis six heures[12] et ai etée dune agitation affreuse. Vous m'avée percée le coeur en me disant ce que vous m'avée dit. Je vois ma mort certaine. Venée passée la journée avec moi. Helas! Je n'existe que quand je suis avec vous, que j'aime uniquement. Croiée le une fois bien sincerement et vous me rendrée la vie. Je ne vous contrarierai jamais mais de grace ne me donnée pas la mort. Adieu tout ce que j'aime. Vivre et vous adorée n'êst pour moi qu'une même chose.

20. *(32)*

[*? mid-December 1747*]

Je vous avoue mon cher amour que vôtre deraison me dessespere et que je ne m'accoutume pas que vous voulliée m'abandonnée sans nulle raison et que vous disiée toujours que vous avée une femme toutte prête. Pour moi qui n'aurois pas d'homme prets—car je vous jure que si je vous perdois jamais aucun homme ne me sera de rien et je vous puis assurée que cela me couteroit la vie. Aiée donc pitiée de moi et de mon etat. Adieu cher amour. A ce soir a minuit. Malgré touts vos torts je vous adore plus que jamais.

21. *(33)*

[*? mid-December 1747*]

Jai etée enchantée cher amour de la nuit que jai passée. Elle m'a rendu la vie. Je vous attendrai avec la plus grande impasience ce soir. Je me flatte que vous viendrée cet aprés disnée. Je ne connois de plaisir que celui d'êstre avec vous. Oui cher amour vous êstes mon tout. Rien ne me plait sans vous. Mde de g.... ne montera pas ici de la journée, ainsi venée. Adieu cher coeur d'amour. Je vous embrasse milles fois et bien tendrement.

22.* *(24)*

[*? mid-December 1747*]

Je suis plus morte que vive mon cher amour. Mde de g..... vient de dire en pleine table que l'on entendoit touttes les nuits du bruit chez elle.[13] D'aujourduy elle fera veillée un de ses gens et toute la maison doit êstre aux aguais. Il y a eu beaucoup d'autres propos tenûs avec un air qui doit me faire tout craindre. Je sent trop que voila une rude epreuve pour notre amour; je m'en meurs de douleur. Je ne vous prescris rien mais j'espere tout, connaissant votre amour pour moi, et il s'agit de ne me pas perdre. Nous serons plus heureux a st ouen;[14] la nuit et le jour je serai a vous et je vous jure que je ferai l'impossible pour que cela soit bientôt et que, parole d'honneur, Mr de M.....[15] n'aprochera pas de moi et je serai toujours a vous uniquement. Je suis plus a plaindre que je ne puis vous le dire. Vous adorant, adieu. Je n'ai pas la force de vous en dire davantage. Au nom de dieu ne me sachée pas mauvais gré et n'imaginée pas que cela soit une deffaite, il s'en faut bien. Si vous voiée l'etat ou je suis je vous ferois pitié. Adieu milles fois cher amour.

23.* *(24A)*

[*? mid-December 1747*]

C'êst la plus malheureuse de touttes les creatures cher amour qui se jette a vos pieds. Ma vie êst entre vos mains. Si vous m'abandonnée mon parti est pris: je me tuerai et mon malheureux enfant. Si vous voullée me rendre la [vie] venée ce soir, venant a 2 heures. Nous tromperons les espions.[16] Au nom de l'amour le plus tendre ne me refusée pas cette grace et de ma vie je ne vous contrarierai.

Mon pauvre Chretien[17] est plus mort que vif. Il n'êst assurement pas coupable. Ma vie êst entre vos mains. Au nom de dieu cher amour venée ce soir me rendre la vie. Jai la fievre. Je n'ai pris qu'un bôle que jai revomis. J'attends mon sort. De grace, quil me soit favorable! Voici a vos pieds la plus tendre des maitresses. Oui, cher amour, je serai toutte ma vie a vous. Je me meurs. Je n'ai pas la force d'ecrire.

24. (20)

[? late December 1747]

Il ny aura point d'esclande cher amour mais il êst impossible que vous veniée davantage. Si vous faisiée la moindre esclande ma vie en repondroit. Ne me scachée pas mauvais gré cher amour. Ma mort vous montrera a quel point je vous aime. Laissons tombée touts les propos et au mois de may nous serons les maitres de nous voir. Venée souvent dans les aprés disnée et donnée moi tous les jours de vos nouvelles si vous voullée que je vive. Je serai toujours vôtre maitresse la plus tendre. Il viendra des tems ou nous serons heureux [...][18] dans quelquetemp mes entours. De grace, venée cet aprés disnée avec mylord.[19] Je pourrai vous parlée. Aimons nous toujours. Pour moi cela sera jusqu'au tombeau. Rendée moi la pareille si vous voullée que vôtre pauvre enfant vive. Au mois de may nous serons heureux mais jai bien peur de ne pouvoir pas vivre jusqu'a ce temp là. Je n'ai point a me plaindre de ce que m'a dit la femme de chambre. Je crois quelle est bien fachée de ce quelle a fait. Faites nul esclande, au nom de dieu! Il êst encore temp de ne me pas perdre. Adieu mon cher amour; je n'ai pas la force de tenir ma plume. Je sent bien la douleur ou vous allée êstre. De grace, menagée vous pour celle qui n'aime que vous dans le monde. Venée tantôt si vous voullée que je vive. Adieu donc tant d'heureuses nuits que jai passée! Il faut les attendre jusqu'au mois de may. Alors nous serons heureux. Ne m'abandonnée pas ou, sinon, je me tue. Mon parti est pris.

25. (23)

[? late December 1747]

Je suis dans un etat qui ne se peut depeindre. Je me suis mis dans mes quatres rideaux en recevant vôtre premiere lettre et n'ai pas pû avaler un verre d'eau. Au nom de dieu soiée raisonable! Je vous jure que dans quelques jours que l'on aura observée si on espionne que nous pourrons nous revoir et cela me rendra la vie. Je ne peut vivre sans vous. Je suis comme une folle. La pauvre Carteret[20] etoit aussi presente aux propos de Mde de g.... et nous avons cherchée les moyens dy remediée et je vous jure que quelques jours d'intervalle feront tous et quil ny aura pas d'eclat. Mais de grace, si vous voullée conservée celle qui vous adore et vôtre pauvre petit enfant menagée vous et venée me voir demain dans l'aprés disnée. Il ny aura personne et avec cela, au nom de dieu, songée que ce n'êst qu'une privation, et qu'apres, cela yra comme auparavant et mieux car nous serons sans inquietude. Si vous voulée que je vive faites moi une reponse favorable qui puisse me tranquilisée. Je vous ferois pitiée. J'espere bien que vous n'êstes pas venû cette nuit. Je l'avois passée a baisée et arrosée de mes larmes touts mon lit ou a etée mon cher amour. Oui je te jure que tant que je respirerai je serai votre plus fidelle maitresse et que vous serée mon plus fidel amant. Je vais tachée de me menagée pour mon cher amour et son cher enfant mais jai bien peur dy succombée. Menagée vous si vous ne voullée pas que je meure et ne me refusée pas de venir demain l'aprés disnée et je vous jure que dans peu de nuits nous serons ensemble et je me flatte que vous ne me le refuserée pas, quand cela se pourra. Adieu cher coeur, tout ce que j'aime. Je n'ai pas la force de tenir ma plume, mes larmes effacent toutte l'ecriture. Je vous baise milles fois. Ah dieu que je vous aime! Pouvez vous en douttée? C'êst me donnée la mort! Adieu cent fois tout ce que j'aime.

26.* (17)

[? *late December 1747*]

Quel etat est le mien cher amour! Tout ce que je pourrois vous le dire ne scauroit vous le depeindre. Cependant cela m'a etée d'une grande consolation de vous avoir vû hier mais l'assurance que vous m'avée donnée que vous passeriée la nuit dehors m'a donnée le coup de poignard dans le coeur. Je n'ai pris nulle nouriture. Jai passée la nuit dans une agitation de quelqu'un separée de ce qu'elle aime uniquement et de vous scavoir courir tous les dangers pour vôtre vie et vôtre santée. Si vous voullée me conservée et mon enfant, si cela se peut encore, j'exige de votre amour de ne plus sortir les nuits que celle que nous passerons ensemble, ce qui sera bientot. Mais je vous jure que cela ne sera pas si vous venée encore passée une nuit dehors. Pouriée vous me refusée dans l'etat ou je suis. Oui cher coeur d'amour, menagée vous pour n'êstre pas malade le jour que nous serons heureux. Ah dieu, quel moment! Je crois que j'en mourrai de plaisir. Faites depecher le plus que vous pourrée vôtre portrait.[21] Allez y un moment demain matin. Jattend de vos nouvelles avec une impasience sans egalle. Helas! c'est tout mon bonheur d'en recevoir; donner m'en encore ce soir sur les huit heures comment vous aurée passée la journée. Songée que je n'existe pas et la seule consolation que je puisse avoir êst que vous menagiée cette santée qui m'êst si chere. Sans vous je ne peut vivre. Que jai etée sensible que vous m'aiée avouée que vous m'aimiée dés avant l'ecosse! Je vous jure le reciproque mais je suis dans le même cas que vous de ne vouloir pas vous le dire de peur d'augmentée vôtre amour. Mais nous pouvons tout nous dire de plus tendre, cela ne peut plus augmentée. Je n'aurois jamais crû que cela put êstre a ce point là mais je ne m'en repent. Quelque chagrin que cela me donne cela fait la douceur de ma vie. Conservez vous donc pour faire mon bonheur et vous devée songée que vous naites pas a vous. Vous vous devée a trois royaumes et a la plus tendre et plus fidelle maitresse. Adieu cher coeur, cher amour; c'êst mon unique plaisir de pouvoir vous ecrire. Donnons nous deux fois par jour de nos nouvelles. Je tembrasse un million de fois et de bon coeur. Je decachete ma lettre recevant dans l'instant la vôtre. Vous êstes adorable de ne pas venir les nuits. Vous en aurée la recompense.

27. *(44)*

[*? late December* 1747]

Au nom de l'amour le plus tendre cher amour venée me voir un instant cet après disnée si vous voullée que je vive. Sans cela je ne prendrai aucune nouriture. Si vous venée et que vous ne me donniée pas l'inquietude de passée les nuits dans la rûe je vous donne cette parole d'honneur que vous m'avée tant demendé hier et je vous jure que dans quelques jours nous passerons une nuit ensemble et si vous êstes raisonable nous en passerons plus d'une. Depuis le malheureux moment que je vous ai quittée je n'ai pas cessée de repandre un torrent de larmes ny ne cesserai si vous ne venée me voir. Je serai exprés enfermée dans mes rideaux. L...[22] ny sera pas et je vous jure que vous serée enchantée de me voir. Je ferai dire a c....[23] de ne plus venir que tres rarement. Je ne verrai que les gens que vous voudrée. En un mot je vivrai uniquement pour vous côme le dois la plus tendre et fidelle maitresse qui exige de vous de vous menagée si vous voullée que nous soions heureux. Envoiée moi votre portrait au plutôt. De grace, donnée moi touttes les consolations que je peut avoir pour gagnée quelques jours et vous verrée si je vous manquerai de parole. Mais au nom de mon amour faites ce que je veux cher amour, cher coeur, cher ange! Que ne puisje êstre toujours avec vous! Les larmes m'empechent de pouvoir tenir ma plume. Si je vous vois cet après disnée je viverai, ou sinon, je me laisserai mourir sans prendre nulle nouriture. J'attend mon sort; il êst entre vos mains. Je tembrasse milles fois par tout. Dans peu de jours cela sera nul. Je te le jure mon cher amour je suis comme une folle. Je nexiste pas mais ne vous occupée pas de ma douleur et tacher de la diminuer en diminuant la vôtre. C'êst l'amour qui vous en fait la loy. Adieu cher coeur d'amour, faites moi vivre en me venant voir. Si il m'etoit aussi aisée pour ce soir cela seroit bientot. Mais ce n'est une privation que de quelques jours. Soiée raisonable. Je te baise milles fois cette charmante bouche qui m'a tant dit quelle m'aime. La mienne vous le redira sans cesse. Adieu tout ce que j'aime.

Dans l'instant arrive mon maitre anglois. De parlée la langue de ce que j'aime me donne la force de pouvoir lui parlée.[24]

28. *(44A)*

[*? late December 1747*]

Ce n'êst en veritée pas une deffaite cher amour, de ce que je vous ai mandée. Je vous en dirai les raisons ce soir. Vous êstes le maitre de venir a minuit. Pouvée vous toujours êstre de cette injustice lâ pour celle qui vous adore et qui vous donne tous les jours de nouvelles preuves de mon amour? Adieu cher coeur je vous attend a minuit avec la plus grande impasience.

29. *(25)*

[*? late December 1747*]

Vous me rendée la vie cher amour en venant passée la nuit avec moi. Je vous aime uniquement. Je sacrifierai pour vous ma vie, ma reputation et tout. De grace, cher amour, soiée sure de la joie que j'aurois de vous voir. C'êst passée de la mort a la vie!

30. *(26)*

[*? late December 1747*]

Vous m'avée rendu la vie cher amour. Jamais nuit n'a etée si delicieuse pour moi que celle que jai passée. Vous y mettrée le comble en me venant voir cet aprés disnée, ce qui fera tout mon bonheur. Adieu cher amour. Vous aimée toutte ma vie sera mon unique plaisir. De ma vie vous n'aurée a vous plaindre de moi.

31. *(53)*

[*? late December 1747*]

Puisje conſée cher amour que vous ne me soupçonnerée plus d'en aimée quelqu'autres que vous? Oui cher coeur je vous le jure sur tout ce que vous voudrée que je n'aime et n'aimerai que vous dans le monde et je ferai l'impossible pour vous le prouvée.[25] A ce soir a la même heure; venée dans mes bras me jurée que vous ne serée plus injuste pour celle qui vous adore. Mon dieu que la journée me vâ paroitre longue! Je t'embrasse milles fois et bien tendrement.

32. (27)

[*? late December 1747*]

Jai etée malade comme une bêste; je n'ai pas fermée l'oeil. Jai etée d'une agitation horrible mais tout cela ne seroit rien si vous ne douttiée pas de ma tendresse et de l'amour que jai pour vous. Mais je vous avoue que les douttes que vous en avée me mettent au dessespoir. Si vous voullée me rendre la tranquilitée soiée sur de ma facon de pensée pour vous qui est l'amour le plus tendre et qui ne finira qu'avec ma vie. A ce soir, le comble de mes plaisirs. Si vous pouviée volée M Watter[26] vous me feriée grand plaisir. Adieu cher coeur d'amour; je vous aime uniquement.

33. (28)

[*? late December 1747*]

Je suis en veritée bien inquiette de touts vos maux.[27] Vous scavée copiée a merveille. Pour moi je me porte tres bien et n'ai mal nul part. Je me porterai encore bien mieux a minuit quand je verrai tout ce que j'aime dans le monde. Adieu cher coeur; je suis folle plus que jamais. Je tembrasse milles fois. Songée a volée Mr watter.

34. (49)

[*? late December 1747*]

Je vais faire dire vos ordres au suisse,[28] mon cher amour, quil executera; et je compte sur vos bontées. Je suis dans une inquietude horrible de vôtre santée. Rien dans le monde ne m'êst plus chere. Oui cher amour menagée vous car je ne vous survivrois pas. Vous êstes l'unique dans le monde que j'aime et c'êst pour la vie. Adieu mon cher coeur; a ce soir a minuit. C'est le moment le plus doux de ma vie.

35. (5)

[*? 31 December 1747 or 1 January 1748*]

Bon jour, bon an,[29] mon cher amour. Aimée moi toujours, c'êst tout ce que je desire. Au nom de dieu venée me voir cet aprés disnée! Je suis toutte malade. Je crois que je serai saigné. De vous voir me gueriroit. Je serai seule toutte la journée. Adieu cher coeur d'amour; je vous aime a la folie. A cet aprés disnée, et a minuit je serai contente.

36. *(50)*

[*? early January 1748*]
Je vais êstre saignée mon cher coeur. Je vous ecris avant, de peur de l'estre du bras droit. Je me flatte que je vous verrai cet aprés disnée. Je vous le demande en grace; je mourrois de douleur d'êstre si l'ongtemp sans vous voir. Adieu cher coeur; je vous aime uniquement. Cela êst plus fort que jamais.

37.* *(31)*

[*? early January 1748*]
Je vous jure, mon cher amour, si vous avée etée facher de couchée seule j'en ai etée outrée et n'en ai pas dormi de la nuit. Je suis encore fatiguée de ma saignée. Venée passée l'aprés disnée avec moi. Cela fera mon bonheur et ce soir a minuit le comble de mes plaisirs. J'aurai ce soir a vous parlée[30] mais ne manquée pas de venir cet aprés disnée. Adieu cher coeur. Je vous aime plus que je ne peut dire.

38.* *(43)*

[*? early January 1748*]
Ne finirée vous jamais de m'accablée de choses dures aprés touttes les promesses que vous m'avée faites de ne faire que ce que je voudrois et ce quil faut pour que je continue a vous aimée? Ce n'êst ni conseil ni entêtement, mais pure raison. Vous êstes le maitre de venir a quel heure vous voudrée au rendée vous mais certainement vous n'entrerée pas que l'epoux ne soit rentrée et couchée. Si vous voullée recomençée vos duretées vous êstes le maitre, mais ne venée plutot pas que de m'en acablée—moi qui suis prêt a mourir d'amour et de tendresse pour vous. La plus grande preuve et l'unique que vous me puissiée donnée êst de faire ce qui m'êst convenable et ce que je veux. Donnée moi de vos nouvelles cet aprés disnée et si vous êstes resolû de continuée vos duretés...adieu. Ne manquée pas de m'ecrire cet aprés disnée.

39.* *(40)*

[*? early January 1748*]
Votre lettre[31] m'etonne plus que je ne peut dire. Estce de cette façon que vous paiée l'amour le plus tendre et qui ne finira jamais? Jai apris depuis tantôt que Mr de M.... alloit au bal. Ainsi soiée au rendez vous a une heure et demie. Je vous avoue que jai l'ame perçee, cher amour. Faites moi un mot de reponse a celle cy. Je suis dans un etat affreux. Ne cesserée vous jamais de me mettre le poignard dans le coeur? Je vous jure, jai peu de tems a vivre mais il me semble

que vous en serée aisément consolée. J'avoue ma foiblesse,[32] les larmes m'empêchent d'en dire davantage. Oui je vous adore et je vous le prouverai ce soir mais de grace ne m'accablée pas de duretés car je n'ai pas la force de les soutenir. Adieu, le plus ingrat et le plus adorée de tous les hommes. Passée vôtre fureur et songée que je vous aime uniquement. Faites moi un mot de reponse pour me rendre la vie. Je n'ai pas la force d'en dire davantage. Envoiée moi reponse mais non pas par le porteur parce quil êst trop connû.[33] Je n'en peut plus; vous serez satisfait.

40.* (21)

[? *mid-January 1748*][34]
Puisque vous voullée venir vous êstes le maitre, je vous attendrai. Ma vie êst fort hasardée mais n'importe. Je suis resolû d'avouer tout a mon pere. Il me sera bien utile. Je vous demande en grace de le trouvée bon. Je n'ai pas voulu le faire sans vôtre permission. Je l'enverrai chercher sur le champ. Je suis dans un etat horrible. Je vous attend cet apres disnée et ce soir.

41. (34)

[? *mid-January 1748*]
Vous ne cessérée donc pas de doutée de mon amour. Daniel vous dira ma façon de pensée mais au nom de dieu nachevée pas de me perdre! Daniel vous dira si jai des raisons essentielles. Je ne conçois pas comment vous voullée m'eprouvée. Il me semble que je suis toutte eprouvée. A ce soir, cher amour; a minuit precise venée vivre dans mes bras.

42. (47)

[? mid-January 1748]
Doutterée vous toujours de mon amour le plus tendre? Cela manque au comble de mon bonheur. Non cher amour, je n'aimerai que vous dans le monde, tant que je vivrai. Songée que vous m'avée promis de venir passée la soirée avec moi. Ny manquée pas, de grace, et que jaie vôtre portrait! Ces jours cy cela sera mon unique consolation.[35] Adieu cher amour. A tantôt et a ce soir. Vous verrée si je vous aime!

43. (46)

[*Saturday morning*,[36] 20 January 1748]
Je vous jure mon cher amour que mon impasience egale la vôtre. Je n'ai ni bû ni mangée et fort peu dormi. A demain. Nous serons heureux et je vous jure que

nous le serons souvent. Je suis toujours fort inquiette sur mon etat. De grace, tacher de prendre sur vous aujourduy! Ecrivée moi aussi tôt que vous serée de retour. Je serai d'une inquietude horrible si le voiage ne vous aura pas fatiguée. Soiée sure, cher coeur d'amour, que vous ne pourrée pas m'aimée plus que je vous aime mais croiée quil faut scavoir prendre sur soi. Adieu tout ce que j'aime. J'attend midi avec une impasience sans egale pour avoir vôtre portrait et encore de vos nouvelles. J'en attend ce soir vers les huit heures. Je tembrasse milles fois cher coeur et bien tendrement.

44. *(48)*

[*Saturday evening, 20 January 1748*]

Jattend des nouvelles de vôtre voiage avec impasience craignant que, ne vous portant pas bien, cela vous êst fort fatiguée. Je suis comme une folle depuis que jai vôtre portrait. Je ne cesse de le regardé. Il me semble quil me dit toujours quil m'aime et je lui dit sans cesse que je l'adore. Un instant aprés que je vous ai eu ecrit ce matin jai apris que Mr de M... n'alloit pas a marli que lundi.[37] Si mon cher amour ecoutoit la prudence et qu'il se ressouvienne que je lui ai jurée que je ne le verrois jamais quand l'epoux y seroit. Mais comme jai donnée ma parole pour demain je scai la tenir et je ne fait que mes representations. Mais du moins mon cher coeur si vous voullée absolument venir demain il ne faut venir qu'a trois heures[38] parceque surement Mr de M... ne rentrera pas avant deux heures ou deux heures et demies. Vous scavée quil faut que je vous soiée raisonable pour que je vous aime toutte ma vie. Ne me mettée jamais a portée du contraire. Je suis malade côme un chien. Estre separée de ce que j'aime en [est la][39] seul cause. Oui cher roi je t'adore. Je ne scaurois trop te [le dire]. Adieu mon amour; je te baise mille fois et partout.

45. *(54)*

[*late afternoon, Sunday, 21 January 1748*]

Jai etée dans une inquietude que je ne peut exprimer de n'avoir pas eu de vos nouvelles hier au soir. Jai attendû Mr de M... pour scavoir de vos nouvelles.[40] Je vous avois ecris et je vous l'envoie. Vous y verrée le depart de Mr de M... differée mais mon cher coeur au moins si vous voullée venir ce soir ne venée qu'a trois heures car il êst restée pour un soupée dont il ne rentrera pas surement avant deux heures et demie. Rendée moi reponse aussi tôt celle cy reçûe comment vous avéz passée la nuit. Pour moi tres mal et je me suis reveillée de tres grand matin pour regardée sans cesse ce que j'adore. Non cher amour je ne me detacherai jamais de vous. J'espere que vous ne ferée jamais rien pour cela. Il ny a que la mort qui puisse nous desunir. Je taime, je le jure, plus que jamais!

Jattend de vos nouvelles avec impassience et mendez moi si vous vous trouverée a 3 heures au rendez vous. J'imagine que oui. Ah quel plaisir nous gouterons, je crois que j'en mourrai! Ne manquée pas de m'ecrire aussi tôt celle cy recûe et soiée sure que vôtre fidelle maitresse ne cessera jamais de vous adorée. Vous verrée quand je serai dans vos bras si je vous aime! C'êst a la folie. Je scai que vous avée etée charmant hier. Je vous suis bien obligé de la contrainte que vous vous êstes faites.[41] De vos nouvelles, tout a l'heure. Adieu tout ce que j'aime—et c'êst pour la vie.

46.* *(45)*

[*Tuesday morning, 23 January 1748*]

Soiée donc parfaitement content mon cher amour. Je vous jure que je vous adore plus que je ne peut dire. Je serai seule toutte la journée. La maman reste chez elle.[42] Il seroit bien joli a vous de me venir voir un moment dans l'aprés disnée. Il ny a que vous dans le monde que je soie bien aise de voir car du reste je suis enchantée d'êstre seule[43] pour pensée plus a mon aise a tout ce que j'aime. Jai fort mal a la tête. Cela me sera un pretexte pour me couchée de bonne heure mais je serois comblée que vous me vinsiée voir dans l'aprés disnée. Adieu cher coeur d'amour. Je suis plus folle que jamais aujourdui. Je vous en donnerai des marques ce soir.[44] Je vous baise milles fois tout.

47.* *(41)*

[*late evening, 23 January 1748*][45]

Ce que je n'ai que trop prevû êst arrivée. Ma belle mere scait touttes vos demarches et vient de venir avec mon pere. Ils m'ont parlée l'un et l'autre comme deux amies. Ainsi, Monseigneur, je suis obligée de vous en avertir et vous scavée depuis l'ongtemp ce que je vous ai dit. Ainsi je leur dois non seulement de ne vous jamais voir mais même de recevoir de vos nouvelles. Si vous me faites l'honneur de me venir de tems en tems côme je crois que vous le ferée pour ne pas achevée de me perdre—cela êst bien avançée—vous serée reçû côme a l'ordinaire. Adieu, Monseigneur. C'êst une rude epreuve pour ma tendresse pour vous qui ne finira qu'avec ma vie.

48.* *(13)*

[*ce 28 janvier 1748*][46]

Il ne m'a pas etée possible depuis l'autre jour de vous ecrire. L'on me guête continuellement. Vous êstes bien cruel de m'avoir refusée de m'faire reponse a la derniere que je vous ai ecri aprés ma malheureuse avanture. J'etois si troublée que je n'avois pas la force de tenir ma plume. Puis-je me flattée que vous serée encore bien aise d'entendre parlée de la plus infortunée de touttes les creatures? Je vais cher amour vous rendre un compte exact de ce qui m'êst arrivée mardi qui êst le jour que je vous ai ecri. Je vous attendois a une heure aprés minuit avec impasience. J'etois fort tranquille. Je vis arrivée a dix heures ma belle mere qui avoit envoyée cherchée mon pere pour lui rendre compte de ma conduite. Elle me dit quil y avoit long temps quelle en etoit instruite mais quelle avoit esperée quelle finiroit. Cependant [elle] me parla sans fureur et avec beaucoup d'amitié quelle le cacherait a tout l'univers[47] mais quil falloit finir et vous ecrire. Jamais le coup de la mort ne m'accablera davantage! Je vous ecrivis côme une troublée. Elle a renvoyée son suisse et mon valet de chambre sort aussi.[48] On m'a fait promettre que je ne vous recrirois plus mais je n'ai pû attendre plus longtems. Je conte sur vôtre amitiée et que surement personne ne scaura que je vous ai ecri. Cela mettroit le comble a mes malheurs. Je vais menée une vie affreuse. On ne m'a pas pû faire prendre de nouriture. Mais tous les maux que l'on me fera endurée ne me seront de rien si vous me conservée de l'amitiée. Sans cela je cesserai de vivre. Songée que jai dans mon sein un enfant de vous, que ce n'êst que pour vous que j'essuie tant de chagrin. Ny mettée pas le comble en cessant de m'aimée. Si vous m'aimée encore, tant que je pourrai je vous donnerai de mes nouvelles et vous me donnerée des vôtres. Cela me soutiendra dans mes malheurs. Je passe mes jours et mes nuits les yeux baignée de larmes, les aiant toujours sur vôtre portrait, et a baisée vos cheveux. En un mot, la teste me tourne. Je n'ai pas dormi deux heures depuis mardi. Je suis dun changemens affreux. Jespere que vous me rendrée la vie en me donnant ce soir de vos nouvelles. Ah dieu, quelle bonheur si vous songée encore a vôtre tendre maitresse! De ma vie je ne cesserai d'estre a vous. Je vous le jure, il viendra des tems heureux. Promettée moi d'en profitée. Mes larmes couvrent mon papier. Puis-je esperée que mon portrait vous êst de quelque consolation? Regardée le souvent: vous y verrée l'image de celle qui vous aime a l'adoration. De grace, pour ne me pas perdre dans le public venée quelque fois[49]—sans cela je serai perdûe. Si vous voule parlée a ma belle mere cela ferait tout mon bonheur. Je n'ai pas la force d'ecrire davantage. Que qui que ce soit ne scache que je vous ai écri. Rendée moi la vie, tout ce que j'aime! Je suis bien a plaindre mais si vous continuée a m'aimée je serai contente. Adieu, cher coeur d'amour.

49. (13A)

[28 January 1748]
Je r'ouvre ma lettre, elle n'a pû vous êstre rendû. Il ny avoit personne chez vous. Jhasarderai encore demain matin. Je vais me couchée bien tristement—il

y a aujourduy huit jours que j'etois au comble de mes voeux,[50] mais, helâs! c'êst bien different. Si vous m'aimée encore, je vivrai. Jai encore de la fievre ce soir et je ne prend rien. Songée a mes malheurs et a vôtre malheureux enfant! Je le conserve parce quil est a vous. Mes larmes m'empêchent de tenir ma plume, rien n'egale l'etat ou je suis. Adieu, tout ce que j'aime. Il faudroit que vous fussiée bien cruel pour me refusée de vos nouvelles! Ne dittes pas même a d....[51] que cette lettre est de moi. On[52] attendra la reponse. C'êst pour moi de la derniere consequence et brulez là sur le champ—et de grace venée dans le jour si vous ne voulée pas achevée de me perdre. Adieu. Je suis si foible que je ne peut ecrire davantage.

50. *(42)*

[*c. 1 February 1748*]

Vous mettée le comble a mes malheurs, refusant de me donnée de vos nouvelles et par consequent ne desirant pas d'en recevoir des miennes. De grace, soiée plus juste pour quelqu'un qui vous adore et qui ne cessera jamais jusqu'au dernier soupir de ma vie de vous adorée. Jai bien senti que la premiere lettre[53] que je vous ai ecri a dû vous deplaire mais cela m'etoit impossible autrement. Mais celle[54] que je vous ai ecri vous depeignoit bien au juste ma situation qui êst affreuse. Mais rien ne me paroitra dûre si vous rendée justice a mon amour et que vous me soiée fidel et que vous me donniée de vos nouvelles par touttes les occasions que j'aurai de vous donnée des miennes. Voiée une miserable creature embrassée vos genoux, qui porte en son sein un enfant qui êst de vous et pour lequel seul je tache de vivre! Mais cela ne peut êstre long, ne dormant ni ne mangeant, passant ma triste vie les yeux attachée sur vôtre portrait et baignée dans mes larmes qui couvrent actuellement mon papier. Rien ne me dissipe; puisje vivre quand tout ce que j'aime dans le monde êst injuste pour moi? Ma mort vous prouvera si jai des torts et mon coeur, que je vous ferai portée, vous parlera encore pour moi. Oui, je vous le jure sur tout de plus sacré, je serai a vous tant que je vivrai! Rendée moi la vie en me rendant vos bontées. Cêst a vos genoux que je vous les demende. Me permettée vous encore de vous apellée mon cher amour? Oui je ne vous crois pas assée injuste pour ne me pas rendre vôtre tendresse. Il viendra des tems ou nous serons heureux, je vous le jure, mais, de grace, venée ici pour le public si vous ne voullée pas me perdre. Jai crû sentir remuée mon malheureux enfant; il semble vouloir vous parlée pour sa malheureuse mere. N'oubliée pas que vous lui avée promis de l'aimée toutte vôtre vie. Je vous ferois compassion si je vous voiois—ma vie est entre vos mains. J'en attend mon arrêst. Si il êst dictée par vôtre ancienne tendresse, que je serai heureuse! Adieu cher coeur, tout ce que j'aime. Mes sanglots m'ôtent la force d'en dire davantage. Rendée moi la vie et a mon cher enfant en me continuant vôtre amitiée et en me donnant de vos nouvelles. J'espere tout de vôtre bonté. J'espere que l'amour parlera pour moi. J'en suis bien digne.

51. (15)

[c. 6 February 1748]

Quoique vous ne m'aiée donner aucune reponse je ne puis m'empecher de vous mander mon etat. Helas! jai cependant bien des raisons pour croire que cela vous interesse peu. A force de chagrin, de ne prendre aucune nouriture et de ne pas dormir, jai sucombée a la fin. Jai la fievre tres forte. Je crains plus pour mon malheureux enfant que pour moi. Que peut m'estre la vie separée de tout ce que j'aime, qui me refuse jusqu'a la consolation de le voir et même de me donnée de ses nouvelles? Si vous aviée la charitée pour l'etat ou je suis de m'acordée l'un et l'autre vous me rendriée la vie. Je ne serai peut êstre plus en etat de vous ecrire. Helas! vous en serée peut êstre bien aise. Je ne peut que trainée car le coup de la mort m'est donnée. Je suis d'une foiblesse horrible—je ne puis vous en dire davantage. Jusqu'a mon dernier soupir je ne cesserai jamais de vous adorée. Oui, cher amour, je serai a vous tant que je vivrai. Que l'etat ou je suis vous attendrisse! Je porte en mon sein un enfant qui êst a vous et qui êst le gage du plus tendre amour. C'êst a vos genoux que je vous demande la vie en venant et en m'ecrivant mais, surtout, brulez sur le champ mes lettres! Cela êst pour moi bien essential. Puisje me flattée que vous regardée quelquefois mon portrait? Pour moi, jour et nuit je fonds en larmes, les yeux attachée sur le vôtre. Adieu. Je sent que je vous suis a charge mais ma vie est entre vos mains. Il ne tient qu'a vous de me faire vivre. Vous serée toujours reçu comme vous le devée êstre et songée que je ne peut vivre sans vous voir. Si ma maladie augmente voila peut êstre la derniere que je vous ecrirai mais je mourrai en vous aimant uniquement.

52. (14)

[c. 8 February 1748]

Je reçois dans le moment la vôtre.[55] Je vous jure cher amour que je n'ai tenû aucun propos, ni personne. C'êst sur ma vie que je vous le jure! De grace, venée—je mourrai de joie de vous voir! Et ecrivée moi souvent, vous me rendrée la vie. Je n'ai le tems que de vous ecrire ce petit mot mais soiée sure que je n'ai tenû aucun propos, come j'existe. Je vous [demande][56] en embrassant vos genoux de venir au plutot et continuée de m'aimée. Je vous serai toutte ma vie fidelle. Jai toujours la fievre. Jai cru mourir de joie en voiant de vôtre ecriture.

53. (9)

[c. 15 February 1748]

Je hasarde encore celle cy. Si cela vous deplait je me priverai de cette consolation. Vous voullée donc que je cesse de vivre. Vous ne voullée plus revenir. Vous me perdée a jamais et vous me privée de vous voir. C'est bien me prouvée que vous ne m'aimée plus! Au nom de cette amour tendre dont vous m'avée flattée tant de fois ne m'otée pas la seule consolation que je puisse avoir dans le monde qui êst de vous voir quelquefois et de ne me pas deshonorée! Vous serée reçu comme si rien ne s'étoit passée. De grace, rendée moi la vie en venant. Je suis dans un etat affreux. Vous serée bien tôt defait de la personne du monde qui vous aime le plus et qui est la plus malheureuse. Me refuserée vous de me donnée de vos nouvelles? J'attend ces deux graces de vous mon cher amour. Permettée moi encore ce mot—c'est a vos genoux que je vous les demende. Mes larmes couvrent mon papier. Aiée pitié de mon malheureux enfant et donnée moi de vos nouvelles. Je me meurs de peur de vous deplaire en vous aimant. J'attend vos ordres. Adieu, le plus aimée de tous les hommes. Rendée moi la vie et venée. Je vous ferois compassion si vous me voiée. Je baise milles fois cette main que j'adore. Je passe ma vie a pleurée et a pensée a mon bonheur passée. Helas! peut êstre ne vous en occupée vous plus? Je me trouve mal et n'ai plus la force de tenir ma plume. Ma vie est entre vos mains. Je crains bien que l'amour ne vous parle plus pour moi et peut êstre la haine a telle pris sa place. Je ne peut resistée a tous les malheurs qui m'environne. Songée encore que j'existe pour vous adorée.

54. (10)

[*c. 18 February 1748*]

Jai vû da... et cela a etée pour moi un grand plaisir de lassurance quil m'a donnée que vous aviée toujours pour moi de lamitiée. Celle que jai pour vous et mon attachement ne finiront qu'avec ma vie. Vous feriée ma seule consolation de vouloir bien me donnée de vos nouvelles. Vous pouvée estre sur que cela sera ignorée de tout le monde, de même que la lettre que je vous ecris. Je me flatte que mon ecriture vous sera connu comme de quelqu'un qui vous êst attachée depuis bien des années.

55. (57)

[*c. 22 February 1748*]

Rien ne peut vous depeindre l'etat de douleur ou je suis de voir que vous me refusée encore de me donnée de vos nouvelles et on veut me flattée que vous m'aimée encore—mais le puisje croire? Si vous m'aimiée vous m'auriée ecrit. On[57] dit, cher coeur d'amour—permettée moi ces noms qui me sont si cheres— que vous voudriée me voir en particulier. Il m'êst impossible de vous allée trouver mais si vous voulliée venir un jour a versailles quand j'y serois, en partant a onze heures du soir vous arriveriée juste a l'heure ou je pourrais vous voir. Il me sera impossible de ne le pas dire a ma femme de chambre. Je suis sure qu'elle ne le dira pas. Ainsi, mon cher amour, acceptée cette seule façon de me voir. Jai vû un temp ou vous n'auriée pas refusée de faire ce chemin là pour moi. Pour moi, que ne feroisje pas pour vous? Je le sent puisque touts mes malheurs ne me font rien si vous m'aimé. Si vous en aimée d'autre je cesserai de vivre. Donnée moi vos ordres pour samedy en reponse a celle cy. Si vous m'aimée encore je le verrai. Si vous m'aimée vous ne refuserée pas loccasion de me voir. Que j'aurai de choses a vous dire! Je vais commencé a sondée ma femme de chambre. Je suis sure delle. Jai des raisons pour cela—en tout cas c'êst mon affaire. Je mourrai de joie le moment que je vous apercevrai! On ne peut pas adorée au point que je vous adore. Adieu mon cher amour; jattens ma consolation de la reponse de samedy. Pour versailles j'yrois le plutôt que je pourrois. Si vous me refusée cette grace et celle de me donnée de vos nouvelles je [ne] peut survivre a ma douleur qui êst inexprimable. Au nom de l'amour le plus tendre, acceptée de me voir a versailles! Jamais cela ne se scaura, je vous le jure sur ma vie. Vous ne pourrée pas refusée cela si vous desirée voir l'amante la plus tendre.

56. *(59)*

[*? Ash Wednesday, 28 February 1748*]

ce mercredy

Puisje esperer que j'aurai demain de vos nouvelles? Que cela sera un moment heureux pour moi si jai ce bonheur lâ! Je ne pourrai y faire reponse que samedy, que je peut encore recevoir de vos nouvelles si vous le voullée bien. Oui cher amour, ne me refusée pas cette grace ny celle de revenir ici. Rien n'êst si faux que l'on tienne aucun propos, je vous le jure sur ma vie! Helas! jai peut êstre si peu de tems a vous voir. Cela seroit un miracle que je revins de mes couches avec tous les chagrins que jai—et avec cela si vous quittée ce pais cy[58] je ne survivrai pas a me séparée de vous pour la vie. Helas! malheureusement, vous n'en êstes pas convaincûe. On ne peut aimée au point que je vous aime, et c'êst pour la vie! Ne me refusée donc pas de me voir et de me donnée de vos nouvelles. Jamais qui que ce soit ne le scaura. Cela me fera tout mon bonheur. Soions toujours deux amants les plus tendres. Je scai que cela seroit trop exigée de vous—ne pouvant vous voir comme je le desirerois—de vous empechée de voir quelqu'un, mais du moins conservée moi vôtre coeur.[59] Il peut venir des tems heureux. Pour pendant mes couches je serai seule. Si vous aviée la bontée de revenir avant, nous nous verrions tout a nôtre aise. Naurée vous pas pitiée de moi quand je mettrai au monde un enfant qui m'êst aussi chere? Les larmes couvrent mon papier, je crains de vous importunée. Si vous me deffendée de vous ecrire, j'attens vos ordres, mais cela seroit m'otée la vie que de ne me pas donnee de vos nouvelles et des nouvelles qui puissent me consolée. Je suis dans des etats affreux. Que vous seriée bon de venir samedy a la comedie françoise![60] Je vous verrois. Je serois dans un balcon. Vous devriée vous mettre vis a vis, je vous verrois a mon aise. Ah dieu, que je serois heureuse que vous vous souciée encore de me voir cher coeur d'amour! Permettée ces noms a l'amante la plus tendre. Je vous adore et c'êst pour la vie. Rien ne me detachera de vous. Aimons nous tant que nous vivrons. Mon sort êst entre vos mains. C'êst en embrassant vos genoux que je vous le demande et que je baise milles fois cette main que j'adore. Si vous aviée la bontée denvoyée un jour Mr ox...[61] dire a Mme de g.... que vous reviendrée—le jour que vous viendrée vous donnerée quelque pretexte pour n'estre pas venû; il ne sera question de rien et vous serée toujours reçû comme vous le devée. C'êst a vos genoux que je vous demende cette grace.

57.* (60)

[c. 6 March 1748]

Je risque peut êstre d'achever de vous deplaire mais je ne puis me refusée la consolation de vous demendée une derniere grace et cela sera pour la vie. L'on ne tient des propos que sur ce que vous ne venée plus ici. Pouvée vous me refusée dy revenir et pouvée vous desirée faire le comble de mes malheurs en me perdant dans le public? Je vous jure sur ma vie qu'il nêst venû aucun propos dici. La conduitte que l'on tient êst admirable et on ne cherche qu'a me consolée et on desire ardemment que vous reveniée pour faire cessée les propos du public— c'êst le seul moyen—et si vous continuée a ne pas venir je suis perdû. Il êst encore temp. Ne me refusée pas. Cêst la vie que je vous demande. Il ne sera question de rien et vous serée reçû côme vous le devée. Pouvée vous refusée cette unique consolation a quelqu'un qui vous a tout sacrifiée, la vie et la reputation et le bonheur de la vie? Je scai que l'on vous dît les dernieres horreurs de moi, que vous m'accusée d'avoir dit beaucoup de choses.[62] Helas! on n'en scavoit que trop. Je n'ai rien a me reprochée. Qui pouvoit me faire sacrifiée tout—que l'amour le plus tendre que javois pour vous? Vos proçedées pour moi devroient bien me faire changer mais je vous aimerai tant que je vivrai. Je crois que cela ne sera pas long dans l'etat ou je suis. On m'a fait sortir pour me distraire mais je ne sort plus ni ne sortirai de l'ongtemp. On êst même obligée de me faire saignée pour sauvée mon malheureux enfant. Ce dernier pourroit il vous attendrir? Car je crois que pour moi que vous m'avée deja peut êstre sacrifiée a d'autres.[63] En un mot il ny a sorte de malheurs qui m'accablent si il vous reste encore un peu d'amitiée pour moi. Ne me refusée pas de revenir tout au plus tôt. Je ne sortirai point. Vous me rendrée la vie. Elle êst entre vos mains. Si vous pouviée dés aujourduy ou demain. Je vous ferai compassion. Ma seule consolation êst de ne vous avoir manquée en rien. Je n'ai que trop cherchée a me rendre coupable mais je scai que l'on vous persuade le contraire. Il faut que je soie bien malheureuse! Il me semble que je vous ai donnée d'assée fortes preuves de mon amour pour que vous n'en puissiée pas doutée. Mon sort êst entre vos mains. C'êst a vos genoux que je vous demende de conservée ma reputation en revenant et me prouvant le seul plaisir que je puisse goutée dans ma vie qui sera celui de vous voir. Si l'on vous persuade que pour faire finir les propos il ne faut plus revenir, ce sont des gens qui ont resolû ma perte et de vous detacher de moi. Je crois quils ont bien reussi. La reponse de celle cy fera le bonheur ou le malheur de ma vie. Si vous reveniée je retournerois chez vous—en un mot je serois la plus heureuse des creatures et il ne seroit question de rien. Si vous me refusée, la vie ne peut que m'êstre odieux—voiant faire le malheur de ma vie par tout ce que j'aime et que j'aimerai toutte ma vie, qui ne sera pas longue. Il êst encore tems si vous voullée revenir ces jours. J'attens tous des sentiments dont vous m'avée flattée si longtemps. Les larmes me font quittée. Au nom de dieu rendez moi la vie en revenant tout au plus tot!

58. (61) To Chrétien

[c. 6 March 1748]

Je vous envoie une lettre pour le p.... qui sera la derniere de ma vie si il me refuse de revenir. C'êst tout ce qu'on desire ici, quil revienne; je ne peut trop admirer la conduitte qu'on a pour moi. On ne cherche qu'a me consolée. Il m'êst impossible de voir le p... en particulier, ni d.... Je nyrai pas si tot au spetacle et quant j'yrai je ne pourois pas le risquée. Quil me mette sur un morceau de papier les noms de mes ennemis, le cachetée, et que vous me l'envoyée. Il peut êstre sur du plus grand secret. Quelque mal ecrit que cela soit je le lirai.[64] Je meurs d'impasience de le scavoir. Je ne sortirai pas de l'ongtemp. Jai fort mal a la poitrine. Je vais êstre saignée. Coment le p... peut il dire que jai tout gatée? Je n'ai jamais cherchée qu'a le justifiée et a me comdamnée, vous le scavée.[65] Quil revienne—il me rendra la vie! On craint fort pour mon etat. Je pleure et suis dans des saisissements continuels. Jai vû le pri. aux spetacles. Il m'a refusée la reverence. Cela m'a penetrée de douleur. Le seul moyen de faire finir les propos êst quil revienne au plus tot. J'attend vôtre reponse avec une impasience sans egale. Je n'entend pas ce quil veut dire—que personne nauroit scu quil me voioit. Vraiment, si il l'avoit voulûe, personne ne s'en seroit apercû! Recomendez bien a d.... mes intêrests, et quil revienne! Que d.... m'ecrive les noms. Il peut êstre sur quil ne risque rien—et quil ne me cache rien! Si il peut engagé le p...; a revenir je lui en marquerai ma reconnoissance. Quil aie soin qu'on brûle ma lettre sur le cham. On lui fera peut êstre quelque jours redemendé mes lettres. Il êst essentiel quil ne les garde pas. Je l'aime toujours tendrement, dittes le bien a d.... Peut êstre cet etée trouveroisje les moyens de le voir. Il ne tient qu'a lui[66] de me rendre heureuse. Je vous enverrai de l'argent incessament.[67] J'ai encore ecri a mon pere. Priée en grace Mr J...[68] de m'aportée vôtre reponse lindi a midi. Dittes lui que c'est bien pressée. Cela me rendra la vie si il revient. Il ne m'est pas possible de le voir. Je ne suis sure de personne—cela acheveroit de me perdre. Mais par la suitte cela se pourroit. L'on peut lui dire—et qu'on lui dise que reellement—je suis serieusement malade et cela êst vrai. Il pourra êstre sure quil sera la cause de ma mort. Faites voir ma lettre a d... Je me meurs de douleur. Vous sentée bien quil m'êst impossible de voir le p.... mais si il veut bien continuée a venir ici j'aurai bien des momens a lui parlée et je lui ecrirai tous les jours. Quil me donne ses derniers ordres; je les attend avec impasience. Faites rendre un pacquet[69] que je vous envoie a son adresse. Je scai que le p... dit que le seul moyen de faire finir les propos êst de ne pas revenir. Ce seroit me perdre si il veut continuée cette conduitte. Surtout, quil ne me refuse pas—cela me donnera le coup de la mort!

59. (63)

[c. 10 March 1748]

Puisje me flattée que vous voudrée bien encore entendre parlée de moi? Je n'osée m'en flattée puisque vous n'avée pas eu la bontée de me donnée de vos nouvelles mais je ne puis cessée de vous redemendée vos bontées que je ne vois que trop que vous m'avée otée. Je scai que vous dittes que je ne vous ai jamais aimée. Ce n'êst que l'amour le plus tendre qui a pû m'engagée a risquée et a sacrifié tout pour vous. Vous scavée que je ne vous ai jamais rien refusée. L'etat ou je suis vous en êst une preuve et, j'ose dire, devroit vous attendrir. Vous dittes[70] que c'êst moi qui ai tout gatée. Si j'ai dit quelque chose—ce que je ne crois pas—j'etois bien pardonable, je n'avois pas ma raison.[71] La mort m'auroit moins frapée que de [me] voir privée de vivre avec vous comme j'y vivois—et c'êst vous qui me privée de la consolation de vous voir et de me donnée de vos nouvelles. Oui cher amour (me permettée vous encore ce nom?) rapellée vos sentiments pour moi sans lesquels je ne peut vivre. L'on me force d'allée pour me tirée de l'etat ou je suis; je vais aux spectacles uniquement pour vous y voir mais ce sont autans de coups de poignard puisque vous ne me regardée pas et montrée au public que mes malheurs sont vraies. Je ne puis presque pas douttée que d'autres ont pris ma place dans vôtre coeur. Les malheurs m'accablent. J'y succomberai mais jusqu'au dernier soupir je vous serai fidelle. Je vous ai adorée dés l'instant que je vous ai connû[72] et je vous adorerai jusqu'au tombeau! Je suis persuadée que si vous pouviez croire l'etat ou je suis il vous attendriroit. Rien dans le monde ne me distrait de vous. Je porte vos cheveux jour et nuit sur moi et passe ma vie les yeux attachés sur vôtre portrait, a fondre en larmes—uniquement occupée de mon bonheur passée et des malheurs qui m'accablent et que vous seul causée si vous ne me continuée pas vos bontées. C'êst a vos genoux que je vous les demende. Si vous me les continuée et me donée de vos nouvelles, et que vous me disiée que vous m'aimée encore, cêst me rendre la vie et a mon pauvre enfant pour lequel il y a tout a craindre par le chagrin qui m'accablent. Je vous jure que je ne suis pas coupable d'avoir fait aucune imprudence. L'amour ne vous parlera til jamais pour moi? Je cesserai de vivre si vous cessée de m'aimée. J'attens larrêst de mon sort en reponse a celle cy. Je conte allée encore une fois[73] a l'opera pour vous apperçevoir. Du moins ne me refusée pas quelques regards! En un mot, continuée a m'aimée, cher coeur d'amour. Permettéz moi ces noms. Puisje croire que vous profiterée si il y venoit des tems ou nous puissions nous voir? Non, je ne puis m'en flattée. Je ne vous fais pas la moitiée du detail de l'etat ou je suis. De ne se croire plus aimée de quelqu'un qu'on adore êst ma situation. Je n'en scache pas de plus affreuses. Adieu. Permettéz moi de baisée milles fois cette main. J'attend quelle me prescrive mon sort. C'êst a vos genoux que je vous le demende et vous jure un amour eternel. Je me menage pour mon malheureux enfant que j'adorerai. Sans cela, si vous ne m'aimée plus, je me deferois d'une vie qui me devient odieuse. Mais au nom de l'amour le plus tendre, aimée moi toujours et pardonnée a l'amante la plus tendre de vous importunée encore—et rendée moi la vie!

60. *(62)* To Chrétien

[*c. 15 March 1748*]

Je suis penetrée de douleur de l'effet qu'a fait ma derniere lettre. J'esperois que l'on auroit pitiée de mon etat, du moins de mon malheureux enfant. J'avois lieu d'esperée que ce dernier attendriroit mais je n'ai rien a me reprochée—je n'ai tenû aucun propos ni on en a tenû ici. Jai fait tout ce qui a pû plaire au p.... et c'êst ce qui met le comble a mes malheurs de la façon dont il me traite— quelqu'un du même sang que lui et qui s'êst sacrifiée pour lui. Je sent que je ne cesserai jamais [de] l'aimée jusqu'a mon dernier soupir. De ma vie je ne lui ferai de reproches et je vois bien qu'il ne faut plus que je l'importune de mes lettres puisque la derniere ne l'a pû attendrir. Je passe ma vie a pleurer sur son portrait. Jour et nuit je suis occupée de lui. Puisje vivre separée de la seule personne que j'aime dans le monde? Je suis dans un etat affreux. Faite moi donnée de vos nouvelles; c'êst une consolation pour moi. Je crois que ma vie sera peu longue. Helas! peut êstre le p... en sera bien aise. Quil soit heureux, c'êst tout ce que je desire. Je defie quil trouve personne qui l'aime plus que moi. Que peut til avoir fait de mon portrait? Il lui êst sans doutte odieux! Le sien fait ma consolation. Je ne peut resistée a toute l'horreur des idées qui m'accablent. Je n'ai pas la force d'en dire davantage, les larmes couvrent mon papier. Mon pauvre enfant ne remue pas—jai tout a craindre. Helas! il êst malheureux avant de venir au monde. Quand je pense que si le p.... avoit voulû jaurois joui du seul bonheur que je puisse avoir dans le monde, sans que l'on l'aie pû jamais scavoir! Mais j'etois faitte pour êstre malheureuse et je le serai tant que je vivrai. Je crois que cela ne sera pas long, etant dans un etat affreux et rien ne peut me dissipée.

61. (11) To Chrétien

[c. 24 March 1748]

Jai eu deux coups de poignards avant hier et hier que je rencontrai le p.... a l'opera et a la comedie. Il a donc resolu de me perdre totalement puisqu'en public il m'a refusée la reverence. C'êst bien vouloir [...]⁷⁴ de mes malheurs. On me force a aller pour m'empecher de tomber malade tout a fait. Touttes les nuits je suis dans des etats qu'on croie que je vais mourir. On est fort inquiette pour moi et mon malheureux enfant. Helas! ce dernier ne pourroit il pas l'attendrir? Je me meurs de chagrin. Je n'ai pû retenir mes larmes a l'opera et a la comedie. Il na pas daignée me regardée. Pour moi j'avois les yeux attachée sur lui. Je n'ai que trop vû que l'aversion avoit pris la place des sentiments dont il m'a flattée. Peut il dire que je ne l'ai jamais aimée? Et qui auroit pû, que l'amour le plus tendre, me faire risquer ma vie et ma reputation? J'oublierai tous mes malheurs si il veut me donnée de ses nouvelles et revenir. C'êst tout ce qu'on desire, il ne sera question de rien. Ma vie est entre ses mains, helas! Refuseroit-on une malheureuse dans l'etat ou je suis—a plus forte raison quelqu'un qui l'adore et l'adorera toutte sa vie? Faites lui voir ma lettre si cela peut l'attendrir; quil me rende la vie et a mon enfant. Je scai que l'on lui dit le diable de moi. Il m'a peut êstre sacrifiée a d'autres. Pour moi, jamais rien ne le remplacera dans mon coeur. Mais si il ne veut pas me rendre la vie je suis capable par le desespoir ou je suis de m'en defaire. En un mot, la tête me tourne. De l'avoir vû m'a mis dans un etat affreux. J'attens vôtre reponse avec impasience—tachez quelle me rende la tranquilitée. Tachez quil voie ma lettre. Je n'ose lui ecrire. Si il le permet je lui ecrirai; mais quil vienne! C'êst la derniere grace que je lui demendrai de ma vie, qui ne sera pas longue. Surtout que Mr oxboro ne scache pas que jai aucun comerce avec vous ni personne. Au nom de dieu tachez de faire voir cette lettre cy et quelle me rende mon bonheur!

62. (56)

[c. 28 March 1748]

J'attend demain avec une impassience sans egale la reponse aux deux dernieres lettres que je vous ai ecrittes. Puisje me flattée quelles me sera favorable? Je suis dans un etat pis que jamais. Je n'ai plus de plaisir qu'a êstre seule, livrée a mon malheur. Je ne cherche aucun plaisir que quand on me force de me dissipée. Mais puisje l'êstre quand je suis séparée de mon cher amour? Si vous m'aimée

encore, permetée moi ces noms de celui que j'adore—et c'est pour la vie!
Donnée moi de vos nouvelles. Si vous vous attachée a quelque autre je cesserai
de vivre. Que je serois heureuse si je pouvois espérer que vous m'aimerée
toujours—mais le puisje croire aux procedées que vous avée pour moi de me
refusée de vous voir et de recevoir de vos nouvelles? Il ny a nulle raison qui
puisse vous empechée de m'en donnée—il ny a que celle que vous ne m'aimée
plus. Les larmes s'emparent de moi a cette idée et je ne la puis soutenir. Je vous
adore cher coeur d'amour. Un amour que tous les malheurs que jai soufert n'a pû
diminuée ne vous attendrira til pas? Jai a peine la force d'ecrire. Helas! c'êst peut
être vous deplaire que de vous importunée d'entendre parlée de moi. Si vous me
le deffendée je me priverai de cette consolation. Je ne peut survivre l'ongtemp a
l'etat ou je suis. Je ne puis le depeindre—sans cesse occupée de vous et pensant
que vous ne m'aimée plus. Je n'ai rien a me reprochée. Je me suis sacrifiée pour
vous et n'ai rien fait qui ait pû jamais vous deplaire. Mes ennemis seront bientôt
content. Ils m'arracheront une vie dont il font le malheur. Mes larmes couvrent
mon papier. Adieu. J'embrasse milles fois vos genoux et mon malheureux
enfant semble sentir son malheur.

63.* (66)

[4 April 1748][75]

Vous avée donc resolû ma mort en me confirmant ce dont je n'etois que trop
persuadée, qui êst vôtre façon de pensée. Pour moi, je n'en peut plus doutée
puisque vous refusée jusqu'aux occasions sures[76] que je vous donne de me voir.
Me refuserée vous aussi de vous ecrire? Jattend vos derniers ordres. Je ne peut
plus vivre si je n'ai pas de vos nouvelles. Je suis pire que je n'ai jamais etée. De
vous avoir rencontrée aujourduy[77] m'a mis hors de moi. En un mot, je suis dans
l'etat de quelqun qui êst haï de ce quelle adore. Rien ne me fera regrettée ce que
jai fait pour vous puisque cela a pû vous plaire. Vous me croiée donc toujours
coupable? C'êst ce qui me met le dernier poignard dans le coeur. Rendée moi
donc justice cher amour et mendée moi mon pardon en me rendant vos bontées,
sans lesquelles je ne peut rien. Je suis deçidée a tout si vous continuée a me les
refusée. Helas! le pouvée vous sans injustice? Mon malheureux enfant vous
parle pour moi. Cela seroit un miracle si il peut venir a bien. Il y a tout a craindre:
ma vie êst entre vos mains—je vous le jure avec veritée, embrassant vos genoux
et en les arrosant de mes larmes. De grace donnée moi de vos nouvelles, sans
quoi le coup de la mort m'êst portée. Je n'en puis dire davantage; jai cherchée
tous les moyens de pouvoir allée vous trouvée[78] mais cela m'êst impossible. Peut
être le pourrois je dans deux mois. Helas! peut êstre ne le voudré vous pas.
Jattend mon sort. L'amour, l'attachement, la tendresse la plus sincere—tout doit
vous parlée pour moi.

64. *(65)* To Chrétien

[*Thursday, 4 April 1748*][79]

Le p... veut donc me frapée le dernier coup de la mort puisquil met le comble a mon desespoir en refusant de me voir a v....[80] ou, sur ma vie, il ny avoit rien a risquée. Il refuse jusqu'a me donnée de ses nouvelles. Si il continue, mon parti êst pris; il sera delivrée de moi. La reponse a celle cy me decidera. Puisque je lui suis si odieuse il faut le debarrassée de moi. Ma mort fera son bonheur. Je suis, je l'avoue, hors de moi. Je ne peut baisée son portrait. Si il m'aimoit encore je lui demenderois en grace de l'avoir en petit. Voiée si il me le refusera. Je ne veut plus absolument sortir. On m'a forcée aujourduy d'allé. Jai rencontrée [le] p.... Il n'a pas daignée me regardée. Je l'ai suivi des yeux tant que jai pû. Je suis comme une folle! Ma grossesse ne paroit pas—il y a tout a craindre.[81] Mais tous mes malheurs ne me feront jamais regrettée ce que jai fait pour le p... puisque cela a pû lui plaire. Je ne sort plus du tout. Je jette des torrents de larmes touttes les nuits. Jai cherchée touts les moyens de l'allée trouvé chez lui mais cela êst impossible; je le pourrai dans deux mois. Scachez si il le voudra si vous voulée que je vive! Quil m'ecrive! Sans cela mon parti êst pris. Il me croit donc toujours coupable? Vous scavée comme je la suis! Jai bien des ennêmis: ma mort les contentera! Faites voir cette lettre au p.... Ma vie êst entre ses mains. Tout me rapele mon bonheur passée. On croit toujours que je vais mourir dans quelques saisissemens. J'adore le p..., pour la vie si il le veut. Elle sera courte si je n'ai pas de ses nouvelles—et des nouvelles qui puisse me consolée! Je dois voir m...[82] aprés demain pour vous faire paiée. Je vous enverrai aussi de l'argent le plutôt que je pourrai. J'attend mon arrêst decisive en reponse a celle cy. Passée mardi qui vient je ne pourrai plus avoir de vos nouvelles que le jeudi de l'autre semaine.[83] Cela me met au dessespoir. Du moins si d'ici a ce tems lâ jai des nouvelles de mon cher p... je vivrai. Mais je prie le prin, si il me refuse en reponse a celle que je vous envoie pour lui rendre, qu'il me rende la vie.

65. *(65A)* To Chrétien

[*6 April 1748*]

Je n'ai pas pu vous faire tenir cette lettre jeudi; je n'ai pas vû Mr J...[84] Cela m'a mis au dessespoir. Je me flatte le voir aujourduy et avoir de vos nouvelles. Je ne peut plus vivre sans voir une fois le p.... Jai trouvée une occasion pour allée chez lui la nuit. Il faut que t....[85] le scache. Je suis sure quil ne le dira pas et assurement le p... ne risque rien puisque cela êst moi qui yrai le trouvée. Cela seroit pour jeudi prochain[86] que je dois allée passée la soirée chez mon oncle[87] et que je dois prendre un carosse de remise le soir. Au lieu de cela, cela en seroit un que d...[88] m'enverroit. J'yrois passée une heure ou deux avec le p.... J'entrerois chez lui ou, si il ne vouloit pas, nous resterions dans le carosse, tout comme il voudroit. Cela sera le comble de mon bonheur. J'espere quil ne me refusera pas. Il ny a aucun risque pour moi, ainsi il ny a pas d'excuse a me donnée. Je ne lui mande pas ceci dans ma lettre.[89] Je vous charge de lui faire voir celle cy. J'attendrai ces ordres mardi qui sera le dernier jour que j'aurai de vos nouvelles jusqu'au jeudi de pasques.[90] Jespere que je l'apercevrai quelques jours aux concerts.[91] Jai etée hier aux thuilleries, esperant quil y seroit. Enfin je suis comme une folle. Si je peux tout arrangée pour jeudi je le ferai dire de bonne heure a d..... Ny paroissée pas. Si le p.... me refuse cela je me donne le coup de la mort. Je ne suis pas encore sur que cela se puisse arrangée. Si je ne fais rien dire a d... c'êst que cela ne se pourra, mais j'espere que le p... me laissera libre, si je le peut, de profitée de l'occassion. Il ne doit pas me refusée si il m'aime encore. Il scaura aprés si je suis coupable! Je ne peut plus vivre si je ne le vois pas. Personne ne le scaura, ni ma femme de chambre. Il ny aura que t.... Jai des raisons pour êstre sure qu'il ne le dira pas—j'en fais mon affaire. En tout cas, cela ne regarde que moi et le p... n'y êst pour rien. Je suis dans un etat pis que jamais. Je n'existe que pour adorer mon cher p.... Quil me donne de ses nouvelles mardi—pour êstre ma consolation tout le tems que je ne pourai pas en avoir. Si il veut, a la fin du mois prochain je pourrai quelquefois allée chez lui. J'attend ses derniers ordres mardi. Jai vû megrot qui vous fera paiée. Que le p.... me rende la vie en voulant bien me voir chez lui jeudi, si cela se peut, et me donne de ses nouvelles. Je l'adore plus que jamais et le prie, si je manque pour jeudi, [...][92]

66. *(89)* To Daniel

[*6 April 1748*]

Jai trouvée un moyen admirable que le porteur de celle cy vous dira. Je me meurs d'impasience que ce moment lâ arrive. Rassurée bien le p... que jamais cela ne se scaura—et si reellement il m'aime encore ecrivée moi un mot.[93] Cela ne sera peut êstre pas la seule foi que je pourrai le voir. Je n'ose lui ecrire. Mendé moi pour vrai si il reviendra sur mon comte aprés ma visitte. C'êst tout ce que je desire. Je l'adore. De vos nouvelles! Tachée de lui faire voir celle cy.

67. *(86)*

[*6 April 1748*]

Puisje me flattée que vous desirée me voir? La tête m'en tourne d'impasience, mon cher amour, cela me rendra la vie. Mais il faut que vous aiée la bontée de m'ecrire un mot pour scavoir si l'arrangement que j'ecris a d...[94] vous convient. Je crois que c'êst le seul qui cachera bien tout. De grace, mandée moi si vous êstes bien aise de l'expedient que jai trouvée. Vous pouvée en toutte suretée me repondre a celle cy. Elle me sera rendû en main propre. Si je n'ai pas de vos

nouvelles, je n'oserai ni ne scaurai si je peut allée chez vous. Donnée moi vos
ordres aussi tôt que vous recevrée celle cy. Cela fera le bonheur de ma vie de vous
voir un moment!

68. *(64)* To Chrétien

ce lundi [*8 April 1748*]

J'attend avec la derniere impasience vôtre reponse de demain. Si le p...
continue a ne me pas ecrire et naccepte pas que j'aille, si je le peut, chez lui je ne
survivrai pas a ma douleur, qui êst pis que jamais. Il faut que je prenne le parti de
me renfermée chez moi; tout l'univers m'ennuie. Je n'aurois de plaisir qu'a
parlée du p... On me dit quelquefois d'en parlée parce que l'on voit l'etat horrible
ou je suis. Tout me rapelle mon ancien bonheur. Rien ne peut depeindre a quel
point cela êst. Surement la tête m'en tournera; plus je vais et pis cela êst. J'ai étée
hier au concert;[95] j'y ai vû mon cher p... Il n'a pas daignée me regardée! Je m'en
suis trouvée mal. Je voudrois quil put imaginée l'etat ou je suis. Il en seroit
surement attendri. Je l'adore. Quoi! On a eu l'horreur de dire que j'avois
montrée de ses lettres? Vous scavée bien le contraire! Je jure sur ma vie que je
n'en ai montrée aucun. Si il a la bontée de m'ecrire je les brulerai sur le
champ—côme jespere quil fait des miennes. Je vais êstre dix jours sans avoir de
vos nouvelles, la tête vâ m'en tournée. Megrot a parlé a mon pere. Il estoit de
mauvaise humeur mais je vous repons que je le ferai changé quand je pourrai le
voir. Il m'a promis d'honneur quil vous donneroit. Pour de contract—il ne faut
pas lui en parlée;[96] j'en suis au desespoir. Surement tant que je vivrai vous ne
manquerée pas—mais si je mourrois c'êst toutte mon inquiétude. Je conte vous
envoiée incessament de l'argent. Je conte en emprunter pour cela. Si le p.... avoit
encore de l'amitié pour moi il ne vous auroit pas abandonnée.[97] Je vous jure que
vôtre etat me met au desespoir. Ne vous chagrinez pas si vous ne voullée pas me
mettre au desespoir—je suis assée malheureuse. Si le p.. accepte pour jeudi, et
que je le puisse, d.. aura de mes nouvelles jeudi. Je crois que si je voiois le p... je
mourrois de joie. Tacher quil me rende justice si il veut que je vive! J'espere que
je pourrai samedy avoir de vos nouvelles. Jai tant pleurée en ecrivant au p..... que
je n'en peut plus. Faites lui voir celle cy et faites lui rendre celle[98] que je vous
envoie pour lui. On m'a dit quil alloit en flandres.[99] La tête m'en tourne
d'inquietude. Tacher de scavoir ce qui en êst. En un mot je ne suis occupée que
de lui. C'êst tout ce que j'aime dans le monde et c'êst lui qui fait mon malheur!

69.* *(76)*

[*8 April 1748*]

Vous continuée donc a me perçée le coeur de douleur en continuant de ne me
pas donnée de vos nouvelles. Vous dittes que jai montrée vos lettres: je vous jure

sur ma vie que non. Je scai qu'on vous l'a dit et bien d'autres horreurs. On a reussi, a ce qui me paroit, a ce que l'on desiroit—qui êst de vous detachée de moi. Que ne peut on me rendre le même service en me detachant de vous? Mais rien n'êst capable de m'en detachée que la mort. J'attend demain mon sort, mon cher amour—permettée moi ces noms qui me sont si cheres. Ce sera mon arrêst prononcée si vous refusée de me donnée de vos nouvelles, et l'occasion de me voir. Si l'un et l'autre malheur m'arrive je n'y survivrai pas. Jai etée hier au conçert exprés pour vous voir. Helas! vous ne m'avée seulement pas regardée. De la contrainte que je me suis faite je me suis trouvée mal, donnant le chaud pour pretexte. Je suis dans un etat pis que jamais. Touts les endroits ou je vous ai vû—en un mot, tout me rapelle mon ancien bonheur et ne me fait que plus sentir l'horreur de ma situation. Oui, cher coeur, ce n'êst que la veritée la plus grande que je ne peut vivre si vous cessée de m'aimée. L'amour le plus tendre, la tendresse la plus vive et l'attachement le plus inviolable sont des sentiments qui ne sortiront jamais de mon coeur pour vous.[100] Il ne manque plus a mon malheur que vous alliée a l'armée! Je ne survivrois pas aux inquietudes que cela me donneroit dans mes couches. Si vous avée encore un peu d'amitiée pour moi.... Je ne puis m'en flattée puisque vous me refusée de me donnée de vos nouvelles. Si vous m'aimiée encore vous devriée bien me rassurée sur cette inquiétude là. Songée a vôtre malheureux enfant—oui, jose vous le dire, il êst a vous![101] Ne peut il vous attendrir pour sa malheureuse mere? Les larmes s'emparent de moi et m'ote la force d'ecrire. Si je ne reçois pas demain de vos nouvelles,[102] et que vous m'empechiée d'allée vous voir quand je le pourrai, je ne pourrai survivre a ma douleur. Je n'ai de plaisir que quand je suis seule. Je ne sort que dans l'esperance de vous rencontrée. Je passe les nuits et les jours a fondre en larmes. C'êst un miracle comment je peut y resistée! C'êst plus fort que moi: je vous adore et cela sera pour ma vie. Je vais estre dix jours sans avoir de vos nouvelles: la tête vâ me tournée. De grace, aiée pitiée de moi! Si vous ne m'aviée jamais aimée je ne serois pas si malheureuse. Je vient d'interrompre ma lettre, fondant en larmes regardant vôtre portrait. Helas! je crois que vous naviée pas jetté les yeux sur moi. Vous me detestée et vous me croiée coupable; je suis innocente et je vous adore; je sent que je vous importune; je finis.[103] Si vous me laissée la libertée et que je puisse vous voir jeudi cela me rendra la vie. Adieu cher amour; je baise mille fois tout ce qui m'est si chere. Mon enfant semble vouloir dire dans mon sein quil vous adore.

70. *(88)* *To Daniel*

[*9 April 1748*]

Jai reçû mon cher daniel la reponse de ch...[104] sur jeudi mais on ne me mande pas si le p... l'aprouve. Cela ne sera surement pas si il ne le desire pas mais je me flatte quil le voudra bien et comme vous ne scavée pas ecrire supliée le p... de m'ecrire ses ordres.[105] Je ne trouve pas l'arrangement du pont tournant bon; tout simplement, j'aurai un carosse de remise qui me menera a la fin du rempart a minuit ou vous m'attendrez et vous y monterée et cela fera tres bien.[106] Mendée moi vôtre reponse sur le champ pour que je m'arrange et rendée la lettre que je vous envoie pour le p.... Quelle joie j'aurai de le voir! Je ne puis l'exprimée!

71. (3) To Chrétien

[? 13 April 1748]

J'ai recû hier vôtre lettre. Je vois avec la plus vive douleur que le p.... croit que c'êst ma faute si je n'ai pas etée jeudi. Cela êst le comble de l'injustice! Scachant même que j'avois des espions, je risquois tout, mais rien ne me faisoit pourvû que je l'eut vû. Mais, dans le moment que j'y contois, arrive ma femme de chambre, un carosse de mon quartier et touts mes gens. Je laisse a jugée au p.... si cela m'etoit possible. Quelques temps auparavant je ne menois plus ma femme de chambre pour pouvoir allée un jour chez le p. et jai pris des carosses de remises. Mde de g.... s'êst mis dans une fureur horrible et a deffendû que je fasse un pas sans ma femme de chambre et touts mes gents. Je nai plus la libertée de voir ni de recevoir des nouvelles de Mme C....[107] Que le p... juge apres si je suis ma maitresse! Je ne desirerois l'êstre que pour lui prouvée que je l'adorerai tant que je vivrai. Comment peut il dire que jai voulû lui faire un afront? Je ne lui ai jamais manquée en rien. Vous scavée mieux que personne si la lettre que jai ecrite venoit de moi.[108] Je n'ai jamais dit un mot de rien. Comment peut on imaginée que je cherche a instruire de mon malheur? Vous scavée que touts les domestiques le scavoient. Ce n'êst pas le moyen que cela soit cachée. Si j'avois pû tout cachée entre ma chair et ma chemise je l'aurois fait. Et comment peut on imaginée le contraire? En un mot si le p.... veut avoir la charité de prendre part a ma situation je pourrai dans un mois le voir a st ou...[109] ou il conte allée. Il ny aura rien de si aisée. Si il vouloit plutôt a v...[110] jamais personne ne pourroit le scavoir et ce seroit la vie quil me donneroit. Il ny a rien que je ne fasse pour le voir. Jai etée hier au concert[111] pour le voir. Il n'a pas daignée me regardée. Je m'en suis trouvée mal en sortant. Je suis comme une folle. Si il ne veut plus recevoir de mes nouvelles, ni me donnée des siennes, quil m'envoye un verre de poison. Je le boirai avec plaisir et mon malheureux enfant perira. Il êst pourtant le gage dun amour que le p.... m'avoit jurée eternelle! Pour le mien, jamais [il] ne changera. Si il change, ce sera pour l'ofrir a dieu[112]—mais je n'en ai pas la force. Allée encore vous jettée aux pieds du p... et lisée lui cette lettre. Quil se resouviene que jamais je ne lui ai rien refusée—que c'êst pour lui que je suis la plus infortunée des creatures, car je lui cache le plus que je peut mes malheurs! Il[s] ne feroient que l'ennuiée. Mon ventre ne grossit pas. On ne conçoit rien a mon etat. C'êst un miracle comme je vis. Ne voiée que d... le soir. On vous guete aussi bien que moi. De vos nouvelles. Donnée moi la mort [ou] la vie; je l'attend du p....

72. *(3.1)*

[*? 13 April 1748*]

Vous ne voullée donc plus cher p... entendre parlée de moi? Si vôtre parti êst pris, envoiée moi un verre de poison. Je suis resolû de me donnée la mort. Je ne peut plus vivre. Vous dittes que je ne vous ai jamais aimé. Et pour qui donc me suis je perdue et portaije dans mon sein le gage de l'amour que vous m'avée tant juré [de]voir[113] estre eternelle? Le mien le sera malgré [vos] injustices pour moi. Donnée moi [la] [mo]rt ou me voiée a v... et a [st o]. Ce sont les deux seuls moyens p[uisque] les autres me sont otés. Jai ma[ndé] tout mes malheurs pour que l'o[n] [vous] les dise. Depuis jeudi je suis come [une folle]. Vous avée l'injustice de dire que je suis ma maitresse. Helas! non. Si je l'etois vous me verriée a vos genoux vous jurée que je ne vous ai jamais manqué en rien! Mon sort êst prononcée—la mort ou la vie pour moi et vôtre malheureux enfant. Jai etée hier au concert pour vous voir. Vous n'avée pas daignée me regardé! Je me suis evanouie en sortant. Je meurs d'amour pour vous et c'êst en embrassant vos genoux que [je] vous demende de m'acordée, si je trouve [une occa]sion de vous voir. Sans cela la mort [me] sera donnée en prononçant que [je] vous adore. Je scai que jai des ennemis [près] de vous. Ils seront contents quand je nexisterai plus. Je me trouve mal et finis en vous baisant milles fois les mains.

73. *(3A)* To Daniel

[*? 13 April 1748*]

Je ne vous ecris qu'un mot mon cher d... J'ecris a Chretien pour quil vous montre sa lettre. Tacher que le p... la voie. Il verra si c'êst ma faute pour jeudi! Si il veut à v.... il me rendroit la vie. Je suis hors de moi. Certainement je me tuerai. Je vous ferois compassion—je vous ecrirai tant que je pourrai. J'ai tant d'espions quil faut que je me mefie de tout! Si le p... vouloit m'accordée dans un mois, je le verrois a st oue.... les nuit tres aisement. Si il ne veut plus entendre parlée de moi je suis resolû a me donnée la mort. Je n'ai pas la force de vous en dire davantage. Je vais ecrire un mot au p...—risquée de lui donnée.

74. *(87)* To Daniel

[*? 14 April 1748*]

Mon parti êst pris mon cher d.... Ne pouvant pas voir le p... chez lui, puisque je ne vais plus seul, si il me refuse encore un jour d'allée a v... j'avalle du poison.

Je ne peut plus vivre—je me meurs de douleur. Ainsi, si il me refuse, j'avallerai le poison en prononçant son nom—et même sans lui reprochée ma mort ni celle de son enfant. Je lui ecris.[114] Demain matin j'enverrai cherchée la reponse; elle decidera mon sort. J'ai a cette heure un apartement a v.. que jai exprés ou il êst impossible que jamais personne ne puisse voir. Si je pouvais l'allée trouvée surement je ne lui donnerai pas cette peine. Elle est legere, si il m'aime. Que ne feroisje pas pour lui? Je n'ai a me reprochée que de trop l'aimée. La reponse êst la vie ou la mort. Ce n'êst pas un discours, c'êst un parti pris. Je me meurs.

75.* (80)

[? 14 April 1748]

Je vous ai mandée les raisons qui m'ont empechée d'allée chez vous jeudi et que les moyens m'en etoient otée. On me flatte que vous avée pitiée de mon sort.... Et comment puisje m'en flattée—vous me refusée de me voir a v...! C'êst le seul moyen—et je vous le demende en grace. Jamais qui que ce soit ne peut s'en douttée. Pouvée vous me refusée cette grace? Si vous me la refusée mon parti êst pris: javalerai un verre de poison. Je ne peut plus vivre traitée comme je la suis de tout ce que j'aime dans le monde. C'êst a vos genoux que je vous demende en grace d'allée un jour a v... Helas! il y a eu un tems ou vous ne me l'auriée pas refusée. Je n'ai point dû demeritée auprés de vous depuis ce tems là. Songée que je porte dans mon sein le gage d'un amour eternel! Aiée pitiée de mon etat! Je me meurs de douleur et c'êst la vie que vous me donnerée en me voiant un moment. Je vous jure sur ma vie que personne n'en scaura rien! C'êst le seul moyen que j'aie—aiée en pitiée! La reponse de celle cy me decidera a me donnée la mort. J'y suis resolû. Je ne peut plus vivre sans voir un moment mon cher amour.

76. (85) To Daniel

[? 15 April 1748]

Je ne m'attendois pas au comble du procedée du p...! Il met le comble a ma douleur. Faites moi ecrire au juste par ch... a qui je vous prie de remettre la lettre[115]que je vous envoie. Qu'êstce qui a pu determinée la derniere fureur? Il n'est plus douteux que le p... n'en aime quelqu'autre. Vous scavée que vous m'avée promis de me le mandée[116] et vous pouvée contée, sur ma vie, sur un secret inviolable. Brulée mes lettres sur le champ. Je me donnerai la consolation de vous ecrire. Je me meurs de douleur mais ne me cachée rien. Je l'exige de vous. Je serois bien fachez que vous vous expossasiée encore a des desagremen. Vous en avée assée essuiée.[117] Si par hasard il parloit de moi, dittes lui que dans un mois je pourrois le voir. Mais il n'êst plus douteux quil aime quelqu'un.

J'attend votre reponse avec une impasience extrême. Selon ce que vous m'avée mandée, si je l'avois vû jeudi cela lui auroit fait beaucoup de peine et il m'auroit fort mal traittée. De vos nouvelles, souvent! C'êst ma seule consolation. Il sera bientôt debarrassée de moi car je ne peut vivre.

77. *(67)* To Chrétien

Ce lundi au soir [*15 April 1748*]
Il ne m'êst possible que de vous ecrire un mot ce soir—aiant etée toutte la soirée dans un etat affreux, dans des saississemens, et jettant des torrents de larmes sans pouvoir rien avalée; a craindre tout pour moi. Le p... me donne le dernier coup de poignard en ne m'ecrivant pas. Je ne peut plus resistée a l'etat ou je suis. Je demende a cette heure, par grace, qu'on me laisse seul. Je ne veux plus sortir; je suis dans un etat que je ne peut vous depeindre. Si le p... veut absolument ma mort—comme je l'imagine, puisque je scai quil lui êst odieux d'entendre prononçée mon nom—il n'a qu'a dire si il me refuse la derniere grace que je lui demende, qui êst de me donnée de ses nouvelles. Il ne sera plus importunée de moi. Je me deferai d'une vie qui m'êst odieuse puisque tout ce que j'adore fait le malheur de ma vie. Je n'ai pas la force de vous en dire davantage. Faites voir cette lettre au p.... Je lui ecris un mot:[118] sa reponse decidera mon sort. En mourant pour lui je mourrai l'adorant. Rien ne peut exprimer l'etat ou je suis et re[e]llement il y a tout a craindre. Ainsi le p..... sera bientôt defait de moi, il sera content. Jai vû aujourduy mon pere qui m'a dit quil ne pouroit pas vous assurée par contract mais que tant quil vivroit il vous feroit une pension, que vous n'aviée qu'a l'allée touchée tous les mois ou touts les quartiers, côme vous voudriée. J'enverrai cherchée megrot; jespere même que cela sera 250. Tachée que le p... m'ecrive! Sans cela vous aprendrée bientôt ma mort. Voila mon saisissement qui me reprend; je ne peut pas en dire davantage. Je me meurs pour ce que j'adore. Je viens de lui ecrire—je ne scai comment je l'ai pû—le papier êst trempé de mes larmes. Comment peut til dire quil ne m'ecrit pas pour les proçedée que lon a eu pour lui, et êst-ce moi qui en serois coupable? Je crois que je soufre assée. N'import, ma vie êst entre ses mains; mon parti êst pris. Aprés la reponse a celle cy je me donnerai la mort. Je suis hors de moi. Que le p.. aie la bontée de brulée mes lettres! Sans doute en a til fait autant de mon portrait. Faites lui voir cette lettre. Je vous enverrai incessament de l'argent, et le plus que je pourrai. A la mort même je ne vous oublierai pas. Je suis bien sensible a tous les soins de d...; je voudrois êstre en etat de les reconnoitre. Qu'il tache que le p... me rend la vie![119]

78. *(68)*

[*15 April 1748*][120]

L'etat ou je suis me met hors d'état de n'ecrire qu'un mot. Il êst court a dire: le dernier coup de la mort m'êst donnée par ce que j'adore. Vous me faites paiée pour touts les torts que vous dittes que l'on a eu avec vous. Quand même cela seroit, en seroije coupable et cela devroit til vous empechée de me donnée de vos nouvelles? Mais vous avée prononcée l'arrest de ma mort. Il êst deçidée, si vous refusée de m'ecrire. Oui, cher amour, je mourrai puisque je vous suis odieuse—et je mourrai vous adorant. Prononcée! Cela sera bientôt executée; cela êst deja bien avançée. Rien ne pouroit vous depeindre l'etat ou je suis. Il êst pis que jamais. En me donnant le coup de la mort je ne regretterai que vous dans le monde—et que ma mort ne puisse vous êstre d'aucune utilitée! Je vous lai dit souvent: je n'aurois jamais hesitée a vous la sacrifiée et je vous la sacrifierai puisque je vous suis odieuse. Les larmes inondent mon papier; je me trouve mal—ce qui me fait finir en vous assurant milles fois que je vous adore. Si vous me refusée de m'ecrire vous n'aurée plus de nouvelles de moi que celle de ma mort. Ne vous ressouvenée vous plus de vos serments pour moi? Mon age, mon enfant, rien ne peut til vous attendrir? Les larmes me font finir en vous demendant a vos genoux le dernier arrêst de mon sort.

79. *(73)*

[*17 April 1748*]

Je vous avois ecris il y a deux jours mon cher p... mais ma lettre[121] n'a pû vous êstre rendû. Je suis au dessespoir que vous ne voulliée pas me voir a v... mais je serois bien fachez de vous en parlée: ce seroit vous deplaire et ce n'êst surement pas mon intention. Elle êst uniquement de vous prouvée que je vous adore. Si il m'etoit possible actuellement, j'yrois vous le jurée a vos genoux; mais cela m'êst impossible puisque l'on veut que j'aie toujours ma femme de chambre avec moi. Aiée pitiée de l'etat ou je suis et permettée moi que j'y aille quand on sera parti ce qui sera le 20 du mois.[122] D'abord je me deferai un soir de ma femme de chambre—ce que je ne peut faire tant qu'on sera ici—et j'yrai jurée a mon cher amour que mon coeur n'êst qu'a lui. Jai tout lieu de craindre que le vôtre ne soit a d'autre qu'a moi. Ne me le cachée pas. Ce sera pour moi le coup de la mort. Aiée la compassion pour moi d'attendre le 20 du mois prochain—je vous le demende pour moi et mon enfant... c'êst deux fois vôtre sang qui vous parle![123] J'attend de vôtre propre main vos ordres. Il y a assée l'ongtemps que vous me refusée la seule consolation que je puisse avoir qui êst de recevoir de vos nouvelles. Je ne peut plus vivre sans cela et si vous m'accordée cette grace cela me soutiendra dans mes malheurs jusqu'a l'instant ou sans faute j'yrai vous jurée que je serai a vous tant que je respirerai. Non, rien ne peut vous depeindre a quel point je vous aime et si vous me refusée de me conservée vôtre coeur et de me voir le mois prochain je me donnerai la mort. Rendée moi la vie en m'ecrivant un mot de vôtre main qui puisse me consolée. En veritée, je suis digne de pitiée et vôtre pauvre enfant aussi! Songée quil êst le gage d'un amour que vous m'avée tant jurée devoir êstre eternel—et de n'aimée jamais d'autre que moi! Helas! je ne vois que trop que vous ne m'aimée plus—et peut êstre en aimée vous d'autres? Je succombe a toutes les idées qui m'accablent. Je vous vis hier a la promenade et vous suivit des yeux tant que je put. Je ne puit retenir mes larmes! Mendée moi le jour que vous yréz a l'opera[124] pour que je tache d'y allée pour vous y voir. Si vous m'ecrivée un mot cela me rendra la vie. Ne me le refusée pas plus l'ongtemps. Je suis dans un etat affreux. Jamais qui que ce soit ne le scauroit. Je brulerai vos lettres sur le champ.[125] Je vous jure sur la vie que je n'en ai jamais montrée. J'attend demain vos ordres de vivre. Puisje esperée que vous serée bien aise de me voir le mois prochain? Ce sera sans faute. Adieu, mon cher amour; je ne peut vivre sans vous voir. Si je vous vois a l'opera, regardée moi avec ces yeux que j'adore. Cela me rendra la vie. Je baise mille fois vos mains.

80. (83)

[? 20 April 1748]

Je m'etois flattée, mon cher p..., que vous auriée eu enfin compassion de celle qui vous adore, et que vous lui auriée donnée la seule consolation quelle peut avoir qui êst celle de recevoir de vos nouvelles. Ne me la refusée plus. Je suis dans un etat pis que jamais. Jai etée au concert[126] pour vous voir; je n'ai pas pû y avoir de place. La semaine prochaine, si je scavois les jours que vous yrée a l'opera, j'yrois. Je ne peut pas vivre sans vous voir. Quand je pense quil y a trois mois!... La tête me tourne, je me rapelle tant d'heureux moments. Helas! peut êstre ne vous en ressouvenée vous plus et peut êstre me detestée vous? Je passe mes jours tant que je le peut enfermée dans ma chambre, a fondre en larmes vis a vis vôtre portrait et en baisant mille fois vos cheveux que je porte jour et nuit sur mon coeur. En un mot, je n'aime que vous dans le monde et ne suis pas un instant sans êstre occupée de vous. Je ne peut plus vivre. Mon malheureux enfant se ressent de mes malheurs. Aiée pitiée de lui et ressouvenée vous d'un tems ou vous lui avée tant dit dans mon sein que vous l'aimeriée. Plus je me represente mon bonheur passée plus mes malheurs en sont grands. Aiée pitiée de la plus infortunée des creatures! Donnée moi de vos nouvelles de cette chere main que j'adore. Je vous ai peut êstre deplû en vous mandant que le mois prochain j'yrois chez vous. J'attend vos ordres, qui seront pour moi des loix tant que je vivrai. Je conte allée a st o... cet etée. Que cela me rapellera d'heureux jours! Cela fera mon martir. On ne peut pas aimée au point que je vous aime. De vos nouvelles! C'êst la vie que je vous demende. Il y a trois mois que je suis dans un martir continuel. Aiée en pitiée! Je n'ai rien a me reprochée—je le jure sur ma vie! Adieu cher amour; adieu tout ce que j'adore. J'attens touts de vos bontées. Ne me les refusée plus si vous vous soucié que je vive, et vôtre enfant.

81. *(77) To Daniel*

[*? 27 April 1748*][127]

Je ne conçois pas comment vous pouvée me proposée de dire a ma femme de chambre mon projet d'allée chez le p...! Cela perdroit tout sur des propos quelle m'a tenû et cela ne m'avanceroit de rien. Je ne pourrois toujours pas y allée avant qu'on fût parti. Vous ne me mandée pas si le p... le veut bien. Il refuse encore de m'ecrire, j'en suis malade de chagrin. J'etois bien vis a vis de lui a l'opera: il ne m'a pas regardée! Jai fondû en larmes tout le tems. Mendez moi donc si il veut bien que j'y aille quand on sera parti. En un mot, si il a quelqu'un, ne me le cachez pas![128] Et si il ne veut plus que je lui ecrive je mourrai de douleur, c'est certain—et mon enfant, je crains le sang. Peut il refusée de m'ecrire un mot? C'êst la vie que je lui demande! Faites moi une reponse positive demain; je l'enverrai cherchée a dix heures du matin. J'ecris a mon cher p.... Si cela lui deplait, cela ne sera plus mais je suis dans un etat affreux! Je me meurs de douleur. Quil aie pitiée de moi! Si il ne m'ecrit pas un mot je me donnerais la mort. J'y suis resolû.

82. *(74)*

[*? 27 April 1748*][129]

Vous me refusée encore de m'ecrire mon cher p.... Il faut donc que vous ne m'aimiée plus. Avouée le moi et je ne vous importunerai plus d'entendre jamais parlée de moi. Je mourrai—oui je me donnerai la mort, et a vôtre enfant! Je me meurs. De grace, ecrivée moi un mot! Qu'est-ce qui peut vous empecher si vous m'aimée? Jai etée hier a l'opera.... Je n'ai pas otée les yeux de dessus vous. Vous ne m'avée pas regardée! Je fondois en larmes. En un mot, je me meurs d'amour pour vous. J'attends vos derniers ordres si vous voullée bien me voir quand je le pourrai—c'êst a dire aussi tôt qu'on sera parti.[130] Si cela vous deplait je vous deferai de moi et je me donnerai la mort. Ne pouvée vous pas avoir pitiée de vôtre sang? Jattends demain mon sort: un mot de vous me rendra la vie; je me jette a vos genoux comme la plus infortunée des creatures. Vous ne pouvée pas vous imaginée a quel point je vous adore! Oui, cher coeur d'amour, je ne vis que pour vous adorée. Ne me donne pas la mort! Il viendra des tems heureux et je serai toujours a vous. J'yrai peut êstre demain a l'opera pour vous voir. De grace, regardée moi avec ces yeux que j'adore! J'attendrai demain vos ordres. Rendée moi la vie!

83. *(58)* To Daniel

[*Monday, 29 April 1748*]

Jai etée hier a l'o... ou jai etée temoin de ce que [je] scavois deja bien de l'amour du p... et de Mde de t....[131] Cela m'a parû êstre fait. J'aurois bien voulû que cela me fut indifferent mais il s'en faut bien; jai eu peine a retenir mes larmes jusqu'au moment ou j'en suis sorti, après quoi elles n'ont pû finir de la soirée, ni de la nuit. En un mot, je suis dans un etat qui ne se peut exprimer. Le seul plaisir que jaie a l...[132] êst de voir le p.... mais hier j'etois si penetrée de douleur que je lui donnerai le moins que je pourrai le plaisir que je sois temoin des siens. Que ne puije me detachée de lui? Cela feroit mon bonheur mais je ne puis.[133] Je l'aime a l'adoration. Jai peine a croire que Mme de t... l'aime de même—sa santée ne s'en trouvera pas bien. Mais que je suis malheureuse de m'en occupée! Il ne porte plus la veste que jai faite—aparament parce quelle vient de moi. C'êst une bien forte aversion! J'y succomberai et je lui donnerai bientôt le plaisir d'êstre debarrassée de moi. Helas! il ny a que mon malheureux enfant pour qui je crains. On me force continuellement d'aller pour me tirée de l'état de douleur ou je suis mais rien ne m'en tire. Quel plaisir puije prendre puisque la seule personne que j'aime dans le monde me met le poignard dans l'ame? Je n'ai pas la force de tenir ma plume. Donnée moi de ses nouvelles. Helas! c'êst ma seule consolation—et son portrait que j'arrose de mes larmes. En un mot, je suis plus deresonné que jamais. Quoi! Il me deteste—moi qui nai rien refusée de tout ce quil a voulû? L'etat ou je suis ne peut lattendrir, mes larmes couvrent mon papiée.

84. *(78)* To Daniel

[*? 3 May 1748*]

Je vous envoye mon cher d... une lettre[134] pour le p... pour scavoir ses ordres parceque jai trouvé un moyen pour allée dans quinze jours un soir chez lui. J'espere quil ne me refusera pas. Il me déteste donc? Je me meurs de douleur—on craint tout pour moi. Mais que m'importe de vivre? J'enverrai cherchée aprés demain[135] vôtre reponse. Si vous vouléz me rendre la vie, quelle me soit favorable! Les quinze jours vont me paroitre un siecle! Je mourrai de joie aux genoux de mon cher p... en lui jurant un amour eternel. Mendée moi si son depart pour dans quelque temp êst vrai.[136] J'en suis malade et peut êstre seroije morte avant. Je l'adore plus que jamais; je ne peut vivre come cela. Je scait que l'on lui a dit que j'aimais quelqun.[137] Ah dieu! Je n'adore que mon p... dans le monde! Ecrivée moi. Tacher que le p... m'ecrive un mot. J'espere quil ne me refusera pas sa port[e]. Quil me donne ses ordres de sa main, cela me rendra a la vie! Tout ce que je peut dire ne peut vous depeindre l'etat ou je suis. Mendée moi un peu ce que devient c....[138] Jai parlée pour lui a mon oncle[139]—j'espere quil tachera de lui faire avoir quelque chose. Ecrivée moi un peu longuement[140] et ne me cachée rien. Jettée vous pour moi aux genoux du p... pour quil fasse finir mes malheurs en me rendant ses bontés. Je n'ai meritée en rien quil me les ôtât; je n'ai rien a me reprochée. Je ne lui reproche que son injustice pour moi. Je me trouve mal; je suis obligé de quittée.

85. *(82) To Daniel*

[? *5 May 1748*]

J'envoie cherchée la reponse a la lettre[141] que je vous ai ecris. Puije esperer que le p... l'aie lû? Je suis dans un etat affreux: jai eu la fievre encore hier; je serai saignée. Il y a a craindre pour mon état mais je vois bien que cela êst egal au p.... Mendée moi si il me permet de lui ecrire encore. Ne se laissera til pas touchée pour m'ecrire un mot? Si il part je mourrai, c'êst sur. Je l'adore plus que jamais. J'attend de vos nouvelles avec une impasience sans egale. J'attend les ordres du p.... Faites lui voir celle cy qu[il] me rende enfin justice.

86. *(75)*

[? *6 May 1748*]

Je vous avois ecrit il y a quelques jours cher p... mais malheureusement ma lettre ne vous a pas etée rendû.[142] Les bruits que vous partiée m'ont mis dans un etat affreux, jen suis malade. Jai etée saignée[143] hier et demain je prend medecine — ce qui êst for dangereux dans l'etat ou je suis, mais je suis dans un etat horrible. On a beau me faire des remedes, le coup de la mort m'êst frapée. Vous me refusée de me donnée de vos nouvelles! Vous ne m'aimée plus! Que m'êst la vie? Je ne songe plus qu'a mourir si vous ne me rendée vos bontés. Je scai que l'on vous a dit que j'aimois quelqu'un. Je ne m'attendois pas a ce comble d'horreur! Je vous jure que je n'adore que vous dans le monde! Ma mort vous le prouvera — c'êst vous qui me la donnée. Aiée enfin pitiée de la plus malheureuse des creatures! Un mot de votre main me rendra la vie. Pouvez vous me le refusée? Me refuserée vous aussi la seule consolation que j'aime dans ma vie? Je pourrai dans quinze jours qu'on sera parti, moyennant un expedient que jai trouvée — je pourrais allée un soir chez vous mais je n'ose sans vos ordres. Me refuserée vous cette grace? Songée que cela sera peut êstre la derniere fois de ma vie que je vous verrai! Ainsi j'espere que vous ne me refuserée pas la porte. Je ne perdrai pas un instan dés qu'on sera parti a allée a vos genoux vous jurée un amour eternel — et vôtre malheureux[144] enfant semble vouloir vous parlée pour moi. Aiée donc la charitée de me donnée vos ordres et de me faire dire si il êst vrai que vous partiée. Je me meurs de douleur mais au moins ne m'otée pas la consolation de vous voir une fois. Ces quinze jours la me vont paroitre des siecles! Adieu, cher coeur d'amour—tout ce que j'adore dans le monde, malgré vos injustices. Faites finir mes malheurs en me rendant vos bontés! C'êst me rendre la vie, et a vôtre enfant. La reponse a celle cy decidera mon sort.[145]

87. (90)

[c. 13 May 1748]

Je n'osois vous ecrire, craignant que cela ne vous importune, mais je ne peut resistée a vous marquée ma joie qui êst inexprimable de voir arrivée le moment ou j'yrai me justifiée a vos genoux et vous jurer un amour eternel et vous prouvée touttes les faussetez que l'on vous a dit contre moi. Je conte dans cinq ou six jours pouvoir allez un soir chez vous.[146] Je vous le manderai la veille et vous suplierai de vous retirée un peu de bonne heure pour que j'aie plus de tems a êstre avec vous.[147] Helas! ce sera le premier moment que j'aurai eu d'agreable depuis quatre mois.[148] Je ne pourrois vivre plus longtemp sans voir tout ce que j'aime. Je ne vous suplie pas de m'ecrire, puisque cela vous deplait, mais ordonnez a d... de me mandée si reellement je peut me flattée que vous serée bien aise de me voir. Cela me soutiendra d'ici au moment que je serai heureuse. Adieu, mon cher amour; faites moi donnée la consolation de scavoir si vous m'aimée encore. Je baise mille fois votre main et espere dans peu de jours la baisée reellement et l'arrosée de mes larmes. Certainement vôtre enfant sentira son bonheur par la joie que j'aurai. Depuis le moment que jai trouvée les moyens de vous voir la tête me tourne! Adieu, mon cher amour.

88. (71) To Daniel

[? 17 May 1748]

On m'a averti aujourduy que j'avois des espions autour de la maison du p..., ainsi je serois perdûe mais si il veut bien se trouvée a minuit au pont tournant, envelopée dans une redingote dans un carosse avec vous, je m'y trouverai et nous nous verrons sans nulle danger. Je me flatte quil ne me refusera pas cette grace. Je n'aurai n'y laquais ni personne avec moi, ainsi cela êst bien sûre. Pour d'aller dans la maison, cela ne me sera possible que quand Mde de g... sera parti. Pour lors, j'yrai. Jattend vôtre reponse et jespere quelle me sera favorable. Le desir que jai de revoir le p... ne peut s'exprimée! Il jugera bien demain de ma façon de pensée! A minuit precise je serai au pont tournant.

89. *(69)*

[*early morning, 19 May 1748*]

Tout ce que je pourrois vous dire ne pourroit vous depeindre la joie que jai eu de vous voir! J'attend de vos nouvelles avec [une] impasience sans egalle. Donnée m'en touts les jours; je vous en donnerai des miennes. Je vous adore plus que jamais! Je n'ai que le tems de vous ecrire un mot. Daniel vous dira ce qui m'est arrivée ce matin:[149] je suis plus morte que vive! Adieu, cher amour, je n'ai pas fermée l'oeil. Je suis comme une folle! Rendée moi la vie en me rendant tout vôtre amour. Demain je vous ecrirai plus longuement.[150] Mais, de grace, voiée moins Mde t...!—et ne prenée personne: j'en mourrois de douleur.[151]

90.* *(81)*

[*? 20 May 1748*]

Le saississement de joie que jai eu, mon cher amour, de vous voir ma mis hors de moi mais touts les saississemens du monde ne me feroient rien—au contraire feroit mon bonheur—si je pouvois vous voir comme je le voudrois. Vous pouvée êstre sur que [si] je peut trouvée des occasions de vous voir j'en profitterai, ne pouvant pas venir sans cela. Je vous aime plus que je ne peut dire et c'êst bien sincere. Depuis l'heureux moment que jai passée avec vous je ne cesse de me rapellée tout ce que vous m'avée dit. Il y a quelque chose qui m'a mis le poignard dans le coeur, je te l'avoue cher coeur d'amour, de l'aveu que vous m'avée fait que vous ne m'aimiée plus tant et que vous voulliée prendre quelqu'un. Je ne resisterai pas a ce coup la: pour moi, tant que j'existerai, je vous serai fidelle—et je n'ai jamais manquée un instant d'êstre a vous. Je me rapelle aussi les choses agreables que vous m'avée dit en t'rautres, en parlant des propos de la gazette.[152] Vous m'avée dit que [vous] ne m'abandonneriée pas plus que vous [ne ren]onçeriée a vos droits. C'êst tout dire, et si vous voullée que je vive n'aimée que moi! Vous m'avée promis, mon cher amour, en me quittant dans la rue, que j'aurois touts les jours de vos nouvelles. Helas! ce sera mon unique consolation. Jai passée mes nuits a baisée mes mains parcequelle vous avoit touchée. En un mot, je vous adore! La lettre que je vous ai envoyée m'a fait une peur horrible.[153] Mendée moi si vous nyrée pas a st o... Regardée souvent mon portrait. Sur tout plus tant Mde t...; elle me fera mourir de chagrin! De vos nouvelles, cher amour; je baise mille fois tout ce que jai baisée hier. Si vous alliez a st o... je vous verrois souvent.

91. *(79)*

[*Tuesday, 21 May 1748*]

Je me flattoit bien ce matin avoir de vos nouvelles comme vous me l'avée promis en me quittant. Helâs! ne me refusée pas la seule consolation que je puisse avoir dans le monde. Je ne dessesperes pas de vous revoir si vous voullée vous pretée. On a parlée a mon espion qui a dit que j'en avois un autre mais il tachera de m'avertir les jours quil ne gaietera pas et si vous voulliée ces jours là venir en carosse de remise me trouvée dans un endroit bien écartée [je monterois] dans le vôtre et nous passerions deux heures ensemble et nous y ferions tout ce que nous avons fait l'heureux jour que je vous ai vû, sans rien craindre. Jespere qu'aprés la preuve que je vient de vous donnée de mon amour vous ne pouvée me refuser cette grace pour que je vous voie sans rien risquée. Je ne peut rien sans cela. On m'a dit aujourduy que vous aviée eu des nouvelles de Mr de puisieux.[154] Cela me fait tremblée. De grace, rassurée moi et donnée moi touts les jours de vos nouvelles! Aujourd'hui, mardi,[155] me tourne la tête. D'imaginée que vous passiée la journée avec Mde t... me dessespere! Cependant, vous m'avée dit quil ny avoit rien. Vous m'avée même dit que vous m'aimiée encore a la folie. Assurée m'en! Cela fera mon bonheur et mendez moi si je peut tachée de m'arrangée pour nous rencontrer quelque jour. Je ne peut vivre sans cela! Je n'ai ni bû ni mangée depuis que je vous ai vû. Si je pouvois, j'yrois chez vous mais vous voiée les dangers que je coure. Aion—aiée pitiée de mon etat! Songée que jai peu de temps a vous voir[156] et que c'êst pour la vie surement. Je ne survivrai pas a vôtre depart! Je vous aime plus que jamais et n'aimerai que vous dans le monde. Avée vous etée bien aise de me voir? Pour moi, la tête m'en tourne! Ne me laissée pas ignorer les choses qui font ma consolation. J'espere avoir de vos nouvelles. Vous me l'avée promis en m'embrassant en me quittant. Si je suis assez heureuse pour que vous ne partiez pas, mendée moi si vous irée à st o...; cela feroit mon bonheur. Adieu, cher amour. Jai passée mes nuits a baisée les endroits ou jai etée si heureuse. Dans le carosse je vous donnerai vôtre petit plaisir, tant que vous voudrée. Adieu, mon amour. J'attens de vos nouvelles demain. Vous n'avée qu'une parole. Rendée moi vôtre amour si vous voullée que je vive!

92. *(91)*

[*? 22 May 1748*]

Jai recû vôtre lettre, cher coeur d'amour, [en] sortant de table. Ma joie a etée [in]exprimable[157] puisque vous m'assurée que vous m'aimée mais, helas! ma joie a bien diminuée de ce quil me paroit que vous ne comptée pas m'ecrire touts les jours. Je m'en suis trouvée tres mal de la revolution que cela m'a fait. De grace, songée quil s'agit de ma vie! Je ne vous parlerai jamais ni de mes parents ni de rien qui puisse vous deplaire. Vous jurée un amour eternel êst tout ce dont je vous parlerai—et de l'empressement que jai de vous revoir. La demarche que jai faite peut vous en êstre une preuve et si vous voullée avoir la charitée de vous pretée a l'arrangement que je vous ai mandée[158] je pourrai vous [voir]. Pourquoi vouloir ne plus m'aimer? La conduitte de mes parents, helas! [je][159] n'y ai nulle part—et pourquoi me reprochée que je me laisse menée par la lisiére? Si vous etiez libre vous n'auriée qu'a m'emmenée—je serois pour la vie avec vous et je ne pourrois être contente que comme cela. Vous ne pouvée pas croire a quel point je vous aime! Si vous ne voullée pas que je tombe malade, ecrivée moi touts les jours et de la façon dont vous m'avée ecrit tant de fois, sans cela je ne peut vivre. Oui, cher amour, je vous [aime]—et si vous voullée que je vive, que je reçoive touts les [jours] un mot que vous m'aimée toujours. Je vous ai demendée l'autre jour[160] la même grace a vos genoux et vous me l'avée promis en me quittant. C'êst, d'honneur, la vie que je vous demende! Mendée moi si vous yrée aprés demain aux thuilleries. J'yrai pour vous y voir. Je suis comme une folle! Pretée vous par bontée a vouloir me rencontrée dans un carosse. Adieu, mon cher amour, vivre et vous aimer êst pour moi la meme chose. Je ne vous parlerai jamais de choses qui peuvent vous deplaire. Jai brulée vôtre lettre sur le champ, côme je ferai des autres[161]—car je connois trop vôtre bon coeur pour ne pas me flattée que vous m'ecrirée. Ce sera ma vie! Vous m'avée mis le poignard dans le coeur en me parlant que jai eu pour vous de l'ingratitude: je me donnerois le coup de la mort si javois quelque chose a me reprochée, mais heureusement cela n'êst pas. C'êst a vos genoux que je vous demende de vos nouvelles. Il s'agit de ma vie, en véritée! Regardée souvent mon portrait—et je vous demande en grace de me donnée le vôtre en petit. De vos nouvelles!

93. *(72)*

[*? 25 May 1748*][162]

Vous vous êstes trouvée incomodée cher amour? Jugée de l'inquietude ou je suis et rien ne peut m'en tirée si vous ne me donnée pas de vos nouvelles. Je ne puis oubliée que vous me l'avée promis en me quittant. Vous m'assurée que vous m'aimée toujours: donnée m'en donc la plus grande preuve en m'écrivant touts les jours un mot—cela me soutiendra dans ma douleur. Depuis que je vous ai vû je ne boit ni ne mange et suis reellement dans un etat affreux. Et de vous scavoir malade y met le comble. J'espere bien vous revoir, si vous le voullée; je ne peut vivre sans cela. Je ne veux pas vous ecrire plus longuement de peur de vous importunée et de vous fatiguée mais si vous voullée que je vive, donnée moi de vos nouvelles—sinon je scais que vous aiant vû je ne peut vivre sans cela. Adieu, tout ce que j'adore dans le monde! Je me meurs pour vous d'amour et c'êst pour la vie. Que ne puije êstre auprés de vous côme j'y etois quand vous etiée malade![163] Ce seroit la seule chose qui pourroit me tranquilisée. Je me meurs d'inquietude.

94.* (84)

[*c. 28 May 1748*]

Pourquoi vouloir faire la resolution de ne plus m'ecrire cher amour? Je ne pourrois vivre sans cela! Vous douttée encore de mon amour? Est il possible que cela se puisse? Si vous voullée que je vive ecrivée moi un mot touts les jours. Si vous pouviée lire dans mon coeur vous verriée quil n'êst qu'a vous et je ne suis pas un instant sans êstre occupée de vous. Ne m'accussée pas d'enfance — je n'en ai pas. Si vous pouviée trouver un moyen pour que je passe ma vie avec vous vous verriée si je vous aime! Je suis dans la plus grande inquietude de vôtre santée. Si je pouvois j'aurois etée ce soir chez vous mais cela m'êst impossible. Il faut laissée un peu trompér mes espions. Avec cela, mon pere êst ici et je pourois le rencontrer. Je serois perdû. Ce n'êst pas que touts les tourmens qu'on me feroit endurée me fassent rien — car la mort même m'êst egal, ne vivant pas avec vous. Je vous ai donnée la plus grande preuve de mon amour. Donnée m'en une qui êst de venir me trouvée dans un carosse avec d.... De cette façon là je ne risque rien, il n'y a qu'autour de vôtre maison qu'on me guete. Vous avée bien vû que jaie tout risquée. Aiee pitiée de mon etat et pretée vous a cet arrangement pour le jour que vous voudrée. Vous n'avée qu'a dire, je serai a vos ordres. Si vous m'aimée vous ne pouvée me refusée loccasion de me voir sans rien risquée. Je me meurs d'amour pour vous, j'en suis malade. Aiée pitiée de moi et de vôtre enfant! Que cela soit au plus tôt! Que je vous voie! Je ne peut vivre sans cela. J'enverrai demain cherchée vos ordres. Ecrivée moi et menagée vôtre santée si vous voullée que je vive. Vous ne pouvée croire a quel point je vous aime. Si vous vous pretée a cet arrangement, ou vous ne risquée rien, jai des choses tres pressantes a vous dire. Songée que je serai peut êstre morte dans deux mois![164] Ne me refusée pas cette grace — je vous la demande a vos genoux. Et de vos nouvelles!

95.* (70)

[*c. 29 May 1748*][165]

La proposition du carosse vous a deplû, cher amour. Je suis au dessespoir de vous l'avoir faite mais pardonnée au desir extrême que jai de vous revoir encore. Vous sçavée tout ce que je risque pour allée chez vous. N'importe, je ferai l'impossible pour y allée dans quelques jours mais, du moins, donnée moi de vos nouvelles, si vous m'aimée, et ne douttée plus de mon amour; il augmente, je vous jure, touts les jours. Que ne puisje êstre jour et nuit avec vous! Si vous trouvée quelque moyen, vous n'avée qu'a dire — mais de grace ne douttée plus de ma tendresse et n'imputée pas ni a manque de tendresse ni a enfance si je ne vais pas chez vous comme je le voudrois! Je n'ai d'autre plaisir que celui de vous voir et malheureusement il y a quatre mois que je suis la plus malheureuse de touttes les creatures! Songée que dans peu j'accoucherai et peut êstre y mourraije. Mais que m'importe, si je ne vous vois pas! Du moins, ne me mettée pas le poignard dans le coeur en me refusant de vos nouvelles! Je ny peut resister. Je suis dans une inquietude horrible de vôtre santée. Je vais chercher touts les moyens a pouvoir vous allée faire quelques moment de plaisir. Helas! je n'en peut contée qu'avec vous. Adieu, mon cher amour; ecrivée moi comme vous me l'avée promis. Si vous pouviée lire dans mon coeur vous y verriée le plaisir que j'ai de recevoir de vos nouvelles. Il est inexprimable! Je vous jure que je ne vous parlerai jamais de rien qui puisse vous deplaire—au moment que je pourrai allée causée avec vous et vous embrassée milles fois. Adieu amour! De vos nouvelles! Je me suis trouvée tres mal aujourduy de douleur de ce que vous n'avée pas voulû m'ecrire.[166]

NOTES TO THE LETTERS

1. Capitalization and punctuation—entirely absent in the letters—have been added minimally in the interests of intelligibility. The Princess's spelling has otherwise been left unchanged.
2. The number in parentheses is that originally given each letter in RA SP Volume 316.
3. Unless otherwise indicated, all subsequent letters are to the Prince.
4. Because of the almost total absence of external clues, dating of the pre-crisis (before 23 January 1748) letters is very approximate. The lovers often exchanged two letters per day, beginning around the first week of December 1747, when the Prince moved from St Ouen to the house on the Rue du Chemin du Rempart near the present-day Place de la Madeleine.
5. The first of several references to nausea, related no doubt to the early stages of Louise's pregnancy. The child, born 28 July 1748, was presumably conceived around the end of October.
6. *l'époux*.
7. During the initially happy and untroubled stages of her affair with the Prince, Louise wrote typically short notes. This is the first letter to extend beyond one page, that is, beyond one side of a folded half sheet.
8. Like most eighteenth-century ladies of fashion, Louise, it seems, rarely rose before one or two o'clock in the afternoon.
9. Mme de Guéméné, Louise's mother-in-law.
10. *Après-dîner*: essentially, the time between dinner and supper reserved for normal social visits.
11. Daniel O'Brien, Charles Edward's personal valet.
12. Presumably, six o'clock in the morning, when the Prince left her bedroom.
13. See p. 196
14. Even after moving to his new house in town, the Prince continued to make intermittent use of the large summer residence placed at his disposal in July 1747 by the Rohan family. He spent part of the Christmas holiday there, for example (D. Flyn to James Edgar, 29 December 1747, RA SP 288/155). Louise's easy access to St Ouen is perhaps explained by the fact that her granduncle, the Comte d'Evreux, owned a large summer residence just next to the Rohan property.
15. Louise's husband, the Duc de Montbazon. Charles Edward's violent jealousy erupted soon after *l'époux* returned from the campaign.

16. Mme de Guéméné's servants (see preceding letter).
17. The Princess's valet and confidant, an important intermediary in the affair and counterpart of Daniel O'Brien on the Prince's side. The near catastrophe referred to resulted in a self-imposed but short-lived period of *privation* which provoked even more violent symptoms of jealousy and insecurity in the inexperienced Prince.
18. Word illegible.
19. Possibly, Lord Clare (Charles, Earl of Thomond) or Lord Lewis Gordon.
20. Mlle Anne-Françoise de Carteret, confidante of the Princess (see pp. 195-98).
21. Charles Edward sat for the Louis Tocqué portrait in question during December 1747 and early January 1748. It was completed by 20 January 1748, when George Waters, Jr., Charles Edward's banker in Paris, made a partial payment of 744 livres to Tocqué for it (see RA SP 289/97). The Prince probably gave the painting that same day to Louise (see Letter 43). An engraving of the work by J.G. Wille, also completed in 1748, appears above, Pl. 25.
22. *L'époux.*
23. Not identified; another of the jealous Prince's imagined rivals.
24. This postscript is inverted on the last (fourth) page of the letter. Louise's enthusiasm for learning English is in sharp contrast with her earlier views on Polish (see pp. 67-68).
25. The success of Louise's efforts to reassure her jealous lover were short-lived. See Charles Edward's letter to Mlle de Carteret of 10 January 1748 and de Carteret's reply of the following day (pp. 197-98 and RA SP 289/46 and 47).
26. Waters was to take delivery of the Tocqué portrait on the Prince's behalf as soon as it was completed.
27. An apothecary's account dated 5 January 1748 indicates that Charles Edward purchased various stomach and toothache remedies around this time (RA SP 291/182).
28. Deeply implicated in the Princess's clandestine love affair, Mme de Guéméné's porter at the house on the Place Royale was dismissed immediately after the 23 January incident (see p. 206).
29. Probably a combined birthday (31 December) and New Year's greeting.
30. Perhaps regarding her new rule (see Letter 38) that, henceforth, their assignations could take place only well after her husband had retired for the night to his own apartment.
31. Perhaps RA SP Box 2/97 (see p. 194, and translation, *Appendix B*, II, 6).
32. That is, she admits she is too weak to enforce her resolution of Letter 38.
33. The notation, *pour Daniel*, appears on the back of this letter.
34. But probably before 14 January when the Court removed to Marly for its annual two-week saturnalia of gambling (see pp. 199-200). Louise's statement regarding her father ("Je l'enverrai chercher sur le champ") suggests that the Grand Chambellan was still in Paris. The Princess's motive for speaking so trustingly to her father is explained by de Carteret in a long letter addressed to the Prince several days after the 23 January crisis (see pp. 205-07 and RA SP Box 4, folder 1/114). A translation of it appears in *Appendix B*, II, 8.
35. Because the Prince was planning to be away from Paris for several days. On Thursday, 18 January, he rented a coach and six and travelled to Luciennes near Marly to visit the Princesse de Conti. On the day following, he went to Versailles (RA SP 289/68) where he remained until late on Saturday.
36. Waters paid Tocqué for the portrait on 20 January (RA SP 289/97), and Louise was expecting to receive it at "noon."
37. That is, 22 January, when he left to take part in the gambling revels as one of the many *salonistes.*

38. That is, 3:00 *a.m.* on Monday, 22 January.

39. The manuscript is torn at this point. Words supplied are enclosed in brackets.

40. Jules presumably saw Charles Edward socially at Versailles on the Friday or Saturday.

41. Perhaps in dealing with Mme de Guéméné at one of the Versailles functions Charles Edward attended. Worth noting is the fact that on the very eve of the great crisis, their passion is still at its height.

42. In her own apartment; that is, on a lower floor of the Hôtel de Guéméné.

43. Mlle de Carteret had turned up at the Hôtel de Guéméné the day before to begin her long-promised visit (see p. 205) but had gone out for the day.

44. The incongruity of Louise's words with the situation that was about to occur presents a moving example of tragic irony. Neither the Prince nor the Princess could have known that their secret intimacies at the Place Royale were now forever at an end.

45. Letter dictated by Louise's father, the Duc de Bouillon, aided by her mother-in-law, Mme de Guéméné.

46. This is the only dated letter in the entire correspondence. No longer able to communicate directly with the Prince, Louise now begins to smuggle out, at irregular intervals, letters three and four pages long.

47. Including, of course, her son, Jules.

48. To avoid additional scandal, Chrétien's dismissal was delayed in order to give him time to find other employment. The faithful valet continued to be useful as an intermediary for some time, however, and in the next several months Louise made determined efforts to compensate him for his sacrifice (see Letters 64, 65 and 77).

49. During the *après-dîner* public visiting period, that is.

50. When they last saw each other in the Princess's bedroom on Sunday "night," that is, after 3:00 a.m. on Monday, 22 January.

51. Imprudently, perhaps, the Princess soon came to trust the Prince's valet implicitly. Such cautionary statements, along with frequent pleas that her letters be burned, indicate a good sense on her part of the very real risks involved. The Prince, on the other hand, either did not realize the extent of the danger, or, more likely, did not care.

52. I have not identified this messenger (who was probably, in any case, ignorant of the contents of the message delivered).

53. Letter 47.

54. Letter 48.

55. On 16 January 1748, James sent from Rome a Latin memorial (Archives Nationales, 273AP427) and an ostensible letter relating to the Bouillon family's claims on the Sobieski jewels to Charles Edward in Paris (see RA SP 289/60 and pp. 184-86). The Prince was to forward the whole to Louise, but along with the memorial, which he sent around 8 February, Charles Edward apparently included another of his accusing personal notes to which Letter 52 is an answer. Louise's *formal* acknowledgement of the memorial was sent on 10 February (see p. 186).

56. Word supplied.

57. Daniel was obviously the Prince's messenger here. During this same period, Charles Edward was also doing his best to snub and offend Mme de Montauban (Mme de Guéméné's sister-in-law) as well as other important members of the Rohan family (see pp. 214-18). It is unlikely that he had any wish to see Louise, however safely, at Versailles and the pleasures of a sexual encounter, unaccompanied by some form of symbolic constraint or punitive victory, were by now of little interest to him. He wanted Louise to come to him on his own terms, even if it meant her risking utter catastrophe.

58. Preliminary peace negotiations were already under way at Aix-la-Chapelle, and it was universally accepted that George II's representatives would insist on renewing the old prohibition against harbouring Stuarts on French territory.

59. Louise seems perilously close here to accepting, for her royal lover's benefit, the indulgent perspectives of Abbé Prévost's Manon: "car la fidélité que je souhaite de vous est celle du coeur." But the Princess was no Manon and soon proved it when she confessed her inability to accept Charles Edward's later dalliance with the Princesse de Talmont (see, for example, Letters 90 and 91).

60. Possibly 2 March when Marmontel's *Denis le Tyran* attracted nearly one thousand spectators (see H. Carrington Lancaster, *The Comédie Française 1701-1774, Plays, Actors, Spectators, Finances*, in *Transactions of the American Philosophical Society*, New Series, Philadelphia, 1951, XL, 757).

61. Colonel James Oxburgh, a member of the Prince's household. Mme de Guéméné wrote to Oxburgh on 7 March, urgently requesting a meeting (see p. 217 and RA SP 297/80).

62. See, for example, the Prince's tale (*Appendix C*).

63. Although rumours of the Prince's new flirtation with Mme de Talmont may already have reached her ears, Louise, in all likelihood, is only probing here.

64. Daniel normally claimed, and quite truthfully, that he was unable to write but he did occasionally manage to scribble words phonetically.

65. Chrétien, Louise's former valet, would have been uniquely well-placed to know the truth of the Princess's assertions.

66. That is, the Prince. Louise's use of pronouns in the preceding lines is especially confusing.

67. Another indication that the recipient of this letter is Chrétien, the former valet, now unemployed and in need.

68. Not identified.

69. Perhaps the waistcoat she made for him (see Letter 83).

70. Presumably a verbal complaint passed on by way of Daniel or Chrétien.

71. That is, in her letter of 23 January.

72. Louise first set eyes on Charles Edward at the Hôtel de Bouillon, Quai Malaquais, on Saturday, 9 January 1745 (see p. 112).

73. *Encore une fois*: Louise was perhaps thinking of attending at least *one more time* before the normal Easter closing performance on Saturday, 30 March. The official closing of the Paris theatres, including the Opéra, extended from Passion Sunday to Quasimodo Monday (in 1748, from 31 March to 22 April). The *concerts* [spirituels] to which Louise refers in subsequent letters were exempt from the general prohibition.

74. Word illegible.

75. See dating of Letter 64 to Chrétien, written on the same day.

76. For example, her plan to meet secretly with the Prince at Versailles.

77. During the Prince's daily promenade in the Tuileries gardens, an event that regularly attracted crowds of admiring spectators.

78. That is, at the Prince's house, as he had repeatedly insisted.

79. See Letter 65, in effect, a long postscript to Letter 64: "Je n'ai pas pu vous faire tenir cette lettre jeudi." Letter 64, after referring to the "mardi qui vient," speaks of the "jeudi de l'autre semaine." Letter 65 identifies that Thursday as the "jeudi de pasques" (i.e., 18 April, since Easter in 1748 fell on 14 April).

80. Versailles, where Louise had access to a private apartment.

81. The Princess was now in her 23rd week of pregnancy.

82. Guillaume-Jean-Louis Maigrot, the Duc de Bouillon's *Trésorier Général* (see Archives Nationales, Minutier Central, LXVIII, 436). Louise had apparently succeeded in extracting a promise from her father to compensate her former valet for his dismissal. Voltaire, interested in details regarding the history of the Bouillon family for the

revision of his *Siècle de Louis XIV*, exchanged a number of letters with Maigrot during the period 1767-1771 (see Best. D. 14614, 14677, 14699, 14748, 15363 and 16960).

83. From 9 April to 18 April, a ten-day period during which time Chrétien's own intermediary, "Mr J...", would apparently be away (see also Letters 65A and 68).

84. See Letter 58.

85. Not identified but probably one of the servants at the Hôtel de Guéméné.

86. 11 April.

87. Possibly, the Comte d'Evreux, Louise's granduncle who lived in what has today become the Elysée Palace, conveniently located near the Prince's house. More likely, however, Louise is referring to Charles-Just de Beauvau, Prince du St. Empire and husband of her "aunt," Marie-Sophie-Charlotte (the Messalina's daughter), who lived in the Grande Rue du Faubourg St. Honoré.

88. The Princess is no doubt thinking of a stratagem similar to that employed by Daniel when Charles Edward was living in St Ouen (see pp. 178-82).

89. Letter 67.

90. 18 April, the Thursday following Easter.

91. During the official Easter closing of the Paris theatres, *concerts spirituels* were presented in the Salle des Suisses of the Tuileries Palace. Though "spiritual" in the beginning, they had by the mid-century come to resemble the more worldly productions of the Opéra (see Henri Lagrave, *Le Théâtre et le public à Paris de 1715 à 1750*, Paris, 1972, p. 94).

92. Illegible.

93. As on other occasions, in spite of Daniel's relative lack of writing skills, the Princess counts on his ability to make himself understood in a short note. That Letter 66 is to Daniel seems probable from the nature of Louise's plea: "Mendé moi *pour vrai*, etc." Among Louise's few confidants, only Daniel was close enough to the Prince to be able to answer such a question.

94. Via Chrétien; see Letter 65.

95. At the Palm Sunday *concert spirituel* performed at the Louvre, Louise and the Prince heard Jean-Joseph Cassanéa de Mondonville's motet, *Magnus Dominus*, followed by Michel-Richard Delalande's *Miserere* (*Mercure de France*, April 1748, p. 125).

96. Louise was apparently hoping that her father would grant Chrétien a legally constituted annuity rather than a less secure informal allowance.

97. The Princess was probably unaware of the extremely precarious nature of Charles Edward's own finances at this time (see pp. 164-65). Still, when it served his purpose, he could always manage, it seems, to provide a strategic financial inducement, as in the case of Mlle de Carteret.

98. Letter 69, obviously not returned as requested.

99. Though the Prince on several occasions had hoped to join the French campaign, there was really never any question of Louis XV and the Ministers permitting it, for fear of offending the British. Louise seems to have been considerably less worried, on the other hand, about the safety of her husband and her brother.

100. A rare example of Louise's better style. The Abbé Prévost himself might have gladly accepted responsibility for such a sentence!

101. Had she now heard through Chrétien or Daniel that the Prince was having unworthy doubts on that point as well?

102. Because Chrétien's intermediary would be absent and, as events would soon show, she was being too closely watched to attempt more direct methods of communication.

103. See note 100.

104. Chrétien.

105. The matter being rather too complicated, no doubt, even for Daniel's most earnestly literate efforts.
106. Louise's counterproposal amounted to meeting at today's Place de la Madeleine rather than Place de la Concorde (Tuileries gardens side).
107. Possibly, Lady Clifford, a frequent visitor to the Prince's house, who may have helped Chrétien and Daniel get their messages through to the Hôtel de Guéméné on the Place Royale.
108. The Prince is still complaining about the letter of 23 January!
109. St Ouen, at the Rohan summer residence, despite the fact that, only the month before, the Prince had snubbed the Princesse de Rohan-Montauban, the person responsible for arranging his free accommodation there!
110. Versailles.
111. The Good Friday performance on the 12th included, among other pieces, a repeat of Delalande's *Miserere* and de Mondonville's new motet, *De profundis* (*Mercure de France*, April 1748, p. 126).
112. The solitary piety of her later years is foreshadowed here.
113. Lower portions of page torn. Words missing, recto and verso.
114. Letter 75.
115. Letter 77.
116. Not surprisingly, Daniel did not keep this promise to Louise, having failed to inform her of the Prince's new love, Mme de Talmont. Obviously, he did not see to the burning of her letters as she requested, either.
117. There is no evidence to suggest that Daniel—ever the Prince's fiercely loyal private valet—incurred Charles Edward's displeasure in any way at this time. In fact, we now know enough about his own character (see pp. 276-77) and Louise's trusting naiveté to guess that such stories of suffering and retribution were probably intended, if not to create additional mischief and obfuscation, to distract the Princess from her own obsessive concerns.
118. Letter 78.
119. This seems to be Louise's last letter to her former valet, Chrétien. Perhaps with his new pension he was able to leave the intrigues of Paris behind him. On the other hand, it is possible that Mme de Guéméné's prohibition concerning "Mme C..." (Lady Clifford?) may have blocked his only safe avenue of communication with the Princess (see also Letter 84).
120. Not delivered, apparently, until later (see Letter 79).
121. Letter 78.
122. 20 May.
123. Both Louise and her child being blood relations of the Prince.
124. Presumably, the Princess writes "*le* jour" because the season was scheduled to resume the following week.
125. Unfortunately, it seems that the Princess was as good as her word.
126. The last of the *concerts spirituels* was performed at the Louvre on Quasimodo Sunday, 21 April, but it is likely that Louise is referring here to the second-last performance, given on Friday, 19 April, since her remark concerning the Prince's attendance at the Opéra is still in the perspective of "next week" (see Letter 79, note 124).
127. In Letter 82 Louise speaks of having seen the Prince at the Opéra "hier," and mentions as well the possibility of her attending again "demain." Since Tuesday, Thursday, Friday and Sunday were opera days, she could have been writing only on Wednesday the 24th, Saturday the 27th or Monday the 29th. Saturday seems most likely.
128. A clue to the probable identity of the recipient: normally that familiar plea was directed to Daniel.

129. See Letter 81, note 127.
130. Louise expected that Mme de Guéméné would leave Paris around 20 May (see Letter 79). Jules was probably already with his regiment.
131. The Princesse de Talmont (see pp. 219-21).
132. *l'Opéra*.
133. The essence of the Princess's tragic passion.
134. Not delivered (see Letter 86).
135. Letter 85 was written on that occasion.
136. The common assumption was that the Prince would be required to leave France soon after the preliminary articles of peace, signed at Aix-la-Chapelle on 30 April, were ratified and made public.
137. An accusation probably reported to Louise by Mlle de Carteret.
138. Proof that Chrétien had dropped out of sight from mid-April on.
139. See note 87.
140. More evidence that the Princess was not deterred by Daniel's inability to write. Occasionally, Daniel used John Stewart, Charles Edward's second valet, as an amanuensis (see pp. 259-60), and he may have done so in his communications with the Princess as well.
141. Letter 84, written two days before.
142. See Letter 84, note 134.
143. The day on which Letter 85 was written ("je serai saignée").
144. Louise had at first written *misérable*.
145. Grudging assent seems to have followed this last entreaty, although the Prince's motives for relenting (very temporarily) remain unclear. Was it the attraction of a symbolic victory—having finally forced Louise to risk everything by coming to his house?—Perhaps a defiant wish to deny to her in person that Louis XV's negotiators at Aix-la-Chapelle could drive him out of France?—Genuine concern (at last!) at her suicide threats? —Renewed affection for his first mistress, his vanity now having recovered from Mme de Guéméné's attempt to teach him good manners and "give him laws"?
146. Louise finally succeeded in meeting with the Prince (but not at his house) late on the night of Saturday, 18 May (see Letter 89).
147. We recognize the value of the hidden backstairs entrance (through Daniel's room) at the Prince's house on the Rue du Chemin du Rempart (see p. 191). The stratagem of "early retirement" had already been used by the Prince and Louise at St Ouen.
148. Their last meeting had taken place on Sunday, 21 January (Letter 45).
149. Perhaps a narrow escape from Mme de Guéméné's spies when Daniel was escorting her back to the Place Royale?
150. Letter 90.
151. See Letter 56, note 59.
152. The *Gazette* for 18 May 1748 (No. 21, pp. 244-45) revealed, finally, that preliminary articles of peace had been signed at Aix-la-Chapelle on 30 April. It also reported that news of the signing had caused "une joye aussi vive que générale" in London. The Prince, even at this late date, refused to believe that the war (which represented his only hope to stay on in Paris) was over (see pp. 229-30).
153. Perhaps Letter 89?
154. Regarding the peace negotiations at Aix-la-Chapelle. Louis-Philogène Brulart, Marquis de Puisieux (1702-1771) was Louis XV's Foreign Minister. Charles Edward had already come to look upon him as a mortal enemy, in the pay of the British Ministry.
155. The question of the Prince's seeing Mme de Talmont on Tuesday, 21 May (first Opéra day of the week), must have come up during their discussions at the Saturday meeting.
156. Whatever the Prince's own view, Louise recognized (along with nearly everyone else)

that final ratification of the peace treaty would necessitate the Young Pretender's departure.

157. Edge of paper torn.

158. Her *carosse de remise* proposal in Letter 91.

159. Edge of paper torn.

160. In the carriage.

161. Those she hoped he would write to her in the days to come. She had, at his insistence, already burned all of his earlier letters to her.

162. Written, possibly, early on Saturday, 25 May, after learning that the Prince had been unable, because of illness, to turn up for his Tuileries promenade on the 24th as she had hoped (Letter 92).

163. Probably at St Ouen around mid-July 1747, just before they became lovers. The Prince, at the time, was suffering from a severe mental depression, triggered by the news of Henry's "betrayal."

164. As a result of giving birth to their child (born, however, without incident on Sunday, 28 July 1748).

165. Written the day after Letter 94 ("J'enverrai demain cherchée vos ordres"), upon learning that the Prince had rejected the idea of meeting again in a carriage. He had apparently insisted instead that she "act like a grown-up" and risk visiting him at his house.

166. The correspondence ends abruptly here. For a few conjectures on what happened next, see pp. 226-27.

Appendix B

I. Louise to the Prince:

1. (16)

[? late November 1747]

If you were pleased with your night, my love, I own to you that, for my part, I was enchanted. My fond hope is that we shall enjoy many more of the same. That will be my only source of happiness. I await your news with impatience. Good-bye, my darling; I am very well. Come spend this night in the arms of one who, in the whole world, adores only her dearest love.

2. (22)

[? late November 1747]

Your letter has not yet arrived, my dearest love, but I hope it will tell me that you are coming to spend the day with me. Remember that I have no other pleasure in the world. Good-bye, my dearest love; I am feeling very well. Come have supper with me; from then until midnight I shall be the happiest of all creatures.

3. (19)

[? late November 1747]

I confess I am delighted, my darling love, at your having told me everything you had against me. Since all the tales you have been told are false, I am not distressed by them. On the contrary, they are proof that you must be on your guard against those who tell you tales. I love you more than ever. I swear that I am sincere and that I shall love you forever. Yes, my beloved, I shall live only to adore you. My dear King, good-bye; till tonight and my crowning joys.

4. (51)

[? early December 1747]

Oh Lord, dearest love, how you pierced my very heart yesterday! But if you conduct yourself now as I have begged you to, we shall avoid further sorrow and enjoy pleasures unmixed with pain. I shall wait for you tonight at midnight, as we agreed. My husband is expected. Today I am sick as a dog from the same condition as yesterday, but I hope that you will cure me tonight. Count on my love and my tenderness: they have no equal. Goodbye, my darling; let us live happily our few remaining hours together. I kiss you a thousand times.

12. (12)

[? mid-December 1747)

I have only now been able to read your letter, my dearest love, and I reply, without losing another moment. Yes, I do swear to you that my love will never end and that never again will I complain or be out of humour. I shall live only for my darling love and solely to please him. Let us spend happily these few remaining hours we have together. Alas, they will be all too brief! Till tonight at midnight; come and find joy in the arms of the woman who adores you and will adore you all her life. Oh Lord! how I long to be in your arms!

22. (24)

[? mid-December 1747]

I am more dead than alive, my darling love! Mme de G[ueméné] has just announced at table that she has been hearing noises in the house every night. Starting today, one of her servants will be posted on guard and the entire household is required to be on the watch. Many other remarks were made in a manner which must cause me to fear the worst. I sense only too well that our love will be sorely tested and I am simply miserable because of it. I do not presume to direct your conduct but, sensible of your love for me, I hope for the best—for otherwise I am undone. Greater happiness awaits us at Saint-Ouen; there, day and night, I shall be yours and I am determined to do the impossible to hasten that time. You have my word of honour that M. de M[ontbazon] will not be allowed to come near me and I shall forever be yours alone. I cannot tell you how pitiful is my state. I adore you and bid you adieu. I have not the strength to tell you more. In the name of God do not think ill of me and do not take this as a defeat; far from it! It would reduce you to tears to see the state I am in. Good-bye a thousand times, my dearest love.

23. *(24 A)*

[? mid-December 1747]
It is the unhappiest of creatures who throws herself at your feet, my darling love. My life is in your hands ; if you abandon me, my mind is made up—I will kill myself, along with my unfortunate child. If you wish to restore me to life, come to me tonight at two o'clock and we will elude our spies. In the name of the most tender love I beg you; do not deny me this kindness and never for the rest of my days will I give you cause for vexation. Poor Chrétien is more dead than alive. Most assuredly he is not at fault. My life is in your hands. In the name of God, dearest love, come tonight and restore me to life. I have a fever. I have taken nothing, but only physic which I threw up immediately. I await my fate. Pray God that it may be favourable! You see at your feet the fondest of mistresses. Yes, my beloved, I shall forever be yours. I am dying; I have not strength enough to write.

26. *(17)*

[? late December 1747]
What a state I am in, my dearest love! I could not even begin to describe it. Seeing you yesterday was a great comfort to me, though when you vowed to spend the night waiting in the street it was like a dagger through my heart. I have not been able to eat anything. I had a very troubled night, separated from you, my only love, and knowing that you were exposing your health and your life to danger. If you wish to safeguard mine and my child's, if that is still possible, I charge you on your love not to come at night except when we can be together, which will be soon. But I swear to you that it will not happen at all if you insist on spending another night outside the house. Can you refuse me in the state I am in? Yes, my dearest love, you must spare yourself so as not to be ill on our day of happiness. Oh Lord, how I look forward to that moment! I shall die of pleasure, I think. You must hurry along your portrait. Go for a short time tomorrow

morning. I await your letters with an impatience that cannot be equalled. Hearing from you is my only source of happiness. Write to me again this evening, around eight o'clock, and tell me how you spent the day. Remember that without you I am nothing, and that my only comfort lies in the hope that you will take care of your health which is so precious to me. Without you I cannot live. I was so touched when you confided to me that you loved me even before Scotland. I swear that the same is true for me but I too must refrain from telling you that, for fear of augmenting your love. But no, we can tell each other whatever tender things we like for our love cannot possibly increase more. I would never have believed it could be so intense but I have no regrets. No matter what sorrow it brings me, it is the joy of my life. Keep well then, for my sake, and remember that you belong to others, that you are dedicated to three kingdoms and to the most loving and faithful mistress in the world. Good-bye my darling, my dearest love; writing to you is my only pleasure. We must write to each other twice a day. I kiss you a million times and with all my heart.

I have just unsealed my letter, having now received yours. You are adorable not to wait around at night. You will have your reward.

37. *(31)*

[? early January 1748]
You were angry, my dearest love, at having to sleep alone.... For my part, I swear to you, I was beside myself, and I did not sleep a wink all night because of it! I am still weak from being bled. Come spend the afternoon with me; it will make me very happy and tonight at midnight my joy will be more than complete. I shall have something to tell you tonight but do not fail to come this afternoon. Good-bye, my beloved; I love you more than I can say.

38. *(43)*

[? early January 1748]
Will your cruelties never cease — and after all your promises to do only what I wish and what is essential if I am to continue loving you? This is neither advice nor stubbornness, but pure reason. You are free to be at the rendezvous at whatever time you like, but you will most certainly not come into the house before my husband has returned and has retired for the night. You are free to begin your tortures again, if that is your wish, but in that case I would prefer that you not come at all, even though I am ready to die of love and tenderness for you. The greatest and only proof of love you can give me is to do as I ask and what befits my situation.

Write me this afternoon, but if you are determined to continue your cruelties... adieu. Write to me this afternoon, without fail!

39. (40)

[? early January 1748)
Your letter leaves me speechless! Is this how you reward my most tender love, a love that will never end? I have just learned that M. de M[ontbazon] will be attending the ball, so be at the rendezvous at half-past one. I confess I am stricken with grief, my dearest love. Send me a reply to this. I am in a frightful state. Will you never cease putting daggers through my heart? My end is not far off, I swear to you, but it seems to me that you will be easily consoled. I admit that I cannot resist any longer; my tears will not allow me to say more. I adore you, yes, and you shall have proof enough of that tonight. But have pity! Do not grind me down with so much unkindness. I have not the strength to bear it. Good-bye, most ungrateful and most adored of men. Let your anger pass, and remember that I love only you. Restore me to life by sending me a word in reply. I have not the strength to say more. Send me an answer but not by the bearer of this; he is too well known. I cannot continue; you will be satisfied.

40. (21)

[? mid-January 1748]
Since you insist on coming, I shall expect you; you are the master. My life will be placed at great risk, but no matter. I have decided to tell my father everything; he will be of great help to me and I beg your approval. I did not want to tell him without your leave. I shall send for him immediately. I am in a dreadful state. I shall expect you this afternoon, and tonight.

46. (45)

[23 January 1748, in the morning]
Be entirely happy, my darling love! I swear that I adore you more than words can say. I shall be by myself all day. My mother-in-law will remain in her apartment. It would be very sweet of you to come for a moment this afternoon. You are the only person in the world I am glad to see, for otherwise I delight in being alone in order to devote all my attention to thinking about you my love. I have a horrible headache. It will serve me as an excuse for retiring early but I shall still be overjoyed to see you this afternoon. Good-bye, my beloved darling. I am more delirious today than ever and you shall have proof of that tonight. I kiss you a thousand times, all of you.

47. *(41)*

[23 January 1748, late evening]

What I foresaw only too clearly has indeed come about. My mother-in-law knows everything of your proceedings and she has just come here, accompanied by my father. They have both spoken to me as friends. I am thus obliged, Your Royal Highness, to advise you of this, and you have long been aware of what I told you. I am required by my duty to them never to see you again nor even to receive your letters. If you will do me the honour of coming to visit from time to time, as I believe you will, so as not to ruin me entirely — it is nearly so already — you will be welcomed as before. Adieu, Your Royal Highness. This is a cruel test of my affection for you which will end only with my life.

48. *(13)*

28 January [1748]

It has not been possible to write to you since the other day, for I am being constantly watched. It was very cruel of you to refuse to answer the letter I wrote after my unfortunate experience. I was so agitated that I had not strength enough to hold my pen. May I flatter myself that you will still be pleased to hear from the unhappiest of all creatures? I will give you, my dearest love, an exact account of what happened to me on Tuesday, the day I wrote to you. I was eagerly looking forward to seeing you at one hour past midnight and feeling quite easy in my mind. At ten o'clock, in walked my mother-in-law and my father whom she had sent for in order to apprise him of my conduct. She told me that she had long since been aware of what was going on but that she had hoped it would end. She spoke to me, for all that, without anger and told me in a most friendly way that she would keep my secret from everyone, but that I had to break off with you and tell you so by letter. A death blow could not have been more crushing! I was in a state of complete distraction when I wrote to you. She has dismissed her porter, and my valet de chambre will also be leaving. I was made to promise that I would never again write to you but I could not wait any longer. I rely on your affection and I trust that no one will discover I have written to you. That would crown my misfortunes! A dreadful life lies ahead for me. They have not been able to make me take any food. But all the evils I shall be required to endure will be as nothing if you continue to love me. Without that, I shall cease to live. Remember that I carry your child in me and that it is for your sake alone that I suffer such affliction. Do not complete my destruction by withholding your love. If you love me still, I will get word to you as often as I can, and you will do the same. That will sustain me in my sorrow. I spend my days and nights weeping, gazing constantly at your portrait and kissing the lock of hair you gave me. I have gone quite mad, in other words, and I have not slept two hours since Tuesday. I am so frightfully changed as to be unrecognizable. I hope that you will bring me back to life, this evening, by sending me word of yourself. Oh Lord, how happy I will be if your fond mistress remains still in your thoughts! I shall be yours as long as I live. I swear to you that there will be a happier time. Promise me that you will be there to enjoy it. My paper is wet with tears. May I hope that my portrait is of some comfort to you? Look upon it often and you will see the likeness of one who loves you to the point of adoration. I beseech you to come and visit from time to time to prevent my public ruin; otherwise I am lost. It would make me very happy if you were to talk to my mother-in-law. I have not the strength to go on writing. Let no one know that I have written to you. Grant me life once more my darling love! I am greatly to be pitied but if you continue to love me that will be happiness enough. Good-bye my dearest beloved.

57. *(60)*

[c. 6 March 1748]

Perhaps I risk your complete displeasure but I cannot help begging one last favour of you, the last of my life. It is only because you have stopped your visits that people are talking. Have you the heart to refuse me? Can you possibly want to crown my misfortunes by ruining me in public? Upon my life, I swear that none of the talk comes from here. Everyone has behaved admirably and has tried only to comfort me. All are eager to see you return and so put an end to the gossip. It is the only way, and if you continue to remain aloof, I am lost. There is still time. Do not refuse me. I am asking you for my life! No one will say anything and you will be welcomed as befits you. Can you deny me this last bit of comfort when I have sacrificed everything for you: life, reputation, and life's happiness? I know that people have told you the vilest things about me, and that you accuse me of having tattled. Alas, people knew only too well what was going on! I have nothing to reproach myself for. What could have persuaded me to sacrifice everything if not the tenderest love I have for you? Your conduct toward me ought indeed cause me to change but I shall love you for as long as I live. In my present state, I think that may not be very long. They have made me go out in order to divert me, but I no longer leave the house, nor shall I for a long time to come. They were even obliged to have me bled in order to save my unfortunate child. Can *he* not soften your heart? As for myself, I think you have perhaps already sacrificed me to others. I could bear any misfortune if only you still felt some little kindness toward me. Please come as soon as possible. I shall not be going out. You would be saving my life. It is in your hands. If only you could come today, or tomorrow! You will see how pitiful I am. My only consolation is that I have never failed you in anything. I have racked my brains to find a reason for blaming myself but I know that people have persuaded you otherwise. I must be very unfortunate indeed! I have given you, it seems to me, sufficient proofs of my love to dispel all your doubts. My fate is in your hands. I beseech you, on my knees, to preserve my reputation by coming back and by granting me the only joy I can experience in life which is that of seeing you. If some persuade you that to put an end to the rumours you must never come here again, it is because they are bent upon ruining me and causing our separation; indeed, I believe they have managed it rather well. Your reply will decide my life's misery or happiness. If you came, I would go back to your house. In short, I would be the happiest of creatures, and not a word would be said. If you refuse me this, my life can only be abhorrent to me, since the cause of my misery is my only love, whom I shall love all my life—which will not be long. There is still time, if only you return soon. The affection you so often expressed to me gives me hope. My tears prevent me from continuing. In God's name, restore me to life by coming back soon!

63. *(66)*

[4 April 1748]

You have chosen death for me, then, by confirming what I already suspected was your way of thinking. I can no longer have doubts since you reject even the safest opportunities I suggest for seeing me. Will you also refuse me permission to write you? I await your last commands. I can no longer live without hearing from you. I am in the worst state ever. Meeting you today drove me frantic—it is the effect of knowing I am hated by the one I adore. Nothing will make me repent what I have done for you, since it made you happy. You still believe me to be guilty? That is what drives the last dagger through my heart! Be just, my darling love, and send me my pardon by restoring your kindness. Without it I can do nothing and I am determined to end everything if you continue to deny me. Alas, can you do that without being unjust? My unhappy child pleads my case before you. It will be miraculous if everything goes well with him. I fear the worst. My life is in your hands—truly I swear it to you, embracing your knees and covering them with tears. I beseech you to send me word of yourself; you will otherwise decree my death. I can say no more. I have sought out every means of going to you but nothing is possible. Perhaps in two months' time a way can be found. Alas, you may not want to see me then! I await my fate. My love, affection, and most sincere tenderness cry out to you in my defense.

69. *(76)*

[8 April 1748]

You continue to destroy me with grief by not writing. You say that I have shown your letters; I swear to you upon my life that it is not so. I know you have

been told this and many other vile things. My enemies have apparently succeeded in their purpose, which is to separate you from me. Can they not render
me the same service and separate me from you? But nothing, save death, can
accomplish that. Tomorrow I await my fate, dearest love—allow me to use those
words, they are so dear to me! My fate will be sealed if you refuse to write and if
you reject the opportunity to see me. I shall not survive if those two misfortunes
befall me. I went to the concert yesterday, only to see you. Alas, you did not even
look at me! My efforts to disguise my mortification were such that I became ill
and I had to say it was because of the heat. I am in the worst possible state. All
the places where I used to see you, everything, in short, reminds me of my
former happiness and increases my sense of horror at my situation. Yes, my
beloved, I speak only the purest truth when I tell you that I cannot go on living if
you stop loving me. My fondest love, my warmest affection, my most inviolable
attachment for you are feelings that my heart can never abandon. All that is
lacking to complete my unhappiness is that you go to the Army. I would not
survive the anxiety it would cause me during my lying-in. If you have yet a little
kindness for me.... But no, I cannot flatter myself it is so, for you refuse to write
me. You should indeed dispel that worry if you still love me. Think of your
unfortunate child—yes, I dare to tell you that he is yours. Is he not able to soften
your heart toward his unhappy mother? My tears seize hold of me and rob me of
the strength to write. If tomorrow I receive no word of you, and if you prevent
me from going to see you when an opportunity arises, I shall not survive my
grief. I take no pleasure in company. I go out only in the hope of meeting you. I
spend my days and nights weeping. It is a miracle that I survive. But I cannot
help myself: I adore you, and I shall continue to adore you for the remainder of
my days. I will be without any news of you for ten days.... I shall be frantic. Please
have pity on me. If you had never loved me, I would not be so unhappy.

I have just interrupted my letter, having burst into tears as I was gazing at your
portrait. I fear, alas, that you have not been looking at mine. You detest me and
think me guilty; I am innocent and I adore you. I sense that I am a bother to you
and so I shall end here. If you allow me to see you, and if I am able to do so on
Thursday, it will give me back my life. Good-bye, my dearest love, I kiss a
thousand times everything that is so dear to me. The child inside me seems to be
saying that he adores you.

75. *(80)*

[? 14 April 1748]
I wrote to explain how I was prevented from going to your house on Thursday
and that the means of doing so have been taken from me. I am told that you now
have pity on me, but how can I believe that when you refuse to see me at

V[ersailles]? It is the only way, and I beg it of you as a favour. No one will ever suspect. Can you refuse me this? If you refuse me, my mind is made up: I shall drink a glass of poison. I cannot go on living, treated as I am by my only love. I beg you, on my knees, to meet me one day at V[ersailles]. There was a time, alas, when you would not have refused me that, and I have done nothing since to forfeit your esteem. Remember that I bear within me the pledge of an everlasting love. Have pity on my condition; I am dying of sorrow and by seeing me for a moment you would restore me to life. I swear to you upon my life that no one will ever know anything about it; it is the only way open to me. Be compassionate! If you deny me this, I am resolved to take my own life. I have reached my decision. I can no longer live without seeing for a moment my dearest love.

90. *(81)*

[? 20 May 1748]

I was so seized with joy at our meeting, my dearest love, that it drove me to distraction. But all the seizures in the world would not trouble me—indeed, they would make me completely happy—if I could see you as I wished. You may be certain that I shall not let slip any safe opportunity. I cannot come unless it is safe. I love you, quite sincerely, more than I can say. I keep remembering, since the happy moment I spent with you, everything that you told me. I admit to you, my beloved, that one thing did hurt me terribly, and that was your admission that you no longer loved me as much as before and that you wanted to take another. I could not survive such a blow! For my part, I shall be faithful to you as long as I live, and I have never ceased being totally yours. But I recall also the pleasant things you said, as when you spoke of the rumours in the gazette. You told me that you would no more abandon me than you would surrender your birth right. That is assurance enough. Love only me, my darling, if you would have me live! You promised when we parted in the street, my beloved, that you would write every day. Alas, it will be my only comfort! I have spent the night kissing my hands because they touched you. I do adore you! The letter I sent you caused me a dreadful fright. Let me know if you are going to St O[uen]. Look often at my portrait. Above all, see less of Mme T[almont]; I shall die of grief because of her. Write me my dearest love. I kiss a thousand times everything that I kissed yesterday. If you went to St O[uen] I would see you often.

94. *(84)*

[c. 28 May 1748]

Why are you resolved to write me no more, my beloved? I could not live without your letters. You still doubt my love? Can that possibly be? If you would have me live, write me a note every day. If you could see into my heart you would know that it belongs to you alone and that there is not a moment when I do not think of you. Do not accuse me of childishness. My childhood is gone. If you could find a way for me to spend my life with you, you would soon discover whether or not I love you! I am greatly concerned about your state of health. I would have gone to your house tonight but it was impossible. We must, for a time, lull the vigilance of our spies. My father is here, moreover, and I might run into him. I would be ruined, although all the tortures inflicted on me would be as nothing, for if I cannot live with you I am indifferent to death itself. I have given you the greatest proof of my love. Give me proof in return by coming to meet me in a carriage with D[aniel]. That way there would be no danger, since it is only around your house that they are watching for me. You have seen that I am prepared to risk everything. Take pity on my condition and lend yourself to this arrangement, for any day you like. You have only to choose and I shall obey your command. If you love me, you cannot refuse the opportunity of seeing me without risk. I am dying for love of you; I am ill with it. Have pity on me and on your child. Let me see you soon! Let me see you! Otherwise I cannot live. I shall send round tomorrow for your orders.Write to me and, if you would have me live, be careful of your health. You cannot imagine how much I love you! If you agree to this arrangement, which offers no risk, I shall have some very pressing things to tell you. Remember that in two months I may well be dead! Do not refuse the favour I ask; I beg you on my knees. Write to me!

95. *(70)*

[c. 29 May 1748]

You were annoyed at my carriage proposal, dearest love. I am in total despair at having suggested it. You must forgive my intense desire to see you again. You know all the risks I run when I go to your house. No matter; I shall do the impossible to visit you there within a day or two. But if you love me, please write, and do not doubt my love any longer. I swear to you that it increases every day. Oh why can I not be with you day and night? If you discover some means, you have only to tell me. But do not, I beg you, doubt any longer my affection for you. If I do not go to your house as I would like, do not ascribe it to a lack of love or to childish obedience on my part. I have no pleasures other than seeing you and it has been four months, unfortunately, since I became the unhappiest of creatures. Soon I shall be giving birth to our child and perhaps I shall not survive. But that matters little to me if I cannot see you! At least do not drive a dagger through my heart by refusing to write. I cannot bear it. I am horribly uneasy about your health. I shall seek out every possible means to go to you and give you a few moments of pleasure. It is only with you that I can count on it, alas! Good-bye my darling love; write me as you promised. If you could see into my heart you would know how delighted I am to receive your letters. My pleasure is beyond words. I promise solemnly that I shall at no time say anything that displeases you when we meet and it becomes possible for us to chat and for me to kiss you a thousand times. Good-bye, my beloved! Send me a letter! Today I was taken ill with sorrow on hearing that you have refused to write to me.

II. Translations from the text.

1

The marriage of Mademoiselle de Bouillon and the Prince de Guéméné was celebrated at the home of Cardinal d'Auvergne who lent them his bed.

Seeing their old-fashioned proceedings and nose-to-nose love-making, the bed of a sudden spoke, and told them that they lacked experience—that Monsieur le Cardinal went about it differently....

2

Great efforts will be made in the North, and the way through the seas will be opened. The island's reign will be reintegrating and London will tremble at the sight of sails.

3

Navarre, 12 June 1745

Dear Uncle and Cousin,

Since you know what brought me to France, you should not be surprised to see me leave in the same manner as I arrived, that is, secretly. It was not to view the country that I came here, nor to be a burden on His Most Christian Majesty, but only to be closer to those kingdoms over which my birth gives me legitimate rights and which I am determined to defend at least by showing that I am not unworthy of them. That is almost all I can contribute of my own. As you have the honour of approaching His Majesty so closely, I beg you to find the most favourable times to represent to him the situation in which I shall soon find myself, and the opportunity that situation will provide him to demonstrate his generosity by granting me the aid for which I shall forever be in his debt.

To provide the help I ask, few. adjustments will be required in arrangements already made for the campaign and even if such changes must be greater, they would soon be counterbalanced by the advantages they bring. There, dear uncle, is the favour I flatter myself I will presently receive through your affection for me. You have already shown me that I can hope you will do everything possible to advance my cause. I write you this from your castle of Navarre which you so graciously lent me. I find it a delightful place and would willingly enjoy all its pleasures if the project I have just announced to you did not call me elsewhere. But no matter where I may find myself you can depend on the friendship and affection that I shall always have for you.

Your Affectionate Nephew and Cousin
Charles P.

4

From Edinburgh, 25 October (Old Style) 1745

Dear Uncle and Cousin,

As you can well imagine, the letter I had the pleasure of receiving from you about two months ago made me very impatient to see the effects of His Most Christian Majesty's generosity toward me. It is true that I received recently some supply of arms and money for which I beg you to tender many thanks on my behalf. But the aid that has reached me does not meet my needs, and time is short. My enemies have added to their strength and brought from across the seas as many troops as they wished, whereas I have not been sent a single regiment. If it is yet the intention to profit from such a fine opportunity, there is not a moment to lose. I am resolved, for my part, to press ever onwards, and to risk another battle at the earliest opportunity. As before, Providence and the valour of my soldiers promise to carry the day. But all that does not prevent my hoping to receive aid from those Princes I have every reason to believe I can count on. Reflect on this, I beg you, and omit nothing in your efforts to obtain what I request. I shall also rely for this on the Chevalier Stuart to whom I have entrusted this letter and whom I have, at the same time, commanded to give you assurances of my special friendship for you.

Your Affectionate Nephew and Cousin
Charles P.R.

5

Sunday at four o'clock

I have just received yours. I am not one for waiting. Tell me at what time I am to be at the rendezvous and I shall be there. And though I love you to distraction, be persuaded that I am my own man and when I am pushed too far, all must give way. Compare your reason to mine. Come, woman! You must understand that you are agreeable to us only insofar as you yield to our pleasures. This may be my last visit. Adieu.

6

Monday noon.

It is not possible to be more vexed or wearied than I am with all the hypocrisy and harassment one encounters at your house. On the one hand, it has been useful in diminishing my love, which was extreme; on the other hand, I am truly ashamed at having already suffered so much. But I swear to you that this will be my last letter and that neither tears nor simpering will do if the slightest repetition occurs. I shall be at the rendezvous. See to it that your man attends me there at half past eleven.

I have just received your note and have nothing more to say except that my resolve is fixed and unskakeable. I shall come this night and not before, and if I meet with the slightest obstacle I swear to take my revenge, and with all suitable commotion. Till tonight at eleven-thirty then, when we shall see each other, or never again!

7

Your Royal Highness

I shall obey the command of Your Royal Highness and give you an exact account of my reasons for not staying when I was last in Paris. The person in question had planned for me to stay with her but as I knew how things stood at her house where I had no desire to remain because of the ill-temper of the mother and, I shall be quite frank, the childishness of the daughter, I hit upon several reasons for leaving. The first was my straitened circumstances but when Your Royal Highness supplied me with funds that reason no longer held and so I confided to the person in question that an affair of the heart drew me here and that I could not bring myself to desist. She accepted my explanation and promised to find some pretext to justify my leaving. That, Your Royal Highness, is indeed what happened but the true reason was that I thought Your Royal Highness suspected me of giving her bad counsel. I can assure you that if she had followed all of the advice I have given her you would not have cause to complain about her and she would be the happier for it. I am distressed to find that you are troubled. I am entirely ignorant of the cause and you have my word of honour, given with all respect, that she has told me nothing of it and that I surely must forever disapprove her not seeing to the happiness of Your Royal Highness, as she ought. In all fairness, I must do her the justice of saying that she has always assured me that you were the sole object of her love and that she could never love anyone else. She is a most unhappy creature if she has thought otherwise! I am so bold as to entreat Your Royal Highness not to confuse me among the causes for complaint that she has given you and to grant me the favour of always looking upon me as a faithful and zealous subject whose most ardent wish will ever be a desire to prove my profound respect .

This eleventh day of January 1748 at 4:30 in the afternoon.

8

Your Royal Highness,

The person Your Royal Highness sent to me yesterday found me on my way and thus unable to thank you for your kindness. I am most happy that you do me the honour of not confusing me with one who has had the misfortune of displeasing you. I can swear that I am not a party to any of it and that I was no more than an unfortunate spectator at the most horrible scene ever witnessed.

I shall give Your Royal Highness the exact truth of the matter. The person in question had been pressing me for more than a fortnight to visit with her, writing me the most insistent letters. One day she even sent round a carriage, which I sent back, being absolutely determined to stay away for I realized from her letters that what has come about would soon happen and I feared still that Your Royal Highness might think I was involved. I am entirely innocent, I swear, for if the person in question had chosen to take my advice, things would not have come to such a pass or caused such a frightful and indecent commotion.

I thus arrived on Monday, being unable to hold out any longer against her entreaties, firmly resolved to leave if what I feared actually came about. You had just left the house when I arrived. She informed me that she was the unhappiest creature on earth, that you showed her no consideration, that her reputation was ruined, that you accused her of indifference, that she loved you to distraction but that you refused to believe it. In truth, she was in a grievous state and she told me that she had been obliged to confess everything to her father so that he would see you and secure your promise not to visit so often, thereby putting an end to all the gossip in Paris about your spending every night there. That indeed is the rumour not only in Paris, but at Marly as well, and everywhere. Finally, the day after my arrival, I called on Your Royal Highness to pay my respects but, unhappily, discovered you had gone out. When I returned that evening to her house, I found her father and her mother-in-law closeted together. I repaired to the daughter-in-law's rooms and found her in deepest despair. She was convinced that her father and mother were talking about her and that everything was undone. In fact, a moment later, the father and mother came up to her bedroom. I was alone with her. On entering, the mother-in-law asked me to leave, saying that she had certain matters to discuss with her daughter-in-law and the father. I withdrew and immediately heard the poor creature cry out, sobbing most frightfully. The three of them remained together for at least an hour and a half, after which I was invited to join them. I found them all in tears. "You are not unaware, Mademoiselle," the father said to me as I entered, "of what has gone on between the Prince and my daughter...; her reputation is absolutely ruined. The Prince has displayed a total lack of consideration for her and has treated her as though she were the lowest of fallen creatures, showing no respect either for himself or for his first cousin, nor any gratitude for the many proofs of affection granted him by her family since his arrival in this country. He has dishonoured his cousin under her own roof. There is but one course to follow in such a calamity and that is to break off the affair entirely. My daughter must write immediately and tell him to come no more and she must break off forthwith. Only in that manner will the reputation of this poor woman be restored, by showing the public that all the rumours were false."—"I hope," the father added, addressing me directly, "that the Prince will have enough self-respect to keep up his visits during the day, for if his outward behaviour does not continue as before people will be convinced that the rumours were true and it will signify that dishonouring her is of little account to him, and that would be most unworthy of a person like the Prince."

I was more dead than alive during this conversation for the poor creature was on the point of expiring in her bed. Never have I witnessed such extreme agitation. Finally, she was made to write the letter that she sent you and, in truth, Your Royal Highness, I must be frank: she was so beside herself that she did not know what she was doing and if the letter is lacking in some terms of the respect owed you, you ought to overlook the fault for I can attest that she was in such an agitated state that it would have been impossible for her to write.

Finally, the mother-in-law adopted a more soothing manner with her, reassuring her that everything could be forgiven, that she felt compassion for her situation and that she should set her mind at ease. To help in calming her, all blame will fall on Your Royal Highness's shoulders. The porter was dismissed the very next day and the valet will soon be sent packing. It is only out of consideration for her that he has been kept on for a time to avoid stirring up more gossip. They are all in despair at your not having answered the last letter and are saying that your show of contempt is only too obvious, that to repair all possible wrongs you ought at least to observe the proprieties that any decent man owes to himself in respecting what he has loved.

The mother-in-law, seeing her daughter in such misery from which she may never recover, talks to her gently enough face to face but reviles her with every species of horror behind her back. In short, you may be sure that this poor woman will lead a most dreadful and sorrowful life for the remainder of her days. She is not without fault, admittedly, and if she had conducted herself properly, all this would not have happened, but given her character, she is more to be pitied than censured: exceedingly intense in her passions, blindly and thoughtlessly giving herself over to them, immature, lacking experience though believing otherwise, totally ignorant of social usage and insisting always on following her own lights which are very limited; but with all that a very kind heart, capable of friendship, and loving what she loves with the utmost intensity, but so imprudent that those whom she loves must put right the balance with sterner examples. There we have, Your Royal Highness, our subject. But have pity on her! Remember that you have loved her passionately and that you cannot so soon tear from your heart what has been so deeply rooted there. Show her a little kindness still. Do not abandon her in her frightful despair. Be charitable enough to call on her from time to time in the afternoon, if only for a quarter of an hour, to convince the public that it has been mistaken. When it is seen that Your Royal Highness comports himself in that manner, her reputation will be restored. I am driven to despair by her ill-considered conduct toward you. She has acted with the greatest possible extravagance and folly but, for all that, she adores you, and of that I am certain. Take pity, in Heaven's name, on the condition you have placed her in! Do not be the ruin of her. Perhaps there will come a happier time when she can conduct herself more wisely and be able to enjoy your love in peace. You and she are not the first to have met storms and setbacks in these circumstances but if you love each other truly such obstacles will be without effect, for love prevails even in separation. Many have found it to be so and find it so every day.

My respect and my fondness have perhaps caused me to address Your Royal Highness too freely but the confidence with which you have honoured me emboldens me to speak as truthfully and as candidly as I can. Please forgive my zeal and be assured, I beg you most humbly, that nothing can equal the profound respect with which I remain,

Your most faithful and most zealous subject.

I am so bold as to entreat you to throw this long letter into the fire. I humbly ask your pardon for its length but I thought it my duty to give Your Royal Highness an account of everything that happened while I was present.

Appendix C

CONTE FAITE A PARIS PAR MR.......
SUR UN JEUNE ETRANGE APELE MR.........

Histoire d'un home d'Excelante Famille arrivé d'un Pais exotick y étant Chassé par les Ennemis de son Roi Ligitime; Il arrive a Gene, et la il est parfaitment bien recu; en abordant tant par La Noblesse hote que Base, Des Diné et Soupe en abondance qui occasion ordinairement que de la fumé et chacun for Curieux de savoire Come il avoit echape de tan de Dangers que La fin d'une Geure Civille doite Naturellement engendre; il y rest quelque tems; enfin voient (c'est qui arrive pour le plus au Malheureux sans pouvoir) que La Soupe se rafroidisé, et qu'apré que la premiere quriosité etoit satisfaite il ny avoit plus a gagnie que du degout, il resolut de Changer d'aire, en effet il alla de la a Avignion en son Chemin pour Espagne, Ou il recut tout le meme bon Aceule qu'il avoit recu a Gene au Commencement; mais il prit bien gard de ny pas rester assé longtems pour avoire la fin, Car il partit immediatment pour Paris, ou il se mit entre les Mains, et sou la protection de Robens Croient se tirer mieu d'affaire par la dans un pais ou il avoit intention de rester autent que la Geure dureroit; enfin il devint Amoureux (etant dans une Maison de Campagne dont j'oublie le Nom) d'un aimable personne apelle Roudeboulon—(s'etoit le nom du vilage ou elle etoit né) dont le Pere etoit un sote, et la bone Mere une Vielle Folle (Come l'on vera par la suite); toute se paset for segretment particulierment du Cote de notre Viageure (car il etoit accoutumé dans son pais d'etre fort cautionné d'ans les Galantries) ce qui a la Verité n'est pas fort en usage icy Car l'on se vante non sullement c'est qui est, mais for souvent c'est qui n'est pas; enfin pour retourner a notre Comte, La Belle Mere, Le Pere, et la pauvre Fille, resolure malgre lui de vouloire rendre cette intrigue publique, et ils y reusire en party, Comme se sorte de Chose se Crois esement; Je plains se pauvre Etrange de ces Malheurs et Notre Pauvre Pais de la Mauvaise opinion que cette Jeune Homme en aura; je crois pouvoire finire icy le Premier Tome des avanture de M........ Comme je crois qu'il a eté asse Maltreté en Galantrie pour l'en degouter autent qui nous fera l'honneur de Reste icy; a son retour che lui, je ne manquerai pas de Publier le second Tome qui tretera probablement de la Geure.[1]

Index

BOUILLON

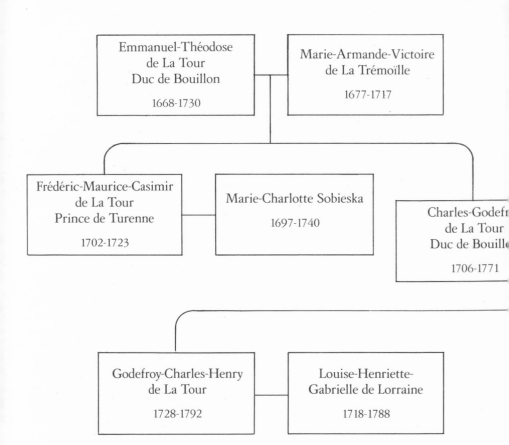

Emmanuel-Théodose
de La Tour
Duc de Bouillon

1668-1730

Marie-Armande-Victoire
de La Trémoïlle

1677-1717

Frédéric-Maurice-Casimir
de La Tour
Prince de Turenne

1702-1723

Marie-Charlotte Sobieska

1697-1740

Charles-Godefr
de La Tour
Duc de Bouill

1706-1771

Godefroy-Charles-Henry
de La Tour

1728-1792

Louise-Henriette-
Gabrielle de Lorraine

1718-1788